MODERN SCHOOL ATLAS

98th Edition

IN ASSOCIATION WITH
THE ROYAL GEOGRAPHICAL SOCIETY
WITH THE INSTITUTE OF BRITISH GEOGRAPHERS

MAP SYMBOLS

- National park boundary
- Administrative area name
- River name
- Place of interest
- Road
- Perennial river
- Railway tunnel
- Motorway
- Built-up area
- Island name
- Airport
- Administrative boundary
- Sea feature name
- Cape name
- Permanent ice and glacier
- Mountain range name
- Mountain pass (m)
- Regional name
- Dam name
- Capital city
- Lake name
- Perennial lake
- Railway under construction
- Disputed international boundary
- Dam
- International boundary
- Canal
- National park name
- Aqueduct
- Mountain peak name
- Valley name
- Depth (m)
- Intermittent lake
- Desert name
- Railway
- Height of lake surface (m)
- Intermittent river
- Sand desert
- Line of longitude
- Elevation (m)
- Line of latitude

Settlement symbols and type styles vary according to the scale of each map and indicate the relative importance of towns rather than specific population figures

SUBJECT LIST

Agriculture 38, 136–7
Aid (international) 152
AIDS and HIV 61, 153
Air quality 36
Air travel 42, 61, 142
Alternative energy 139
Arctic ice cap 130
Armed conflicts 153
Biomes 58, 74, 92, 100, 106, 118, 134–5
BRICS countries 151
Bush fires 101
Carbon dioxide emissions 37, 61, 130
Climate 34–5, 58, 74, 92, 100,
                        106, 118, 128–9, 132–3
Climate change 35, 130–1
Coal 41, 61, 101, 138
Conservation 37
Continental drift 124
Crime rate 48
Debt (international) 152
Deforestation 131
Desertification 131
Drought 10, 101
Drug traffic 153
Earthquakes 12, 81, 83, 115, 125
Education 48, 61, 145
Electricity generation 41, 139
El Niño 129
Employment 39, 80, 140
Energy 40–1, 61, 101, 138
European Union (EU) 60–1
Eurozone 60
Exports 39, 141
Family size 149
Fishing 38, 136–7
Flood risk 36
Food production 38, 136–7
Forestry 136–7
Fuel 40–1, 138
Gender Inequality Index (GII) 145
Geology 32, 124
Global warming 35, 130
Greenhouse gases 37, 130
Gross National Income (GNI) 61, 144
Group of Eight (G8) 151
Hadley Cell 128
Health care 61, 145
Heatwaves 101
Human Development Index (HDI) 144
Hurricanes 116
Hydroelectricity 41, 61, 80, 101, 139
Illiteracy 145
Imports 39

Industry 39, 80, 140
Infant mortality 149
Internet 48, 141
Inter-tropical convergence zone (ITCZ) ..127–8
Languages 59, 150
La Niña 129
Latitude and longitude 4
LEDCs 146
Life expectancy 146
Manufacturing 39, 80, 140
Map projections 5
Maternal mortality 148
MEDCs 146
Migration 47, 152
Minerals 101, 139
Monsoon 85
National parks 37
Natural vegetation 37, 134–5
Nuclear power 12, 41, 61, 139
Ocean conveyor belt 126
Ocean currents 126
Oil and gas 40–1, 61, 88, 101, 138
Plate tectonics 124–5
Population 46–7, 59, 75, 93, 101,
                        107, 119, 146–7
Refugees 152
Religions 150
Remote sensing 6–7
Renewable energy 41, 139
Research and development 140
Satellite imagery 6–17
Scale 4
Services 39, 140
Shale gas 41
Soils 37, 134–5
Standards of living 48, 61, 144
Telecommunications 141
Time zones 142
Tourism 43, 61, 113, 143
Trade 39, 141
Transport 42, 61
Travel 36, 42–3, 142
Tsunamis 12, 81, 83
Unemployment 48
United Nations (UN) 151
Urban population 148
Urban regeneration 16–7, 37
Volcanoes 81, 115, 125
Waste recycling 36
Water supply 36, 88, 144
Wealth 48, 61, 144
Wind power 41
World Heritage Sites 37, 143

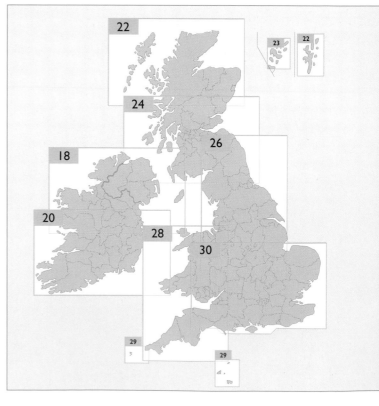

CONTENTS

SCALE, LATITUDE AND LONGITUDE 4
MAP PROJECTIONS 5

REMOTE SENSING 6–17

INTRODUCTION 6–7
COLOUR COMPOSITES 8
VEGETATION AND LANDFORMS 9
GLOBAL MONITORING 10–11
ENVIRONMENTAL MONITORING 12–13
GEOLOGICAL INTERPRETATION 14
SYNTHETIC APERTURE RADAR 15
URBAN REGENERATION 16–17

UNITED KINGDOM AND IRELAND 18–48

IRELAND – NORTH 18–19
IRELAND – SOUTH 20–21
NORTHERN SCOTLAND 22–23
SOUTHERN SCOTLAND 24–25
NORTHERN ENGLAND 26–27
WALES AND SOUTH-WEST ENGLAND 28–29
SOUTH AND SOUTH-EAST ENGLAND 30–31
UK AND IRELAND: GEOLOGY 32
UK AND IRELAND: RELIEF OF LAND 33
UK AND IRELAND: CLIMATE 34–35
UK AND IRELAND: ENVIRONMENT 36–37
UK AND IRELAND: AGRICULTURE,
   INDUSTRY AND TRADE 38–39
UK AND IRELAND: ENERGY 40–41
UK AND IRELAND: TRANSPORT
   AND TOURISM 42–43
UK AND IRELAND: COUNTIES AND
   REGIONS 44–45
UK AND IRELAND: POPULATION TRENDS 46–47
UK AND IRELAND: STANDARDS OF LIVING 48

THE WORLD 49–122

THE WORLD: RELIEF OF LAND 50–51
THE WORLD: COUNTRIES 52–53
ARCTIC OCEAN AND ANTARCTICA 54–55

EUROPE: RELIEF OF LAND 56
EUROPE: COUNTRIES 57
EUROPE: CLIMATE AND BIOMES 58
EUROPE: POPULATION 59
EUROPEAN UNION 60–61
UK AND IRELAND 62
SCANDINAVIA AND THE BALTIC LANDS 63
CENTRAL EUROPE 64–65
FRANCE 66
SPAIN AND PORTUGAL 67
ITALY AND THE BALKAN STATES 68–69
EASTERN EUROPE AND TURKEY 70–71
ASIA: RELIEF OF LAND 72
ASIA: COUNTRIES 73
ASIA: CLIMATE AND BIOMES 74
ASIA: POPULATION AND WEALTH 75
RUSSIA AND NORTHERN ASIA 76–77
CHINA AND THE FAR EAST 78–79
CHINA: INDUSTRY AND HYDROELECTRICITY 80
JAPAN 81
SOUTH-EAST ASIA 82–83
SOUTH ASIA 84–85
THE MIDDLE EAST 86–87
THE MIDDLE EAST: OIL AND WATER 88
ARABIA AND THE HORN OF AFRICA 89
AFRICA: RELIEF OF LAND 90
AFRICA: COUNTRIES 91
AFRICA: CLIMATE AND BIOMES 92
AFRICA: POPULATION AND WEALTH 93
NORTHERN AFRICA 94–95
CENTRAL AND SOUTHERN AFRICA 96–97
OCEANIA 98–99
OCEANIA: CLIMATE AND POPULATION 100–101
PACIFIC OCEAN 102–103
NORTH AMERICA: RELIEF OF LAND 104
NORTH AMERICA: COUNTRIES 105
NORTH AMERICA: CLIMATE AND BIOMES 106
NORTH AMERICA: POPULATION AND
   WEALTH 107
CANADA 108–109

UNITED STATES 110–111
NORTH-EAST UNITED STATES AND
   THE ST LAWRENCE 112–113
MEXICO, CENTRAL AMERICA AND
   THE CARIBBEAN 114–115
CARIBBEAN: HURRICANES 116
SOUTH AMERICA: RELIEF OF LAND 117
SOUTH AMERICA: CLIMATE AND BIOMES 118
SOUTH AMERICA: POPULATION AND
   WEALTH 119
SOUTH AMERICA 120–121
SOUTH-EAST BRAZIL 122

WORLD THEMES 123–160

THE WORLD: VOLCANOES
   AND EARTHQUAKES 124–125
THE WORLD: TEMPERATURE AND
   OCEAN CURRENTS 126
THE WORLD: PRESSURE, WINDS
   AND PRECIPITATION 127
THE WORLD: CLIMATE 128–129
THE WORLD: CLIMATE CHANGE 130–131
THE WORLD CLIMATE STATISTICS 132–133
THE WORLD: BIOMES 134–135
THE WORLD: AGRICULTURE 136–137
THE WORLD: ENERGY AND MINERALS 138–139
THE WORLD: INDUSTRY AND TRADE 140–141
THE WORLD: TRAVEL AND TOURISM 142–143
THE WORLD: STANDARDS OF LIVING 144–145
THE WORLD: POPULATION DISTRIBUTION 146–147
THE WORLD: POPULATION TRENDS 148–149
THE WORLD: LANGUAGES AND RELIGION 150
THE WORLD: INTERNATIONAL
   ORGANIZATIONS 151
THE WORLD: HUMAN CONCERNS 152–153
THE WORLD: SOCIAL AND
   ECONOMIC STATISTICS 154–159
THE WORLD: PHYSICAL DIMENSIONS 160

INDEX 161–184

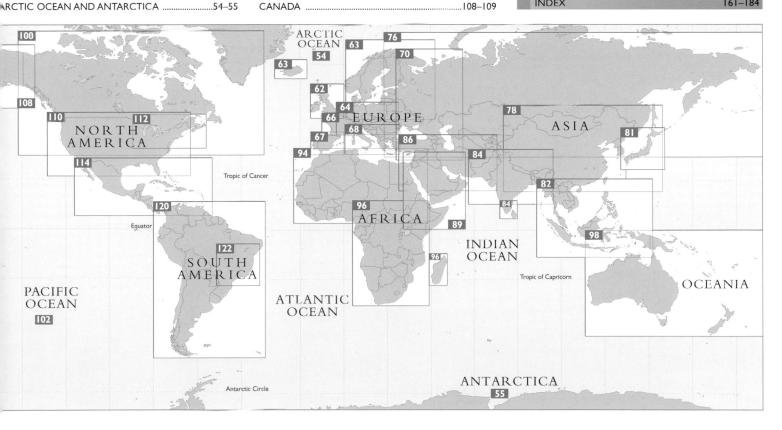

SCALE

The scale of a map is the relationship of the distance between two points shown on the map and the distance between the same two points on the Earth's surface. For instance, 1 inch on the map represents 1 mile on the ground, or 10 kilometres on the ground is represented by 1 centimetre on the map.

Instead of saying 1 centimetre represents 10 kilometres, we could say that 1 centimetre represents 1 000 000 centimetres on the map. If the scale is stated so that the same unit of measurement is used on both the map and the ground, then the proportion will hold for any unit of measurement. Therefore, the scale is usually written 1:1 000 000. This is called a 'representative fraction' and usually appears at the top of the map page, above the scale bar.

Calculations can easily be made in centimetres and kilometres by dividing the second figure in the representative fraction by 100 000 (i.e. by deleting the last five zeros). Thus at a scale of 1:5 000 000, 1 cm on the map represents 50 km on the ground. This is called a 'scale statement'. The calculation for inches and miles is more laborious, but 1 000 000 divided by 63 360 (the number of inches in a mile) shows that 1:1 000 000 can be stated as 1 inch on the map represents approximately 16 miles on the ground.

Many of the maps in this atlas feature a scale bar. This is a bar divided into the units of the map – miles and kilometres – so that a map distance can be measured with a ruler,

dividers or a piece of paper, then placed along the scale bar, and the distance read off. To the left of the zero on the scale bar there are usually more divisions. By placing the ruler or dividers on the nearest rounded figure to the right of the zero, the smaller units can be counted off to the left.

The map extracts below show Los Angeles and its surrounding area at six different scales. The representative fraction, scale statement and scale bar are positioned above each map. Map 1 is at 1:27 000 and is the largest scale extract shown. Many of the individual buildings are identified and most of the streets are named, but at this scale only part of central Los Angeles can be shown within the given area. Map 2 is much smaller in scale at 1:250 000. Only a few important buildings and streets can be named, but the whole of central Los Angeles is shown. Maps 3, 4 and 5 show how greater areas can be depicted as the map scale decreases, down to Map 6 at 1:35 000 000. At this small scale, the entire Los Angeles conurbation is depicted by a single town symbol and a large part of the south-western USA and part of Mexico is shown.

The scales of maps must be used with care since large distances on small-scale maps can be represented by one or two centimetres. On certain projections scale is only correct along certain lines, parallels or meridians. As a general rule, the larger the map scale, the more accurate and reliable will be the distance measured.

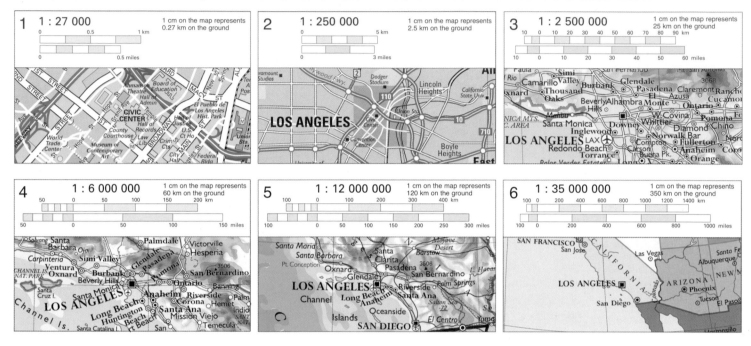

LATITUDE AND LONGITUDE

Accurate positioning of individual points on the Earth's surface is made possible by reference to the geometric system of latitude and longitude.

Latitude is the distance of a point north or south of the Equator measured at an angle with the centre of the Earth, whereby the Equator is latitude 0 degrees, the North Pole is 90 degrees north and the South Pole 90 degrees south. Latitude parallels are drawn west–east around the Earth, parallel to the Equator, decreasing in diameter from the Equator until they become a point at the poles. On the maps in this atlas the lines of latitude are represented by blue lines running across the map in smooth curves, with the degree figures in blue at the sides of the maps. The degree interval depends on the scale of the map.

Lines of longitude are meridians drawn north–south, cutting the lines of latitude at right angles on the Earth's surface and intersecting with one another at the poles. Longitude is measured by an angle at the centre of the Earth from the prime meridian (0 degrees), which passes through Greenwich in London. It is given as a measurement east or west of the Greenwich Meridian from 0 to 180 degrees. The meridians are

normally drawn north–south vertically down the map, with the degree figures in blue in the top and bottom margins of the map.

In the index each place name is followed by its map page number, its letter-figure grid reference, and then its latitude and longitude. The unit of measurement is the degree, which is subdivided into 60 minutes. An index entry states the position of a place in degrees and minutes. The latitude is followed by N(orth) or S(outh) and the longitude E(ast) or W(est).

For example:
Helston, U.K.   29 G3   50 7N   5 17W
Helston is on map page 29, in grid square G3, and is 50 degrees 7 minutes north of the Equator and 5 degrees 17 minutes west of Greenwich.

McKinley, Mt., U.S.A.   108 C4   63 4N   151 0W
Mount McKinley is on map page 108, in grid square C4, and is 63 degrees 4 minutes north of the Equator and 151 degrees west of Greenwich.

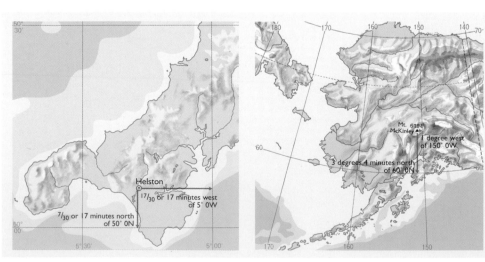

HOW TO LOCATE A PLACE OR FEATURE

The two diagrams (left) show how to estimate the required distance from the nearest line of latitude or longitude on the map page, in order to locate a place or feature listed in the index (such as Helston in the UK and Mount McKinley in the USA, as detailed in the above example).

In the left-hand diagram there are 30 minutes between the lines and so to find the position of Helston an estimate has to be made: 7 parts of the 30 minutes north of the 50 0N latitude line, and 17 parts of the 30 minutes west of the 5 0W longitude line.

In the right-hand diagram it is more difficult to estimate because there is an interval of 10 degrees between the lines. In the example of Mount McKinley, the reader has to estimate 3 degrees 4 minutes north of 60 0N and 1 degree west of 150 0W.

MAP PROJECTIONS

A map projection is the systematic depiction of the imaginary grid of lines of latitude and longitude from a globe on to a flat surface. The grid of lines is called the 'graticule' and it can be constructed either by graphical means or by mathematical formulae to form the basis of a map. As a globe is three dimensional, it is not possible to depict its surface on a flat map without some form of distortion. Preservation of one of the basic properties listed below can only be secured at the expense of the others and thus the choice of projection is often a compromise solution.

Correct area
In these projections the areas from the globe are to scale on the map. This is particularly useful in the mapping of densities and distributions. Projections with this property are termed 'equal area', 'equivalent' or 'homolographic'.

Correct distance
In these projections the scale is correct along the meridians, or in the case of the 'azimuthal equidistant', scale is true along any line drawn from the centre of the projection. They are called 'equidistant'.

Correct shape
This property can only be true within small areas as it is achieved only by having a uniform scale distortion along both the 'x' and 'y' axes of the projection. The projections are called 'conformal' or 'orthomorphic'.

Map projections can be divided into three broad categories – **'azimuthal'**, **'conic'** and **'cylindrical'**. Cartographers use different projections from these categories depending on the map scale, the size of the area to be mapped, and what they want the map to show.

AZIMUTHAL OR ZENITHAL PROJECTIONS
These are constructed by the projection of part of the graticule from the globe on to a plane tangential to any single point on it. This plane may be tangential to the equator (equatorial case), the poles (polar case) or any other point (oblique case). Any straight line drawn from the point at which the plane touches the globe is the shortest distance from that point and is known as a 'great circle'. In its 'gnomonic' construction any straight line on the map is a great circle, but there is great exaggeration towards the edges and this reduces its general uses. There are five different ways of transferring the graticule on to the plane and these are shown below. The diagrams below also show how the graticules vary, using the polar case as the example.

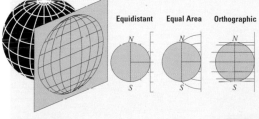

Equidistant   Equal Area   Orthographic   Gnomonic   Stereographic (conformal)

Polar case
The polar case is the simplest to construct and the diagram on the right shows the differing effects of all five methods of construction, comparing their coverage, distortion, etc, using North America as the example.

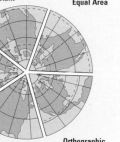

Equidistant   Equal Area
Stereographic
Gnomonic   Orthographic

Oblique case
The plane touches the globe at any point between the Equator and poles. The oblique orthographic uses the distortion in azimuthal projections away from the centre to give a graphic depiction of the Earth as seen from any desired point in space.

Equatorial case
The example shown here is Lambert's Equivalent Azimuthal. It is the only projection which is both equal area and where bearing is true from the centre.

CONICAL PROJECTIONS
These use the projection of the graticule from the globe on to a cone which is tangential to a line of latitude (termed the 'standard parallel'). This line is always an arc and scale is always true along it. Because of its method of construction, it is used mainly for depicting the temperate latitudes around the standard parallel, i.e. where there is least distortion. To reduce the distortion and include a larger range of latitudes, the projection may be constructed with the cone bisecting the surface of the globe so that there are two standard parallels, each of which is true to scale. The distortion is thus spread more evenly between the two chosen parallels.

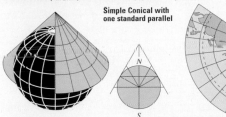
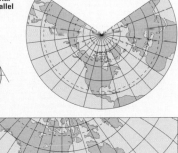

Simple Conical with one standard parallel

Bonne
This is a modification of the simple conic, whereby the true scale along the meridians is sacrificed to enable the accurate representation of areas. However, scale is true along each parallel but shapes are distorted at the edges.

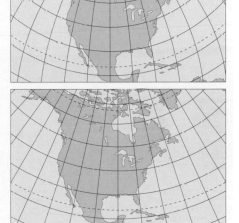

Albers Conical Equal Area
This projection uses two standard parallels. The selection of these relative to the land area to be mapped is very important. It is equal area and is especially useful for large land masses oriented east–west, such as the USA.

CYLINDRICAL AND OTHER WORLD PROJECTIONS
This group of projections are those which permit the whole of the Earth's surface to be depicted on one map. They are a very large group of projections and the following are only a few of them. Cylindrical projections are constructed by the projection of the graticule from the globe on to a cylinder tangential to the globe. Although cylindrical projections can depict all the main land masses, there is considerable distortion of shape and area towards the poles. One cylindrical projection, Mercator, overcomes this shortcoming by possessing the unique navigational property that any straight line drawn on it is a line of constant bearing ('loxodrome'). It is used for maps and charts between 15° either side of the Equator. Beyond this, enlargement of area is a serious drawback, although it is used for navigational charts at all latitudes.

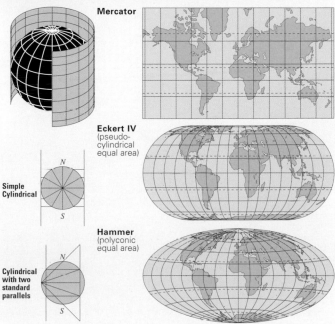

Mercator

Eckert IV (pseudo-cylindrical equal area)

Simple Cylindrical

Cylindrical with two standard parallels

Hammer (polyconic equal area)

The first satellite to monitor our environment systematically was launched as long ago as April 1961. It was called TIROS-1 and was designed specifically to record atmospheric change. The first of the generation of Earth resources satellites was Landsat-1, launched in July 1972. The succeeding decades have seen a revolution in our ability to survey and map our environment. Digital sensors mounted on satellites now scan vast areas of the Earth's surface day and night and at a range of resolutions from 0.3 m to several kms depending on the type of satellite. At any one time, up to 50 satellites may be in orbit. They collect and relay back to Earth huge volumes of geographical data, which is processed and stored by computers.

Satellite imagery and remote sensing

An ability to collect data of large areas at high resolution and the freedom from national access restrictions, have meant that sensors on these satellite platforms are increasingly replacing surface and airborne data-gathering techniques. Twenty-four hours a day, satellites are scanning the Earth's surface and atmosphere, adding to an ever-expanding range of geographic and geophysical data available to help us understand and manage our human and physical environments. Remote sensing is the science of extracting information from such images.

Satellite orbits

Most high resolution Earth-observation satellites are in a near-polar, Sun-synchronous orbit *(see diagram below right)*. At altitudes of between 400–900 km the satellites revolve around the Earth approximately every 100 minutes and on each orbit cross the equator at a similar local (solar) time, usually late morning. This helps ensure the sun is at a high elevation yet atmospheric moisture, which commonly increases throughout the day in warm climates, is relatively low. High resolution sensors can be pointed sideways from the orbital path, resulting in a 1–3 day interval, or 'revisit' time, between imaging opportunities.

Exceptions to these Sun-synchronous orbits include the geostationary meteorological satellites, such as the European Meteosat, American GOES and Russian Elektro satellites. These have an approximate 36,000 km high orbit and rotate around the Earth every 24 hours, thus remaining above the same point on the Equator. These satellites acquire frequent images showing cloud and atmospheric moisture movements for almost a full hemisphere.

In addition, there are constellations of global navigation satellite systems, each comprising 20 – 30 satellites, such as the American Global Positioning System (GPS), Russian GLONASS and, under development, the European Galileo system. These satellites

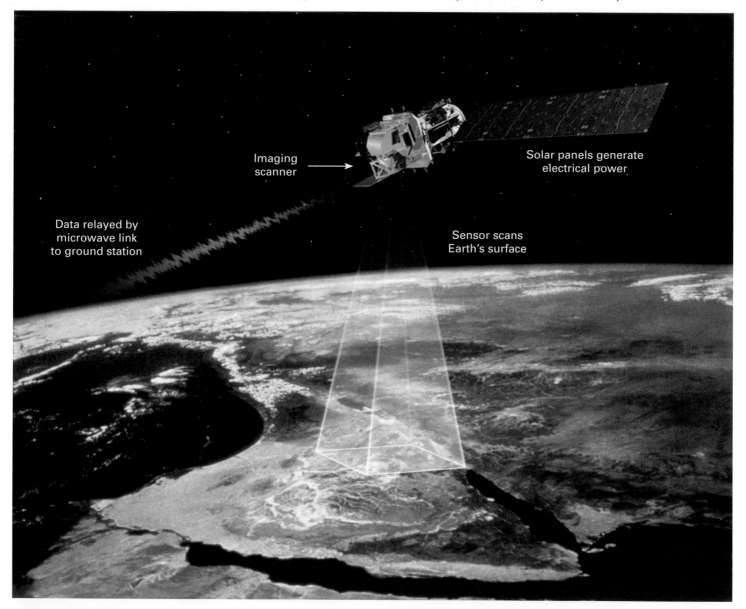

Imaging scanner

Solar panels generate electrical power

Data relayed by microwave link to ground station

Sensor scans Earth's surface

Landsat-8
This is the latest addition to the Landsat Earth-observation satellite programme, orbiting at 710 km above the Earth. With onboard recorders, the satellite can store data until it passes within range of a ground station. Basic geometric and radiometric corrections are then applied before distribution of the imagery to users.

circle the Earth at a height of 20,200 km in different orbital planes, enabling us to fix our position on the Earth's surface to an accuracy of a few centimetres. Although initially developed for military use, these systems now assist everyday life used by smart phones and in-car navigation systems. More precise corrections to location accuracy improves both terrestrial and aerial surveys, aircraft and marine navigation as well as guidance for precision agriculture.

Digital sensors

Early satellite designs involved images being exposed to photographic film and returned to Earth by capsule for processing. However, even the first commercial satellite imagery, from Landsat-1, used digital imaging sensors and transmitted the data back to ground stations (see diagram opposite).

Optical, or passive, sensors record the radiation reflected from the Earth for specific wavebands. Radar, or active, sensors transmit their own microwave radiation, which is reflected from the Earth's surface back to the satellite and recorded. This allows this type of sensor to operate twenty-four hours a day and in all weather. The SAR (Synthetic Aperture Radar) images on page 15 are examples of the latter.

Whichever scanning method is used, each satellite records image data of constant width but potentially several thousand kilometres in length. Once the data has been received on Earth, it may be split into approximately square sections or 'scenes' for distribution or, increasingly, customers provide a polygon of their 'Area of Interest' which is extracted from the full image strip.

Spectral resolution, wavebands and false-colour composites

Satellites can record data from many sections of the electro-magnetic spectrum (wavebands) simultaneously. Since we can only see images made from the three primary colours (red, green and blue), a selection of any three wavebands needs to be made in order to form a picture that will enable visual interpretation of the scene to be made. When any combination other than the visible bands are used, such as near or middle infrared, the resulting image is termed a 'false-colour composite'.
The selection of these wavebands depends on the purpose of the final image – geology, hydrology, agronomy and environmental needs each have their own optimum waveband combinations.

GEOGRAPHIC INFORMATION SYSTEMS

A Geographic Information System (GIS) enables any available geospatial data to be compiled, presented and analysed using specialized computer software.

Many aspects of our lives now benefit from the use of GIS – from the management and maintenance of the networks of pipelines and cables that supply our homes, to the exploitation or protection of the natural resources that we use. Much of this is at a regional or national scale and the data collected from satellites form an important part of our interpretation and understanding of the world around us.

GIS systems are used for many aspects of central planning and modern life, such as defence, land use, reclamation, telecommunications and the deployment of emergency services. Commercial companies can use demographic and infrastructure data within a GIS to plan marketing strategies, identifying where their services would be most needed, and thus decide where best to locate their businesses. Insurance companies use GIS to determine premiums based on population distribution, crime figures and the likelihood of natural disasters, such as flooding or subsidence.

Whatever the application, all the relevant data can be prepared in a GIS so that a user can extract and display the information of particular interest on a map, or compare it with other material in order to help analyse and resolve a specific problem. From analysis of the data that has been acquired, it is often possible to use a GIS to create a computer 'model' of possible future situations and see what impact various actions may have. A GIS can also monitor change over time, aiding the interpretation of long-term trends.

A GIS may also use satellite data to extract useful information and map large areas, which would otherwise take many man-years using other methods. For applications such as hydro-carbon and mineral exploration, forestry, agriculture, environmental monitoring and urban development, these developments have made it possible to undertake projects on a global scale unheard of before.

To find out more about how GIS works and how it affects our lives, why not go the Ordnance Survey's Mapzone website at: http://mapzone.ordnancesurvey.co.uk/mapzone/giszone.html

EXAMPLES OF OPTICAL AND RADAR SATELLITES

OPTICAL SATELLITES

High Resolution (0.3 m–1.5 m resolution): Since 1999

Application:	• Detailed infrastructure mapping • Logistics planning • Environmental mapping

Satellite examples: Ikonos, GeoEye, Worldview-1/2/3, Pleiades, SPOT6

Medium Resolution (1.5 m–10 m): Since 1981

Application:	• Land use / Land cover mapping • Logistics planning • Daily monitoring

Satellite examples: RapidEye, SPOT 1-5, Formosat, Cosmos

Low Resolution (10 m–30 m): Since 1982

Application:	• Regional scale mapping • Environmental mapping

Satellite examples: Landsat, SPOT 1-4, ASTER

RADAR SATELLITES

High Resolution (1 m–3 m resolution): Since 2007

Application:	• Oil slick mapping • Ice mapping • Geology

Satellite examples: Radarsat-2, CosmoSkymed, TerraSAR-X, ALOS-2

Medium Resolution (3 m–10 m): Since 2006

Application:	• Oil slick mapping • Ice mapping • Geology

Satellite examples: Radarsat-2, CosmoSkymed, TerraSAR-X, ALOS-1, ALOS-2, Sentinel-1A

Low Resolution (10 m–30 m): Since 1991

Application:	• Oil slick mapping • Ice mapping • Geology

Satellite examples: ERS-1/2, Envisat, JERS-1

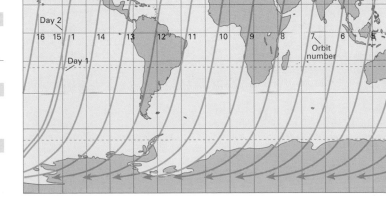

Satellite orbits

Landsat-8 makes over 14 orbits per day in its Sun-synchronous orbit. During the full 16 days of a repeat cycle, coverage of the areas between those shown is achieved.

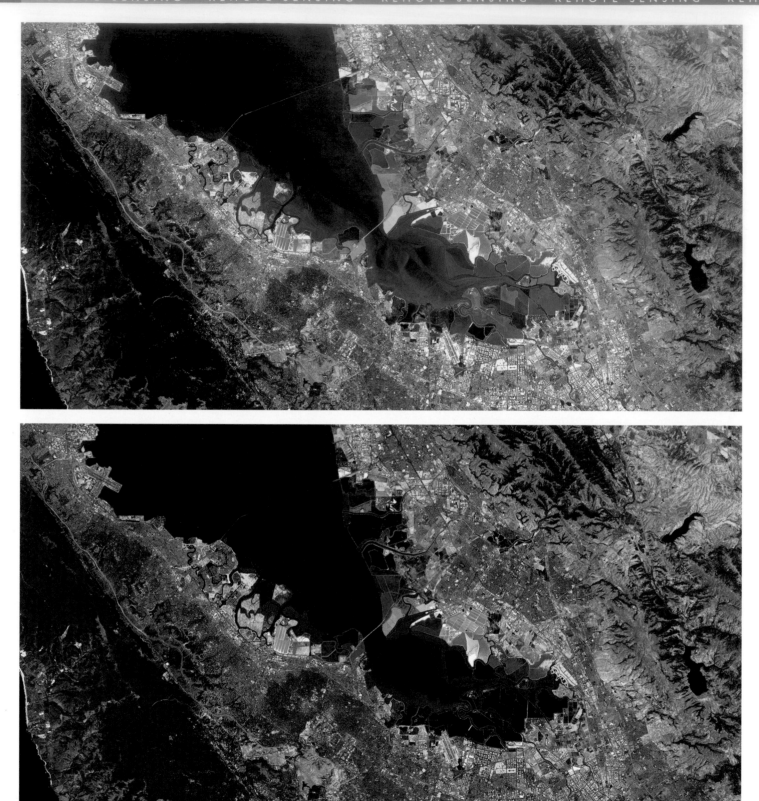

Natural-colour and false-colour composites

These images show the salt ponds at the southern end of San Francisco Bay, which now form the San Francisco Bay National Wildlife Refuge. They demonstrate the difference between 'natural colour' (*top*) and 'false colour' (*bottom*) composites.

The top image is made from visible red, green and blue wavelengths. The colours correspond closely to those one would observe from an aircraft. The salt ponds appear green or orange-red due to the colour of the sediments they contain. The urban areas appear grey and vegetation is either dark green (trees) or light brown (dry grass).

The bottom image is made up of near-infrared, visible red and visible green wavelengths. These wavebands are represented here in red, green and blue, respectively. Since chlorophyll in healthy vegetation strongly reflects near-infrared light, this is clearly visible as red in the image.

False-colour composite imagery is therefore very sensitive to the presence of healthy vegetation. The bottom image thus shows better discrimination between the 'leafy' residential urban areas, such as Palo Alto (south-west of the Bay), and other urban areas by the 'redness' of the trees. The high chlorophyll content of watered urban grass areas shows as bright red, contrasting with the dark red of trees and the brown of natural, dry grass. *(USGS)*

Nishino-shima, Japan

This small volcanic island, in the Ogasawara chain, erupted into the world at the end of 2013 in the western Pacific Ocean some 1,000 km south of Tokyo. This natural-colour image was captured by Landsat 8 in August 2014 and shows the long white plume of volcanic gases. The continuing flowing out of lava on the eastern side of the island makes this a dangerous island to approach until conditions settle. *(NASA)*

Piqiang Fault, China

By recording and processing the amount of energy reflected or emitted from the Earth in different ways, satellite images can help scientists see patterns in land-forms that otherwise might be hard to make out with the naked eye. The colours assigned here clearly show the movement of the bands of sedimentary rocks along the fault line. The land has moved by about 3km along the fault. *(NASA)*

Kazakhstan/China

The startling contrast in land-use across the international border between Kazakstan, to the west, and China, to the east, is made clear in this Landsat 8 image. There is huge pressure on China to extract the maximum agricultural output from any suitable land, even when it requires irrigation. In the corresponding area of Kazakhstan, there is less need for intensive agriculture and therefore no irrigation. *(NASA)*

Niger Delta, West Africa

The River Niger is the third longest river in Africa after the Nile and Congo, and this false-colour image shows the different vegetation types. Deltas are by nature constantly evolving sedimentary features and often contain many ecosystems within them. In the case of the Niger Delta, there are also vast hydrocarbon reserves beneath it with associated wells and pipelines. Satellite imagery helps to plan activity and monitor this fragile and changing environment. *(USGS)*

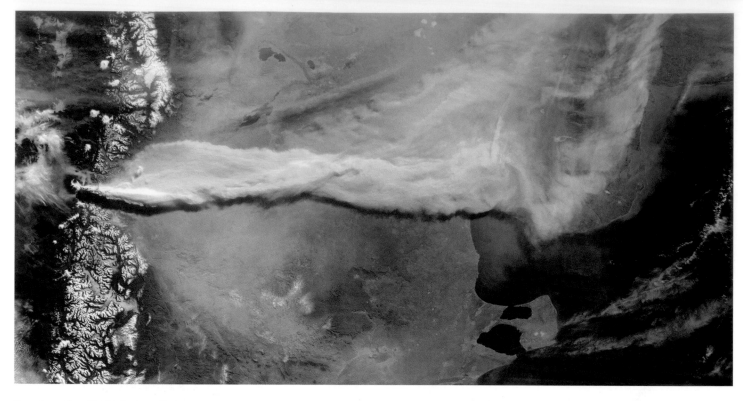

Puyehue-Cordón Volcano, Chile
Part of the ash plume from the June 2011 major eruption from this strato-volcano in the Andes can be seen drifting eastwards at high altitude across the coast of Argentina, to the north of the distinctive shape of the Valdés Peninsula. The ash eventually travelled in the upper atmosphere as far as Australia and New Zealand, causing disruption to commercial flights. *(Jeff Schmaltz, MODIS Rapid Response Team at NASA GSFC)*

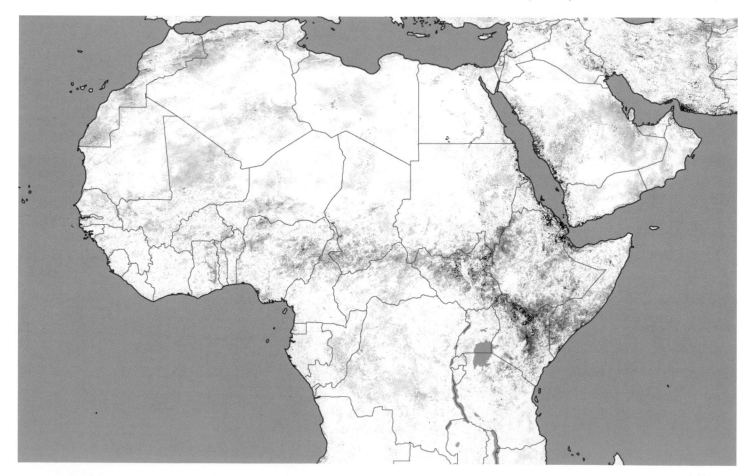

East African drought
The colours on the image represent the 'vegetation anomaly', i.e. the deviation from what would be considered normal growth, between April and June 2011. Brown indicates poor plant growth and highlights the severe drought in Somalia, South Sudan and northern Kenya. *(NASA GIMMS Group at GSFC)*

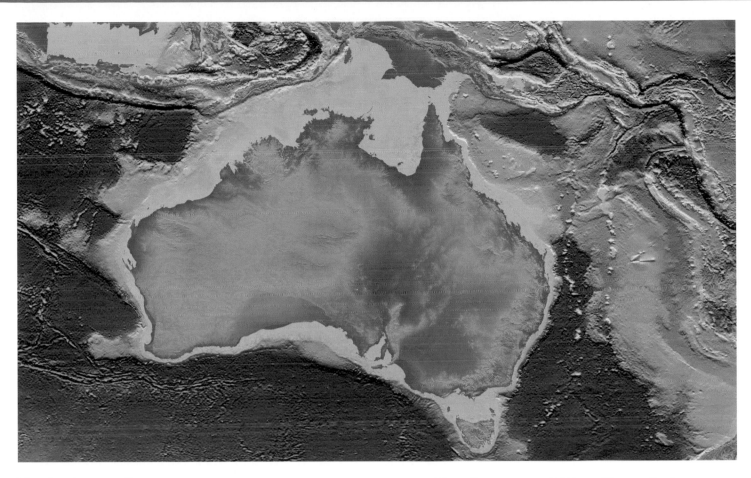

Mapping the ocean floors

The accurate global mapping of whole ocean floors has only been possible since the advent of satellite radar altimetry. From a known orbit, microwave pulses measure the ocean surface. The effects of tides, waves and currents can mathematically be removed from these measurements and the resultant ocean-surface shape reflects that of the ocean floor beneath, due to the gravitational effects of the water over the sea-floor topography. However, for large-scale navigational charts, shipboard echo soundings are still used. (NPA Satellite Mapping, CGG)

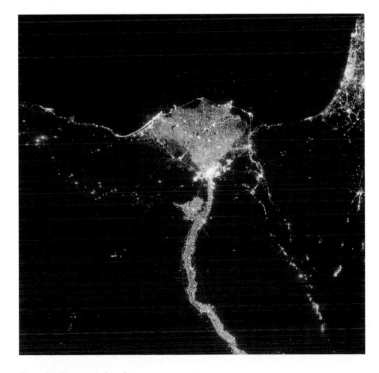

Population monitoring

The most effective way of monitoring human location is to view the lights from settlements. This image shows the towns along the course of the Nile to its delta. It was captured using a visible infrared sensor. (Suomi National Polar-orbiting Partnership)

Typhoon 'Phanfone'

On October 3rd, 2014, this typhoon is seen approaching the southern Japanese island of Kyushu, just visible at the top right of this image. Maximum wind speeds of 204 km per hour were estimated. (Jeff Schmaltz, LANCE/EOSDIS Rapid Response)

Zhugpu, China
On 10 August 2010, after intense monsoon rains, this remote region suffered disastrous flooding, followed by a series of landslides, which together claimed over 1,500 lives. Access to the area was very difficult and satellite imagery helped focus and direct rescue efforts, using scarce resources. *(WorldView-2 courtesy DigitalGlobe)*

Fukushima Nuclear Power Station, Japan
This image was captured by the GeoEye-1 satellite, travelling at 6 km/sec and 680 km above the Earth. In front of the pylons, in the centre of the image, the damaged reactors in the heart of the irradiated area can be seen, following the March 2011 Japanese earthquake and tsunami. It allowed initial assessment of a very dangerous area to take place with minimum risk to human life. *(©DigitalGlobe, Inc. All Rights Reserved)*

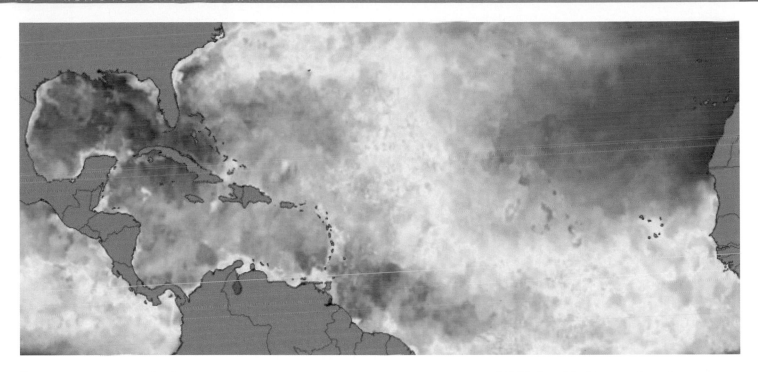

Ocean temperature monitoring

Part of a global dataset, the central Atlantic Ocean from West Africa across to Central America is shown during the hurricane season in Central and North America, in August 2011. The yellow and orange colours indicate surface water temperatures over 27.8°C, the critical temperature above which tropical storms are fuelled and intensified. The powerful Hurricane Irene hit the eastern United States later in the month. (*NASA image created by Jesse Allen, using merged AMSR-E/MODIS data*)

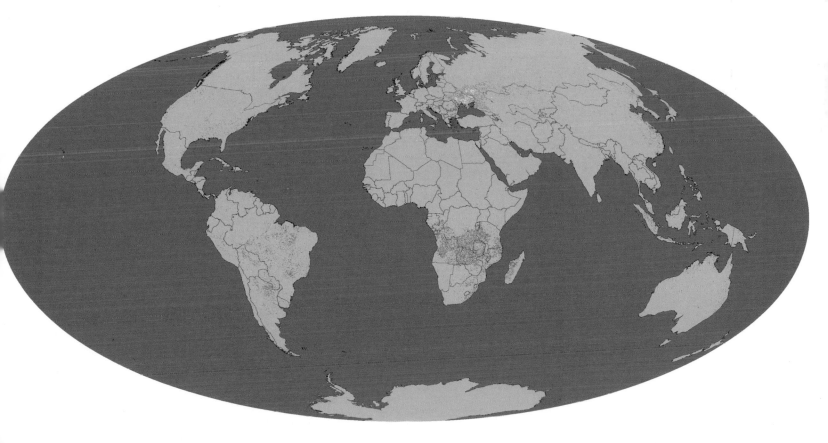

World fires

This image shows all the fires worldwide that were burning during August 2008, whether they were man-made to clear ground for crops, for example, or occurred naturally from, say, lightning strikes. The orange tint indicates where fires are at their fiercest. Over any given year the areas affected by the fires move with the seasons, February being the month with most fires in the tropics. Acquiring this data from satellites allows efficient management of scarce resources in remote and environmentally threatened areas. (*NASA image by Reto Stockli and Jesse Allen using data courtesy of the MODIS Land Science Team at NASA GSFC*)

Sichuan Basin, China

The north-east/south-west trending ridges in this image are anticlinal folds developed in the Earth's crust as a result of plate collision and compression. Geologists map these folds and the lowlands between them formed by synclinal folds, as they are often the areas where oil or gas are found in commercial quantities. The river shown in this image is the Yangtse, near Chongqing. *(China RSGS)*

Pingualuit Crater, Canada

The circular feature is a meteorite crater in the Ungava Peninsula, Québec, formed by an impact over 1.4 million years ago. It is 3.4 km wide and 264 m deep. The lake within has no link to any water sources and has been formed only by rain and snow. Thus the water is among the world's clearest and least saline. Sediments in the lake have been unaffected by ice sheets and are important for scientific research. *(NPA Satellite Mapping, CGG)*

Wadi Hadramaut, Yemen

Yemen is extremely arid – however, in the past it was more humid and wet, enabling large river systems to carve out the deep and spectacular gorges and dried-out river beds (*wadis*) seen in this image. The erosion has revealed many contrasting rock types. The image has been processed to exaggerate this effect, producing many shades of red, pink and purple, which make geological mapping easier and more cost-effective. *(USGS)*

Zagros Mountains, Iran

These mountains were formed as Arabia collided with Southern Eurasia. The upper half of this colour-enhanced image shows an anticline that runs east–west. The dark grey features are called diapirs, which are bodies of viscous rock salt that are very buoyant and sometimes rise to the surface, spilling and spreading out like a glacier. The presence of salt in the region is important as it stops oil escaping to the surface. *(USGS)*

Pollution monitoring

In April 2010, an explosion and subsequent fire occurred on the oil rig 'Deepwater Horizon'. The accident resulted in the deaths of 11 workers and caused a massive, uncontrolled oil release into the Gulf of Mexico. The oil flow was finally stopped on the 15th July 2010, with an estimated 4.9 million barrels discharged into the local environment.

The slick produced was so large, remote sensing was the only viable method to measure its true extent. When oil slicks on the sea, it dampens small surface waves which allow it to be distinguished from the surrounding rougher surface.

The image shown here is a Envisat SAR (Synthetic Aperature Radar) scene from the European Space Agency, acquired 6 days after the explosion. The Mississippi Delta can be seen extending into the Gulf of Mexico towards the centre of the image. The oil slick is the large dark feature to the east of the delta. *(ESA)*

Environmental monitoring

Synthetic Aperture Radar (SAR) uses microwaves to penetrate cloud and needs no solar illumination, so is ideal for monitoring remote and difficult areas. In the middle of this image the David Glacier in Antarctica is seen flowing to the sea. Here it floats onwards and is known as the Drygalski Ice Tongue. At its end, a tabular iceberg is breaking off, or 'calving', whilst to the right is part of a 120 km long iceberg that almost collided with it. *(ESA)*

West India Docks, 1983

This vertical image shows the derelict site of the West India Docks, which were built between 1802 and 1870, as part of the London Docks which eventually stretched from Tower Bridge downstream to Beckton in the east.

The most successful year for the London Docks, in terms of tonnage handled, was 1961. However, by the 1970s they could no longer compete with coastal ports due to the containerisation of cargo and increased size of ships. This resulted in their rapid closure, consequent high unemployment and the economic decline in the area.

By 1981 the docks had closed. These images were taken as part of an aerial survey for the London Docklands Development Corporation, a new government Enterprise Zone covering all of the London Docks. Planning regulations were relaxed, transport infrastructure (the Docklands Light Railway) was constructed and financial incentives offered to attract businesses and property developers.

In this mosaic, made up of eight separate images and taken in 1983, the three docks making up the West India group can be seen. In the south dock empty Thames lighters, once used to move cargo from larger ships, are still visible. The warehouse at the western end of the middle spur was called 'Canary Wharf', where ships from the Canary Islands unloaded cargo, principally bananas and tomatoes. The name was subsequently adopted for the whole area. The building in the northeast corner, with the visible external roof supports, is Billingsgate Fish Market which moved from the City of London into this new building in 1982.

Aerial surveys from aircraft are still used by organisations such as the Ordnance Survey since they are efficient for large areas, provide higher resolution imagery than satellites and can be more flexible in areas such as the UK, where cloud cover often limits imaging opportunities. *(©Tower Hamlets Local History Library and Archives)*

Canary Wharf, 2014

Regeneration of the West India Docks site started in 1988. The whole 39 hectare area was renamed 'Canary Wharf' by the developers. The rapid construction of buildings such as One Canada Square (Canary Wharf Tower, the highest building in the area), and the extension of the Jubilee tube line from Green Park to Stratford attracted many companies to relocate from the City of London and elsewhere.

The satellite image, dating from 2014, shows how much the area has been developed. Over 100,000 people now work there, primarily in the financial and insurance sectors. To support these businesses, many others work in IT, retail and the legal profession.

Very little of what can be seen in the top image, in 1983, is visible here, with the newer buildings being constructed over parts of the North Dock. Billingsgate still occupies its place and is still London's fish market, most of its produce arriving by road from all over the country. In the northwest, the roofs of a group of the original former warehouses can be seen in both images. These are the earliest buildings on the site, dating from the early nineteenth century, and now partially house the Museum of London Docklands. The long shadows cast by the new buildings show how high they are.

Future developments include the planned opening of Crossrail in 2018 and the construction of more residential property, to the east of the main business centre, as well as the further commercial development of high-rise offices.

Satellite imagery is most useful for mapping areas in remote or inaccessible areas of the world, particularly where cloud cover is not too persistent. The ability to revisit and monitor small sites without the high cost of aircraft mobilisation is another benefit. *(NPA Satellite Mapping, CGG)*

1:1 000 000

COPYRIGHT PHILIP'S

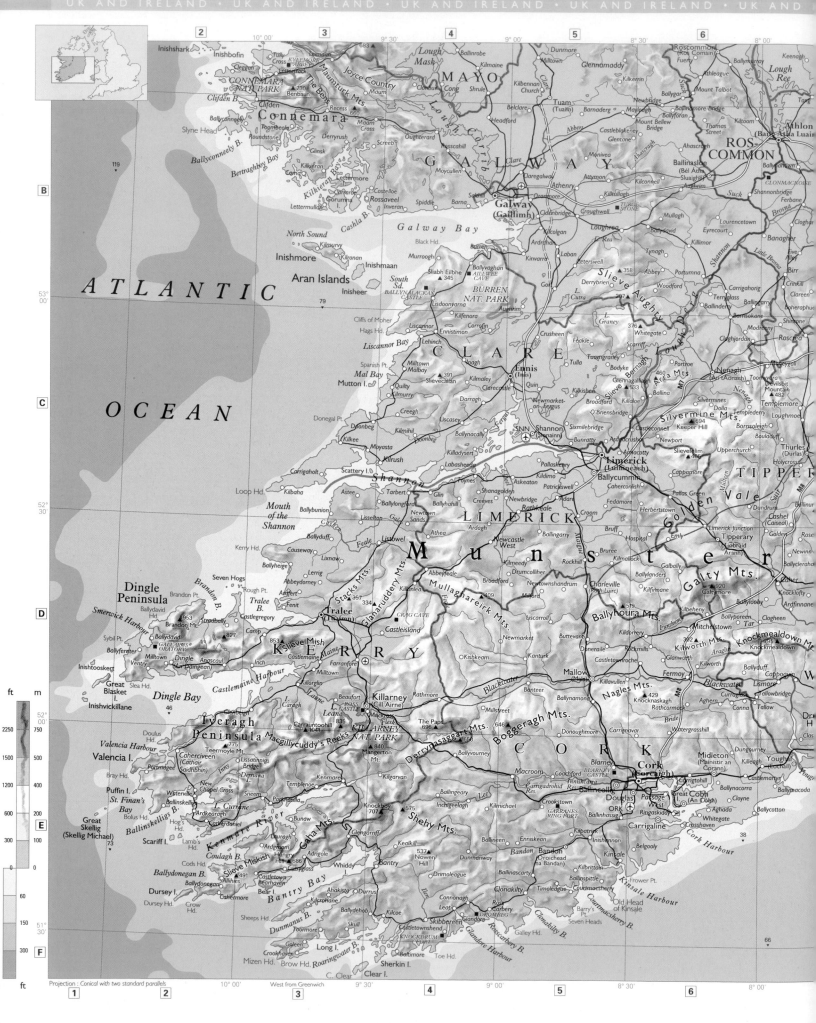

ATLANTIC

OCEAN

Projection : Conical with two standard parallels

West from Greenwich

1:1 000 000

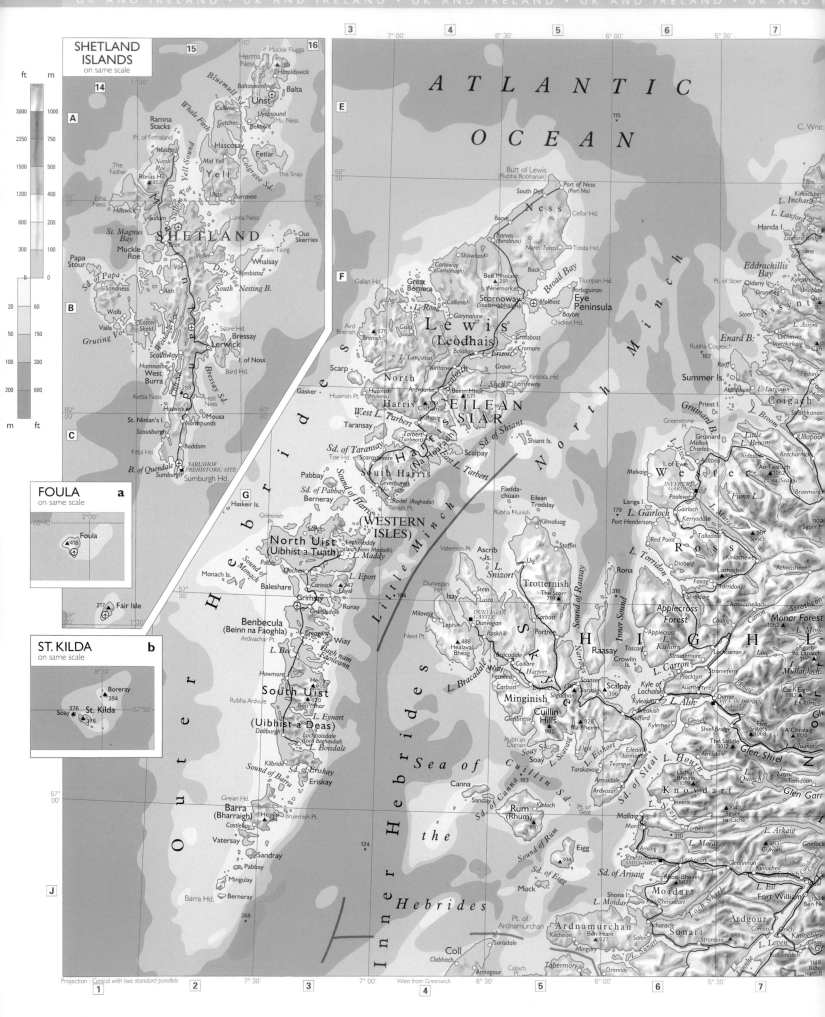

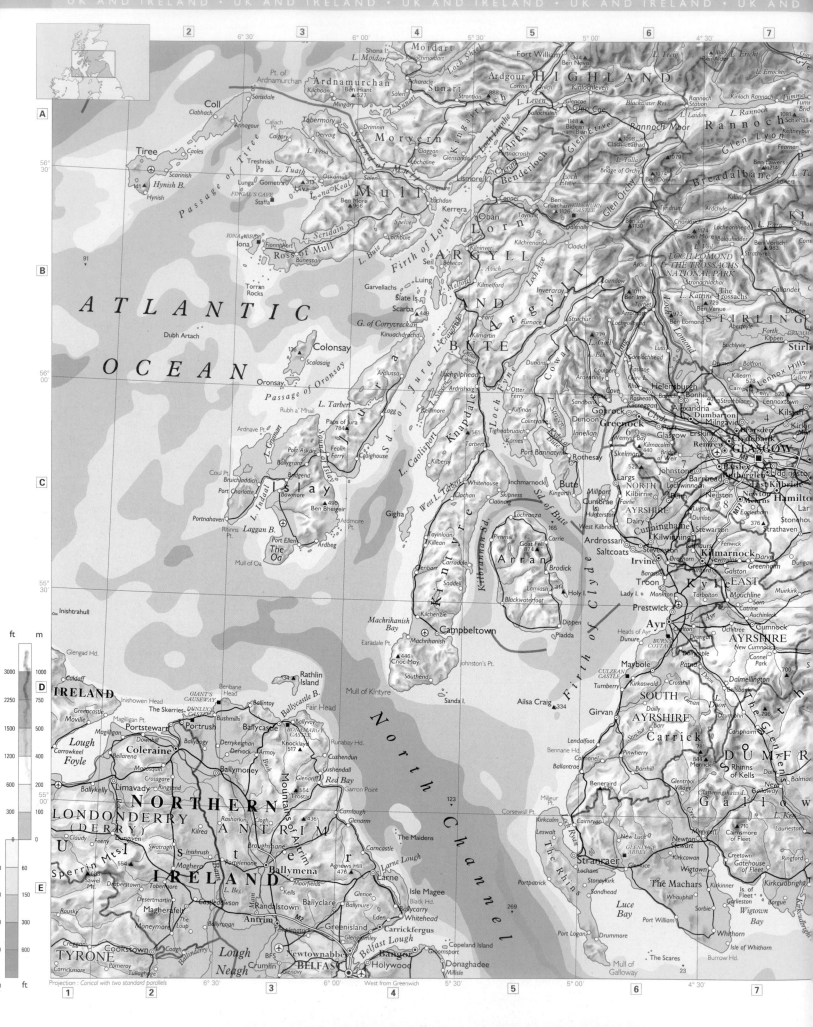

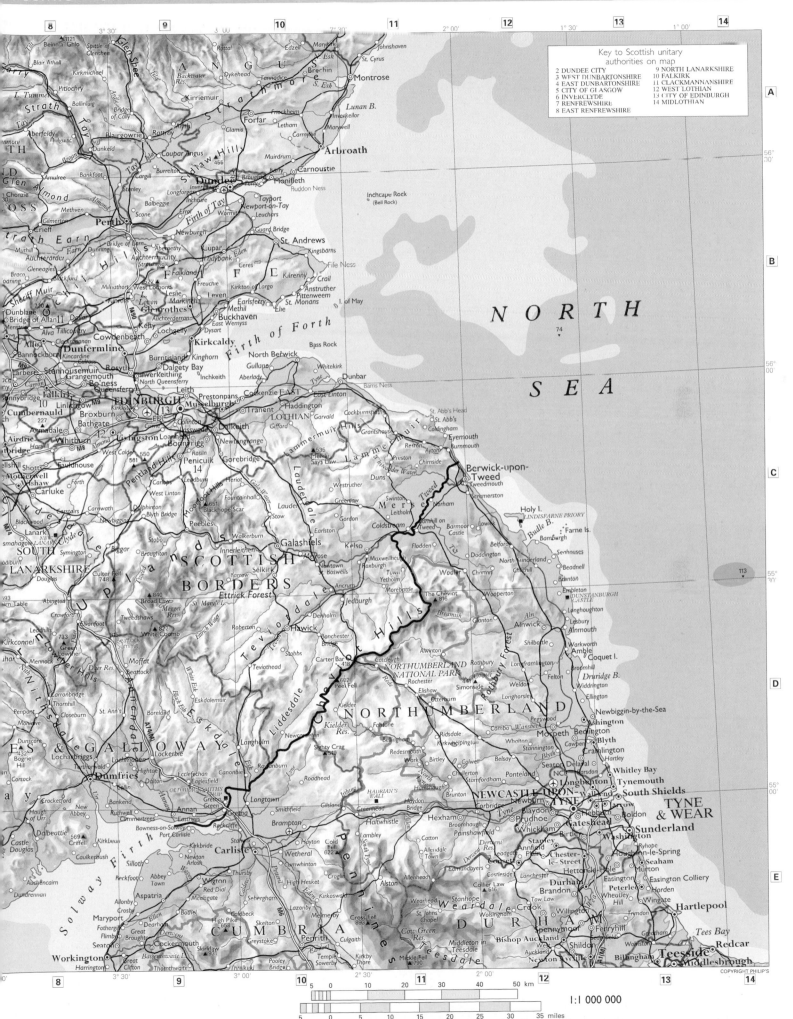

Key to Scottish unitary
authorities on map
2 DUNDEE CITY
3 WEST DUNBARTONSHIRE
4 EAST DUNBARTONSHIRE
5 CITY OF GLASGOW
6 INVERCLYDE
7 RENFREWSHIRE
8 EAST RENFREWSHIRE
9 NORTH LANARKSHIRE
10 FALKIRK
11 CLACKMANNANSHIRE
12 WEST LOTHIAN
13 CITY OF EDINBURGH
14 MIDLOTHIAN

NORTH SEA

COPYRIGHT PHILIP'S

1:1 000 000

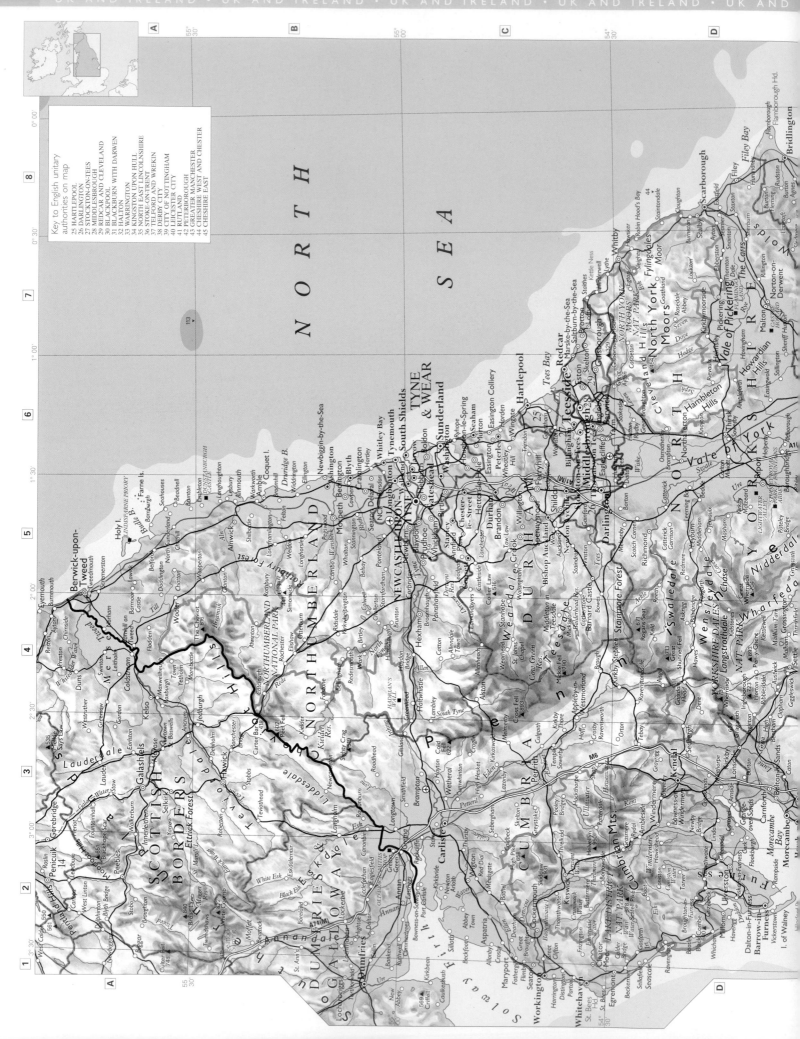

Key to English unitary
authorities on map
25 HARTLEPOOL
26 DARLINGTON
27 STOCKTON-ON-TEES
28 MIDDLESBROUGH
29 REDCAR AND CLEVELAND
30 BLACKPOOL
31 BLACKBURN WITH DARWEN
32 HALTON
33 WARRINGTON
34 KINGSTON UPON HULL
35 NORTH EAST LINCOLNSHIRE
36 STOKE-ON-TRENT
37 TELFORD AND WREKIN
38 DERBY CITY
39 CITY OF NOTTINGHAM
40 LEICESTER CITY
41 RUTLAND
42 PETERBOROUGH
43 GREATER MANCHESTER
44 CHESHIRE WEST AND CHESTER
45 CHESHIRE EAST

NORTH SEA

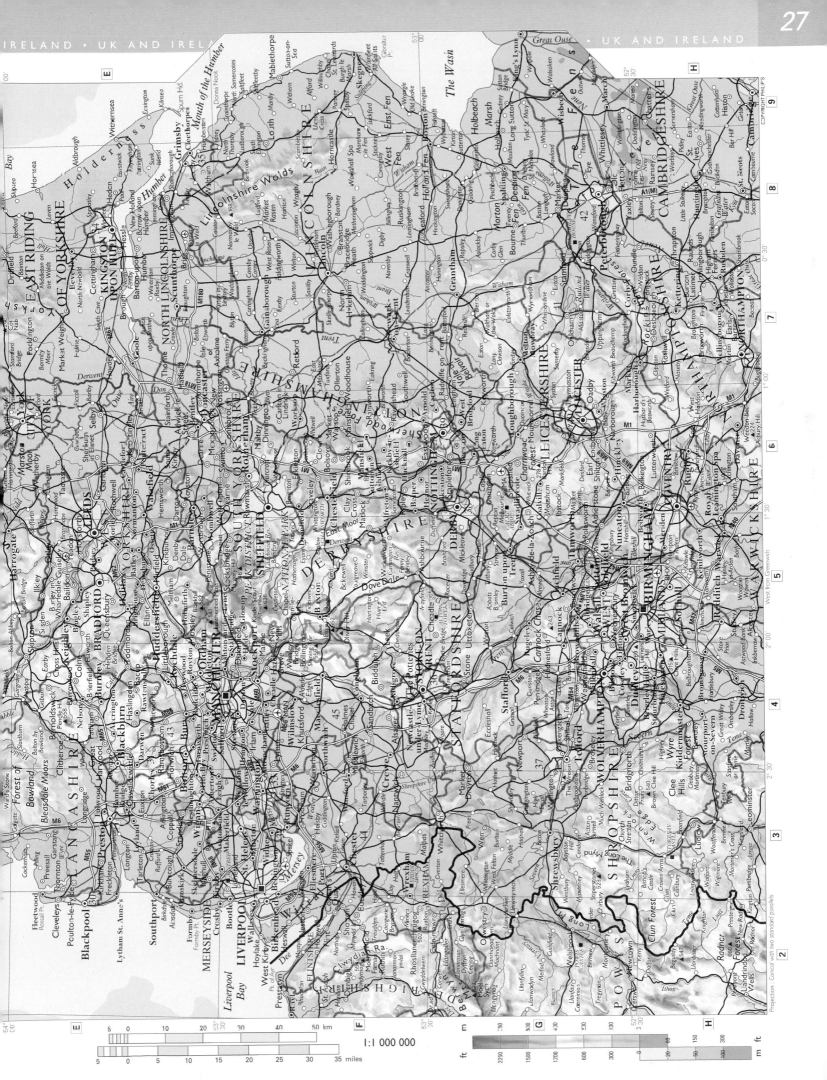

1:1 000 000

Projection · Conical with two standard parallels

CHANNEL ISLANDS
on same scale

FRANCE

Passage de la Déroute

Jersey

Guernsey

Alderney

Sark

CHANNEL ISLANDS

ISLES OF SCILLY
on same scale

Isles of Scilly

Tresco   St. Martin's
Hugh Town St. Mary's
Bryher   Crow Sound
            St. Mary's Sd.
St. Agnes

Key to Welsh unitary
authorities on map
15 SWANSEA
16 NEATH PORT TALBOT
17 BRIDGEND
18 RHONDDA CYNON TAFF
19 MERTHYR TYDFIL
20 CAERPHILLY
21 BLAENAU GWENT
22 TORFAEN
23 CARDIFF
24 NEWPORT

Key to English unitary
authorities on map
32 HALTON
33 WARRINGTON
37 TELFORD AND WREKIN
45 NORTH SOMERSET
46 CITY OF BRISTOL
47 BATH AND NORTH EAST SOMERSET
57 PLYMOUTH
58 TORBAY
59 CHESHIRE WEST AND CHESTER
60 CHESHIRE EAST

Projection: Conical with two standard parallels

COPYRIGHT PHILIP'S

West from Greenwich

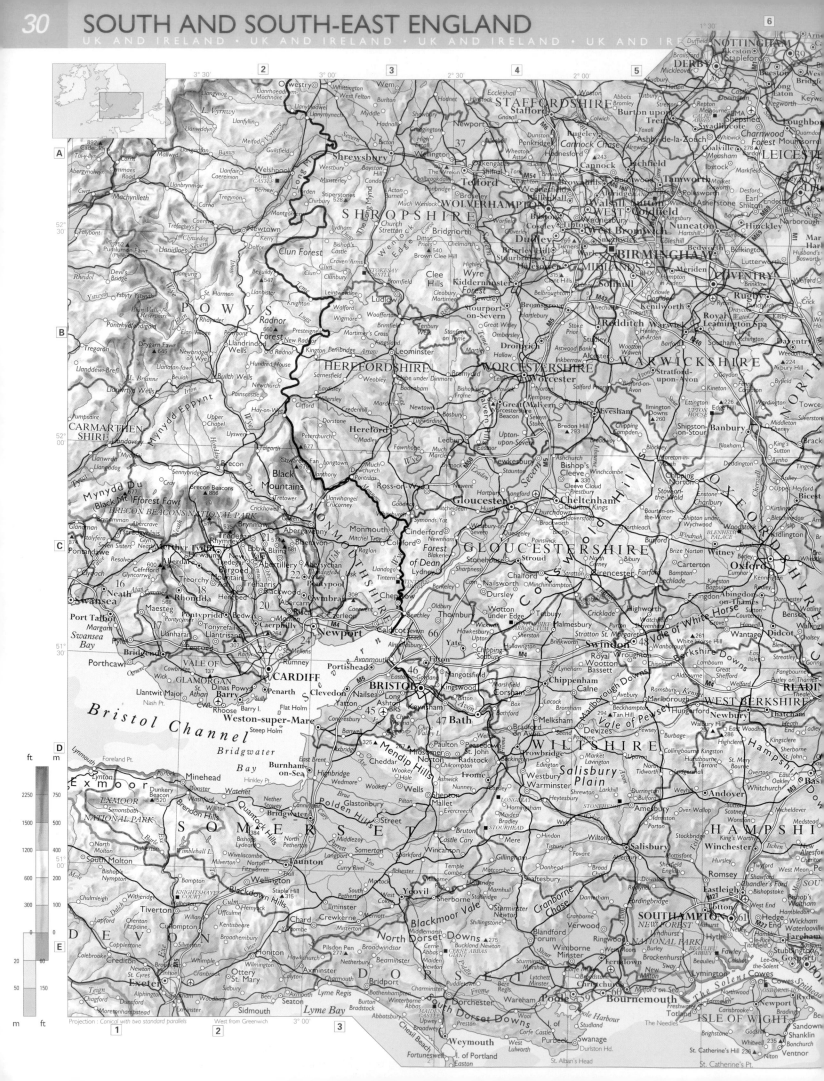

Key to English unitary
authorities on map
37 TELFORD AND WREKIN
38 DERBY CITY
39 CITY OF NOTTINGHAM
40 LEICESTER CITY
41 RUTLAND
42 PETERBOROUGH
43 MILTON KEYNES
44 LUTON
45 NORTH SOMERSET
46 CITY OF BRISTOL
47 BATH AND NORTH EAST SOMERSET
48 SWINDON
49 READING
50 WOKINGHAM
51 WINDSOR AND MAIDENHEAD
52 SLOUGH
53 BRACKNELL FOREST
54 THURROCK
55 SOUTHEND-ON-SEA
56 MEDWAY
59 POOLE
60 BOURNEMOUTH
61 SOUTHAMPTON
62 PORTSMOUTH
63 BRIGHTON AND HOVE
64 BEDFORD
65 CENTRAL BEDFORDSHIRE
66 SOUTH GLOUCESTERSHIRE

Key to Welsh unitary
authorities on map
16 NEATH PORT TALBOT
17 BRIDGEND
18 RHONDDA CYNON TAFF
19 MERTHYR TYDFIL
20 CAERPHILLY
21 BLAENAU GWENT
22 TORFAEN
23 CARDIFF
24 NEWPORT

1:1 000 000

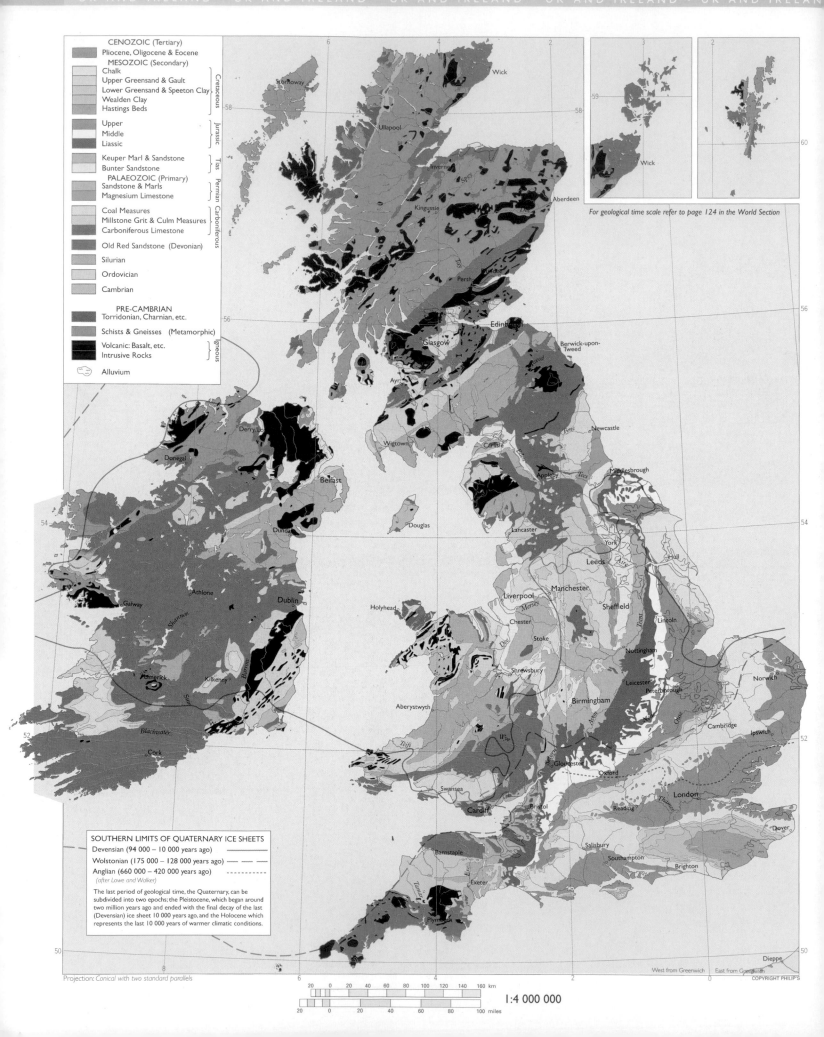

CENOZOIC (Tertiary)
Pliocene, Oligocene & Eocene

MESOZOIC (Secondary)
Chalk — Cretaceous
Upper Greensand & Gault
Lower Greensand & Speeton Clay
Wealden Clay
Hastings Beds

Upper — Jurassic
Middle
Liassic

Keuper Marl & Sandstone — Trias
Bunter Sandstone

PALAEOZOIC (Primary)
Sandstone & Marls — Permian
Magnesium Limestone

Coal Measures — Carboniferous
Millstone Grit & Culm Measures
Carboniferous Limestone

Old Red Sandstone (Devonian)

Silurian

Ordovician

Cambrian

PRE-CAMBRIAN
Torridonian, Charnian, etc.

Schists & Gneisses (Metamorphic)

Volcanic: Basalt, etc. — Igneous
Intrusive Rocks

Alluvium

For geological time scale refer to page 124 in the World Section

SOUTHERN LIMITS OF QUATERNARY ICE SHEETS
Devensian (94 000 – 10 000 years ago) ————
Wolstonian (175 000 – 128 000 years ago) — — —
Anglian (660 000 – 420 000 years ago) ·········
(after Lowe and Walker)

The last period of geological time, the Quaternary, can be subdivided into two epochs; the Pleistocene, which began around two million years ago and ended with the final decay of the last (Devensian) ice sheet 10 000 years ago, and the Holocene which represents the last 10 000 years of warmer climatic conditions.

Projection: Conical with two standard parallels

West from Greenwich   East from Greenwich

COPYRIGHT PHILIP'S

1:4 000 000

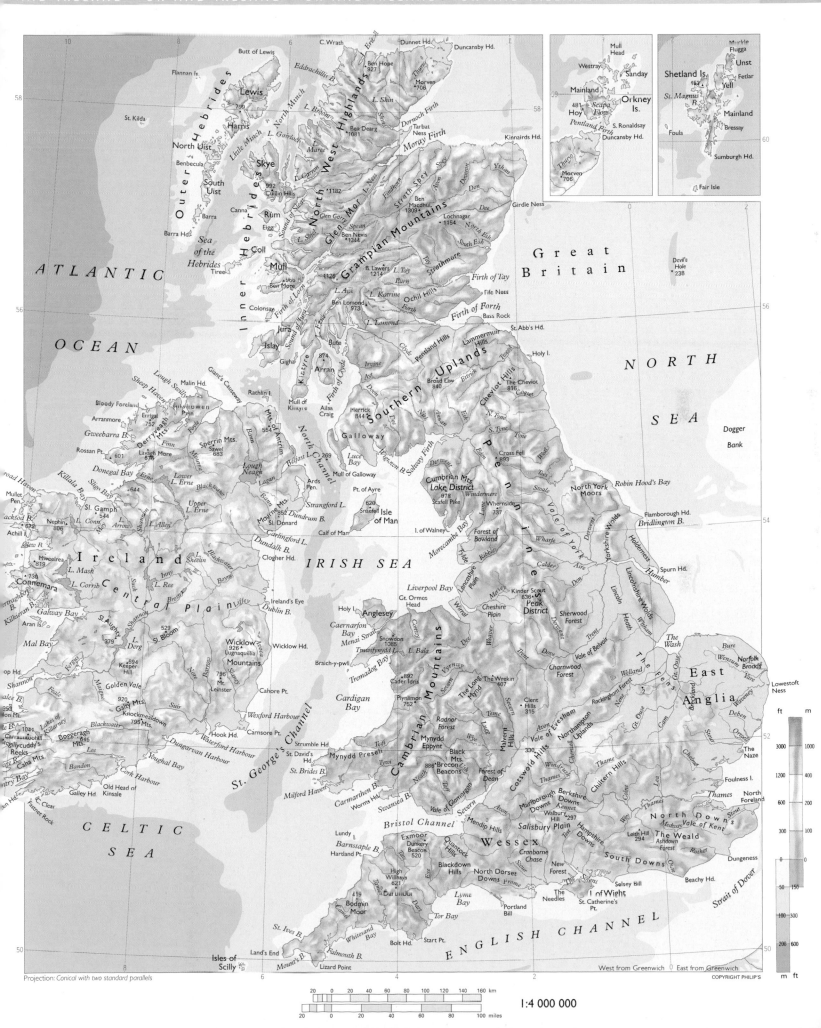

Projection: Conical with two standard parallels

1:4 000 000

COPYRIGHT PHILIP'S

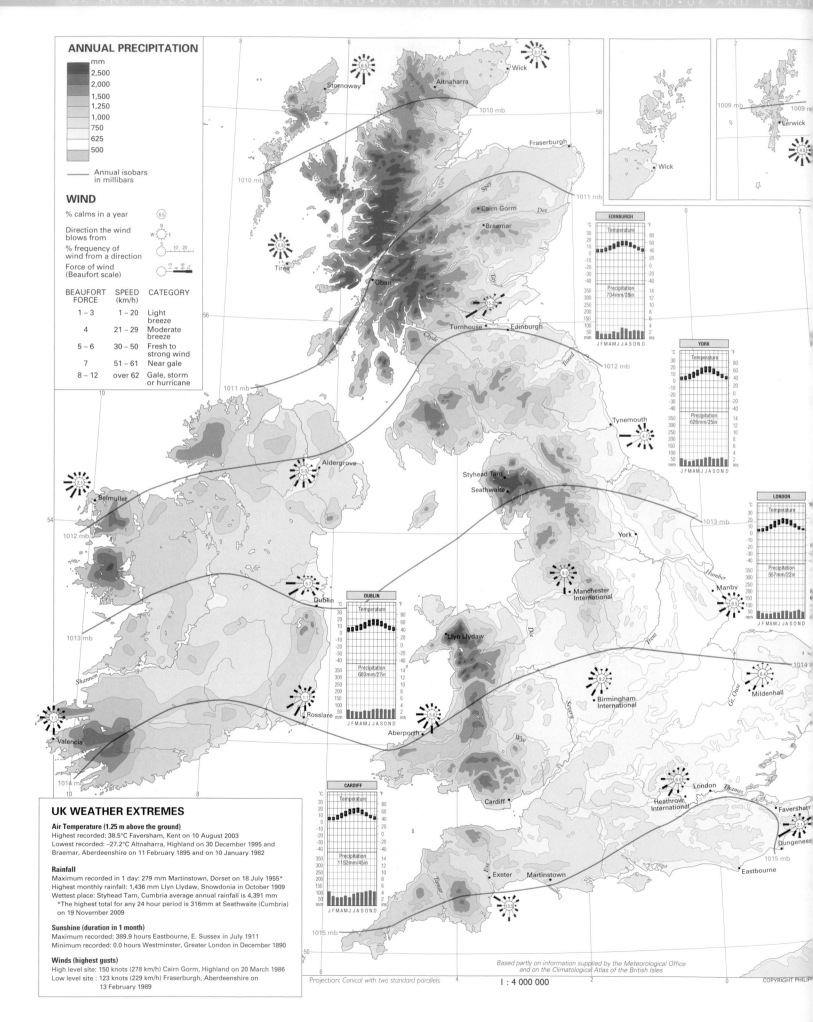

ANNUAL PRECIPITATION

mm
2,500
2,000
1,500
1,250
1,000
750
625
500

—— Annual isobars in millibars

WIND

% calms in a year

Direction the wind blows from

% frequency of wind from a direction

Force of wind (Beaufort scale)

BEAUFORT FORCE	SPEED (km/h)	CATEGORY
1 – 3	1 – 20	Light breeze
4	21 – 29	Moderate breeze
5 – 6	30 – 50	Fresh to strong wind
7	51 – 61	Near gale
8 – 12	over 62	Gale, storm or hurricane

UK WEATHER EXTREMES

Air Temperature (1.25 m above the ground)
Highest recorded: 38.5°C Faversham, Kent on 10 August 2003
Lowest recorded: –27.2°C Altnaharra, Highland on 30 December 1995 and Braemar, Aberdeenshire on 11 February 1895 and on 10 January 1982

Rainfall
Maximum recorded in 1 day: 279 mm Martinstown, Dorset on 18 July 1955*
Highest monthly rainfall: 1,436 mm Llyn Llydaw, Snowdonia in October 1909
Wettest place: Styhead Tarn, Cumbria average annual rainfall is 4,391 mm
  *The highest total for any 24 hour period is 316mm at Seathwaite (Cumbria) on 19 November 2009

Sunshine (duration in 1 month)
Maximum recorded: 389.9 hours Eastbourne, E. Sussex in July 1911
Minimum recorded: 0.0 hours Westminster, Greater London in December 1890

Winds (highest gusts)
High level site: 150 knots (278 km/h) Cairn Gorm, Highland on 20 March 1986
Low level site: 123 knots (229 km/h) Fraserburgh, Aberdeenshire on 13 February 1989

Projection: Conical with two standard parallels

Based partly on information supplied by the Meteorological Office and on the Climatological Atlas of the British Isles

1 : 4 000 000

COPYRIGHT PHILIP'S

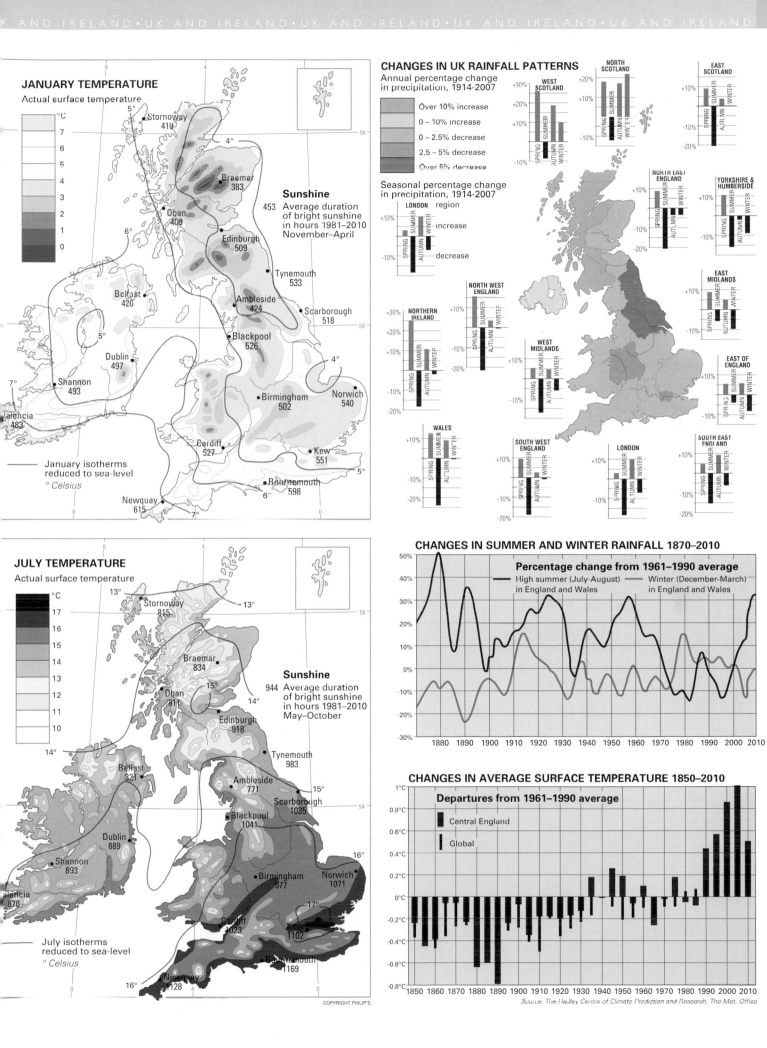

JANUARY TEMPERATURE
Actual surface temperature

°C
7
6
5
4
3
2
1
0

Stornoway 410
Braemar 383
Oban 408
Edinburgh 509
Tynemouth 533
Belfast 420
Ambleside 424
Scarborough 518
Blackpool 526
Dublin 497
Shannon 493
Valencia 483
Birmingham 502
Norwich 540
Cardiff 527
Kew 551
Bournemouth 598
Newquay 615

Sunshine
453 Average duration of bright sunshine in hours 1981–2010 November–April

— January isotherms reduced to sea-level
° Celsius

JULY TEMPERATURE
Actual surface temperature

°C
17
16
15
14
13
12
11
10

Stornoway 815
Braemar 834
Oban 811
Edinburgh 918
Tynemouth 983
Belfast 821
Ambleside 771
Scarborough 1035
Blackpool 1041
Dublin 889
Shannon 893
Valencia 878
Birmingham 1077
Norwich 1071
Cardiff 1023
Kew 1102
Bournemouth 1169
Newquay 1128

Sunshine
944 Average duration of bright sunshine in hours 1981–2010 May–October

— July isotherms reduced to sea-level
° Celsius

COPYRIGHT PHILIP'S

CHANGES IN UK RAINFALL PATTERNS
Annual percentage change in precipitation, 1914–2007

Over 10% increase
0 – 10% increase
0 – 2.5% decrease
2.5 – 5% decrease
Over 5% decrease

Seasonal percentage change in precipitation, 1914–2007
region
increase
decrease

WEST SCOTLAND
NORTH SCOTLAND
EAST SCOTLAND
LONDON
NORTH EAST ENGLAND
YORKSHIRE & HUMBERSIDE
NORTHERN IRELAND
NORTH WEST ENGLAND
WEST MIDLANDS
EAST MIDLANDS
EAST OF ENGLAND
WALES
SOUTH WEST ENGLAND
LONDON
SOUTH EAST ENGLAND

CHANGES IN SUMMER AND WINTER RAINFALL 1870–2010
Percentage change from 1961–1990 average
— High summer (July–August) in England and Wales
— Winter (December–March) in England and Wales

CHANGES IN AVERAGE SURFACE TEMPERATURE 1850–2010
Departures from 1961–1990 average
Central England
Global

Source: The Hadley Centre of Climate Prediction and Research, The Met. Office

WATER SUPPLY

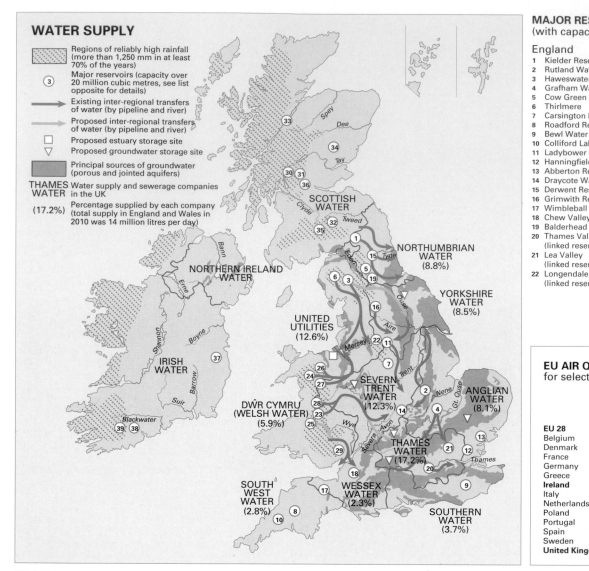

Regions of reliably high rainfall (more than 1,250 mm in at least 70% of the years)

③ Major reservoirs (capacity over 20 million cubic metres, see list opposite for details)

Existing inter-regional transfers of water (by pipeline and river)

Proposed inter-regional transfers of water (by pipeline and river)

□ Proposed estuary storage site

▽ Proposed groundwater storage site

Principal sources of groundwater (porous and jointed aquifers)

THAMES WATER Water supply and sewerage companies in the UK

(17.2%) Percentage supplied by each company (total supply in England and Wales in 2010 was 14 million litres per day)

MAJOR RESERVOIRS
(with capacity in million m³)

England

1	Kielder Reservoir	198
2	Rutland Water	123
3	Haweswater	85
4	Grafham Water	59
5	Cow Green Reservoir	41
6	Thirlmere	41
7	Carsington Reservoir	36
8	Roadford Reservoir	35
9	Bewl Water Reservoir	31
10	Colliford Lake	29
11	Ladybower Reservoir	28
12	Hanningfield Reservoir	27
13	Abberton Reservoir	25
14	Draycote Water	23
15	Derwent Reservoir	22
16	Grimwith Reservoir	22
17	Wimbleball Lake	21
18	Chew Valley Lake	20
19	Balderhead Reservoir	20
20	Thames Valley (linked reservoirs)	
21	Lea Valley (linked reservoirs)	
22	Longendale (linked reservoirs)	

Wales

23	Elan Valley	
24	Llyn Celyn	
25	Llyn Brianne	
26	Llyn Brenig	
27	Llyn Vyrnwy	
28	Llyn Clywedog	
29	Llandegfedd Reservoir	

Scotland

30	Loch Lomond	
31	Loch Katrine	
32	Megget Reservoir	
33	Loch Ness	
34	Blackwater Reservoir	
35	Daer Reservoir	
36	Carron Valley Reservoir	

Ireland

37	Poulaphouca Reservoir	16
38	Inishcarra Reservoir	8
39	Carrigadrohid Reservoir	3

EU AIR QUALITY Greenhouse gas emissions for selected EU countries 2012

	million tonnes of CO2 equivalent 2012	Share of total EU 28 emissions 2012
EU 28	**4,544.2**	**100%**
Belgium	116.5	2.6%
Denmark	51.6	1.1%
France	490.1	10.8%
Germany	939.1	20.7%
Greece	111.0	2.4%
Ireland	**58.5**	**1.3%**
Italy	460.1	10.1%
Netherlands	191.7	4.2%
Poland	399.3	8.8%
Portugal	68.8	1.5%
Spain	340.8	7.5%
Sweden	57.6	1.3%
United Kingdom	**580.8**	**12.8%**

WASTE RECYCLING
The percentage of total household waste recycled in 2013

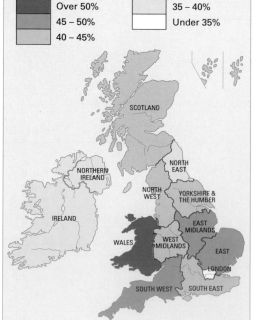

- Over 50%
- 45 – 50%
- 40 – 45%
- 35 – 40%
- Under 35%

JOURNEY TO SCHOOL IN THE UK
Mode of travel to school by children aged 5–16 in 2012

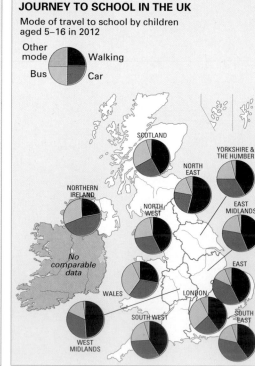

Other mode — Walking
Bus — Car

FLOOD RISK IN ENGLAND AND WALES

■ Areas at greatest risk from flooding (as designated by the Environment Agency)

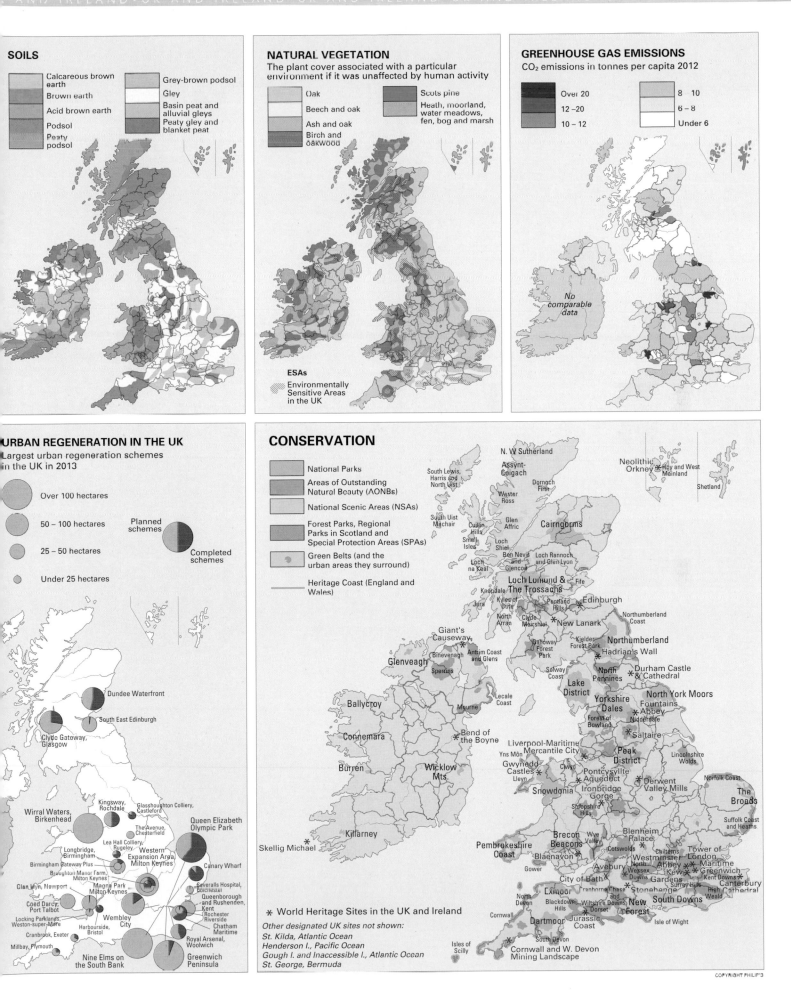

SOILS

- Calcareous brown earth
- Brown earth
- Acid brown earth
- Podsol
- Peaty podsol
- Grey-brown podsol
- Gley
- Basin peat and alluvial gleys
- Peaty gley and blanket peat

NATURAL VEGETATION

The plant cover associated with a particular environment if it was unaffected by human activity

- Oak
- Beech and oak
- Ash and oak
- Birch and oakwood
- Scots pine
- Heath, moorland, water meadows, fen, bog and marsh

ESAs Environmentally Sensitive Areas in the UK

GREENHOUSE GAS EMISSIONS

CO$_2$ emissions in tonnes per capita 2012

- Over 20
- 12–20
- 10–12
- 8–10
- 6–8
- Under 6

No comparable data

URBAN REGENERATION IN THE UK

Largest urban regeneration schemes in the UK in 2013

- Over 100 hectares
- 50–100 hectares
- 25–50 hectares
- Under 25 hectares
- Planned schemes
- Completed schemes

Dundee Waterfront, South East Edinburgh, Clyde Gateway Glasgow, Kingsway Rochdale, Glasshoughton Colliery Castleford, The Avenue Chesterfield, Lea Hall Colliery Rugeley, Queen Elizabeth Olympic Park, Canary Wharf, Longbridge Birmingham, Birmingham Gateway Plus, Western Expansion Area Milton Keynes, Broughton Manor Farm Milton Keynes, Magna Park Milton Keynes, Glan Llyn Newport, Coed Darcy Port Talbot, Locking Parklands Weston-super-Mare, Wembley City, Harbourside Bristol, Cranbrook Exeter, Millbay Plymouth, Nine Elms on the South Bank, Greenwich Peninsula, Royal Arsenal Woolwich, Chatham Maritime, Rochester Riverside, Queenborough and Rushenden Kent, Severalls Hospital Colchester, Wirral Waters Birkenhead

CONSERVATION

- National Parks
- Areas of Outstanding Natural Beauty (AONBs)
- National Scenic Areas (NSAs)
- Forest Parks, Regional Parks in Scotland and Special Protection Areas (SPAs)
- Green Belts (and the urban areas they surround)
- Heritage Coast (England and Wales)

✳ World Heritage Sites in the UK and Ireland

Other designated UK sites not shown:
St. Kilda, Atlantic Ocean
Henderson I., Pacific Ocean
Gough I. and Inaccessible I., Atlantic Ocean
St. George, Bermuda

COPYRIGHT PHILIP'S

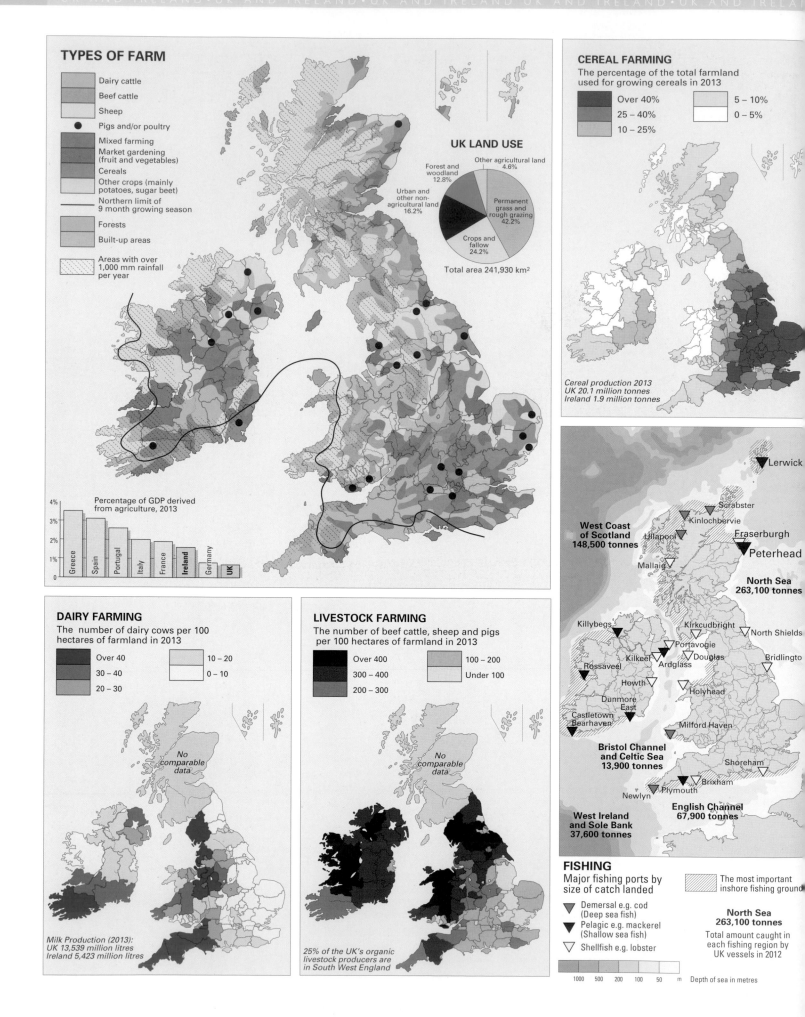

TYPES OF FARM

- Dairy cattle
- Beef cattle
- Sheep
- ● Pigs and/or poultry
- Mixed farming
- Market gardening (fruit and vegetables)
- Cereals
- Other crops (mainly potatoes, sugar beet)
- ⎯ Northern limit of 9 month growing season
- Forests
- Built-up areas
- Areas with over 1,000 mm rainfall per year

UK LAND USE

Other agricultural land 4.6%
Forest and woodland 12.8%
Urban and other non-agricultural land 16.2%
Permanent grass and rough grazing 42.2%
Crops and fallow 24.2%

Total area 241,930 km²

Percentage of GDP derived from agriculture, 2013

Greece, Spain, Portugal, Italy, France, Ireland, Germany, UK

CEREAL FARMING

The percentage of the total farmland used for growing cereals in 2013

- Over 40%
- 25 – 40%
- 10 – 25%
- 5 – 10%
- 0 – 5%

Cereal production 2013
UK 20.1 million tonnes
Ireland 1.9 million tonnes

DAIRY FARMING

The number of dairy cows per 100 hectares of farmland in 2013

- Over 40
- 30 – 40
- 20 – 30
- 10 – 20
- 0 – 10

No comparable data

Milk Production (2013):
UK 13,539 million litres
Ireland 5,423 million litres

LIVESTOCK FARMING

The number of beef cattle, sheep and pigs per 100 hectares of farmland in 2013

- Over 400
- 300 – 400
- 200 – 300
- 100 – 200
- Under 100

No comparable data

25% of the UK's organic livestock producers are in South West England

FISHING

Major fishing ports by size of catch landed

- ▼ Demersal e.g. cod (Deep sea fish)
- ▼ Pelagic e.g. mackerel (Shallow sea fish)
- ▽ Shellfish e.g. lobster

The most important inshore fishing ground

North Sea 263,100 tonnes

Total amount caught in each fishing region by UK vessels in 2012

1000 500 200 100 50 m Depth of sea in metres

Lerwick
Scrabster
Kinlochbervie
Ullapool
Fraserburgh
Peterhead
Mallaig

West Coast of Scotland 148,500 tonnes

North Sea 263,100 tonnes

Killybegs
Kirkcudbright
North Shields
Portavogie
Rossaveel
Kilkeel
Douglas
Bridlington
Ardglass
Howth
Holyhead
Dunmore East
Castletown
Bearhaven
Milford Haven

Bristol Channel and Celtic Sea 13,900 tonnes

Shoreham
Brixham
Newlyn Plymouth

West Ireland and Sole Bank 37,600 tonnes

English Channel 67,900 tonnes

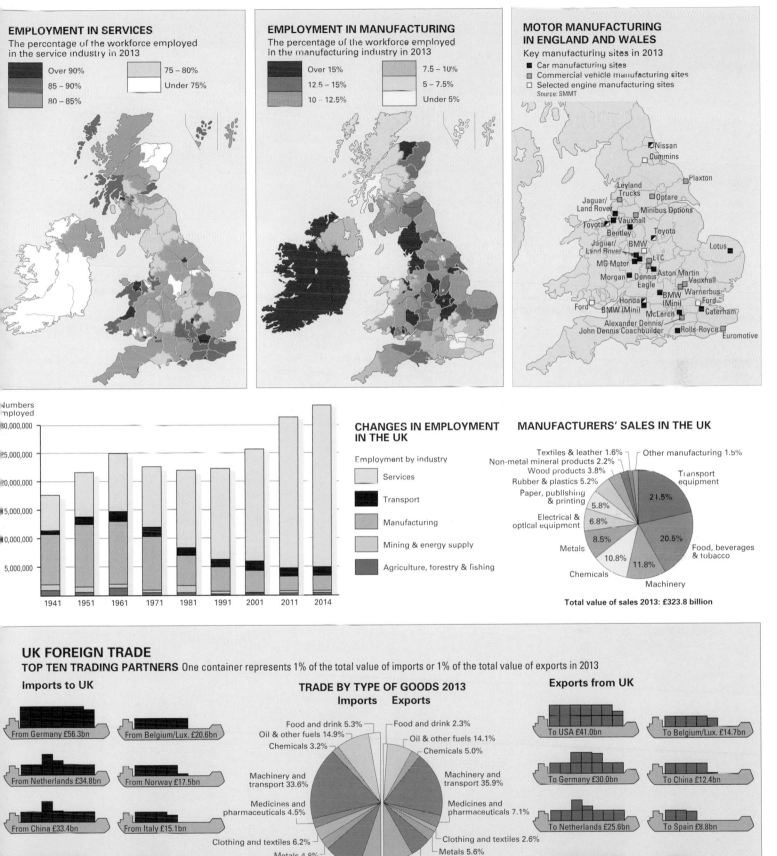

EMPLOYMENT IN SERVICES

The percentage of the workforce employed in the service industry in 2013

- Over 90%
- 85 – 90%
- 80 – 85%
- 75 – 80%
- Under 75%

EMPLOYMENT IN MANUFACTURING

The percentage of the workforce employed in the manufacturing industry in 2013

- Over 15%
- 12.5 – 15%
- 10 – 12.5%
- 7.5 – 10%
- 5 – 7.5%
- Under 5%

MOTOR MANUFACTURING IN ENGLAND AND WALES

Key manufacturing sites in 2013

- ■ Car manufacturing sites
- ■ Commercial vehicle manufacturing sites
- □ Selected engine manufacturing sites

Source: SMMT

Nissan, Cummins, Plaxton, Leyland Trucks, Optare, Jaguar/Land Rover, Minibus Options, Toyota, Vauxhall, Bentley, Toyota, Jaguar/Land Rover, BMW, Lotus, MG Motor, LTC, Morgan, Dennis Eagle, Aston Martin, Vauxhall, Warnerbus, Ford, Honda, BMW (Mini), Ford, BMW (Mini), McLaren, Caterham, Alexander Dennis/John Dennis Coachbuilder, Rolls-Royce, Euromotive

CHANGES IN EMPLOYMENT IN THE UK

Employment by industry

- Services
- Transport
- Manufacturing
- Mining & energy supply
- Agriculture, forestry & fishing

Numbers employed

30,000,000
25,000,000
20,000,000
15,000,000
10,000,000
5,000,000

1941 1951 1961 1971 1981 1991 2001 2011 2014

MANUFACTURERS' SALES IN THE UK

- Textiles & leather 1.6%
- Non-metal mineral products 2.2%
- Wood products 3.8%
- Rubber & plastics 5.2%
- Paper, publishing & printing 5.8%
- Electrical & optical equipment 6.8%
- Metals 8.5%
- Chemicals 10.8%
- Machinery 11.8%
- Food, beverages & tobacco 20.5%
- Transport equipment 21.5%
- Other manufacturing 1.5%

Total value of sales 2013: £323.8 billion

UK FOREIGN TRADE

TOP TEN TRADING PARTNERS One container represents 1% of the total value of imports or 1% of the total value of exports in 2013

Imports to UK

- From Germany £56.3bn
- From Belgium/Lux. £20.6bn
- From Netherlands £34.8bn
- From Norway £17.5bn
- From China £33.4bn
- From Italy £15.1bn
- From USA £27.7bn
- From Ireland £12.4bn
- From France £24.3bn
- From Spain £12.3bn

TRADE BY TYPE OF GOODS 2013

Imports | Exports

Imports:
- Food and drink 5.3%
- Oil & other fuels 14.9%
- Chemicals 3.2%
- Machinery and transport 33.6%
- Medicines and pharmaceuticals 4.5%
- Clothing and textiles 6.2%
- Metals 4.8%
- Other manufactures 16.5%
- Miscellaneous goods 11.0%

Exports:
- Food and drink 2.3%
- Oil & other fuels 14.1%
- Chemicals 5.0%
- Machinery and transport 35.9%
- Medicines and pharmaceuticals 7.1%
- Clothing and textiles 2.6%
- Metals 5.6%
- Other manufactures 11.5%
- Miscellaneous goods 15.9%

Total value of imports 2013: £368.0 billion **Total value of exports 2013: £282.2 billion**

Exports from UK

- To USA £41.0bn
- To Belgium/Lux. £14.7bn
- To Germany £30.0bn
- To China £12.4bn
- To Netherlands £25.6bn
- To Spain £8.8bn
- To France £21.3bn
- To Italy £8.6bn
- To Ireland £19.0bn
- To UAE £6.2bn

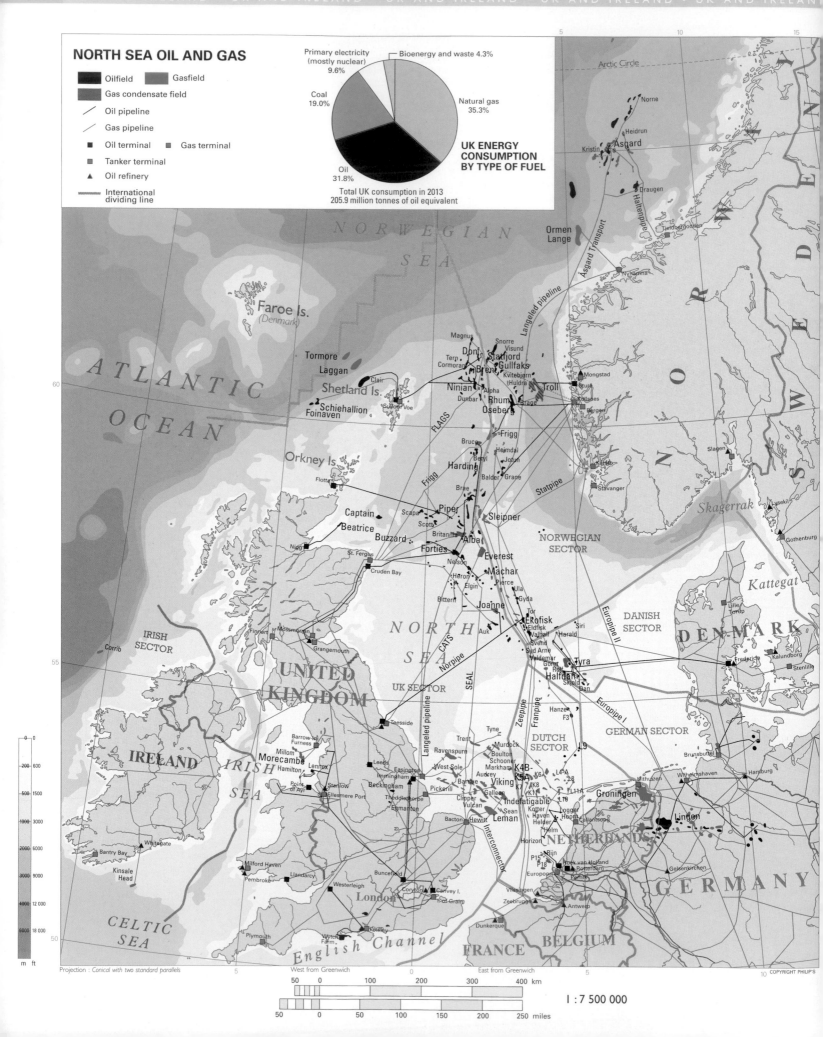

NORTH SEA OIL AND GAS

■ Oilfield	■ Gasfield
■ Gas condensate field	

- / Oil pipeline
- / Gas pipeline
- ■ Oil terminal   ■ Gas terminal
- ■ Tanker terminal
- ▲ Oil refinery
- ══ International dividing line

UK ENERGY CONSUMPTION BY TYPE OF FUEL

Primary electricity (mostly nuclear) 9.6%
Bioenergy and waste 4.3%
Natural gas 35.3%
Coal 19.0%
Oil 31.8%

Total UK consumption in 2013
205.9 million tonnes of oil equivalent

Projection : Conical with two standard parallels

West from Greenwich   East from Greenwich

1 : 7 500 000

COPYRIGHT PHILIP'S

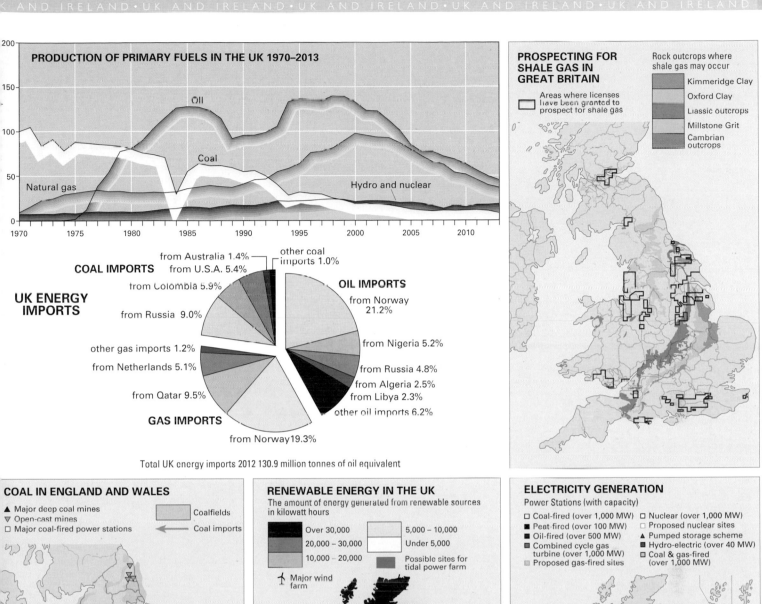

PRODUCTION OF PRIMARY FUELS IN THE UK 1970–2013

Oil

Coal

Natural gas

Hydro and nuclear

UK ENERGY IMPORTS

COAL IMPORTS
- from Australia 1.4%
- from U.S.A. 5.4%
- from Colombia 5.9%
- from Russia 9.0%
- other coal imports 1.0%

GAS IMPORTS
- other gas imports 1.2%
- from Netherlands 5.1%
- from Qatar 9.5%
- from Norway 19.3%

OIL IMPORTS
- from Norway 21.2%
- from Nigeria 5.2%
- from Russia 4.8%
- from Algeria 2.5%
- from Libya 2.3%
- other oil imports 6.2%

Total UK energy imports 2012 130.9 million tonnes of oil equivalent

PROSPECTING FOR SHALE GAS IN GREAT BRITAIN

Areas where licenses have been granted to prospect for shale gas

Rock outcrops where shale gas may occur
- Kimmeridge Clay
- Oxford Clay
- Liassic outcrops
- Millstone Grit
- Cambrian outcrops

COAL IN ENGLAND AND WALES

- ▲ Major deep coal mines
- ▽ Open-cast mines
- ☐ Major coal-fired power stations
- ▨ Coalfields
- ← Coal imports

Kellingley, Drax, Ferrybridge, Hatfield, Fiddler's Ferry, Maltby, Wolbeck, Eggborough, Thoresby, West Burton, Cottam, Daw Mill, Rugeley, Ratcliffe, Didcot, Tilbury, Aberthaw, Kingsnorth

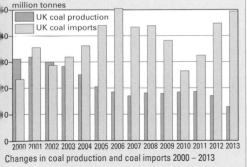

million tonnes
- ▨ UK coal production
- ▨ UK coal imports

2000 2001 2002 2003 2004 2005 2006 2007 2008 2009 2010 2011 2012 2013

Changes in coal production and coal imports 2000 – 2013

RENEWABLE ENERGY IN THE UK

The amount of energy generated from renewable sources in kilowatt hours

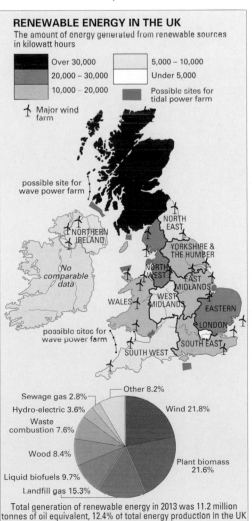

- Over 30,000
- 20,000 – 30,000
- 10,000 – 20,000
- 5,000 – 10,000
- Under 5,000
- Possible sites for tidal power farm
- Major wind farm

possible site for wave power farm

NORTHERN IRELAND

(No comparable data)

NORTH EAST, YORKSHIRE & THE HUMBER, NORTH WEST, EAST MIDLANDS, WEST MIDLANDS, WALES, EASTERN, LONDON, SOUTH EAST, SOUTH WEST

possible sites for wave power farm

(renewable energy pie chart)
- Sewage gas 2.8%
- Hydro-electric 3.6%
- Waste combustion 7.6%
- Wood 8.4%
- Liquid biofuels 9.7%
- Landfill gas 15.3%
- Other 8.2%
- Wind 21.8%
- Plant biomass 21.6%

Total generation of renewable energy in 2013 was 11.2 million tonnes of oil equivalent, 12.4% of total energy production in the UK

ELECTRICITY GENERATION

Power Stations (with capacity)
- ☐ Coal-fired (over 1,000 MW)
- ■ Peat-fired (over 100 MW)
- ■ Oil-fired (over 500 MW)
- ■ Combined cycle gas turbine (over 1,000 MW)
- ▨ Proposed gas-fired sites
- ☐ Nuclear (over 1,000 MW)
- ☐ Proposed nuclear sites
- ▲ Pumped storage scheme
- ■ Hydro-electric (over 40 MW)
- ☐ Coal & gas-fired (over 1,000 MW)

Fasnakyle, Foyers, Peterhead, Bannoch, Errochty, Cruachan, Clunie, Lochay, Clachan, Sloy, Cockenzie, Longannet, Torness, Hunterston, Ballylumford, Hartlepool, Thor Cogeneration, Braystones, Sellafield, Teesside, Kirksanton, Lough Ree, Heysham, Saltend, South Humber Bank, West Offaly, Drax, Fiddler's Ferry, Ferrybridge, Cottam, Moneypoint, Edenderry, Poolbeg, Wylfa, West Burton, Eggborough, Dinorwig, Staythorpe, Tarbert, Turlough Hill, Ffestiniog, Connahs Quay, Ratcliffe-on-Soar, King's Lynn, Aghada, Ardnacrusha, Rugeley, Sizewell, Rheidol, Pembroke, Oldbury, Didcot, Barking, Bradwell, Aberthaw, Littlebrook, Tilbury, Hinkley Point, Seabank, Kingsnorth, Grain, Fawley, Dungeness

Fuel used in the generation of electricity in the UK 1980–2010 (2013 percentages are in brackets)

	0%	20%	40%	60%	80%	100%
1980						
1990						
2000						
2010						

Coal (28%) — Oil — Natural gas (37%) — Nuclear (11%) — Hydro-electric (3%) — Net imports / Other fuels

COPYRIGHT PHILIP'S

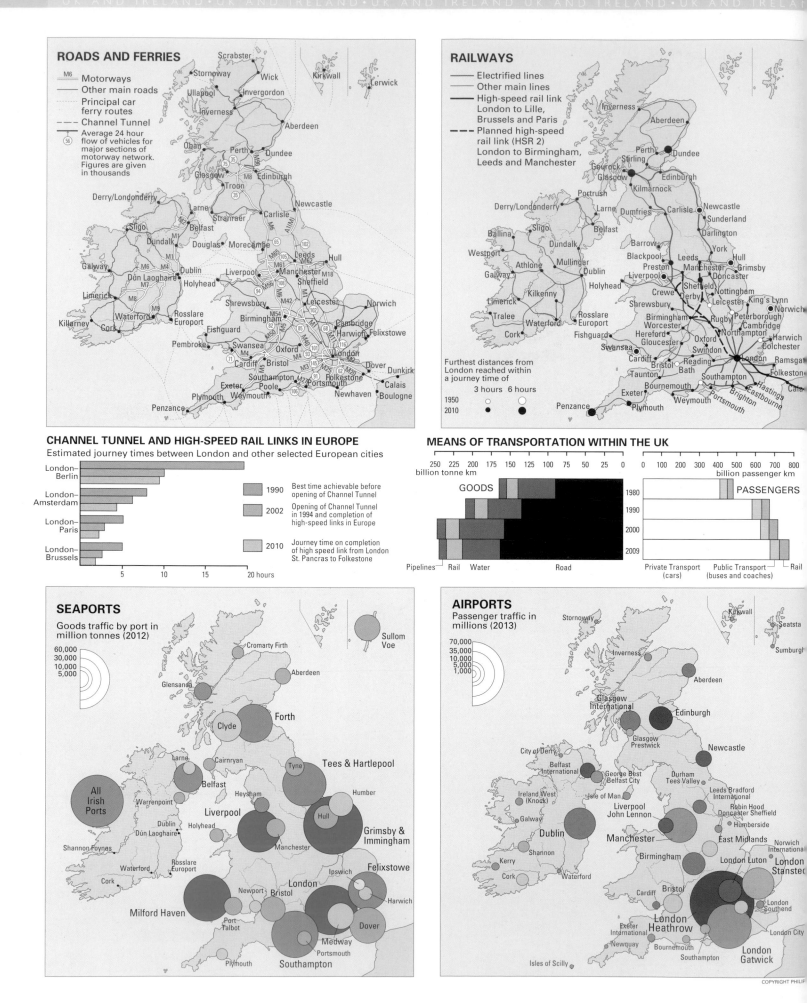

ROADS AND FERRIES

- **M6** Motorways
- Other main roads
- Principal car ferry routes
- Channel Tunnel
- Average 24 hour flow of vehicles for major sections of motorway network. Figures are given in thousands

RAILWAYS

- Electrified lines
- Other main lines
- High-speed rail link London to Lille, Brussels and Paris
- Planned high-speed rail link (HSR 2) London to Birmingham, Leeds and Manchester

Furthest distances from London reached within a journey time of

	3 hours	6 hours
1950	○	○
2010	●	●

CHANNEL TUNNEL AND HIGH-SPEED RAIL LINKS IN EUROPE

Estimated journey times between London and other selected European cities

- 1990 — Best time achievable before opening of Channel Tunnel
- 2002 — Opening of Channel Tunnel in 1994 and completion of high-speed links in Europe
- 2010 — Journey time on completion of high speed link from London St. Pancras to Folkestone

MEANS OF TRANSPORTATION WITHIN THE UK

GOODS — billion tonne km
Pipelines, Rail, Water, Road

PASSENGERS — billion passenger km
Private Transport (cars), Public Transport (buses and coaches), Rail

SEAPORTS

Goods traffic by port in million tonnes (2012)
60,000 / 30,000 / 10,000 / 5,000

AIRPORTS

Passenger traffic in millions (2013)
70,000 / 35,000 / 10,000 / 5,000 / 1,000

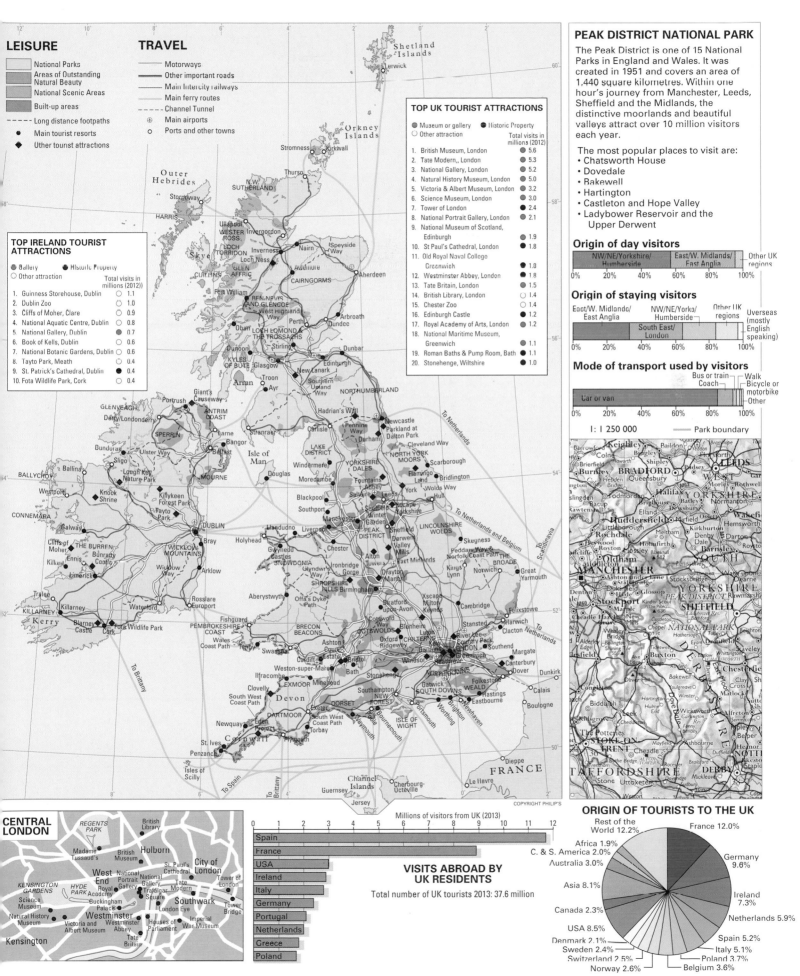

LEISURE

- National Parks
- Areas of Outstanding Natural Beauty
- National Scenic Areas
- Built-up areas
- ---- Long distance footpaths
- • Main tourist resorts
- ◆ Other tourist attractions

TRAVEL

- —— Motorways
- —— Other important roads
- —— Main Intercity railways
- —— Main ferry routes
- ----- Channel Tunnel
- ⊕ Main airports
- ○ Ports and other towns

TOP IRELAND TOURIST ATTRACTIONS

- ● Gallery   ◆ Historic Property
- ○ Other attraction

		Total visits in millions (2012)
1.	Guinness Storehouse, Dublin	○ 1.1
2.	Dublin Zoo	○ 1.0
3.	Cliffs of Moher, Clare	○ 0.9
4.	National Aquatic Centre, Dublin	○ 0.8
5.	National Gallery, Dublin	● 0.7
6.	Book of Kells, Dublin	○ 0.6
7.	National Botanic Gardens, Dublin	○ 0.6
8.	Tayto Park, Meath	○ 0.4
9.	St. Patrick's Cathedral, Dublin	● 0.4
10.	Fota Wildlife Park, Cork	○ 0.4

TOP UK TOURIST ATTRACTIONS

- ● Museum or gallery   ● Historic Property
- ○ Other attraction

		Total visits in millions (2012)
1.	British Museum, London	● 5.6
2.	Tate Modern,, London	● 5.3
3.	National Gallery, London	● 5.2
4.	Natural History Museum, London	● 5.0
5.	Victoria & Albert Museum, London	● 3.2
6.	Science Museum, London	● 3.0
7.	Tower of London	● 2.4
8.	National Portrait Gallery, London	● 2.1
9.	National Museum of Scotland, Edinburgh	● 1.9
10.	St Paul's Cathedral, London	● 1.8
11.	Old Royal Naval College Greenwich	● 1.0
12.	Westminster Abbey, London	● 1.8
13.	Tate Britain, London	● 1.5
14.	British Library, London	○ 1.4
15.	Chester Zoo	○ 1.4
16.	Edinburgh Castle	● 1.2
17.	Royal Academy of Arts, London	● 1.2
18.	National Maritime Museum, Greenwich	● 1.1
19.	Roman Baths & Pump Room, Bath	● 1.1
20.	Stonehenge, Wiltshire	● 1.0

PEAK DISTRICT NATIONAL PARK

The Peak District is one of 15 National Parks in England and Wales. It was created in 1951 and covers an area of 1,440 square kilometres. Within one hour's journey from Manchester, Leeds, Sheffield and the Midlands, the distinctive moorlands and beautiful valleys attract over 10 million visitors each year.

The most popular places to visit are:
- Chatsworth House
- Dovedale
- Bakewell
- Hartington
- Castleton and Hope Valley
- Ladybower Reservoir and the Upper Derwent

Origin of day visitors

Origin of staying visitors

Mode of transport used by visitors

1: 1 250 000   —— Park boundary

COPYRIGHT PHILIP'S

CENTRAL LONDON

VISITS ABROAD BY UK RESIDENTS

Millions of visitors from UK (2013)

Spain
France
USA
Ireland
Italy
Germany
Portugal
Netherlands
Greece
Poland

Total number of UK tourists 2013: 37.6 million

ORIGIN OF TOURISTS TO THE UK

- Rest of the World 12.2%
- France 12.0%
- Africa 1.9%
- Germany 9.6%
- C. & S. America 2.0%
- Australia 3.0%
- Ireland 7.3%
- Asia 8.1%
- Netherlands 5.9%
- Canada 2.3%
- Spain 5.2%
- USA 8.5%
- Italy 5.1%
- Denmark 2.1%
- Poland 3.7%
- Sweden 2.4%
- Belgium 3.6%
- Switzerland 2.5%
- Norway 2.6%

Total number of foreign tourists 2013: 32.8 million

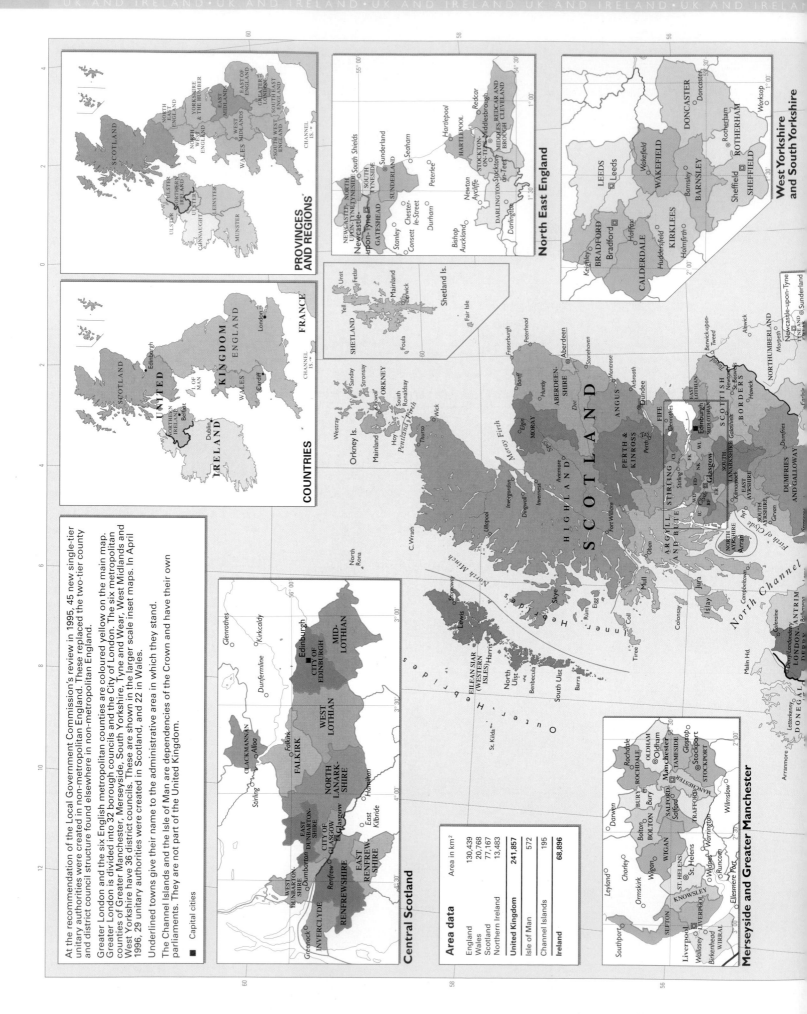

At the recommendation of the Local Government Commission's review in 1995, 45 new single-tier unitary authorities were created in non-metropolitan England. These replaced the two-tier county and district council structure found elsewhere in non-metropolitan England.

Greater London and the six English metropolitan counties are coloured yellow on the main map. Greater London is divided into 32 borough councils and the City of London. The six metropolitan counties of Greater Manchester, Merseyside, South Yorkshire, Tyne and Wear, West Midlands and West Yorkshire have 36 district councils. These are shown in the larger scale inset maps. In April 1996, 29 unitary authorities were created in Scotland, and 22 in Wales.

Underlined towns give their name to the administrative area in which they stand.

The Channel Islands and the Isle of Man are dependencies of the Crown and have their own parliaments. They are not part of the United Kingdom.

■ Capital cities

PROVINCES AND REGIONS

COUNTRIES

North East England

West Yorkshire and South Yorkshire

Central Scotland

Area data

	Area in km²
England	130,439
Wales	20,768
Scotland	77,167
Northern Ireland	13,483
United Kingdom	**241,857**
Isle of Man	572
Channel Islands	195
Ireland	**68,896**

Merseyside and Greater Manchester

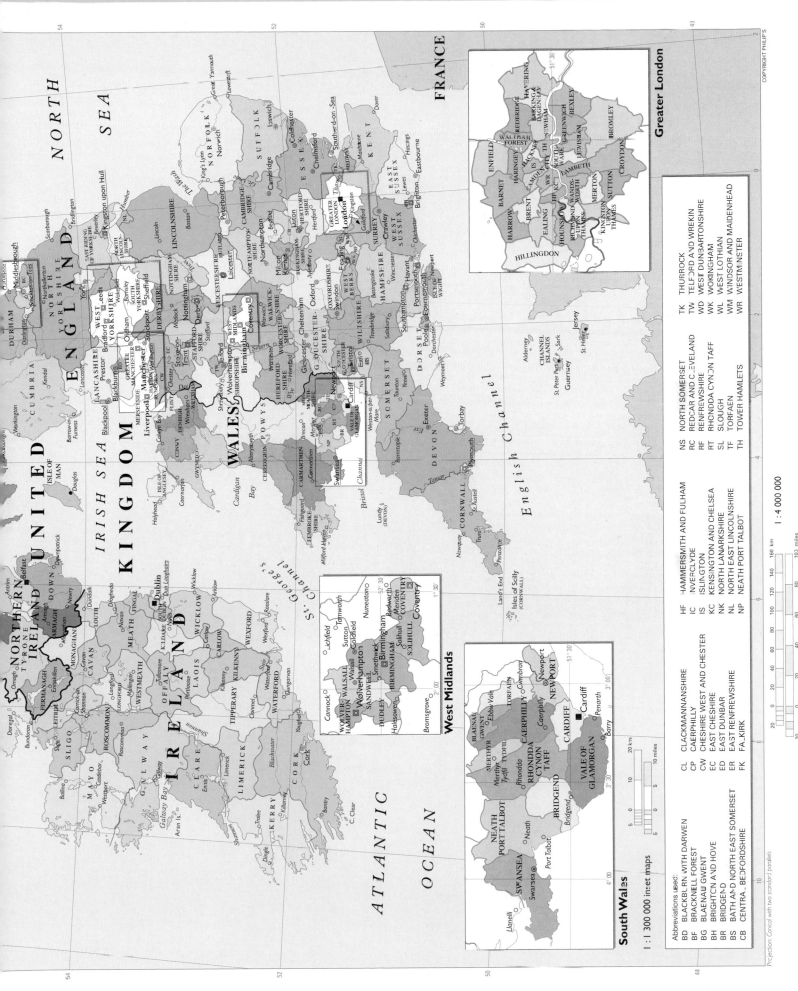

Greater London

West Midlands

South Wales
1 : 1 300 000 inset maps

Abbreviations used:
BD BLACKBURN WITH DARWEN
BF BRACKNELL FOREST
BG BLAENAU GWENT
BH BRIGHTON AND HOVE
BR BRIDGEND
BS BATH AND NORTH EAST SOMERSET
CB CENTRAL BEDFORDSHIRE

CL CLACKMANNANSHIRE
CP CAERPHILLY
CW CHESHIRE WEST AND CHESTER
EC CHESHIRE WEST AND CHESTER
ED EAST DUNBAR
ER EAST RENFREWSHIRE
FK FALKIRK

HF HAMMERSMITH AND FULHAM
IC INVERCLYDE
IS ISLINGTON
KC KENSINGTON AND CHELSEA
NK NORTH LANARKSHIRE
NL NORTH EAST LINCOLNSHIRE
NP NEATH PORT TALBOT

NS NORTH SOMERSET
RC REDCAR AND CLEVELAND
RF RENFREWSHIRE
RT RHONDDA CYNON TAFF
SL SLOUGH
TF TORFAEN
TH TOWER HAMLETS

TK THURROCK
TW TELFORD AND WREKIN
WD WEST DUNBARTONSHIRE
WK WOKINGHAM
WL WEST LOTHIAN
WM WINDSOR AND MAIDENHEAD
WR WESTMINSTER

1 : 4 000 000

Projection: Conical with two standard parallels

COPYRIGHT PHILIP'S

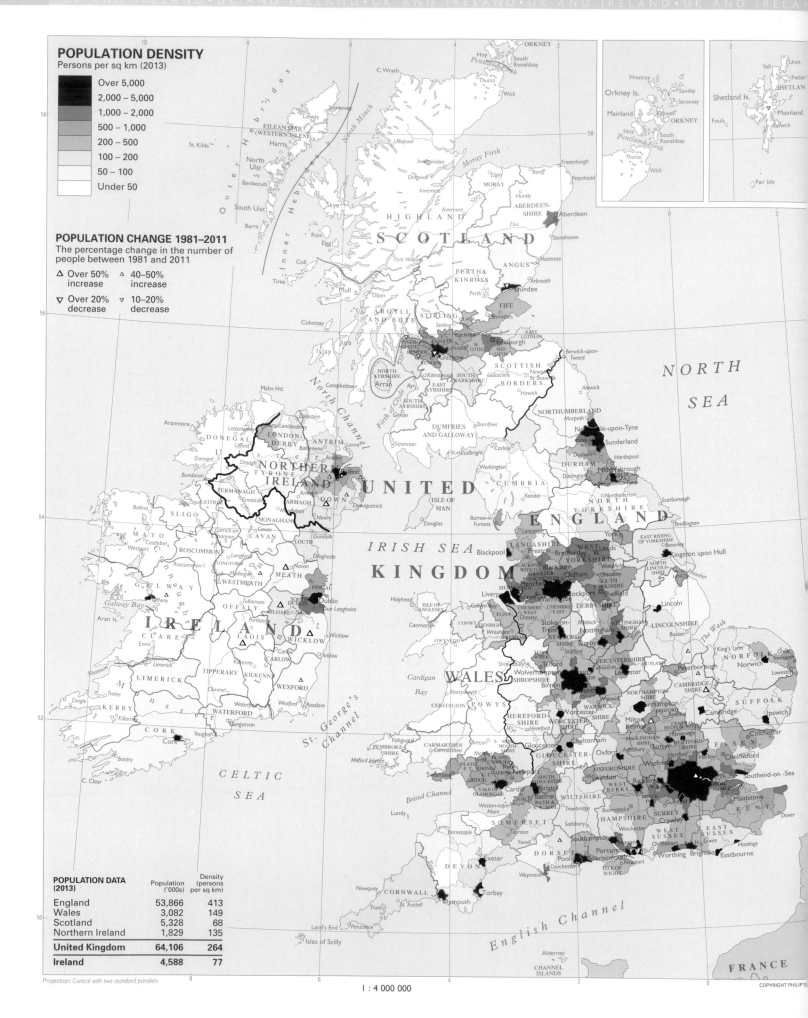

POPULATION DENSITY
Persons per sq km (2013)

- Over 5,000
- 2,000 – 5,000
- 1,000 – 2,000
- 500 – 1,000
- 200 – 500
- 100 – 200
- 50 – 100
- Under 50

POPULATION CHANGE 1981–2011
The percentage change in the number of people between 1981 and 2011

- △ Over 50% increase
- △ 40–50% increase
- ▽ Over 20% decrease
- ▽ 10–20% decrease

POPULATION DATA (2013)	Population ('000s)	Density (persons per sq km)
England	53,866	413
Wales	3,082	149
Scotland	5,328	68
Northern Ireland	1,829	135
United Kingdom	64,106	264
Ireland	4,588	77

Projection: Conical with two standard parallels

1 : 4 000 000

COPYRIGHT PHILIP'S

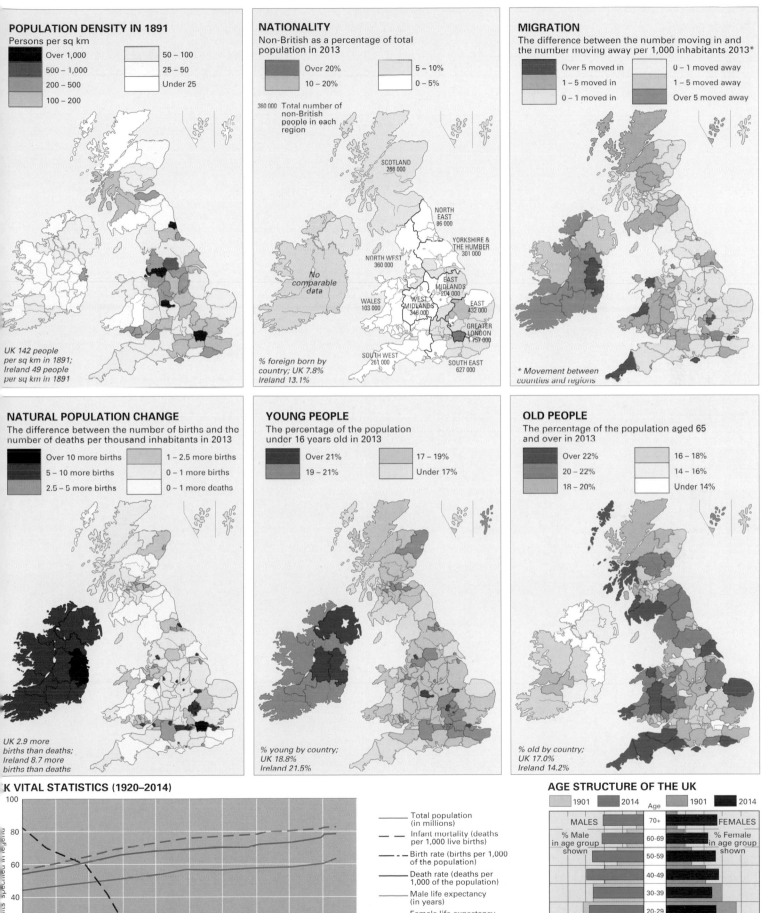

POPULATION DENSITY IN 1891
Persons per sq km

- Over 1,000
- 500 – 1,000
- 200 – 500
- 100 – 200
- 50 – 100
- 25 – 50
- Under 25

UK 142 people per sq km in 1891; Ireland 49 people per sq km in 1891

NATIONALITY
Non-British as a percentage of total population in 2013

- Over 20%
- 10 – 20%
- 5 – 10%
- 0 – 5%

360 000 Total number of non-British people in each region

SCOTLAND 266 000
NORTH EAST 86 000
YORKSHIRE & THE HUMBER 301 000
NORTH WEST 360 000
EAST MIDLANDS 204 000
WALES 103 000
WEST MIDLANDS 346 000
EAST 432 000
GREATER LONDON 1 757 000
SOUTH WEST 261 000
SOUTH EAST 627 000

No comparable data

% foreign born by country; UK 7.8% Ireland 13.1%

MIGRATION
The difference between the number moving in and the number moving away per 1,000 inhabitants 2013*

- Over 5 moved in
- 1 – 5 moved in
- 0 – 1 moved in
- 0 – 1 moved away
- 1 – 5 moved away
- Over 5 moved away

* Movement between counties and regions

NATURAL POPULATION CHANGE
The difference between the number of births and the number of deaths per thousand inhabitants in 2013

- Over 10 more births
- 5 – 10 more births
- 2.5 – 5 more births
- 1 – 2.5 more births
- 0 – 1 more births
- 0 – 1 more deaths

UK 2.9 more births than deaths; Ireland 8.7 more births than deaths

YOUNG PEOPLE
The percentage of the population under 16 years old in 2013

- Over 21%
- 19 – 21%
- 17 – 19%
- Under 17%

% young by country; UK 18.8% Ireland 21.5%

OLD PEOPLE
The percentage of the population aged 65 and over in 2013

- Over 22%
- 20 – 22%
- 18 – 20%
- 16 – 18%
- 14 – 16%
- Under 14%

% old by country; UK 17.0% Ireland 14.2%

UK VITAL STATISTICS (1920–2014)

Units specified in legend

—— Total population (in millions)
– – – Infant mortality (deaths per 1,000 live births)
–·–·– Birth rate (births per 1,000 of the population)
—— Death rate (deaths per 1,000 of the population)
—— Male life expectancy (in years)
– – – Female life expectancy (in years)

1920 1940 1960 1980 2000 2020

COPYRIGHT PHILIP'S

AGE STRUCTURE OF THE UK

1901 2014 Age 1901 2014

MALES   70+   FEMALES
% Male in age group shown   60-69   % Female in age group shown
            50-59
            40-49
            30-39
            20-29
            10-19
            0-9

25 20 15 10 5   5 10 15 20 25

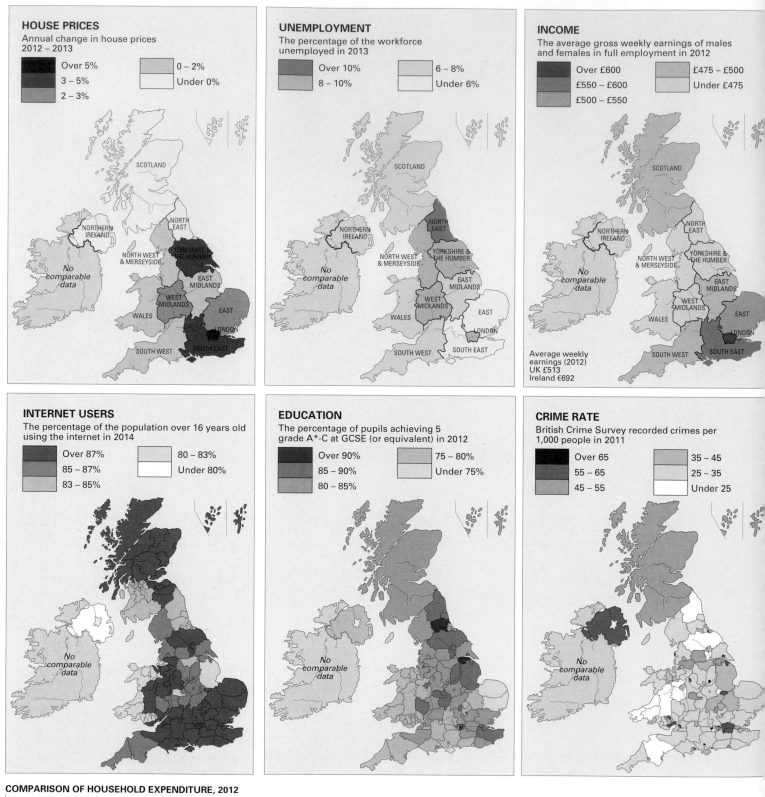

HOUSE PRICES
Annual change in house prices
2012 – 2013

Over 5%	0 – 2%
3 – 5%	Under 0%
2 – 3%	

UNEMPLOYMENT
The percentage of the workforce
unemployed in 2013

Over 10%	6 – 8%
8 – 10%	Under 6%

INCOME
The average gross weekly earnings of males
and females in full employment in 2012

Over £600	£475 – £500
£550 – £600	Under £475
£500 – £550	

Average weekly
earnings (2012)
UK £513
Ireland €692

INTERNET USERS
The percentage of the population over 16 years old
using the internet in 2014

Over 87%	80 – 83%
85 – 87%	Under 80%
83 – 85%	

EDUCATION
The percentage of pupils achieving 5
grade A*-C at GCSE (or equivalent) in 2012

Over 90%	75 – 80%
85 – 90%	Under 75%
80 – 85%	

CRIME RATE
British Crime Survey recorded crimes per
1,000 people in 2011

Over 65	35 – 45
55 – 65	25 – 35
45 – 55	Under 25

COMPARISON OF HOUSEHOLD EXPENDITURE, 2012

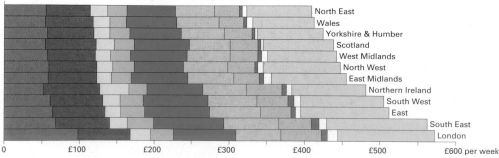

North East
Wales
Yorkshire & Humber
Scotland
West Midlands
North West
East Midlands
Northern Ireland
South West
East
South East
London

0   £100   £200   £300   £400   £500   £600 per week

Housing, fuel & power	Recreation & culture
Food, beverages & tobacco	Restaurants & hotels
Clothing & footwear	Health
Household goods & services	Education
Transport & communication	Miscellaneous goo & services

Average household expenditure per week in UK in 2012: £48

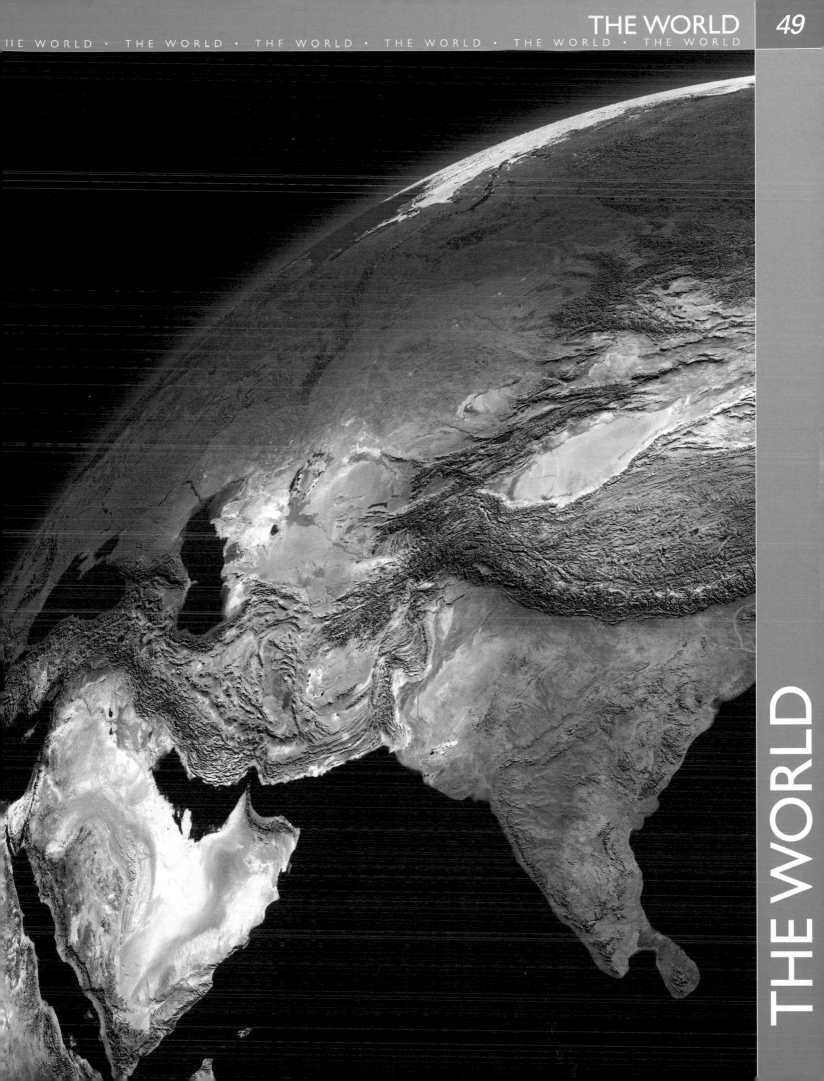

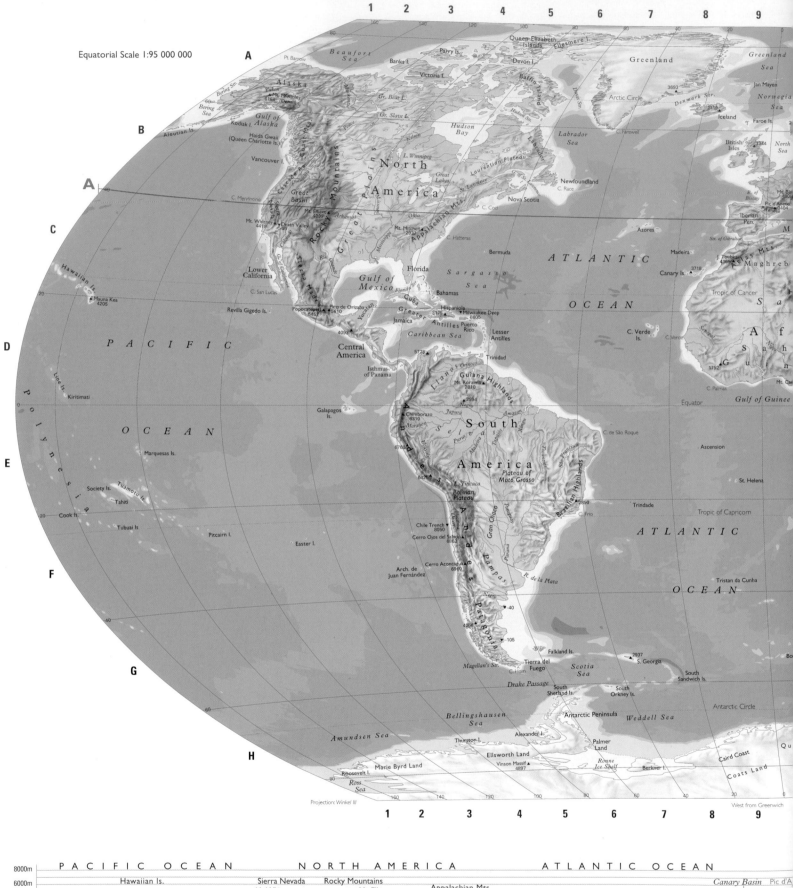

Equatorial Scale 1:95 000 000

Projection: Winkel III

West from Greenwich

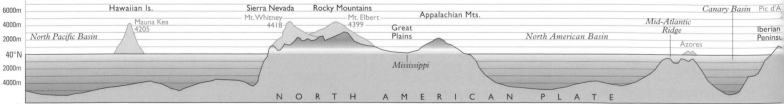

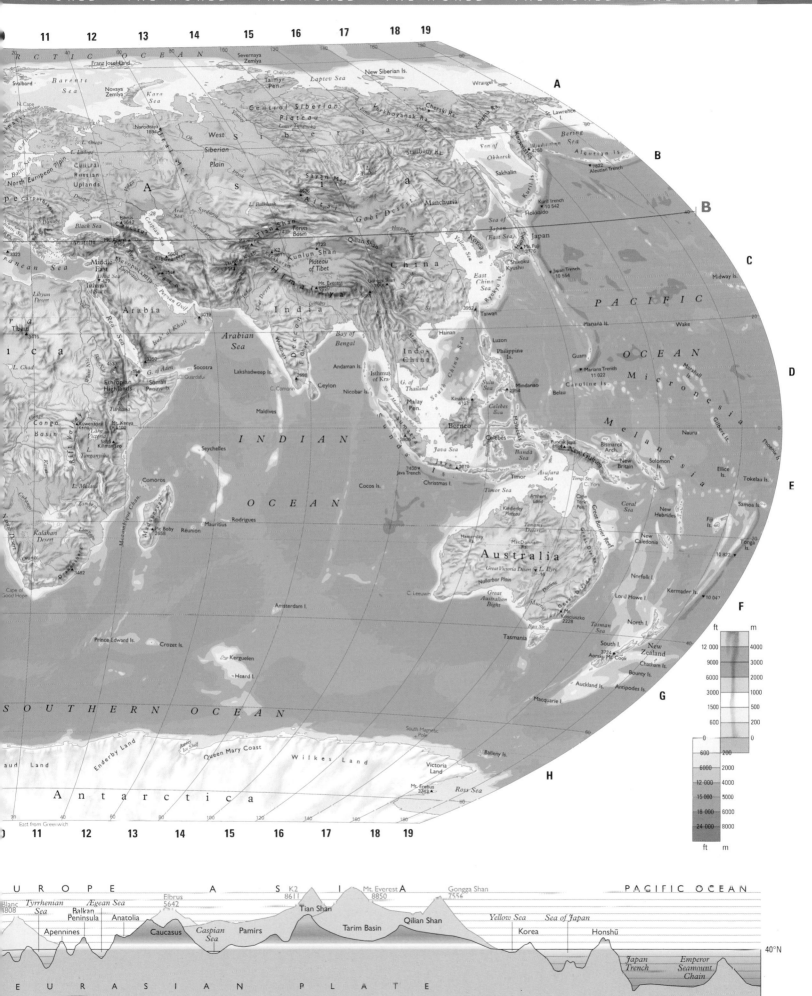

The maps below have been constructed on an Oblique Azimuthal Equidistant projection, on which all distances measured through the centre point are true to scale. The green lines are drawn at 5,000, 10,000 and 15,000 km from the central city.

Projection: Winkel III

West from Greenwich

MEXICO CITY
19° 26'N 99° 04'W

NEW YORK
40° 43'N 74° 00'W

RIO DE JANEIRO
22° 50'S 43° 15'W

LONDON
51° 28'N 00° 27'W

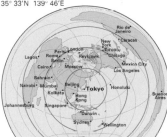

CAPE TOWN
33° 55′S 18° 35′E

DELHI
28° 39′N 77° 13′E

TOKYO
35° 33′N 139° 46′E

SYDNEY
33° 56′S 151° 10′E

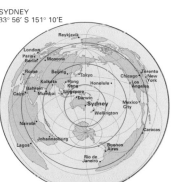

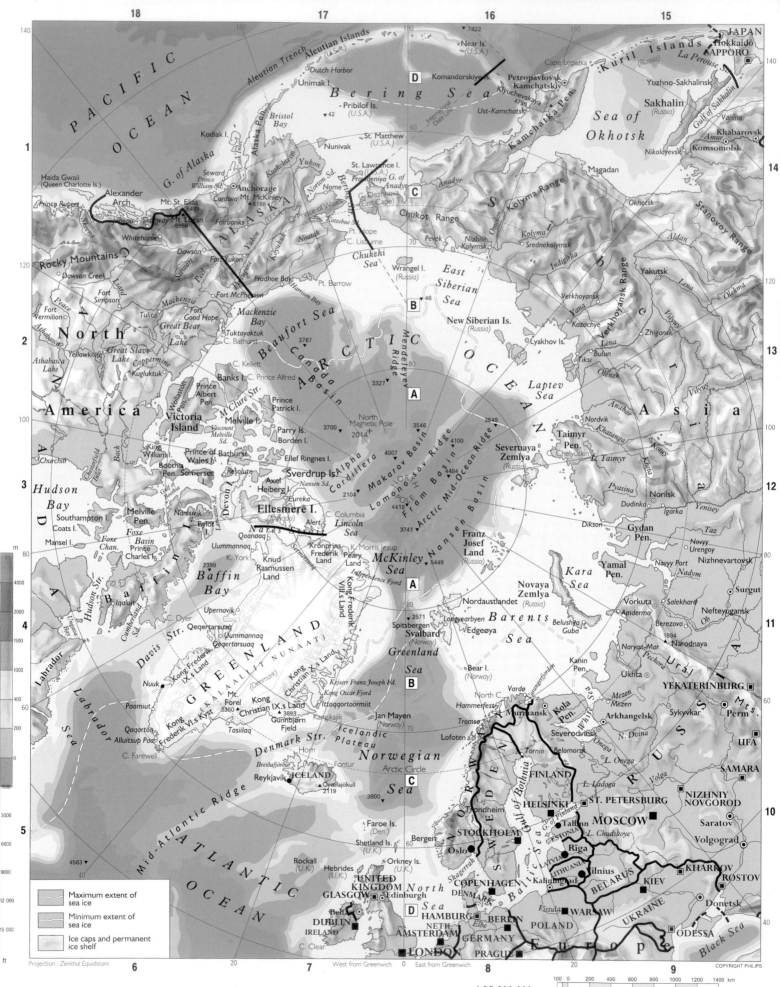

Maximum extent of sea ice

Minimum extent of sea ice

Ice caps and permanent ice shelf

Projection : Zenithal Equidistant

1:35 000 000

COPYRIGHT PHILIPS

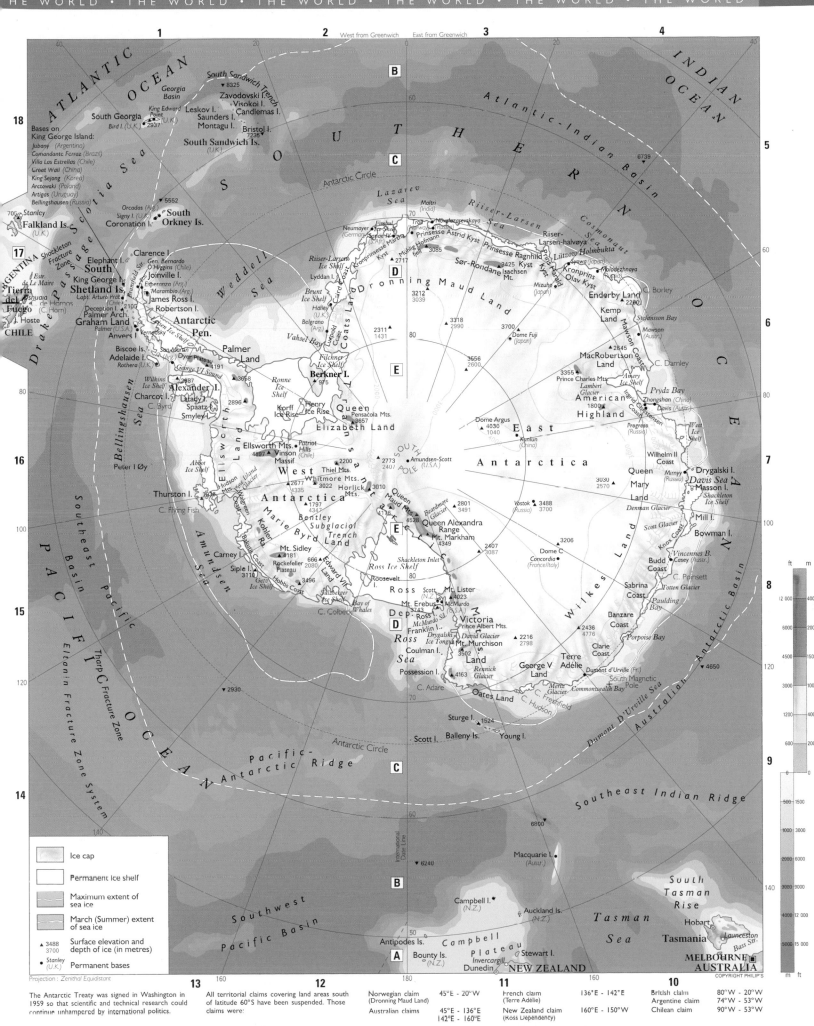

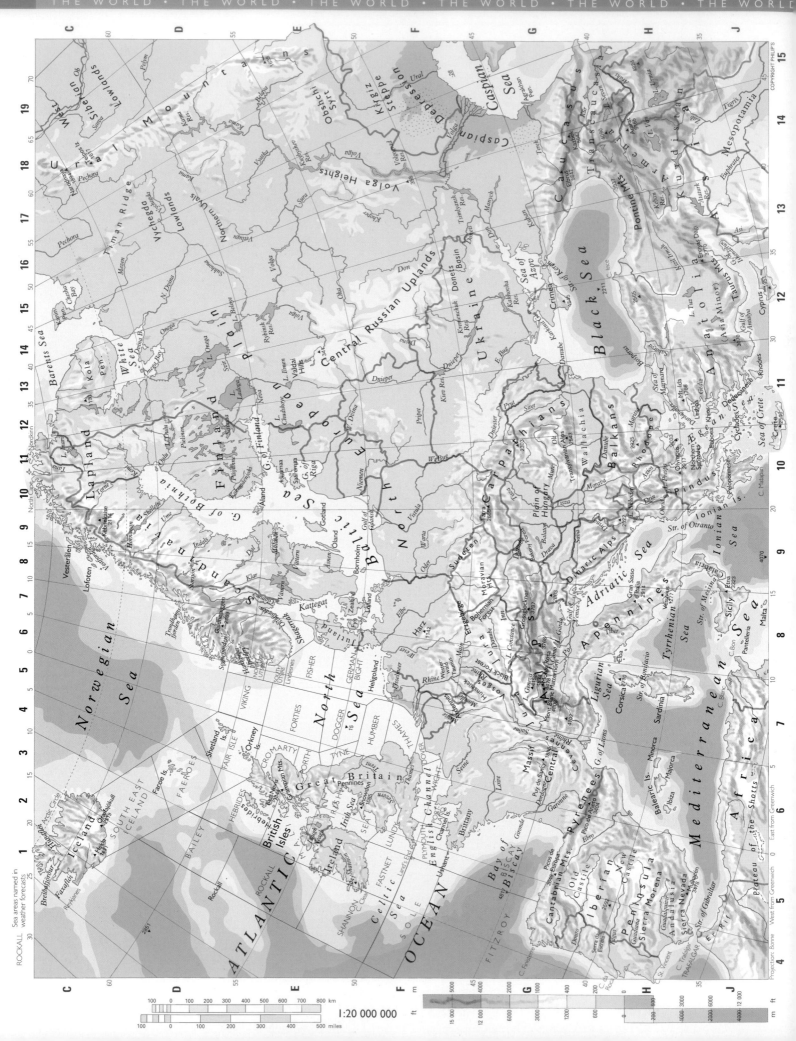

1:20 000 000

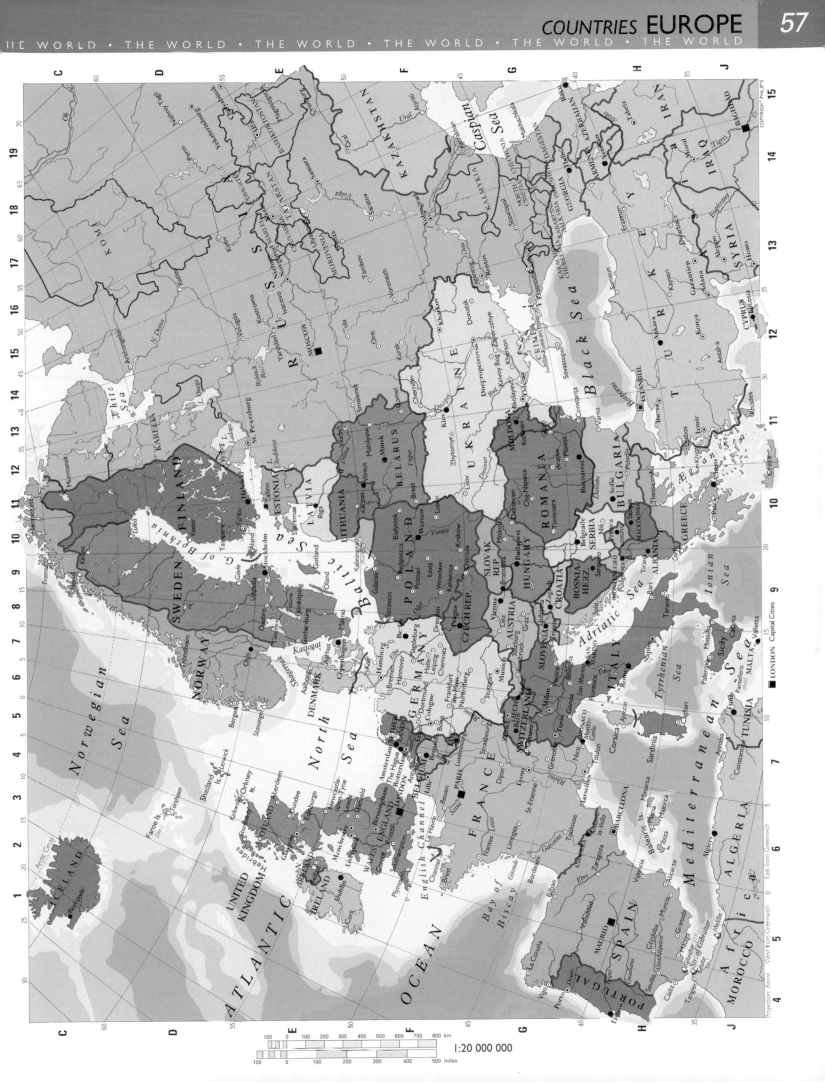

1:20 000 000

■ LONDON Capital Cities

Projection: Bonne

COPYRIGHT PHILIP'S

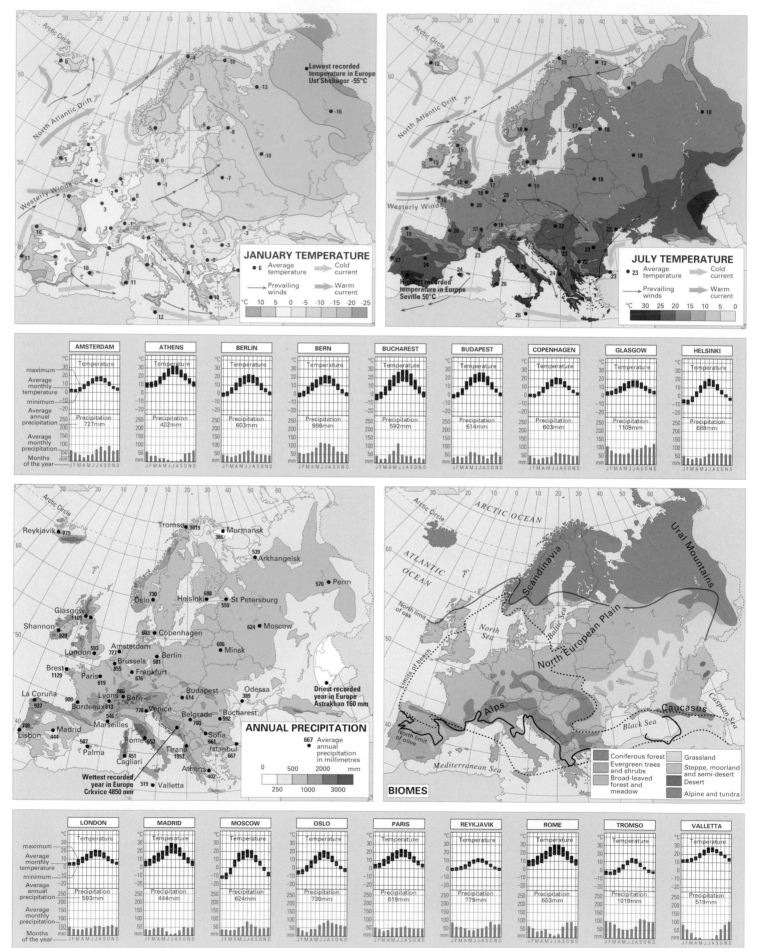

JANUARY TEMPERATURE

Lowest recorded temperature in Europe Ust'Shchugor -55°C

- 6 Average temperature
→ Prevailing winds
⟹ Cold current
⟹ Warm current

°C 10 5 0 -5 -10 -15 -20 -25

JULY TEMPERATURE

Highest recorded temperature in Europe Seville 50°C

- 23 Average temperature
→ Prevailing winds
⟹ Cold current
⟹ Warm current

°C 30 25 20 15 10 5 0

ANNUAL PRECIPITATION

- 667 Average annual precipitation in millimetres

Driest recorded year in Europe Astrakhan 160 mm

Wettest recorded year in Europe Crkvice 4850 mm

0   500   2000   mm
     250   1000   3000

BIOMES

■ Coniferous forest
■ Evergreen trees and shrubs
■ Broad-leaved forest and meadow
□ Grassland
■ Steppe, moorland and semi-desert
■ Desert
■ Alpine and tundra

Scandinavia · Ural Mountains · North European Plain · Alps · Caucasus · North limit of oak · Limits of beech · North limit of olive

Climate graphs (temperature and precipitation):
AMSTERDAM 727mm · ATHENS 402mm · BERLIN 603mm · BERN 986mm · BUCHAREST 592mm · BUDAPEST 614mm · COPENHAGEN 603mm · GLASGOW 1109mm · HELSINKI 688mm

LONDON 593mm · MADRID 444mm · MOSCOW 624mm · OSLO 730mm · PARIS 619mm · REYKJAVIK 779mm · ROME 653mm · TROMSO 1019mm · VALLETTA 519mm

Projection: Bonne

COPYRIGHT PHILIP'S

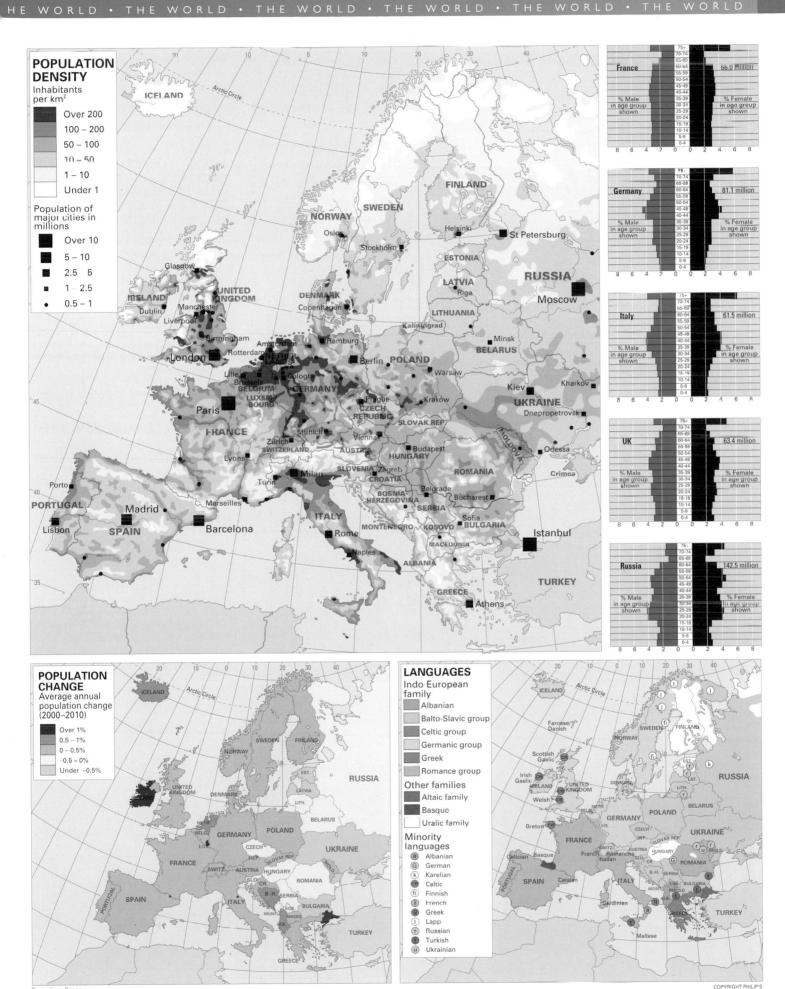

POPULATION DENSITY

Inhabitants per km²

- Over 200
- 100 – 200
- 50 – 100
- 10 – 50
- 1 – 10
- Under 1

Population of major cities in millions

- Over 10
- 5 – 10
- 2.5 – 5
- 1 – 2.5
- 0.5 – 1

France — 66.0 million
Germany — 81.1 million
Italy — 61.5 million
UK — 63.4 million
Russia — 142.5 million

% Male in age group shown — % Female in age group shown

POPULATION CHANGE

Average annual population change (2000–2010)

- Over 1%
- 0.5 – 1%
- 0 – 0.5%
- -0.5 – 0%
- Under -0.5%

LANGUAGES

Indo-European family

- Albanian
- Balto-Slavic group
- Celtic group
- Germanic group
- Greek
- Romance group

Other families

- Altaic family
- Basque
- Uralic family

Minority languages

- a Albanian
- G German
- k Karelian
- Ce Celtic
- fi Finnish
- f French
- g Greek
- l Lapp
- r Russian
- t Turkish
- u Ukrainian

Projection: Bonne

COPYRIGHT PHILIP'S

GROWTH OF THE EU

€ Euro-zone ○ EU headquarters

- Founder members (Treaty of Rome 1957)
- Admission in 1973
- Admission in 1981
- Admission in 1986
- Admission in 1990 (German unification)
- Admission in 1995
- Admission in 2004
- Admission in 2007
- Admission in 2013

EU COUNTRY COMPARISONS	Population (thousands)	Annual Income (US$ per capita)
Germany	81,147	39,500
France	65,952	35,700
United Kingdom	63,396	37,300
Italy	61,482	29,600
Spain	47,371	30,100
Poland	38,384	21,100
Romania	21,790	13,200
Netherlands	16,805	41,400
Portugal	10,799	22,900
Greece	10,773	23,600
Belgium	10,444	37,800
Czech Republic	10,163	27,200
Hungary	9,939	19,800
Sweden	9,119	40,900
Austria	8,222	42,600
Bulgaria	6,982	14,400
Denmark	5,556	37,800
Slovak Republic	5,488	24,700
Finland	5,266	35,900
Ireland	4,776	41,300
Croatia	4,476	17,800
Lithuania	3,516	22,600
Latvia	2,178	19,100
Slovenia	1,993	27,400
Estonia	1,266	22,400
Cyprus	1,155	24,500
Luxembourg	515	77,900
Malta	411	27,500
Total EU 2013 (28 countries)	**509,364**	**30,571**

REGIONS OF THE EU

Austria *(States)* — **A**
1 Niederösterreich
2 Oberösterreich
3 Burgenland
4 Kärnten
5 Salzburg
6 Steiermark
7 Tirol
8 Wien
9 Vorarlberg

Belgium *(Regions)* — **B**
1 Bruxelles
2 Vlaanderen
3 Wallonie

Bulgaria *(Regions)* — **BG**
1 Severen tsentralen
2 Severoiztochen
3 Severozapaden
4 Yugoiztochen
5 Yugozapaden
6 Yuzhen tsentralen

Croatia — **HR**

Cyprus *(member state with no corresponding division)* — **CY**

Czech Republic *(Regions)* —
1 Jihovychod
2 Jihozapad
3 Moravskoslezsko
4 Praha
5 Severovychod
6 Severozapad
7 Stredni Cechy
8 Stredni Morava

Denmark *(member state with no corresponding division)* — **DK**

Estonia *(member state with no corresponding division)* — **EST**

Finland *(Provinces)* — **FIN**
1 Åland
2 Itä-Suomi
3 Väli-Suomi
4 Pohjois-Suomi
5 Etelä-Suomi

France *(Regions)* — **F**
1 Alsace
2 Aquitaine
3 Auvergne
4 Bourgogne
5 Bretagne
6 Centre
7 Champagne-Ardenne
8 Corse
9 Franche-Comté
10 Ile-de-France
11 Languedoc-Roussillon
12 Limousin
13 Loire (Pays de la)
14 Lorraine
15 Midi-Pyrénées
16 Nord-Pas-de-Calais
17 Normandie (Basse-)
18 Normandie (Haute-)
19 Picardie
20 Poitou-Charentes
21 Provence-Alpes-Côte d'Azur
22 Rhône-Alpes

Germany *(Länder)* — **D**
1 Baden-Württemberg
2 Niedersachsen
3 Bayern
4 Berlin
5 Brandenburg
6 Bremen
7 Hamburg
8 Hessen
9 Mecklenburg-Vorpommern
10 Nordrhein-Westfalen
11 Rheinland-Pfalz
12 Saarland
13 Sachsen
14 Sachsen-Anhalt
15 Schleswig-Holstein
16 Thüringen

Greece *(Regions)* — **GR**
1 Anatoliki Makedonia kai Thraki
2 Kriti
3 Voreio Aigaio
4 Notio Aigaio
5 Epiros
6 Attiki
7 Sterea Ellas
8 Dytiki Ellas
9 Ionioi Nisoi
10 Dytiki Makedonia
11 Kentriki Makedonia
12 Peloponnese
13 Thessaly

Hungary *(Megyék)* — **H**
1 Del-Alfold
2 Del-Dunantul
3 Eszak-Alfold
4 Eszak-Magyarorszag
5 Kozep-Dunantul
6 Kozep-Magyarorszag
7 Nyugat-Dunantul

Ireland *(Regions)* — **IRL**
1 Border, Midland & Western
2 Southern & Eastern

Italy *(Regions)* — **I**
1 Abruzzo
2 Basilicata
3 Calábria
4 Campánia
5 Emilia-Romagna
6 Friuli-Venézia Giulia
7 Lazio
8 Liguria
9 Lombardia
10 Marche
11 Molise
12 Umbria
13 Piemonte
14 Puglia
15 Sardegna
16 Sicilia
17 Toscana
18 Trentino-Alto Adige/Südtirol
19 Valle d'Aosta
20 Véneto

Latvia *(member state with no corresponding division)* — **LV**

Lithuania *(member state with no corresponding division)* — **LT**

Luxembourg *(member state with no corresponding division)* — **L**

Malta *(member state with no corresponding division)* — **M**

Netherlands *(Regions)* — **NL**
1 Noord-Nederland
2 Oost-Nederland
3 West-Nederland
4 Zuid-Nederland

Poland *(Voivodships)* — **PL**
1 Dolnoślaskie
2 Kujawsko-Pomorskie
3 Łódzkie
4 Lubelskie
5 Lubuskie
6 Małopolskie
7 Mazowieckie
8 Opolskie
9 Podkarpackie
10 Podlaskie
11 Pomorskie
12 Śląskie
13 Swietokrzyskie
14 Warmińsko-Mazurskie
15 Wielkopolskie
16 Zachodniopomorskie

Portugal *(Autonomous regions)* — **P**
1 Alentejo
2 Algarve
3 Centro
4 Lisboa
5 Norte

Romania *(Regions)* — **RO**
1 Bucureşti-Ilfov
2 Centru
3 Nord-Est
4 Nord-Vest
5 Sud
6 Sud-Est
7 Sud-Vest
8 Vest

Slovak Republic *(Kraj)* — **SK**
1 Bratislavsky Kraj
2 Stredne Slovensko
3 Vychodne Slovensko
4 Zapadne Slovensko

Slovenia *(member state with no corresponding division)* — **SLO**

Spain *(Autonomous communities)* — **E**
1 Andalucía
2 Aragon
3 Asturias
4 Islas Baleares
5 País Vasco
6 Islas Canarias
7 Cantabria
8 Castilla y Léon
9 Castilla-La Mancha
10 Cataluña
11 Extremadura
12 Galicia
13 Madrid
14 Murcia
15 Navarra
16 Rioja (La)
17 Valencia

Sweden *(Regions)* — **S**
1 Stockholm
2 Östra Mellansverige
3 Sydsverige
4 Västsverige
5 Norra Mellansverige
6 Mellersta Norrland
7 Övre Norrland
8 Småland med öarna

United Kingdom *(Regions)* — **GB**
1 North East England
2 North West England
3 Yorkshire & The Humber
4 East Midlands
5 West Midlands
6 East of England
7 Greater London
8 South East England
9 South West England
10 Wales
11 Scotland
12 Northern Ireland

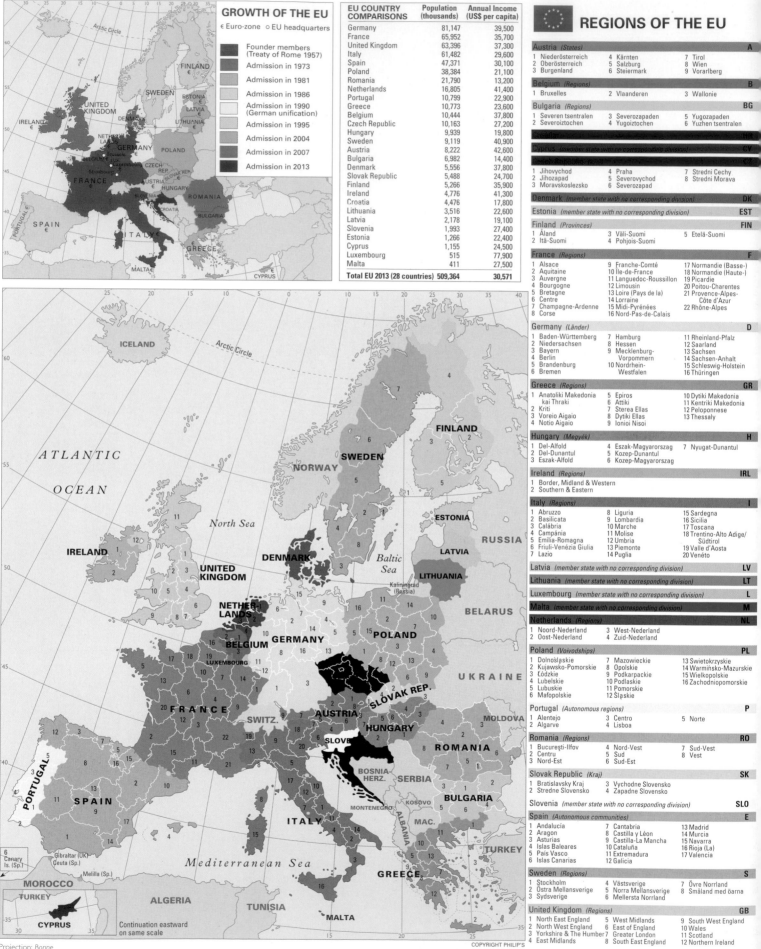

Continuation eastward on same scale

Projection: Bonne

COPYRIGHT PHILIP'S

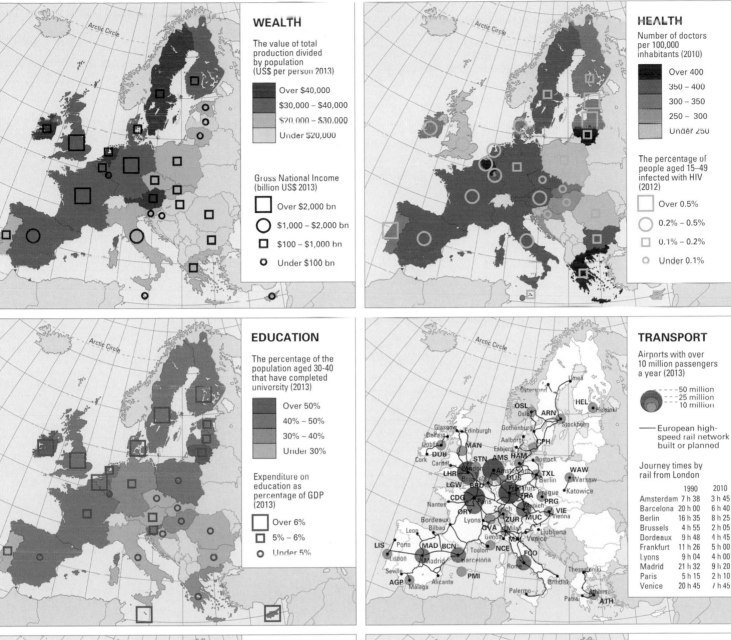

WEALTH

The value of total production divided by population (US$ per person 2013)

- Over $40,000
- $30,000 – $40,000
- $20,000 – $30,000
- Under $20,000

Gross National Income (billion US$ 2013)

- Over $2,000 bn
- $1,000 – $2,000 bn
- $100 – $1,000 bn
- Under $100 bn

HEALTH

Number of doctors per 100,000 inhabitants (2010)

- Over 400
- 350 – 400
- 300 – 350
- 250 – 300
- Under 250

The percentage of people aged 15–49 infected with HIV (2012)

- Over 0.5%
- 0.2% – 0.5%
- 0.1% – 0.2%
- Under 0.1%

EDUCATION

The percentage of the population aged 30-40 that have completed university (2013)

- Over 50%
- 40% – 50%
- 30% – 40%
- Under 30%

Expenditure on education as percentage of GDP (2013)

- Over 6%
- 5% – 6%
- Under 5%

TRANSPORT

Airports with over 10 million passengers a year (2013)

- 50 million
- 25 million
- 10 million

— European high-speed rail network built or planned

Journey times by rail from London

	1990	2010
Amsterdam	7 h 38	3 h 45
Barcelona	20 h 00	6 h 40
Berlin	16 h 35	8 h 25
Brussels	4 h 55	2 h 05
Dordeaux	9 h 48	4 h 45
Frankfurt	11 h 26	5 h 00
Lyons	9 h 04	4 h 00
Madrid	21 h 32	9 h 20
Paris	5 h 15	2 h 10
Venice	20 h 45	7 h 45

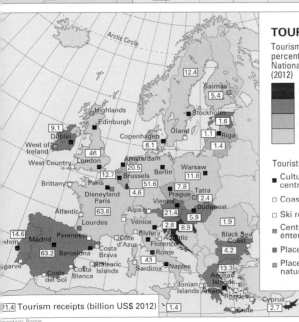

TOURISM

Tourism receipts as a percentage of Gross National Income (GNI) (2012)

- Over 10%
- 5% – 10%
- 2.5% – 5%
- Under 2.5%

Tourist destinations

- Cultural & historical centres
- Coastal resorts
- Ski resorts
- Centres of entertainment
- Places of pilgimage
- Places of great natural beauty

21.4 Tourism receipts (billion US$ 2012)

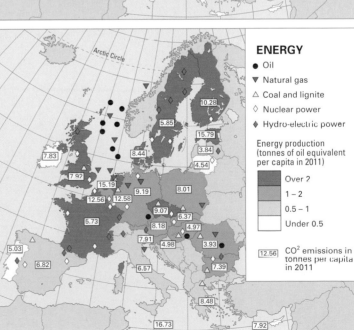

ENERGY

- Oil
- Natural gas
- Coal and lignite
- Nuclear power
- Hydro-electric power

Energy production (tonnes of oil equivalent per capita in 2011)

- Over 2
- 1 – 2
- 0.5 – 1
- Under 0.5

12.56 CO_2 emissions in tonnes per capita in 2011

Projection: Bonne

COPYRIGHT PHILIP'S

ICELAND on same scale

1:10 000 000

COPYRIGHT PHILIP'S

Projection: Conical with two standard parallels

18 East from Greenwich

50   0   25   50   75   100   125   150   175 km

1:5 000 000

50   0   25   50   75   100 miles

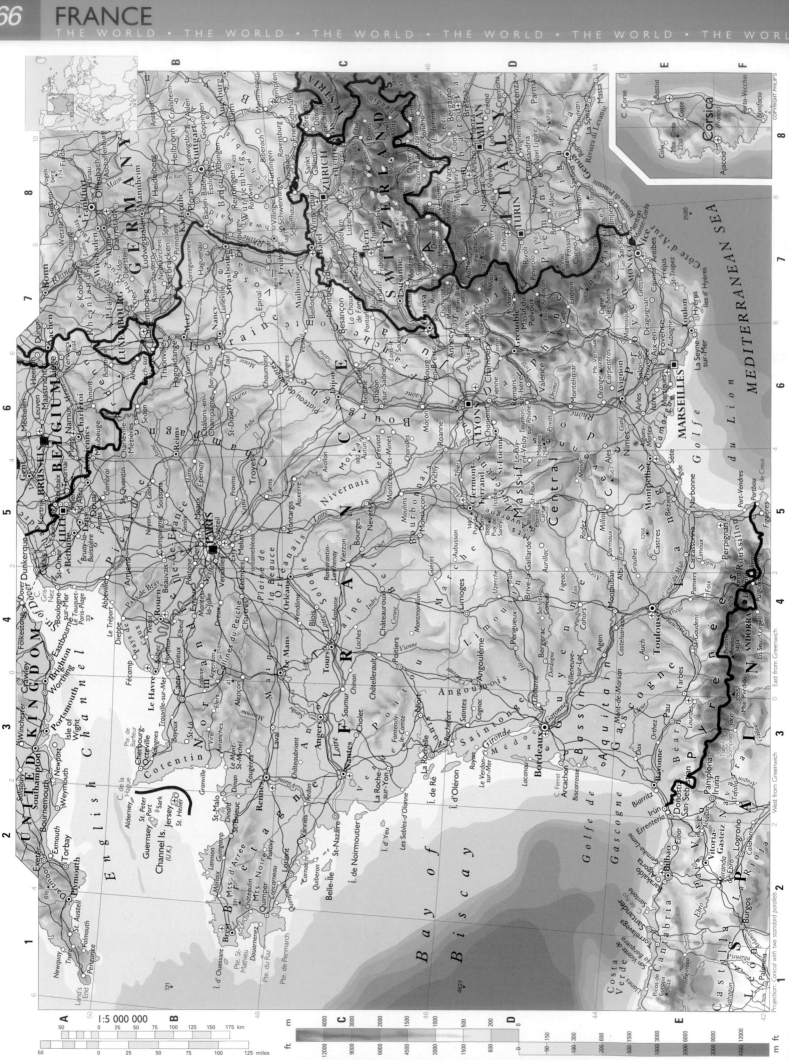

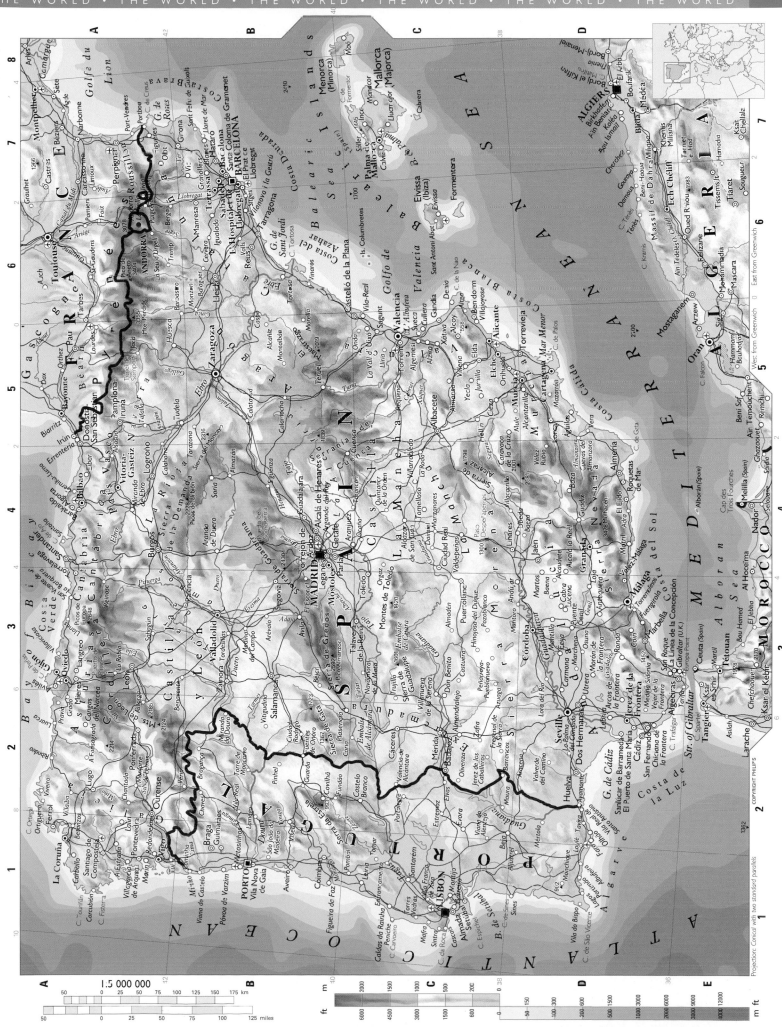

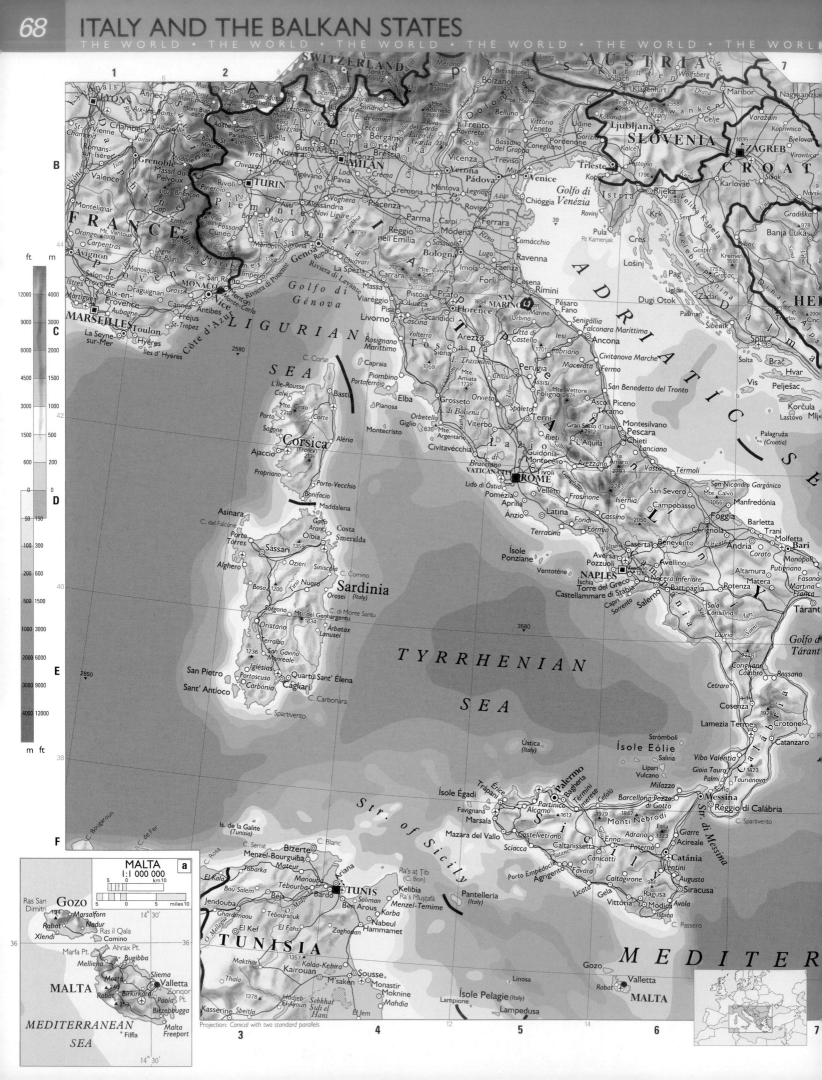

FRANCE

SWITZERLAND

AUSTRIA

SLOVENIA

ZAGREB

CROAT

MILAN

TURIN

MONACO

MARSEILLES

LIGURIAN SEA

Corsica *(France)*

SAN MARINO

Florence

ADRIATIC SEA

VATICAN CITY

ROME

Sardinia *(Italy)*

NAPLES

TYRRHENIAN SEA

BARI

TÁRANT

Golfo di Tárant

Ísole Éolie

Palermo

Messina

Sicily

Catánia

Siracusa

Str. of Sicily

TUNISIA

TUNIS

Pantelleria *(Italy)*

Ísole Pelagie *(Italy)*

MEDITER

MALTA

MALTA
1:1 000 000

5   0   km 10

5   0   miles 10

Gozo

MALTA

Valletta

MEDITERRANEAN SEA

Projection: Conical with two standard parallels

1:5 000 000

East from Greenwich

50 0 25 50 75 100 125 150 175 km

50 0 25 50 75 100 125 miles

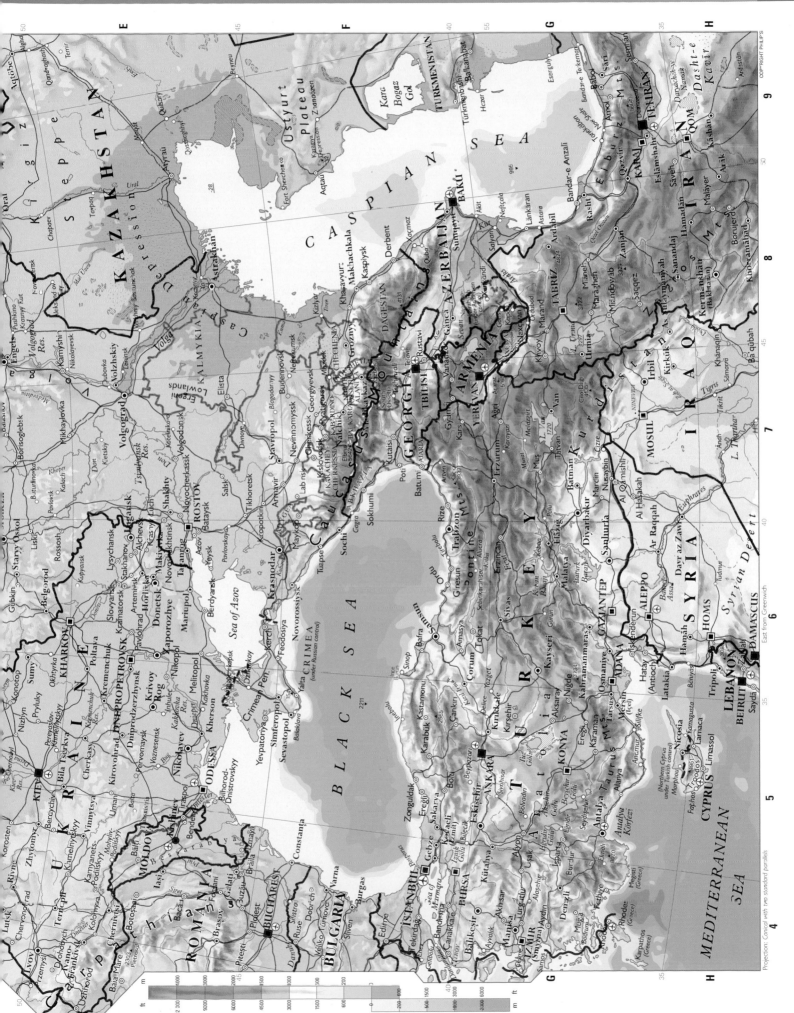

Projection: Conical with two standard parallels

East from Greenwich

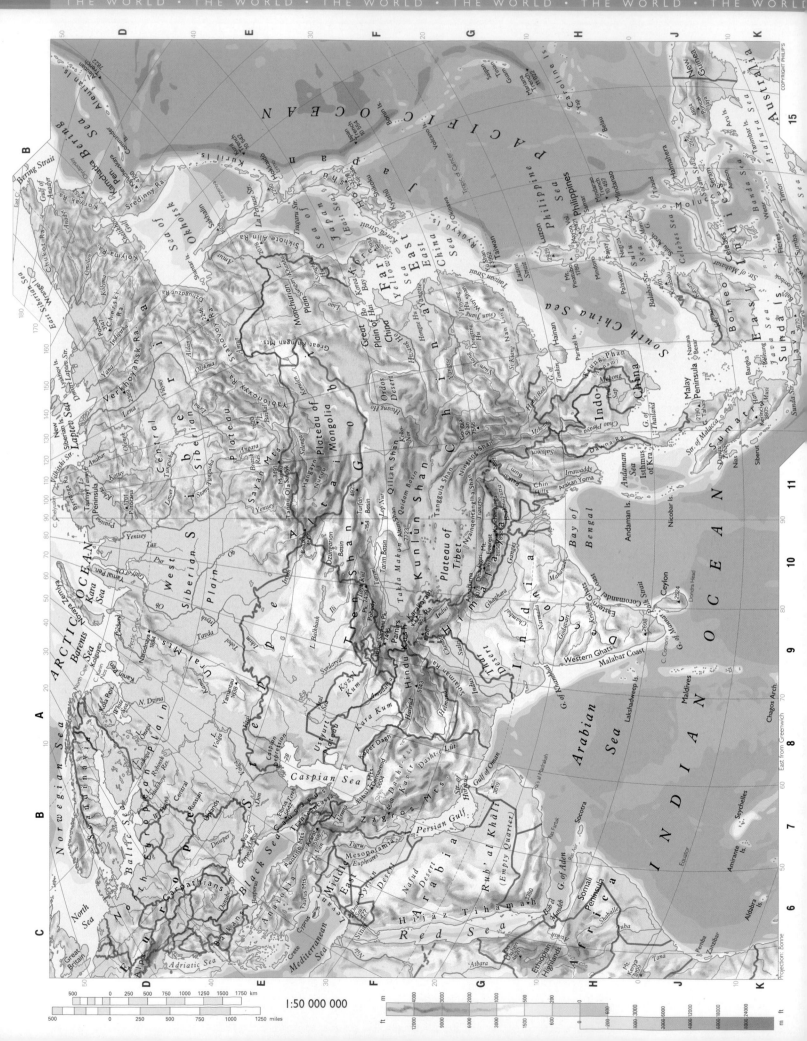

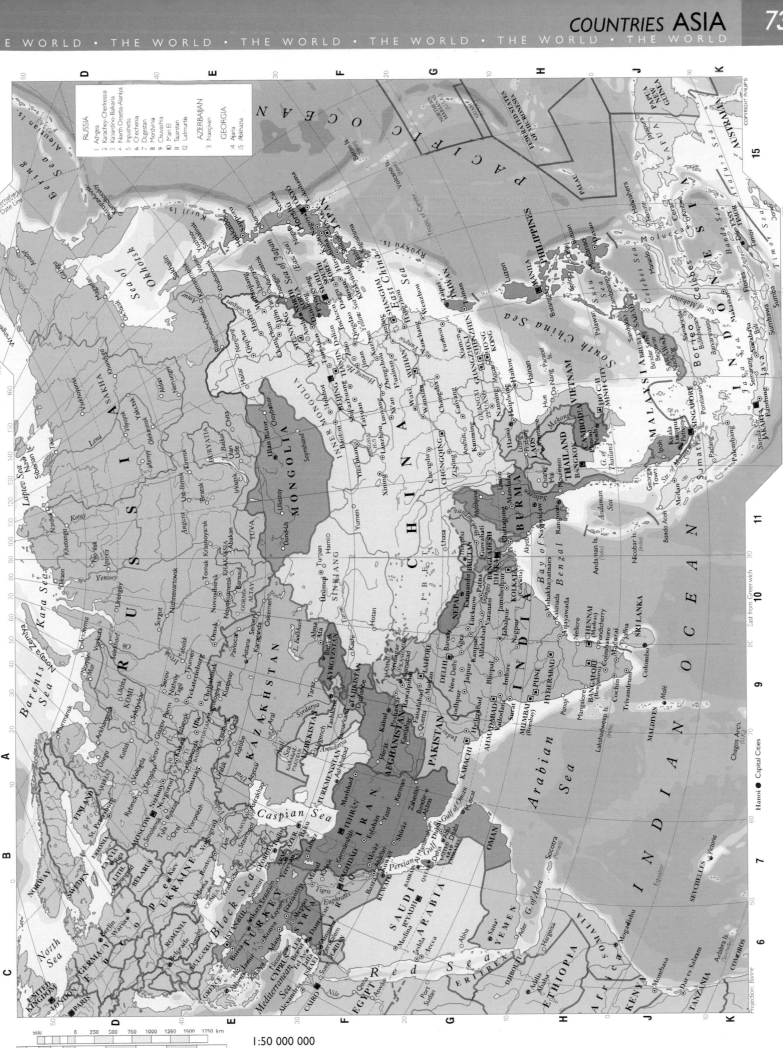

RUSSIA
1 Adygea
2 Karachev-Cherkessia
3 Kabardino-Balkaria
4 North Ossetia-Alaniya
5 Ingushetia
6 Chechenia
7 Dagestan
8 Mordvinia
9 Chuvashia
10 Pari El
11 Tatarstan
12 Udmurtia

AZERBAIJAN
3 Naxçıvan

GEORGIA
4 Ajaria
5 Abkhazia

COPYRIGHT PHILIP'S

Hanoi ● Capital Cities

1:50 000 000

Projection: Borre

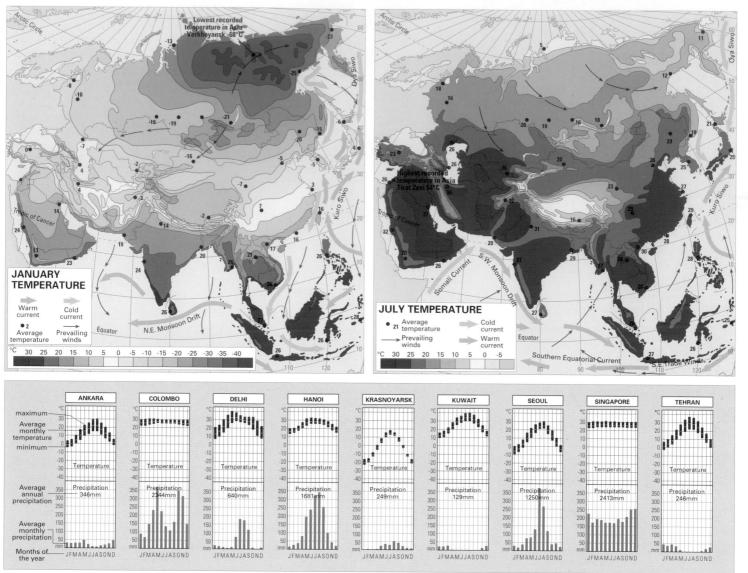

JANUARY TEMPERATURE

Lowest recorded temperature in Asia Verkhoyansk -68°C

Warm current
Cold current
• 2 Average temperature
Prevailing winds

°C 30 25 20 15 10 5 0 -5 -10 -15 -20 -25 -30 -35 -40

JULY TEMPERATURE

Highest recorded temperature in Asia Tirat Zevi 54°C

Somali Current
S.-W. Monsoon Drift
Southern Equatorial Current
S.E. Trade Winds

• 21 Average temperature
Cold current
Prevailing winds
Warm current

°C 30 25 20 15 10 5 0 -5

Climate graphs: ANKARA, COLOMBO, DELHI, HANOI, KRASNOYARSK, KUWAIT, SEOUL, SINGAPORE, TEHRAN

- maximum
- Average monthly temperature
- minimum
- Average annual precipitation
- Average monthly precipitation
- Months of the year

ANKARA — Temperature; Precipitation 346mm
COLOMBO — Temperature; Precipitation 2344mm
DELHI — Temperature; Precipitation 640mm
HANOI — Temperature; Precipitation 1681mm
KRASNOYARSK — Temperature; Precipitation 249mm
KUWAIT — Temperature; Precipitation 129mm
SEOUL — Temperature; Precipitation 1250mm
SINGAPORE — Temperature; Precipitation 2413mm
TEHRAN — Temperature; Precipitation 246mm

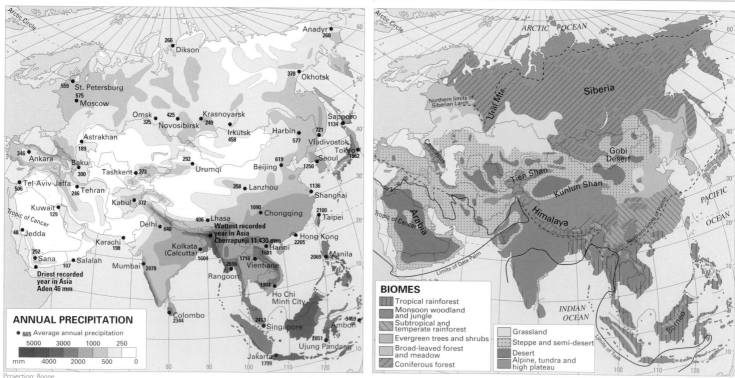

ANNUAL PRECIPITATION

Anadyr 260
Dikson 266
Okhotsk 378
St. Petersburg 559
Moscow 575
Omsk 325, 425
Novosibirsk
Krasnoyarsk 249
Irkutsk 458
Sapporo 1134
Harbin
Vladivostok 577, 721
Astrakhan 189
Ankara 346
Baku
Tashkent 300, 373
Urumqi 292
Beijing 619
Tokyo 1562
Seoul 1250
Tel-Aviv-Jaffa 506
Tehran 246
Kabul 372
Lanzhou 358
Shanghai 1136
Chongqing 1090
Lhasa 406
Kuwait 129
Delhi 640
Taipei 2100
Jedda 48
Karachi 198
Kolkata (Calcutta) 1604
Hanoi 1681
Hong Kong 2265
Sana 252
Salalah 107
Mumbai 2078
Vientiane 1716, 2616
Manila 2069
Rangoon
Wettest recorded year in Asia Cherrapunji 11,430 mm
Driest recorded year in Asia Aden 46 mm
Ho Chi Minh City 1984
Colombo 2344
Singapore 2413
Ambon 3459
Ujung Pandang
Jakarta 1799
2851

• 665 Average annual precipitation

mm 5000 4000 3000 2000 1000 500 250 0

BIOMES

- Tropical rainforest
- Monsoon woodland and jungle
- Subtropical and temperate rainforest
- Evergreen trees and shrubs
- Broad-leaved forest and meadow
- Coniferous forest
- Grassland
- Steppe and semi-desert
- Desert
- Alpine, tundra and high plateau

ARCTIC OCEAN
Siberia
Ural Mts.
Northern limits of Siberian Larch
Caucasus
Gobi Desert
Tien Shan
Kunlun Shan
Arabia
Himalaya
Tropic of Cancer
Limits of Date Palm
Northern limits of Palm
Limits of Teak
PACIFIC OCEAN
INDIAN OCEAN
Borneo

Projection: Bonne

COPYRIGHT PHILIP'S

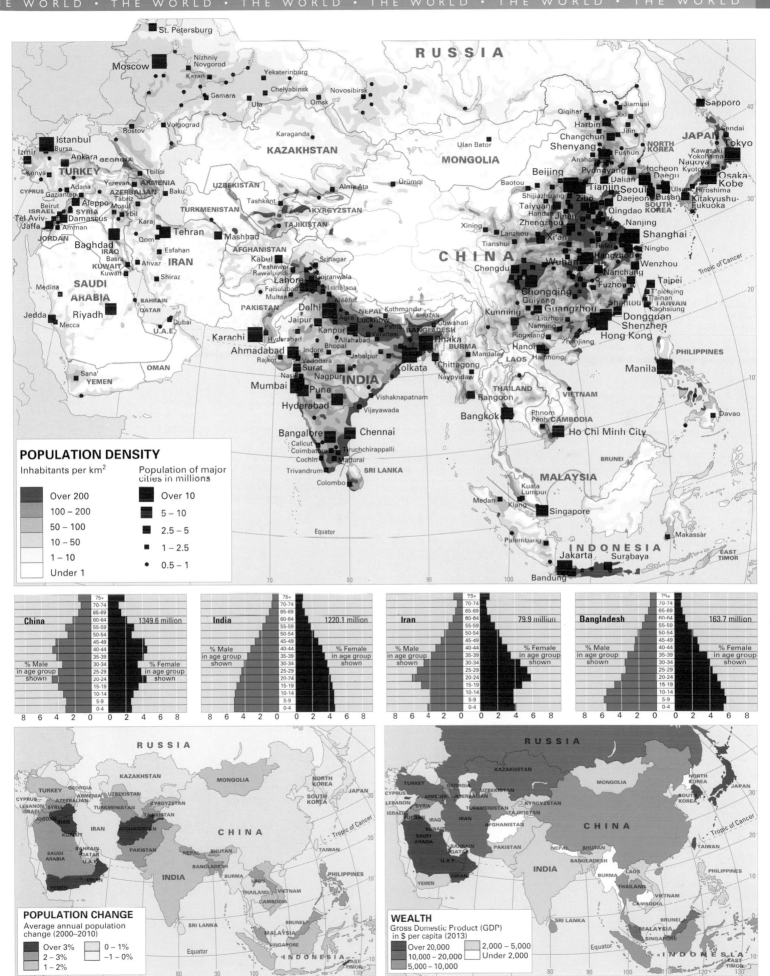

St. Petersburg
Moscow
Nizhniy Novgorod
Yekaterinburg
Kazan
Chelyabinsk
Novosibirsk
Samara
Ufa
Omsk
Volgograd
Rostov
Karaganda

RUSSIA

KAZAKHSTAN

MONGOLIA

Ulan Bator

Qiqihar
Jiamusi
Jixi
Harbin
Jilin
Changchun
Fushun
Shenyang
Anshan
NORTH KOREA
JAPAN
Sapporo
Sendai
Tokyo

Istanbul
Izmir
Bursa
Ankara
Konya
GEORGIA
TURKEY
Adana
Tbilisi
ARMENIA
Yerevan
AZERBAIJAN
Baku
UZBEKISTAN
Tashkent
Alma Ata
Ürümqi
Baotou
Beijing
Pyongyang
Incheon
Seoul
Daegu
Ulsan
SOUTH KOREA
Busan
Kawasaki
Yokohama
Nagoya
Kyoto
Osaka
Kobe
Hiroshima
Kitakyushu
Fukuoka

CYPRUS
Gaziantep
Aleppo
Beirut
Mosul
Irbil
ISRAEL
SYRIA
Tabriz
TURKMENISTAN
KYRGYZSTAN
Shijiazhuang
Taiyuan
Zibo
Tianjin
Jinan
Daejeon
Qingdao
Nanjing
Shanghai

Tel Aviv-Jaffa
Damascus
Amman
JORDAN
Karaj
Tehran
TAJIKISTAN
Xining
Lanzhou
Zhengzhou
Handan
Xi'an
Ningbo
Hangzhou
Wenzhou

Baghdad
IRAQ
Basra
KUWAIT
Kuwait
Qom
Esfahan
Mashhad
Tianshui
Chengdu
Wuhan
Hefei
Nanchang
Fuzhou
Taipei
T'aichung

AFGHANISTAN
Kabul
Srinagar
Kunming
Chongqing
Guiyang
Guangzhou
Shantou
Tainan
TAIWAN
Kaohsiung

SAUDI ARABIA
Medina
BAHRAIN
QATAR
Dubai
U.A.E.
Ahvaz
Shiraz
IRAN
Peshawar
Rawalpindi
Faisalabad
Multan
Lahore
Gujranwala
Ludhiana
PAKISTAN
Delhi
Meerut
NEPAL
Kathmandu
BHUTAN
Liuzhou
Nanning
Pingxiang
Zhanjiang
Dongguan
Shenzhen
Hong Kong

Jedda
Mecca
Riyadh
Karachi
Hyderabad
Jaipur
Agra
Lucknow
Kanpur
Allahabad
Patna
Varanasi
Guwahati
BANGLADESH
Dhaka
Hanoi
Haiphong
PHILIPPINES

OMAN
Sana'
YEMEN
Ahmadabad
Rajkot
Indore
Bhopal
Vadodara
Jabalpur
Chittagong
BURMA
Mandalay
LAOS
VIETNAM
Manila

Mumbai
Surat
Nasik
Nagpur
INDIA
Vishaknapatnam
Naypyidaw
Rangoon
THAILAND

Pune
Hyderabad
Vijayawada

Bangalore
Calicut
Coimbatore
Cochin
Chennai
Tiruchchirappalli
Madurai
Bangkok
Phnom Penh
CAMBODIA
Ho Chi Minh City
Davao

Trivandrum
Colombo
SRI LANKA
MALAYSIA
BRUNEI

Kuala Lumpur
Medan
Klang
Singapore
Makassar

Palembang
INDONESIA
EAST TIMOR

Equator
Jakarta
Surabaya
Bandung

Tropic of Cancer

POPULATION DENSITY

Inhabitants per km²

- Over 200
- 100 – 200
- 50 – 100
- 10 – 50
- 1 – 10
- Under 1

Population of major cities in millions

- Over 10
- 5 – 10
- 2.5 – 5
- 1 – 2.5
- 0.5 – 1

China — 1349.6 million

| | 75+ |
| 70-74 |
| 65-69 |
| 60-64 |
| 55-59 |
| 50-54 |
| 45-49 |
| 40-44 |
| 35-39 |
% Male in age group shown | 30-34 | % Female in age group shown
| 25-29 |
| 20-24 |
| 15-19 |
| 10-14 |
| 5-9 |
| 0-4 |

8 6 4 2 0 0 2 4 6 8

India — 1220.1 million

75+
70-74
65-69
60-64
55-59
50-54
45-49
% Male in age group shown | 40-44 | % Female in age group shown
35-39
30-34
25-29
20-24
15-19
10-14
5-9
0-4

8 6 4 2 0 0 2 4 6 8

Iran — 79.9 million

75+
70-74
65-69
60-64
55-59
50-54
45-49
% Male in age group shown | 40-44 | % Female in age group shown
35-39
30-34
25-29
20-24
15-19
10-14
5-9
0-4

8 6 4 2 0 0 2 4 6 8

Bangladesh — 163.7 million

75+
70-74
65-69
60-64
55-59
50-54
45-49
% Male in age group shown | 40-44 | % Female in age group shown
35-39
30-34
25-29
20-24
15-19
10-14
5-9
0-4

8 6 4 2 0 0 2 4 6 8

RUSSIA
KAZAKHSTAN
MONGOLIA
NORTH KOREA
JAPAN
SOUTH KOREA
TURKEY
GEORGIA
CYPRUS
LEBANON
ARMENIA
AZERBAIJAN
UZBEKISTAN
ISRAEL
SYRIA
JORDAN
IRAQ
KUWAIT
TURKMENISTAN
KYRGYZSTAN
TAJIKISTAN
CHINA
SAUDI ARABIA
BAHRAIN
QATAR
IRAN
AFGHANISTAN
PAKISTAN
NEPAL
BHUTAN
U.A.E.
YEMEN
OMAN
INDIA
BANGLADESH
BURMA
LAOS
VIETNAM
THAILAND
TAIWAN
PHILIPPINES
CAMBODIA
SRI LANKA
BRUNEI
MALAYSIA
SINGAPORE
INDONESIA
EAST TIMOR

Tropic of Cancer
Equator

POPULATION CHANGE

Average annual population change (2000–2010)

- Over 3%
- 2 – 3%
- 1 – 2%
- 0 – 1%
- –1 – 0%

WEALTH

Gross Domestic Product (GDP) in $ per capita (2013)

- Over 20,000
- 10,000 – 20,000
- 5,000 – 10,000
- 2,000 – 5,000
- Under 2,000

Projection: Bonne

COPYRIGHT PHILIP'S

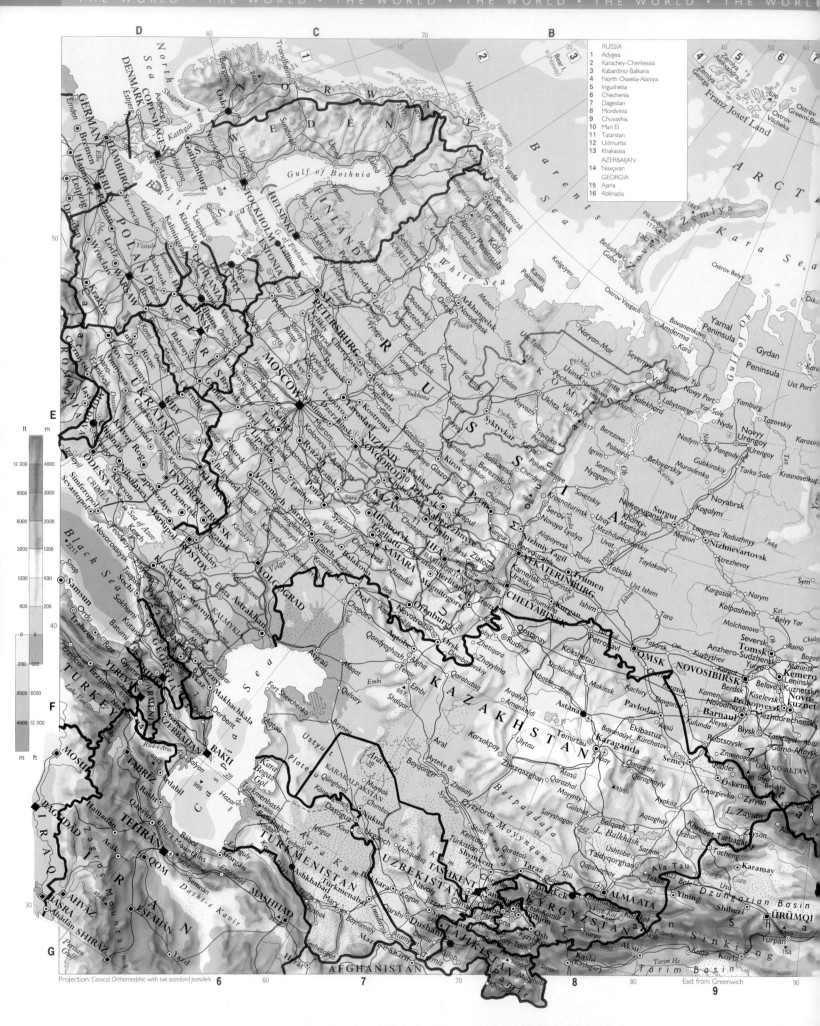

RUSSIA
1 Adygea
2 Karachey-Cherkessia
3 Kabardino-Balkaria
4 North Ossetia-Alaniya
5 Ingushetia
6 Chechenia
7 Dagestan
8 Mordvinia
9 Chuvashia
10 Mari El
11 Tatarstan
12 Udmurtia
13 Khakassia
AZERBAIJAN
14 Naxçıvan
GEORGIA
15 Ajaria
16 Abkhazia

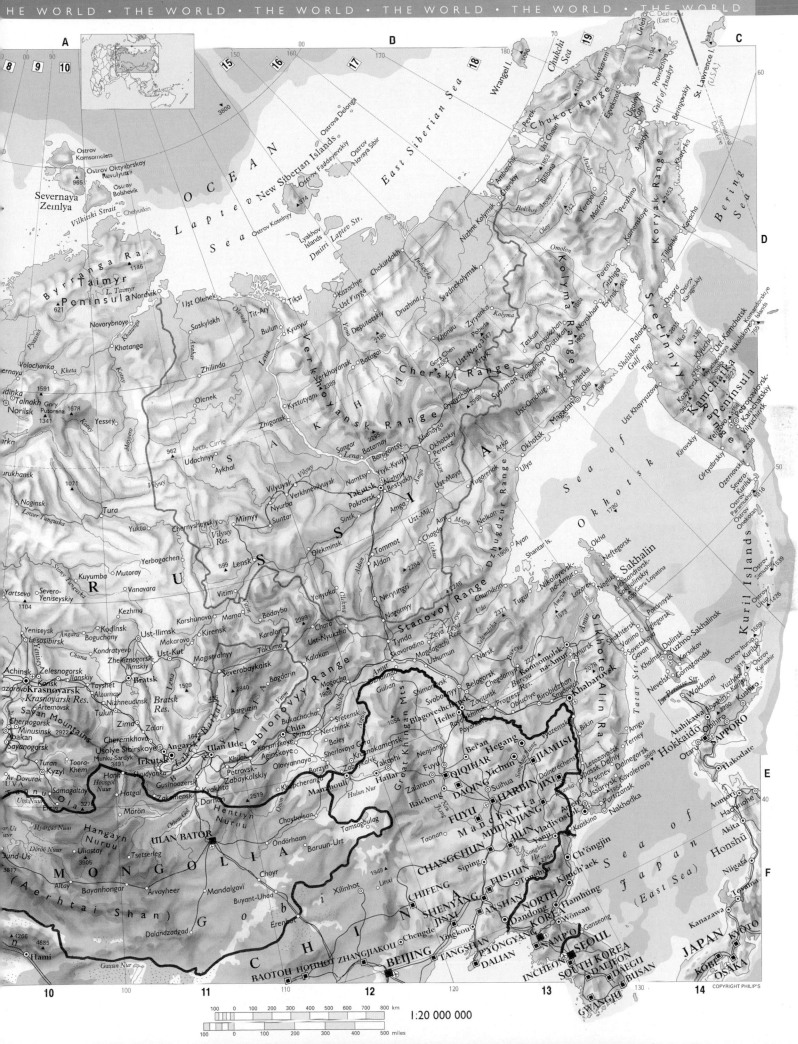

1:20 000 000

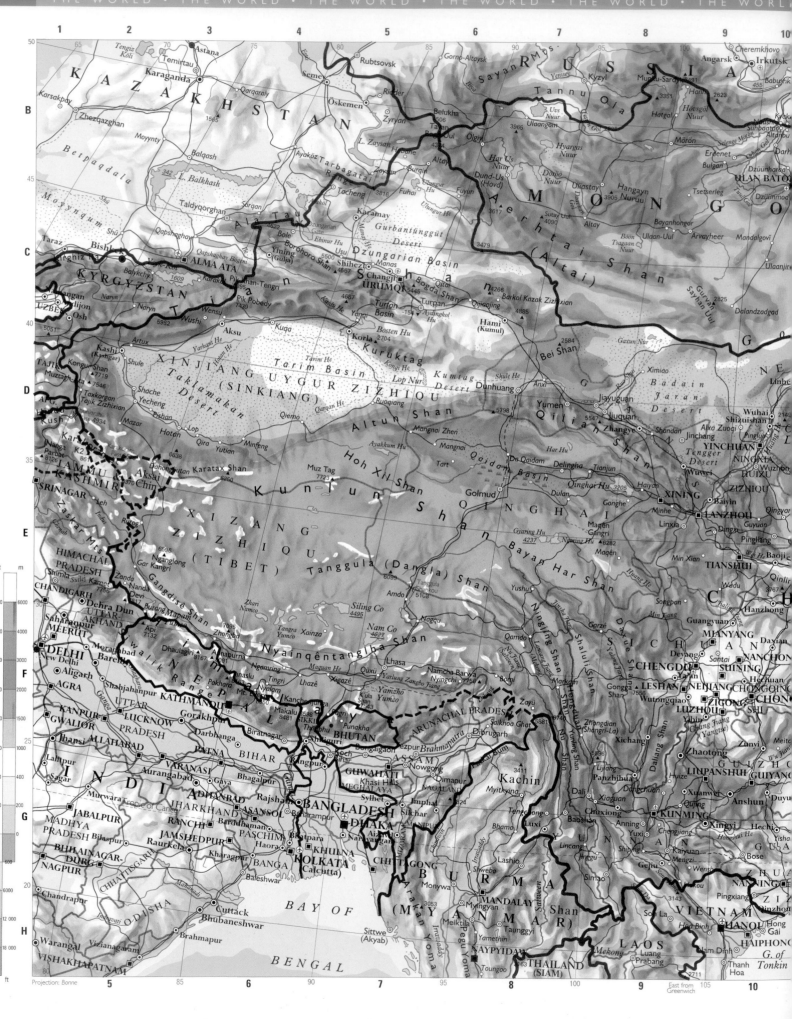

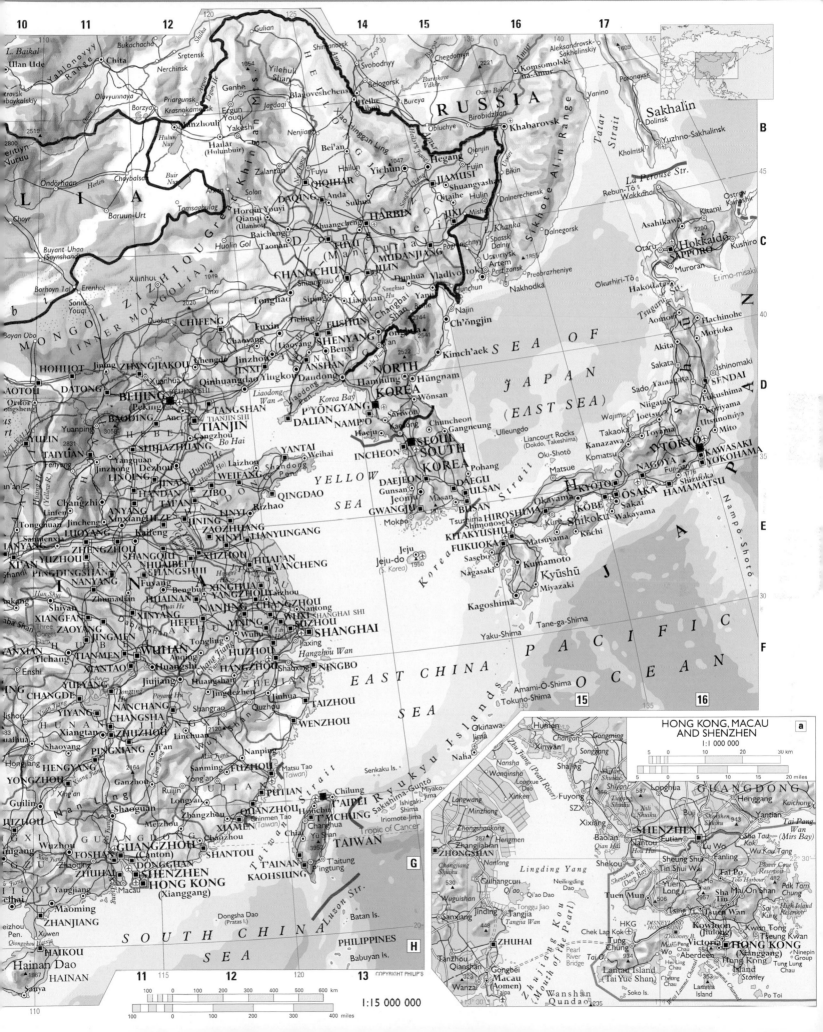

HONG KONG, MACAU AND SHENZHEN

1:1 000 000

1:15 000 000

COPYRIGHT PHILIP'S

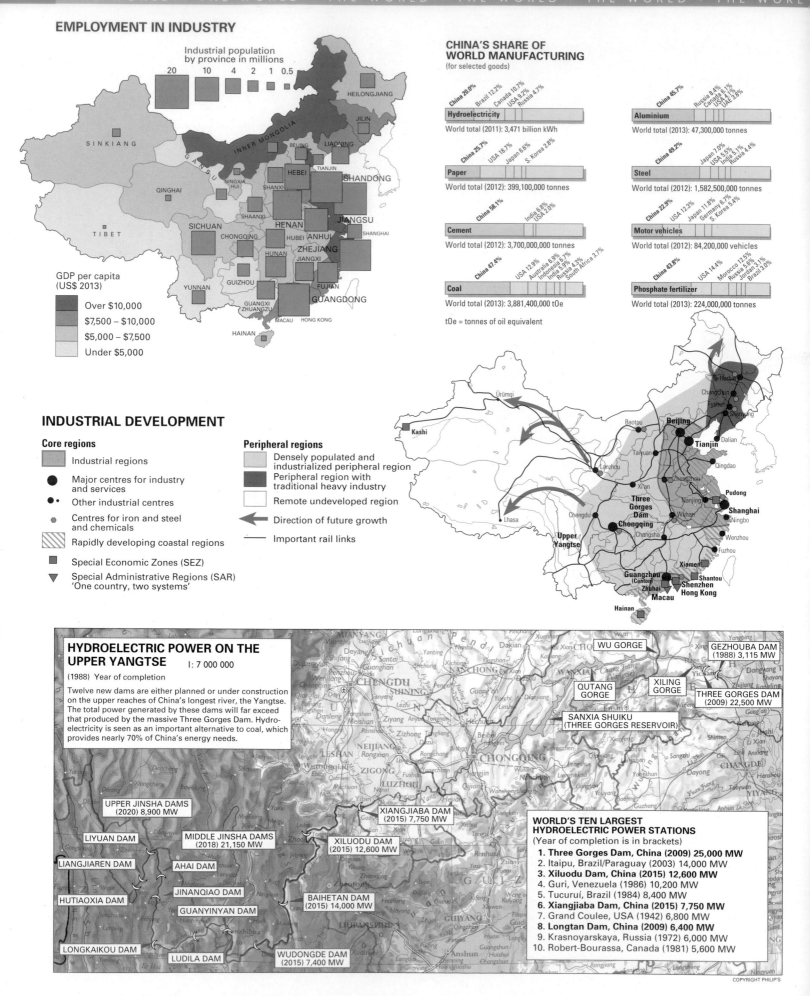

EMPLOYMENT IN INDUSTRY

Industrial population
by province in millions
20 10 4 2 1 0.5

GDP per capita
(US$ 2013)

Over $10,000
$7,500 – $10,000
$5,000 – $7,500
Under $5,000

CHINA'S SHARE OF WORLD MANUFACTURING
(for selected goods)

Hydroelectricity
China 20.0% Brazil 12.2% Canada 10.7% USA 9.2% Russia 4.7%
World total (2011): 3,471 billion kWh

Paper
China 25.7% USA 18.7% Japan 6.6% S. Korea 2.8%
World total (2012): 399,100,000 tonnes

Cement
China 58.1% India 6.8% USA 2.0%
World total (2012): 3,700,000,000 tonnes

Coal
China 47.4% USA 12.9% Australia 6.9% Indonesia 8.7% India 5.5% Russia 4.3% South Africa 3.7%
World total (2013): 3,881,400,000 tOe

Aluminium
China 45.7% Russia 8.4% Canada 6.1% USA 5.1% UAE 3.8%
World total (2013): 47,300,000 tonnes

Steel
China 49.2% Japan 7.0% USA 5.5% India 5.1% Russia 4.4%
World total (2012): 1,582,500,000 tonnes

Motor vehicles
China 22.9% USA 12.3% Japan 11.8% Germany 6.7% S. Korea 5.4%
World total (2012): 84,200,000 vehicles

Phosphate fertilizer
China 43.8% USA 14.4% Morocco 12.5% Russia 5.5% Jordan 3.1% Brazil 3.0%
World total (2013): 224,000,000 tonnes

tOe = tonnes of oil equivalent

INDUSTRIAL DEVELOPMENT

Core regions

Industrial regions

● Major centres for industry and services

•●• Other industrial centres

● Centres for iron and steel and chemicals

▨ Rapidly developing coastal regions

■ Special Economic Zones (SEZ)

▼ Special Administrative Regions (SAR) 'One country, two systems'

Peripheral regions

Densely populated and industrialized peripheral region

Peripheral region with traditional heavy industry

Remote undeveloped region

← Direction of future growth

— Important rail links

HYDROELECTRIC POWER ON THE UPPER YANGTSE
1: 7 000 000

(1988) Year of completion

Twelve new dams are either planned or under construction on the upper reaches of China's longest river, the Yangtse. The total power generated by these dams will far exceed that produced by the massive Three Gorges Dam. Hydroelectricity is seen as an important alternative to coal, which provides nearly 70% of China's energy needs.

UPPER JINSHA DAMS (2020) 8,900 MW

LIYUAN DAM

LIANGJIAREN DAM

HUTIAOXIA DAM

LONGKAIKOU DAM

LUDILA DAM

MIDDLE JINSHA DAMS (2018) 21,150 MW

AHAI DAM

JINANQIAO DAM

GUANYINYAN DAM

WUDONGDE DAM (2015) 7,400 MW

XIANGJIABA DAM (2015) 7,750 MW

XILUODU DAM (2015) 12,600 MW

BAIHETAN DAM (2015) 14,000 MW

WU GORGE

QUTANG GORGE

XILING GORGE

SANXIA SHUIKU (THREE GORGES RESERVOIR)

GEZHOUBA DAM (1988) 3,115 MW

THREE GORGES DAM (2009) 22,500 MW

WORLD'S TEN LARGEST HYDROELECTRIC POWER STATIONS
(Year of completion is in brackets)

1. **Three Gorges Dam, China (2009) 25,000 MW**
2. Itaipu, Brazil/Paraguay (2003) 14,000 MW
3. **Xiluodu Dam, China (2015) 12,600 MW**
4. Guri, Venezuela (1986) 10,200 MW
5. Tucuruí, Brazil (1984) 8,400 MW
6. **Xiangjiaba Dam, China (2015) 7,750 MW**
7. Grand Coulee, USA (1942) 6,800 MW
8. **Longtan Dam, China (2009) 6,400 MW**
9. Krasnoyarskaya, Russia (1972) 6,000 MW
10. Robert-Bourassa, Canada (1981) 5,600 MW

COPYRIGHT PHILIP'S

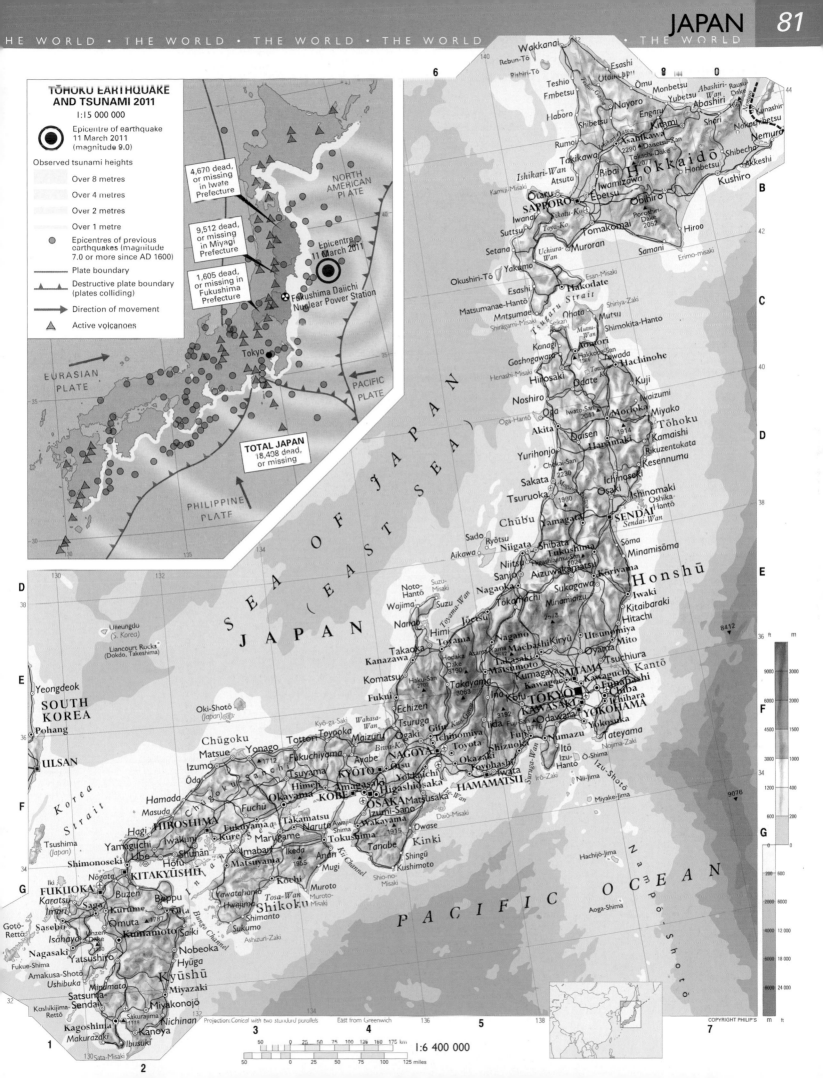

TŌHOKU EARTHQUAKE AND TSUNAMI 2011

1:15 000 000

◉ Epicentre of earthquake
11 March 2011
(magnitude 9.0)

Observed tsunami heights

Over 8 metres

Over 4 metres

Over 2 metres

Over 1 metre

● Epicentres of previous earthquakes (magnitude 7.0 or more since AD 1600)

Plate boundary

Destructive plate boundary (plates colliding)

→ Direction of movement

▲ Active volcanoes

4,670 dead, or missing in Iwate Prefecture

9,512 dead, or missing in Miyagi Prefecture

1,605 dead, or missing in Fukushima Prefecture

Epicentre 11 March 2011

Fukushima Daiichi Nuclear Power Station

NORTH AMERICAN PLATE

TOTAL JAPAN
18,408 dead, or missing

EURASIAN PLATE

PACIFIC PLATE

PHILIPPINE PLATE

Tokyo

Projection: Conical with two standard parallels

East from Greenwich

1:6 400 000

COPYRIGHT PHILIP'S

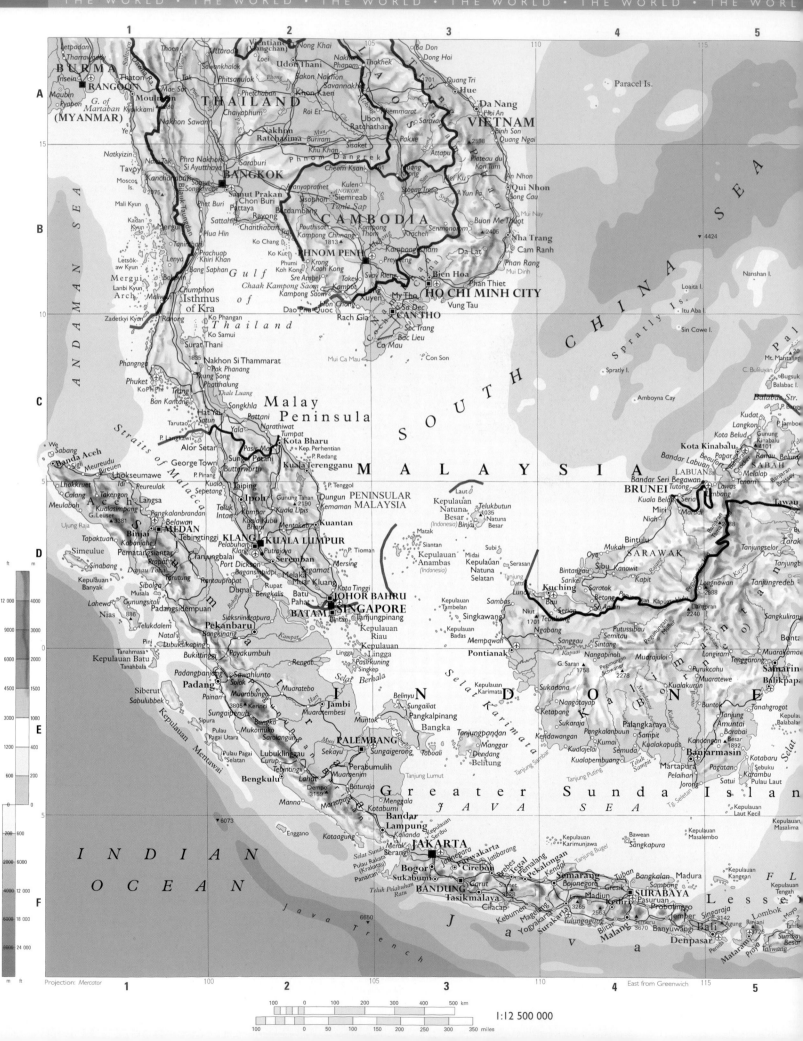

Projection: Mercator

East from Greenwich

1:12 500 000

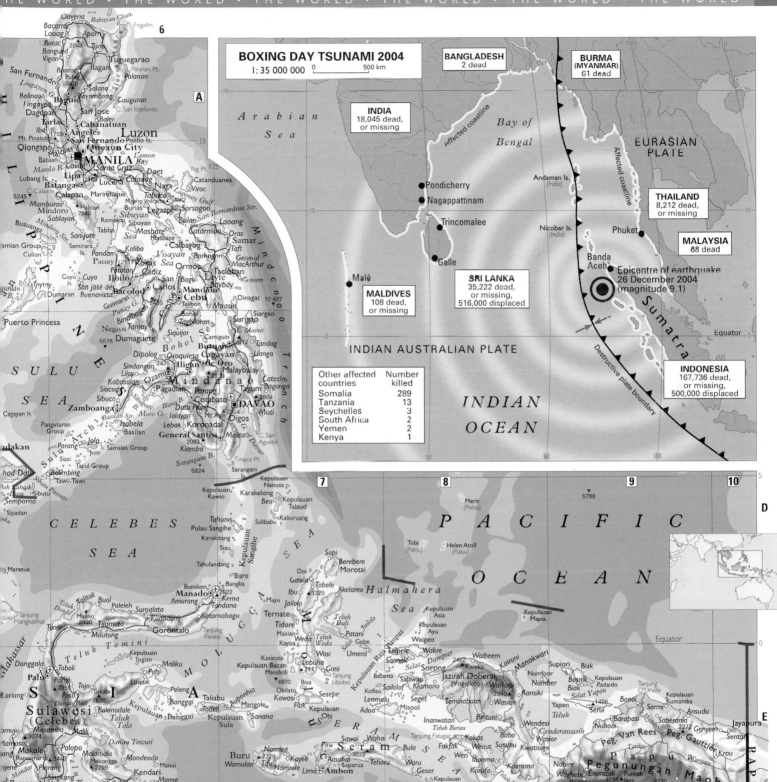

BOXING DAY TSUNAMI 2004

1 : 35 000 000   0 — 500 km

BANGLADESH 2 dead

BURMA (MYANMAR) 61 dead

INDIA 18,045 dead, or missing

THAILAND 8,212 dead, or missing

MALAYSIA 68 dead

SRI LANKA 35,222 dead, or missing, 516,000 displaced

MALDIVES 108 dead, or missing

INDONESIA 167,736 dead, or missing, 500,000 displaced

Epicentre of earthquake 26 December 2004 (magnitude 9.1)

EURASIAN PLATE

INDIAN AUSTRALIAN PLATE

Destructive plate boundary

Other affected countries	Number killed
Somalia	289
Tanzania	13
Seychelles	3
South Africa	2
Yemen	2
Kenya	1

COPYRIGHT PHILIP'S

continuation southwards
on same scale

Projection: Conical with two standard parallels

THE MONSOON 1:100 000 000

Monthly rainfall

mm		mm
400		50
200		25
100		0

→ Wind direction

━ ITCZ (intertropical convergence zone)

In early March, which normally marks the end of the subcontinent's cool season and the start of the hot season, winds blow outwards from the mainland. But as the overhead sun and the ITCZ move northwards, the land is intensely heated, and a low-pressure system develops. The south-east trade winds, which are drawn across the Equator, change direction and are sucked into the interior to become south-westerly winds, bringing heavy rain. By November, the overhead sun and the ITCZ have again moved southwards and the wind directions are again reversed. Cool winds blow from the Asian interior to the sea, losing any moisture on the Himalayas before descending to the coast.

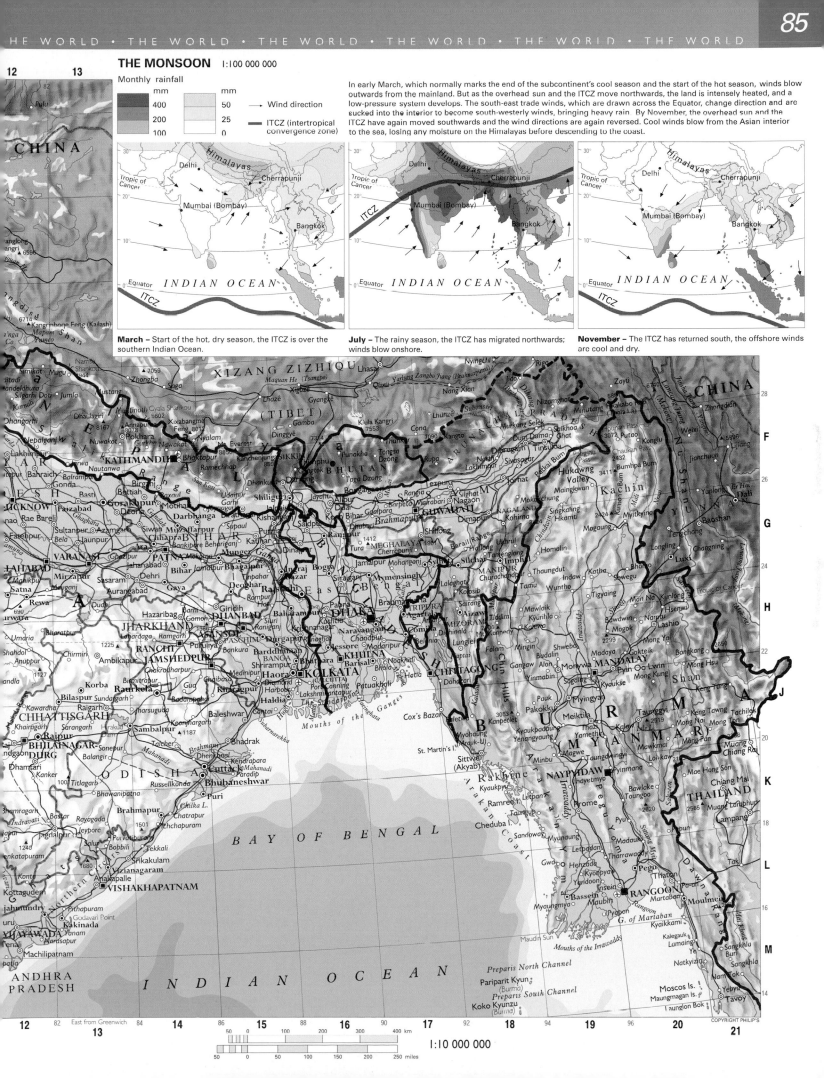

March – Start of the hot, dry season, the ITCZ is over the southern Indian Ocean.

July – The rainy season, the ITCZ has migrated northwards; winds blow onshore.

November – The ITCZ has returned south, the offshore winds are cool and dry.

Projection: Conical Orthomorphic with two standard parallels

1:10 000 000

v v v v v v
v v v v v v   Lava fields
v v v v v v

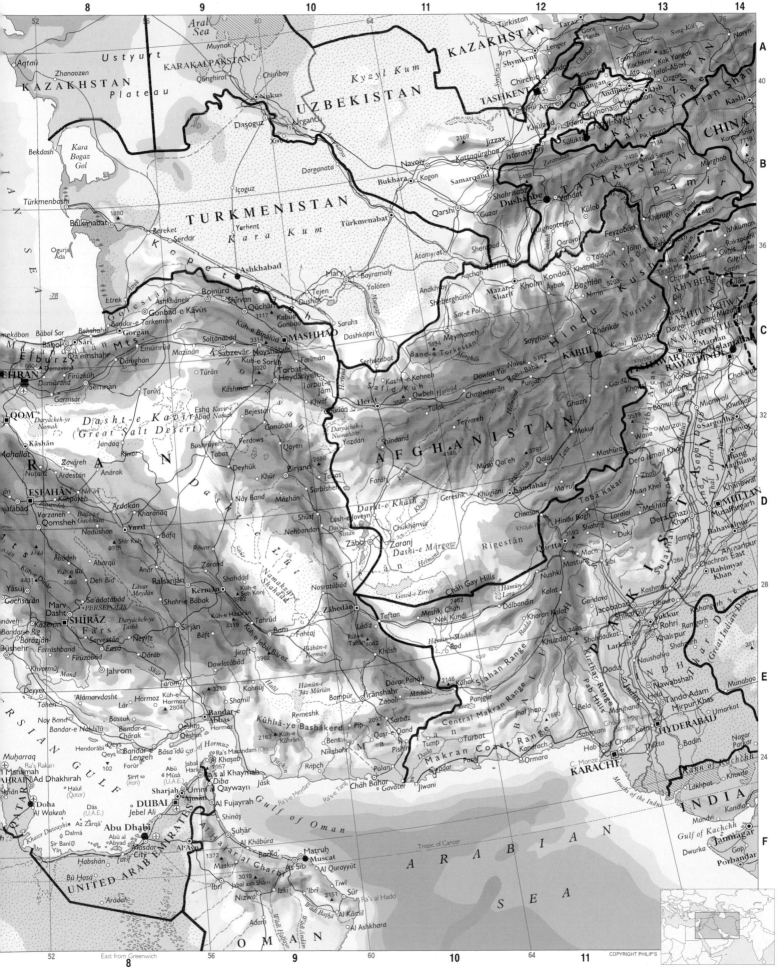

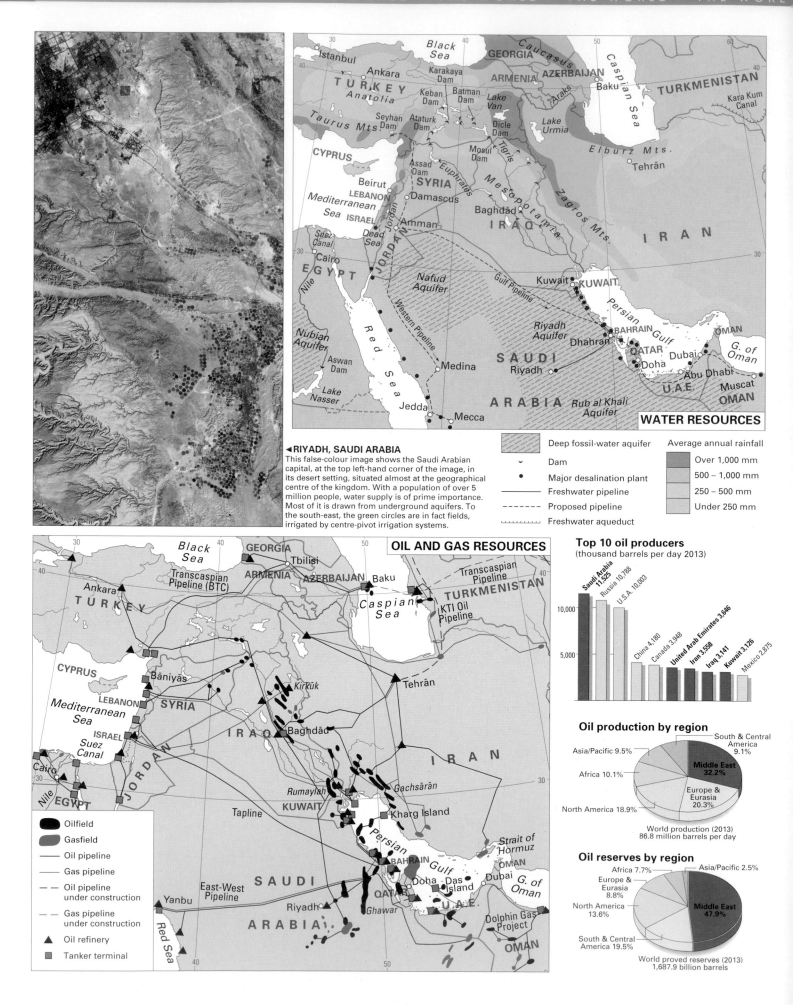

◄ RIYADH, SAUDI ARABIA

This false-colour image shows the Saudi Arabian capital, at the top left-hand corner of the image, in its desert setting, situated almost at the geographical centre of the kingdom. With a population of over 5 million people, water supply is of prime importance. Most of it is drawn from underground aquifers. To the south-east, the green circles are in fact fields, irrigated by centre-pivot irrigation systems.

WATER RESOURCES

Deep fossil-water aquifer
Dam
Major desalination plant
Freshwater pipeline
Proposed pipeline
Freshwater aqueduct

Average annual rainfall
Over 1,000 mm
500 – 1,000 mm
250 – 500 mm
Under 250 mm

OIL AND GAS RESOURCES

Oilfield
Gasfield
Oil pipeline
Gas pipeline
Oil pipeline under construction
Gas pipeline under construction
▲ Oil refinery
■ Tanker terminal

Top 10 oil producers
(thousand barrels per day 2013)

Saudi Arabia 11,525
Russia 10,788
U.S.A. 10,003
China 4,180
Canada 3,948
United Arab Emirates 3,646
Iran 3,558
Iraq 3,141
Kuwait 3,126
Mexico 2,875

Oil production by region

Asia/Pacific 9.5%
Africa 10.1%
North America 18.9%
Europe & Eurasia 20.3%
Middle East 32.2%
South & Central America 9.1%

World production (2013)
86.8 million barrels per day

Oil reserves by region

Africa 7.7%
Europe & Eurasia 8.8%
North America 13.6%
South & Central America 19.5%
Middle East 47.9%
Asia/Pacific 2.5%

World proved reserves (2013)
1,687.9 billion barrels

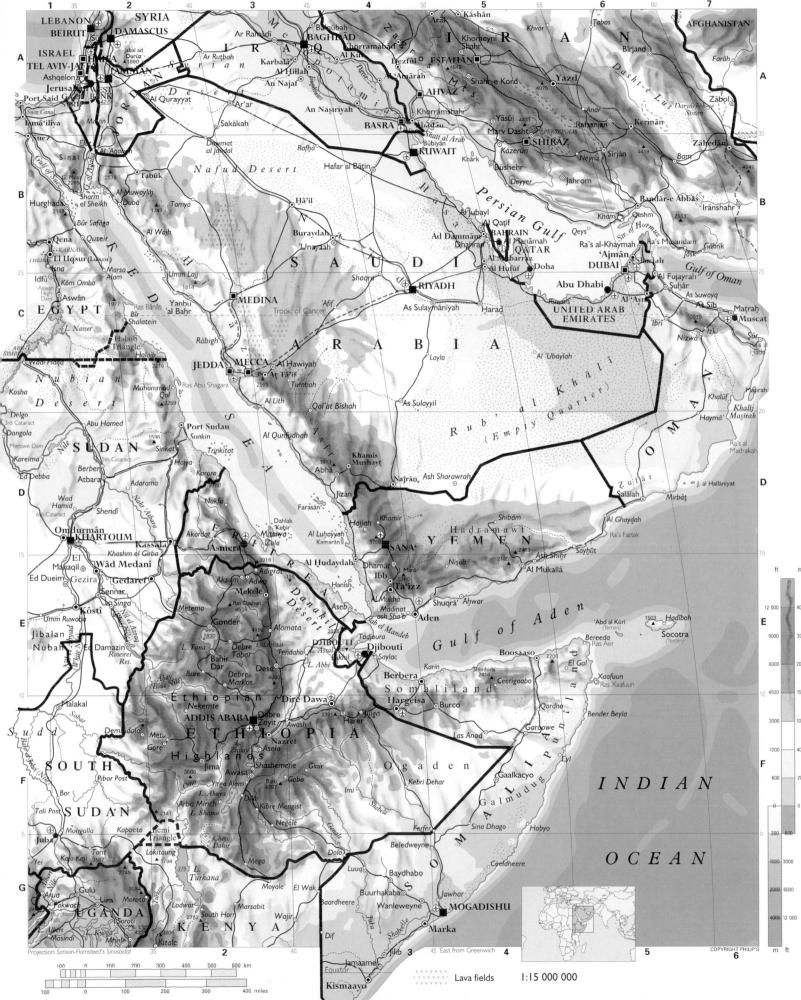

Projection: Sanson-Flamsteed's Sinusoidal

Lava fields

1:15 000 000

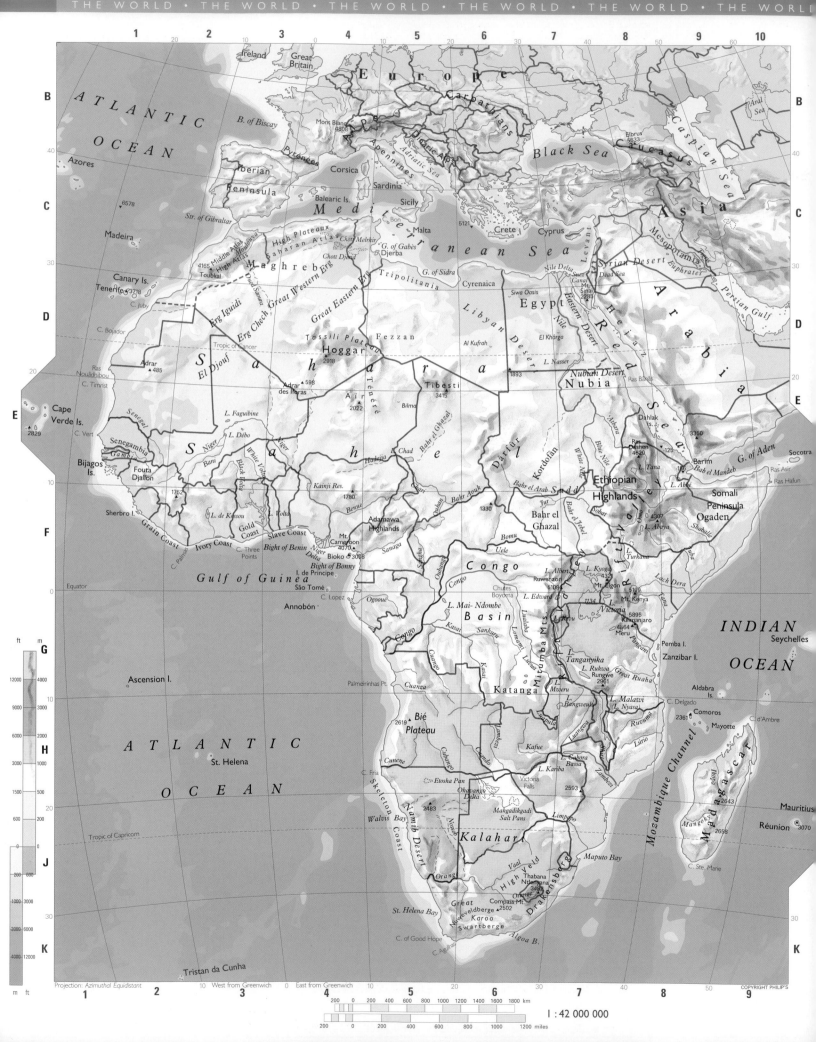

Projection: Azimuthal Equidistant

1 : 42 000 000

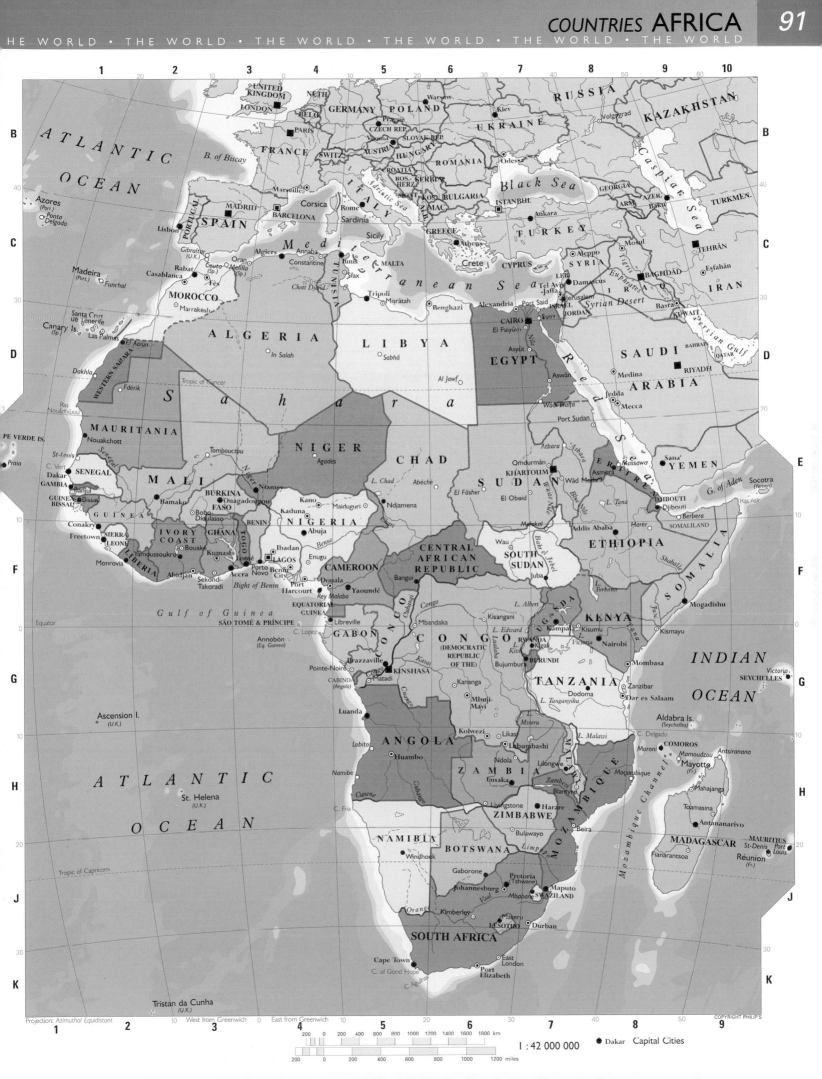

Projection: Azimuthal Equidistant

COPYRIGHT PHILIP'S

200 0 200 400 600 800 1000 1200 1400 1600 1800 km

200 0 200 400 600 800 1000 1200 miles

1 : 42 000 000   ● Dakar Capital Cities

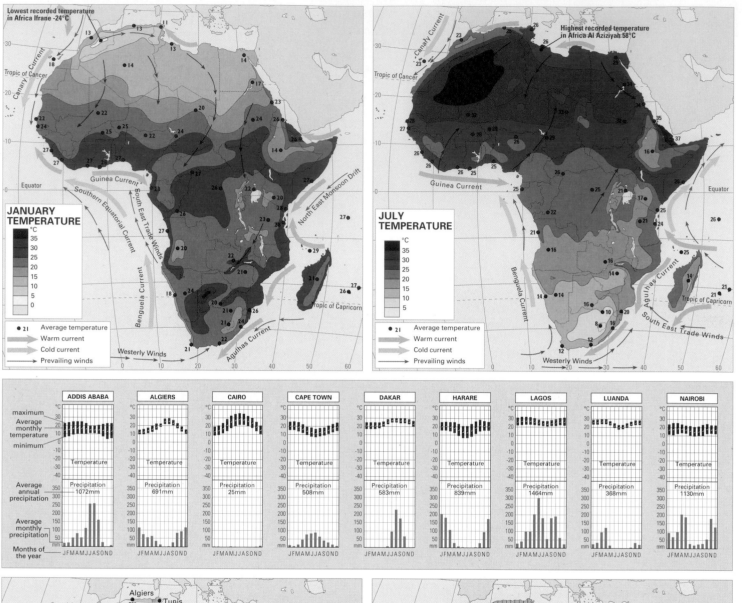

JANUARY TEMPERATURE

Lowest recorded temperature in Africa Ifrane -24°C

°C
35
30
25
20
15
10
5
0

• 21 Average temperature
Warm current
Cold current
Prevailing winds

JULY TEMPERATURE

Highest recorded temperature in Africa Al Aziziyah 58°C

°C
35
30
25
20
15
10
5

• 21 Average temperature
Warm current
Cold current
Prevailing winds

Climate graphs: ADDIS ABABA, ALGIERS, CAIRO, CAPE TOWN, DAKAR, HARARE, LAGOS, LUANDA, NAIROBI

maximum
Average monthly temperature
minimum
Average annual precipitation
Average monthly precipitation
Months of the year

ADDIS ABABA — Precipitation 1072mm
ALGIERS — Precipitation 691mm
CAIRO — Precipitation 25mm
CAPE TOWN — Precipitation 508mm
DAKAR — Precipitation 583mm
HARARE — Precipitation 839mm
LAGOS — Precipitation 1464mm
LUANDA — Precipitation 368mm
NAIROBI — Precipitation 1130mm

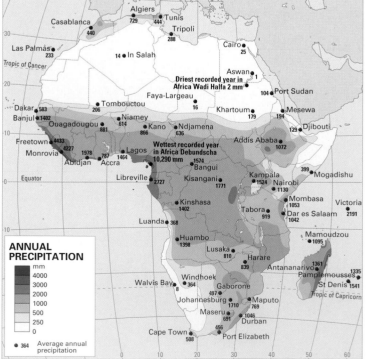

ANNUAL PRECIPITATION

Driest recorded year in Africa Wadi Halfa 2 mm
Wettest recorded year in Africa Debundscha 10,290 mm

mm
4000
3000
2000
1000
500
250
0

• 364 Average annual precipitation

Algiers 729
Tunis 444
Tripoli 288
Casablanca 440
Las Palmás 233
Cairo 25
In Salah 14
Aswan 1
Faya-Largeau 16
Port Sudan 104
Dakar 583
Tombouctou 206
Khartoum 179
Mesewa 194
Banjul 1402
Niamey 614
Ndjamena 636
Djibouti 129
Ouagadougou 881
Kano 866
Freetown 4433
Addis Ababa 1072
Monrovia 4227
Abidjan 1978
Accra 787
Lagos 1574
Lagos 1464
Bangui ...
Libreville 2727
Kisangani ...
Kampala 1524
Nairobi 1771
Nairobi 1130
Mogadishu 399
Mombasa 1053
Kinshasa 1402
Tabora 919
Dar es Salaam 1042
Victoria 2191
Luanda 368
Mamoudzou 1095
Huambo 1398
Lusaka 810
Antananarivo 1361
Pamplemousses 1335
Harare 839
Walvis Bay 8
Windhoek 364
Gaborone ...
St Denis 1541
Johannesburg 497
Maputo 769
Maseru 1710
Durban 1046
691
Cape Town 508
Port Elizabeth 456

Projection: *Zenithal Equidistant*

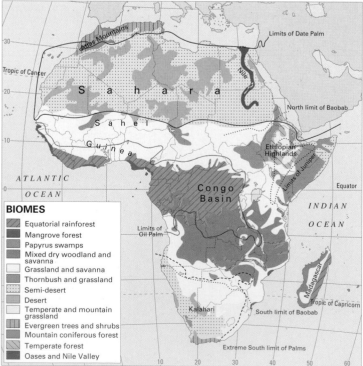

BIOMES
Equatorial rainforest
Mangrove forest
Papyrus swamps
Mixed dry woodland and savanna
Grassland and savanna
Thornbush and grassland
Semi-desert
Desert
Temperate and mountain grassland
Evergreen trees and shrubs
Mountain coniferous forest
Temperate forest
Oases and Nile Valley

Atlas Mountains
Sahara
Sahel
Guinea
Congo Basin
Ethiopian Highlands
Kalahari
Madagascar

Limits of Date Palm
North limit of Baobab
Limits of Juniper
Limits of Oil Palm
South limit of Baobab
Extreme South limit of Palms

ATLANTIC OCEAN
INDIAN OCEAN

COPYRIGHT PHILIP'S

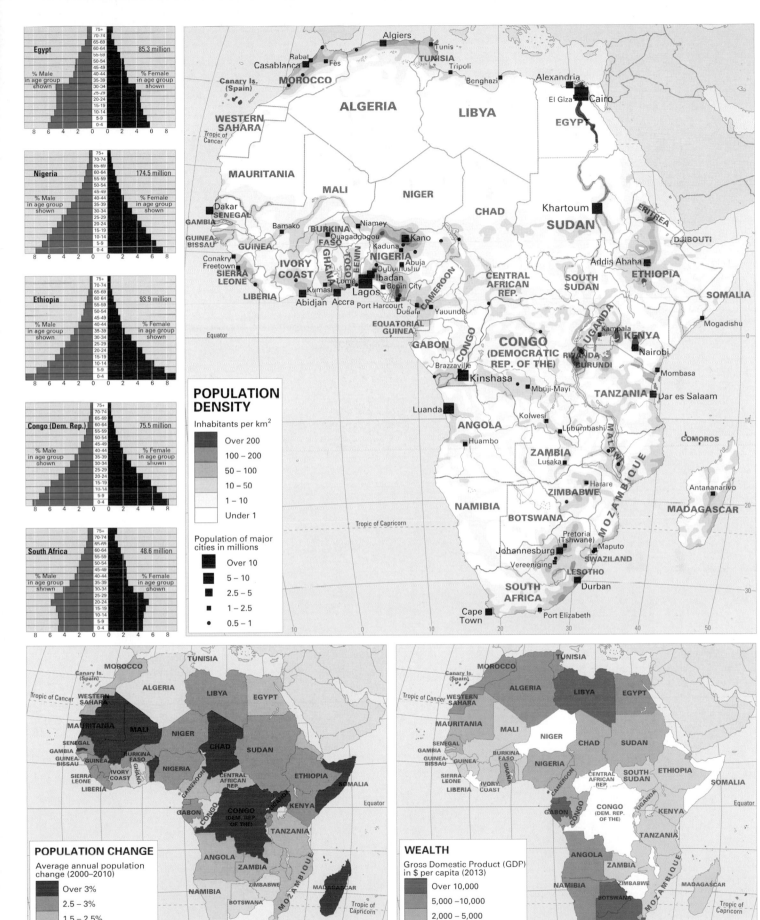

Egypt 85.3 million

% Male in age group shown | % Female in age group shown

75+ / 70-74 / 65-69 / 60-64 / 55-59 / 50-54 / 45-49 / 40-44 / 35-39 / 30-34 / 25-29 / 20-24 / 15-19 / 10-14 / 5-9 / 0-4

8 6 4 2 0 2 4 6 8

Nigeria 174.5 million

% Male in age group shown | % Female in age group shown

8 6 4 2 0 2 4 6 8

Ethiopia 93.9 million

% Male in age group shown | % Female in age group shown

8 6 4 2 0 2 4 6 8

Congo (Dem. Rep.) 75.5 million

% Male in age group shown | % Female in age group shown

8 6 4 2 0 2 4 6 8

South Africa 48.6 million

% Male in age group shown | % Female in age group shown

8 6 4 2 0 2 4 6 8

POPULATION DENSITY

Inhabitants per km²

- Over 200
- 100 – 200
- 50 – 100
- 10 – 50
- 1 – 10
- Under 1

Population of major cities in millions

- ■ Over 10
- ■ 5 – 10
- ■ 2.5 – 5
- ■ 1 – 2.5
- • 0.5 – 1

POPULATION CHANGE

Average annual population change (2000–2010)

- Over 3%
- 2.5 – 3%
- 1.5 – 2.5%
- 0 – 1.5%
- –1 – 0%

WEALTH

Gross Domestic Product (GDP) in $ per capita (2013)

- Over 10,000
- 5,000 – 10,000
- 2,000 – 5,000
- 1,000 – 2,000
- Under 1,000

Projection: Zenithal Equidistant

COPYRIGHT PHILIP'S

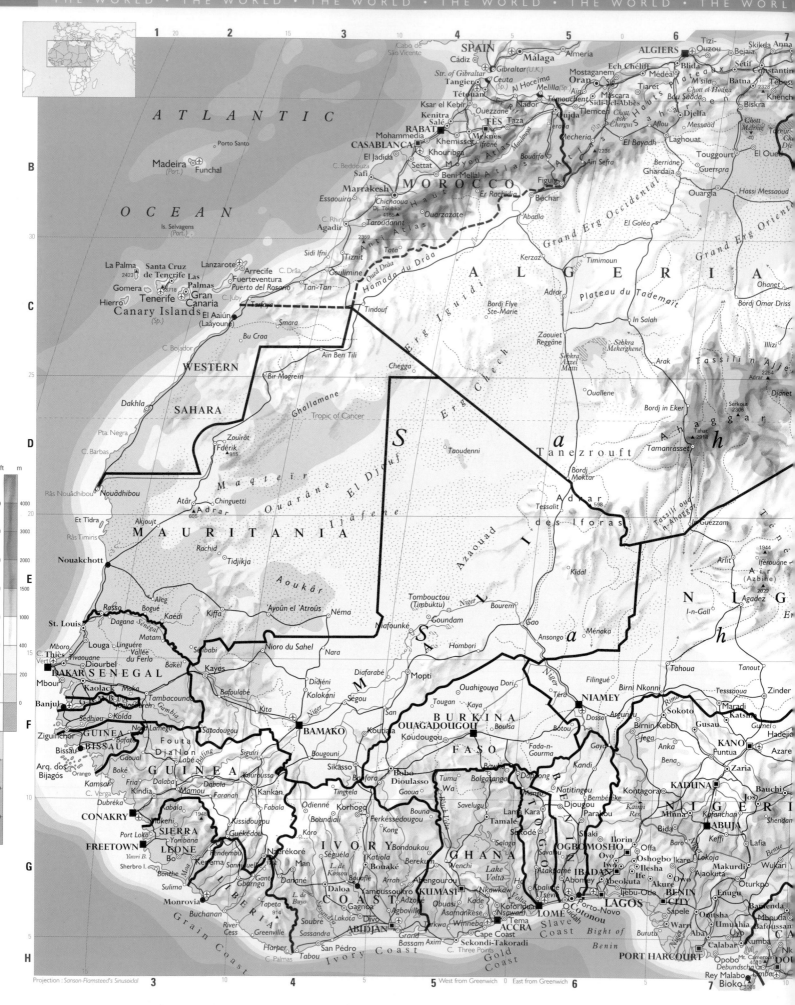

Lava fields

100   0   100   200   300   400   500   600 km

100   0   100   200   300   400 miles

1:15 000 000

COPYRIGHT PHILIPS

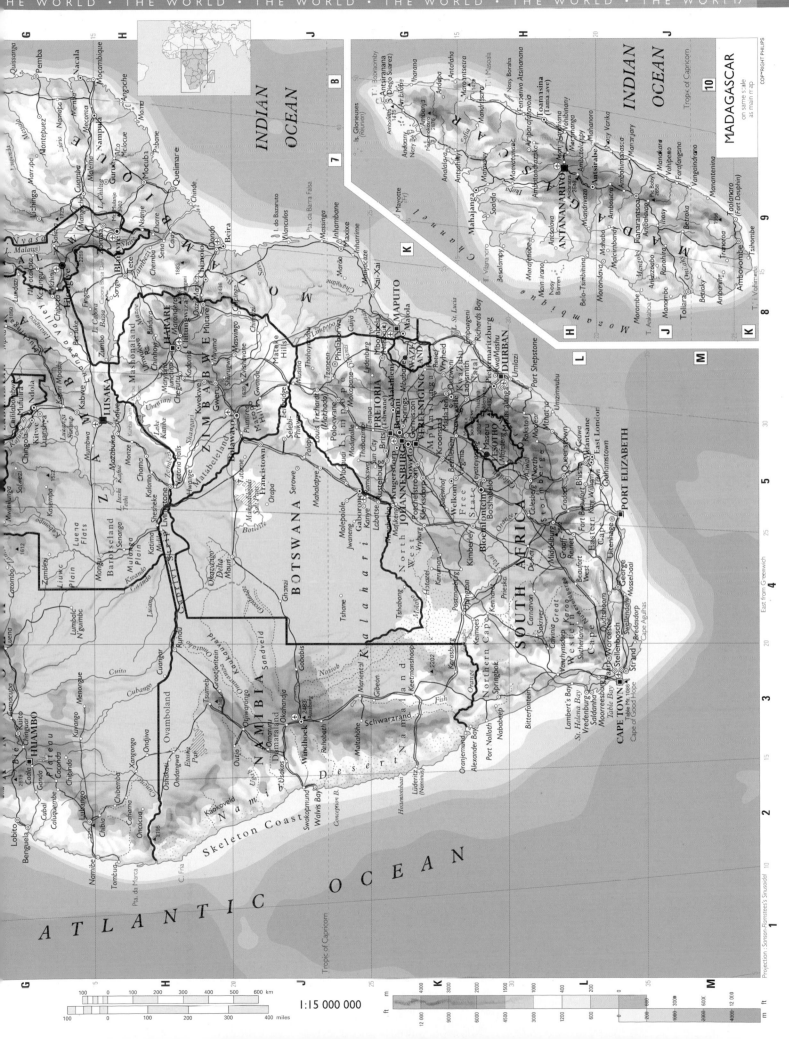

MADAGASCAR
on same scale
as main map

INDIAN OCEAN

INDIAN OCEAN

ATLANTIC OCEAN

SOUTH AFRICA

NAMIBIA

BOTSWANA

ZAMBIA

ZIMBABWE

ANGOLA

Kalahari Desert

Namib Desert

Skeleton Coast

1:15 000 000

Projection: Sanson-Flamsteed's Sinusoidal

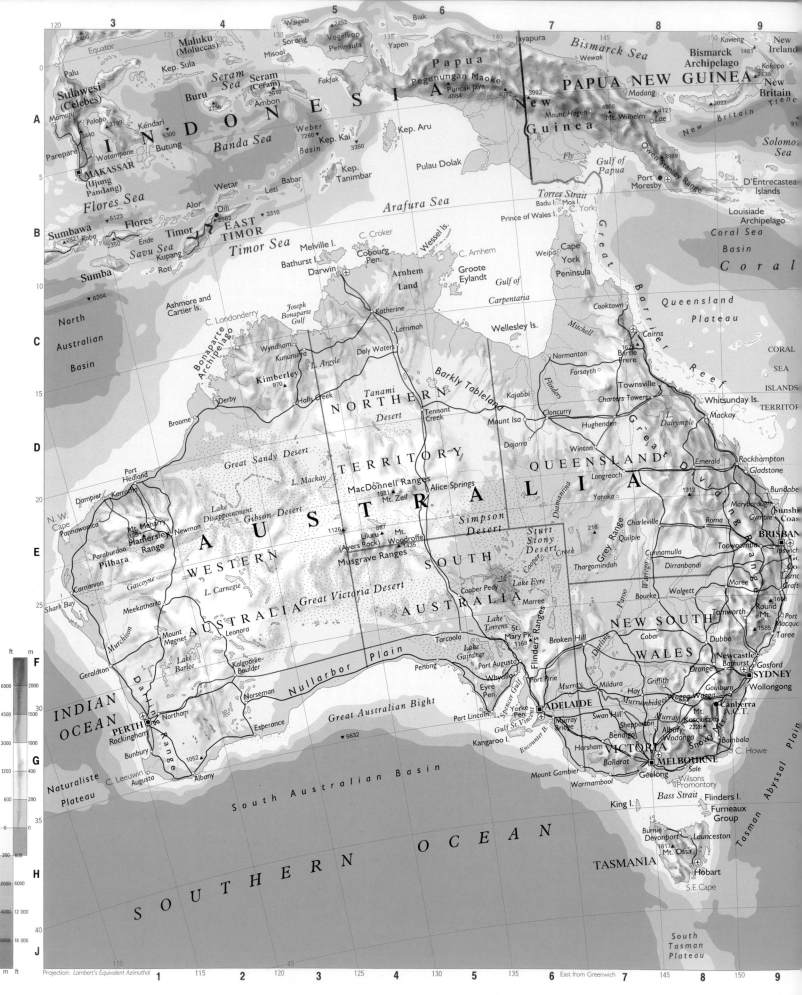

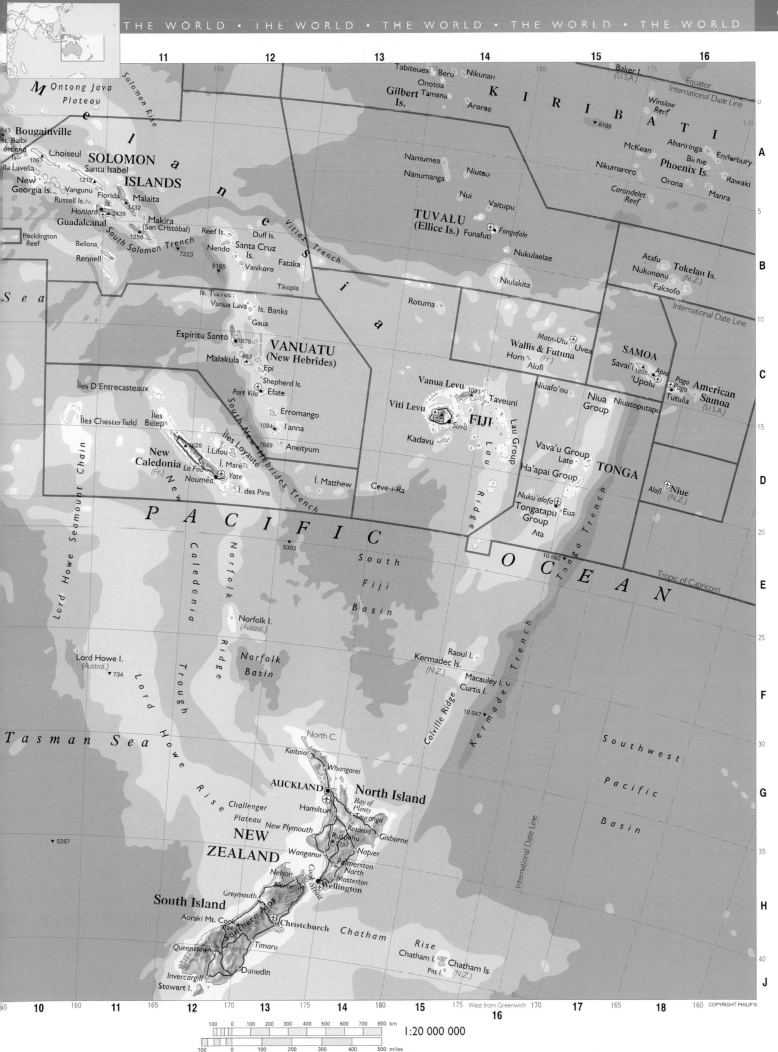

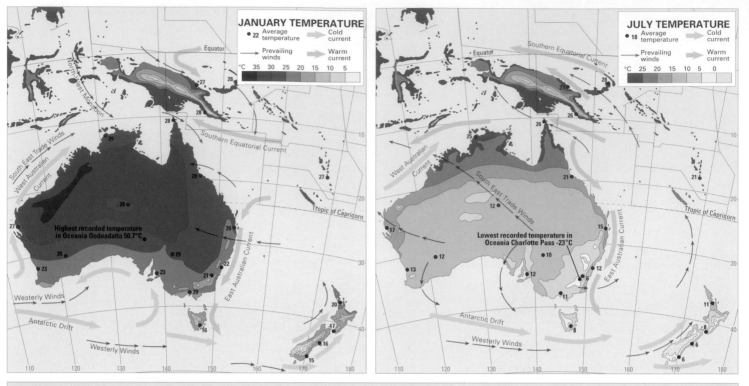

JANUARY TEMPERATURE

- 22 Average temperature
- Prevailing winds
- Cold current
- Warm current

°C 35 30 25 20 15 10 5

Highest recorded temperature in Oceania Oodnadatta 50.7°C

North-West Monsoon
South East Trade Winds
West Australian Current
Westerly Winds
Antarctic Drift
Westerly Winds
Equator
Southern Equatorial Current
Tropic of Capricorn
East Australian Current

JULY TEMPERATURE

- 18 Average temperature
- Prevailing winds
- Cold current
- Warm current

°C 25 20 15 5 0

Lowest recorded temperature in Oceania Charlotte Pass -23°C

Southern Equatorial Current
West Australian Current
South East Trade Winds
Equator
Tropic of Capricorn
East Australian Current
Antarctic Drift
Westerly Winds

Climate graphs

maximum
Average monthly temperature
minimum

Average annual precipitation

Average monthly precipitation

Months of the year

Station	Precipitation
ALICE SPRINGS	282mm
DARWIN	1488mm
DUNEDIN	937mm
PERTH	881mm
PORT MORESBY	1011mm
PORT VILA	2103mm
SYDNEY	1181mm
TOWNSVILLE	1093mm
WELLINGTON	1124mm

Temperature °C: 30 20 10 0 -10 -20 -30 -40
Precipitation mm: 350 300 250 200 150 100 50
JFMAMJJASOND

ANNUAL PRECIPITATION

627 Average annual precipitation

mm 2000 500 0
3000 1000 250

Wettest recorded year in Oceania Bellenden Ker 11,251 mm

Driest recorded year in Oceania Mulka 103 mm

Equator
Tropic of Capricorn

- Madang 3508
- Kokopo 2259
- Thursday I 900
- Port Moresby 1011
- Darwin 1488
- Townsville 1093
- Port Vila 2103
- Alice Springs 282
- Carnarvon 236
- Kalgoorlie 238
- Perth 881
- Broken Hill 233
- Adelaide 535
- Canberra 585
- Sydney 1182
- Brisbane 1136
- Melbourne 648
- Hobart 627
- Auckland 1243
- Wellington 1124
- Christchurch 669
- Dunedin 937

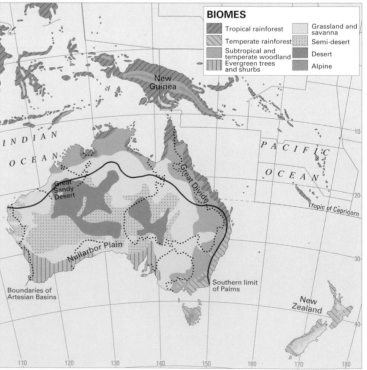

BIOMES

- Tropical rainforest
- Temperate rainforest
- Subtropical and temperate woodland
- Evergreen trees and shrubs
- Grassland and savanna
- Semi-desert
- Desert
- Alpine

INDIAN OCEAN
PACIFIC OCEAN
New Guinea
New Zealand
Great Sandy Desert
Great Divide
Nullarbor Plain
Boundaries of Artesian Basins
Southern limit of Palms
Tropic of Capricorn

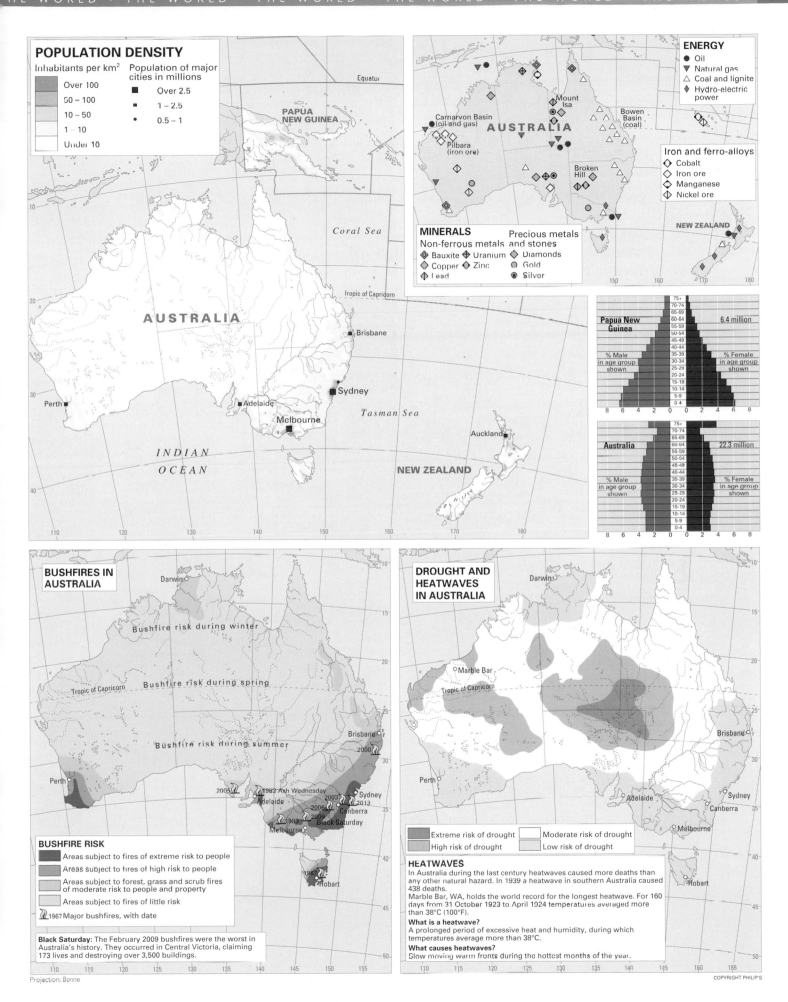

POPULATION DENSITY

Inhabitants per km²

	Over 100
	50 – 100
	10 – 50
	1 – 10
	Under 10

Population of major cities in millions

- ■ Over 2.5
- ▪ 1 – 2.5
- • 0.5 – 1

PAPUA NEW GUINEA

Equator

Coral Sea

Tropic of Capricorn

AUSTRALIA

● Brisbane

■ Sydney

● Adelaide

■ Melbourne

Tasman Sea

Perth ■

INDIAN OCEAN

● Auckland

NEW ZEALAND

ENERGY

- ● Oil
- ▼ Natural gas
- △ Coal and lignite
- ◆ Hydro-electric power

Mount Isa

Carnarvon Basin (oil and gas)

AUSTRALIA

Bowen Basin (coal)

Pilbara (iron ore)

Broken Hill

Iron and ferro-alloys

- ◇ Cobalt
- ◇ Iron ore
- ◇ Manganese
- ◇ Nickel ore

NEW ZEALAND

MINERALS
Non-ferrous metals

- ◆ Bauxite
- ◇ Copper
- ◖ Lead

- ▼ Uranium
- ◆ Zinc

Precious metals and stones

- ◇ Diamonds
- ○ Gold
- ◉ Silver

Population pyramids

Papua New Guinea — 6.4 million

% Male in age group shown / % Female in age group shown

Age groups: 75+, 70-74, 65-69, 60-64, 55-59, 50-54, 45-49, 40-44, 35-39, 30-34, 25-29, 20-24, 15-19, 10-14, 5-9, 0-4

Scale: 8 6 4 2 0 0 2 4 6 8

Australia — 22.3 million

% Male in age group shown / % Female in age group shown

Age groups: 75+, 70-74, 65-69, 60-64, 55-59, 50-54, 45-49, 40-44, 35-39, 30-34, 25-29, 20-24, 15-19, 10-14, 5-9, 0-4

Scale: 8 6 4 2 0 0 2 4 6 8

BUSHFIRES IN AUSTRALIA

Darwin

Bushfire risk during winter

Tropic of Capricorn

Bushfire risk during spring

Bushfire risk during summer

Brisbane

2000

Perth

2005

1983 Ash Wednesday

2003

2013

Adelaide

2006

Sydney

2009

Canberra

1983

Black Saturday

Melbourne

1967

Hobart

BUSHFIRE RISK

	Areas subject to fires of extreme risk to people
	Areas subject to fires of high risk to people
	Areas subject to forest, grass and scrub fires of moderate risk to people and property
	Areas subject to fires of little risk
〰1967	Major bushfires, with date

Black Saturday: The February 2009 bushfires were the worst in Australia's history. They occurred in Central Victoria, claiming 173 lives and destroying over 3,500 buildings.

DROUGHT AND HEATWAVES IN AUSTRALIA

Darwin

Tropic of Capricorn

○ Marble Bar

Brisbane

Perth ○

Adelaide

Sydney

Canberra

Melbourne

Hobart

	Extreme risk of drought		Moderate risk of drought
	High risk of drought		Low risk of drought

HEATWAVES

In Australia during the last century heatwaves caused more deaths than any other natural hazard. In 1939 a heatwave in southern Australia caused 438 deaths.

Marble Bar, WA, holds the world record for the longest heatwave. For 160 days from 31 October 1923 to April 1924 temperatures averaged more than 38°C (100°F).

What is a heatwave?
A prolonged period of excessive heat and humidity, during which temperatures average more than 38°C.

What causes heatwaves?
Slow moving warm fronts during the hottest months of the year.

Projection: Bonne

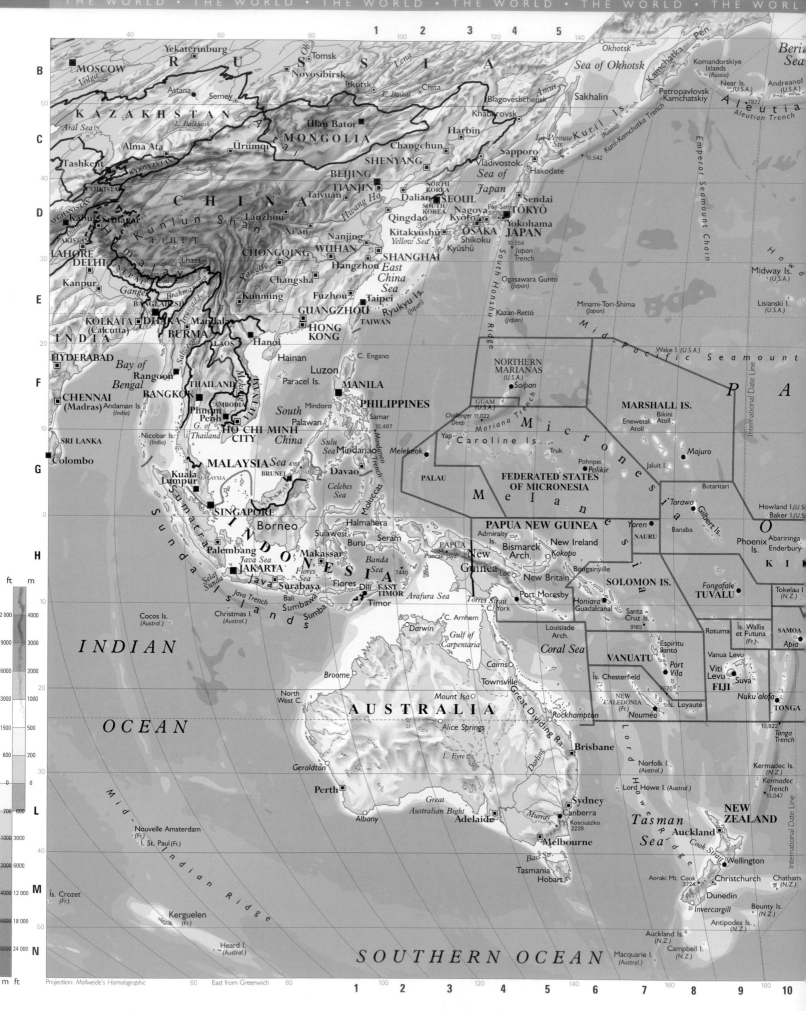

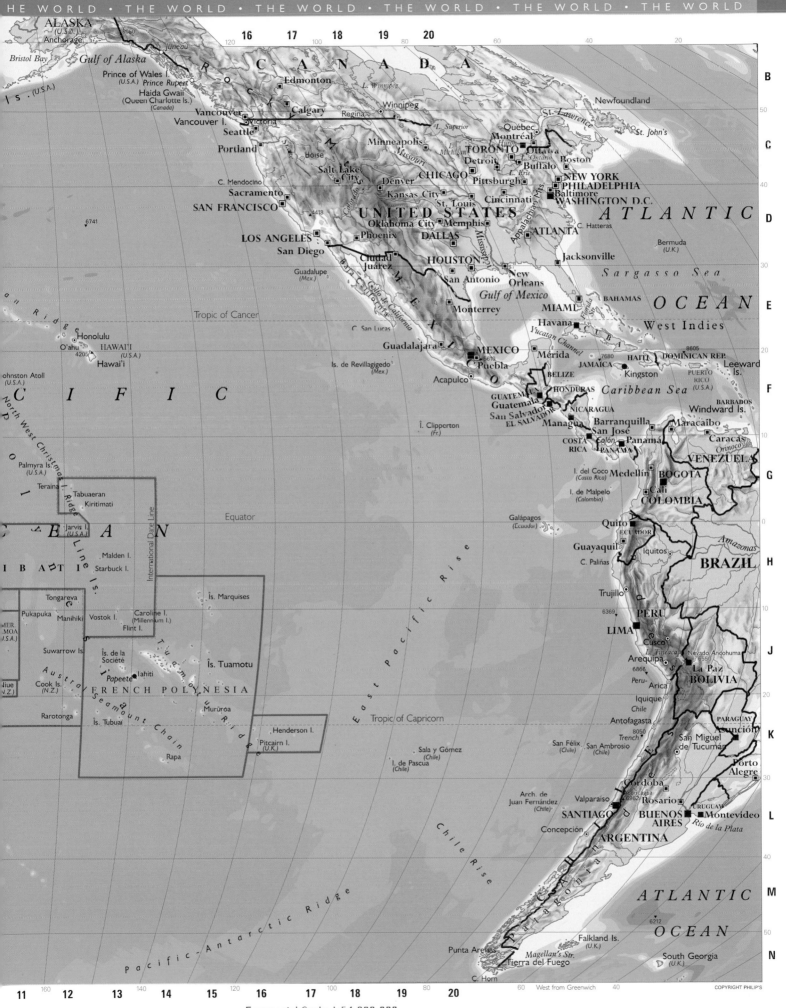

ALASKA
(U.S.A.)
Anchorage
Bristol Bay
Gulf of Alaska
Juneau
Prince of Wales I.
(U.S.A.) Prince Rupert
Haida Gwaii
(Queen Charlotte Is.)
(Canada)
Vancouver
Vancouver I. Victoria
Seattle
Portland
Boise
C. Mendocino
Sacramento
SAN FRANCISCO
6741
LOS ANGELES
San Diego
Guadalupe
(Mex.)

CANADA
Edmonton
L. Winnipeg
Calgary
Regina
Winnipeg
Newfoundland

Minneapolis
L. Superior
St. Lawrence
Québec
Montréal
St. John's
TORONTO Ottawa
Detroit Buffalo Boston
L. Michigan L. Erie
Salt Lake City
Denver
Kansas City
St. Louis
CHICAGO
Pittsburgh
Cincinnati
NEW YORK
PHILADELPHIA
Baltimore
WASHINGTON D.C.
4418
UNITED STATES
Oklahoma City
Memphis
Phoenix
DALLAS
Ciudad Juárez
HOUSTON
San Antonio
Monterrey
New Orleans
Gulf of Mexico
MIAMI
BAHAMAS
Jacksonville
ATLANTA
C. Hatteras
Bermuda
(U.K.)
Sargasso Sea
OCEAN
ATLANTIC
D

Tropic of Cancer
Honolulu
O'ahu
HAWAI'I
4205
Hawai'i
(U.S.A.)
Johnston Atoll
(U.S.A.)
Is. de Revillagigedo
(Mex.)
C. San Lucas
Guadalajara
MEXICO
6610
Puebla
Acapulco
Mérida
Yucatan Channel
Havana
CUBA
West Indies
8605
HAITI
JAMAICA
Kingston
DOMINICAN REP.
PUERTO RICO
(U.S.A.)
Leeward Is.
BELIZE
GUATEMALA
Guatemala
San Salvador
EL SALVADOR
HONDURAS
NICARAGUA
Managua
Caribbean Sea
BARBADOS
Windward Is.

North West Christmas Ridge
Palmyra Is.
(U.S.A.)
Teraina
Tabuaeran
Kiritimati
Jarvis I.
(U.S.A.)
Malden I.
Starbuck I.
Î. Clipperton
(Fr.)
Barranquilla
Maracaibo
San José
COSTA RICA
Colón
Panamá
PANAMA
Caracas
Orinoco
VENEZUELA
I. del Coco
(Costa Rica)
Medellín
BOGOTÁ
Cali
COLOMBIA
I. de Malpelo
(Colombia)
Equator
Galápagos
(Ecuador)
Quito
ECUADOR
Guayaquil
Iquitos
C. Palinas
Amazonas
BRAZIL
Trujillo

PACIFIC
CIBATI
Tongareva
Pukapuka Manihiki
Suwarrow Is.
AMER.
SAMOA
(U.S.A.)
Niue
(N.Z.)
Cook Is.
(N.Z.)
Vostok I.
Flint I.
Îs. Marquises
Caroline I.
(Millennium I.)
Îs. de la Société
Papeete Tahiti
Îs. Tuamotu
FRENCH POLYNESIA
Mururoa
Rarotonga
Îs. Tubuai
Australes Seamount Chain
Tuamotu Ridge
Henderson I.
Pitcairn I.
(U.K.)
Rapa

6369
PERU
LIMA
Cusco
L. Titicaca
Arequipa
6866
Peru-
Arica
Nevado Ancohuma
6550
La Paz
BOLIVIA
Iquique
Chile
Tropic of Capricorn
Antofagasta
8050
Trench
PARAGUAY
Asunción
San Miguel de Tucumán
Porto Alegre

East Pacific Rise
Sala y Gómez
(Chile)
San Félix
(Chile)
San Ambrosio
(Chile)
Córdoba
Arch. de Juan Fernández
(Chile)
Aconcagua
6962
Valparaíso
Rosario
URUGUAY
Montevideo
SANTIAGO
BUENOS AIRES
Río de la Plata
Concepción
ARGENTINA
Chile Rise
Patagonia
ATLANTIC
OCEAN

Pacific-Antarctic Ridge
Punta Arenas
Magellan's Str.
Tierra del Fuego
C. Horn
Falkland Is.
(U.K.)
South Georgia
(U.K.)
6212

Equatorial Scale 1:54 000 000

West from Greenwich

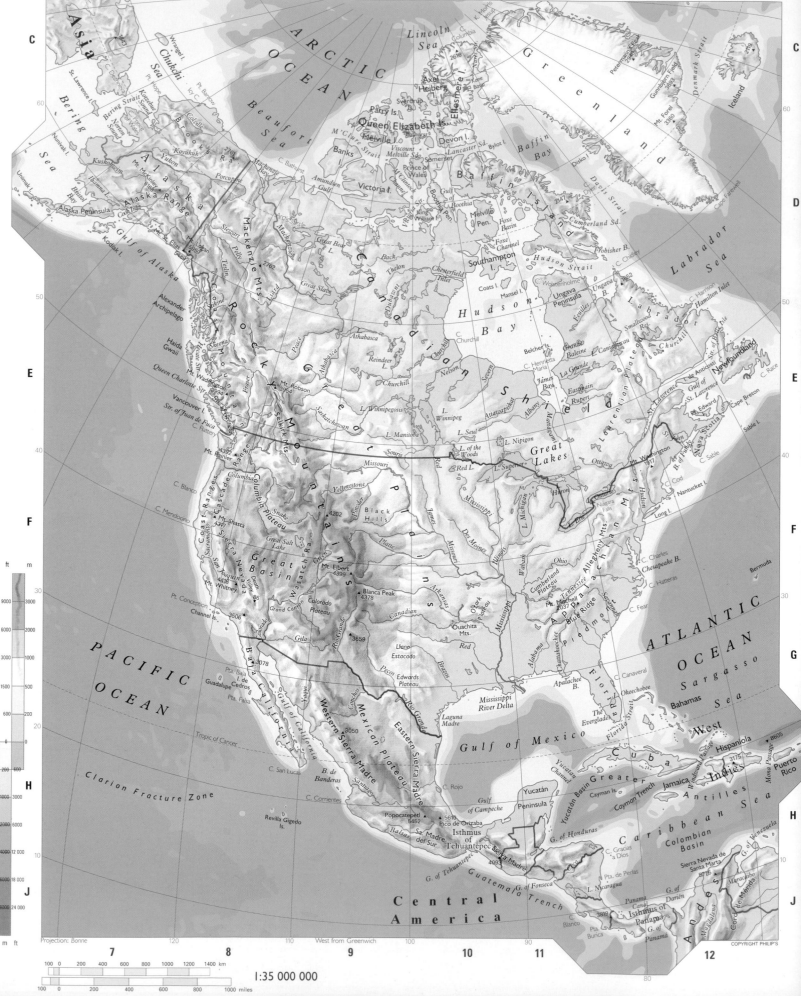

Projection: Bonne

■ MÉXICO Capital Cities

1:35 000 000

West from Greenwich

COPYRIGHT PHILIP'S

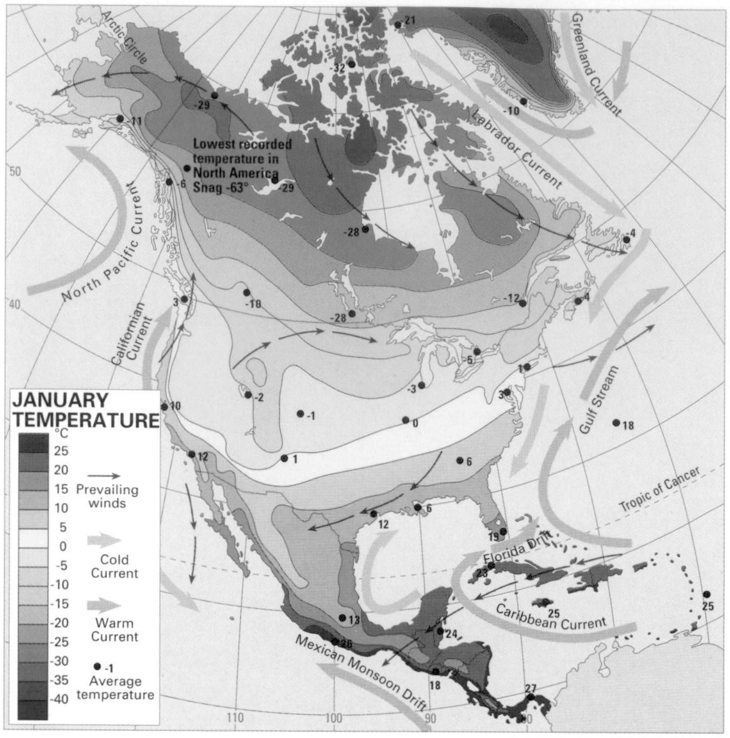
JANUARY TEMPERATURE
°C
25
20
15
10
5
0
-5
-10
-15
-20
-25
-30
-35
-40
Prevailing winds
Cold Current
Warm Current
-1 Average temperature
Lowest recorded temperature in North America Snag -63°
Arctic Circle
Greenland Current
Labrador Current
North Pacific Current
Californian Current
Gulf Stream
Florida Drift
Caribbean Current
Mexican Monsoon Drift
Tropic of Cancer

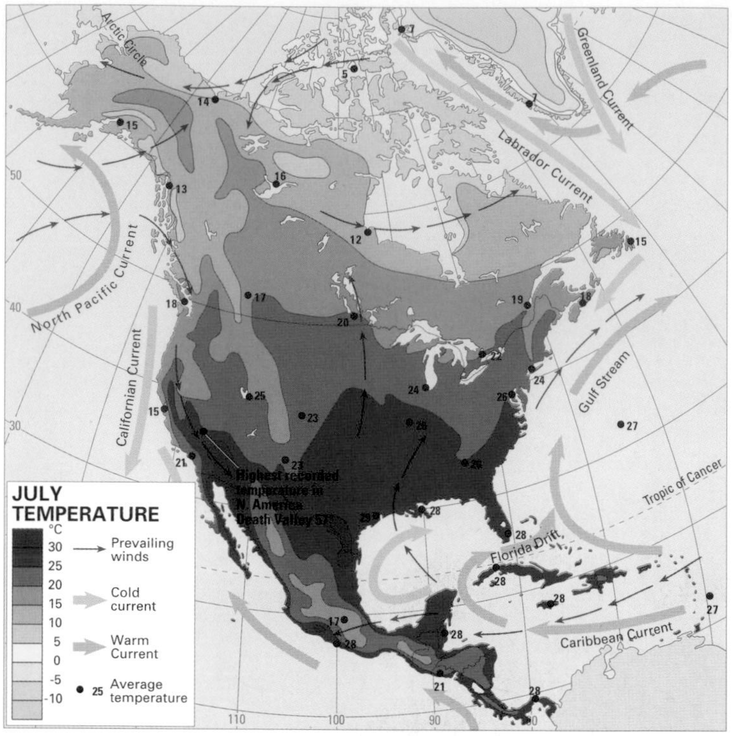
JULY TEMPERATURE
°C
30
25
20
15
10
5
0
-5
-10
Prevailing winds
Cold current
Warm Current
25 Average temperature
Highest recorded temperature in N. America Death Valley 57°
Arctic Circle
Greenland Current
Labrador Current
North Pacific Current
Californian Current
Gulf Stream
Florida Drift
Caribbean Current
Tropic of Cancer

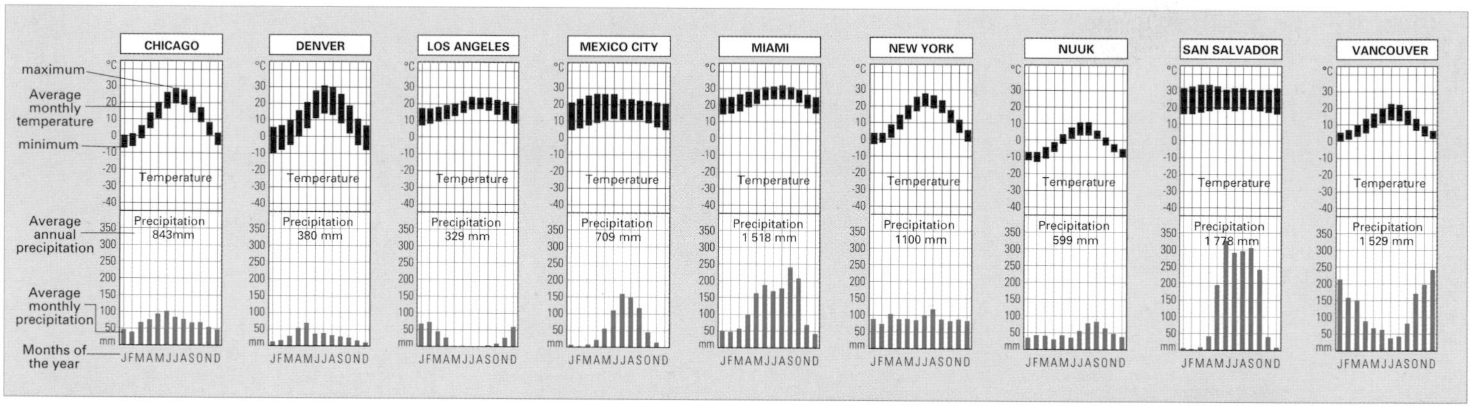
CHICAGO
DENVER
LOS ANGELES
MEXICO CITY
MIAMI
NEW YORK
NUUK
SAN SALVADOR
VANCOUVER
maximum
Average monthly temperature
minimum
Temperature
Average annual precipitation
Average monthly precipitation
Months of the year
JFMAMJJASOND
Precipitation 843mm
Precipitation 380 mm
Precipitation 329 mm
Precipitation 709 mm
Precipitation 1 518 mm
Precipitation 1100 mm
Precipitation 599 mm
Precipitation 1 778 mm
Precipitation 1 529 mm

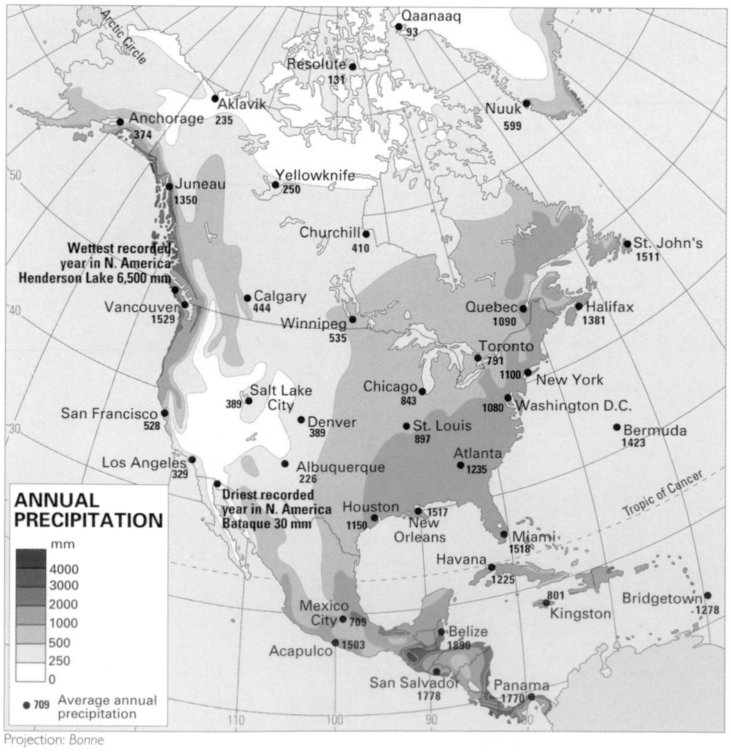
ANNUAL PRECIPITATION
mm
4000
3000
2000
1000
500
250
0
709 Average annual precipitation
Wettest recorded year in N. America Henderson Lake 6,500 mm
Driest recorded year in N. America Bataque 30 mm
Qaanaaq 93
Resolute 131
Aklavik 235
Anchorage 374
Nuuk 599
Juneau 1350
Yellowknife 250
Churchill 410
St. John's 1511
Calgary 444
Vancouver 1529
Quebec 1090
Halifax 1381
Winnipeg 535
Toronto 791
New York 1100
Salt Lake City 389
Chicago 843
Washington D.C. 1080
San Francisco 528
Denver 389
St. Louis 897
Bermuda 1423
Atlanta 1235
Los Angeles 329
Albuquerque 226
Houston 1150
New Orleans 1517
Miami 1518
Havana 1225
Kingston 801
Bridgetown 1278
Mexico City 709
Belize 1890
Acapulco 1503
San Salvador 1778
Panama 1770
Tropic of Cancer

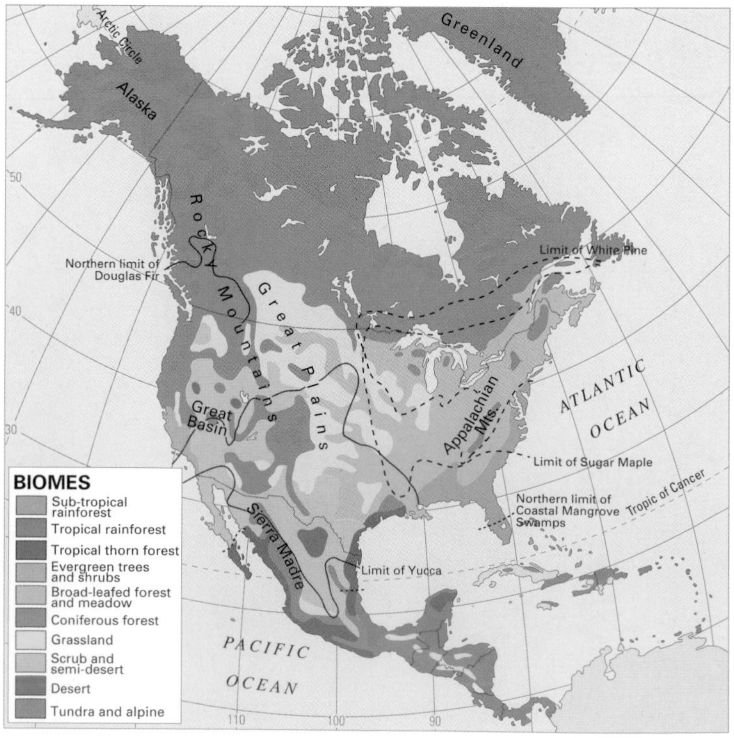
BIOMES
Sub-tropical rainforest
Tropical rainforest
Tropical thorn forest
Evergreen trees and shrubs
Broad-leafed forest and meadow
Coniferous forest
Grassland
Scrub and semi-desert
Desert
Tundra and alpine
Greenland
Alaska
Rocky Mountains
Great Plains
Great Basin
Sierra Madre
Appalachian Mts.
Northern limit of Douglas Fir
Limit of White Pine
Limit of Sugar Maple
Northern limit of Coastal Mangrove Swamps
Limit of Yucca
ATLANTIC OCEAN
PACIFIC OCEAN
Tropic of Cancer

Projection: *Bonne*

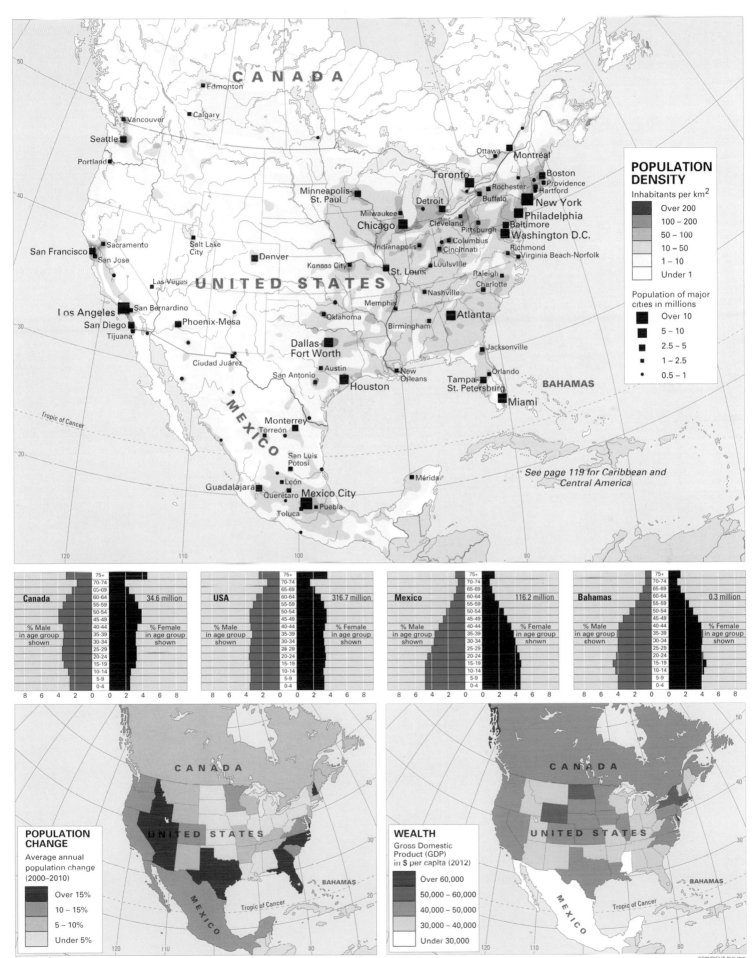

POPULATION DENSITY

Inhabitants per km²

- Over 200
- 100 – 200
- 50 – 100
- 10 – 50
- 1 – 10
- Under 1

Population of major cities in millions

- Over 10
- 5 – 10
- 2.5 – 5
- 1 – 2.5
- 0.5 – 1

See page 119 for Caribbean and Central America

Canada — 34.6 million
% Male in age group shown / % Female in age group shown

USA — 316.7 million
% Male in age group shown / % Female in age group shown

Mexico — 116.2 million
% Male in age group shown / % Female in age group shown

Bahamas — 0.3 million
% Male in age group shown / % Female in age group shown

POPULATION CHANGE

Average annual population change (2000–2010)

- Over 15%
- 10 – 15%
- 5 – 10%
- Under 5%

WEALTH

Gross Domestic Product (GDP) in $ per capita (2012)

- Over 60,000
- 50,000 – 60,000
- 40,000 – 50,000
- 30,000 – 40,000
- Under 30,000

Projection: Bonne

COPYRIGHT PHILIP'S

ALASKA
1:30 000 000

Projection : Bonne

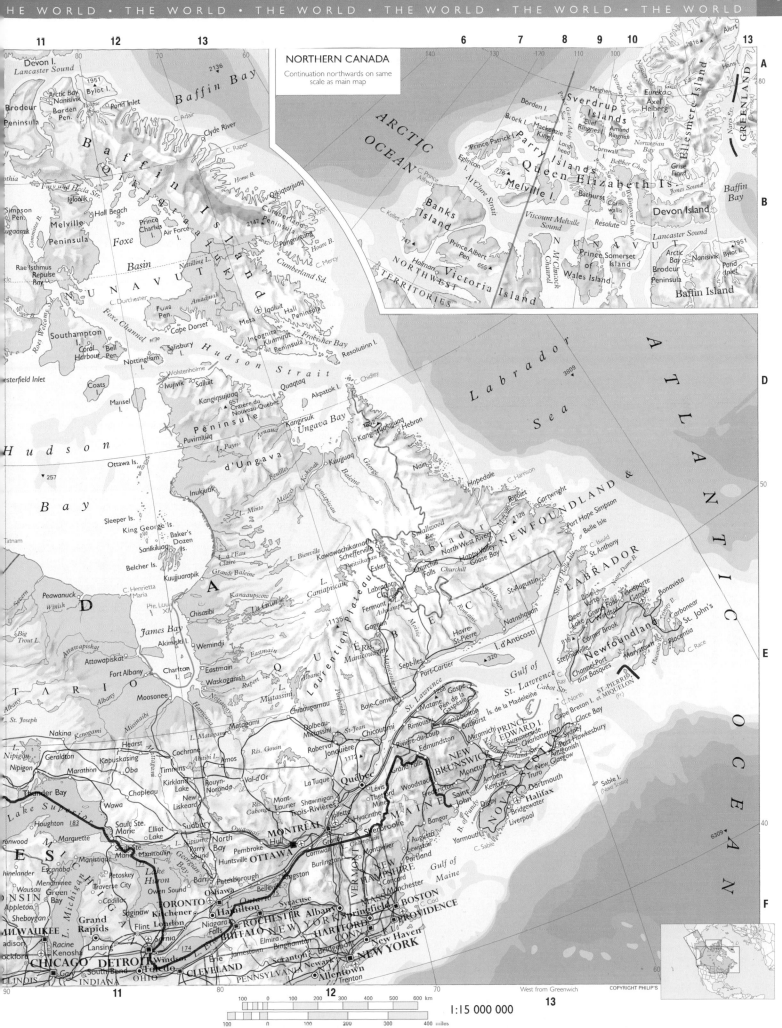

NORTHERN CANADA

Continuation northwards on same
scale as main map

1:15 000 000

West from Greenwich

COPYRIGHT PHILIP'S

Projection: Albers' Equal Area with two standard parallels

West from Greenwich

See page 108 for map of Alaska

1:12 000 000

Projection: Albers' Equal Area with two standard parallels

1:6 000 000

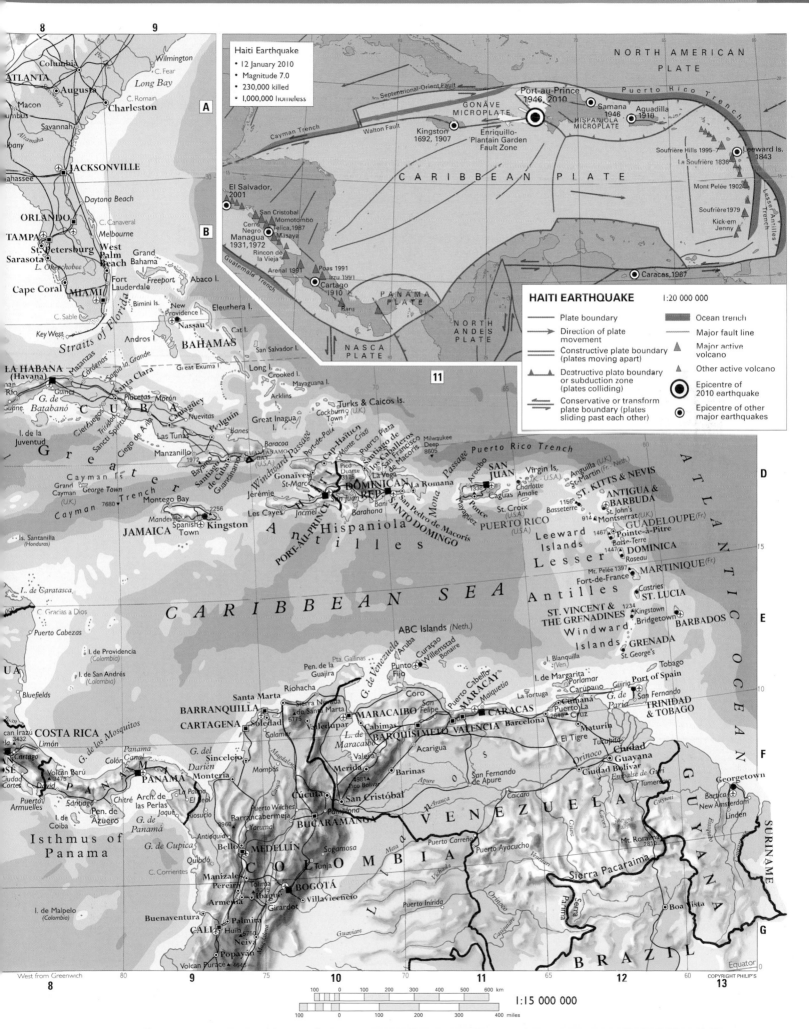

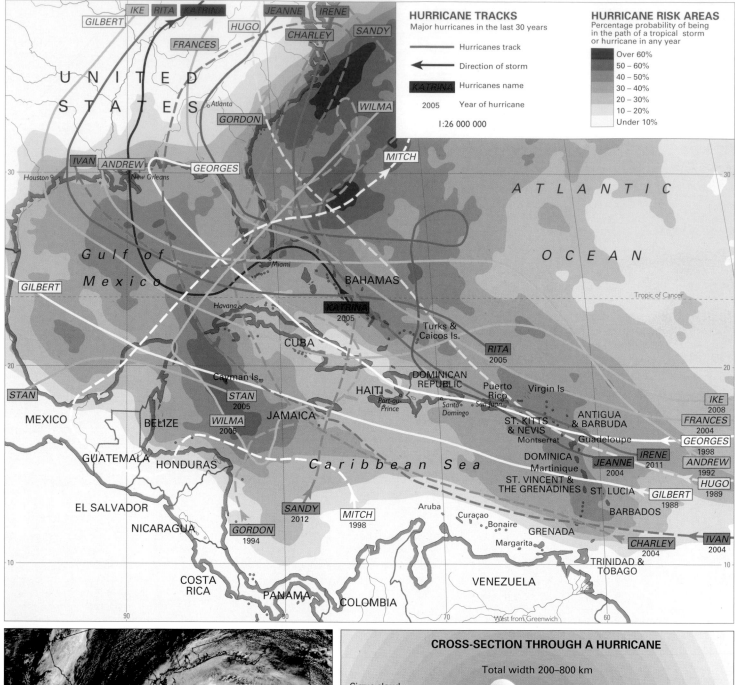

HURRICANE TRACKS
Major hurricanes in the last 30 years

——— Hurricanes track

⟵ Direction of storm

KATRINA Hurricanes name

2005 Year of hurricane

1:26 000 000

HURRICANE RISK AREAS
Percentage probability of being
in the path of a tropical storm
or hurricane in any year

Over 60%
50 – 60%
40 – 50%
30 – 40%
20 – 30%
10 – 20%
Under 10%

UNITED STATES

GILBERT IKE RITA KATRINA JEANNE IRENE

HUGO SANDY

FRANCES CHARLEY

Atlanta

GORDON

WILMA

IVAN ANDREW GEORGES

Houston New Orleans

MITCH

A T L A N T I C

30

Gulf of Mexico

Miami

O C E A N

BAHAMAS

GILBERT

Havana

Tropic of Cancer

KATRINA 2005

CUBA

Turks & Caicos Is.

RITA 2005

Cayman Is.

20

STAN

STAN 2005

WILMA 2005

JAMAICA

HAITI

Port-au-Prince

DOMINICAN REPUBLIC

Santo Domingo

Puerto Rico

San Juan

Virgin Is

IKE 2008

MEXICO

BELIZE

ANTIGUA & BARBUDA

FRANCES 2004

ST. KITTS & NEVIS

Guadeloupe

GEORGES 1998

GUATEMALA HONDURAS

Montserrat

C a r i b b e a n   S e a

DOMINICA

Martinique

JEANNE 2004

IRENE 2011

ANDREW 1992

EL SALVADOR

ST. VINCENT & THE GRENADINES

ST. LUCIA

HUGO 1989

SANDY 2012

MITCH 1998

Aruba

Curaçao

Bonaire

ST. LUCIA

GILBERT 1988

BARBADOS

NICARAGUA

GORDON 1994

Margarita

GRENADA

CHARLEY 2004

IVAN 2004

10

COSTA RICA

PANAMA

COLOMBIA

VENEZUELA

TRINIDAD & TOBAGO

West from Greenwich

90 *80* *70* *60*

▲ Hurricane Katrina hit the USA's Gulf Coast on 29th August 2005. It was
the costliest and one of the five deadliest hurricanes ever to strike the
United States. This satellite image shows the storm approaching the US
coastline.

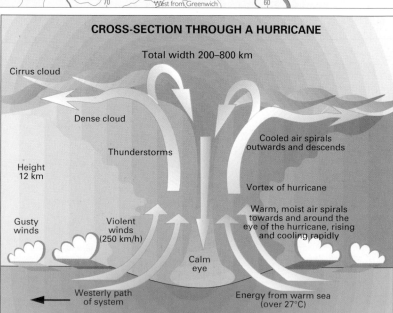

CROSS-SECTION THROUGH A HURRICANE

Total width 200–800 km

Cirrus cloud

Dense cloud

Thunderstorms

Cooled air spirals
outwards and descends

Vortex of hurricane

Height
12 km

Warm, moist air spirals
towards and around the
eye of the hurricane, rising
and cooling rapidly

Gusty
winds

Violent
winds
(250 km/h)

Calm
eye

Westerly path
of system

Energy from warm sea
(over 27°C)

COPYRIGHT PHILIP'S

Bahamas

Gulf of Campeche

Yucatán Peninsula

Isthmus of Tehuantepec

Central America

Guatemala Trench

L. Nicaragua

G. de Honduras

C. Gracias a Dios

Greater Antilles

Cuba

West Indies

Jamaica

Hispaniola

Puerto Rico

Leeward Islands

Guadeloupe
Dominica
Martinique
St. Lucia
St. Vincent
Barbados
Grenada
Tobago
Trinidad

Lesser Antilles

Caribbean Sea

Panama Canal

Isthmus of Panama

Gulf of Panamá

G. of Darién

I. del Coco

I. de Malpelo

B. de Buenaventura

C. de San Francisco

Pen. de la Guajira

C. de la Aguja

Sierra Nevada de Santa Marta

Pen. de Paraguaná

L. de Maracaibo

Cauca

Magdalena

Orinoco

Apure

Meta

Guaviare

Putumayo

Caquetá

Vaupés

Napo

Marañón

Galapagos Is.

G. of Guayaquil

Pta. Pariñas

Pta. Negra

Cotopaxi
5897

Chimborazo
6267

Huascarán
6768

Nevado Coropuna
6425

Chincha Alta

ATLANTIC OCEAN

Pen. de la Guajira

Llanos

Guiana Highlands

Sierra Pacaraima

Mt. Roraima
2810

Pico da Neblina
2994

Negro

Amazon

Amazon

Basin

Selva

Juruá

Purus

Madeira

Roosevelt

Madre de Dios

Beni

Mamoré

Guaporé

Sa. dos Parecis

Plateau of Mato Grosso

Cuyuni

Angel Falls

Devil's I.

C. Orange

I. de Maracá

Serra Tumucumaque

Represa de Balbina

Marajó

B. de Marajó

Equator

B. de São Marcos

C. de São Roque

Plat. of Borborema

Represa de Sobradinho

Sertão

Brazilian Highlands

Tocantins

Xingu

Tapajós

Teles Pires

Arinos

Araguaia

Paranaíba

São Francisco

Serra do Espinhaço

Serra Geral

Abrolhos Bank

B. de Todos os Santos

PACIFIC

OCEAN

Altiplano (Bolivian Plateau)

L. Titicaca
3812

Nevado Ancohuma
6550

L. de Poopó

Salar de Uyuni

Pta. Tetas

8050

Atacama Desert

Cerro Ojos del Salado
6863

Monte Pissis
6793

Cerro Bonete
6759

Cerro Mercedario
6770

Mt. Aconcagua
6962

San Félix

San Ambrosio

Arch. de Juan Fernández

Pta. Lengua da Vaca

Chaco Boreal

Chaco Austral

Gran Chaco

Pampas

Entre Ríos

Salinas Grandes

Sa. de Córdoba

L. Mar Chiquita

Dulce

Salado

Paraná

Paraguay

Pilcomayo

Bermejo

Rep. de Itaipú

Iguaçu

Paraná

Grande

Paranapanema

Serra do Mar

Serra da Mantiqueira

Pico da Bandeira
2890

I. de São Sebastião

C. de São Tomé

C. Frio

C. Santa Marta Grande

L. dos Patos

Mirim

Negro

Uruguay

Rio de la Plata

B. Samborombón

C. San Antonio

Tropic of Capricorn

Pta. Lavapié

Chile Rise

Chiloé I.

Chonos Archipelago

Mte. San Valentín
4058

Taitao Peninsula

G. de Penas

Wellington I.

Madre de Dios I.

Magellan's Str.

Riesco I.

Santa Inés I.

Canal Cockburn

C. Horn

Pta. Lavapié

Colorado

Negro

Limay

Neuquén

Chubut

G. San Matías

Valdés Peninsula

Bahía Blanca

G. San Jorge

C. Tres Puntas

Chico

Patagonia

L. Buenos Aires

Santa Cruz

L. Argentino

C. Vírgenes

West Falkland

East Falkland

Falkland Is.

Tierra del Fuego

Staten I.

Scotia Sea

Argentine

Abyssal

Plain
6212

ATLANTIC

OCEAN

South Georgia
2935

Andes

Cordillera de Calalaste

Cordillera de Domeyko

Peru-Chile Trench

ft   m

12000   4000

9000   3000

6000   2000

3000   1000

1500   500

600   200

0   0

0   0

200   600

1000   3000

2000   6000

4000   12000

6000   18000

8000   24000

m   ft

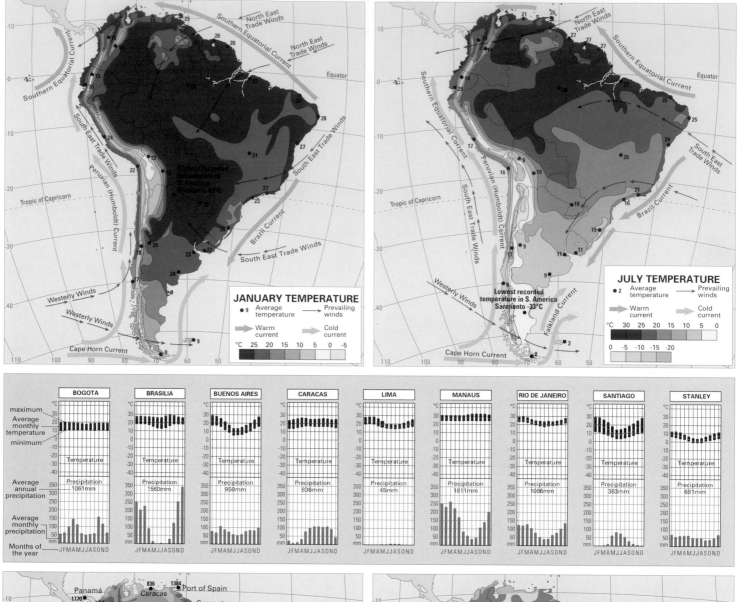

JANUARY TEMPERATURE

- 9   Average temperature
- →   Prevailing winds
- ⟶   Warm current
- ⟶   Cold current

°C   25   20   15   10   5   0   -5

Highest Recorded Temperature in S. America Rivadavia 49°C

JULY TEMPERATURE

- 2   Average temperature
- →   Prevailing winds
- ⟶   Warm current
- ⟶   Cold current

°C   30   25   20   15   10   5   0

0   -5   -10   -15   -20

Lowest recorded temperature in S. America Sarmiento -33°C

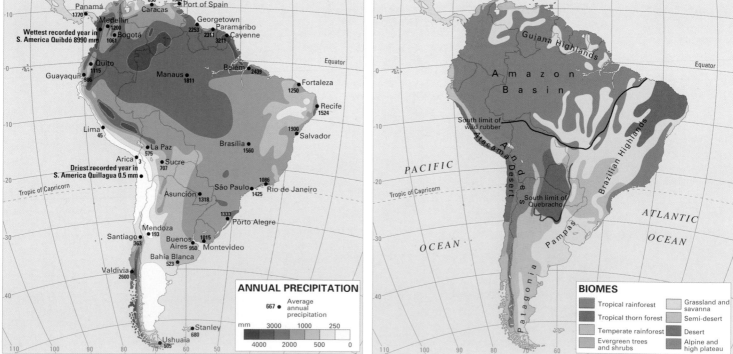

Climate graphs for: BOGOTA, BRASILIA, BUENOS AIRES, CARACAS, LIMA, MANAUS, RIO DE JANEIRO, SANTIAGO, STANLEY

- maximum
- Average monthly temperature
- minimum
- Temperature
- Average annual precipitation
- Precipitation
- Average monthly precipitation
- Months of the year — JFMAMJJASOND

Average annual precipitation:
- BOGOTA 1061mm
- BRASILIA 1560mm
- BUENOS AIRES 950mm
- CARACAS 836mm
- LIMA 45mm
- MANAUS 1811mm
- RIO DE JANEIRO 1086mm
- SANTIAGO 363mm
- STANLEY 681mm

ANNUAL PRECIPITATION

- 667   Average annual precipitation

mm   3000   1000   250
4000   2000   500   0

Panamá 1770
Medellín 1200
Caracas 836
Port of Spain 1384
Bogotá 1061
Georgetown 2253
Paramaribo 2311
Cayenne 3211
Quito 1115
Guayaquil 995
Manaus 1811
Belém 2439
Fortaleza 1250
Recife 1524
Lima 45
Salvador 1900
La Paz 575
Brasília 1560
Arica 3
Sucre 707
São Paulo 1425
Rio de Janeiro 1086
Asunción 1318
Pôrto Alegre 1333
Mendoza 193
Santiago 363
Buenos Aires 950
Montevideo 1015
Bahía Blanca 523
Valdivia 2600
Stanley 680
Ushuaia 505

Wettest recorded year in S. America Quibdó 8990 mm
Driest recorded year in S. America Quillagua 0.5 mm

BIOMES

- Tropical rainforest
- Tropical thorn forest
- Temperate rainforest
- Evergreen trees and shrubs
- Grassland and savanna
- Semi-desert
- Desert
- Alpine and high plateau

Guiana Highlands
Amazon Basin
South limit of wild rubber
Andes
Atacama Desert
Brazilian Highlands
South limit of Quebracho
Pampas
Patagonia

PACIFIC OCEAN
ATLANTIC OCEAN

Projection: Lambert's Equivalent Azimuthal

COPYRIGHT PHILIP'S

Venezuela   28.5 million

% Male in age group shown   % Female in age group shown

75+ 70-74 65-69 60-64 55-59 50-54 45-49 40-44 35-39 30-34 25-29 20-24 15-19 10-14 5-9 0-4

8 6 4 2 0 2 4 6 8

POPULATION DENSITY
Inhabitants per km²

Over 200	10 – 50
100 – 200	1 – 10
50 – 100	Under 1

WEALTH
Gross Domestic Product (GDP) in $ per capita (2013)

Over 20,000	2,000 – 5,000
10,000 – 20,000	Under 2,000
5,000 – 10,000	

Population of major cities in millions

■ Over 10	■ 1 – 2.5
■ 5 – 10	• 0.5 – 1
■ 2.5 – 5	

Brazil   201.0 million

% Male in age group shown   % Female in age group shown

75+ 70-74 65-69 60-64 55-59 50-54 45-49 40-44 35-39 30-34 25-29 20-24 15-19 10-14 5-9 0-4

8 6 4 2 0 2 4 6 8

Argentina   42.6 million

% Male in age group shown   % Female in age group shown

75+ 70-74 65-69 60-64 55-59 50-54 45-49 40-44 35-39 30-34 25-29 20-24 15-19 10-14 5-9

8 6 4 2 0 2 4 6 8

Projection: Lambert's Equivalent Azimuthal

COPYRIGHT PHILIP'S

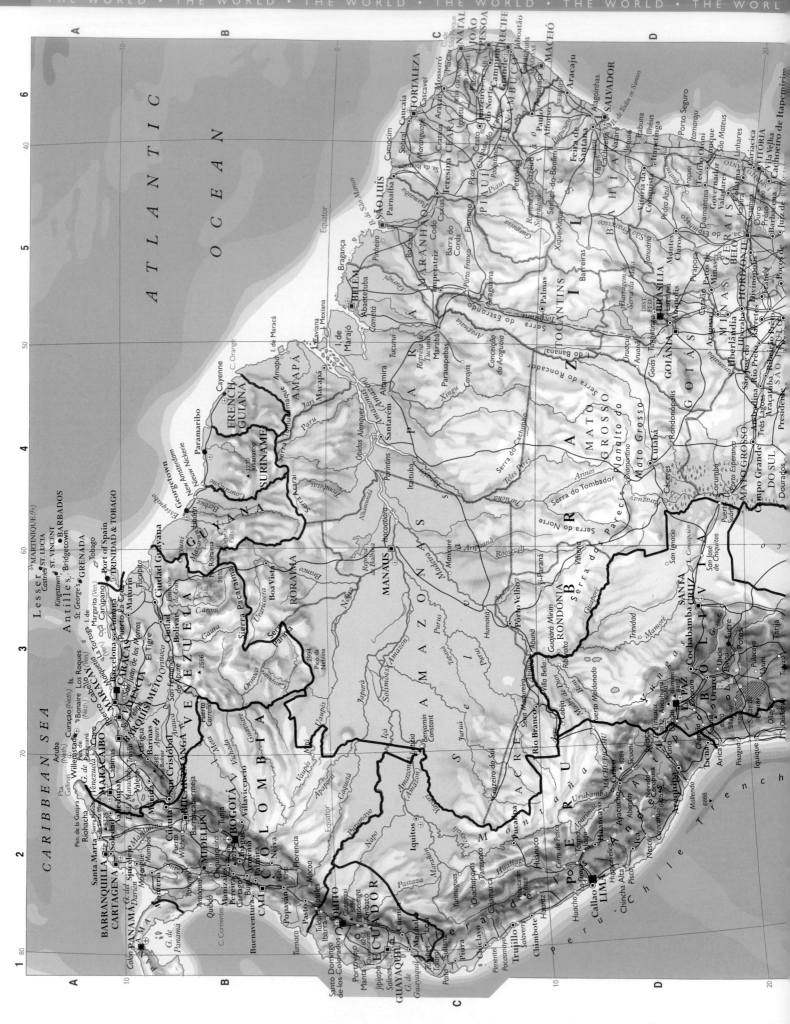

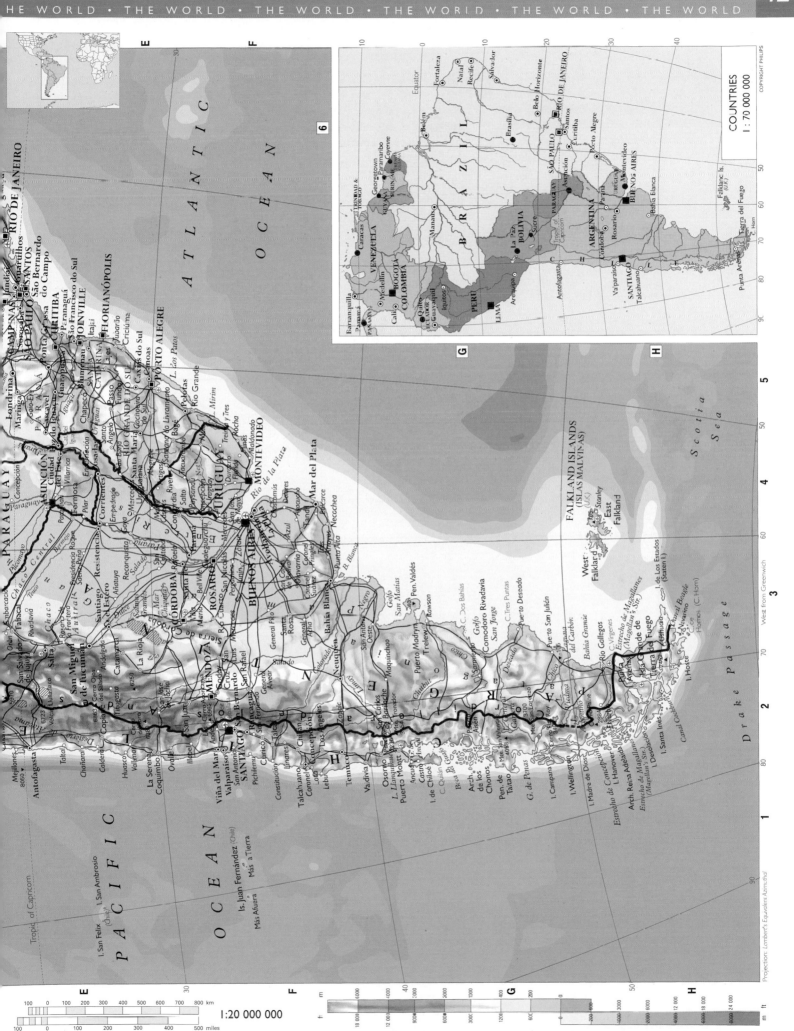

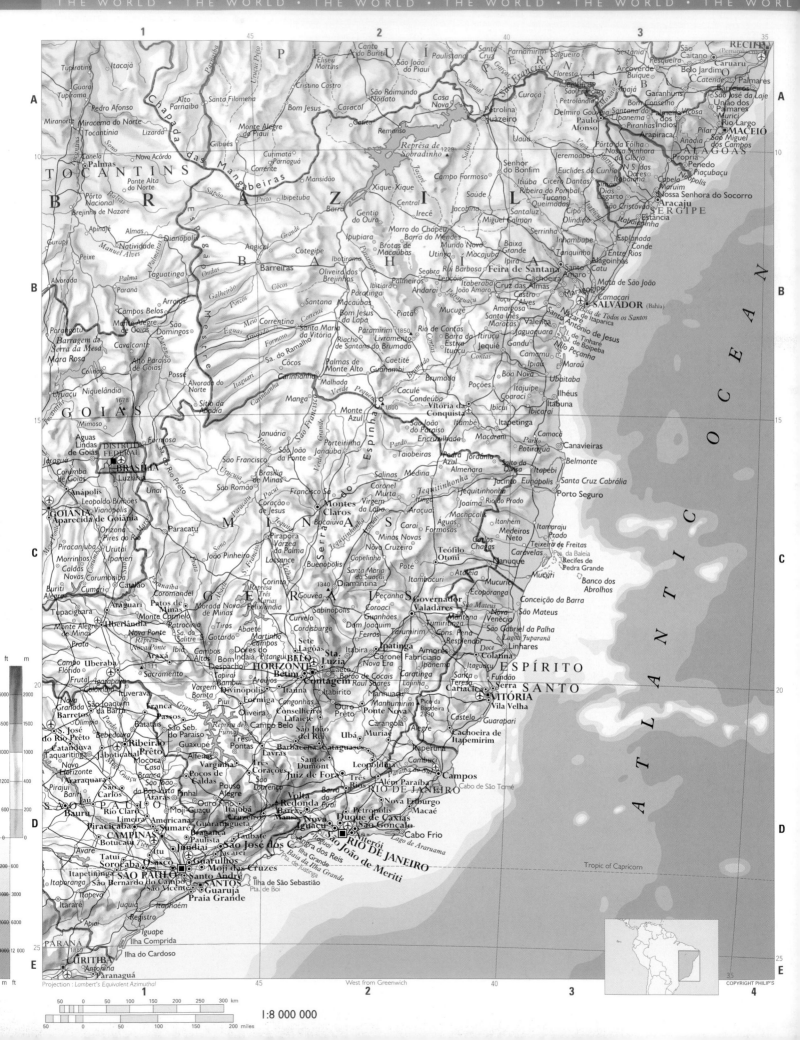

Projection : Lambert's Equivalent Azimuthal

West from Greenwich

1:8 000 000

50   0   50   100   150   200   250   300 km

50   0   50   100   150   200 miles

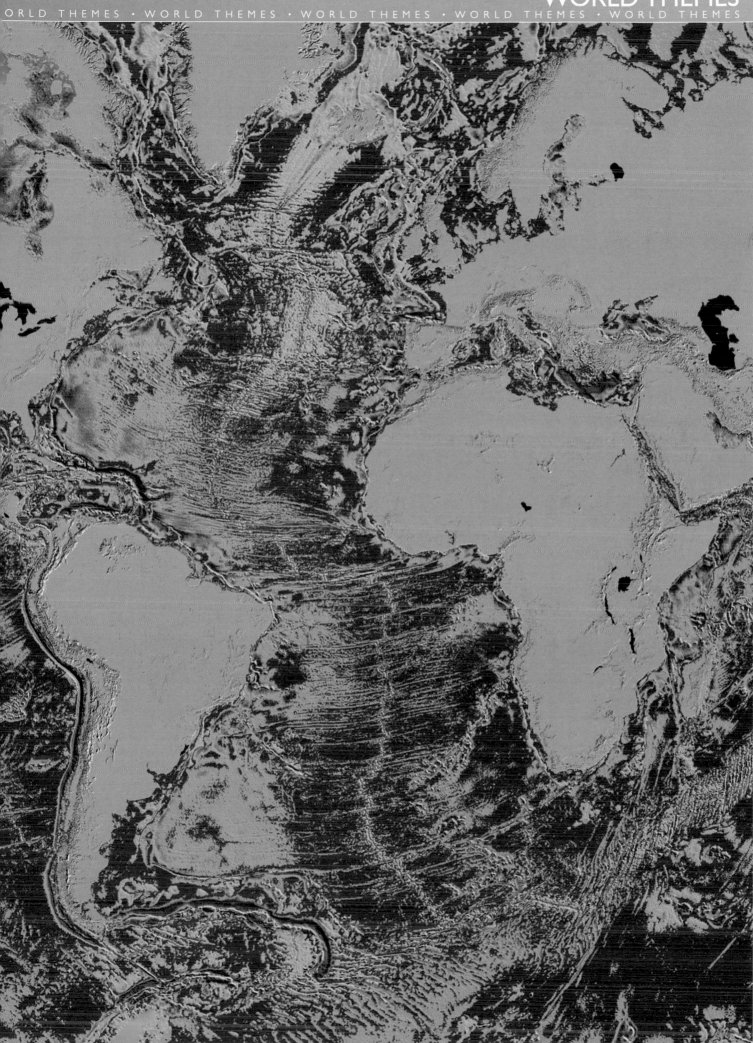

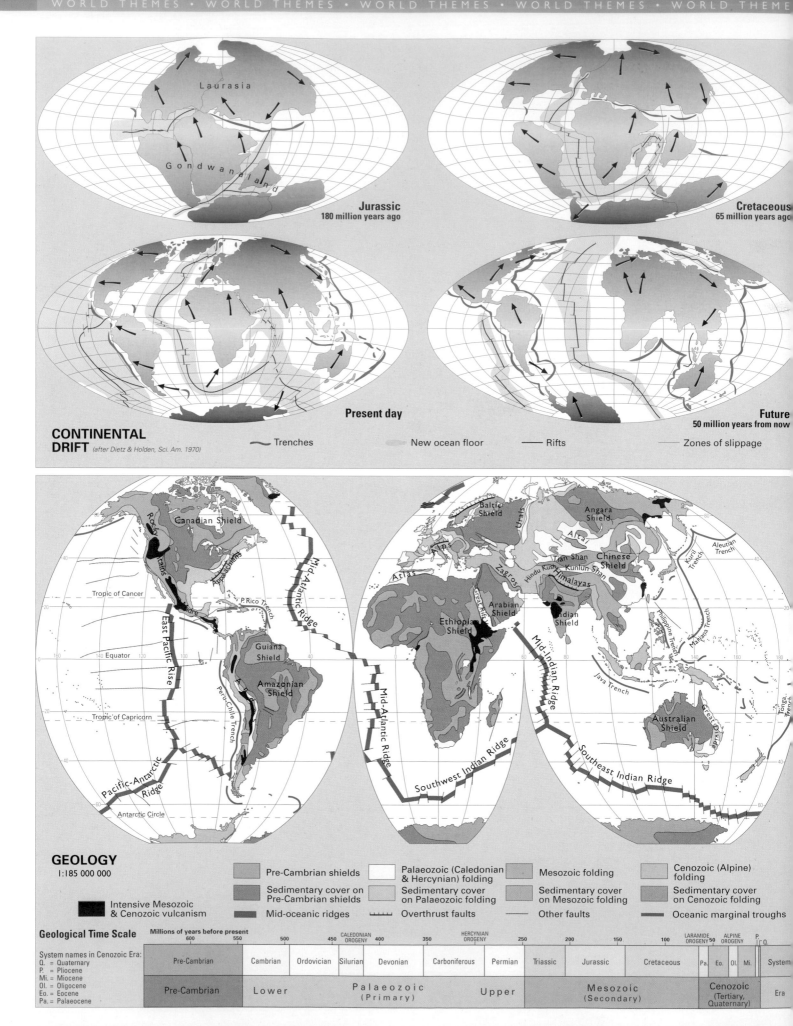

Jurassic
180 million years ago

Laurasia

Gondwanaland

Cretaceous
65 million years ago

Present day

Future
50 million years from now

CONTINENTAL DRIFT (after Dietz & Holden, Sci. Am. 1970)

⌒ Trenches   New ocean floor   — Rifts   Zones of slippage

GEOLOGY
1:185 000 000

Canadian Shield · Rocky Mountains · Appalachians · Tropic of Cancer · Sierra Madre · P. Rico Trench · East Pacific Rise · Guiana Shield · Equator · Amazonian Shield · Andes · Peru-Chile Trench · Tropic of Capricorn · Mid-Atlantic Ridge · Pacific-Antarctic Ridge · Antarctic Circle

Baltic Shield · Urals · Angara Shield · Altai · Atlas · Tian Shan · Chinese Shield · Aleutian Trench · Zagros · Hindu Kush · Kunlun Shan · Kuril Trench · Atlas · Arabian Shield · Himalayas · Indian Shield · Ethiopian Shield · Great Rift · Philippine Trench · Mariana Trench · Mid-Indian Ridge · Java Trench · Mid-Atlantic Ridge · Southwest Indian Ridge · Australian Shield · Great Divide · Southeast Indian Ridge · Tonga Trench

Intensive Mesozoic & Cenozoic vulcanism

Pre-Cambrian shields	Palaeozoic (Caledonian & Hercynian) folding	Mesozoic folding	Cenozoic (Alpine) folding
Sedimentary cover on Pre-Cambrian shields	Sedimentary cover on Palaeozoic folding	Sedimentary cover on Mesozoic folding	Sedimentary cover on Cenozoic folding
Mid-oceanic ridges	Overthrust faults	Other faults	Oceanic marginal troughs

Geological Time Scale

Millions of years before present

System names in Cenozoic Era:		600	550	500	450 CALEDONIAN OROGENY	400	350	HERCYNIAN OROGENY	250	200	150	100	LARAMIDE OROGENY 50	ALPINE OROGENY	P. P. Q.	
Q. = Quaternary		Pre-Cambrian		Cambrian	Ordovician	Silurian	Devonian	Carboniferous	Permian	Triassic	Jurassic	Cretaceous	Pa.	Eo.	Ol. Mi.	System
P. = Pliocene																
Mi. = Miocene																
Ol. = Oligocene																
Eo. = Eocene		Pre-Cambrian		Lower			Palaeozoic (Primary)		Upper		Mesozoic (Secondary)		Cenozoic (Tertiary, Quaternary)			Era
Pa. = Palaeocene																

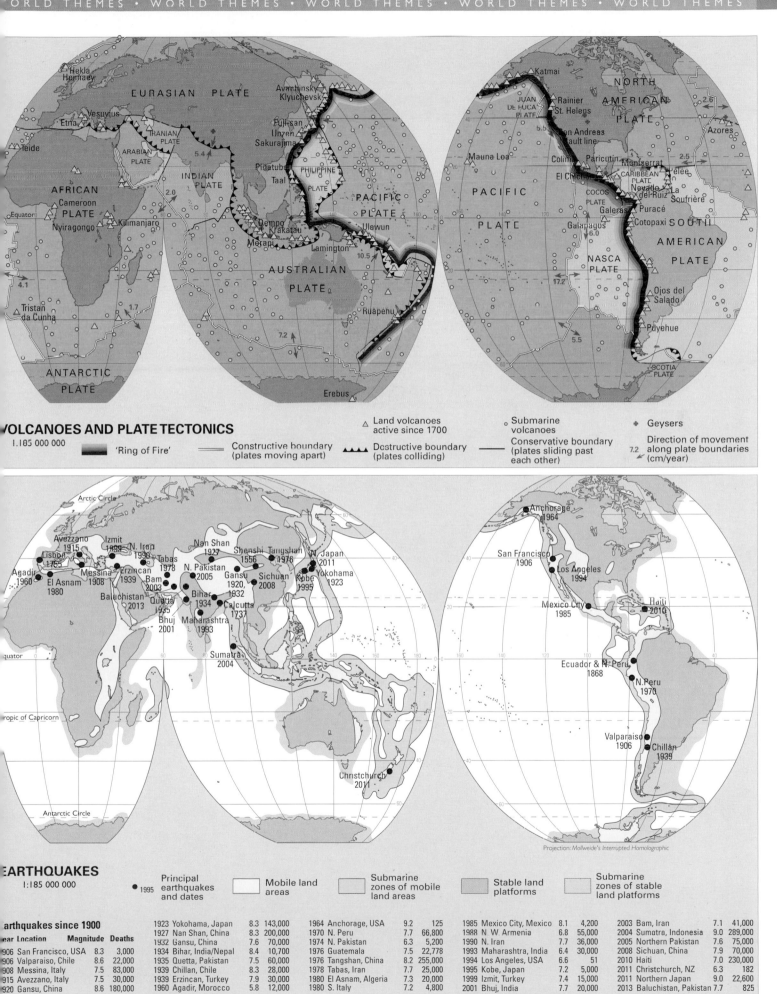

VOLCANOES AND PLATE TECTONICS

1:185 000 000

'Ring of Fire'	
Constructive boundary (plates moving apart)	
Destructive boundary (plates colliding)	
Conservative boundary (plates sliding past each other)	
△ Land volcanoes active since 1700	
○ Submarine volcanoes	
✦ Geysers	
7.2 ↙ Direction of movement along plate boundaries (cm/year)	

EARTHQUAKES

1:185 000 000

- ● 1995 Principal earthquakes and dates
- Mobile land areas
- Submarine zones of mobile land areas
- Stable land platforms
- Submarine zones of stable land platforms

Projection: Mollweide's Interrupted Homolographic

Earthquakes since 1900

Year	Location	Magnitude	Deaths
1906	San Francisco, USA	8.3	3,000
1906	Valparaiso, Chile	8.6	22,000
1915	Avezzano, Italy	7.5	30,000
1920	Gansu, China	8.6	180,000
1923	Yokohama, Japan	8.3	143,000
1927	Nan Shan, China	8.3	200,000
1932	Gansu, China	7.6	70,000
1934	Bihar, India/Nepal	8.4	10,700
1935	Quetta, Pakistan	7.5	60,000
1939	Chillan, Chile	8.3	28,000
1939	Erzincan, Turkey	7.9	30,000
1960	Agadir, Morocco	5.8	12,000
1964	Anchorage, USA	9.2	125
1970	N. Peru	7.7	66,800
1974	N. Pakistan	6.3	5,200
1976	Guatemala	7.5	22,778
1976	Tangshan, China	8.2	255,000
1978	Tabas, Iran	7.7	25,000
1980	El Asnam, Algeria	7.3	20,000
1980	S. Italy	7.2	4,800
1985	Mexico City, Mexico	8.1	4,200
1988	N.W. Armenia	6.8	55,000
1990	N. Iran	7.7	36,000
1993	Maharashtra, India	6.4	30,000
1994	Los Angeles, USA	6.6	51
1995	Kobe, Japan	7.2	5,000
1999	Izmit, Turkey	7.4	15,000
2001	Bhuj, India	7.7	20,000
2003	Bam, Iran	7.1	41,000
2004	Sumatra, Indonesia	9.0	289,000
2005	Northern Pakistan	7.6	75,000
2008	Sichuan, China	7.9	70,000
2010	Haiti	7.0	230,000
2011	Christchurch, NZ	6.3	182
2011	Northern Japan	9.0	22,600
2013	Baluchistan, Pakistan	7.7	825

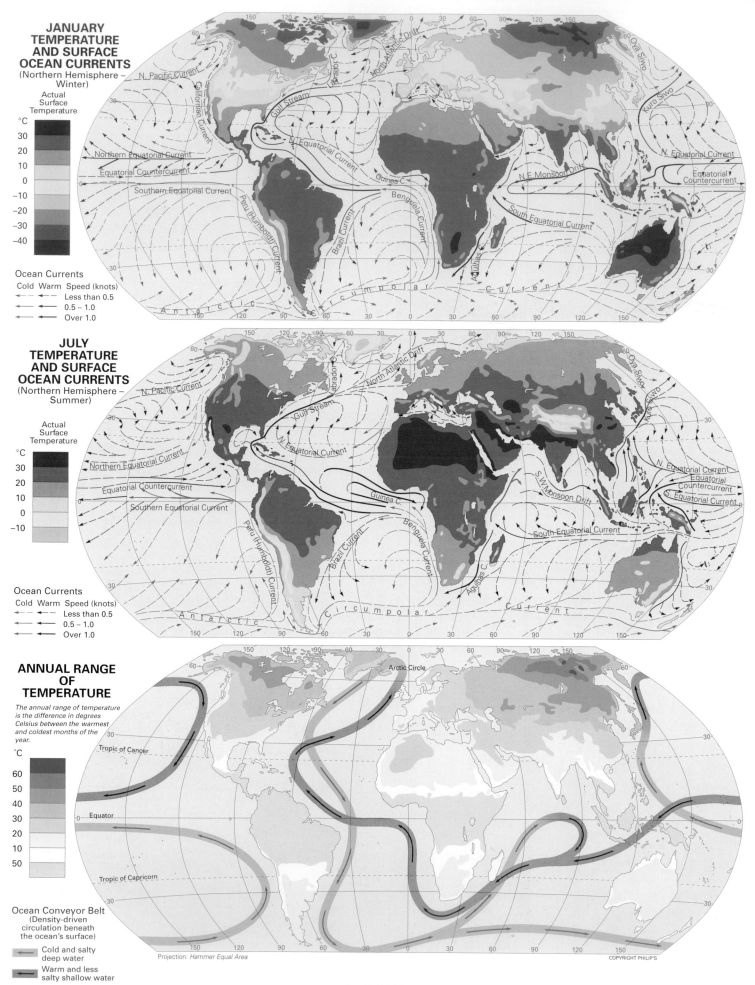

JANUARY TEMPERATURE AND SURFACE OCEAN CURRENTS
(Northern Hemisphere – Winter)

Actual Surface Temperature

°C
30
20
10
0
−10
−20
−30
−40

Ocean Currents

Cold Warm Speed (knots)
Less than 0.5
0.5 – 1.0
Over 1.0

JULY TEMPERATURE AND SURFACE OCEAN CURRENTS
(Northern Hemisphere – Summer)

Actual Surface Temperature

°C
30
20
10
0
−10

Ocean Currents

Cold Warm Speed (knots)
Less than 0.5
0.5 – 1.0
Over 1.0

ANNUAL RANGE OF TEMPERATURE

The annual range of temperature is the difference in degrees Celsius between the warmest and coldest months of the year.

°C
60
50
40
30
20
10
50

Ocean Conveyor Belt
(Density-driven circulation beneath the ocean's surface)

Cold and salty deep water

Warm and less salty shallow water

Projection: Hammer Equal Area

COPYRIGHT PHILIP'S

1 : 190 000 000

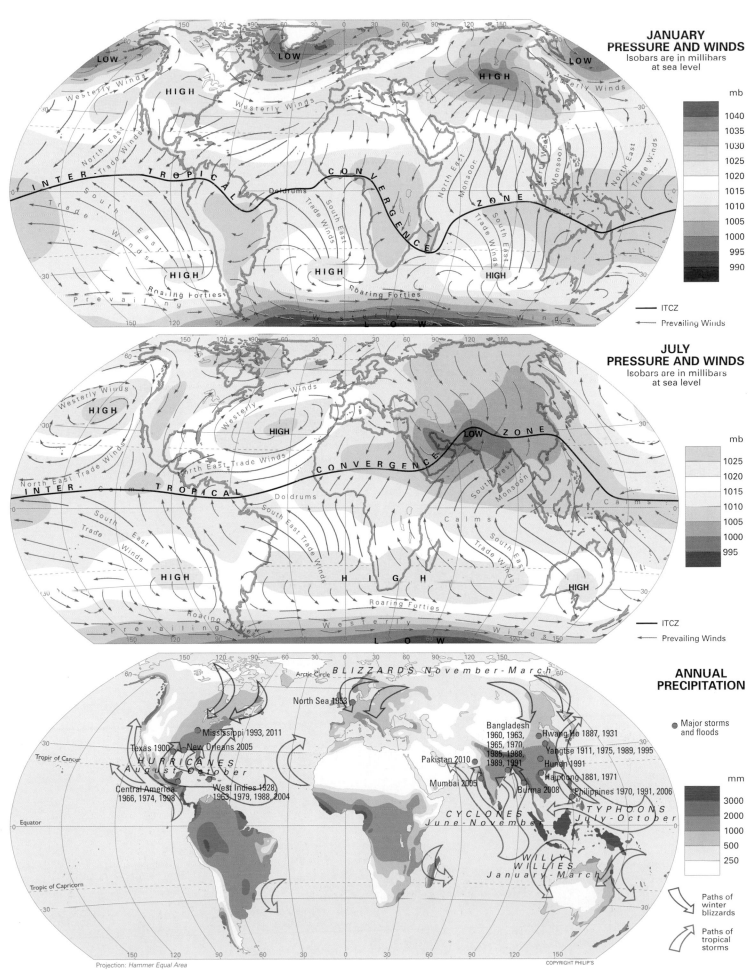

JANUARY PRESSURE AND WINDS
Isobars are in millibars at sea level

mb
1040
1035
1030
1025
1020
1015
1010
1005
1000
995
990

—— ITCZ

←— Prevailing Winds

JULY PRESSURE AND WINDS
Isobars are in millibars at sea level

mb
1025
1020
1015
1010
1005
1000
995

—— ITCZ

←— Prevailing Winds

ANNUAL PRECIPITATION

● Major storms and floods

mm
3000
2000
1000
500
250

Paths of winter blizzards

Paths of tropical storms

Projection: Hammer Equal Area

COPYRIGHT PHILIP'S

KEY TO CLIMATE REGIONS MAP

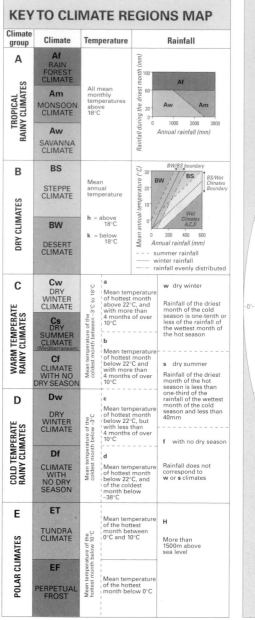

Climate group	Climate	Temperature	Rainfall	
A TROPICAL RAINY CLIMATES	**Af** RAIN FOREST CLIMATE	All mean monthly temperatures above 18°C		
	Am MONSOON CLIMATE			
	Aw SAVANNA CLIMATE			
B DRY CLIMATES	**BS** STEPPE CLIMATE	Mean annual temperature **h** = above 18°C **k** = below 18°C	--- summer rainfall — winter rainfall -·- rainfall evenly distributed	
	BW DESERT CLIMATE			
C WARM TEMPERATE RAINY CLIMATES	**Cw** DRY WINTER CLIMATE	**a** Mean temperature of the coldest month between −3°C to 18°C / Mean temperature of hottest month above 22°C, and with more than 4 months of over 10°C	**w** dry winter / Rainfall of the driest month of the cold season is one-tenth or less of the rainfall of the wettest month of the hot season	
	Cs DRY SUMMER CLIMATE (Mediterranean)	**b** Mean temperature of hottest month below 22°C and with more than 4 months of over 10°C	**s** dry summer / Rainfall of the driest month of the hot season is less than one-third of the rainfall of the wettest month of the cold season and less than 40mm	
	Cf CLIMATE WITH NO DRY SEASON			
D COLD TEMPERATE RAINY CLIMATES	**Dw** DRY WINTER CLIMATE	**c** Mean temperature of the coldest month below −3°C / Mean temperature of hottest month below 22°C, but with less than 4 months of over 10°C	**f** with no dry season	
	Df CLIMATE WITH NO DRY SEASON	**d** Mean temperature of hottest month below 22°C, and of the coldest month below −38°C	Rainfall does not correspond to **w** or **s** climates	
E POLAR CLIMATES	**ET** TUNDRA CLIMATE	Mean temperature of the coldest month below 10°C / Mean temperature of the hottest month between 0°C and 10°C	**H** More than 1500m above sea level	
	EF PERPETUAL FROST	Mean temperature of the hottest month below 0°C		

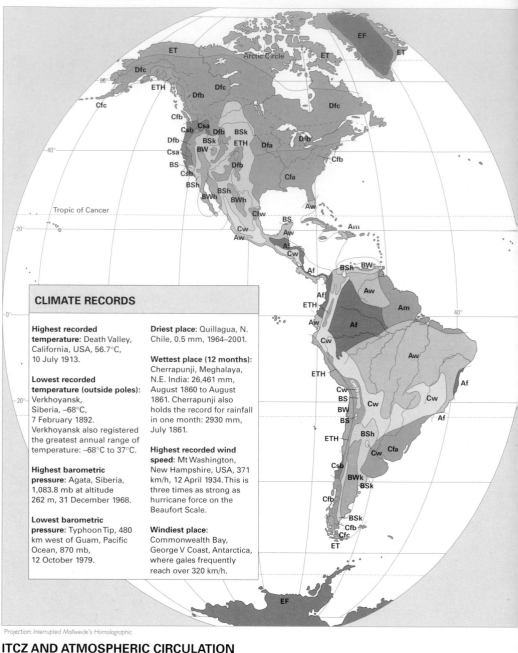

Projection: *Interrupted Mollweide's Homolographic*

CLIMATE RECORDS

Highest recorded temperature: Death Valley, California, USA, 56.7°C, 10 July 1913.

Lowest recorded temperature (outside poles): Verkhoyansk, Siberia, −68°C, 7 February 1892. Verkhoyansk also registered the greatest annual range of temperature: −68°C to 37°C.

Highest barometric pressure: Agata, Siberia, 1,083.8 mb at altitude 262 m, 31 December 1968.

Lowest barometric pressure: Typhoon Tip, 480 km west of Guam, Pacific Ocean, 870 mb, 12 October 1979.

Driest place: Quillagua, N. Chile, 0.5 mm, 1964–2001.

Wettest place (12 months): Cherrapunji, Meghalaya, N.E. India, 26,461 mm, August 1860 to August 1861. Cherrapunji also holds the record for rainfall in one month: 2930 mm, July 1861.

Highest recorded wind speed: Mt Washington, New Hampshire, USA, 371 km/h, 12 April 1934. This is three times as strong as hurricane force on the Beaufort Scale.

Windiest place: Commonwealth Bay, George V Coast, Antarctica, where gales frequently reach over 320 km/h.

WINDCHILL FACTOR

In sub-zero weather, even moderate winds significantly reduce effective temperatures. The chart below shows the windchill effect across a range of speeds.

	Wind speed in kilometres per hour				
	16	**32**	**48**	**64**	**80**
0°C	−8	−14	−17	−19	−20
−5°C	−14	−21	−25	−27	−28
−10°C	−20	−28	−33	−35	−36
−15°C	−26	−36	−40	−43	−44
−20°C	−32	−42	−48	−51	−52
−25°C	−38	−49	−56	−59	−60
−30°C	−44	−57	−63	−66	−68
−35°C	−51	−64	−72	−74	−76
−40°C	−57	−71	−78	−82	−84
−45°C	−63	−78	−86	−90	−92
−50°C	−69	−85	−94	−98	−100

ITCZ AND ATMOSPHERIC CIRCULATION

The Trade Winds converge on the Earth's surface at the Inter-Tropical Convergence Zone (ITCZ), where the hot and moist air rises rapidly to the upper limit of the Earth's troposphere to be carried by the Hadley Cell towards the mid-latitudes where it descends as dry air. Two lesser circulation cells – the Ferrel Cell and the Polar Cell carry the air further towards the Poles. The pattern of this circulation may vary from year to year and may affect the huge Pacific Cell, resulting in El Niño or La Niña events – see diagrams opposite.

High pressure
Low pressure
Warm air
Cold air
Surface winds
Clouds

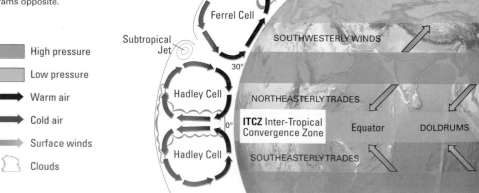

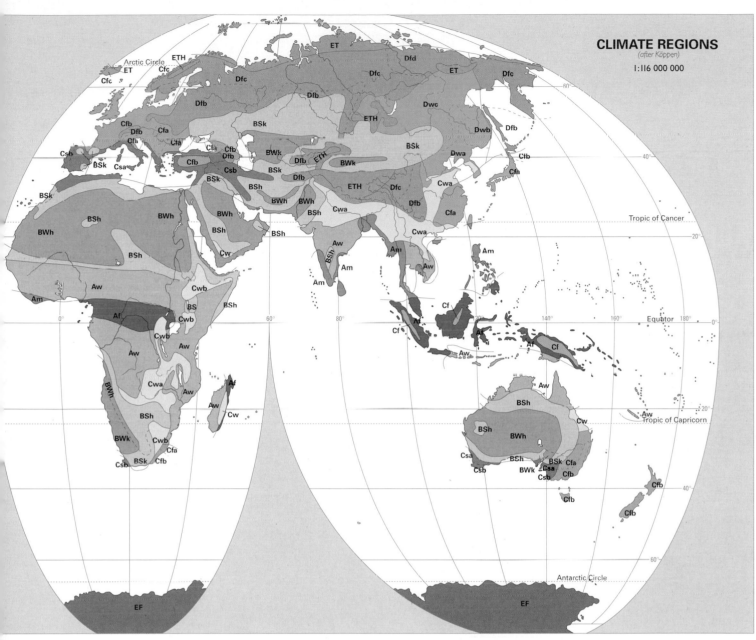

CLIMATE REGIONS
(after Köppen)

1:116 000 000

EL NIÑO

El Niño, 'The Little Boy' in Spanish, was the name given by local fishermen to the warm current that can appear off the Pacific coast of South America. In a normal year, south-easterly trade winds drive surface waters westwards off the coast of South America, drawing cold, nutrient-rich water up from below. In an El Niño year, warm water from the west Pacific suppresses upwelling in the east, depriving the region of nutrients and driving the fish away. The water is warmed by as much as 7°C, disturbing the circulation of the Pacific Cell. During an intense El Niño, the south-east trade winds change direction and become equatorial westerlies, resulting in climatic extremes in many regions of the world, such as drought in parts of Australia and India, and heavy rainfall in the SE USA.

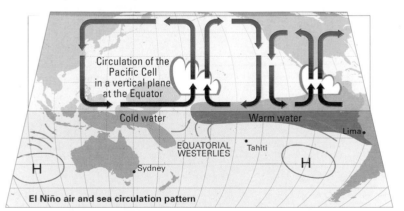

El Niño air and sea circulation pattern

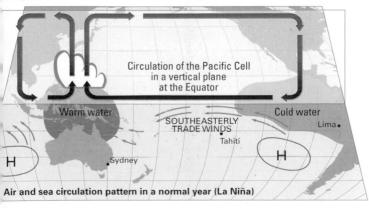

Air and sea circulation pattern in a normal year (La Niña)

El Niño events occur about every 4 to 7 years and typically last for around 12 to 18 months. El Niño usually results in reduced rainfall across northern and eastern Australia. This can lead to widespread and severe drought, as well as increased temperatures and bushfire risk. However, each El Niño event is unique in terms of its strength as well as its impact. It is measured by the Southern Oscillation Index (SOI) and the changes in ocean temperatures.

La Niña, or 'The Little Girl', is associated with cooler waters in the central and eastern Pacific. A La Niña year can result in cooler land temperatures across the tropics and subtropics and more storms in the North Atlantic.

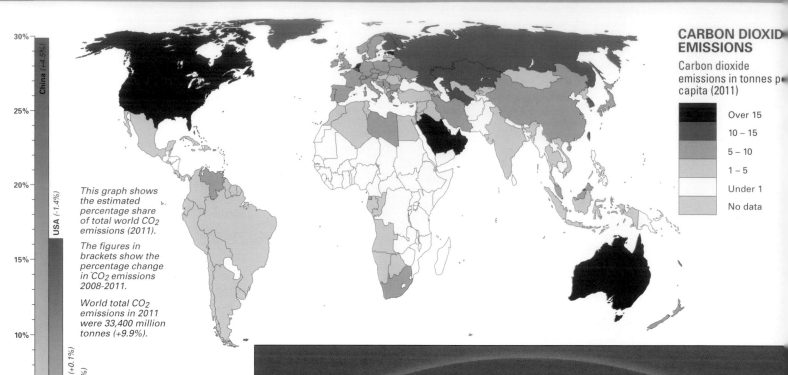

CARBON DIOXIDE EMISSIONS

Carbon dioxide emissions in tonnes per capita (2011)

■	Over 15
■	10 – 15
■	5 – 10
■	1 – 5
□	Under 1
■	No data

This graph shows the estimated percentage share of total world CO₂ emissions (2011).

The figures in brackets show the percentage change in CO₂ emissions 2008-2011.

World total CO₂ emissions in 2011 were 33,400 million tonnes (+9.9%).

Bar chart data (percentage share of total world CO₂ emissions):
- China (+4.5%)
- USA (-1.4%)
- Russia (+0.1%)
- India (0%)
- Japan (-0.1%)
- Germany (-0.1%)
- Iran (+0.1%)
- South Korea (+0.1%)
- Canada (0%)
- Saudi Arabia (+0.2%)
- Brazil (-0.1%)
- Mexico (-0.1%)
- South Africa (-0.1%)
- UK (0%)
- Australia (-0.2%)

Arctic Ice Cap

This image shows the extent of sea-ice in the Arctic in September 2012. The sea-ice area expands and contracts seasonally and September, at the end of the northern hemisphere summer, represents its smallest extent. The year 2012 showed the biggest reduction in sea-ice since satellite surveillance began in 1979 and this is believed to be related to climate change and global warming. Although dramatic, the sea-ice itself is thought to be quite thin, on average about 3 m (10 ft) thick. Even large reductions would not in themselves involve any sea-level change since the ice is floating and displaces the sea water. One by-product of this is the opening-up of clear sea. This would enable shipping in the northern hemisphere to move between the Atlantic and Pacific Oceans using the much shorter routes around the north coasts of Canada and of Russia, rather than heading south to do this.

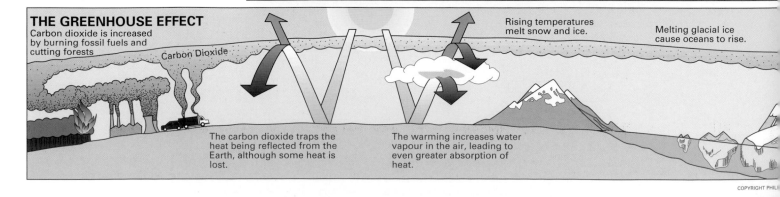

THE GREENHOUSE EFFECT

Carbon dioxide is increased by burning fossil fuels and cutting forests

Carbon Dioxide

Rising temperatures melt snow and ice.

Melting glacial ice cause oceans to rise.

The carbon dioxide traps the heat being reflected from the Earth, although some heat is lost.

The warming increases water vapour in the air, leading to even greater absorption of heat.

PREDICTED CHANGE IN TEMPERATURE

The difference between actual annual average surface air temperature, 1960–90, and predicted annual average surface air temperature, 2070–2100. This map shows the predicted increase, assuming a 'medium growth' of the global economy and assuming that no measures to combat the emission of greenhouse gases are taken.

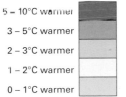

- 5 – 10°C warmer
- 3 – 5°C warmer
- 2 – 3°C warmer
- 1 – 2°C warmer
- 0 – 1°C warmer

Source: The Hadley Centre of Climate Prediction and Research, The Met. Office.

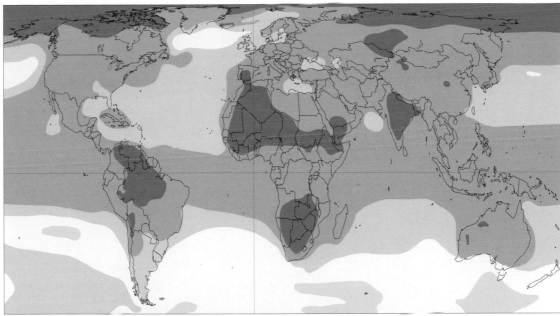

PREDICTED CHANGE IN PRECIPITATION

The difference between actual annual average precipitation, 1960–90, and predicted annual average precipitation, 2070–2100. It should be noted that these predicted annual mean changes mask quite significant seasonal detail.

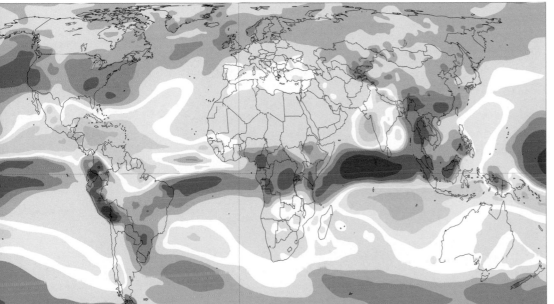

- Over 2 mm more rain per day
- 1 – 2 mm more rain per day
- 0.5 – 1 mm more rain per day
- 0.2 – 0.5 mm more rain per day
- No change
- 0.2 – 0.5 mm less rain per day
- 0.5 – 1 mm less rain per day
- 1 – 2 mm less rain per day
- Over 2 mm less rain per day

DESERTIFICATION AND DEFORESTATION

- Existing deserts and dry areas
- Areas with a high risk of desertification
- Areas with a moderate risk of desertification
- Former extent of rainforest
- Existing rainforest

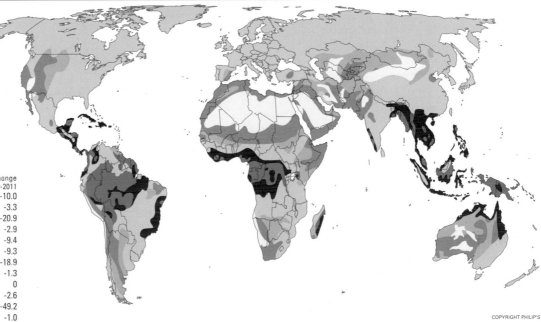

Deforestation 1990–2011

	Total forest cover in million ha 1990	Total forest cover in million ha 2011	% change 1990–2011
Brazil	574.8	517.3	-10.0
Australia	153.4	148.4	-3.3
Indonesia	118.5	93.7	-20.9
Peru	69.9	67.8	-2.9
Bolivia	62.8	56.9	-9.4
Papua New Guinea	31.5	28.6	-9.3
Cameroon	24.3	19.7	-18.9
Congo	22.7	22.4	-1.3
Malaysia	20.4	20.4	0
Thailand	19.5	19.0	-2.6
Nigeria	17.0	8.6	-49.2
Madagascar	13.5	12.5	-1.0

	Jan
Addis Ababa, Ethiopia 2,410 m	
Temperature Daily max. °C	23
Daily min. °C	6
Average monthly °C	14
Rainfall Monthly total mm	13
Sunshine Hours per day	8.7

- Height of meteorological station above sea level in metres
- Average monthly maximum temperature in degrees Celsius
- Average monthly minimum temperature in degrees Celsius
- Average monthly temperature in degrees Celsius
- Average monthly precipitation in millimetres
- Average daily duration of bright sunshine per month in hours

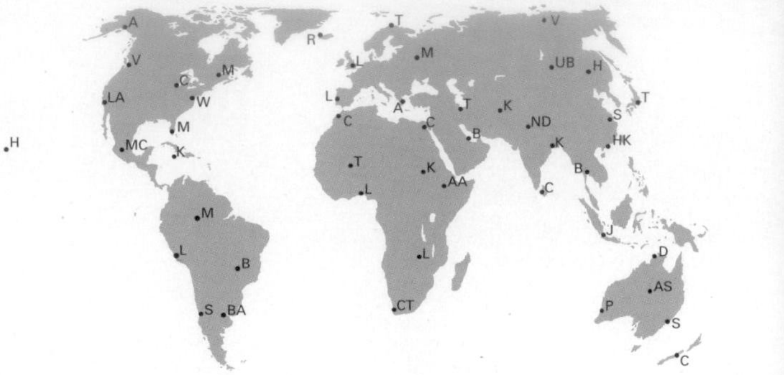

	Jan	Feb	Mar	Apr	May	June	July	Aug	Sept	Oct	Nov	Dec	Year
Addis Ababa, Ethiopia 2,410 m													
Temperature Daily max. °C	23	24	25	24	25	23	20	20	21	22	23	22	23
Daily min. °C	6	7	9	10	9	10	11	11	10	7	5	5	8
Average monthly °C	14	15	17	17	17	16	16	15	15	15	14	14	15
Rainfall Monthly total mm	13	35	67	91	81	117	247	255	167	29	8	5	1,115
Sunshine Hours per day	8.7	8.2	7.6	8.1	6.5	4.8	2.8	3.2	5.2	7.6	6.7	7	6.4
Alice Springs, Australia 580 m													
Temperature Daily max. °C	35	35	32	27	23	19	19	23	27	31	33	35	28
Daily min. °C	21	20	17	12	8	5	4	6	10	15	18	20	13
Average monthly °C	28	27	25	20	15	12	12	14	18	23	25	27	21
Rainfall Monthly total mm	44	33	27	10	15	13	7	8	7	18	29	38	249
Sunshine Hours per day	10.3	10.4	9.3	9.2	8	8	8.9	9.8	10	9.7	10.1	10	9.5
Anchorage, USA 183 m													
Temperature Daily max. °C	−7	−3	0	7	13	18	19	17	13	6	−2	−6	−6
Daily min. °C	−15	−12	−9	−2	4	8	10	9	5	−2	−9	−14	−2
Average monthly °C	−11	−7	−4	3	9	13	15	13	9	2	−5	−10	−4
Rainfall Monthly total mm	20	18	13	11	13	25	47	64	64	47	28	24	374
Sunshine Hours per day	2.4	4.1	6.6	8.3	8.3	9.2	8.5	6	4.4	3.1	2.6	1.6	5.4
Athens, Greece 107 m													
Temperature Daily max. °C	13	14	16	20	25	30	33	33	29	24	19	15	23
Daily min. °C	6	7	8	11	16	20	23	23	19	15	12	8	14
Average monthly °C	10	10	12	16	20	25	28	28	24	20	15	11	18
Rainfall Monthly total mm	62	37	37	23	23	14	6	7	15	51	56	71	402
Sunshine Hours per day	3.9	5.2	5.8	7.7	8.9	10.7	11.9	11.5	9.4	6.8	4.8	3.8	7.3
Bahrain City, Bahrain 2 m													
Temperature Daily max. °C	20	21	25	29	33	36	37	38	36	32	27	22	30
Daily min. °C	14	15	18	22	25	29	31	32	29	25	22	16	23
Average monthly °C	17	18	21	25	29	32	34	35	32	29	25	19	26
Rainfall Monthly total mm	18	12	10	9	2	0	0	0	0	0.4	3	16	70
Sunshine Hours per day	5.9	6.9	7.9	8.8	10.6	13.2	12.1	12	12	10.3	7.7	6.4	9.5
Bangkok, Thailand 10 m													
Temperature Daily max. °C	32	33	34	35	34	33	32	32	32	31	31	31	33
Daily min. °C	20	23	24	26	25	25	25	24	24	24	23	20	24
Average monthly °C	26	28	29	30	30	29	28	28	28	28	27	26	28
Rainfall Monthly total mm	9	30	36	82	165	153	168	183	310	239	55	8	1,438
Sunshine Hours per day	8.2	8	8	10	7.5	6.1	4.7	5.2	5.2	6.1	7.3	7.8	7
Brasilia, Brazil 910 m													
Temperature Daily max. °C	28	28	28	28	27	27	27	29	30	29	28	27	28
Daily min. °C	18	18	18	17	15	13	13	14	16	18	18	18	16
Average monthly °C	23	23	23	22	21	20	20	21	23	24	23	22	22
Rainfall Monthly total mm	252	204	227	93	17	3	6	3	30	127	255	343	1,560
Sunshine Hours per day	5.8	5.7	6	7.4	8.7	9.3	9.6	9.8	7.9	6.5	4.8	4.4	7.2
Buenos Aires, Argentina 25 m													
Temperature Daily max. °C	30	29	26	22	18	14	14	16	18	21	25	28	22
Daily min. °C	17	17	16	12	9	5	6	6	8	10	14	16	11
Average monthly °C	23	23	21	17	13	10	10	11	13	15	19	22	16
Rainfall Monthly total mm	79	71	109	89	76	61	56	61	79	86	84	99	950
Sunshine Hours per day	9.2	8.5	7.5	6.8	4.9	3.5	3.8	5.2	6	6.8	8.1	8.5	6.6
Cairo, Egypt 75 m													
Temperature Daily max. °C	19	21	24	28	32	35	35	35	33	30	26	21	28
Daily min. °C	9	9	12	14	18	20	22	22	20	18	14	10	16
Average monthly °C	14	15	18	21	25	28	29	28	26	24	20	16	22
Rainfall Monthly total mm	4	4	3	1	2	1	0	0	1	1	3	7	27
Sunshine Hours per day	6.9	8.4	8.7	9.7	10.5	11.9	11.7	11.3	10.4	9.4	8.3	6.4	9.5
Cape Town, South Africa 44 m													
Temperature Daily max. °C	26	26	25	23	20	18	17	18	19	21	24	25	22
Daily min. °C	15	15	14	11	9	7	7	7	8	10	13	15	11
Average monthly °C	21	20	20	17	14	13	12	12	14	16	18	20	16
Rainfall Monthly total mm	12	19	17	42	67	98	68	76	36	45	12	13	505
Sunshine Hours per day	11.4	10.2	9.4	7.7	6.1	5.7	6.4	6.6	7.6	8.6	10.2	10.9	8.4
Casablanca, Morocco 59 m													
Temperature Daily max. °C	17	18	20	21	22	24	26	26	26	24	21	18	22
Daily min. °C	8	9	11	12	15	18	19	20	18	15	12	10	14
Average monthly °C	13	13	15	16	18	21	23	23	22	20	17	14	18
Rainfall Monthly total mm	78	61	54	37	20	3	0	1	6	28	58	94	440
Sunshine Hours per day	5.2	6.3	7.3	9	9.4	9.7	10.2	9.7	9.1	7.4	5.9	5.3	7.9

	Jan	Feb	Mar	Apr	May	June	July	Aug	Sept	Oct	Nov	Dec	Year
Chicago, USA 186 m													
Temperature Daily max. °C	1	2	6	14	21	26	29	28	24	17	8	2	15
Daily min. °C	−7	−6	−2	5	11	16	20	19	14	8	0	−5	−6
Average monthly °C	−3	−2	2	9	16	21	24	23	19	13	4	−2	4
Rainfall Monthly total mm	47	41	70	77	96	103	86	80	69	71	56	48	844
Sunshine Hours per day	4	5	6.6	6.9	8.9	10.2	10	9.2	8.2	6.9	4.5	3.7	7
Christchurch, New Zealand 5 m													
Temperature Daily max. °C	21	21	19	17	13	11	10	11	14	17	19	21	16
Daily min. °C	12	12	10	7	4	2	1	3	5	7	8	11	7
Average monthly °C	16	16	15	12	9	6	6	7	9	12	13	16	11
Rainfall Monthly total mm	56	46	43	46	76	69	61	58	51	51	51	61	669
Sunshine Hours per day	7	6.5	5.6	4.7	4.3	3.9	4.1	4.7	5.6	6.1	6.9	6.3	5.5
Colombo, Sri Lanka 10 m													
Temperature Daily max. °C	30	31	31	31	30	30	29	29	30	29	29	30	30
Daily min. °C	22	22	23	24	25	25	25	25	25	24	23	22	24
Average monthly °C	26	26	27	28	28	27	27	27	27	27	26	26	27
Rainfall Monthly total mm	101	66	118	230	394	220	140	102	174	348	333	142	2,368
Sunshine Hours per day	7.9	9	8.1	7.2	6.4	5.4	6.1	6.3	6.2	6.5	6.4	7.8	6.9
Darwin, Australia 30 m													
Temperature Daily max. °C	32	32	33	33	33	31	31	32	33	34	34	33	33
Daily min. °C	25	25	25	24	23	21	19	21	23	25	26	26	24
Average monthly °C	29	29	29	29	28	26	25	26	28	29	30	29	28
Rainfall Monthly total mm	405	309	279	77	8	2	0	1	15	48	108	214	1,466
Sunshine Hours per day	5.8	5.8	6.6	9.8	9.3	10	9.9	10.4	10.1	9.4	9.6	6.8	8.6
Harbin, China 175 m													
Temperature Daily max. °C	−14	−9	0	12	21	26	29	27	20	12	−1	−11	9
Daily min. °C	−26	−23	−12	−1	7	14	18	16	8	0	−12	−22	−3
Average monthly °C	−20	−16	−6	6	14	20	23	22	14	6	−7	−17	3
Rainfall Monthly total mm	4	6	17	23	44	92	167	119	52	36	12	5	577
Sunshine Hours per day	6.4	7.8	8	7.8	8.3	8.6	8.6	8.2	7.2	6.9	6.1	5.7	7.5
Hong Kong, China 35 m													
Temperature Daily max. °C	18	18	20	24	28	30	31	31	30	27	24	20	25
Daily min. °C	13	13	16	19	23	26	26	26	25	23	19	15	20
Average monthly °C	16	15	18	22	25	28	28	28	27	25	21	17	23
Rainfall Monthly total mm	30	60	70	133	332	479	286	415	364	33	46	17	2,265
Sunshine Hours per day	4.7	3.5	3.1	3.8	5	5.4	6.8	6.5	6.6	7	6.2	5.5	5.3
Honolulu, Hawaii 5 m													
Temperature Daily max. °C	26	26	26	27	28	29	29	29	30	29	28	26	28
Daily min. °C	19	19	19	20	21	22	23	23	23	22	21	20	21
Average monthly °C	23	22	23	23	24	26	26	26	26	26	24	23	24
Rainfall Monthly total mm	96	84	73	33	25	8	11	23	25	47	55	76	556
Sunshine Hours per day	7.3	7.7	8.3	8.6	8.8	9.1	9.4	9.3	9.2	8.3	7.5	6.2	8.3
Jakarta, Indonesia 10 m													
Temperature Daily max. °C	29	29	30	31	31	31	31	31	31	31	30	29	30
Daily min. °C	23	23	23	24	24	23	23	23	23	23	23	23	23
Average monthly °C	26	26	27	27	27	27	27	27	27	27	27	26	27
Rainfall Monthly total mm	300	300	211	147	114	97	64	43	66	112	142	203	1,799
Sunshine Hours per day	6.1	6.5	7.7	8.5	8.4	8.5	9.1	9.5	9.6	9	7.7	7.1	8.1
Kabul, Afghanistan 1,791 m													
Temperature Daily max. °C	2	4	12	19	26	31	33	33	30	22	17	8	20
Daily min. °C	−8	−6	1	6	11	13	16	15	11	6	1	−3	5
Average monthly °C	−3	−1	6	13	18	22	25	24	20	14	9	3	12
Rainfall Monthly total mm	28	61	72	117	33	1	7	1	0	1	37	14	372
Sunshine Hours per day	5.9	6	5.7	6.8	10.1	11.5	11.4	11.2	9.8	9.4	7.8	6.1	8.5
Khartoum, Sudan 380 m													
Temperature Daily max. °C	32	33	37	40	42	41	38	36	38	39	35	32	37
Daily min. °C	16	17	20	23	26	27	26	25	25	25	21	17	22
Average monthly °C	24	25	28	32	34	34	32	30	32	32	28	25	30
Rainfall Monthly total mm	0	0	0	1	7	5	56	80	28	2	0	0	179
Sunshine Hours per day	10.6	11.2	10.4	10.8	10.4	10.1	8.6	8.6	9.6	10.3	10.8	10.6	10.2
Kingston, Jamaica 35 m													
Temperature Daily max. °C	30	30	30	31	31	32	32	32	32	31	31	31	31
Daily min. °C	20	20	20	21	22	24	23	23	23	23	22	21	22
Average monthly °C	25	25	25	26	26	28	28	28	27	27	26	26	26
Rainfall Monthly total mm	23	15	23	31	102	89	38	91	99	180	74	36	801
Sunshine Hours per day	8.3	8.8	8.7	8.7	8.3	7.8	8.5	8.5	7.6	7.3	8.3	7.7	8.2

		Jan	Feb	Mar	Apr	May	June	July	Aug	Sept	Oct	Nov	Dec	Year
Kolkata (Calcutta), India 5 m														
Temperature	Daily max. °C	27	29	34	36	35	34	32	32	32	32	29	26	31
	Daily min. °C	13	15	21	24	25	26	26	26	26	23	18	13	21
	Average monthly °C	20	22	27	30	30	30	29	29	29	28	23	20	26
Rainfall	Monthly total mm	10	30	34	44	140	297	325	332	253	114	20	5	1,604
Sunshine	Hours per day	8.6	8.7	8.9	9	8.7	5.4	4.1	4.1	5.1	6.5	8.3	8.4	7.1
Lagos, Nigeria 40 m														
Temperature	Daily max. °C	32	33	33	32	31	29	28	28	29	30	31	32	31
	Daily min. °C	22	23	23	23	23	22	22	21	22	22	23	22	22
	Average monthly °C	27	28	28	28	27	26	25	24	25	26	27	27	26
Rainfall	Monthly total mm	28	41	99	99	203	300	180	56	180	190	63	25	1,464
Sunshine	Hours per day	5.9	6.8	6.3	6.1	5.6	3.8	2.8	3.3	3	5.1	6.6	6.5	5.2
Lima, Peru 120 m														
Temperature	Daily max. °C	28	29	29	27	24	20	20	19	20	22	24	26	24
	Daily min. °C	19	20	19	17	16	15	14	14	14	15	16	17	16
	Average monthly °C	24	24	24	22	20	17	17	16	17	18	20	21	20
Rainfall	Monthly total mm	1	1	1	1	5	5	8	8	8	3	3	1	45
Sunshine	Hours per day	6.3	6.8	6.9	6.7	4	1.4	1.1	1	1.1	2.5	4.1	5	3.9
Lisbon, Portugal 77 m														
Temperature	Daily max. °C	14	15	17	20	21	25	27	28	26	22	17	15	21
	Daily min. °C	8	8	10	12	13	15	17	17	17	14	11	9	13
	Average monthly °C	11	12	14	16	17	20	22	23	21	18	14	12	17
Rainfall	Monthly total mm	111	76	109	54	44	16	3	4	33	62	93	103	708
Sunshine	Hours per day	4.7	5.9	6	8.3	9.1	10.6	11.4	10.7	8.4	6.7	5.2	4.6	7.7
London (Kew), UK 5 m														
Temperature	Daily max. °C	6	7	10	13	17	20	22	21	19	14	10	7	14
	Daily min. °C	2	2	3	6	8	12	14	13	11	8	5	4	7
	Average monthly °C	4	5	7	9	12	16	18	17	15	11	8	5	11
Rainfall	Monthly total mm	54	40	37	37	46	45	57	59	49	57	64	48	593
Sunshine	Hours per day	1.7	2.3	3.5	5.7	6.7	7	6.6	6	5	3.3	1.9	1.4	4.3
Los Angeles, USA 30 m														
Temperature	Daily max. °C	18	18	18	19	20	22	24	24	24	23	22	19	21
	Daily min. °C	7	8	9	11	13	15	17	17	16	14	11	9	12
	Average monthly °C	12	13	14	15	17	18	21	21	20	18	16	14	17
Rainfall	Monthly total mm	69	74	46	28	3	3	0	0	5	10	28	61	327
Sunshine	Hours per day	6.9	8.2	8.9	8.8	9.5	10.3	11.7	11	10.1	8.6	8.2	7.6	9.2
Lusaka, Zambia 1,154 m														
Temperature	Daily max. °C	26	26	26	27	25	23	23	26	29	31	29	27	27
	Daily min. °C	17	17	16	15	12	10	9	11	15	18	18	17	15
	Average monthly °C	22	22	21	21	18	17	16	19	22	25	23	22	21
Rainfall	Monthly total mm	224	173	90	19	3	1	0	1	1	17	85	196	810
Sunshine	Hours per day	5.1	5.4	6.9	8.9	9	9	9.1	9.6	9.5	9	7	5.5	7.8
Manaus, Brazil 45 m														
Temperature	Daily max. °C	31	31	31	31	31	31	32	33	34	34	33	32	32
	Daily min. °C	24	24	24	24	24	24	24	24	24	25	25	24	24
	Average monthly °C	28	28	28	27	28	28	28	29	29	29	29	28	28
Rainfall	Monthly total mm	278	278	300	287	193	99	61	41	62	112	165	220	2,096
Sunshine	Hours per day	3.9	4	3.6	3.9	5.4	6.9	7.9	8.2	7.5	6.6	5.9	4.9	5.7
Mexico City, Mexico 2,309 m														
Temperature	Daily max. °C	21	23	26	27	26	25	23	24	23	22	21	21	24
	Daily min. °C	5	6	7	9	10	11	11	11	11	9	6	5	8
	Average monthly °C	13	15	16	18	18	18	17	17	17	16	14	13	16
Rainfall	Monthly total mm	8	4	9	23	57	111	160	149	119	46	16	7	709
Sunshine	Hours per day	7.3	8.1	8.5	8.1	7.8	7	6.2	6.4	5.6	6.3	7	7.3	7.1
Miami, USA 2 m														
Temperature	Daily max. °C	24	25	27	28	30	31	32	32	31	29	27	25	28
	Daily min. °C	14	15	16	19	21	23	24	24	24	22	18	15	20
	Average monthly °C	19	20	21	23	25	27	28	28	27	25	22	20	24
Rainfall	Monthly total mm	51	48	58	99	163	188	170	178	241	208	71	43	1,518
Sunshine	Hours per day	7.7	8.3	8.7	9.4	8.9	8.5	8.7	8.4	7.1	6.5	7.5	7.1	8.1
Montreal, Canada 57 m														
Temperature	Daily max. °C	−6	−4	2	11	18	23	26	25	20	14	5	−3	11
	Daily min. °C	−13	−11	−5	2	9	14	17	16	11	6	0	−9	3
	Average monthly °C	−9	−8	−2	6	13	19	22	20	16	10	3	−6	7
Rainfall	Monthly total mm	87	76	86	83	81	91	98	87	96	84	89	89	1,047
Sunshine	Hours per day	2.8	3.4	4.5	5.2	6.7	7.7	8.2	7.7	5.6	4.3	2.4	2.2	5.1
Moscow, Russia 156 m														
Temperature	Daily max. °C	−6	−4	1	9	18	22	24	22	17	10	1	−5	9
	Daily min. °C	−14	−16	−11	−1	5	9	12	9	4	−2	−6	−12	−2
	Average monthly °C	−10	−10	−5	4	12	15	18	16	10	4	−2	−8	4
Rainfall	Monthly total mm	31	28	33	35	52	67	74	74	58	51	36	36	575
Sunshine	Hours per day	1	1.9	3.7	5.2	7.8	8.3	8.4	7.1	4.4	2.4	1	0.6	4.4
New Delhi, India 220 m														
Temperature	Daily max. °C	21	24	29	36	41	39	35	34	34	34	28	23	32
	Daily min. °C	6	10	14	20	26	28	27	26	24	17	11	7	18
	Average monthly °C	14	17	22	28	33	34	31	30	29	26	20	15	25
Rainfall	Monthly total mm	25	21	13	8	13	77	178	184	123	10	2	11	665
Sunshine	Hours per day	7.7	8.2	8.2	8.7	9.2	7.9	6	6.3	6.9	9.4	8.7	8.3	8

		Jan	Feb	Mar	Apr	May	June	July	Aug	Sept	Oct	Nov	Dec	Year
Perth, Australia 60 m														
Temperature	Daily max. °C	29	30	27	25	21	18	17	18	19	21	25	27	23
	Daily min. °C	17	18	16	14	12	10	9	9	10	11	14	16	13
	Average monthly °C	23	24	22	19	16	14	13	13	15	16	19	22	18
Rainfall	Monthly total mm	8	13	22	44	128	189	177	145	84	58	19	13	900
Sunshine	Hours per day	10.4	9.8	8.8	7.5	5.7	4.8	5.4	6	7.2	8.1	9.6	10.4	7.8
Reykjavik, Iceland 18 m														
Temperature	Daily max. °C	2	3	5	6	10	13	15	14	12	8	5	4	8
	Daily min. °C	−3	−3	−1	1	4	7	9	8	6	3	0	−2	3
	Average monthly °C	0	0	2	4	7	10	12	11	9	5	3	1	5
Rainfall	Monthly total mm	89	64	62	56	42	42	50	56	67	94	78	79	779
Sunshine	Hours per day	0.8	2	3.6	4.5	5.9	6.1	5.8	5.4	3.5	2.3	1.1	0.3	3.7
Santiago, Chile 520 m														
Temperature	Daily max. °C	30	29	27	24	19	15	15	17	19	22	26	29	23
	Daily min. °C	12	11	10	7	5	3	3	4	6	7	9	11	7
	Average monthly °C	21	20	18	15	12	9	9	10	12	15	17	20	15
Rainfall	Monthly total mm	3	3	5	13	64	84	76	56	31	15	8	5	363
Sunshine	Hours per day	10.8	8.9	8.5	5.5	3.6	3.3	3.3	3.6	4.8	6.1	8.7	10.1	6.4
Shanghai, China 5 m														
Temperature	Daily max. °C	8	8	13	19	24	28	32	32	27	23	17	10	20
	Daily min. °C	−1	0	4	9	14	19	23	23	19	13	7	2	11
	Average monthly °C	3	4	8	14	19	23	27	27	23	18	12	6	15
Rainfall	Monthly total mm	48	59	84	94	94	180	147	142	130	71	51	36	1,136
Sunshine	Hours per day	4	3.7	4.4	4.8	5.4	4.7	6.9	7.5	5.3	5.6	4.7	4.5	5.1
Sydney, Australia 40 m														
Temperature	Daily max. °C	26	26	25	22	19	17	17	18	20	22	24	25	22
	Daily min. °C	18	19	17	14	11	9	8	9	11	13	16	17	14
	Average monthly °C	22	22	21	18	15	13	12	13	16	18	20	21	18
Rainfall	Monthly total mm	89	101	127	135	127	117	117	76	74	71	74	74	1,182
Sunshine	Hours per day	7.5	7	6.4	6.1	5.7	5.3	6.1	7	7.3	7.5	7.5	7.5	6.8
Tehran, Iran 1,191 m														
Temperature	Daily max. °C	9	11	16	21	29	30	37	36	29	24	16	11	22
	Daily min. °C	−1	1	4	10	16	20	23	23	18	12	6	1	11
	Average monthly °C	4	6	10	15	22	25	30	29	23	18	11	6	17
Rainfall	Monthly total mm	37	23	36	31	14	2	1	1	1	5	29	27	207
Sunshine	Hours per day	5.9	6.7	7.5	7.4	8.6	11.6	11.2	11	10.1	7.6	6.9	6.3	8.4
Timbuktu, Mali 269 m														
Temperature	Daily max. °C	31	35	38	41	43	42	38	35	38	40	37	31	37
	Daily min. °C	13	16	18	22	26	27	25	24	24	23	18	14	21
	Average monthly °C	22	25	28	31	34	34	32	30	31	31	28	23	29
Rainfall	Monthly total mm	0	0	0	1	4	20	54	93	31	3	0	0	206
Sunshine	Hours per day	9.1	9.6	9.6	9.7	9.8	9.4	9.6	9	9.3	9.5	9.5	8.9	9.4
Tokyo, Japan 5 m														
Temperature	Daily max. °C	9	9	12	18	22	25	29	30	27	20	16	11	19
	Daily min. °C	1	−1	3	4	13	17	22	23	19	13	7	1	10
	Average monthly °C	4	4	8	11	18	21	25	26	23	17	11	6	14
Rainfall	Monthly total mm	48	73	101	135	131	182	146	147	217	220	101	61	1,562
Sunshine	Hours per day	6	5.9	5.7	6	6.2	5	5.8	6.6	4.5	4.4	4.8	5.4	5.5
Tromsø, Norway 100 m														
Temperature	Daily max. °C	−2	−2	0	3	7	12	16	14	10	5	2	0	5
	Daily min. °C	−6	−6	−5	−2	1	6	9	8	5	1	−2	−4	0
	Average monthly °C	−4	−4	−3	0	4	9	13	11	7	3	0	−2	3
Rainfall	Monthly total mm	96	79	91	65	61	59	56	80	109	115	88	95	994
Sunshine	Hours per day	0.1	1.6	2.9	6.1	5.7	6.9	7.9	4.8	3.5	1.7	0.3	0	3.5
Ulan Bator, Mongolia 1,305 m														
Temperature	Daily max. °C	−19	−13	−4	7	13	21	22	21	14	6	−6	−16	4
	Daily min. °C	−32	−29	−22	−8	−2	7	11	8	2	−8	−20	−28	−11
	Average monthly °C	−26	−21	−13	−1	6	14	16	14	8	−1	−13	−22	−4
Rainfall	Monthly total mm	1	1	2	5	10	28	76	51	23	5	5	2	209
Sunshine	Hours per day	6.4	7.8	8	7.8	8.3	8.6	8.6	8.2	7.2	6.9	6.1	5.7	7.5
Vancouver, Canada 5 m														
Temperature	Daily max. °C	6	7	10	14	17	20	23	22	19	14	9	7	14
	Daily min. °C	0	1	3	5	8	11	13	12	10	7	3	2	6
	Average monthly °C	3	4	6	9	13	16	18	17	14	10	6	4	10
Rainfall	Monthly total mm	214	161	151	90	69	65	39	44	83	172	198	243	1,529
Sunshine	Hours per day	1.6	3	3.8	5.9	7.5	7.4	9.5	8.2	6	3.7	2	1.4	5
Verkhoyansk, Russia 137 m														
Temperature	Daily max. °C	−47	−40	−20	−1	11	21	24	21	12	−8	−33	−42	−8
	Daily min. °C	−51	−48	−40	−25	−7	4	6	1	−6	−20	−39	−50	−23
	Average monthly °C	−49	−44	−30	−13	2	12	15	11	3	−14	−36	−46	−16
Rainfall	Monthly total mm	7	5	5	4	5	25	33	30	13	11	10	7	155
Sunshine	Hours per day	0	2.6	6.9	9.6	9.7	10	9.7	7.5	4.1	2.4	0.6	0	5.4
Washington, D.C., USA 22 m														
Temperature	Daily max. °C	7	8	12	19	25	29	31	30	26	20	14	8	19
	Daily min. °C	−1	−1	2	8	13	18	21	20	16	10	4	−1	9
	Average monthly °C	3	3	7	13	19	24	26	25	21	15	9	4	14
Rainfall	Monthly total mm	84	68	96	85	103	88	108	120	100	78	75	75	1,080
Sunshine	Hours per day	4.4	5.7	6.7	7.4	8.2	8.8	8.6	8.2	7.5	6.5	5.3	4.5	6.8

Tropical Rain Forest
Tall broadleaved evergreen forest, trees 30–50m high with climbers and epiphytes forming continuous canopies. Associated with wet climate, 2–3000mm precipitation per year and high temperatures 24–28°C. High diversity of species, typically 100 per ha, including lianas, bamboo, palms, rubber, mahogany. Mangrove swamps form in coastal areas.

Subtropical and Temperate Rain Forest
Precipitation, which is less than in the Tropical Rain Forest, falls in the long wet season interspersed with a season of reduced rainfall and lower temperatures. As a result there are fewer species, thinner canopies, fewer lianas and denser ground level foliage. Vegetation consists of evergreen oak, laurel, bamboo, magnolia and tree ferns.

Monsoon Woodland and Open Jungle
Mostly deciduous trees, because of the long dry season and lower temperature. Trees can reach 30m but are sparser than in the rain forests. There is les competition for light and thick jungle vegetation grows at lower levels. Hig species diversity includes lianas, bamboo, teak, sandalwood, sal and banya

This diagram shows the highly stratified nature of the tropical rain forest. Crowns of trees form numerous layers at different heights and the dense shade limits undergrowth.

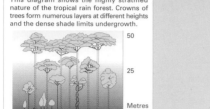

Temperate Deciduous and Coniferous Forest
A transition zone between broadleaves and conifers. Broadleaves are better suited to the warmer, damper and flatter locations.

Coniferous Forest (Taiga or Boreal)
Forming a large continuous belt across Northern America and Eurasia with a uniformity in tree species. Characteristically trees are tall, conical with short branches and wax-covered needle-shaped leaves to retain moisture. Cold climate with prolonged harsh winters and cool summers where average temperatures are under 0°C for more than six months of the year Undergrowth is sparse with mosses and lichens. Tree species include pine, fir, spruce, larch, tamarisk.

Mountainous Forest, mainly Coniferous
Mild winters, high humidity and high levels of rainfall throughout the year provide habitat for dense needle-leaf evergreen forests and the largest trees in the world, up to 100m, including the Douglas fir, redwood and giant sequoia.

High Plateau Steppe and Tundra
Similar to arctic tundra with frozen ground for the majority of the year. Very sparse ground coverage of low, shallow-rooted herbs, small shrubs, mosses, lichens and heather interspersed with bare soil.

Arctic Tundra
Average temperatures are 0°C, precipitation is mainly snowfall and the ground remains frozen for 10 months of the year. Vegetation flourishes when the shallow surface layer melts in the long summer days. Underlying permafrost remains frozen and surface water cannot drain away, making conditions marshy. Consists of sedges, snow lichen, arctic meadow grass, cotton grasses and dwarf willow.

Polar and Mountainous Ice Desert
Areas of bare rock and ice with patches of rock-strewn lithosols, low in organic matter and low water content. In sheltered patches only a few mosses, lichens and low shrubs can grow, including woolly moss and purple saxifrage.

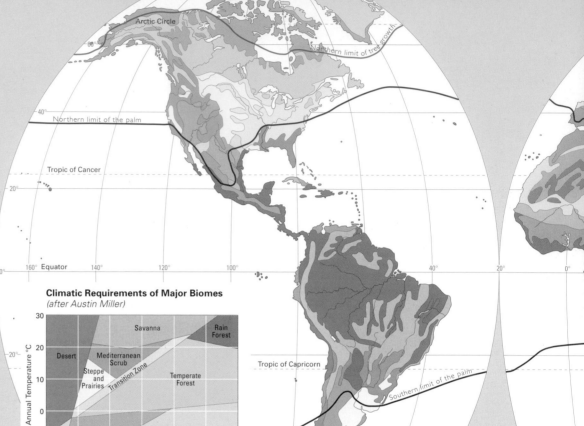

Climatic Requirements of Major Biomes
(after Austin Miller)

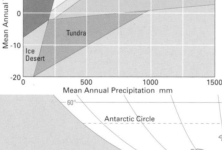

SOIL REGIONS
1:220 000 000

- Tundra soil
- Podzols
- Brown forest soil
- Lightly leached dry forest soil
- Red and yellow subtropical forest soil
- Reddish savanna soil and tropical red earths
- Laterites
- Chernozem
- Degraded chernozem
- Black savanna soil
- Chestnut steppe soil
- Desertic (arid) soil
- Alluvium
- Mountain and high plateau soils
- Oases soil
- Tropical and mangrove swamp

(after Glinka, Stremme, Marbut, and others)

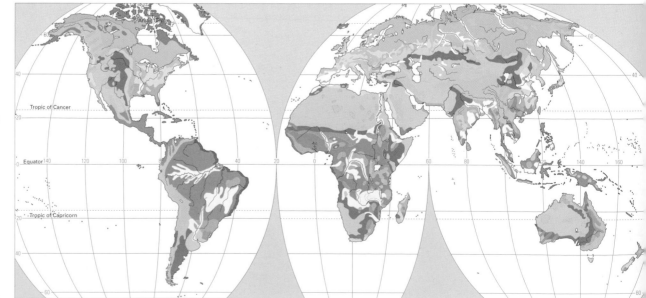

Projection: *Interrupted Mollweide's Homolographic*

ubtropical and Temperate Woodland, Scrub and Bush
at clearings with woody shrubs and tall grasses. Trees are fire-resistant and
ther deciduous or xerophytic because of long dry periods. Species include
ucalyptus, acacia, mimosa and euphorbia.

Tropical Savanna with Low Trees and Bush
Tall, coarse grass with enough precipitation to support a scattering of short
deciduous trees and thorn scrub. Vegetation consists of elephant grass, acacia,
palms and baobab and is limited by aridity, grazing animals and periodic fires;
trees have developed thick, woody bark, small leaves or thorns.

Tropical Savanna and Grassland
Areas with a hot climate and long dry season. Extensive areas of tall grasses
often reach 3.5m with scattered fire and drought resistant bushes, low trees
and thickets of elephant grass. Shrubs include acacia, baobab and palms.

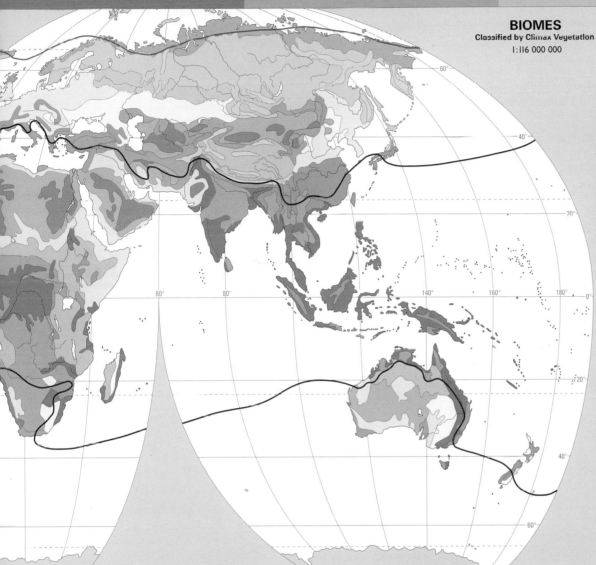

BIOMES
Classified by Climax Vegetation
1:116 000 000

Dry Semi-desert with Shrub and Grass
Xerophytic shrubs with thin grass cover and few trees, limited by a long dry season and short, hot, rainy period. Sagebrush, bunch grass and acacia shrubs are common.

Desert Shrub
Scattered xerophytic plants able to withstand daytime extremes in temperature and long periods of drought. There is a large diversity of desert flora such as cacti, yucca, tamarisk, hard grass and artemisia.

Desert
Precipitation less than 250mm per year. Vegetation is very sparse, mainly bare rock, sand dunes and salt flats. Vegetation comprises a few xerophytic shrubs and ephemeral flowers.

Dry Steppe and Shrub
Semi-arid with cold, dry winters and hot summers. Bare soil with sparsely distributed short grasses and scattered shrubs and short trees. Species include acacia, artemisia, saksaul and tamarisk.

Temperate Grasslands, Prairie and Steppe
Continuous, tall, dense and deep-rooted swards of ancient grasslands, considered to be natural climax vegetation as determined by soil and climate. Average precipitation 250–750mm, with a long dry season, limits growth of trees and shrubs. Includes Stipa grass, buffalo grass, blue stems and loco weed.

Mediterranean Hardwood Forest and Scrub
Areas with hot and arid summers. Sparse evergreen trees are short and twisted with thick bark, interspersed with areas of scrub land. Trees have waxy leaves or thorns and deep root systems to resist drought. Many of the hardwood forests have been cleared by man, resulting in extensive scrub formation – maquis and chaparral. Species found are evergreen oak, stone pine, cork, olive and myrtle.

Temperate Deciduous Forest and Meadow
Areas of relatively high, well-distributed rainfall and temperature favourable for forest growth. The tall broadleaved trees form a canopy in the summer, but shed their leaves in the winter. The undergrowth is sparse and poorly developed, but in the spring, herbs and flowers develop quickly. Diverse species, with up to 20 per ha, including oak, beech, birch, maple, ash, elm, chestnut and hornbeam. Many of these forests have been cleared for urbanization and farming.

SOIL DEGRADATION
1:220 000 000

Areas of Concern
- Areas of serious concern
- Areas of some concern
- Stable terrain
- Non-vegetated land

Causes of soil degradation (by region)
- Grazing practices
- Other agricultural practices
- Industrialization
- Deforestation
- Fuelwood collection

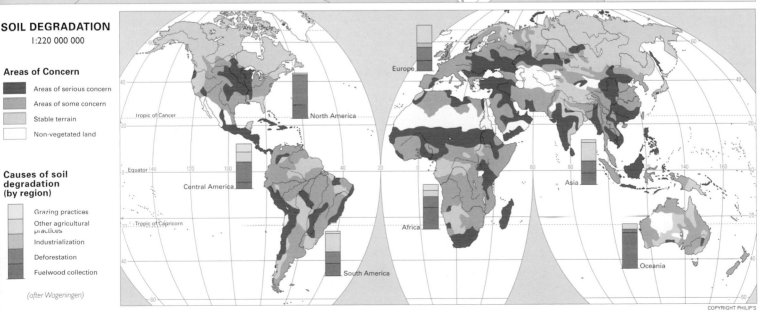

(after Wageningen)

COPYRIGHT PHILIP'S

AGRICULTURAL PRODUCTION

Crops

Wheat

China 18.0% | India 14.1% | USA 9.2% | France 6.0% | Russia 5.6% | Canada 4.0% | Germany 3.3%

World total (2012): 670,875,110 tonnes

Rice

China 28.6% | India 21.2% | Indonesia 9.6% | Vietnam 6.1% | Thailand 5.3% | Bangladesh 4.7% | Burma (Myanmar) 4.6%

World total (2012): 719,738,273 tonnes

Cassava

Nigeria 20.6% | Indonesia 9.1% | Brazil 8.8% | Thailand 8.6% | Congo (D.R.) 6.1% | Ghana 5.5%

World total (2012): 262,585,741 tonnes

Barley

Russia 10.5% | France 8.5% | Germany 7.8% | Australia 6.2% | Canada 6.0% | Ukraine 5.2%

World total (2012): 132,886,519 tonnes

Maize

USA 31.4% | China 23.9% | Brazil 8.1%

World total (2012): 872,066,770 tonnes

Potatoes

China 23.6% | India 12.3% | Russia 8.1% | Ukraine 6.4% | USA 5.3%

World total (2012): 364,808,768 tonnes

Soybeans

USA 33.9% | Brazil 27.2% | Argentina 16.6% | China 5.3%

World total (2012): 241,841,416 tonnes

Millet

India 34.6% | Nigeria 16.7% | Niger 12.9% | Mali 5.9% | China 5.4%

World total (2012): 29,866,016 tonnes

Sugar Cane

Brazil 39.3% | India 19.0% | China 6.8% | Thailand 5.3% | Pakistan 3.2% | Mexico 2.8%

World total (2012): 1,832,541,194 tonnes

Sugar Beet

Russia 16.7% | France 12.5% | USA 11.8% | Germany 10.3% | Ukraine 6.8% | Turkey 5.6% | Poland 4.6% | UK 2.7%

World total (2012): 269,865,481 tonnes

Animal Products

Milk

India 16.6% | USA 12.1% | China 5.7% | Pakistan 5.0% | Brazil 4.3% | Russia 4.2%

World total (2012): 753,924,958 tonnes

Eggs

China 37.4% | USA 8.2% | India 5.6% | Japan 3.6%

World total (2012): 66,372,549 tonnes

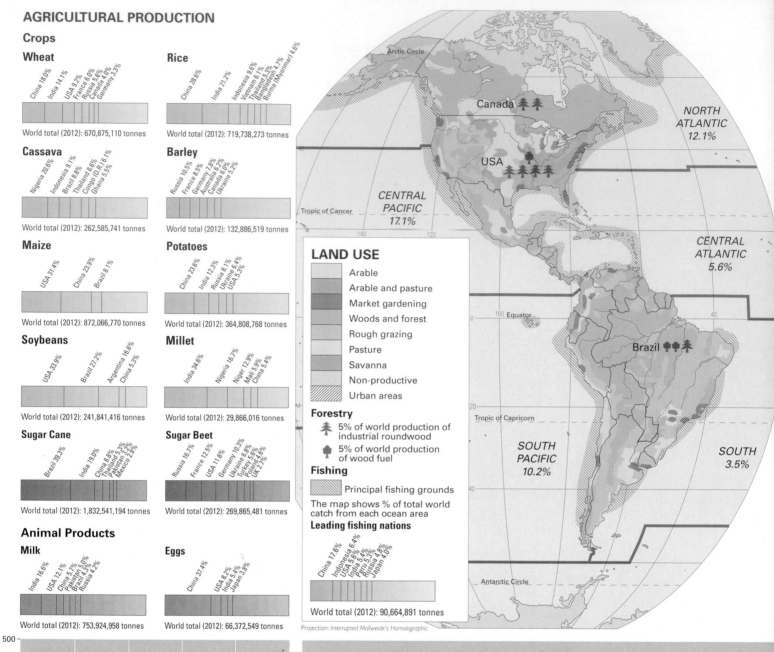

LAND USE

- Arable
- Arable and pasture
- Market gardening
- Woods and forest
- Rough grazing
- Pasture
- Savanna
- Non-productive
- Urban areas

Forestry

🌲 5% of world production of industrial roundwood

🌳 5% of world production of wood fuel

Fishing

Principal fishing grounds

The map shows % of total world catch from each ocean area

Leading fishing nations

China 17.6% | Indonesia 6.4% | USA 5.6% | India 5.3% | Peru 5.1% | Russia 4.8% | Japan 4.0%

World total (2012): 90,664,891 tonnes

Projection: Interrupted Mollweide's Homolographic

Ocean areas on map:
- NORTH ATLANTIC 12.1%
- CENTRAL PACIFIC 17.1%
- CENTRAL ATLANTIC 5.6%
- SOUTH PACIFIC 10.2%
- SOUTH 3.5%

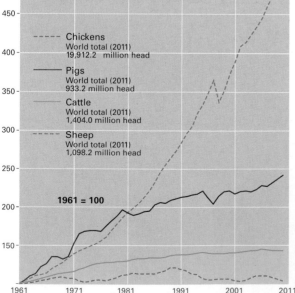

World Livestock Production

1961 = 100

- - - - Chickens
World total (2011)
19,912.2 million head

———— Pigs
World total (2011)
933.2 million head

———— Cattle
World total (2011)
1,404.0 million head

- - - - Sheep
World total (2011)
1,098.2 million head

Y-axis: 150, 200, 250, 300, 350, 400, 450, 500
X-axis: 1961, 1971, 1981, 1991, 2001, 2011

WILL THE WORLD RUN OUT OF FOOD?

At present-day rates, the world's population is predicted to reach at least 9 billion people by 2050. To sustain this population there will have to be a 70% increase in food production.

Currently, many people struggle to achieve the minimum food intake to sustain life. Globally, about 1 billion people are malnourished compared with 1 billion who are overweight.

Over 30% of the world's grain is fed to livestock because more and more people like to eat meat. But animals (and humans) are very inefficient in their utilization of nutrients; generally less than 20% of the nitrogen in their food is used; the rest is excreted, causing air and water pollution.

Meat is also very expensive in terms of water consumption: 0.5 kg of beef requires 8,442 litres of water to produce it. By 2030 there will be a 30% increase in water demand. Over 71% of the Earth's surface is covered in water but less than 3% of this is fresh water, of which over two-thirds is frozen in ice-caps and glaciers. Its over-exploitation in developed areas and availability in regions where it is scarce are major problems. For example, China currently has 20% of the world's population, but only 11% of its water.

How can we feed 9 billion people adequately and sustainably? The Royal Society has said that we need 'Sustainable Intensification', that is, to produce more using less and with less of an impact on the environment through good soil management, maintaining or enhancing crop genetic diversity, and introducing pest and disease resistance, as well as better fertiliser use.

Some, however, reject technological approaches and advocate extensive systems described as 'organic', 'bio-dynamic' or 'ecological', objecting to the reliance on chemical fertilisers and pesticides.

We need to reduce the 30% of the world's crop yield lost to pests, diseases and weeds; protect the fertile soil that irregularly covers only 11% of the global land surface and is a non-renewable asset; and cut back on food waste. In the UK it is estimated that 8.3 million tonnes of food worth £20 billion is sent to landfill each year. Some people now live on the food thrown away by shops – called 'skipping'.

If we adopt appropriate techniques and modify our behaviour, we stand a good chance of feeding the future, predominantly urban, population.

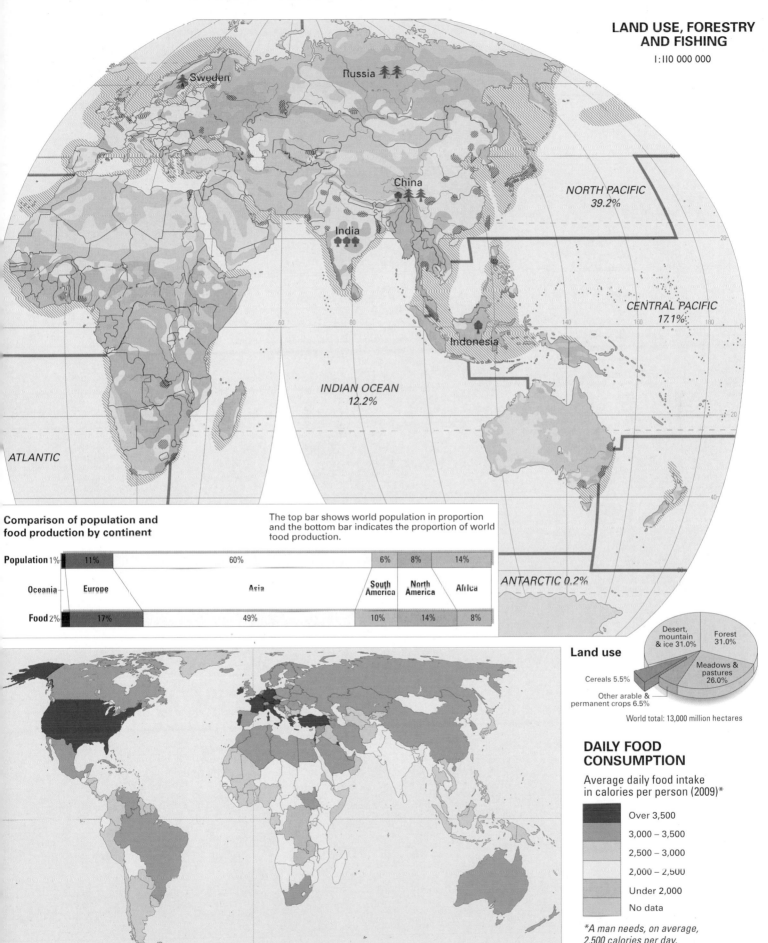

LAND USE, FORESTRY AND FISHING
1:110 000 000

Sweden

Russia

China

India

Indonesia

NORTH PACIFIC
39.2%

CENTRAL PACIFIC
17.1%

INDIAN OCEAN
12.2%

ATLANTIC

ANTARCTIC 0.2%

Comparison of population and food production by continent

The top bar shows world population in proportion and the bottom bar indicates the proportion of world food production.

Population	1%	11%	60%	6%	8%	14%
	Oceania	Europe	Asia	South America	North America	Africa
Food	2%	17%	49%	10%	14%	8%

Land use

Desert, mountain & ice 31.0%

Forest 31.0%

Meadows & pastures 26.0%

Cereals 5.5%

Other arable & permanent crops 6.5%

World total: 13,000 million hectares

DAILY FOOD CONSUMPTION

Average daily food intake in calories per person (2009)*

- Over 3,500
- 3,000 – 3,500
- 2,500 – 3,000
- 2,000 – 2,500
- Under 2,000
- No data

*A man needs, on average, 2,500 calories per day, a woman needs 2,000.

Projection: Eckert IV

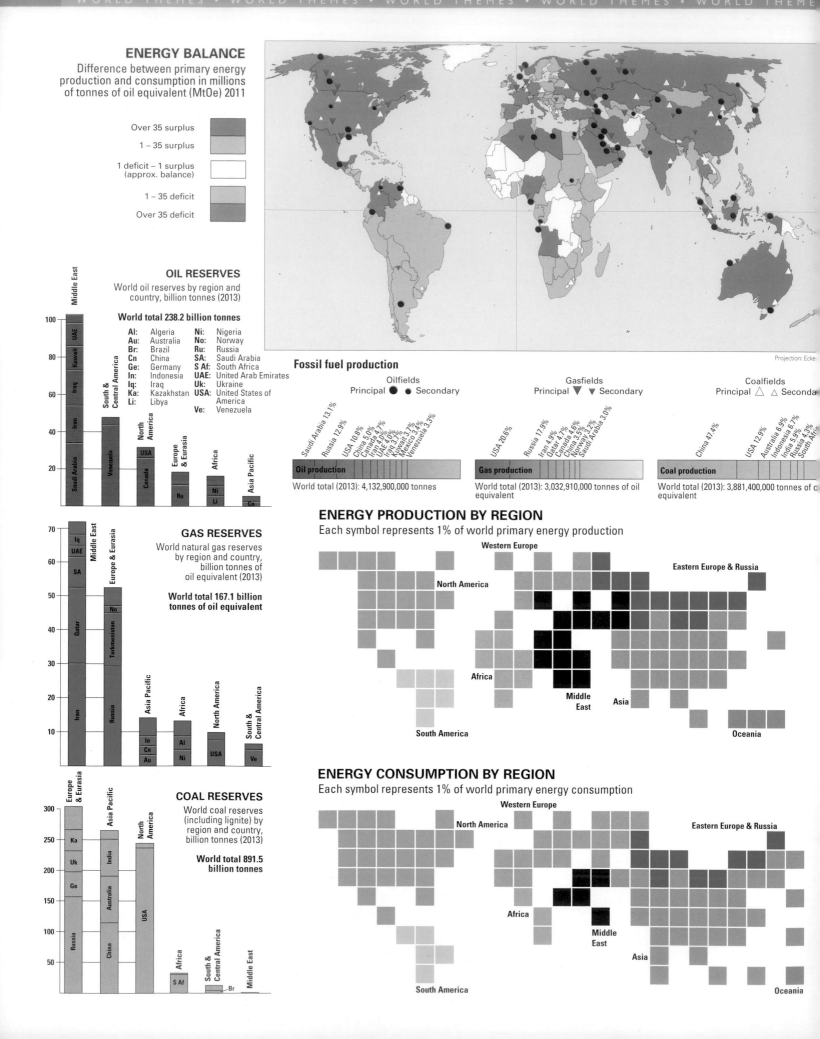

ENERGY BALANCE

Difference between primary energy production and consumption in millions of tonnes of oil equivalent (MtOe) 2011

- Over 35 surplus
- 1 – 35 surplus
- 1 deficit – 1 surplus (approx. balance)
- 1 – 35 deficit
- Over 35 deficit

OIL RESERVES

World oil reserves by region and country, billion tonnes (2013)

World total 238.2 billion tonnes

Al: Algeria	**Ni:** Nigeria
Au: Australia	**No:** Norway
Br: Brazil	**Ru:** Russia
Cn: China	**SA:** Saudi Arabia
Ge: Germany	**S Af:** South Africa
In: Indonesia	**UAE:** United Arab Emirates
Iq: Iraq	**Uk:** Ukraine
Ka: Kazakhstan	**USA:** United States of America
Li: Libya	**Ve:** Venezuela

GAS RESERVES

World natural gas reserves by region and country, billion tonnes of oil equivalent (2013)

World total 167.1 billion tonnes of oil equivalent

COAL RESERVES

World coal reserves (including lignite) by region and country, billion tonnes (2013)

World total 891.5 billion tonnes

Projection: Ecke

Fossil fuel production

Oilfields
Principal ● ● Secondary

Gasfields
Principal ▼ ▼ Secondary

Coalfields
Principal △ △ Seconda

Oil production
Saudi Arabia 13.1% | Russia 12.9% | USA 10.8% | China 5.0% | Canada 4.7% | Iran 4.0% | UAE 4.0% | Iraq 3.7% | Kuwait 3.3% | Mexico 3.3% | Venezuela 3.3%

World total (2013): 4,132,900,000 tonnes

Gas production
USA 20.6% | Russia 17.9% | Iran 4.9% | Qatar 4.7% | Canada 4.6% | China 3.5% | Norway 3.2% | Saudi Arabia 3.0%

World total (2013): 3,032,910,000 tonnes of oil equivalent

Coal production
China 47.4% | USA 12.9% | Australia 6.9% | Indonesia 6.7% | India 5.9% | Russia 4.3% | South Afr

World total (2013): 3,881,400,000 tonnes of c equivalent

ENERGY PRODUCTION BY REGION

Each symbol represents 1% of world primary energy production

Western Europe
North America
Eastern Europe & Russia
Africa
Middle East
Asia
South America
Oceania

ENERGY CONSUMPTION BY REGION

Each symbol represents 1% of world primary energy consumption

Western Europe
North America
Eastern Europe & Russia
Africa
Middle East
Asia
South America
Oceania

ELECTRICITY GENERATION
Percentage of electricity generated by source (latest available data)

Over 75% from thermal

50 – 75% from thermal

Over 75% from hydro

50 – 75% from hydro

Over 50% from nuclear

No dominant source

No data

● Selected geothermal plants

◆ Selected hydroelectric plants

(see page 80 for list of world's ten largest hydroelectric plants)

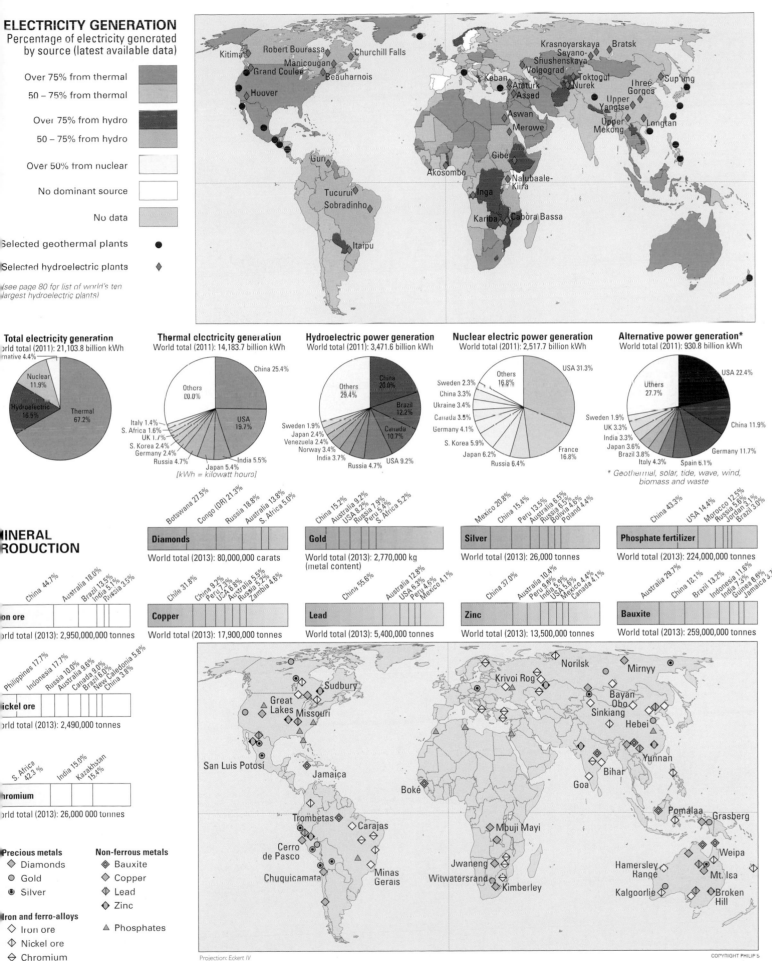

Total electricity generation
World total (2011): 21,103.8 billion kWh

- Alternative 4.4%
- Nuclear 11.9%
- Hydroelectric 16.5%
- Thermal 67.2%

Thermal electricity generation
World total (2011): 14,183.7 billion kWh

- China 25.4%
- Others 20.0%
- USA 19.7%
- India 5.5%
- Japan 5.4%
- Russia 4.7%
- Germany 2.4%
- S. Korea 2.4%
- UK 1.7%
- S. Africa 1.6%
- Italy 1.4%

[kWh = kilowatt hours]

Hydroelectric power generation
World total (2011): 3,471.6 billion kWh

- China 20.0%
- Others 29.4%
- Brazil 12.2%
- Canada 10.7%
- USA 9.2%
- Russia 4.7%
- India 3.7%
- Norway 3.4%
- Venezuela 2.4%
- Japan 2.4%
- Sweden 1.9%

Nuclear electric power generation
World total (2011): 2,517.7 billion kWh

- USA 31.3%
- Others 16.8%
- France 16.8%
- Russia 6.4%
- Japan 6.2%
- S. Korea 5.9%
- Germany 4.1%
- Canada 3.5%
- Ukraine 3.4%
- China 3.3%
- Sweden 2.3%

Alternative power generation*
World total (2011): 930.8 billion kWh

- USA 22.4%
- Others 27.7%
- China 11.9%
- Germany 11.7%
- Spain 6.1%
- Italy 4.3%
- Brazil 3.8%
- Japan 3.6%
- India 3.3%
- UK 3.3%
- Sweden 1.9%

*Geothermal, solar, tide, wave, wind, biomass and waste

MINERAL PRODUCTION

Diamonds					
Botswana 27.5%	Congo (DR) 21.3%	Russia 18.8%	Australia 13.8%	S. Africa 5.0%	

World total (2013): 80,000,000 carats

Gold							
China 15.2%	Australia 9.2%	USA 8.2%	Russia 7.9%	Peru 5.4%	S. Africa 5.2%	

World total (2013): 2,770,000 kg (metal content)

Silver							
Mexico 20.8%	China 15.4%	Peru 13.5%	Australia 6.5%	Russia 6.5%	Bolivia 4.6%	Poland 4.4%

World total (2013): 26,000 tonnes

Phosphate fertilizer					
China 43.3%	USA 14.4%	Morocco 12.5%	Russia 5.6%	Jordan 3.3%	Brazil 3.0%

World total (2013): 224,000,000 tonnes

Iron ore				
China 44.7%	Australia 18.0%	Brazil 13.5%	India 5.1%	Russia 3.5%

World total (2013): 2,950,000,000 tonnes

Copper						
Chile 31.8%	China 9.2%	Peru 7.3%	USA 6.8%	Australia 5.5%	Russia 5.2%	Zambia 4.6%

World total (2013): 17,900,000 tonnes

Lead				
China 55.6%	Australia 12.8%	USA 6.3%	Peru 4.5%	Mexico 4.1%

World total (2013): 5,400,000 tonnes

Zinc					
China 37.0%	Australia 10.4%	Peru 9.0%	India 5.6%	USA 4.4%	Canada 4.1%

World total (2013): 13,500,000 tonnes

Bauxite						
Australia 29.7%	China 18.1%	Brazil 13.2%	Indonesia 11.6%	India 7.9%	Guinea 6.8%	Jamaica 3.7%

World total (2013): 259,000,000 tonnes

Nickel ore							
Philippines 17.7%	Indonesia 17.7%	Russia 10.0%	Australia 9.6%	Canada 9.0%	Brazil 6.0%	New Caledonia 5.8%	China 3.8%

World total (2013): 2,490,000 tonnes

Chromium		
S. Africa 42.3%	India 15.0%	Kazakhstan 15.4%

World total (2013): 26,000,000 tonnes

Precious metals
- ◇ Diamonds
- ● Gold
- ◉ Silver

Iron and ferro-alloys
- ◇ Iron ore
- ◊ Nickel ore
- ◇ Chromium

Non-ferrous metals
- ◆ Bauxite
- ◇ Copper
- ◈ Lead
- ◇ Zinc

- ▲ Phosphates

Projection: Eckert IV

COPYRIGHT PHILIP'S

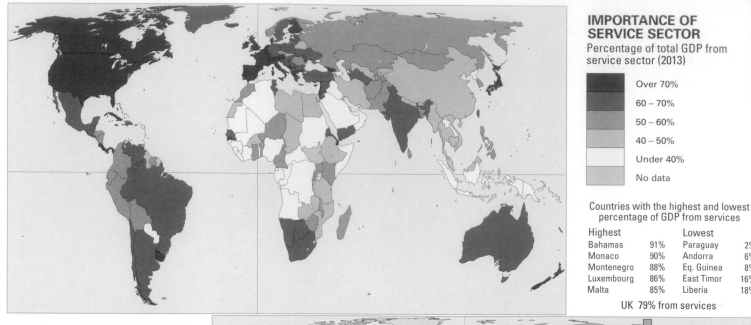

IMPORTANCE OF SERVICE SECTOR

Percentage of total GDP from service sector (2013)

- Over 70%
- 60 – 70%
- 50 – 60%
- 40 – 50%
- Under 40%
- No data

Countries with the highest and lowest percentage of GDP from services

Highest		Lowest	
Bahamas	91%	Paraguay	2%
Monaco	90%	Andorra	6%
Montenegro	88%	Eq. Guinea	8%
Luxembourg	86%	East Timor	16%
Malta	85%	Liberia	18%

UK 79% from services

IMPORTANCE OF MANUFACTURING SECTOR

- **Steel**
  World total (2012): 1,582.5 million tonnes

- **Cement**
  World total (2012): 3,700 million tonnes

- **Motor vehicles**
  World total (2012): 84.2 million vehicles

- **Paper**
  World total (2012): 399.1 million tonnes

Percentage of total GDP from industrial sector (2012)

- Over 50%
- 40 – 50%
- 30 – 40%
- 20 – 30%
- Under 20%
- No data

40%
30%
20%
10%
Production of manufactured goods as a percentage of world total (for selected goods and countries)

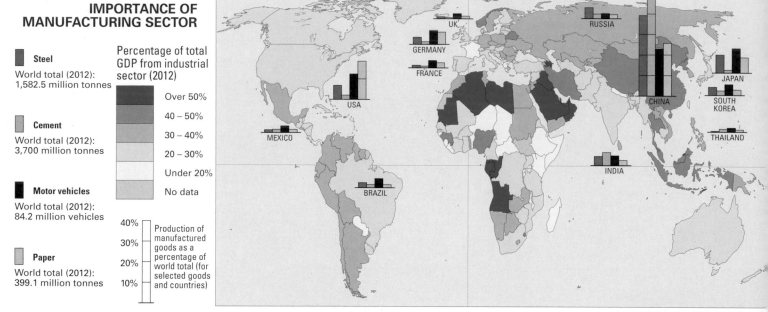

DIVISION OF EMPLOYMENT Distribution of workers by sector for selected countries (2012)

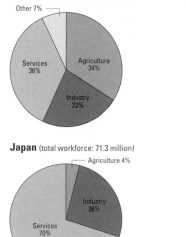

China (total workforce: 913.4 million)
- Other 7%
- Services 36%
- Agriculture 34%
- Industry 23%

Bangladesh (total workforce: 109.5 million)
- Services 40%
- Agriculture 47%
- Industry 13%

Germany (total workforce: 46.3 million)
- Agriculture 2%
- Other 10%
- Industry 15%
- Services 74%

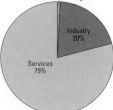

Japan (total workforce: 71.3 million)
- Agriculture 4%
- Industry 26%
- Services 70%

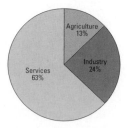

USA (total workforce: 178.9 million)
- Agriculture 1%
- Industry 20%
- Services 79%

Mexico (total workforce: 67.8 million)
- Agriculture 13%
- Industry 24%
- Services 63%

RESEARCH & DEVELOPMENT

Expenditure on R&D as a percentage of GDP (2011)

Country	Percentage
Israel	4.4
Finland	3.8
South Korea	3.7
Sweden	3.4
Japan	3.3
Denmark	3.1
Germany	2.8
USA	2.8
Austria	2.8
Slovenia	2.5
Estonia	2.4
France	2.3
Belgium	2.0
Netherlands	2.0
China	1.8
Czech Republic	1.8
UK	1.8
Ireland	1.8
Canada	1.7
Norway	1.7
Portugal	1.5
Luxembourg	1.4
Spain	1.3
New Zealand	1.3
Italy	1.3

WORLD TRADE

Percentage share of total
world exports by value (2013)

- Over 10%
- 5 – 10%
- 2.5 – 5%
- 1.0 – 2.5%
- 0.1 – 1.0%
- Under 0.1%
- No data

● Top ten container ports

International trade is dominated by a
handful of powerful maritime nations;
the members of 'G8' (Canada, France,
Germany, Italy, Japan, Russia, UK and
USA) and the 'BRICS' nations (Brazil,
Russia, India, China and South Africa).

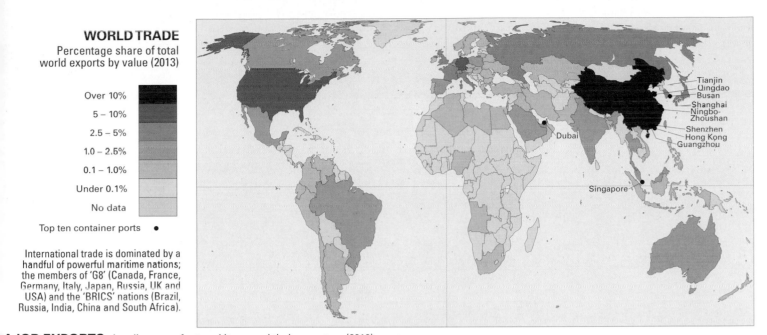

AJOR EXPORTS Leading manufactured items and their exporters (2010)

Motor Vehicles
World total: US$ 1,315,597 million

- Germany 18.5%
- Japan 11.3%
- USA 10.2%
- Mexico 5.9%
- S. Korea 5.5%
- Canada 4.5%
- China 4.5%
- UK 3.9%
- gium 3.7%
- ain 3.7%
- co 3.5%
- ly 2.0%
- Rep. 2.2%
- Other 19.8%

Telecommunications Gear
World total: US$ 1,989,113 million

- China 28.2%
- USA 8.3%
- Germany 7.2%
- South Korea 6.8%
- Singapore 6.2%
- Japan 5.4%
- Mexico 3.9%
- Malaysia 3.1%
- Netherlands 2.3%
- France 2.2%
- UK 1.6%
- Thailand 1.5%
- Other 23.3%

Petrol Products
World total: US$ 2,071,603 million

- Russia 18.0%
- USA 7.2%
- Canada 5.8%
- Netherlands 5.5%
- Norway 5.0%
- Singapore 3.4%
- India 3.4%
- Belgium 3.2%
- Australia 3.1%
- Algeria 3.1%
- UK 3.0%
- Kazakhstan 3.0%
- Other 36.3%

Computers
World total: US$ 315,695 million

- China 51.2%
- USA 8.4%
- Mexico 5.5%
- lands 4.9%
- nd 3.9%
- any 3.5%
- ore 3.1%
- Rep. 2.9%
- laysia 2.8%
- UK 1.3%
- Other 12.5%

Electronic Equipment
World total: US$ 1,989,120 million

- China 28.2%
- USA 8.3%
- Germany 7.2%
- S. Korea 6.8%
- Singapore 6.2%
- Japan 5.4%
- Mexico 3.9%
- Malaysia 3.1%
- Netherlands 2.3%
- France 2.2%
- UK 1.6%
- Other 24.8%

Pharmaceuticals
World total: US$ 474,014 million

- Germany 15.8%
- Switzerland 12.1%
- Belgium 10.6%
- USA 8.4%
- France 7.8%
- UK 6.8%
- Ireland 5.5%
- Italy 5.0%
- Netherlands 1.0%
- Spain 2.7%
- Other 20.5%

Top Ten Container Ports

Total container traffic,
in million TEU (2012)
('TEU' stands for Twenty-foot
Equivalent Unit, the equivalent
of a standard container)

- Shanghai (China)
- Singapore (Singapore)
- Hong Kong (China)
- Shenzhen (China)
- Busan (S. Korea)
- Ningbo-Zhoushan (China)
- Guangzhou (China)
- Qingdao (China)
- Jebel Ali (Dubai, UAE)
- Tianjin (China)

INTERNET AND TELECOMMUNICATIONS

Percentage of total population
using the Internet (2013)

- Over 75%
- 50 – 75%
- 25 – 50%
- 10 – 25%
- Under 10%
- No data

Telecommunications

Trade in office machines
and telecom equipment,
percentage of world total

IMPORT EXPORT
- 40%
- 30%
- 20%
- 10%

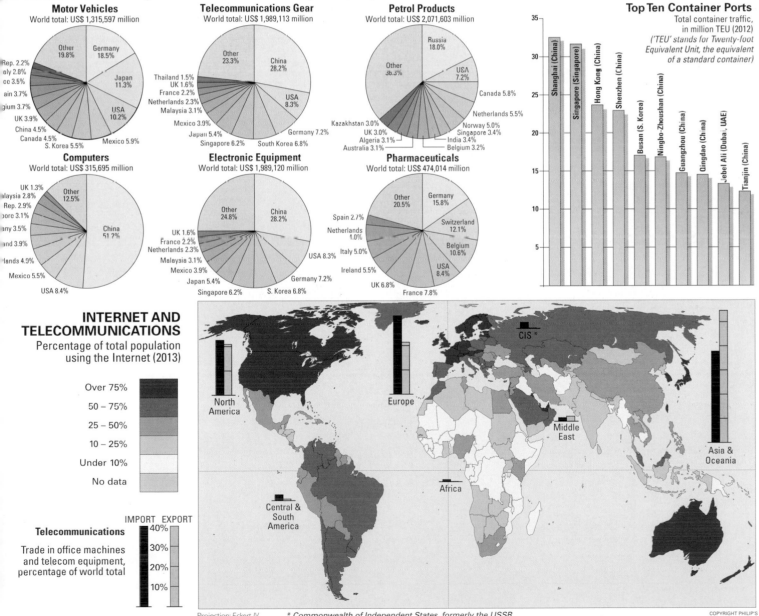

North
America

Europe

CIS *

Middle
East

Asia &
Oceania

Africa

Central &
South
America

Projection: *Eckert IV*   * *Commonwealth of Independent States, formerly the USSR*

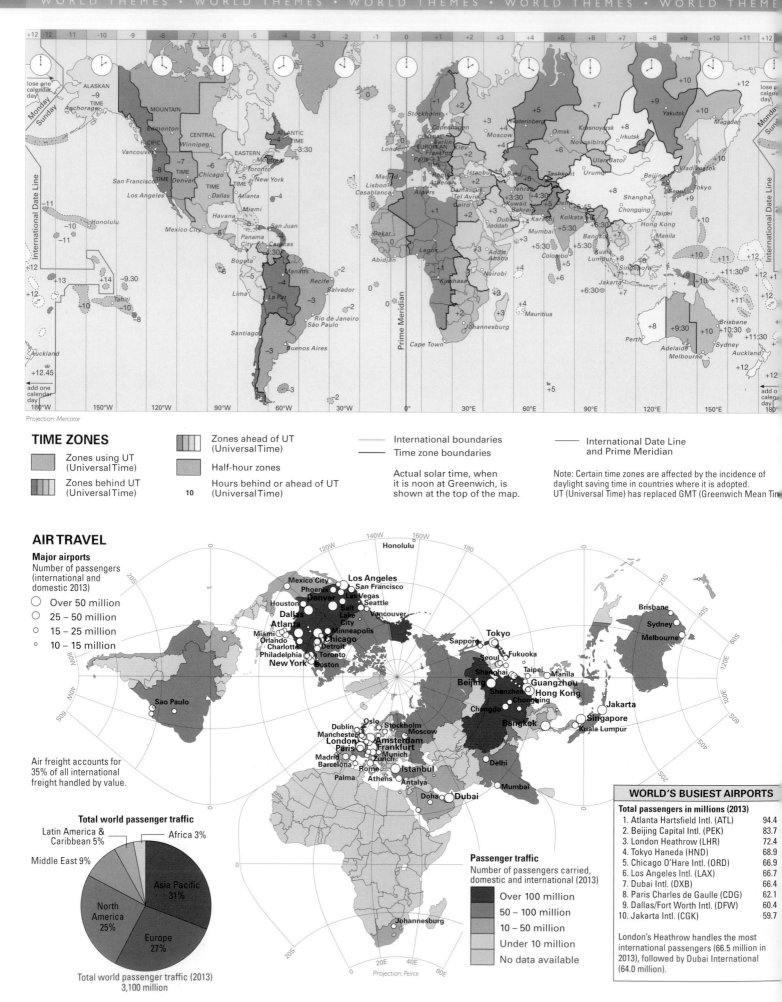

Projection: Mercator

TIME ZONES

Zones using UT (Universal Time)

Zones behind UT (Universal Time)

10 Hours behind or ahead of UT (Universal Time)

Zones ahead of UT (Universal Time)

Half-hour zones

International boundaries

Time zone boundaries

Actual solar time, when it is noon at Greenwich, is shown at the top of the map.

International Date Line and Prime Meridian

Note: Certain time zones are affected by the incidence of daylight saving time in countries where it is adopted. UT (Universal Time) has replaced GMT (Greenwich Mean Tim

AIR TRAVEL

Major airports
Number of passengers (international and domestic 2013)

○ Over 50 million

○ 25 – 50 million

○ 15 – 25 million

○ 10 – 15 million

Air freight accounts for 35% of all international freight handled by value.

Passenger traffic
Number of passengers carried, domestic and international (2013)

Over 100 million

50 – 100 million

10 – 50 million

Under 10 million

No data available

WORLD'S BUSIEST AIRPORTS

Total passengers in millions (2013)

1. Atlanta Hartsfield Intl. (ATL) — 94.4
2. Beijing Capital Intl. (PEK) — 83.7
3. London Heathrow (LHR) — 72.4
4. Tokyo Haneda (HND) — 68.9
5. Chicago O'Hare Intl. (ORD) — 66.9
6. Los Angeles Intl. (LAX) — 66.7
7. Dubai Intl. (DXB) — 66.4
8. Paris Charles de Gaulle (CDG) — 62.1
9. Dallas/Fort Worth Intl. (DFW) — 60.4
10. Jakarta Intl. (CGK) — 59.7

London's Heathrow handles the most international passengers (66.5 million in 2013), followed by Dubai International (64.0 million).

Total world passenger traffic

Latin America & Caribbean 5%

Africa 3%

Middle East 9%

Asia Pacific 31%

North America 25%

Europe 27%

Total world passenger traffic (2013) 3,100 million

Projection: Peirce

UNESCO WORLD HERITAGE SITES 2014

Total sites = 1,007 (779 cultural, 197 natural and 31 mixed)

Region	Cultural sites	Natural sites	Mixed sites
Africa	48	37	4
Arab States	71	4	2
Asia & Pacific	161	59	11
Europe & North America	408	61	10
Latin America & Caribbean	92	36	3

NB Some sites are trans boundary, therefore the total figures may not add up

TOURIST EARNINGS

Countries receiving the most from overseas tourism, US$ million (2012)

USA US$200,092

France, Spain, China, Germany, UK, Macau, Italy, Hong Kong, Thailand, Australia, Turkey

TOURIST SPENDING

Countries spending the most on overseas tourism, US$ million (2012)

USA 6,573

China, Germany, UK, Russia, France, Canada, Japan, Australia, Italy, Brazil, Belgium

IMPORTANCE OF TOURISM

Tourism receipts as a percentage of Gross National Income (2013)

- Over 10%
- 5 – 10%
- 2.5 – 5%
- 1 – 2.5%
- Under 1%
- No data

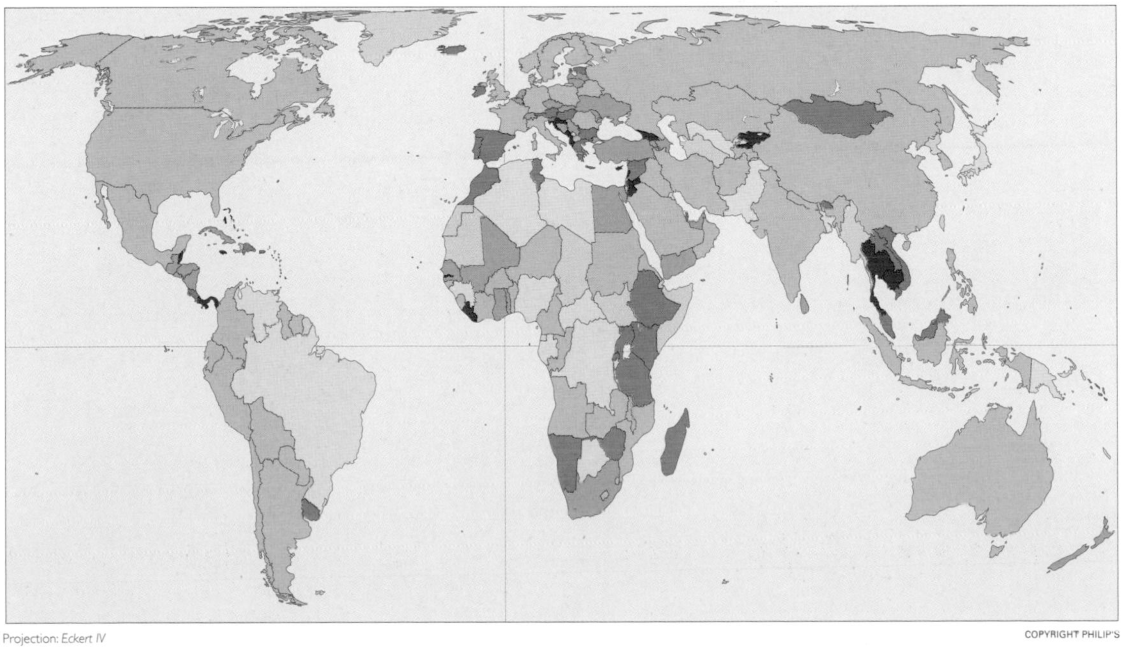

Tourist arrivals in millions (2013)

France	83.0
USA	69.8
Spain	60.7
China	55.7
Italy	47.7
UK	31.2

Projection: Eckert IV

Europe at larger scale

Samøøa, Fjords, St-Petersburg, Øland, Edinburgh, Copenhagen, Dublin, Amsterdam, London, Disneyland, Prague, Brittany, Paris, Paris, Tatra, Vienna, Budapest, Lourdes, Alps, Black Sea Coast, Pyrenees, Costa Brava, Istanbul, Lisbon, Barcelona, Côte d'Azur, Florence, Rome, Algarve, Balearic Islands, Pompeii, Ionian Islands, Costa del Sol, Costa Blanca, Aegean, Athens, Crete, Rhodes

TOURIST DESTINATIONS

Projection: Peirce

Destinations
- ■ Cultural & historical centres
- □ Coastal resorts
- □ Ski resorts
- Centres of entertainment
- Places of pilgrimage
- Places of great natural beauty

Other tourist destinations

Movement of tourists
- More than 10 million
- 5 – 10 million
- 3 – 5 million
- Less than 3 million

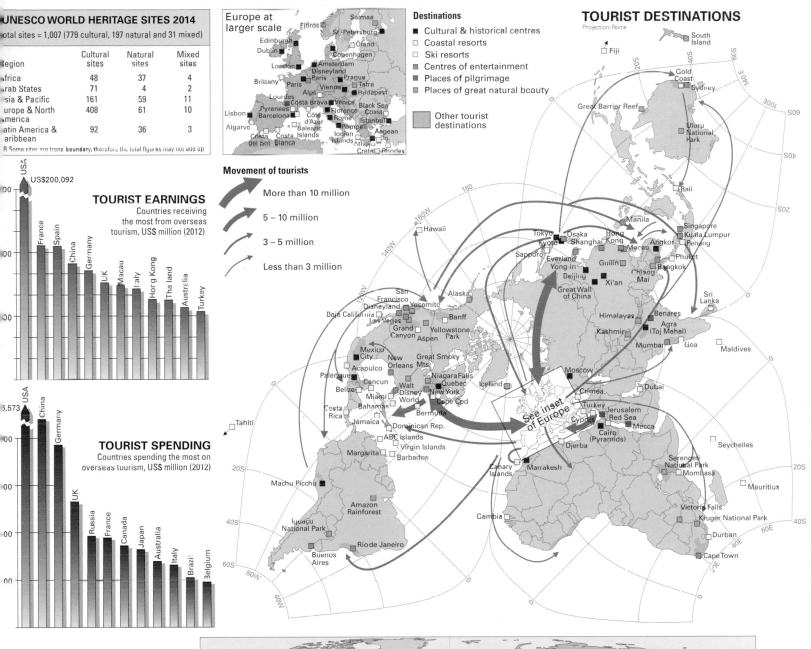

Map labels: South Island, Fiji, Gold Coast, Sydney, Great Barrier Reef, Uluru National Park, Bali, Singapore, Kuala Lumpur, Manila, Penang, Macau, Angkor, Hong Kong, Shanghai, Phuket, Osaka, Kyoto, Tokyo, Chiang Mai, Bangkok, Sapporo, Everland, Yong-in, Guilin, Beijing, Xi'an, Great Wall of China, Sri Lanka, Benares, Agra (Taj Mahal), Himalayas, Kashmir, Mumbai, Goa, Maldives, Hawaii, Alaska, San Francisco, Disneyland, Yosemite, Baja California, Las Vegas, Banff, Grand Canyon, Aspen, Yellowstone Park, Mexico City, Acapulco, New Orleans, Great Smoky Mts, Niagara Falls, Moscow, Palenque, Belize, Cancun, Walt Disney World, Quebec, New York, Iceland, Crimea, Dubai, Costa Rica, Miami, Bahamas, Cape Cod, Bermuda, See inset of Europe, Turkey, Cyprus, Jerusalem, Red Sea, Mecca, Jamaica, Dominican Rep., ABC Islands, Virgin Islands, Cairo (Pyramids), Seychelles, Margarita, Barbados, Canary Islands, Marrakesh, Djerba, Serengeti National Park, Mombasa, Mauritius, Machu Picchu, Gambia, Victoria Falls, Kruger National Park, Amazon Rainforest, Iguaçu National Park, Rio de Janeiro, Durban, Cape Town, Buenos Aires

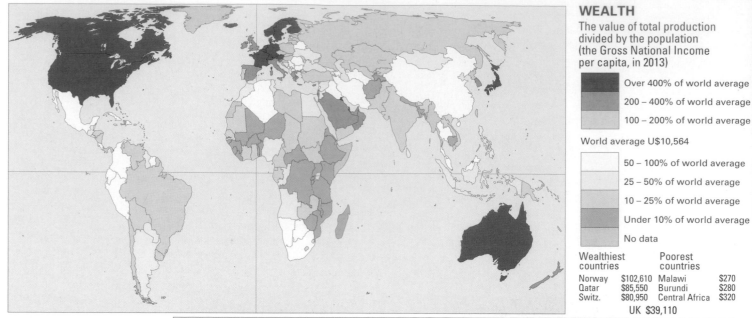

WEALTH

The value of total production divided by the population (the Gross National Income per capita, in 2013)

- Over 400% of world average
- 200 – 400% of world average
- 100 – 200% of world average

World average U$10,564

- 50 – 100% of world average
- 25 – 50% of world average
- 10 – 25% of world average
- Under 10% of world average
- No data

Wealthiest countries		Poorest countries	
Norway	$102,610	Malawi	$270
Qatar	$85,550	Burundi	$280
Switz.	$80,950	Central Africa	$320
		UK $39,110	

WATER SUPPLY

The percentage of total population with access to safe drinking water (2012)

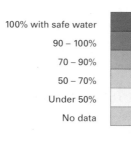

- 100% with safe water
- 90 – 100%
- 70 – 90%
- 50 – 70%
- Under 50%
- No data

Least well-provided countries

Somalia	32%
Papua New Guinea	40%
Congo (DR)	47%
Mozambique	49%

One person in eight in the world has no access to a safe water supply.

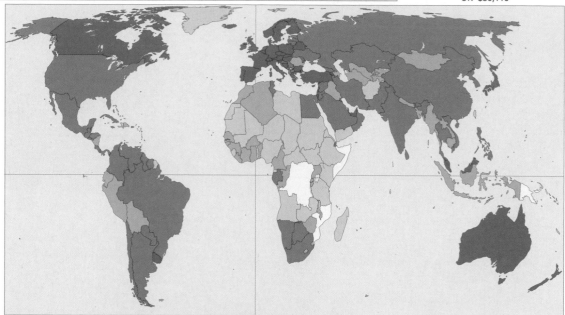

HUMAN DEVELOPMENT INDEX

The Human Development Index (HDI), calculated by the UN Development Programme (UNDP), gives a value to countries using indicators of life expectancy, education and standards of living in 2013 . Higher values show more developed countries.

- Over 0.9
- 0.8 – 0.9
- 0.7 – 0.8
- 0.6 – 0.7
- 0.5 – 0.6
- Under 0.5
- No data

Highest values		Lowest values	
Norway	0.944	Central Africa	0.341
Australia	0.933	Congo (DR)	0.338
Switzerland	0.917	Niger	0.337
		UK 0.892	

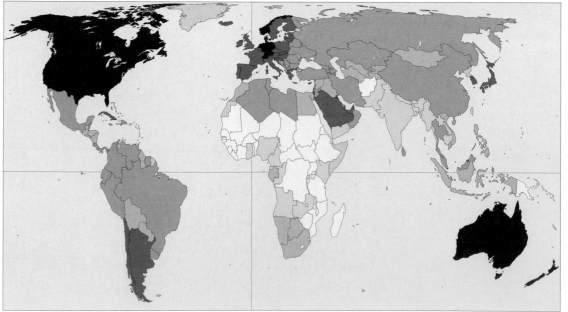
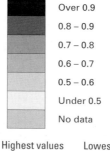

Projection: *Eckert IV*

COPYRIGHT PHILIP'S

HEALTH CARE

Number of qualified doctors
per 100,000 people
(latest available data)

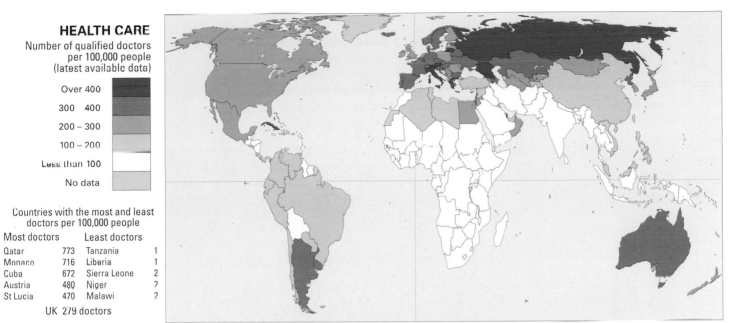

Over 400

300 – 400

200 – 300

100 – 200

Less than 100

No data

Countries with the most and least
doctors per 100,000 people

Most doctors		Least doctors	
Qatar	773	Tanzania	1
Monaco	716	Liberia	1
Cuba	672	Sierra Leone	2
Austria	480	Niger	2
St Lucia	470	Malawi	2

UK 279 doctors

ILLITERACY

Percentage of adult total
population unable to read or
write (2012)

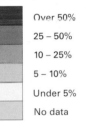

Over 50%

25 – 50%

10 – 25%

5 – 10%

Under 5%

No data

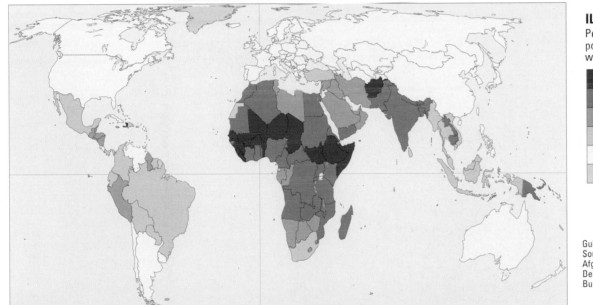

Countries with the highest
illiteracy rates (%)

Guinea	75	Niger	71
South Sudan	73	Mali	67
Afghanistan	72	Chad	65
Benin	71	Somalia	62
Burkina Faso	71	Ethiopia	61

UK 1% adults

GENDER INEQUALITY INDEX

The Gender Inequality Index (GII) is a
composite measure reflecting inequality in
achievements between women and men in
three categories: reproductive health,
empowerment and the labour market.
It varies between 0, when women and men
fare equally, and 1, when women or men
fare poorly compared to the other in all
categories (2013).

Over 0.65

0.5 – 0.65

0.25 – 0.5

Under 0.25

No data

Highest values		Lowest values	
Slovenia	0.021	Yemen	0.733
Switzerland	0.030	Chad	0.707
Germany	0.046	Afghanistan	0.705

UK 0.193

Projection: *Eckert IV*

AGE DISTRIBUTION PYRAMIDS

The bars represent the percentage of the total population (males plus females) in each age group. More Economically Developed Countries (MEDCs), such as New Zealand, have populations spread evenly across age groups and usually a growing percentage of elderly people. Less Economically Developed Countries (LEDCs), such as Kenya, have the great majority of their people in the younger age groups, about to enter their most fertile years.

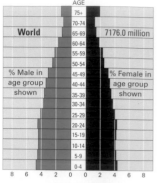

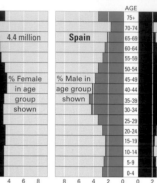

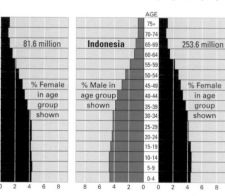

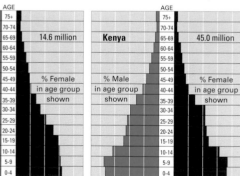

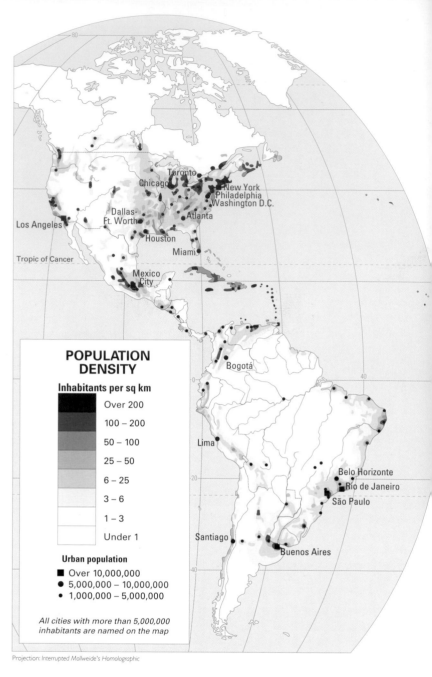

POPULATION DENSITY

Inhabitants per sq km

	Over 200
	100 – 200
	50 – 100
	25 – 50
	6 – 25
	3 – 6
	1 – 3
	Under 1

Urban population
- ■ Over 10,000,000
- ● 5,000,000 – 10,000,000
- • 1,000,000 – 5,000,000

All cities with more than 5,000,000 inhabitants are named on the map

Projection: Interrupted Mollweide's Homolographic

POPULATION CHANGE 1930–2020   Population totals are in millions

Figures in italics represent the percentage average annual increase for the period shown

	1930	1930–1960	1960	1960–1990	1990	1990–2020	2020
World	2,013	*1.4%*	3,019	*1.9%*	5,292	*1.2%*	7,631
Africa	155	*2.0%*	281	*2.9%*	648	*2.5%*	1,286
North America	135	*1.3%*	199	*1.1%*	276	*1.0%*	370
Latin America*	129	*1.8%*	218	*2.4%*	448	*1.3%*	647
Asia	1,073	*1.5%*	1,669	*2.1%*	3,108	*1.3%*	4,542
Europe	355	*0.6%*	425	*0.6%*	508	*0.3%*	549
Oceania	10	*1.4%*	16	*1.8%*	27	*1.3%*	39
CIS†	176	*0.7%*	214	*1.0%*	281	*0.1%*	285

* South America plus Central America, Mexico and the West Indies
† Commonwealth of Independent States, formerly the USSR

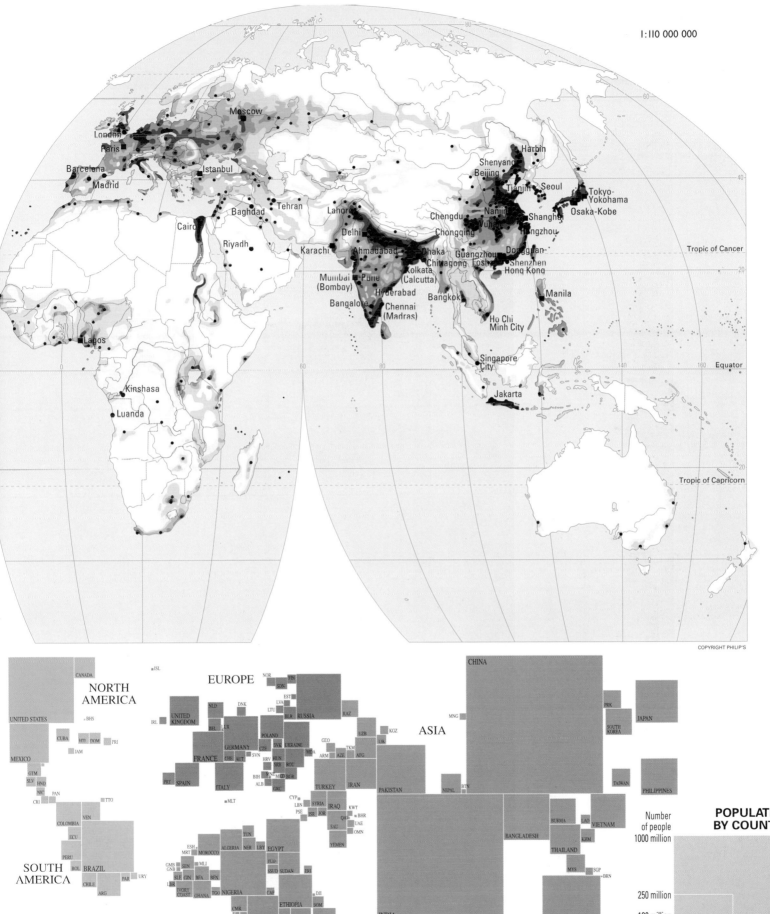

1:110 000 000

Moscow
London
Paris
Barcelona
Madrid
Istanbul
Baghdad
Tehran
Cairo
Riyadh
Lahore
Delhi
Karachi
Ahmadabad
Mumbai (Bombay)
Pune
Hyderabad
Bangalore
Chennai (Madras)
Kolkata (Calcutta)
Dhaka
Chittagong
Harbin
Shenyang
Beijing
Tianjin
Seoul
Chengdu
Nanjing
Wuhan
Shanghai
Chongqing
Hangzhou
Guangzhou
Foshan
Dongguan
Shenzhen
Hong Kong
Tokyo-Yokohama
Osaka-Kobe
Bangkok
Ho Chi Minh City
Manila
Singapore City
Jakarta
Lagos
Kinshasa
Luanda

Tropic of Cancer
Equator
Tropic of Capricorn

COPYRIGHT PHILIP'S

POPULATION BY COUNTRY

NORTH AMERICA
EUROPE
ASIA
SOUTH AMERICA
AFRICA
OCEANIA

CHINA
INDIA
UNITED STATES
INDONESIA
JAPAN
RUSSIA

Number of people
1000 million
250 million
100 million
50 million
10 million
1 million

e squares are in proportion to the total population for
ch country shown. Countries with a population less than
0,000 are not shown. UN standard country codes have
en used to identify smaller squares.

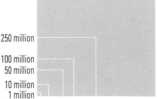

MATERNAL MORTALITY

The number of mothers who died per 100,000 live births (2013)

- Over 500
- 100 – 500
- 50 – 100
- 10 – 50
- Under 10
- No data

Countries with the highest and lowest maternal mortality

Highest		Lowest	
Sierra Leone	1,100	Israel	2
Chad	980	Poland	3
Central Africa	880	Austria	4
Somalia	850	Italy	4
Burundi	740	Sweden	4

UK 8 mothers

POPULATION CHANGE

The projected population change for the years 2004–2050

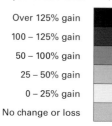

- Over 125% gain
- 100 – 125% gain
- 50 – 100% gain
- 25 – 50% gain
- 0 – 25% gain
- No change or loss

Based on estimates for the year 2050, the ten most populous nations in the world will be, in millions:

India	1,657	Pakistan	291
China	1,304	Bangladesh	250
USA	400	Brazil	232
Indonesia	300	Ethiopia	228
Nigeria	391	Philippines	172

UK (2050) 71 million

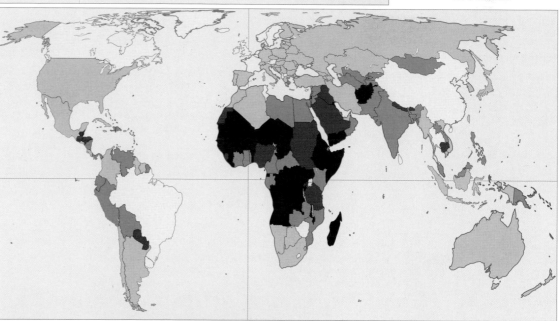

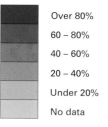

URBAN POPULATION

Percentage of total population living in towns and cities (2013)

- Over 80%
- 60 – 80%
- 40 – 60%
- 20 – 40%
- Under 20%
- No data

Countries that are the most and least urbanized (%)

Most urbanized		Least urbanized	
Singapore	100	Trinidad & Tobago	9
Qatar	99	Burundi	12
Belgium	98	Papua New Guinea	13

UK 82% urban

In 2008, for the first time in history, more than half the world's population lived in urban areas.

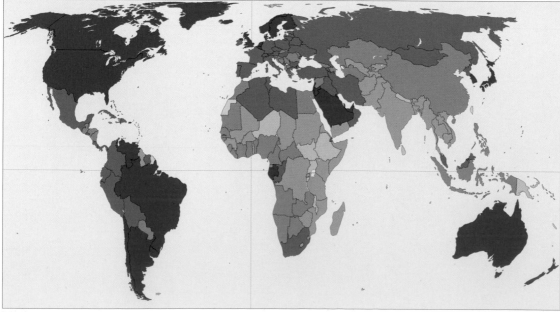

Projection: *Eckert IV*

COPYRIGHT PHILIP'S

INFANT MORTALITY

Number of babies who died under
the age of one, per 1,000 live births
(2014)

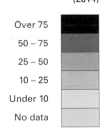

Over 75	
50 – 75	
25 – 50	
10 – 25	
Under 10	
No data	

Countries with the highest and
lowest child mortality

Highest		Lowest	
Afghanistan	117	Monaco	2
Mali	104	Japan	2
Somalia	100	Norway	2

UK 4 babies

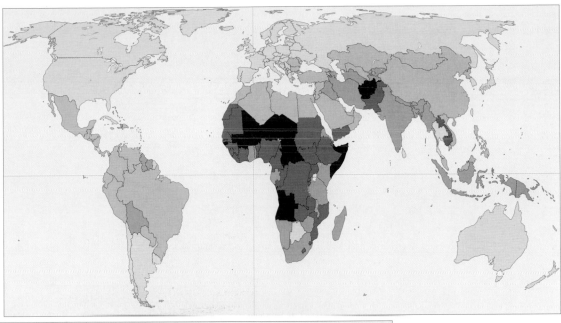

LIFE EXPECTANCY

The average expected lifespan
of babies born in 2014

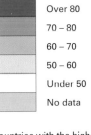

Over 80	
70 – 80	
60 – 70	
50 – 60	
Under 50	
No data	

Countries with the highest and lowest
life expectancy at birth in years

Highest		Lowest	
Japan	84	Afghanistan	50
Singapore	84	Swaziland	51
Switzerland	82	Central Africa	51
Australia	82	Somalia	52
Italy	82	Zambia	52

UK 80 years

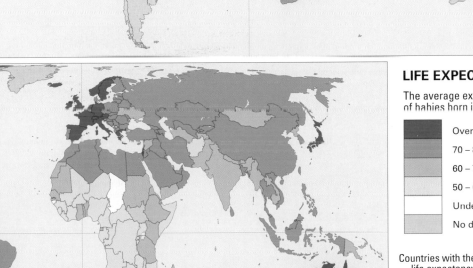

FAMILY SIZE

Children born per woman (2014)

More than 5	
4 – 5	
3 – 4	
2 – 3	
Less than 2	
No data	

Countries with the largest and
smallest family size

Largest		Smallest	
Niger	6.9	Singapore	0.8
Mali	6.2	Taiwan	1.1
Burundi	6.1	South Korea	1.3
Somalia	6.1	Bosnia-Herz.	1.3
Uganda	6.0	Lithuania	1.3

UK 1.9 children

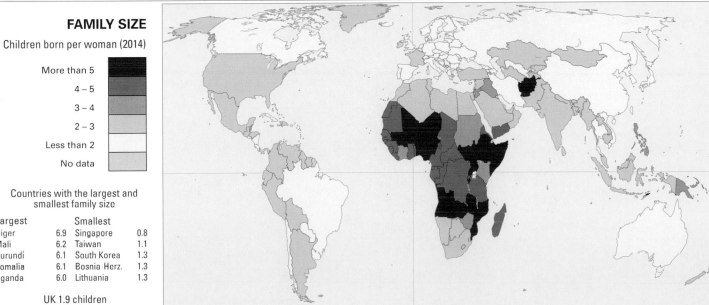

Projection: Eckert IV

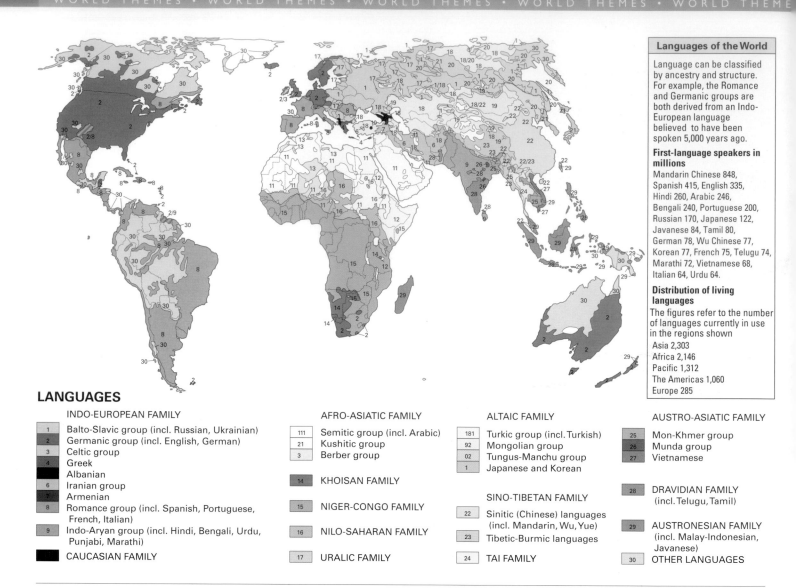

Languages of the World

Language can be classified by ancestry and structure. For example, the Romance and Germanic groups are both derived from an Indo-European language believed to have been spoken 5,000 years ago.

First-language speakers in millions

Mandarin Chinese 848, Spanish 415, English 335, Hindi 260, Arabic 246, Bengali 240, Portuguese 200, Russian 170, Japanese 122, Javanese 84, Tamil 80, German 78, Wu Chinese 77, Korean 77, French 75, Telugu 74, Marathi 72, Vietnamese 68, Italian 64, Urdu 64.

Distribution of living languages

The figures refer to the number of languages currently in use in the regions shown

Asia 2,303
Africa 2,146
Pacific 1,312
The Americas 1,060
Europe 285

LANGUAGES

INDO-EUROPEAN FAMILY

1	Balto-Slavic group (incl. Russian, Ukrainian)
2	Germanic group (incl. English, German)
3	Celtic group
4	Greek
	Albanian
6	Iranian group
7	Armenian
8	Romance group (incl. Spanish, Portuguese, French, Italian)
9	Indo-Aryan group (incl. Hindi, Bengali, Urdu, Punjabi, Marathi)

CAUCASIAN FAMILY

AFRO-ASIATIC FAMILY

111	Semitic group (incl. Arabic)
21	Kushitic group
3	Berber group

14 KHOISAN FAMILY

15 NIGER-CONGO FAMILY

16 NILO-SAHARAN FAMILY

17 URALIC FAMILY

ALTAIC FAMILY

181	Turkic group (incl. Turkish)
92	Mongolian group
02	Tungus-Manchu group
1	Japanese and Korean

SINO-TIBETAN FAMILY

| 22 | Sinitic (Chinese) languages (incl. Mandarin, Wu, Yue) |
| 23 | Tibetic-Burmic languages |

24 TAI FAMILY

AUSTRO-ASIATIC FAMILY

25	Mon-Khmer group
26	Munda group
27	Vietnamese

28 DRAVIDIAN FAMILY (incl. Telugu, Tamil)

29 AUSTRONESIAN FAMILY (incl. Malay-Indonesian, Javanese)

30 OTHER LANGUAGES

RELIGIONS

- Roman Catholicism
- Orthodox and other Eastern Churches
- Protestantism
- Sunni Islam
- Shiite Islam
- Buddhism
- Hinduism
- Confucianism
- Judaism
- Shintoism
- Tribal Religions

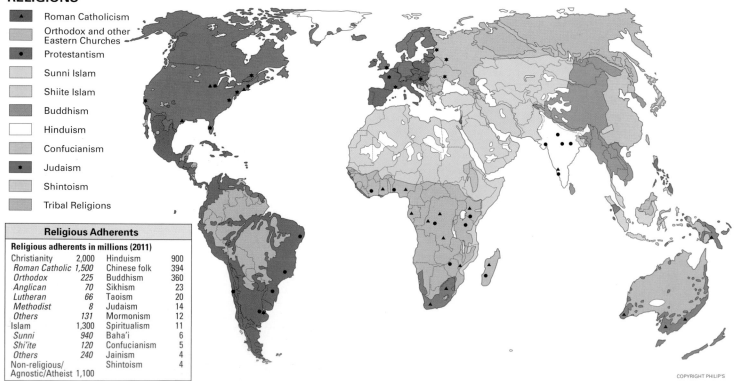

Religious Adherents

Religious adherents in millions (2011)

Christianity	2,000	Hinduism	900
Roman Catholic	1,500	Chinese folk	394
Orthodox	225	Buddhism	360
Anglican	70	Sikhism	23
Lutheran	66	Taoism	20
Methodist	8	Judaism	14
Others	131	Mormonism	12
Islam	1,300	Spiritualism	11
Sunni	940	Baha'i	6
Shi'ite	120	Confucianism	5
Others	240	Jainism	4
Non-religious/		Shintoism	4
Agnostic/Atheist	1,100		

United Nations

Created in 1945 to promote peace and co-operation, and based in New York, the United Nations is the world's largest international organization, with 193 members and a budget for 2014–15 of US \$5.53 billion. Each member of the General Assembly has one vote, while the five permanent members of the 15-nation Security Council – China, France, Russia, the UK and the USA – hold a veto. The Secretariat is the UN's principal administrative arm. The 54 members of the Economic and Social Council are responsible for economic, social, cultural, educational, health and related matters. The UN has 16 specialized agencies – based in Canada, France, Switzerland and Italy, as well as the USA – which help members in fields such as education (UNESCO), agriculture (FAO), medicine (WHO) and finance (IFC). By the end of 1994, all the original 11 trust territories of the Trusteeship Council had become independent.

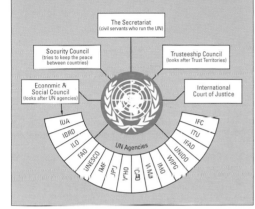

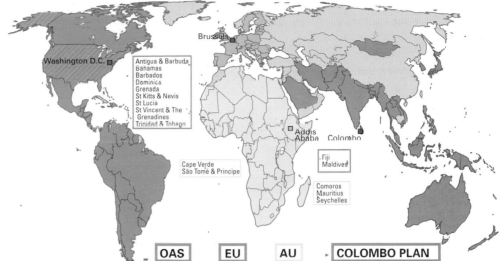

| OAS | EU | AU | COLOMBO PLAN |

AU The African Union was set up in 2002, taking over from the Organization of African Unity (1963). It has 54 members. Working languages are Arabic, English, French and Portuguese.

COLOMBO PLAN (formed in 1951) Its 27 members aim to promote economic and social development in Asia and the Pacific.

OAS Organization of American States (formed in 1948). It aims to promote social and economic co-operation between countries in the developed North America and developing Latin America.

EU European Union (evolved from the European Community in 1993). Cyprus, the Czech Republic, Estonia, Hungary, Latvia, Lithuania, Malta, Poland, the Slovak Republic and Slovenia joined the EU in May 2004, Bulgaria and Romania joined in 2007, Croatia joined in 2013. The other 15 members of the EU are Austria, Belgium, Denmark, Finland, France, Germany, Greece, Ireland, Italy, Luxembourg, Netherlands, Portugal, Spain, Sweden and the UK. Together, the 28 members aim to integrate economies, co-ordinate social developments and bring about political union. Its member states have set up common institutions to which they delegate some of their sovereignty so that decisions on specific matters of joint interest can be made democratically at European level.

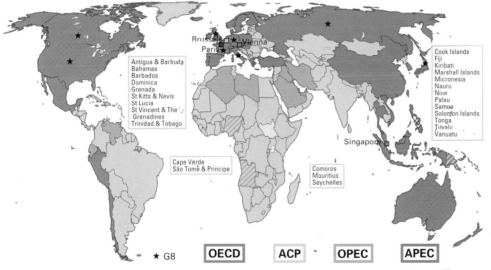

| OECD | ACP | OPEC | APEC |

★ G8

ACP African-Caribbean-Pacific (formed in 1963). Members enjoy economic ties with the EU.

APEC Asia-Pacific Economic Co-operation (formed in 1989). It aims to enhance economic growth and prosperity for the region and to strengthen the Asia-Pacific community. APEC is the only intergovernmental grouping in the world operating on the basis of non-binding commitments, open dialogue, and equal respect for the views of all participants. There are 21 member economies.

G8 Group of eight leading industrialized nations, comprising Canada, France, Germany, Italy, Japan, Russia, the UK and the USA. Periodic meetings are held to discuss major world issues, such as world recessions.

OECD Organization for Economic Co-operation and Development (formed in 1961). It comprises 34 major free-market economies. The 'G8' is its 'inner group' of leading industrial nations, comprising Canada, France, Germany, Italy, Japan, Russia, the UK and the USA.

OPEC Organization of Petroleum Exporting Countries (formed in 1960). It controls about three-quarters of the world's oil supply. Gabon formally withdrew from OPEC in August 1996.

ARAB LEAGUE (1945) Aims to promote economic, social, political and military co-operation. There are 21 member nations.

ASEAN Association of South-east Asian Nations (formed in 1967). Cambodia joined in 1999.

BRICS This acronym refers to the five largest and fastest growing developing economies, Brazil, Russia, India, China and South Africa.

COMMONWEALTH The Commonwealth of Nations evolved from the British Empire. Pakistan was suspended in 1999, but reinstated in 2004. Zimbabwe was suspended in 2002 and, in response to its continued suspension, left the Commonwealth in 2003. Rwanda joined the Commonwealth in 2009, as the 54th member state, becoming only the second country which was not formerly a British colony to be admitted to the group. The Gambia left in 2013.

LAIA The Latin American Integration Association (formed in 1980) superceded the Latin American Free Trade Association formed in 1961. Its aim is to promote freer regional trade.

NATO North Atlantic Treaty Organization (formed in 1949). It continues despite the winding-up of the Warsaw Pact in 1991. Bulgaria, Estonia, Latvia, Lithuania, Romania, the Slovak Republic and Slovenia became members in 2004 and Albania and Croatia in 2009.

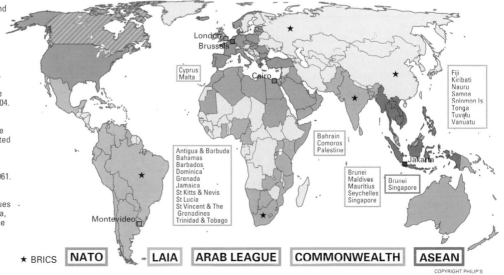

★ BRICS

| NATO | LAIA | ARAB LEAGUE | COMMONWEALTH | ASEAN |

COPYRIGHT PHILIP'S

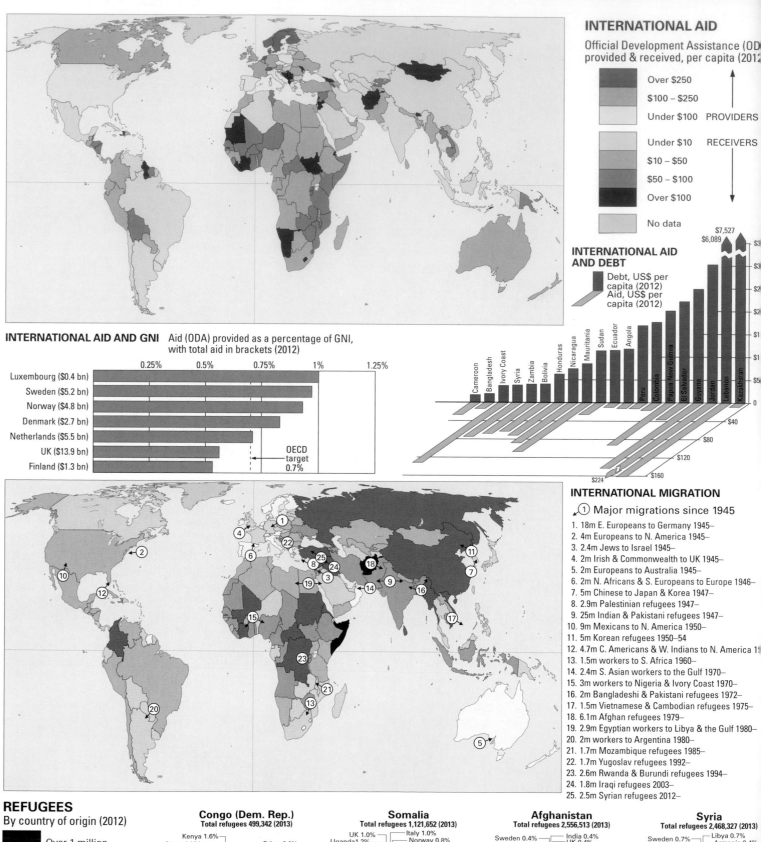

INTERNATIONAL AID

Official Development Assistance (ODA)
provided & received, per capita (2012)

Over $250	
$100 – $250	PROVIDERS
Under $100	
Under $10	RECEIVERS
$10 – $50	
$50 – $100	
Over $100	
No data	

INTERNATIONAL AID AND DEBT

Debt, US$ per capita (2012)
Aid, US$ per capita (2012)

$7,527 $6,089

INTERNATIONAL AID AND GNI

Aid (ODA) provided as a percentage of GNI,
with total aid in brackets (2012)

Luxembourg ($0.4 bn)
Sweden ($5.2 bn)
Norway ($4.8 bn)
Denmark ($2.7 bn)
Netherlands ($5.5 bn)
UK ($13.9 bn)
Finland ($1.3 bn)

0.25%   0.5%   0.75%   1%   1.25%

OECD target 0.7%

INTERNATIONAL MIGRATION

① Major migrations since 1945

1. 18m E. Europeans to Germany 1945–
2. 4m Europeans to N. America 1945–
3. 2.4m Jews to Israel 1945–
4. 2m Irish & Commonwealth to UK 1945–
5. 2m Europeans to Australia 1945–
6. 2m N. Africans & S. Europeans to Europe 1946–
7. 5m Chinese to Japan & Korea 1947–
8. 2.9m Palestinian refugees 1947–
9. 25m Indian & Pakistani refugees 1947–
10. 9m Mexicans to N. America 1950–
11. 5m Korean refugees 1950–54
12. 4.7m C. Americans & W. Indians to N. America 1960–
13. 1.5m workers to S. Africa 1960–
14. 2.4m S. Asian workers to the Gulf 1970–
15. 3m workers to Nigeria & Ivory Coast 1970–
16. 2m Bangladeshi & Pakistani refugees 1972–
17. 1.5m Vietnamese & Cambodian refugees 1975–
18. 6.1m Afghan refugees 1979–
19. 2.9m Egyptian workers to Libya & the Gulf 1980–
20. 2m workers to Argentina 1980–
21. 1.7m Mozambique refugees 1985–
22. 1.7m Yugoslav refugees 1992–
23. 2.6m Rwanda & Burundi refugees 1994–
24. 1.8m Iraqi refugees 2003–
25. 2.5m Syrian refugees 2012–

REFUGEES

By country of origin (2012)

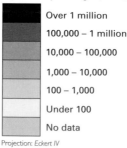

Over 1 million	
100,000 – 1 million	
10,000 – 100,000	
1,000 – 10,000	
100 – 1,000	
Under 100	
No data	

Congo (Dem. Rep.)
Total refugees 499,342 (2013)

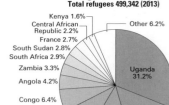

Kenya 1.6%
Central African Republic 2.2%
Other 6.2%
France 2.7%
South Sudan 2.8%
South Africa 2.9%
Zambia 3.3%
Angola 4.2%
Congo 6.4%
Uganda 31.2%
Rwanda 14.6%
Tanzania 12.9%
Burundi 9.0%

Somalia
Total refugees 1,121,652 (2013)

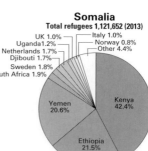

UK 1.0%
Uganda 1.2%
Netherlands 1.7%
Djibouti 1.7%
Sweden 1.8%
South Africa 1.9%
Italy 1.0%
Norway 0.8%
Other 4.4%
Kenya 42.4%
Yemen 20.6%
Ethiopia 21.5%

Afghanistan
Total refugees 2,556,513 (2013)

Sweden 0.4%
Austria 0.5%
Germany 0.9%
India 0.4%
UK 0.4%
Other 2.4%
Iran 31.8%
Pakistan 63.2%

Syria
Total refugees 2,468,327 (2013)

Sweden 0.7%
Germany 0.9%
Egypt 5.3%
Libya 0.7%
Armenia 0.4%
Other 1.5%
Iraq 8.6%
Lebanon 34.5%
Jordan 23.7%
Turkey 23.7%

Projection: *Eckert IV*

COPYRIGHT PHILIP'S

Cameroon · Bangladesh · Ivory Coast · Syria · Zambia · Bolivia · Honduras · Nicaragua · Mauritania · Sudan · Ecuador · Angola · Peru · Colombia · Papua New Guinea · El Salvador · Guyana · Jordan · Lebanon · Kazakhstan

$40 $80 $120 $160 $224

ARMED CONFLICTS

Current military and civilian deaths in countries with conflict, per year (2013)

- Over 10,000
- 1,000 – 10,000
- 100 – 1,000

Countries with at least one armed conflict between 1994 and 2014

Leading arms exporting countries (US $ million)		Leading recipients of arms deliveries (US $ million)	
Russia	$8,283	India	$5,581
USA	$6,153	UAE	$2,245
China	$1,837	China	$1,534
France	$1,489	Saudi Arabia	$1,400
UK	$1,394	Pakistan	$1,002

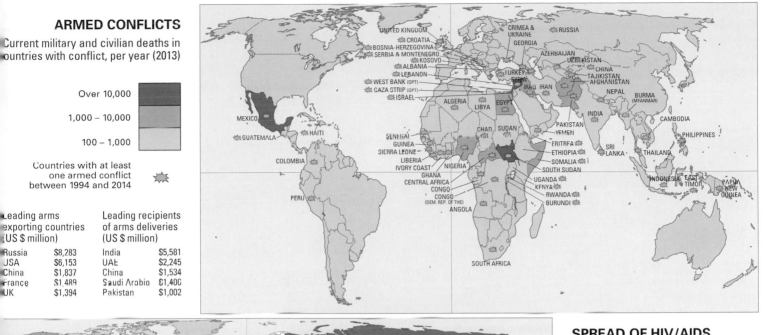

SPREAD OF HIV/AIDS

Percentage of the population living with HIV/AIDS (2012)

- Over 10%
- 1 – 10%
- 0.5 – 1%
- 0.2 – 0.5%
- Under 0.2%
- No data

Caribbean 250,000 — Total number of adults and children living with HIV/AIDS by region (2012)

Human Immunodeficiency Virus (HIV) is passed from one person to another and attacks the body's defence against illness. It develops into the Acquired Immunodeficiency Syndrome (AIDS) when a particularly severe illness, such as cancer, takes hold. The pandemic started about 25 years ago and by 2012 35 million people were living with HIV or AIDS.

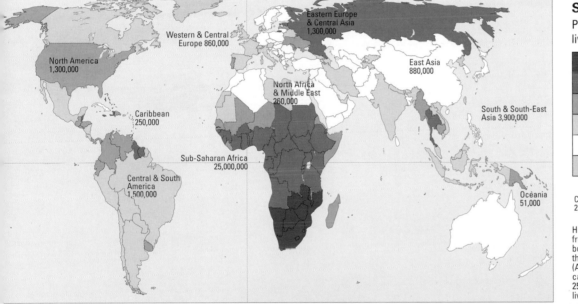

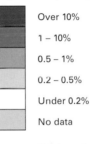

TRAFFIC IN DRUGS

Countries producing illegal drugs

- Cannabis
- Opium poppy
- Coca leaves
- Cocaine
- Amphetamines

Major routes of drug trafficking

- Opium
- Coca leaves
- Cocaine
- Heroin
- Cannabis
- Amphetamines (usually used within producing countries)
- Conflicts relating to drug trafficking

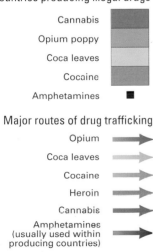

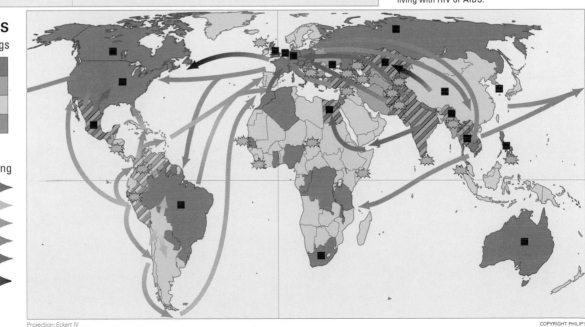

Projection: Eckert IV

	POPULATION						WEALTH						TRADE		
	Total population (millions 2014)	Population density (persons per km² 2014)	Population change (average annual percentage 2014)	Birth rate (births per thousand people 2014)	Death rate (deaths per thousand people 2014)	Urban population (percentage of total 2014)	Gross National income (million US$ 2013)	Gross National Income per capita (PPP US$ 2013)	GDP growth rate (percentage 2013)	GDP from agriculture (percentage of GDP 2013)	GDP from industry (percentage of GDP 2013)	GDP from services (percentage of GDP 2013)	Imports (percentage of GDP 2013)	Exports (percentage of GDP 2013)	Tourism receipts (US$ per capita 2012)
Afghanistan	31.8	49	2.3	39	14	26	21,500	2,000	3.1	20.0	25.6	54.4	47	6	
Albania	3.0	105	0.3	13	6	56	13,043	10,520	0.7	19.5	12.0	68.5	53	35	54
Algeria	38.8	16	1.9	24	4	70	207,535	12,990	3.1	9.4	62.6	28.0	28	37	
Angola	19.1	15	2.8	39	12	43	107,477	6,770	5.6	10.2	61.4	28.4	41	55	
Argentina	43.0	15	1.0	17	7	92	304,070	7,550	3.5	9.3	29.7	61.0	15	14	13
Armenia	3.1	103	−0.1	14	9	63	11,267	8,240	4.6	20.6	37.3	42.1	51	27	16
Australia	22.5	3	1.1	12	7	89	1,515.558	42,540	2.5	3.8	27.4	68.7	21	20	1,55
Austria	8.2	98	0.0	9	10	66	411,731	43,810	0.4	1.6	28.6	69.8	53	57	2,60
Azerbaijan	9.7	112	1.0	17	7	54	69,185	16,180	5.8	6.2	63.0	30.8	27	49	27
Bahamas	0.3	23	0.9	16	7	83	7,661	21,540	1.9	2.1	7.1	90.8	63	45	7,64
Bahrain	1.3	1,904	2.5	14	3	89	25,771	36,140	4.4	0.3	46.7	53.0	48	75	1,39
Bangladesh	166.3	1,155	1.6	22	6	34	140,440	2,810	5.8	17.2	28.9	53.9	31	23	
Barbados	0.3	674	0.3	12	8	32	4,270	15,080	−0.8	3.1	13.9	83.0	54	42	
Belarus	9.6	46	−0.2	11	14	76	63,553	16,940	2.1	9.2	46.2	44.7	64	61	10
Belgium	10.4	343	0.1	10	11	98	506,080	40,280	0.1	0.8	22.6	76.6	84	86	1.2
Belize	0.3	15	1.9	25	6	44	1,546	8,160	2.5	13.0	23.0	64.0	63	61	9
Benin	10.2	90	2.8	37	8	44	8,147	1,780	5.0	31.6	12.9	55.6	27	15	2
Bhutan	0.7	16	1.1	18	7	38	1,854	7,210	5.8	13.8	41.2	45.0	65	38	13
Bolivia	10.6	10	1.6	23	7	68	27,214	5,750	6.8	9.2	38.5	52.3	38	47	5
Bosnia-Herzegovina	3.9	76	−0.1	9	10	40	18,160	9,820	0.8	8.1	26.4	65.5	55	31	17
Botswana	2.2	4	1.3	21	13	57	15,619	15,500	3.9	1.9	35.7	62.4	60	55	
Brazil	202.7	24	0.8	15	7	85	2,342,552	14,750	2.3	5.5	26.4	68.1	15	13	3
Brunei	0.4	73	1.7	17	3	77	12,461	68,090	1.4	0.7	70.9	28.4	32	76	
Bulgaria	6.9	62	−0.8	9	14	74	51,069	15,200	0.5	6.7	30.3	63.0	71	70	59
Burkina Faso	18.4	67	3.1	42	12	29	11,262	1,560	6.5	33.6	23.6	42.8	34	27	
Burma (Myanmar)	55.7	82	1.0	19	8	34	17,766	150	6.8	38.0	20.3	41.7	–	–	
Burundi	10.4	374	3.3	42	10	12	2,828	820	4.5	34.4	18.4	47.2	37	9	
Cambodia	15.5	85	1.6	24	8	21	14,451	2,890	7.0	34.8	24.5	40.7	60	54	13
Cameroon	23.1	49	2.6	37	10	54	28,185	2,660	4.6	20.6	27.3	52.1	31	28	1
Canada	34.8	3	0.8	10	8	82	1,835,341	42,590	1.6	1.7	28.4	69.9	32	30	60
Cape Verde Is.	0.5	135	1.4	21	6	65	1,813	6,220	1.5	9.3	18.8	74.8	52	35	89
Central African Rep.	5.3	8	2.1	35	14	40	1,475	600	−14.5	56.6	14.5	28.9	22	12	
Chad	11.4	9	1.9	37	15	22	13,097	2,000	3.9	46.3	9.9	43.8	39	29	
Chile	17.4	23	0.8	14	6	89	268,296	21,030	4.4	3.6	35.4	61.0	33	33	18
China	1,355.7	141	0.4	12	7	54	8,905,336	11,850	7.7	10.0	43.9	46.1	24	26	4
Colombia	46.2	41	1.1	17	5	76	365,099	11,890	4.2	6.6	37.8	55.6	20	18	2
Comoros	0.8	349	1.9	29	8	28	647	1,560	3.5	51.0	10.0	39.0	52	15	
Congo	4.7	14	1.9	37	10	65	11,833	4,720	5.8	3.3	73.9	22.9	35	87	
Congo (Dem. Rep.)	77.4	33	2.5	36	10	42	26,919	680	6.2	44.3	21.7	34.0	37	27	
Costa Rica	4.8	93	1.2	16	4	76	45,534	13,570	3.5	6.2	21.3	72.5	39	35	54
Croatia	4.5	79	−0.1	9	12	59	56,706	20,370	−1.0	5.0	25.8	69.2	42	43	1,97
Cuba	11.0	100	−0.1	10	8	77	66,397	18,520	3.1	3.8	22.3	73.9	19	20	23
Cyprus	1.2	126	1.5	11	7	67	22,799	29,570	−8.7	2.4	15.9	81.7	47	40	2,38
Czech Republic	10.6	135	0.2	10	10	73	189,976	25,530	−0.9	2.4	37.3	60.3	72	79	76
Denmark	5.6	129	0.2	10	10	88	343,057	44,440	0.1	1.5	21.7	76.8	49	55	1,10
Djibouti	0.8	35	2.2	24	8	77	1,106	1,280	5.0	3.0	17.3	79.7	–	–	2
Dominican Republic	10.4	213	1.3	19	5	78	58,418	11,150	2.0	6.0	29.1	64.9	32	26	46
East Timor	1.2	81	2.4	34	6	32	4,215	6,410	8.1	2.6	81.6	15.8	120	10	1
Ecuador	15.7	55	1.4	19	5	64	86,644	10,310	4.0	5.9	35.1	59.0	33	31	6
Egypt	86.9	87	1.8	23	5	43	258,955	10,850	1.8	14.5	37.5	48.0	578	18	12
El Salvador	6.1	292	0.3	17	6	66	23,556	7,490	1.6	10.3	29.5	60.1	25	26	14
Equatorial Guinea	0.7	26	2.5	34	8	40	10,840	23,240	−1.5	4.6	87.3	8.1	69	88	
Eritrea	6.4	54	2.3	31	8	22	3,121	1,180	7.0	11.7	26.9	61.4	23	14	
Estonia	1.3	28	−0.7	10	14	68	23,005	24,230	1.5	3.9	30.0	66.2	87	88	1,24
Ethiopia	96.6	88	2.9	38	9	19	43,836	1,350	7.0	47.0	10.8	42.2	32	14	2
Fiji	0.9	49	0.7	20	6	53	3,905	7,610	3.0	11.7	18.1	70.2	63	60	1,10
Finland	5.3	16	0.1	10	11	84	256,254	38,480	−0.6	2.9	25.1	71.9	40	40	1,02
France	66.3	120	0.5	12	9	79	2,789,619	37,580	0.3	1.9	18.7	79.4	29	27	96
Gabon	1.7	6	1.9	35	13	87	17,807	17,220	6.6	3.6	63.9	32.5	35	59	
Gambia, The	1.9	170	2.2	32	7	59	941	1,620	6.4	19.7	12.6	67.7	50	28	5
Gaza Strip (OPT)*	1.8	5,045	2.9	32	3	74	11,392	4,900	5.7	4.2	17.9	77.9	63	16	
Georgia	4.9	71	−0.1	13	11	54	15,976	7,040	2.5	8.5	21.6	69.9	58	45	34
Germany	81.0	227	−0.2	8	11	75	3,716,838	44,540	0.5	0.8	30.1	69.0	45	51	63
Ghana	25.8	108	2.2	31	7	53	45,605	3,880	7.9	21.5	28.7	49.8	47	42	4
Greece	10.8	82	0.0	9	11	78	248,597	25,630	−3.8	3.5	16.0	80.5	32	29	1,23

	ENERGY			LAND & AGRICULTURE				SOCIAL INDICATORS							
	Energy Produced (tonnes of oil equivalent per capita 2011)	Energy consumed (tonnes of oil equivalent per capita 2011)	CO$_2$ emissions (tonnes per capita 2011)	Land area (thousand km²)	Arable and permanent crops (% of land area)	Permanent pasture (% of land area)	Forest (% of land area)	Human Development Index (HDI value 2013)	Life expectancy (years 2014)	Food intake (calories per capita per day 2009)	Adults living with HIV/AIDS (percentage 2012)	Gender Inequality Index (GII value 2013)	Adult illiteracy rate (percentage 2012)	Passenger cars (per thousand people 2011)	Internet users (per hundred people 2013)
Afghanistan	0.01	0.01	0.22	652	12	46	2	0.468	50	–	0.1	0.705	72	21	5.9
Albania	0.50	0.77	1.40	28.7	25	18	28	0.716	78	2,903	0.1	0.245	4	94	60.1
Algeria	4.17	1.11	3.20	2,382	4	14	1	0.717	76	3,239	0.1	0.425	27	79	16.5
Angola	6.91	0.67	1.54	1,247	3	43	47	0.526	55	2,079	2.3	–	30	–	19.1
Argentina	1.85	1.97	4.56	2,780	12	36	11	0.808	78	2,918	0.4	0.381	2	–	59.9
Armenia	0.30	0.92	3.96	29.8	18	44	9	0.730	74	2,806	0.2	0.325	1	94	46.3
Australia	13.63	5.50	18.02	7,741	6	49	20	0.933	82	3,261	0.1	0.113	–	559	83.0
Austria	1.40	3.93	8.18	83.9	17	21	47	0.881	80	3,800	0.3	0.056	–	536	80.6
Azerbaijan	7.17	1.37	3.89	86.6	25	32	11	0.747	72	3,072	0.2	0.340	0	95	58.7
Bahamas	0.00	5.56	15.11	13.9	1	0	51	0.789	72	2,750	3.3	0.316	–	–	72.0
Bahrain	14.90	7.35	24.45	0.69	6	5	1	0.815	79	–	0.2	0.253	5	297	90.0
Bangladesh	0.16	0.21	0.37	144	67	5	11	0.558	71	2,481	0.1	0.529	42	2	6.5
Barbados	2.86	1.79	5.03	0.43	40	5	19	0.776	75	3,021	0.9	0.350	–	381	75.0
Belarus	0.45	3.11	6.95	208	27	16	45	0.786	72	3,186	0.4	0.152	0	290	54.2
Belgium	1.74	5.35	12.56	30.5	26	16	22	0.881	80	3,721	0.2	0.068	–	491	82.2
Belize	0.62	1.39	1.67	23	4	2	62	0.732	68	2,680	1.4	0.435	–	–	31.7
Benin	0.23	0.39	0.50	113	26	5	22	0.476	61	2,592	1.1	0.614	71	18	4.9
Bhutan	2.64	2.01	0.47	47	4	11	54	0.584	69	–	0.2	0.495	47	55	29.9
Bolivia	1.78	0.75	1.38	1,099	4	30	53	0.667	69	2,172	0.3	0.472	9	20	39.5
Bosnia-Herzegovina	1.00	1.85	5.72	51.2	21	20	43	0.731	76	3,070	0.1	0.201	2	196	67.9
Botswana	0.48	1.12	1.86	582	0	45	20	0.683	54	2,164	23.0	0.486	15	97	15.0
Brazil	1.22	1.37	2.41	8,514	8	23	62	0.744	73	3,173	–	0.441	10	179	51.6
Brunei	47.34	9.43	21.54	5.8	2	1	73	0.852	77	3,088	0.1	–	5	327	64.5
Bulgaria	1.73	2.62	7.39	111	30	18	35	0.777	74	2,791	0.1	0.627	2	367	53.1
Burkina Faso	0.00	0.03	0.09	274	23	22	21	0.388	55	2,647	1.0	0.607	71	8	4.4
Burma (Myanmar)	0.42	0.27	0.25	677	18	0	50	0.524	66	2,493	0.6	0.430	7	5	1.2
Burundi	0.00	0.00	0.02	27.8	50	35	7	0.389	60	1,604	1.3	0.501	13	2	1.3
Cambodia	0.26	0.37	0.30	181	37	9	51	0.584	64	2,382	0.8	0.505	26	19	6.0
Cameroon	0.42	0.32	0.41	475	15	4	51	0.504	57	2,457	4.5	0.622	29	11	6.4
Canada	12.02	7.33	16.24	9,971	6	2	34	0.902	82	3,399	0.3	0.136	–	420	85.8
Cape Verde Is.	0.00	0.00	0.83	4	17	6	21	0.636	72	2,644	0.2	–	15	74	37.5
Central African Rep.	0.01	0.03	0.06	623	3	5	36	0.341	51	2,181	4.7	0.654	43	1	3.5
Chad	0.67	0.01	0.03	1,284	3	36	9	0.372	49	2,074	2.7	0.707	65	2	2.3
Chile	0.59	1.94	4.74	757	2	19	22	0.822	78	2,908	0.4	0.355	1	137	66.5
China	1.82	2.03	6.52	9,597	13	43	22	0.719	75	3,036	0.1	0.202	5	54	45.8
Colombia	2.69	0.67	1.59	1,139	3	35	55	0.711	75	2,717	0.5	0.460	6	53	51.7
Comoros	0.00	0.06	0.21	2.2	73	8	2	0.488	63	2,139	0.1	–	25	33	6.5
Congo	3.93	0.39	1.62	342	2	29	66	0.564	59	2,056	2.8	0.617	–	26	6.6
Congo (Dem. Rep.)	0.35	0.38	0.04	2,345	3	7	68	0.338	57	1,605	1.1	0.669	39	5	2.2
Costa Rica	0.52	0.98	1.49	51.1	10	25	50	0.763	78	2,886	0.3	0.344	4	145	46.0
Croatia	0.85	1.97	4.98	56.5	17	6	34	0.812	76	3,130	0.1	0.172	1	345	66.7
Cuba	0.51	0.99	2.56	111	37	25	26	0.815	78	3,258	0.1	0.350	0	21	25.7
Cyprus	0.09	2.12	8.48	9.3	12	0	19	0.845	78	2,678	0.1	0.136	1	421	65.5
Czech Republic	3.15	4.14	9.07	78.9	42	13	34	0.861	78	3,305	0.1	0.087	–	437	74.1
Denmark	3.80	3.23	8.44	43.1	57	6	13	0.900	79	3,378	0.2	0.056	–	395	94.6
Djibouti	0.00	1.19	1.52	23.2	0	73	0	0.467	62	2,419	1.2	–	–	–	9.5
Dominican Republic	0.08	0.73	2.07	48.5	27	25	41	0.700	78	2,491	0.7	0.505	10	89	45.9
East Timor	4.40	0.11	0.19	14.9	15	10	51	0.620	67	2,076	–	–	42	–	1.1
Ecuador	1.89	0.85	1.94	284	10	20	41	0.711	76	2,267	0.6	0.429	8	41	40.4
Egypt	1.07	0.98	2.46	1,001	4	0	0	0.682	73	3,349	0.1	0.580	26	34	49.6
El Salvador	0.36	0.69	1.11	21	44	31	14	0.662	74	2,574	0.6	0.441	16	53	23.1
Equatorial Guinea	34.69	0.00	7.83	28.1	7	4	59	0.556	63	–	6.2	–	6	–	16.4
Eritrea	0.10	0.13	0.11	118	7	68	15	0.381	64	1,640	0.7	–	31	6	0.9
Estonia	3.90	4.22	15.79	45.1	14	5	53	0.840	74	3,163	1.2	0.154	0	428	80.0
Ethiopia	0.35	0.38	0.08	1,104	15	20	13	0.435	61	2,097	1.3	0.547	61	1	1.9
Fiji	0.18	1.07	1.64	18.3	14	10	55	0.724	72	2,996	0.2	–	–	118	37.1
Finland	3.25	6.45	10.28	338	7	0	73	0.879	80	3,240	0.1	0.075	–	475	91.5
France	2.08	3.87	5.73	552	35	18	29	0.884	82	3,531	0.4	0.080	–	482	81.9
Gabon	9.07	1.25	3.02	268	2	18	85	0.674	52	2,745	4.0	0.508	11	–	9.2
Gambia, The	0.00	0.08	0.24	11.3	40	26	48	0.441	64	2,643	1.3	0.642	49	5	14.0
Gaza Strip (OPT)*	0.00	0.94	0.59	0.4	36	25	2	–	75	2,130	–	–	8	28	46.6
Georgia	0.24	0.79	1.28	69.7	8	28	40	0.744	76	2,743	0.3	–	0	138	43.1
Germany	1.52	3.81	9.19	357	35	14	32	0.911	80	3,549	0.1	0.046	–	531	84.0
Ghana	0.41	0.43	0.37	239	32	37	23	0.573	66	2,934	1.4	0.549	29	18	12.3
Greece	0.89	2.40	8.48	132	25	11	30	0.853	80	3,661	0.1	0.146	3	460	59.9

	POPULATION						WEALTH						TRADE		
	Total population (millions 2014)	Population density (persons per km² 2014)	Population change (average annual percentage change 2014)	Birth rate (births per thousand people 2014)	Death rate (deaths per thousand people 2014)	Urban population (percentage of total 2014)	Gross National income (million US$ 2013)	Gross National Income per capita (PPP US$ 2013)	GDP growth rate (percentage 2013)	GDP from agriculture (percentage of GDP 2013)	GDP from industry (percentage of GDP 2013)	GDP from services (percentage of GDP 2013)	Imports (percentage of GDP 2013)	Exports (percentage of GDP 2013)	Tourism receipts (US$ per capita 2012)
Guatemala	14.6	134	1.9	25	5	51	51,626	7,130	3.3	13.5	23.8	62.7	35	24	10
Guinea	11.5	47	2.6	36	10	37	5,418	1,160	2.9	22.9	46.5	30.5	54	28	
Guinea-Bissau	1.7	47	1.9	34	15	49	884	1,240	3.5	58.0	13.5	28.5	32	17	
Guyana	0.7	3	−0.1	16	7	29	3,002	6,550	5.3	20.7	38.5	40.8	−	−	8
Haiti	10.0	360	1.1	23	8	57	8,397	1,710	−3.4	24.1	19.9	56.0	48	13	1
Honduras	8.6	77	1.7	24	5	54	17,671	4,270	2.8	14.0	28.2	57.8	70	48	8
Hungary	9.9	107	−0.2	9	13	71	123,100	20,930	0.2	3.4	28.0	68.7	87	94	59
Iceland	0.3	3	0.7	13	7	94	14,190	38,870	1.9	5.9	22.9	71.2	50	58	2,76
India	1,236.3	376	1.3	20	7	32	1,960,072	5,350	3.2	17.4	25.8	56.9	28	25	1
Indonesia	253.6	133	1.0	17	6	53	894,967	9,260	5.3	14.3	46.6	39.1	26	24	3
Iran	80.8	49	1.2	18	6	73	447,534	15,600	−1.5	10.6	44.9	44.5	−	−	
Iraq	32.6	74	2.2	27	5	69	224,177	15,220	4.2	3.3	64.6	32.1	39	42	5
Ireland	4.8	69	1.2	15	6	63	179,390	35,090	−0.6	1.6	28.0	70.4	84	108	1,92
Israel	7.8	380	1.5	18	6	92	275,024	32,140	3.3	2.4	31.2	66.4	36	36	82
Italy	61.7	205	0.3	9	10	69	2,058,172	34,100	−1.8	2.0	24.4	73.5	28	30	70
Ivory Coast	22.8	71	2.0	29	10	54	27,968	2,900	8.0	26.3	21.3	52.4	50	55	
Jamaica	2.9	266	0.7	18	7	55	14,163	8,480	0.4	6.5	29.4	64.1	53	30	71
Japan	127.1	336	−0.1	8	9	93	5,875,019	37,630	2.0	1.1	25.6	73.2	17	15	12
Jordan	7.9	89	3.9	25	4	83	31,973	11,660	3.3	3.2	29.9	67.0	71	42	68
Kazakhstan	17.9	7	1.2	20	8	53	193,810	20,780	5.0	5.2	37.9	56.9	28	40	9
Kenya	45.0	78	2.1	28	7	25	41,220	2,250	5.1	29.3	17.4	53.3	45	28	4
Korea, North	24.9	205	0.5	15	9	61	205,000	8,991	1.3	23.4	47.2	29.4	−	−	
Korea, South	49.0	494	0.2	8	7	82	1,301,575	33,440	2.8	2.6	39.2	58.2	49	54	40
Kosovo	1.9	171	−	−	−	−	7,101	8,940	2.5	12.9	22.6	64.5	53	18	
Kuwait	2.7	154	1.7	20	2	98	140,425	88,170	2.3	0.3	50.6	49.1	23	71	29
Kyrgyzstan	5.6	28	1.0	23	7	36	6,881	3,070	7.4	20.8	34.4	44.8	98	48	13
Laos	6.8	29	1.6	25	8	38	9,880	4,570	8.3	24.8	32.0	37.5	48	36	7
Latvia	2.2	34	−0.6	10	14	67	28,598	21,390	4.0	4.9	25.7	69.4	63	59	48
Lebanon	5.9	566	9.4	15	6	88	44,081	17,390	1.5	4.6	20.0	75.4	76	63	1,52
Lesotho	1.9	64	0.3	26	15	27	3,211	3,320	4.1	7.4	34.5	58.2	114	49	2
Liberia	4.1	37	2.5	35	10	49	1,744	790	8.1	76.9	5.4	17.7	90	32	
Libya	6.2	4	3.1	18	4	78	77,140	28,110	−5.1	2.0	58.3	39.7	−	−	
Lithuania	3.5	54	−0.3	9	12	67	41,289	23,080	3.4	3.7	28.3	68.0	79	77	40
Luxembourg	0.5	200	1.1	12	9	90	38,125	59,750	0.5	0.3	13.3	86.4	143	176	9,06
Macedonia (FYROM)	2.1	81	0.2	12	9	57	10,106	11,520	3.1	10.2	27.5	62.3	73	54	11
Madagascar	23.2	40	2.6	33	7	35	10,163	1,350	2.6	27.3	16.4	56.3	39	29	
Malawi	17.4	147	3.3	42	9	16	4,447	760	5.0	29.4	18.9	51.7	64	46	
Malaysia	30.1	91	1.5	20	5	74	309,047	22,460	4.7	11.2	40.6	48.1	73	82	69
Maldives	0.4	1.312	−0.1	16	4	41	1,934	9,890	3.5	3.0	17.0	80.0	112	111	4,75
Mali	16.5	13	3.0	46	13	39	10,224	1,540	4.8	38.5	24.4	37.0	38	31	
Malta	0.4	1,290	0.3	10	9	95	8,274	26,400	2.4	1.4	25.3	73.3	89	94	3,53
Mauritania	3.5	3	2.3	32	8	59	4,114	2,850	6.4	16.9	54.6	28.5	100	62	
Mauritius	1.3	666	0.7	13	7	40	12,050	17,220	3.4	4.5	22.0	73.4	66	54	1,35
Mexico	120.3	61	1.2	19	5	79	1,216,087	16,110	1.2	3.6	36.6	59.8	32	32	11
Moldova	3.6	106	−1.0	12	13	45	8,772	5,190	8.9	13.8	19.9	66.2	82	44	8
Mongolia	3.0	2	1.4	21	6	71	10,706	8,810	11.8	16.5	32.6	50.9	67	45	15
Montenegro	0.7	46	−0.5	11	9	64	4,514	14.600	1.5	0.8	11.3	87.9	64	44	1,30
Morocco	33.0	74	1.0	18	5	60	101,815	7,000	5.1	15.1	31.7	53.2	50	36	26
Mozambique	24.7	31	2.5	39	12	32	15,190	1,040	7.0	28.7	24.9	46.4	75	32	1
Namibia	2.2	3	0.7	20	14	46	13,452	9,590	4.4	7.7	29.6	62.6	59	44	
Nepal	31.0	211	1.8	21	7	18	20,262	2,260	3.6	36.8	14.5	48.7	38	11	
Netherlands	16.9	407	0.4	11	9	90	797,211	43,210	−0.8	2.6	25.4	72.1	78	88	1,22
New Zealand	4.4	16	0.8	13	7	86	157,463	30,750	2.5	5.0	25.5	69.5	28	30	1,26
Nicaragua	5.8	45	1.0	18	5	59	10,834	4,440	4.6	17.1	25.5	57.5	52	41	7
Niger	17.5	14	3.3	46	13	19	7,292	910	6.2	35.2	14.2	50.6	44	25	
Nigeria	177.2	192	2.5	38	13	47	478,482	5,600	6.2	30.9	43.0	26.0	13	18	
Norway	5.1	16	1.2	12	8	80	521,713	66,520	1.6	1.2	42.3	56.5	28	39	1,13
Oman	3.2	10	2.1	24	3	77	83,686	52,170	5.1	1.0	64.4	34.6	32	62	57
Pakistan	196.2	246	1.5	23	7	38	250,981	4,920	3.6	25.3	21.6	53.1	19	13	
Panama	3.6	48	1.4	19	5	66	41,328	19,290	7.5	3.7	17.9	78.4	67	71	1,078
Papua New Guinea	6.6	14	1.8	25	7	13	14,749	2,430	5.4	27.6	39.1	33.3	−	−	
Paraguay	6.7	16	1.2	17	5	59	27,499	7,640	12.0	20.4	17.7	61.9	43	50	
Peru	30.1	23	1.0	19	6	78	194,084	11,360	5.1	6.2	37.5	56.3	25	24	11
Philippines	107.7	359	1.8	24	5	45	321,296	7,820	6.8	11.2	31.6	57.2	32	28	4
Poland	38.3	119	−0.1	10	10	61	499,481	22,350	1.3	4.0	33.3	62.7	45	48	30

	ENERGY			LAND & AGRICULTURE				SOCIAL INDICATORS							
	Energy produced (tonnes of oil equivalent per capita 2011)	Energy consumed (tonnes of oil equivalent per capita 2011)	CO₂ emissions (tonnes per capita 2011)	Land area (thousand km²)	Arable and permanent crops (% of land area)	Permanent pasture (% of land area)	Forest (% of land area)	Human Development Index (HDI) value 2013	Life expectancy (years 2014)	Food intake (calories per capita per day 2009)	Adults living with HIV/AIDS (percentage 2012)	Gender Inequality Index (GII value 2013)	Adult illiteracy rate (percentage 2012)	Passenger cars (per thousand people 2011)	Internet users (per hundred people 2013)
Guatemala	0.53	0.69	0.85	109	21	18	35	0.628	72	2,244	0.7	0.523	24	38	19.7
Guinea	0.01	0.00	0.13	246	13	44	27	0.392	60	2,652	1.7	–	75	–	1.6
Guinea-Bissau	0.00	0.10	0.29	36.1	19	39	78	0.396	50	2,476	3.9	–	45	29	3.1
Guyana	0.00	0.68	2.25	215	2	6	77	0.638	68	2,718	1.3	0.524	15	60	33.0
Haiti	0.26	0.08	0.22	27.8	47	18	4	0.471	63	1,979	2.1	0.599	51	–	10.6
Honduras	0.28	0.61	0.98	112	13	16	49	0.617	71	2,694	0.5	0.482	15	29	17.8
Hungary	1.08	2.50	4.97	93	53	11	22	0.818	75	3,477	0.1	0.247	1	298	72.6
Iceland	15.43	17.96	12.24	103	0	23	0	0.895	81	3,376	0.3	0.088	–	646	96.5
India	0.45	0.61	1.45	3,287	57	3	23	0.586	68	2,321	0.3	0.563	37	11	15.1
Indonesia	1.61	0.86	1.73	1,905	20	6	53	0.684	72	2,646	0.4	0.500	7	39	15.8
Iran	4.54	2.81	8.02	1,648	12	18	7	0.749	71	3,143	0.2	0.510	15	113	31.4
Iraq	4.67	1.27	4.58	438	12	9	2	0.642	71	–	0.1	0.542	22	28	9.2
Ireland	0.39	2.89	7.83	70.3	16	45	10	0.899	81	3,617	0.2	0.115	–	418	78.2
Israel	0.63	2.99	9.65	20.6	18	6	7	0.888	81	3,569	0.2	0.101	–	282	70.8
Italy	0.52	2.82	6.57	301	33	12	31	0.872	82	3,627	0.3	0.067	1	605	58.5
Ivory Coast	0.55	0.58	0.31	322	22	42	33	0.452	58	2,670	3.2	0.645	43	20	2.6
Jamaica	0.17	1.14	3.33	11	22	21	31	0.715	73	2,807	1.7	0.457	13	142	37.8
Japan	0.41	3.61	9.26	378	13	0	68	0.890	84	2,723	0.1	0.138	–	455	86.3
Jordan	0.05	1.14	2.85	89.3	3	8	1	0.745	74	2,977	0.1	0.488	4	131	44.2
Kazakhstan	10.31	4.72	11.29	2,725	8	69	1	0.757	70	3,284	0.1	0.323	0	215	54.0
Kenya	0.39	0.48	0.30	580	10	37	6	0.535	64	2,092	6.1	0.548	28	14	39.0
Korea, North	1.03	0.77	2.70	121	24	0	49	–	70	2,078	–	–	0	–	–
Korea, South	0.96	5.23	12.53	99.3	18	1	64	0.891	80	3,200	0.1	0.101	–	284	84.8
Kosovo	0.99	1.11	–	10.9				–	74	–	0.1	–	8	–	–
Kuwait	59.44	10.41	31.73	17.8	1	8	0	0.814	78	3,681	0.1	0.288	6	449	75.5
Kyrgyzstan	0.29	0.56	1.43	200	7	49	5	0.628	70	2,791	0.3	0.348	1	63	23.4
Laos	0.17	0.00	0.22	237	6	4	69	0.569	64	2,377	0.3	0.534	27	2	12.5
Latvia	0.95	2.12	3.84	64.6	19	10	54	0.810	73	2,923	0.7	0.222	0	298	75.2
Lebanon	0.05	1.45	4.70	10.4	28	39	13	0.765	77	3,153	0.1	0.413	10	–	70.5
Lesotho	0.02	0.00	0.23	30.4	12	66	1	0.486	53	2,371	23.1	0.557	24	–	5.0
Liberia	0.00	0.07	0.16	111	6	21	46	0.412	58	2,261	0.9	0.655	57	2	4.6
Libya	4.70	2.19	8.61	1,760	1	8	0	0.784	76	3,157	0.3	0.215	11	230	16.5
Lithuania	0.42	2.41	4.54	65.2	30	12	34	0.834	76	3,486	0.1	0.116	0	565	68.5
Luxembourg	0.20	8.05	23.58	2.6	24	26	33	0.881	80	3,637	0.3	0.154	–	667	93.8
Macedonia (FYROM)	0.87	1.48	3.34	25.7	19	24	39	0.732	76	2,957	0.1	0.162	3	152	61.2
Madagascar	0.01	0.06	0.09	587	6	64	22	0.498	65	2,117	0.5	–	36	7	2.2
Malawi	0.03	0.06	0.06	118	38	20	35	0.414	60	2,318	10.8	0.591	39	4	5.4
Malaysia	2.93	2.64	6.66	330	23	1	63	0.773	75	2,902	0.4	0.210	7	341	67.0
Maldives	–	–	2.71	0.3	20	–	–	0.698	75	2,720	0.1	0.283	2	11	44.1
Mali	0.01	0.03	0.05	1,240	4	28	10	0.407	55	2,624	0.9	0.673	67	7	2.3
Malta	0.00	2.06	16.73	0.3	31	0	1	0.829	80	3,438	0.1	0.220	8	595	68.9
Mauritania	0.21	0.29	0.54	1,026	0	38	0	0.487	62	2,856	0.4	0.644	41	–	6.2
Mauritius	0.02	1.22	3.88	2	15	3	17	0.771	75	2,993	1.2	0.375	11	137	39.0
Mexico	2.01	1.56	4.07	1,958	14	39	33	0.756	75	3,146	0.2	0.376	7	195	43.5
Moldova	0.02	0.94	1.75	33.9	65	11	11	0.663	70	2,707	0.7	0.302	1	120	48.8
Mongolia	6.16	1.31	3.26	1,567	1	74	7	0.698	69	2,434	0.1	0.320	3	72	17.7
Montenegro	1.21	1.90	3.27	14	14	24	40	0.789	75	2,887	0.1	–	2	272	56.8
Morocco	0.03	0.54	1.37	447	20	47	11	0.617	77	3,264	0.1	0.460	33	65	56.0
Mozambique	0.56	0.42	0.15	802	6	56	39	0.393	53	2,112	11.1	0.657	49	11	5.4
Namibia	0.14	0.72	1.50	824	1	46	9	0.624	52	2,151	13.3	0.450	24	51	13.9
Nepal	0.31	0.38	0.11	147	17	12	25	0.540	67	2,443	0.3	0.479	43	4	13.3
Netherlands	4.12	4.64	15.19	41.5	33	25	11	0.915	81	3,261	0.2	0.057	–	471	94.0
New Zealand	3.75	4.12	8.66	271	12	41	31	0.910	81	3,172	0.1	0.185	–	597	82.8
Nicaragua	0.26	0.52	0.89	130	18	25	27	0.614	73	2,517	0.3	0.458	22	21	15.5
Niger	0.01	0.03	0.08	1,267	11	23	1	0.337	55	2,489	0.5	0.709	71	6	1.7
Nigeria	1.66	0.72	0.46	924	44	42	11	0.504	53	2,711	3.1	–	49	31	38.0
Norway	41.65	5.68	9.78	324	3	1	32	0.944	82	3,453	0.1	0.068	–	480	95.1
Oman	24.27	8.36	17.40	310	0	5	0	0.783	75	–	0.1	0.348	13	177	66.5
Pakistan	0.35	0.48	0.75	796	28	5	2	0.537	67	2,423	0.1	0.563	45	16	10.9
Panama	0.23	1.09	4.59	75.5	9	21	44	0.765	78	2,606	0.7	0.506	6	102	42.9
Papua New Guinea	0.37	0.31	0.53	463	2	0	64	0.491	67	2,175	0.5	0.617	38	6	6.5
Paraguay	1.13	0.74	0.62	407	11	41	45	0.676	77	2,518	0.3	0.457	6	28	36.9
Peru	0.80	0.70	1.29	1,285	3	13	53	0.737	73	2,563	0.4	0.387	10	39	39.2
Philippines	0.23	0.43	0.80	300	35	5	25	0.660	72	2,580	0.1	0.406	5	9	37.0
Poland	1.78	2.63	8.01	323	43	10	31	0.834	77	3,392	0.1	0.139	0	470	62.8

	POPULATION					WEALTH						TRADE		
	Total population (millions 2014)	Population density (persons per km² 2014)	Population change (average annual percentage 2014)	Birth rate (births per thousand people 2014)	Death rate (deaths per thousand people 2014)	Urban population (percentage of total 2014)	Gross National Income (million US$ 2013)	Gross National Income Per capita (PPP US$ 2013)	GDP growth rate (percentage 2013)	GDP from agriculture (percentage of GDP 2013)	GDP from industry (percentage of GDP 2013)	GDP from services (percentage of GDP 2013)	Imports (percentage of GDP 2013)	Exports (percentage of GDP 2013)	Tourism receipts (US$ per capita 2012)
Portugal	10.8	122	0.1	9	11	63	216,185	25,350	−1.8	2.6	22.2	75.2	40	41	1,3
Qatar	2.1	193	3.6	10	2	99	185,521	123,860	5.5	0.1	72.2	27.7	29	76	3,6
Romania	21.7	91	−0.3	9	12	54	180,846	18,060	3.5	6.4	34.2	59.4	43	42	
Russia	142.5	8	0.0	12	14	74	1,988,216	23,200	1.3	4.2	37.5	58.3	22	28	1
Rwanda	12.3	469	2.6	35	9	28	7,329	1,430	7.5	31.9	14.8	53.3	31	17	
Saudi Arabia	27.3	13	1.5	19	3	83	755,238	53,780	3.6	2.0	62.5	35.5	31	52	3
Senegal	13.6	69	2.5	35	9	43	15,074	2,240	4.0	14.9	22.7	62.4	42	24	
Serbia	7.2	93	−0.5	9	14	56	41,030	12,020	2.0	7.9	31.8	60.3	58	40	1
Sierra Leone	5.7	80	2.3	37	11	40	4,123	1,750	13.3	47.9	18.6	33.5	54	16	
Singapore	5.6	8,187	1.9	8	3	100	291,788	76,850	4.1	0.0	29.4	70.6	168	191	3,5
Slovak Republic	5.4	111	0.0	10	10	54	93,032	24,930	0.8	3.1	30.8	47.0	87	89	4
Slovenia	2.0	98	−0.2	9	11	50	46,965	27,680	−1.1	2.8	28.9	68.3	70	71	1,4
Solomon Is.	0.6	21	2.1	26	4	22	901	1,810	4.0	50.0	10.6	39.4	–	–	1
Somalia	10.4	16	1.8	41	14	39	959	130	2.6	59.3	7.2	33.5	–	–	
South Africa	48.4	40	−0.5	19	17	64	380,700	12,240	2.0	2.6	29.0	68.4	34	31	2
South Sudan	11.6	19	4.1	38	8	19	12,674	2,190	24.7	–	–	–	42	10	
Spain	47.7	96	0.8	10	9	79	1,361,122	31,850	−1.3	3.1	26.0	70.8	32	34	1,3
Sri Lanka	21.9	333	0.9	16	6	18	64,966	9,470	6.3	10.6	32.4	57.0	32	22	
Sudan	35.5	19	1.8	30	8	34	43,079	2,370	3.9	27.4	33.6	39.0	17	6	
Suriname	0.6	4	1.1	17	6	66	4,994	15,860	4.7	8.9	36.6	54.5	–	–	1
Swaziland	1.4	82	1.1	25	14	21	3,843	6,220	0.0	7.6	47.8	44.6	72	64	
Sweden	9.7	22	0.8	12	9	86	567,230	44,660	0.9	2.0	31.3	66.8	40	46	1,3
Switzerland	8.1	195	0.8	10	8	74	647,341	53,920	2.0	0.7	26.8	72.5	42	52	2,4
Syria	18.0	97	−9.7	23	7	57	50,869	2,410	−2.3	17.6	22.2	60.2	–	–	
Taiwan	23.4	649	0.3	9	7	78	1,016,390	44,190	2.2	2.0	29.4	68.6	–	–	
Tajikistan	8.1	56	1.8	25	6	27	8,098	2,500	7.4	21.1	23.2	55.7	68	19	
Tanzania	49.6	53	2.8	37	8	31	30,021	1,750	7.0	27.6	25.0	47.4	44	28	
Thailand	67.7	132	0.4	11	8	49	359,938	13,510	2.9	12.1	43.6	44.2	70	74	56
Togo	7.4	129	2.7	35	7	40	3,625	1,180	5.5	27.6	33.7	38.7	56	39	
Trinidad & Tobago	1.2	240	−0.1	14	8	6	21,133	26,210	1.6	0.3	57.7	42.0	63	88	
Tunisia	10.9	67	0.9	17	6	67	47,498	10,960	2.8	8.6	30.4	61.0	58	49	2
Turkey	81.6	105	1.1	17	6	73	820,622	18,760	3.8	8.9	27.3	63.8	32	26	40
Turkmenistan	5.2	11	1.1	19	6	50	36,051	12,920	12.2	7.2	24.4	68.4	44	73	
Uganda	35.9	149	3.2	44	11	16	19,241	1,370	5.6	23.1	26.9	50.0	33	23	
Ukraine	44.3	73	−0.6	9	16	70	179,944	8,960	0.4	9.9	29.6	60.5	55	47	1
United Arab Emirates	5.6	67	2.7	16	2	85	355,500	58,090	4.0	0.6	61.1	38.2	74	95	
United Kingdom	63.7	263	0.5	12	9	82	2,506,906	35,760	1.8	0.7	20.5	78.9	33	31	72
USA	318.9	33	0.8	13	8	81	16,967,740	53,960	1.6	1.1	19.5	79.4	17	14	6
Uruguay	3.3	19	0.3	13	9	95	51,717	18,930	3.5	7.5	21.5	71.0	30	26	6
Uzbekistan	28.9	65	0.9	17	5	36	57,411	5,340	7.0	19.1	32.2	48.7	30	28	
Vanuatu	0.3	22	2.0	26	4	25	790	2,840	3.3	22.4	9.7	67.9	51	48	1,1
Venezuela	28.9	32	1.4	19	5	89	381,592	17,890	1.6	3.7	35.5	60.8	24	26	
Vietnam	93.4	281	1.0	16	6	33	155,150	5,030	5.3	19.3	38.5	42.2	77	80	7
West Bank (OPT)*	2.7	463	2.0	23	4	74	11,392	4,900	5.7	4.2	17.9	77.9	63	16	
Yemen	26.1	49	2.7	31	6	34	32,582	3,820	3.8	7.7	30.9	61.4	–	–	
Zambia	14.6	19	2.9	42	13	41	21,544	3,070	6.0	19.8	33.8	46.5	48	50	
Zimbabwe	13.8	35	4.4	32	11	33	11,536	1,536	3.2	20.1	25.4	54.5	61	30	5

NOTES

The tables list information for the main states and territories of the world using the latest available data in each category.

OPT*
Occupied Palestinian Territory.

POPULATION TOTAL
These are estimates of the mid-year total in 2014.

POPULATION DENSITY
The total population divided by the land area (both are recorded in the table above).

BIRTH/DEATH RATES
These are 2014 estimates from the CIA World Factbook.

URBAN POPULATION
The urban population shows the percentage of the total population living in towns and cities (each country will differ with regard to the size or type of town that is defined as an urban area).

GNI
Gross National Income is a good indication of a country's wealth. It is the income in US dollars from goods and services in a country for one year, including income from overseas.

GNI PER CAPITA
The GNI (see note) divided by the total population by using the PPP method (see note).

PER CAPITA
An amount divided by the total population of a country or the amount per person.

PPP
Purchasing Power Parity (PPP) is a method used to enable real comparisons to be made between countries when measuring wealth. The UN International Comparison Programme gives estimates of the PPP for each country, so it can be used as an indicator of real price levels for goods and services rather than using currency exchange rates (see GNI and GNI per capita).

AGRICULTURE, INDUSTRY AND SERVICES
The percentage contributions that

each of these three sectors makes to a country's Gross Domestic Product (GDP).

IMPORTS AND EXPORTS
The value of goods and services imported into a country and exported to other countries, given as a percenta, of a country's Gross Domestic Produc (GDP).

TOURISM RECEIPTS
The amount of income generated from tourism in US dollars per capita.

PRODUCTION AND CONSUMPTIO OF ENERGY
The total amount of commercial energ produced or consumed in a country

ENERGY | LAND & AGRICULTURE | SOCIAL INDICATORS

	Energy produced (tonnes of oil equivalent per capita 2011)	Energy consumed (tonnes of oil equivalent per capita 2011)	CO₂ emissions (tonnes per capita 2011)	Land area (thousand km²)	Arable and permanent crops (% of land area)	Permanent pasture (% of land area)	Forest (% of land area)	Human Development Index (HDI) value 2013	Life expectancy (years 2014)	Food intake (calories per capita per day 2009)	Adults living with HIV/AIDS (percentage 2012)	Gender Inequality Index (GII value 2013)	Adult illiteracy rate (percentage 2012)	Passenger cars (per thousand people 2011)	Internet users (per hundred people 2013)
Portugal	0.49	2.19	5.03	88.8	18	20	38	0.822	79	3,617	0.6	0.116	5	446	62.1
Qatar	249.06	17.42	34.86	11	1	4	0	0.851	76	–	0.1	0.524	4	–	85.3
Romania	1.26	1.78	3.93	238	40	19	28	0.785	75	3,487	0.1	0.320	2	203	49.8
Russia	9.48	5.11	12.55	17,075	8	6	49	0.778	70	3,172	1.0	0.314	0	233	61.4
Rwanda	0.00	0.03	0.08	26.3	64	18	17	0.506	59	2,188	2.9	0.410	34	2	8.7
Saudi Arabia	23.03	6.74	19.65	2,150	2	79	0	0.836	75	3,076	0.1	0.321	13	133	60.5
Senegal	0.13	0.26	0.56	197	18	29	44	0.485	61	2,479	0.5	0.537	50	17	20.9
Serbia	1.53	2.24	8.00	77.5	41	16	30	0.745	75	2,823	0.1	–	2	231	51.5
Sierra Leone	0.00	0.07	0.28	71.7	27	31	39	0.374	57	2,162	1.5	0.643	57	5	1.7
Singapore	0.19	6.45	40.48	0.7	1	0	3	0.901	84	–	0.1	0.090	4	117	73.0
Slovak Republic	1.17	3.21	6.37	49	29	11	40	0.830	77	2,881	0.1	0.164	–	324	77.9
Slovenia	1.90	3.53	7.91	20.3	10	15	62	0.874	78	3,275	0.1	0.021	0	520	72.7
Solomon Is.	0.00	0.14	0.36	28.9	3	0	79	0.491	75	2,439	–	–	–	–	8.0
Somalia	0.00	0.03	0.08	638	2	69	11	–	52	–	0.5	–	–	–	1.5
South Africa	3.32	2.74	9.42	1,221	13	69	8	0.658	50	3,017	17.9	0.461	7	112	48.9
South Sudan	–	–	–	620	–	–	–	–	–	–	2.7	–	73	–	–
Spain	0.68	2.69	6.82	498	37	21	29	0.869	81	3,239	0.4	0.100	2	482	71.6
Sri Lanka	0.25	0.50	0.62	65.6	35	7	30	0.750	76	2,426	0.1	0.383	9	20	21.9
Sudan	0.98	0.36	0.42	1,886	9	49	29	0.473	63	2,326	1.1	0.628	28	24	22.7
Suriname	2.30	1.85	4.22	163	0	0	95	0.705	72	2,548	1.1	0.463	5	236	37.4
Swaziland	0.18	0.43	0.75	17.4	11	60	32	0.530	51	2,249	26.5	0.529	12	51	24.7
Sweden	3.58	5.19	5.85	450	6	1	69	0.898	82	3,125	0.1	0.054	–	466	94.8
Switzerland	1.61	3.21	5.52	41.3	11	28	31	0.917	82	3,454	0.4	0.030	–	526	86.7
Syria	1.05	0.91	2.80	185	31	45	3	0.658	68	3,212	0.1	0.556	16	36	26.2
Taiwan	0.52	0.11	12.65	36	23	–	58	–	80	–	–	–	–	–	70.3
Tajikistan	0.20	0.31	0.34	143	6	28	3	0.607	67	2,106	0.3	0.383	0	29	16.0
Tanzania	0.45	0.45	0.16	945	12	27	39	0.488	61	2,137	5.1	0.553	32	4	4.4
Thailand	1.03	1.79	4.04	513	37	2	37	0.722	74	2,862	1.1	0.364	7	74	28.9
Togo	0.34	0.43	0.21	56.8	48	18	6	0.473	64	2,363	2.9	0.579	40	2	4.5
Trinidad & Tobago	34.36	15.69	42.42	5.1	14	1	44	0.766	72	2,751	1.6	0.321	1	–	63.8
Tunisia	0.71	0.89	1.93	164	32	31	6	0.721	76	3,314	0.1	0.265	21	91	43.8
Turkey	0.41	1.54	3.76	775	32	19	14	0.759	73	3,666	0.1	0.360	6	110	46.3
Turkmenistan	13.05	4.84	10.38	488	4	65	9	0.698	69	2,878	0.1	–	0	82	9.6
Uganda	0.01	0.00	0.10	241	40	26	16	0.484	54	2,260	7.2	0.529	27	3	16.2
Ukraine	1.89	2.77	6.75	604	58	14	17	0.734	69	3,198	0.9	0.326	0	151	41.8
United Arab Emirates	36.92	7.41	47.66	83.6	3	4	4	0.827	77	3,245	0.2	0.244	10	237	88.0
United Kingdom	2.07	2.97	7.92	242	25	48	12	0.892	80	3,432	0.2	0.193	–	454	89.8
USA	5.70	7.03	17.62	9,629	19	26	33	0.914	80	3,688	0.6	0.262	–	403	84.2
Uruguay	0.57	1.31	2.52	175	10	75	9	0.790	77	2,808	0.7	0.364	2	195	58.1
Uzbekistan	2.04	1.63	4.12	447	11	52	8	0.661	73	2,618	0.1	–	1	–	38.2
Vanuatu	–	–	0.59	12.2	12	–	–	0.616	73	2,841	–	–	17	–	11.3
Venezuela	7.27	2.38	6.61	912	4	20	53	0.764	74	3,014	0.6	0.464	5	107	54.9
Vietnam	0.74	0.70	1.24	332	30	2	44	0.638	73	2,690	0.4	0.322	7	14	43.9
West Bank (OPT)*	0.00	0.58	0.59	5.9	36	25	2	–	76	2,130	–	–	–	28	46.6
Yemen	0.78	0.31	1.98	528	3	42	1	0.500	65	2,109	0.1	0.733	35	16	20.0
Zambia	0.56	0.62	0.18	753	3	27	57	0.561	52	1,879	12.7	0.617	39	13	15.4
Zimbabwe	0.71	0.70	0.73	391	10	31	42	0.492	56	2,219	14.7	0.516	16	97	18.5

per capita (see note). It is expressed in tonnes of oil equivalent (an energy unit giving the heating value derived from one tonne of oil).

CARBON DIOXIDE EMISSIONS
The amount of carbon dioxide that each country produces per capita.

LAND AREA
This is the total land area of a country, less the area of major lakes and rivers, in square kilometres.

ARABLE AND PERMANENT CROPS
These figures give a percentage of the total land area that is used for crops and fruit (including temporary fallow land or meadows).

PERMANENT PASTURE
This is the percentage of land area that has permanent forage crops for cattle or horses, cultivated or wild. Some land may be classified both as permanent pasture or as forest.

FOREST
Natural/planted trees including cleared land that will be reforested in the near future as a percentage of the land area.

HUMAN DEVELOPMENT INDEX (HDI)
Produced by the UN Development Programme using indicators of life expectancy, knowledge and standards of living to give a value between 0 and 1 for each country. A high value shows a higher human development.

LIFE EXPECTANCY
The average age that a child born today is expected to live to, if mortality levels of today last throughout its lifetime. It is a measure of the overall quality of life.

FOOD INTAKE
The amount of food (measured in calories) supplied, divided by the total population to show the amount each person consumes.

ADULTS LIVING WITH HIV/AIDS
The percentage of all adults (aged 15–49) who have the Human Immuno-deficiency Virus or the Acquired Immunodeficiency Syndrome. The total number of adults and children with HIV/AIDS in 2012 was 35 million.

GENDER INEQUALITY INDEX
Like the HDI (see note), the GII uses the same UNDP indicators but gives a value between 0 and 1 to measure the social and economic differences between men and women. The higher the value, the more equality exists between men and women.

ILLITERACY
The percentage of all adults (over 15 years) who cannot read or write simple sentences. High rates of illiteracy can impede economic development.

PASSENGER CARS AND INTERNET USERS
These are good indicators of a country's development wealth.

Each topic list is divided into continents and within a continent the items are listed in order of size. The bottom part of many of the lists is selective in order to give examples from as many different countries as possible. The figures are rounded as appropriate.

World, Continents, Oceans

	km²	miles²	%
The World	509,450,000	196,672,000	–
Land	149,450,000	57,688,000	29.3
Water	360,000,000	138,984,000	70.7
Asia	44,500,000	17,177,000	29.8
Africa	30,302,000	11,697,000	20.3
North America	24,241,000	9,357,000	16.2
South America	17,793,000	6,868,000	11.9
Antarctica	14,100,000	5,443,000	9.4
Europe	9,957,000	3,843,000	6.7
Australia & Oceania	8,557,000	3,303,000	5.7
Pacific Ocean	155,557,000	60,061,000	46.4
Atlantic Ocean	76,762,000	29,638,000	22.9
Indian Ocean	68,556,000	26,470,000	20.4
Southern Ocean	20,327,000	7,848,000	6.1
Arctic Ocean	14,056,000	5,427,000	4.2

Ocean Depths

Atlantic Ocean	m	ft
Puerto Rico (Milwaukee) Deep	8,605	28,232
Cayman Trench	7,680	25,197
Gulf of Mexico	5,203	17,070
Mediterranean Sea	5,121	16,801
Black Sea	2,211	7,254
North Sea	660	2,165

Indian Ocean	m	ft
Java Trench	7,450	24,442
Red Sea	2,635	8,454

Pacific Ocean	m	ft
Mariana Trench	11,022	36,161
Tonga Trench	10,882	35,702
Japan Trench	10,554	34,626
Kuril Trench	10,542	34,587

Arctic Ocean	m	ft
Molloy Deep	5,608	18,399

Southern Ocean	m	ft
South Sandwich Trench	7,235	23,737

Mountains

Europe		m	ft
Elbrus	*Russia*	5,642	18,510
Dykh-Tau	*Russia*	5,205	17,076
Shkhara	*Russia/Georgia*	5,201	17,064
Koshtan-Tau	*Russia*	5,152	16,903
Kazbek	*Russia/Georgia*	5,047	16,558
Pushkin	*Russia/Georgia*	5,033	16,512
Katyn-Tau	*Russia/Georgia*	4,979	16,335
Shota Rustaveli	*Russia/Georgia*	4,860	15,945
Mont Blanc	*France/Italy*	4,808	15,774
Monte Rosa	*Italy/Switzerland*	4,634	15,203
Dom	*Switzerland*	4,545	14,911
Liskamm	*Switzerland*	4,527	14,852
Weisshorn	*Switzerland*	4,505	14,780
Taschorn	*Switzerland*	4,490	14,730
Matterhorn/Cervino	*Italy/Switzerland*	4,478	14,691
Grossglockner	*Austria*	3,797	12,457
Mulhacén	*Spain*	3,478	11,411
Zugspitze	*Germany*	2,962	9,718
Olympus	*Greece*	2,917	9,570
Galdhøpiggen	*Norway*	2,469	8,100
Kebnekaise	*Sweden*	2,117	6,946
Ben Nevis	*UK*	1,344	4,409

Asia		m	ft
Everest	*China/Nepal*	8,850	29,035
K2 (Godwin Austen)	*China/Kashmir*	8,611	28,251
Kanchenjunga	*India/Nepal*	8,598	28,208
Lhotse	*China/Nepal*	8,516	27,939
Makalu	*China/Nepal*	8,481	27,824
Cho Oyu	*China/Nepal*	8,201	26,906
Dhaulagiri	*Nepal*	8,167	26,795
Manaslu	*Nepal*	8,156	26,758
Nanga Parbat	*Kashmir*	8,126	26,660
Annapurna	*Nepal*	8,078	26,502
Gasherbrum	*China/Kashmir*	8,068	26,469
Broad Peak	*China/Kashmir*	8,051	26,414
Xixabangma	*China*	8,012	26,286
Kangbachen	*Nepal*	7,858	25,781
Trivor	*Pakistan*	7,720	25,328
Pik Imeni Ismail Samani	*Tajikistan*	7,495	24,590
Demavend	*Iran*	5,604	18,386
Ararat	*Turkey*	5,165	16,945
Gunong Kinabalu	*Malaysia (Borneo)*	4,101	13,455
Fuji-San	*Japan*	3,776	12,388

Africa		m	ft
Kilimanjaro	*Tanzania*	5,895	19,340
Mt Kenya	*Kenya*	5,199	17,057
Ruwenzori	*Uganda/Congo (D.R.)*	5,109	16,762
Meru	*Tanzania*	4,565	14,977
Ras Dashen	*Ethiopia*	4,553	14,937
Karisimbi	*Rwanda/Congo (D.R.)*	4,507	14,787
Mt Elgon	*Kenya/Uganda*	4,321	14,176
Batu	*Ethiopia*	4,307	14,130
Toubkal	*Morocco*	4,165	13,665
Mt Cameroun	*Cameroon*	4,070	13,353

Oceania		m	ft
Puncak Jaya	*Indonesia*	4,884	16,024
Puncak Trikora	*Indonesia*	4,730	15,518
Puncak Mandala	*Indonesia*	4,702	15,427
Mt Wilhelm	*Papua New Guinea*	4,508	14,790
Mauna Kea	*USA (Hawaii)*	4,205	13,796
Mauna Loa	*USA (Hawaii)*	4,169	13,678
Aoraki Mt Cook	*New Zealand*	3,724	12,218
Mt Kosciuszko	*Australia*	2,228	7,310

North America		m	ft
Mt McKinley (Denali)	*USA (Alaska)*	6,168	20,237
Mt Logan	*Canada*	5,959	19,551
Pico de Orizaba	*Mexico*	5,610	18,405
Mt St Elias	*USA/Canada*	5,489	18,008
Popocatépetl	*Mexico*	5,452	17,887
Mt Foraker	*USA (Alaska)*	5,304	17,401
Iztaccihuatl	*Mexico*	5,286	17,342
Lucania	*Canada*	5,226	17,146
Mt Steele	*Canada*	5,073	16,644
Mt Bona	*USA (Alaska)*	5,005	16,420
Mt Whitney	*USA*	4,418	14,495
Tajumulco	*Guatemala*	4,220	13,845
Chirripó Grande	*Costa Rica*	3,837	12,589
Pico Duarte	*Dominican Rep.*	3,175	10,417

South America		m	ft
Aconcagua	*Argentina*	6,962	22,841
Ojos del Salado	*Argentina/Chile*	6,863	22,516
Pissis	*Argentina*	6,793	22,288
Mercedario	*Argentina/Chile*	6,770	22,211
Huascarán	*Peru*	6,768	22,204
Bonete	*Argentina*	6,759	22,176
Llullaillaco	*Argentina/Chile*	6,723	22,057
Nevado de Cachi	*Argentina*	6,720	22,047
Yerupaja	*Peru*	6,632	21,758
Sajama	*Bolivia*	6,520	21,391
Chimborazo	*Ecuador*	6,267	20,561
Pico Cristóbal Colón	*Colombia*	5,775	18,948
Pico Bolivar	*Venezuela*	4,981	16,343

Antarctica		m	ft
Vinson Massif		4,897	16,066
Mt Kirkpatrick		4,528	14,855

Rivers

Europe		km	miles
Volga	*Caspian Sea*	3,700	2,300
Danube	*Black Sea*	2,850	1,770
Ural	*Caspian Sea*	2,535	1,575
Dnieper	*Black Sea*	2,285	1,420
Kama	*Volga*	2,030	1,260
Don	*Black Sea*	1,990	1,240
Petchora	*Arctic Ocean*	1,790	1,110
Oka	*Volga*	1,480	920
Dniester	*Black Sea*	1,400	870
Vyatka	*Kama*	1,370	850
Rhine	*North Sea*	1,320	820
North Dvina	*Arctic Ocean*	1,290	800
Elbe	*North Sea*	1,145	710

Asia		km	miles
Yangtse	*Pacific Ocean*	6,380	3,960
Yenisey–Angara	*Arctic Ocean*	5,550	3,445
Huang He	*Pacific Ocean*	5,464	3,395
Ob–Irtysh	*Arctic Ocean*	5,410	3,360
Mekong	*Pacific Ocean*	4,500	2,795
Amur	*Pacific Ocean*	4,442	2,760
Lena	*Arctic Ocean*	4,402	2,735
Irtysh	*Ob*	4,250	2,640
Yenisey	*Arctic Ocean*	4,090	2,540
Ob	*Arctic Ocean*	3,680	2,285
Indus	*Indian Ocean*	3,100	1,925
Brahmaputra	*Indian Ocean*	2,900	1,800
Syrdarya	*Aralkum Desert*	2,860	1,775
Salween	*Indian Ocean*	2,800	1,740
Euphrates	*Indian Ocean*	2,700	1,675
Amudarya	*Aralkum Desert*	2,540	1,575

Africa		km	miles
Nile	*Mediterranean*	6,695	4,160
Congo	*Atlantic Ocean*	4,670	2,900
Niger	*Atlantic Ocean*	4,180	2,595
Zambezi	*Indian Ocean*	3,540	2,200
Oubangi/Uele	*Congo (Dem. Rep.)*	2,250	1,400
Kasai	*Congo (Dem. Rep.)*	1,950	1,210
Shaballe	*Indian Ocean*	1,930	1,200
Orange	*Atlantic Ocean*	1,860	1,155
Cubango	*Okavango Delta*	1,800	1,120
Limpopo	*Indian Ocean*	1,770	1,100
Senegal	*Atlantic Ocean*	1,640	1,020

Australia		km	miles
Murray–Darling	*Southern Ocean*	3,750	2,330
Darling	*Murray*	3,070	1,905
Murray	*Southern Ocean*	2,575	1,600
Murrumbidgee	*Murray*	1,690	1,050

North America		km	miles
Mississippi–Missouri	*Gulf of Mexico*	5,971	3,710
Mackenzie	*Arctic Ocean*	4,240	2,630
Missouri	*Mississippi*	4,088	2,540
Mississippi	*Gulf of Mexico*	3,782	2,350
Yukon	*Pacific Ocean*	3,185	1,980
Rio Grande	*Gulf of Mexico*	3,030	1,880
Arkansas	*Mississippi*	2,340	1,450
Colorado	*Pacific Ocean*	2,330	1,445
Red	*Mississippi*	2,040	1,270
Columbia	*Pacific Ocean*	1,950	1,210
Saskatchewan	*Lake Winnipeg*	1,940	1,205

South America		km	miles
Amazon	*Atlantic Ocean*	6,450	4,010
Paraná–Plate	*Atlantic Ocean*	4,500	2,800
Purus	*Amazon*	3,350	2,080
Madeira	*Amazon*	3,200	1,990
São Francisco	*Atlantic Ocean*	2,900	1,800
Paraná	*Plate*	2,800	1,740
Tocantins	*Atlantic Ocean*	2,750	1,710
Orinoco	*Atlantic Ocean*	2,740	1,700
Paraguay	*Paraná*	2,550	1,580
Pilcomayo	*Paraná*	2,500	1,550
Araguaia	*Tocantins*	2,250	1,400

Lakes

Europe		km²	miles²
Lake Ladoga	*Russia*	17,700	6,800
Lake Onega	*Russia*	9,700	3,700
Saimaa system	*Finland*	8,000	3,100
Vänern	*Sweden*	5,500	2,100

Asia		km²	miles²
Caspian Sea	*Asia*	371,000	143,000
Lake Baikal	*Russia*	30,500	11,780
Tonlé Sap	*Cambodia*	20,000	7,700
Lake Balqash	*Kazakhstan*	18,500	7,100
Aral Sea	*Kazakhstan/Uzbekistan*	17,160	6,625

Africa		km²	miles²
Lake Victoria	*East Africa*	68,000	26,000
Lake Tanganyika	*Central Africa*	33,000	13,000
Lake Malawi/Nyasa	*East Africa*	29,600	11,430
Lake Chad	*Central Africa*	25,000	9,700
Lake Turkana	*Ethiopia/Kenya*	8,500	3,290
Lake Volta	*Ghana*	8,480	3,270

Australia		km²	miles²
Lake Eyre	*Australia*	8,900	3,400
Lake Torrens	*Australia*	5,800	2,200
Lake Gairdner	*Australia*	4,800	1,900

North America		km²	miles²
Lake Superior	*Canada/USA*	82,350	31,800
Lake Huron	*Canada/USA*	59,600	23,010
Lake Michigan	*USA*	58,000	22,400
Great Bear Lake	*Canada*	31,800	12,280
Great Slave Lake	*Canada*	28,500	11,000
Lake Erie	*Canada/USA*	25,700	9,900
Lake Winnipeg	*Canada*	24,400	9,400
Lake Ontario	*Canada/USA*	19,500	7,500
Lake Nicaragua	*Nicaragua*	8,200	3,200

South America		km²	miles²
Lake Titicaca	*Bolivia/Peru*	8,300	3,200
Lake Poopo	*Bolivia*	2,800	1,100

Islands

Europe		km²	miles²
Great Britain	*UK*	229,880	88,700
Iceland	*Atlantic Ocean*	103,000	39,800
Ireland	*Ireland/UK*	84,400	32,600
Novaya Zemlya (N.)	*Russia*	48,200	18,600
Sicily	*Italy*	25,500	9,800

Asia		km²	miles²
Borneo	*South-east Asia*	744,360	287,400
Sumatra	*Indonesia*	473,600	182,860
Honshu	*Japan*	230,500	88,980
Celebes	*Indonesia*	189,000	73,000
Java	*Indonesia*	126,700	48,900
Luzon	*Philippines*	104,700	40,400
Hokkaido	*Japan*	78,400	30,300

Africa		km²	miles²
Madagascar	*Indian Ocean*	587,040	226,660
Socotra	*Indian Ocean*	3,600	1,400
Réunion	*Indian Ocean*	2,500	965

Oceania		km²	miles²
New Guinea	*Indonesia/Papua NG*	821,030	317,000
New Zealand (S.)	*Pacific Ocean*	150,500	58,100
New Zealand (N.)	*Pacific Ocean*	114,700	44,300
Tasmania	*Australia*	67,800	26,200
New Caledonia	*Pacific Ocean*	16,650	6,470

North America		km²	miles²
Greenland	*Atlantic Ocean*	2,175,600	839,800
Baffin I.	*Canada*	508,000	196,100
Victoria I.	*Canada*	212,200	81,900
Ellesmere I.	*Canada*	212,000	81,800
Cuba	*Caribbean Sea*	110,860	42,800
Hispaniola	*Dominican Rep./Haiti*	76,200	29,400
Jamaica	*Caribbean Sea*	11,400	4,400
Puerto Rico	*Atlantic Ocean*	8,900	3,400

South America		km²	miles²
Tierra del Fuego	*Argentina/Chile*	47,000	18,100
Chiloé	*Chile*	8,480	3,275
Falkland I. (E.)	*Atlantic Ocean*	6,800	2,600

How to use the Index

The index contains the names of all the principal places and features shown on the maps. Each name is followed by an additional entry in italics giving the country or region within which it is located. The alphabetical order of names composed of two or more words is governed primarily by the first word and then by the second. This is an example of the rule:

Albert, L. *Africa* 1°30N 31°0E **96** D6
Albert Lea *U.S.A.* 43°39N 93°22W **111** B8
Albert Nile ➔ *Uganda* 3°36N 32°2E **96** D6
Alberta □ *Canada* 54°40N 115°0W **108** D8
Albertville *France* 45°40N 6°22E **66** D7

Physical features composed of a proper name (Erie) and a description (Lake) are positioned alphabetically by the proper name. The description is positioned after the proper name and is usually abbreviated:

Erie, L. *N. Amer.* 42°15N 81°0W **112** D7

Where a description forms part of a settlement or administrative name, however, it is always written in full and put in its true alphabetical position:

Mount Isa *Australia* 20°42S 139°26E **98** E6

Names beginning with M' and Mc are indexed as if they were spelled Mac. Names beginning St. are alphabetized under Saint, but Santa and San are spelled in full and are alphabetized accordingly. If the same place name occurs two or more times in the index and all are in the same country, each is followed by the name of the administrative subdivision in which it is located.

The geographical co-ordinates that follow each name in the index give the latitude and longitude of each place. The first co-ordinate indicates latitude – the distance north or south of the Equator. The second co-ordinate indicates longitude – the distance east or west of the Greenwich Meridian. Both latitude and longitude are measured in degrees and minutes (there are 60 minutes in a degree).

The latitude is followed by N(orth) or S(outh) and the longitude by E(ast) or W(est).

The number in bold type that follows the geographical co-ordinates refers to the number of the map page where that feature or place will be found. This is usually the largest scale at which the place or feature appears.

The letter and figure that are immediately after the page number give the grid square on the map page, within which the feature is situated. The letter represents the latitude and the figure the longitude. A lower case letter immediately after the page number refers to an inset map on that page.

In some cases the feature itself may fall within the specified square, while the name is outside. This is usually the case only with features that are larger than a grid square.

Rivers are indexed to their mouths or confluences, and carry the symbol ➔ after their names. The following symbols are also used in the index: ■ country, ☑ overseas territory or dependency, □ first-order administrative area, △ national park, ✈ (LHR) principal airport (and location identifier).

Abbreviations used in the Index

Afghan. – Afghanistan
Ala. – Alabama
Alta. – Alberta
Amer. – America(n)
Arch. – Archipelago
Ariz. – Arizona
Ark. – Arkansas
Atl. Oc. – Atlantic Ocean
B. – Baie, Bahía, Bay, Bucht, Bugt
B.C. – British Columbia
Bangla. – Bangladesh
C. – Cabo, Cap, Cape, Coast
C.A.R. – Central African Republic
Calif. – California
Cent. – Central
Chan. – Channel
Colo. – Colorado
Conn. – Connecticut
Cord. – Cordillera
Cr. – Creek
D.C. – District of Columbia
Del. – Delaware
Dom. Rep. – Dominican Republic
E. – East
El Salv. – El Salvador
Eq. Guin. – Equatorial Guinea
Fla. – Florida
Falk. Is. – Falkland Is.
G. – Golfe, Golfo, Gulf
Ga. – Georgia
Hd. – Head
Hts. – Heights
I.(s). – Île, Ilha, Insel, Isla, Island, Isle(s)
Ill. – Illinois
Ind. – Indiana
Ind. Oc. – Indian Ocean
Ivory C. – Ivory Coast
Kans. – Kansas
Ky. – Kentucky
L. – Lac, Lacul, Lago, Lagoa, Lake, Limni, Loch, Lough
La. – Louisiana
Lux. – Luxembourg
Madag. – Madagascar
Man. – Manitoba
Mass. – Massachusetts
Md. – Maryland
Me. – Maine
Mich. – Michigan
Minn. – Minnesota
Miss. – Mississippi
Mo. – Missouri
Mont. – Montana
Mozam. – Mozambique
Mt.(s) – Mont, Monte, Monti, Montaña, Mountain
N. – Nord, Norte, North, Northern,
N.B. – New Brunswick
N.C. – North Carolina
N. Cal. – New Caledonia
N. Dak. – North Dakota
N.H. – New Hampshire
N.J. – New Jersey
N. Mex. – New Mexico
N.S. – Nova Scotia
N.S.W. – New South Wales
N.W.T. – North West Territory
N.Y. – New York
N.Z. – New Zealand
Nat. Park – National Park
Nebr. – Nebraska
Neths. – Netherlands
Nev. – Nevada
Nfld. – Newfoundland and Labrador
Nic. – Nicaragua
Okla. – Oklahoma
Ont. – Ontario
Oreg. – Oregon
P.E.I. – Prince Edward Island
Pa. – Pennsylvania
Pac. Oc. – Pacific Ocean
Papua N.G. – Papua New Guinea
Pen. – Peninsula, Péninsule
Phil. – Philippines
Pk. – Peak
Plat. – Plateau
Prov. – Province, Provincial
Pt. – Point
Pta. – Ponta, Punta
Pte. – Pointe
Qué. – Québec
Queens. – Queensland
R. – Rio, River
R.I. – Rhode Island
Ra.(s) – Range(s)
Reg. – Region
Rep. – Republic
Res. – Reserve, Reservoir
S. – San, South
Si. Arabia – Saudi Arabia
S.C. – South Carolina
S. Dak. – South Dakota
Sa. – Serra, Sierra
Sask. – Saskatchewan
Scot. – Scotland
Sd. – Sound
Sib. – Siberia
St. – Saint, Sankt, Sint
Str. – Strait, Stretto
Switz. – Switzerland
Tas. – Tasmania
Tenn. – Tennessee
Tex. – Texas
Trin. & Tob.. – Trinidad & Tobago
U.A.E. – United Arab Emirates
U.K. – United Kingdom
U.S.A. – United States of America
Va. – Virginia
Vic. – Victoria
Vol. – Volcano
Vt. – Vermont
W. – West
W. Va. – West Virginia
Wash. – Washington
Wis. – Wisconsin

A

Aachen *Germany* 50°45N 6°6E **64** C4
Aalborg *Denmark* 57°2N 9°54E **63** F5
Aarau *Switz.* 47°23N 8°4E **64** E5
Aare ➔ *Switz.* 47°33N 8°14E **64** E5
Aarhus *Denmark* 56°8N 10°11E **63** F6
Aba *Nigeria* 5°10N 7°19E **94** G7
Abaco I. *Bahamas* 26°25N 77°10W **115** B9
Ābādān *Iran* 30°22N 48°20E **86** D7
Abaetetuba *Brazil* 1°40S 48°50W **120** C5
Abakan *Russia* 53°40N 91°10E **77** D10
Abancay *Peru* 13°35S 72°55W **120** D2
Abariringa *Kiribati* 2°50S 171°40W **99** A16
Abaya, L. *Ethiopia* 6°30N 37°50E **89** F2
Abbé, L. *Ethiopia* 11°8N 41°47E **89** E3
Abbeville *France* 50°6N 1°49E **66** A4
Abbey Town *U.K.* 54°51N 3°17W **28** C2
Abbot Ice Shelf *Antarctica* 73°0S 92°0W **55** D16
Abbots Bromley *U.K.* 52°50N 1°52W **27** G5
Abbotsbury *U.K.* 50°40N 2°37W **30** E3
ABC Islands *W. Indies* 12°15N 69°0W **115** E11
Abéché *Chad* 13°50N 20°35E **95** F10
Abeokuta *Nigeria* 7°3N 3°19E **94** G6
Aberaeron *U.K.* 52°15N 4°15W **28** C5
Aberchirder *U.K.* 57°34N 2°37W **23** G12
Aberdare *U.K.* 51°43N 3°27W **28** D7
Aberdaugleddau = Milford Haven *U.K.* 51°42N 5°7W **28** D3
Aberdeen *China* 22°14N 114°8E **79** a
Aberdeen *U.K.* 57°9N 2°5W **23** H13
Aberdeen *S. Dak., U.S.A.* 45°28N 98°29W **110** A7
Aberdeen *Wash., U.S.A.* 46°59N 123°50W **110** A2
Aberdeenshire □ *U.K.* 57°17N 2°36W **23** H12
Aberdovey = Aberdyfi *U.K.* 52°33N 4°3W **28** B5
Aberdyfi *U.K.* 52°33N 4°3W **28** B5
Aberfeldy *U.K.* 56°37N 3°51W **25** A8
Aberfoyle *U.K.* 56°11N 4°23W **24** B7
Abergavenny *U.K.* 51°49N 3°1W **28** D7
Abergele *U.K.* 53°17N 3°35W **28** A6
Abergwaun = Fishguard *U.K.* 52°0N 4°58W **28** D4
Aberhonddu = Brecon *U.K.* 51°57N 3°23W **28** D7
Abermaw = Barmouth *U.K.* 52°44N 4°4W **28** B5
Aberpennar = Mountain Ash *U.K.* 51°40N 3°23W **28** D7
Aberporth *U.K.* 52°8N 4°33W **28** C4
Abersoch *U.K.* 52°49N 4°30W **28** B5
Abersychan *U.K.* 51°44N 3°3W **28** D7
Abert, L. *U.S.A.* 42°38N 120°14W **110** B2
Abertawe = Swansea *U.K.* 51°37N 3°57W **29** D6
Aberteifi = Cardigan *U.K.* 52°5N 4°40W **28** C4
Abertillery *U.K.* 51°44N 3°8W **28** D7
Aberystwyth *U.K.* 52°25N 4°5W **28** C5
Abhā *Si. Arabia* 18°0N 42°34E **89** D3
Abidjan *Ivory C.* 5°26N 3°58W **94** G5
Abilene *U.S.A.* 32°28N 99°43W **110** D7
Abingdon-on-Thames *U.K.* 51°40N 1°17W **30** C6
Abitibi, L. *Canada* 48°40N 79°40W **109** E12
Abkhazia □ *Georgia* 43°12N 41°5E **71** F7
Abomey *Benin* 7°10N 2°5E **94** G6
Aboyne *U.K.* 57°4N 2°47W **23** H12
Abrolhos, Banco dos *Brazil* 18°0S 38°0W **122** C3
Absaroka Range *U.S.A.* 44°45N 109°50W **110** B5
Abu Dhabi *U.A.E.* 24°28N 54°22E **87** E8
Abu Hamed *Sudan* 19°32N 33°13E **95** E12
Abuja *Nigeria* 9°5N 7°32E **94** G7
Abunã *Brazil* 9°40S 65°20W **120** C3
Abunã ➔ *Brazil* 9°41S 65°20W **120** C3
Abyei ☑ *Sudan* 9°30N 28°30E **95** G11
Acaponeta *Mexico* 22°30N 105°22W **114** C3
Acapulco *Mexico* 16°51N 99°55W **114** D5
Acaraí, Serra *Brazil* 1°50N 57°50W **120** B4
Acarigua *Venezuela* 9°33N 69°12W **120** B3
Accomac *U.S.A.* 37°43N 75°40W **113** G10
Accra *Ghana* 5°35N 0°6W **94** G5
Accrington *U.K.* 53°45N 2°22W **27** E4
Aceh □ *Indonesia* 4°15N 97°30E **82** D1
Acharnes *Greece* 38°5N 23°44E **69** E10
Acheloos ➔ *Greece* 38°19N 21°7E **69** E9
Achill Hd. *Ireland* 53°58N 10°15W **18** D1
Achill I. *Ireland* 53°58N 10°1W **18** D1
Acklins I. *Bahamas* 22°30N 74°0W **115** C10
Acle *U.K.* 52°39N 1°33E **31** A12
Aconcagua, Cerro *Argentina* 32°39S 70°0W **121** F3
Acre □ *Brazil* 9°1S 71°0W **120** C2
Acre ➔ *Brazil* 8°45S 67°22W **120** C3
Acton Burnell *U.K.* 52°37N 2°41W **27** G3
Ad Dammām *Si. Arabia* 26°20N 50°5E **86** E7
Ad Dīwānīyah *Iraq* 32°0N 45°0E **86** D6
Adair, C. *Canada* 71°30N 71°34W **109** B12
Adak I. *U.S.A.* 51°45N 176°45W **108** D2
Adamaoua, Massif de l' *Cameroon* 7°20N 12°20E **95** G8
Adam's Bridge *Sri Lanka* 9°15N 79°40E **84** Q11
Adana *Turkey* 37°0N 35°16E **71** G6
Adare, C. *Antarctica* 71°0S 171°0E **55** D11
Addis Ababa *Ethiopia* 9°2N 38°42E **89** F2
Adelaide *Australia* 34°52S 138°30E **98** G6
Adelaide I. *Antarctica* 67°15S 68°30W **55** C17
Adelaide Pen. *Canada* 68°15N 97°30W **108** C10
Adélie, Terre *Antarctica* 68°0S 140°0E **55** C10
Aden *Yemen* 12°45N 45°0E **89** E4
Aden, G. of *Ind. Oc.* 12°30N 47°30E **89** E4
Adige ➔ *Italy* 45°9N 12°20E **68** B5
Adigrat *Ethiopia* 14°20N 39°26E **89** E2
Adirondack Mts. *U.S.A.* 44°0N 74°0W **113** D10
Admiralty Is. *Papua N. G.* 2°0S 147°0E **102** H6
Adour ➔ *France* 43°32N 1°32W **66** E3
Adrar *Mauritania* 20°30N 7°30W **94** D3
Adrian *U.S.A.* 41°54N 84°2W **112** E5
Adriatic Sea *Medit. S.* 43°0N 16°0E **68** C6
Adwa *Ethiopia* 14°15N 38°52E **89** E2
Adwick le Street *U.K.* 53°34N 1°10W **27** E6
Adygea □ *Russia* 45°0N 40°0E **71** F7
Ægean Sea *Medit. S.* 38°30N 25°0E **69** E11
Afghanistan ■ *Asia* 33°0N 65°0E **87** C11
Africa 10°0N 20°0E **90** E6
Afyon *Turkey* 38°45N 30°33E **71** G5
Agadez *Niger* 16°58N 7°59E **94** E7
Agadir *Morocco* 30°28N 9°55W **94** B4
Agartala *India* 23°50N 91°23E **85** H17
Agen *France* 44°12N 0°38E **66** D4
Agra *India* 27°17N 77°58E **84** F10
Ağri *Turkey* 39°44N 43°3E **71** G7
Agrigento *Italy* 37°19N 13°34E **68** F5
Agua Prieta *Mexico* 31°18N 109°34W **114** A3
Aguascalientes *Mexico* 21°53N 102°18W **114** C4
Aguja, C. de la *Colombia* 11°18N 74°12W **117** B3
Agulhas, C. *S. Africa* 34°52S 20°0E **97** L4
Ahaggar *Algeria* 23°0N 6°30E **94** D7
Ahmadabad *India* 23°0N 72°40E **84** H8
Ahmadnagar *India* 19°7N 74°46E **84** K9
Ahmadpur East *Pakistan* 29°12N 71°10E **84** E7
Ahvāz *Iran* 31°20N 48°40E **86** D7
Ahvenanmaa *Finland* 60°15N 20°0E **63** E8
Aḩwar *Yemen* 13°30N 46°40E **89** E4
Ailsa Craig *U.K.* 55°15N 5°6W **24** D5
Aimorés *Brazil* 19°30S 41°4W **122** C2
Aïn Témouchent *Algeria* 35°16N 1°8W **94** A5
Ainsdale *U.K.* 53°37N 3°2W **27** E2
Aïr *Niger* 18°30N 8°0E **94** E7
Air Force I. *Canada* 67°58N 74°5W **109** C12
Aird, The *U.K.* 57°25N 4°33W **23** H8
Airdrie *Canada* 51°18N 114°2W **108** D8
Airdrie *U.K.* 55°52N 3°57W **25** C8
Aire ➔ *U.K.* 53°43N 0°55W **27** E7
Aisgill *U.K.* 54°23N 2°21W **26** D4
Aisne ➔ *France* 49°26N 2°50E **66** B5
Aix-en-Provence *France* 43°32N 5°27E **66** E6
Aix-les-Bains *France* 45°41N 5°53E **66** D6
Aizawl *India* 23°40N 92°44E **85** H18
Aizuwakamatsu *Japan* 37°30N 139°56E **81** E6
Ajaccio *France* 41°55N 8°40E **66** F8
Ajanta Ra. *India* 20°28N 75°50E **84** J9
Ajaria □ *Georgia* 41°30N 42°0E **71** F7
Ajdābiyā *Libya* 30°54N 20°4E **95** B10
'Ajmān *U.A.E.* 25°25N 55°30E **87** E8
Ajmer *India* 26°28N 74°37E **84** F9
Aketi *Dem. Rep. of the Congo* 2°38N 23°47E **96** D4
Akhisar *Turkey* 38°56N 27°48E **71** G4
Akimiski I. *Canada* 52°50N 81°30W **109** D11
Akita *Japan* 39°45N 140°7E **81** D7
'Akko *Israel* 32°55N 35°4E **86** C3
Aklavik *Canada* 68°12N 135°0W **108** C6
Akola *India* 20°42N 77°2E **84** J10
Akpatok I. *Canada* 60°25N 68°8W **109** C13
Akranes *Iceland* 64°19N 22°5W **63** B1
Akron *U.S.A.* 41°5N 81°31W **112** E7
Aksai Chin *China* 35°15N 79°55E **84** B11
Aksaray *Turkey* 38°25N 34°2E **71** G5
Akşehir Gölü *Turkey* 38°30N 31°25E **71** G5
Aksu *China* 41°5N 80°10E **78** C5
Aksum *Ethiopia* 14°5N 38°40E **89** E2
Akure *Nigeria* 7°15N 5°5E **94** G7
Akureyri *Iceland* 65°40N 18°6W **63** A2
Al 'Amārah *Iraq* 31°55N 47°15E **86** D6
Al 'Aqabah *Jordan* 29°31N 35°0E **86** D3
Al 'Aramah *Si. Arabia* 25°30N 46°0E **86** E6
Al 'Ayn *U.A.E.* 24°15N 55°45E **87** E8
Al 'Azīzīyah *Libya* 32°30N 13°1E **95** B8
Al Bayḑā *Libya* 32°50N 21°44E **95** B10
Al Fallūjah *Iraq* 33°20N 43°55E **86** C5
Al Fāw *Iraq* 30°0N 48°30E **86** D7
Al Ḩadīthah *Iraq* 34°0N 41°13E **86** C5
Al Ḩasakah *Syria* 36°35N 40°45E **86** B5
Al Ḩillah *Iraq* 32°30N 44°25E **86** C6
Al Hoceïma *Morocco* 35°8N 3°58W **94** A5
Al Ḩudaydah *Yemen* 14°50N 43°0E **89** E3
Al Hufūf *Si. Arabia* 25°25N 49°45E **86** E7
Al Jahrah *Kuwait* 29°25N 47°40E **86** D6
Al Jawf *Libya* 24°10N 23°24E **95** D10
Al Jubayl *Si. Arabia* 27°0N 49°50E **86** E7
Al Khalīl *West Bank* 31°32N 35°6E **86** D3
Al Khums *Libya* 32°40N 14°17E **95** B8
Al Kufrah *Libya* 24°17N 23°15E **95** D10
Al Kūt *Iraq* 32°30N 46°0E **86** C6
Al Manāmah *Bahrain* 26°10N 50°30E **87** E7
Al Mubarraz *Si. Arabia* 25°30N 49°40E **86** E7
Al Mukallā *Yemen* 14°33N 49°2E **89** E4
Al Musayyib *Iraq* 32°49N 44°20E **86** C6
Al Qāmishlī *Syria* 37°2N 41°14E **86** B5
Al Qaţīf *Si. Arabia* 26°35N 50°0E **86** E7
Al Qunfudhah *Si. Arabia* 19°3N 41°4E **89** D3
Al Qurayyāt *Si. Arabia* 31°20N 37°20E **86** D4
Ala Tau *Asia* 45°30N 80°40E **78** B5
Alabama □ *U.S.A.* 33°0N 87°0W **111** D9
Alabama ➔ *U.S.A.* 31°8N 87°57W **111** D9
Alagoas □ *Brazil* 9°0S 36°0W **122** A3
Alagoinhas *Brazil* 12°7S 38°20W **122** B3
Alai Range *Asia* 39°45N 72°0E **87** B13
Alamogordo *U.S.A.* 32°54N 105°57W **110** D5
Alamosa *U.S.A.* 37°28N 105°52W **110** C5
Åland = Ahvenanmaa *Finland* 60°15N 20°0E **63** E8
Alanya *Turkey* 36°38N 32°0E **71** G5
Alappuzha *India* 9°30N 76°28E **84** Q10
Alaşehir *Turkey* 38°23N 28°30E **71** G4
Alaska □ *U.S.A.* 64°0N 154°0W **108** C5
Alaska, G. of *Pac. Oc.* 58°0N 145°0W **108** D5
Alaska Peninsula *U.S.A.* 56°0N 159°0W **108** D4
Alaska Range *U.S.A.* 62°50N 151°0W **108** C4
Alba-Iulia *Romania* 46°8N 23°39E **65** E12
Albacete *Spain* 39°0N 1°50W **67** C5
Albanel, L. *Canada* 50°55N 73°12W **109** D12
Albania ■ *Europe* 41°0N 20°0E **69** D9
Albany *Australia* 35°1S 117°58E **98** H2
Albany *Ga., U.S.A.* 31°35N 84°10W **111** D10
Albany *N.Y., U.S.A.* 42°39N 73°45W **113** D11
Albany *Oreg., U.S.A.* 44°38N 123°6W **110** B2
Albany ➔ *Canada* 52°17N 81°31W **109** D11
Albemarle Sd. *U.S.A.* 36°5N 76°0W **111** C11
Albert, L. *Africa* 1°30N 31°0E **96** D6
Albert Lea *U.S.A.* 43°39N 93°22W **111** B8
Albert Nile ➔ *Uganda* 3°36N 32°2E **96** D6
Alberta □ *Canada* 54°40N 115°0W **108** D8
Albertville *France* 45°40N 6°22E **66** D7
Albi *France* 43°56N 2°9E **66** E5
Albion *U.S.A.* 42°15N 84°45W **112** D5
Alboran Sea *Medit. S.* 36°0N 3°30W **67** E3
Albrighton *U.K.* 52°38N 2°16W **27** G4

Albuquerque · · · Azamgarh

Albuquerque U.S.A. 35°5N 106°39W 110 C5
Albury Australia 36°3S 146°56E 98 H8
Alcalá de Henares Spain 40°28N 3°22W 67 B4
Alcester U.K. 52°14N 1°52W 30 B5
Alchevsk Ukraine 48°30N 38°45E 71 E6
Alcoy Spain 38°43N 0°30W 67 C5
Aldabra Is. Seychelles 9°22S 46°28E 91 G8
Aldan Russia 58°40N 125°30E 77 D13
Aldan → Russia 63°28N 129°35E 77 C13
Aldborough U.K. 54°5N 1°22W 26 D6
Aldbourne U.K. 51°29N 1°37W 30 D5
Aldbrough U.K. 53°49N 0°6W 27 E8
Aldeburgh U.K. 52°10N 1°37E 31 B12
Alderbury U.K. 51°3N 1°44W 30 D5
Alderley Edge U.K. 53°18N 2°13W 27 F4
Alderney U.K. 49°42N 2°11W 29 H9
Aldershot U.K. 51°15N 0°44W 31 D7
Aledo U.S.A. 41°12N 90°45W 112 E2
Alegrete Brazil 29°40S 56°0W 121 E4
Além Paraíba Brazil 21°52S 42°41W 122 D2
Alençon France 48°27N 0°4E 66 B4
Alenquer Brazil 1°56S 54°46W 120 C4
'Alenuihāhā Channel
  U.S.A. 20°30N 156°0W 110 H17
Aleppo Syria 36°10N 37°15E 86 B4
Alert Canada 83°2N 60°0W 109 A13
Alès France 44°9N 4°5E 66 D6
Alessándria Italy 44°54N 8°37E 68 B3
Ålesund Norway 62°28N 6°12E 63 E5
Aleutian Is. Pac. Oc. 52°0N 175°0W 102 D10
Aleutian Trench Pac. Oc. 48°0N 180°0E 102 C10
Alexander Arch. U.S.A. 56°0N 136°0W 108 D6
Alexander I. Antarctica 69°0S 70°0W 55 C17
Alexandria Egypt 31°13N 29°58E 95 B11
Alexandria U.K. 55°59N 4°35W 24 C7
Alexandria La., U.S.A. 31°18N 92°27W 111 D8
Alexandria Va., U.S.A. 38°49N 77°5W 112 F9
Alford Aberds., U.K. 57°14N 2°41W 23 H12
Alford Lincs., U.K. 53°15N 0°10E 27 F9
Alfreton U.K. 53°6N 1°24W 27 F6
Alfriston U.K. 50°48N 0°10E 31 E9
Algarve Portugal 36°58N 8°20W 67 D1
Algeciras Spain 36°9N 5°28W 67 D3
Algeria ■ Africa 28°30N 2°0E 94 C6
Algiers Algeria 36°42N 3°8E 94 A6
Algoa B. S. Africa 33°50S 25°45E 90 E4
Alicante Spain 38°23N 0°30W 67 C5
Alice Springs Australia 23°40S 133°50E 98 E5
Aligarh India 27°55N 78°10E 84 F11
Alipur Duar India 26°30N 89°35E 85 F16
Aliquippa U.S.A. 40°37N 80°15W 112 E7
Aliwal North S. Africa 30°45S 26°45E 97 L5
Alkmaar Neths. 52°37N 4°45E 64 B3
Allahabad India 25°25N 81°58E 85 G12
Allegan U.S.A. 42°32N 85°51W 112 D5
Allegheny → U.S.A. 40°27N 80°1W 112 E8
Allegheny Mts. U.S.A. 38°15N 80°10W 111 C11
Allen → U.K. 54°58N 2°18W 26 C4
Allen, Bog of Ireland 53°15N 7°0W 21 B9
Allen, L. Ireland 54°8N 8°4W 18 C5
Allendale Town U.K. 54°53N 2°14W 26 C4
Allenheads U.K. 54°49N 2°12W 26 C4
Allentown U.S.A. 40°37N 75°29W 113 E10
Alleynes B. Barbados 13°13N 59°39W 114 c
Alliance U.S.A. 42°6N 102°52W 110 B6
Allier → France 46°57N 3°4E 66 C5
Alligator Pond Jamaica 17°52N 77°34W 114 a
Alloa U.K. 56°7N 3°47W 25 B8
Allonby U.K. 54°46N 3°26W 26 C2
Alma U.S.A. 43°23N 84°39W 112 D5
Alma Ata Kazakhstan 43°15N 76°57E 76 E8
Almada Portugal 38°41N 9°8W 67 C1
Almelo Neths. 52°22N 6°42E 64 B4
Almería Spain 36°52N 2°27W 67 D4
Almondsbury U.K. 51°32N 2°34W 30 C4
Aln → U.K. 55°24N 1°37W 26 B5
Alness U.K. 57°41N 4°16W 23 G9
Alnmouth U.K. 55°24N 1°37W 26 B5
Alnwick U.K. 55°24N 1°42W 26 B5
Alor Indonesia 8°15S 124°30E 83 F6
Alor Setar Malaysia 6°7N 100°22E 82 C2
Alpena U.S.A. 45°4N 83°27W 112 C6
Alpes Maritimes Europe 44°10N 7°10E 66 D7
Alphington U.K. 50°42N 3°31W 29 F6
Alpine U.S.A. 30°22N 103°40W 110 D6
Alps Europe 46°30N 9°30E 64 E5
Alrewas U.K. 52°44N 1°44W 27 G5
Alsace □ France 48°15N 7°25E 66 B7
Alsager U.K. 53°6N 2°18W 27 F4
Alston U.K. 54°49N 2°25W 26 C4
Altai Mongolia 46°40N 92°45E 78 B7
Altamira Brazil 3°12S 52°10W 120 C4
Altamura Italy 40°49N 16°33E 68 D7
Altarnun U.K. 50°35N 4°32W 29 F4
Altay China 47°48N 88°10E 78 B6
Altay Mongolia 46°22N 96°15E 78 B8
Altiplano Bolivia 17°0S 68°0W 120 D3
Alton U.K. 51°9N 0°59W 31 D7
Alton U.S.A. 38°53N 90°11W 112 F2
Alton Towers U.K. 52°59N 1°52W 27 G5
Altoona U.S.A. 40°31N 78°24W 112 E8
Altrincham U.K. 53°24N 2°21W 27 F4
Altun Shan China 38°30N 88°0E 78 D6
Altus U.S.A. 34°38N 99°20W 110 D7
Alucra Turkey 40°22N 38°47E 71 F6
Alvechurch U.K. 52°21N 1°57W 30 B5
Alwar India 27°38N 76°34E 84 F10
Alwinton U.K. 55°21N 2°7W 26 B4
Alxa Zuoqi China 38°30N 105°40E 78 D10
Alyth U.K. 56°38N 3°13W 23 J11
Amadjuak L. Canada 65°0N 71°8W 109 C12
Amagasaki Japan 34°42N 135°23E 81 F4
Amapá Brazil 2°5N 50°50W 120 B4
Amapá □ Brazil 1°40N 52°0W 120 B4
Amarillo U.S.A. 35°13N 101°50W 110 C6
Amasya Turkey 40°40N 35°50E 71 F6
Amazon = Amazonas →
  S. Amer. 0°5S 50°0W 120 C4
Amazonas □ Brazil 5°0S 65°0W 120 C3
Amazonas → S. Amer. 0°5S 50°0W 120 C4

Ambala India 30°23N 76°56E 84 D10
Ambergris Cay Belize 18°0N 87°55W 114 D7
Ambikapur India 23°15N 83°15E 85 H13
Ambilobé Madag. 13°10S 49°3E 97 G9
Amble U.K. 55°20N 1°36W 26 B5
Ambleside U.K. 54°26N 2°58W 26 D3
Ambon Indonesia 3°43S 128°12E 83 E7
Amderma Russia 69°45N 61°30E 76 C7
Amdo China 32°20N 91°40E 78 E7
Ameca Mexico 20°33N 104°2W 114 C4
Ameland Neths. 53°27N 5°45E 64 B3
American Highland Antarctica 73°0S 75°0E 55 D6
American Samoa ☑ Pac. Oc. 14°20S 170°0W 99 C16
Americana Brazil 22°45S 47°20W 122 D1
Amersham U.K. 51°40N 0°36W 31 C7
Ames U.S.A. 42°2N 93°37W 111 B8
Amesbury U.K. 51°10N 1°46W 30 D5
Amherst Canada 45°48N 64°8W 109 E13
Amiens France 49°54N 2°16E 66 B5
Amirante Is. Seychelles 6°0S 53°0E 72 J7
Amlwch U.K. 53°24N 4°20W 28 A5
'Ammān Jordan 31°57N 35°52E 86 D3
Ammanford U.K. 51°48N 3°59W 28 D6
Amos Canada 48°35N 78°5W 109 E12
Ampleforth U.K. 54°13N 1°6W 26 D6
Ampthill U.K. 52°2N 0°30W 31 B8
Amravati India 20°55N 77°45E 84 J10
Amreli India 21°35N 71°17E 84 J7
Amritsar India 31°35N 74°57E 84 D9
Amroha India 28°53N 78°30E 84 E11
Amsterdam Neths. 52°23N 4°54E 64 B3
Amsterdam U.S.A. 42°56N 74°11W 113 D10
Amsterdam I. Ind. Oc. 38°30S 77°30E 53 F13
Amudarya → Uzbekistan 43°58N 59°34E 87 A8
Amund Ringnes I. Canada 78°20N 96°25W 109 B10
Amundsen Gulf Canada 71°0N 124°0W 108 B7
Amundsen Sea Antarctica 72°0S 115°0W 55 D15
Amuntai Indonesia 2°28S 115°25E 82 E5
Amur → Russia 52°56N 141°10E 77 D15
An Najaf Iraq 32°3N 44°15E 86 C6
Anaconda U.S.A. 46°8N 112°57W 110 A4
Anadyr Russia 64°35N 177°20E 77 C18
Anadyr, G. of Russia 64°0N 180°0E 77 C19
Anaheim U.S.A. 33°50N 117°55W 110 D3
Anambas, Kepulauan
  Indonesia 3°20N 106°30E 82 D3
Anamur Turkey 36°8N 32°58E 71 G5
Anantapur India 14°39N 77°42E 84 M10
Anápolis Brazil 16°15S 48°50W 122 C1
Anar Iran 30°55N 55°13E 87 D8
Anatolia Turkey 39°0N 30°0E 71 G5
Añatuya Argentina 28°20S 62°50W 121 E3
Ancaster U.K. 52°59N 0°32W 27 G7
Ancholme → U.K. 53°40N 0°32W 27 E7
Anchorage U.S.A. 61°13N 149°54W 108 C5
Anci China 39°20N 116°40E 79 D12
Ancohuma Bolivia 16°0S 68°50W 120 D3
Ancona Italy 43°38N 13°30E 68 C5
Ancrum U.K. 55°31N 2°35W 25 C10
Ancud Chile 42°0S 73°50W 121 G2
Ancud, G. de Chile 42°0S 73°0W 121 G2
Anda China 46°24N 125°19E 79 B14
Andalgalá Argentina 27°40S 66°30W 121 E3
Andalucía □ Spain 37°35N 5°0W 67 D3
Andalusia U.S.A. 31°18N 86°29W 111 D9
Andaman Is. Ind. Oc. 12°30N 92°45E 53 D14
Anderson Alaska, U.S.A. 64°25N 149°15W 108 C5
Anderson Ind., U.S.A. 40°10N 85°41W 112 E5
Anderson S.C., U.S.A. 34°31N 82°39W 111 D10
Anderson → Canada 69°42N 129°0W 108 C7
Andes, Cord. de los S. Amer. 20°0S 68°0W 121 E3
Andhra Pradesh □ India 18°0N 79°0E 84 L11
Andijon Uzbekistan 41°10N 72°15E 87 A13
Andorra ■ Europe 42°30N 1°30E 66 E4
Andorra La Vella Andorra 42°31N 1°32E 66 E4
Andover U.K. 51°12N 1°29W 30 D6
Andradina Brazil 20°54S 51°23W 120 E4
Andreanof Is. U.S.A. 51°30N 176°0W 108 D2
Ándria Italy 41°13N 16°17E 68 D7
Andros Greece 37°50N 24°57E 69 F11
Andros I. Bahamas 24°30N 78°0W 115 C9
Aneityum Vanuatu 20°12S 169°45E 99 E12
Angara → Russia 58°5N 94°20E 77 D10
Angarsk Russia 52°30N 104°0E 77 D11
Ånge Sweden 62°31N 15°35E 63 E7
Angel Falls Venezuela 5°57N 62°30W 120 B3
Angeles Phil. 15°9N 120°33E 83 A6
Ångermanälven → Sweden 63°0N 17°20E 63 E7
Angers France 47°30N 0°35W 66 C3
Anglesey U.K. 53°16N 4°18W 28 A5
Angoche Mozam. 16°8S 39°55E 97 H7
Angola ■ Africa 12°0S 18°0E 97 G3
Angoulême France 45°39N 0°10E 66 D4
Angoumois France 45°50N 0°25E 66 D3
Angra dos Reis Brazil 23°0S 44°10W 122 D2
Angren Uzbekistan 41°1N 70°12E 87 A12
Anguilla ☑ W. Indies 18°14N 63°5W 115 D12
Angus □ U.K. 56°46N 2°56E 23 J11
Angus, Braes of U.K. 56°51N 3°10W 23 J11
Anhui □ China 32°0N 117°0E 79 E12
Anjou France 47°20N 0°15W 66 C3
Ankang China 32°40N 109°1E 79 E10
Ankara Turkey 39°57N 32°54E 71 G5
Ann, C. U.S.A. 42°38N 70°35W 113 D12
Ann Arbor U.S.A. 42°17N 83°45W 112 D6
Annaba Algeria 36°50N 7°46E 94 A7
Annalee → Ireland 54°2N 7°24W 18 C7
Annan U.K. 54°59N 3°16W 25 E9
Annan → U.K. 54°58N 3°16W 25 E9
Annandale U.K. 55°10N 3°25W 25 D9
Annapolis U.S.A. 38°59N 76°30W 112 F9
Annapurna Nepal 28°34N 83°50E 85 E14
Annecy France 45°55N 6°8E 66 D7
Annfield Plain U.K. 54°52N 1°44W 26 C5
Anniston U.S.A. 33°39N 85°50W 111 D9
Annobón Atl. Oc. 1°25S 5°36E 90 G4
Annotto B. Jamaica 18°17N 76°45W 114 a

Anqing China 30°30N 117°3E 79 E12
Anse la Raye St. Lucia 13°55N 61°3W 114 b
Anshan China 41°5N 122°58E 79 C13
Anshun China 26°18N 105°57E 78 F10
Anstey U.K. 52°41N 1°12W 27 G6
Anstruther U.K. 56°14N 2°41W 25 B10
Antalaha Madag. 14°57S 50°20E 97 G10
Antalya Turkey 36°52N 30°45E 71 G5
Antalya Körfezi Turkey 36°15N 31°30E 71 G5
Antananarivo Madag. 18°55S 47°31E 97 H9
Antarctic Pen. Antarctica 67°0S 60°0W 55 C18
Antarctica 90°0S 0°0 55 E3
Anti Atlas Morocco 30°0N 8°30W 94 C4
Antibes France 43°34N 7°6E 66 E7
Anticosti, Î. d' Canada 49°30N 63°0W 109 E13
Antigo U.S.A. 45°9N 89°9W 112 C3
Antigonish Canada 45°38N 61°58W 109 E13
Antigua & Barbuda ■
  W. Indies 17°20N 61°48W 115 D12
Antilles Cent. Amer. 15°0N 65°0W 115 E12
Antioch = Hatay Turkey 36°14N 36°10E 71 G6
Antioquia Colombia 6°40N 75°55W 120 B2
Antipodes Is. Pac. Oc. 49°45S 178°40E 102 M9
Antofagasta Chile 23°50S 70°30W 121 E2
Antrim U.K. 54°43N 6°14W 19 B9
Antrim □ U.K. 54°56N 6°25W 19 B9
Antrim, Mts. of U.K. 55°3N 6°14W 19 A9
Antsirabe Madag. 19°55S 47°2E 97 H9
Antsiranana Madag. 12°25S 49°20E 97 G9
Antwerp Belgium 51°13N 4°25E 64 C3
Anuradhapura Sri Lanka 8°22N 80°28E 84 Q12
Anxi China 40°30N 95°43E 78 C8
Anyang China 36°5N 114°21E 79 D11
Anzhero-Sudzhensk Russia 56°10N 86°0E 76 D9
Ânzio Italy 41°27N 12°37E 68 D5
Aomori Japan 40°45N 140°45E 81 C7
Aoraki Mount Cook N.Z. 43°36S 170°9E 99 J13
Aosta Italy 45°45N 7°20E 68 B2
Aozou Strip Chad 22°0N 19°0E 95 D9
Apalachee B. U.S.A. 30°0N 84°0W 111 E10
Apaporis → Colombia 1°23S 69°25W 120 C3
Aparecida de Goiânia Brazil 16°49S 49°14W 122 C1
Apatity Russia 67°34N 33°22E 70 A5
Apeldoorn Neths. 52°13N 5°57E 64 B3
Apia Samoa 13°50S 171°50W 99 C16
Apostle Is. U.S.A. 47°0N 90°40W 112 B2
Appalachian Mts. U.S.A. 38°0N 80°0W 112 G7
Appennini Italy 44°30N 10°0E 68 B4
Appleby-in-Westmorland
  U.K. 54°35N 2°29W 26 C4
Applecross Forest U.K. 57°27N 5°40W 22 H6
Appledore Devon, U.K. 51°3N 4°13W 29 E5
Appledore Kent, U.K. 51°1N 0°47E 31 D10
Appleton U.S.A. 44°16N 88°25W 112 C3
Apure → Venezuela 7°37N 66°25W 120 B3
Apurímac → Peru 12°17S 73°56W 120 D2
Aqaba, G. of Red Sea 29°0N 34°40E 86 D3
Aqtaū Kazakhstan 43°39N 51°12E 71 F9
Aqtöbe Kazakhstan 50°17N 57°10E 71 D10
Ar Ramādī Iraq 33°25N 43°20E 86 C5
Ar Raqqah Syria 35°59N 39°8E 86 C4
Ara India 25°35N 84°32E 85 G14
'Arab, Bahr el → South Sudan 9°0N 29°30E 95 G11
Arab, Shatt al → Asia 29°57N 48°34E 86 D7
Arabia Asia 25°0N 45°0E 72 F6
Arabian Sea Ind. Oc. 16°0N 65°0E 72 G8
Aracaju Brazil 10°55S 37°4W 122 B3
Aracati Brazil 4°30S 37°44W 120 C6
Araçatuba Brazil 21°10S 50°30W 120 E4
Araçuaí Brazil 16°52S 42°4W 122 C2
Arad Romania 46°10N 21°20E 65 E11
Arafura Sea E. Indies 9°0S 135°0E 98 B5
Aragón □ Spain 41°25N 0°40W 67 B5
Araguacema Brazil 8°50S 49°20W 120 C5
Araguaia → Brazil 5°21S 48°41W 120 C5
Araguari Brazil 18°38S 48°11W 122 C1
Arāk Iran 34°0N 49°40E 86 C7
Arakan Coast Burma 19°0N 94°0E 85 K19
Arakan Yoma Burma 20°0N 94°40E 85 K19
Aral Kazakhstan 46°41N 61°45E 76 E7
Aral Sea Asia 45°0N 58°20E 76 E6
Aran I. = Arranmore Ireland 55°0N 8°30W 18 B4
Aran Is. Ireland 53°6N 9°38W 20 B3
Aransas Pass U.S.A. 27°55N 97°9W 111 E7
Arapiraca Brazil 9°45S 36°39W 122 A3
Ar'ar Si. Arabia 30°59N 41°2E 86 D5
Araraquara Brazil 21°50S 48°0W 122 D1
Araras Brazil 22°22S 47°23W 122 D1
Ararat Turkey 39°50N 44°15E 71 G7
Araripe, Chapada do Brazil 7°20S 40°0W 120 C6
Aras, Rūd-e → Asia 40°5N 48°29E 86 A7
Arauca → Venezuela 7°24N 66°35W 120 B3
Araxá Brazil 19°35S 46°55W 122 C1
Arbroath U.K. 56°34N 2°35W 25 A10
Arcachon France 44°40N 1°10W 66 D3
Arctic Bay Canada 73°1N 85°7W 109 B11
Arctic Ocean Arctic 78°0N 160°0W 54 B18
Ardabil Iran 38°15N 48°18E 86 B7
Ardee Ireland 53°52N 6°33W 19 C8
Ardennes Belgium 49°50N 5°5E 64 D3
Arderin Ireland 53°2N 7°39W 21 B7
Ardgour U.K. 56°45N 5°25W 22 J7
Ardingly U.K. 51°3N 0°4W 31 D8
Ardivachar Pt. U.K. 57°23N 7°26W 22 H3
Ardmore U.S.A. 34°10N 97°8W 111 D7
Ardnamurchan U.K. 56°43N 6°0W 22 J5
Ardnamurchan, Pt. of U.K. 56°43N 6°14W 22 J5
Ardnave Pt. U.K. 55°53N 6°20W 24 D3
Ardrossan U.K. 55°39N 4°49W 24 D6
Ards Pen. U.K. 54°33N 5°34W 19 B10
Arecibo Puerto Rico 18°29N 66°43W 115 D11
Arena, Pt. U.S.A. 38°57N 123°44W 110 C2
Arendal Norway 58°28N 8°46E 63 F5
Arequipa Peru 16°20S 71°30W 120 D2
Arezzo Italy 43°25N 11°53E 68 C4
Argentan France 48°45N 0°1W 66 B3
Argentina ■ S. Amer. 35°0S 66°0W 121 F3
Argentina, L. Argentina 50°10S 73°0W 121 H2
Argostoli Greece 38°11N 20°29E 69 E9

Argun → Russia 53°20N 121°28E 79 A13
Argyle, L. Australia 16°20S 128°40E 98 D4
Argyll U.K. 56°10N 5°20W 24 B5
Argyll & Bute □ U.K. 56°13N 5°28W 24 B4
Ariana Tunisia 36°52N 10°12E 95 A8
Arica Chile 18°32S 70°20W 120 D2
Arinos → Brazil 10°25S 58°20W 120 D4
Aripuanã → Brazil 5°7S 60°25W 120 C3
Arisaig U.K. 56°55N 5°51W 22 J6
Arizona □ U.S.A. 34°0N 112°0W 110 D4
Arkaig, L. U.K. 56°59N 5°10W 22 J7
Arkansas □ U.S.A. 35°0N 92°30W 111 D8
Arkansas → U.S.A. 33°47N 91°4W 111 D8
Arkansas City U.S.A. 37°4N 97°2W 111 C7
Arkhangelsk Russia 64°38N 40°36E 70 B7
Arkle → U.K. 54°24N 1°56W 26 D5
Arklow Ireland 52°48N 6°10E 21 C10
Arles France 43°41N 4°40E 66 E6
Arlington U.S.A. 38°53N 77°7W 112 F9
Arlon Belgium 49°42N 5°49E 64 D3
Armagh U.K. 54°21N 6°39W 19 B8
Armagh □ U.K. 54°18N 6°37W 19 C8
Armavir Russia 45°2N 41°7E 71 E7
Armenia Colombia 4°35N 75°45W 120 B2
Armenia ■ Asia 40°20N 45°0E 71 F7
Arnaud → Canada 59°59N 69°46W 109 D13
Arnhem Neths. 51°58N 5°55E 64 C3
Arnhem, C. Australia 12°20S 137°30E 98 C6
Arnhem Land Australia 13°10S 134°30E 98 C5
Arno → Italy 43°41N 10°17E 68 C4
Arnold U.K. 53°1N 1°7W 27 F6
Arnprior Canada 45°26N 76°21W 112 C9
Arnside U.K. 54°12N 2°49W 26 D3
Arra Mts. Ireland 52°50N 8°22W 20 C6
Arran U.K. 55°34N 5°12W 24 C5
Arranmore Ireland 55°0N 8°30W 18 B4
Arras France 50°17N 2°46E 66 A5
Arrecife Canary Is. 28°57N 13°37W 94 C3
Arrow, L. Ireland 54°3N 8°19W 18 C5
Artemivsk Ukraine 48°35N 38°0E 71 E6
Artigas Uruguay 30°20S 56°30W 121 F4
Artois France 50°20N 2°30E 66 A5
Artux China 39°40N 76°10E 78 D4
Artvin Turkey 41°14N 41°44E 71 F7
Aru, Kepulauan Indonesia 6°0S 134°30E 83 F8
Arua Uganda 3°1N 30°58E 96 D6
Aruanã Brazil 14°54S 51°10W 120 D4
Aruba ☑ W. Indies 12°30N 70°0W 115 E11
Arun → U.K. 50°49N 0°33W 31 E7
Arunachal Pradesh □ India 28°0N 95°0E 85 F19
Arundel U.K. 50°51N 0°33W 31 E7
Arusha Tanzania 3°20S 36°40E 96 E7
Aruwimi →
  Dem. Rep. of the Congo 1°13N 23°36E 96 D4
Arvayheer Mongolia 46°15N 102°48E 78 B9
Arviat Canada 61°6N 93°59W 108 C10
Arxan China 47°11N 119°57E 79 B12
Arzamas Russia 55°27N 43°55E 70 C7
As Sulaymānīyah Iraq 35°35N 45°29E 86 C6
As Sulaymānīyah Si. Arabia 24°9N 47°18E 86 E6
As Suwayq Oman 23°51N 57°26E 89 C6
Aş Şuwayrah Iraq 32°55N 45°0E 86 C6
Asahikawa Japan 43°46N 142°22E 81 B8
Asama-Yama Japan 36°24N 138°31E 81 E6
Asamankese Ghana 5°50N 0°40W 94 G5
Asansol India 23°40N 87°1E 85 H15
Asbestos Canada 45°47N 71°58W 113 C12
Asbury Park U.S.A. 40°13N 74°1W 113 E10
Ascension I. Atl. Oc. 7°57S 14°23W 52 E9
Áscoli Piceno Italy 42°51N 13°34E 68 C5
Ascot U.K. 51°25N 0°40W 31 D7
Aseb Eritrea 13°0N 42°40E 89 E3
Asenovgrad Bulgaria 42°1N 24°51E 69 C11
Asfordby U.K. 52°47N 0°57W 27 G7
Ash Kent, U.K. 51°16N 1°17E 31 D11
Ash Surrey, U.K. 51°15N 0°43W 31 D7
Ashbourne U.K. 53°2N 1°43W 27 F5
Ashburton U.K. 50°30N 3°46W 29 F6
Ashby-de-la-Zouch U.K. 52°46N 1°29W 27 G6
Ashchurch U.K. 52°0N 2°5W 30 C4
Ashdown Forest U.K. 51°3N 0°5E 31 D9
Asheville U.S.A. 35°36N 82°33W 111 C10
Ashford Derby, U.K. 53°14N 1°42W 27 F5
Ashford Kent, U.K. 51°8N 0°53E 31 D10
Ashington U.K. 55°11N 1°33W 26 B5
Ashkhabad Turkmenistan 37°58N 58°24E 87 B9
Ashland Ky., U.S.A. 38°28N 82°38W 112 F6
Ashland Ohio, U.S.A. 40°52N 82°19W 112 E6
Ashland Wis., U.S.A. 46°35N 90°53W 111 A8
Ashqelon Israel 31°42N 34°35E 86 D3
Ashtabula U.S.A. 41°52N 80°47W 112 E7
Ashton-in-Makerfield U.K. 53°30N 2°40W 27 F4
Ashton-under-Lyne U.K. 53°29N 2°6W 27 F4
Ashuanipi, L. Canada 52°45N 66°15W 109 D13
Ashwater U.K. 50°43N 4°19W 29 F5
Ashwick U.K. 51°13N 2°31W 30 D3
Asia 45°0N 75°0E 72 E9
Asinara Italy 41°4N 8°16E 68 D3
'Asīr Si. Arabia 18°40N 42°30E 89 D3
Asir, Ras Somalia 11°55N 51°10E 89 E5
Askrigg U.K. 54°19N 2°6W 26 D4
Aslackby U.K. 52°53N 0°24W 27 G8
Asmara Eritrea 15°19N 38°55E 89 D2
Aspatria U.K. 54°47N 3°19W 26 C2
Aspen U.S.A. 39°11N 106°49W 110 C5
Assal, L. Djibouti 11°40N 42°26E 89 E3
Assen Neths. 53°0N 6°35E 64 B4
Assiniboia Canada 49°40N 105°59W 108 E9
Assiniboine → Canada 49°53N 97°8W 108 E10
Assisi Italy 43°4N 12°37E 68 C5
Assynt U.K. 58°12N 5°12W 22 F7
Assynt, L. U.K. 58°10N 5°3W 22 F7
Astana Kazakhstan 51°10N 71°30E 76 D8
Asti Italy 44°54N 8°12E 68 B3
Astipálaia Greece 36°32N 26°22E 69 F12
Astoria U.S.A. 46°11N 123°50W 110 A2
Astrakhan Russia 46°25N 48°5E 71 E8
Asturias □ Spain 43°15N 6°0W 67 A3
Astwood Bank U.K. 52°15N 1°56W 30 B5

Asunción Paraguay 25°10S 57°30W 121 E4
Aswân Egypt 24°4N 32°57E 95 D12
Aswan High Dam Egypt 23°54N 32°54E 95 D12
Asyût Egypt 27°11N 31°4E 95 C12
Aţ Ţā'if Si. Arabia 21°5N 40°27E 89 C3
Atacama, Desierto de Chile 24°0S 69°20W 121 E3
Atatürk Baraji Turkey 37°28N 38°30E 71 G6
Atbara Sudan 17°42N 33°59E 95 E12
Atbara → Sudan 17°40N 33°56E 95 E12
Atchafalaya B. U.S.A. 29°25N 91°25W 111 E8
Athabasca Canada 54°45N 113°20W 108 D8
Athabasca → Canada 58°40N 110°50W 108 D8
Athabasca, L. Canada 59°15N 109°15W 108 D9
Athboy Ireland 53°36N 6°56W 19 D8
Athenry Ireland 53°18N 8°44W 20 B5
Athens Greece 37°58N 23°43E 69 F10
Athens Ga., U.S.A. 33°57N 83°23W 111 D10
Athens Ohio, U.S.A. 39°20N 82°6W 112 F6
Atherstone U.K. 52°35N 1°33W 27 G5
Atherton U.K. 53°32N 2°30W 27 F4
Athlone Ireland 53°25N 7°56W 20 B7
Atholl, Forest of U.K. 56°51N 3°50W 23 J10
Athos Greece 40°9N 24°22E 69 D11
Athy Ireland 53°0N 7°0W 21 B8
Atikokan Canada 48°45N 91°37W 112 A2
Atka I. U.S.A. 52°7N 174°30E 108 D2
Atlanta U.S.A. 33°45N 84°23W 111 D10
Atlantic City U.S.A. 39°21N 74°27W 113 F10
Atlantic Ocean 0°0 20°0W 50 D8
Atlas Saharien Algeria 33°30N 1°0E 94 B6
Atlin Canada 59°31N 133°41W 108 D6
Attawapiskat Canada 52°56N 82°24W 109 D11
Attawapiskat → Canada 52°57N 82°18W 109 D11
Attleborough U.K. 52°32N 1°1E 31 A11
Attu I. U.S.A. 52°55N 172°55E 108 D1
Atyraū Kazakhstan 47°5N 52°0E 71 E9
Au Sable → U.S.A. 44°25N 83°20W 112 C6
Aube → France 48°34N 3°43E 66 B5
Auburn Ind., U.S.A. 41°22N 85°4W 112 E5
Auburn N.Y., U.S.A. 42°56N 76°34W 112 D9
Aubusson France 45°57N 2°11E 66 D5
Auch France 43°39N 0°36E 66 E4
Auchterarder U.K. 56°18N 3°41W 25 B8
Auchtermuchty U.K. 56°18N 3°13W 25 B9
Auckland N.Z. 36°52S 174°46E 99 H13
Auckland Is. Pac. Oc. 50°40S 166°5E 102 N8
Aude → France 43°13N 3°14E 66 E5
Audlem U.K. 52°59N 2°30W 27 G4
Aughnacloy U.K. 54°25N 6°59W 19 C8
Augsburg Germany 48°25N 10°52E 64 D6
Augusta Australia 34°19S 115°9E 98 G2
Augusta U.S.A. 33°28N 81°58W 111 D10
Aunis France 46°5N 0°50E 66 C3
Aurangabad Bihar, India 24°45N 84°18E 85 G14
Aurangabad Maharashtra,
  India 19°50N 75°23E 84 K9
Aurillac France 44°55N 2°26E 66 D5
Aurora Colo., U.S.A. 39°43N 104°49W 110 C6
Aurora Ill., U.S.A. 41°45N 88°19W 112 E3
Austin U.S.A. 30°17N 97°45W 110 D7
Australia ■ Oceania 23°0S 135°0E 98 E3
Australian Capital Territory □
  Australia 35°30S 149°0E 98 H8
Austria ■ Europe 47°0N 14°0E 64 E8
Autun France 46°58N 4°17E 66 C6
Auvergne □ France 45°20N 3°15E 66 D5
Auvergne, Mts. d' France 45°20N 2°55E 66 D5
Auxerre France 47°48N 3°32E 66 C5
Avallon France 47°30N 3°53E 66 C5
Avaré Brazil 23°4S 48°58W 122 D1
Avebury U.K. 51°26N 1°50W 30 D5
Avellaneda Argentina 34°40S 58°22W 121 F4
Avellino Italy 40°54N 14°47E 68 D6
Aversa Italy 40°58N 14°12E 68 D6
Aveton Gifford U.K. 50°18N 3°50W 29 G6
Aveyron □ France 44°5N 1°16E 66 D4
Aviemore U.K. 57°12N 3°50W 23 H10
Avignon France 43°57N 4°50E 66 E6
Ávila Spain 40°39N 4°43W 67 B3
Avilés Spain 43°35N 5°57W 67 A3
Avoca → Ireland 52°48N 6°10W 21 C10
Avon → Bristol, U.K. 51°29N 2°41W 30 D3
Avon → Dorset, U.K. 50°44N 1°46W 30 E5
Avon → Warks., U.K. 52°0N 2°8W 30 B5
Avonmouth U.K. 51°30N 2°42W 30 D3
Avranches France 48°40N 1°20W 66 B3
Awasa Ethiopia 7°2N 38°28E 89 F2
Awash Ethiopia 9°1N 40°10E 89 F3
Awbārī, Idehan Libya 27°10N 11°30E 95 C8
Awe, L. U.K. 56°17N 5°16W 24 B5
Axbridge U.K. 51°17N 2°49W 30 D3
Axe → U.K. 50°42N 3°4W 29 F7
Axe Edge U.K. 53°14N 1°57W 27 F5
Axel Heiberg I. Canada 80°0N 90°0W 109 B11
Axholme, Isle of U.K. 53°32N 0°50W 27 E7
Axios → Greece 40°57N 22°35E 69 D10
Axminster U.K. 50°46N 3°0W 29 F8
Axmouth U.K. 50°42N 3°3W 29 F7
Ayacucho Argentina 37°5S 58°20W 121 F4
Ayacucho Peru 13°0S 74°0W 120 D2
Ayakkum Hu China 37°30N 89°20E 78 D6
Aydın Turkey 37°51N 27°51E 71 G4
Aydingkol Hu China 42°40N 89°15E 78 C6
Ayers Rock = Uluru Australia 25°23S 131°5E 98 F5
Aylesbury U.K. 51°49N 0°49W 31 C7
Aylesford U.K. 51°18N 0°30E 31 D10
Aylmer, L. Canada 64°5N 108°30W 108 C8
Aylsham U.K. 52°48N 1°15E 31 A11
Aynho U.K. 52°0N 1°15W 30 B6
Ayr U.K. 55°28N 4°38W 24 D6
Ayr → U.K. 55°28N 4°38W 24 D6
Aysgarth U.K. 54°18N 2°1W 26 D4
Ayton Borders, U.K. 55°51N 2°6W 25 C11
Ayton N. Yorks., U.K. 54°15N 0°28W 26 D7
Ayutthaya Thailand 14°25N 100°30E 82 B2
Ayvalık Turkey 39°20N 26°46E 71 G4
Az Zarqā Jordan 32°5N 36°4E 86 C4
Az Zāwiyah Libya 32°52N 12°56E 95 B8
Azad Kashmir □ Pakistan 33°50N 73°50E 84 B8
Azamgarh India 26°5N 83°13E 85 F13

Āzarbāyjān □ *Iran* 37°0N 44°30E **86** B6
Azare *Nigeria* 11°55N 10°10E **94** F8
Azerbaijan ■ *Asia* 40°20N 48°0E **71** F8
Azores *Atl. Oc.* 38°0N 27°0W **91** C1
Azov *Russia* 47°3N 39°25E **71** E6
Azov, Sea of *Europe* 46°0N 36°30E **71** E6
Azuero, Pen. de *Panama* 7°30N 80°30W **115** F8
Azul *Argentina* 36°42S 59°43W **121** F4

B

Bab el Mandeb *Red Sea* 12°35N 43°25E **89** E3
Bābā, Koh-i- *Afghan.* 34°30N 67°0E **84** B5
Babine L. *Canada* 54°48N 126°0W **108** D7
Babol *Iran* 36°40N 52°50E **87** B8
Babruysk *Belarus* 53°10N 29°15E **65** B15
Babuyan Chan. *Phil.* 18°40N 121°30E **83** A6
Babylon *Iraq* 32°34N 44°22E **86** C6
Bac Lieu *Vietnam* 9°17N 105°43E **82** C3
Bacabal *Brazil* 4°15S 44°45W **120** C5
Bacău *Romania* 46°35N 26°55E **65** E14
Back → *Canada* 65°10N 104°0W **108** C9
Bacolod *Phil.* 10°40N 122°57E **83** B6
Bacton *U.K.* 52°52N 1°27E **31** A11
Bacup *U.K.* 53°42N 2°11W **27** E4
Bad Axe *U.S.A.* 43°48N 83°0W **112** D6
Badain Jaran Desert *China* 40°23N 102°0E **78** C9
Badajoz *Spain* 38°50N 6°59W **67** C2
Badakhshān □ *Afghan.* 36°30N 71°0E **87** B12
Badalona *Spain* 41°26N 2°15E **67** B7
Baden-Württemberg □ *Germany* 48°20N 8°40E **64** D5
Badenoch *U.K.* 56°50N 4°15W **23** J9
Badlands *U.S.A.* 43°55N 102°30W **110** B6
Baffin B. *N. Amer.* 72°0N 64°0W **109** B13
Baffin I. *Canada* 68°0N 75°0W **109** C12
Bafoulabé *Mali* 13°50N 10°55W **94** F3
Bafoussam *Cameroon* 5°28N 10°25E **96** C2
Bafra *Turkey* 41°34N 35°54E **71** F6
Bagamoyo *Tanzania* 6°28S 38°55E **96** F7
Bagé *Brazil* 31°20S 54°15W **121** F4
Bagenalstown *Ireland* 52°42N 6°58W **21** C9
Baggy Pt. *U.K.* 51°8N 4°16W **29** E5
Baghdād *Iraq* 33°20N 44°23E **86** C6
Baghlān *Afghan.* 32°12N 68°46E **87** B12
Bagshot *U.K.* 51°22N 0°41W **31** D7
Baguio *Phil.* 16°26N 120°34E **83** A6
Bahamas ■ *N. Amer.* 24°0N 75°0W **115** C10
Baharampur *India* 24°2N 88°27E **85** G16
Bahawalpur *Pakistan* 29°24N 71°40E **84** E7
Bahía = Salvador *Brazil* 13°0S 38°30W **122** B3
Bahía □ *Brazil* 12°0S 42°0W **122** B2
Bahía, Is. de la *Honduras* 16°45N 86°15W **114** D7
Bahía Blanca *Argentina* 38°35S 62°13W **121** F3
Bahir Dar *Ethiopia* 11°37N 37°10E **89** E2
Bahr el Ghazal □ *South Sudan* 7°30N 25°30E **95** G11
Bahraich *India* 27°38N 81°37E **85** F12
Bahrain ■ *Asia* 26°0N 50°35E **87** E7
Baia Mare *Romania* 47°40N 23°35E **65** E12
Baicheng *China* 45°38N 122°42E **79** B13
Baie-Comeau *Canada* 49°12N 68°10W **109** E13
Baie-St-Paul *Canada* 47°28N 70°32W **113** B12
Baie Verte *Canada* 49°55N 56°12W **109** E14
Ba'ījī *Iraq* 35°0N 43°30E **86** C5
Baikal, L. *Russia* 53°0N 108°0E **77** D11
Baildon *U.K.* 53°51N 1°46W **27** E5
Baile Sear = Baleshare *U.K.* 57°31N 7°22W **22** G3
Bain → *U.K.* 53°6N 0°12W **27** F8
Bainbridge *U.K.* 54°18N 2°6W **26** D4
Baja, Pta. *Mexico* 29°58N 115°49W **114** B1
Baja California *Mexico* 31°10N 115°12W **114** A1
Baker, L. *Canada* 64°0N 96°0W **108** C10
Baker City *U.S.A.* 44°47N 117°50W **110** B3
Baker I. *Pac. Oc.* 0°10N 176°35W **99** A15
Baker Lake *Canada* 64°20N 96°3W **108** C10
Bakers Dozen Is. *Canada* 56°45N 78°45W **109** D12
Bakersfield *U.S.A.* 35°23N 119°1W **110** C3
Bakewell *U.K.* 53°13N 1°40W **27** F5
Baku *Azerbaijan* 40°29N 49°56E **71** F8
Bala *U.K.* 52°54N 3°36W **28** B6
Bala, L. *U.K.* 52°53N 3°37W **28** B6
Balabac Str. *E. Indies* 7°53N 117°5E **82** C5
Balaghat Ra. *India* 18°50N 76°30E **84** K10
Balaklava *Ukraine* 44°30N 33°30E **71** F5
Balakovo *Russia* 52°4N 47°55E **70** D8
Balashov *Russia* 51°30N 43°10E **71** D7
Balaton *Hungary* 46°50N 17°40E **65** E9
Balbi, Mt. *Papua N. G.* 5°55S 154°58E **99** B10
Balbina, Represa de *Brazil* 2°0S 59°30W **120** C4
Balbriggan *Ireland* 53°37N 6°11W **19** D9
Balcarce *Argentina* 38°0S 58°10W **121** F4
Balderton *U.K.* 53°3N 0°47W **27** F7
Baldock *U.K.* 52°0N 0°11W **31** C8
Baldoyle *Ireland* 53°24N 6°8W **21** B10
Baldwin *U.S.A.* 43°54N 85°51W **112** D5
Baldy Peak *U.S.A.* 33°54N 109°34W **110** D5
Balearic Is. *Spain* 39°30N 3°0E **67** C7
Baleine → *Canada* 58°15N 67°40W **109** D13
Baleshare *U.K.* 57°31N 7°22W **22** G3
Baleshwar *India* 21°35N 87°3E **85** J15
Bali *Indonesia* 8°20S 115°0E **82** F4
Balıkeşir *Turkey* 39°39N 27°53E **71** G4
Balikpapan *Indonesia* 1°10S 116°55E **82** E5
Balkan Mts. *Bulgaria* 43°15N 23°0E **69** C10
Balkanabat *Turkmenistan* 39°30N 54°22E **87** B8
Balkhash, L. *Kazakhstan* 46°0N 74°50E **76** E8
Ballachulish *U.K.* 56°41N 5°8W **22** J7
Ballaghaderreen *Ireland* 53°55N 8°34W **18** D4
Ballantrae *U.K.* 55°6N 4°59W **24** D6
Ballarat *Australia* 37°33S 143°50E **98** H7
Ballater *U.K.* 57°3N 3°3W **23** H11
Ballenas, B. de *Mexico* 26°45N 113°26W **114** B2
Balleny Is. *Antarctica* 66°30S 163°0E **55** C11
Ballina *Ireland* 54°7N 9°9W **18** C3
Ballinasloe *Ireland* 53°20N 8°13W **20** B6
Ballinincollig *Ireland* 51°33N 8°35W **20** E5
Ballinrobe *Ireland* 53°38N 9°13W **18** D3
Ballinskelligs B. *Ireland* 51°48N 10°13W **20** E2
Ballybunion *Ireland* 52°31N 9°40W **20** C3
Ballycastle *U.K.* 55°12N 6°15W **19** A9
Ballyclare *U.K.* 54°46N 6°0W **19** B10
Ballycroy △ *Ireland* 54°5N 9°50W **18** C2
Ballycummin *Ireland* 52°38N 8°38W **20** C5
Ballyhaunis *Ireland* 53°46N 8°46W **18** D4
Ballyhoura Mts. *Ireland* 52°18N 8°33W **20** D5
Ballymena *U.K.* 54°52N 6°17W **19** B9
Ballymoney *U.K.* 55°5N 6°31W **19** A8
Ballymote *Ireland* 54°5N 8°31W **18** C4
Ballynahinch *U.K.* 54°24N 5°54W **19** C10
Ballyquintin Pt. *U.K.* 54°20N 5°30W **19** C11
Ballyshannon *Ireland* 54°30N 8°11W **18** B5
Balmoral Forest *U.K.* 57°0N 3°15W **23** J11
Balrampur *India* 27°30N 82°20E **85** F13
Balsas → *Mexico* 17°55N 102°10W **114** D4
Baltic Sea *Europe* 57°0N 19°0E **63** F7
Baltimore *Ireland* 51°29N 9°22W **20** F4
Baltimore *U.S.A.* 39°17N 76°36W **112** F9
Baluchistan □ *Pakistan* 27°30N 65°0E **84** F4
Bam *Iran* 29°7N 58°14E **87** D9
Bamako *Mali* 12°34N 7°55W **94** F4
Bambari *C.A.R.* 5°40N 20°35E **96** C4
Bamberg *Germany* 49°54N 10°54E **64** D6
Bamburgh *U.K.* 55°37N 1°43W **26** A5
Bamenda *Cameroon* 5°57N 10°11E **96** C2
Bamford *U.K.* 53°22N 1°41W **27** F5
Bampton *Devon, U.K.* 50°59N 3°29W **29** F7
Bampton *Oxon., U.K.* 51°44N 1°32W **30** C5
Banaba *Kiribati* 0°45S 169°50E **102** H8
Bananal, I. do *Brazil* 11°30S 50°30W **120** D4
Banbridge *U.K.* 54°22N 6°16W **19** C9
Banbury *U.K.* 52°4N 1°20W **30** B6
Banchory *U.K.* 57°3N 2°29W **23** H13
Bancroft *Canada* 45°3N 77°51W **112** C9
Banda *India* 25°30N 80°26E **84** G12
Banda, Kepulauan *Indonesia* 4°37S 129°50E **83** E7
Banda Aceh *Indonesia* 5°35N 95°20E **82** C1
Banda Sea *Indonesia* 6°0S 130°0E **83** F7
Bandar-e Abbās *Iran* 27°15N 56°15E **87** E9
Bandar-e Anzalī *Iran* 37°30N 49°30E **86** B7
Bandar-e Ma'shur *Iran* 30°35N 49°10E **86** D7
Bandar-e Torkeman *Iran* 37°0N 54°10E **87** B8
Bandar Lampung *Indonesia* 5°20S 105°10E **82** F3
Bandar Seri Begawan *Brunei* 4°52N 115°0E **82** C4
Bandeira, Pico da *Brazil* 20°26S 41°47W **122** D2
Bandırma *Turkey* 40°20N 28°0E **71** F4
Bandon *Ireland* 51°44N 8°44W **20** E5
Bandon → *Ireland* 51°43N 8°37W **20** E5
Bandundu *Dem. Rep. of the Congo* 3°15S 17°22E **96** E3
Bandung *Indonesia* 6°54S 107°36E **82** F3
Banes *Cuba* 21°0N 75°42W **115** C9
Banff *Canada* 51°10N 115°34W **108** D8
Banff *U.K.* 57°40N 2°33W **23** G12
Bangalore *India* 12°59N 77°40E **84** N10
Bangassou *C.A.R.* 4°55N 23°7E **96** D4
Banggai, Kepulauan *Indonesia* 1°40S 123°30E **83** E6
Bangka *Indonesia* 2°0S 105°50E **82** E3
Bangkok *Thailand* 13°45N 100°35E **82** B2
Bangladesh ■ *Asia* 24°0N 90°0E **85** H17
Bangor *Down, U.K.* 54°40N 5°40W **19** B10
Bangor *Gwynedd, U.K.* 53°14N 4°8W **28** A5
Bangui *C.A.R.* 4°23N 18°35E **96** D3
Bangweulu, L. *Zambia* 11°0S 30°0E **96** G6
Banham *U.K.* 52°27N 1°2E **31** B11
Baní *Dom. Rep.* 18°16N 70°22W **115** D10
Banja Luka *Bos.-H.* 44°49N 17°11E **68** B7
Banjarmasin *Indonesia* 3°20S 114°35E **82** E4
Banjul *Gambia* 13°28N 16°40W **94** F2
Bankend *U.K.* 55°1N 3°33W **25** D8
Banks I. *Canada* 73°15N 121°30W **108** B7
Banks Is. *Vanuatu* 13°50S 167°30E **99** C12
Bann → *U.K.* 55°8N 6°41W **19** A8
Bannockburn *U.K.* 56°5N 3°55W **25** B8
Bannu *Pakistan* 33°0N 70°18E **84** C7
Banská Bystrica *Slovak Rep.* 48°46N 19°14E **65** D10
Bantry *Ireland* 51°41N 9°27W **20** E4
Bantry B. *Ireland* 51°37N 9°44W **20** E3
Banwell *U.K.* 51°19N 2°52W **30** D3
Banyak, Kepulauan *Indonesia* 2°10N 97°10E **82** D1
Banyuwangi *Indonesia* 8°13S 114°21E **82** F4
Bao'an *China* 22°34N 113°52E **79** a
Baoding *China* 38°50N 115°28E **79** D12
Baoji *China* 34°20N 107°5E **78** E10
Baoshan *China* 25°10N 99°5E **78** F8
Baotou *China* 40°32N 110°2E **79** C11
Ba'qūbah *Iraq* 33°45N 44°50E **86** C6
Bar Harbor *U.S.A.* 44°23N 68°13W **113** C13
Bar-le-Duc *France* 48°47N 5°10E **66** B6
Baraboo *U.S.A.* 43°28N 89°45W **112** D3
Baracoa *Cuba* 20°20N 74°30W **115** C10
Barahona *Dom. Rep.* 18°13N 71°7W **115** D10
Barail Range *India* 25°15N 93°20E **85** G18
Barakaldo *Spain* 43°18N 2°59W **67** A4
Baranavichy *Belarus* 53°10N 26°0E **65** B14
Baranof I. *U.S.A.* 57°0N 135°0W **108** D6
Barbacena *Brazil* 21°15S 43°56W **122** D2
Barbados ■ *W. Indies* 13°10N 59°30W **114** c
Barberton *U.S.A.* 41°1N 81°39W **112** E7
Barcelona *Spain* 41°22N 2°10E **67** B7
Barcelona *Venezuela* 10°10N 64°40W **120** A3
Barddhaman *India* 23°14N 87°39E **85** H15
Bardīyah *Libya* 31°45N 25°5E **95** B10
Bardney *U.K.* 53°13N 0°19W **27** F8
Bardsey I. *U.K.* 52°45N 4°47W **28** B4
Bardstown *U.S.A.* 37°49N 85°28W **112** G5
Bareilly *India* 28°22N 79°27E **84** E11
Barents Sea *Arctic* 73°0N 39°0E **54** B9
Barford *U.K.* 52°16N 1°35W **30** B5
Bargoed *U.K.* 51°42N 3°15W **28** D7
Barham *U.K.* 51°12N 1°11E **31** D11
Barhi *India* 24°15N 85°25E **85** G14
Bari *Italy* 41°0N 16°51E **68** D7
Bari Doab *Pakistan* 30°20N 73°0E **84** D8
Barīm *Yemen* 12°39N 43°25E **90** E8
Barinas *Venezuela* 8°36N 70°15W **120** B2
Baring, C. *Canada* 70°0N 117°30W **108** C8
Barisal *Bangla.* 22°45N 90°20E **85** H17
Barking and Dagenham □ *U.K.* 51°32N 0°10E **31** C9
Barkly Tableland *Australia* 17°50S 136°40E **98** D6
Barlborough *U.K.* 53°17N 1°17W **27** F6
Barlby *U.K.* 53°48N 1°2W **27** E6
Barlee, L. *Australia* 29°15S 119°30E **98** F2
Barletta *Italy* 41°19N 16°17E **68** D7
Barmby Moor *U.K.* 53°56N 0°49W **27** E7
Barmer *India* 25°45N 71°20E **84** G7
Barmoor Castle *U.K.* 55°39N 1°59W **26** A5
Barmouth *U.K.* 52°44N 4°4W **28** B5
Barnard Castle *U.K.* 54°33N 1°55W **26** C5
Barnaul *Russia* 53°20N 83°40E **76** D9
Barnet □ *U.K.* 51°38N 0°9W **31** C8
Barnetby le Wold *U.K.* 53°34N 0°24W **27** E8
Barnoldswick *U.K.* 53°55N 2°11W **27** E4
Barnsley *U.K.* 53°34N 1°27W **27** E6
Barnstaple *U.K.* 51°5N 4°4W **29** E5
Barnstaple Bay = Bideford Bay *U.K.* 51°5N 4°20W **29** E5
Barotseland *Zambia* 15°0S 24°0E **97** H4
Barques, Pt. Aux *U.S.A.* 44°4N 82°58W **112** C6
Barquísimeto *Venezuela* 10°4N 69°19W **120** A3
Barra *Brazil* 11°5S 43°10W **122** B2
Barra *U.K.* 57°0N 7°29W **22** J2
Barra, Sd. of *U.K.* 57°4N 7°25W **22** H3
Barra do Corda *Brazil* 5°30S 45°10W **120** C5
Barra do Piraí *Brazil* 22°30S 43°50W **122** D2
Barra Hd. *U.K.* 56°47N 7°40W **22** J2
Barra Mansa *Brazil* 22°35S 44°12W **122** D2
Barrancabermeja *Colombia* 7°0N 73°50W **120** B2
Barranquilla *Colombia* 11°0N 74°50W **120** A2
Barre *U.S.A.* 44°12N 72°30W **113** C11
Barreiras *Brazil* 12°8S 45°0W **122** B2
Barreiro *Portugal* 38°39N 9°5W **67** C1
Barreiros *Brazil* 8°49S 35°12W **122** A3
Barretos *Brazil* 20°30S 48°35W **122** D1
Barrhead *U.K.* 55°48N 4°23W **24** C7
Barrie *Canada* 44°24N 79°40W **109** E12
Barrow *U.S.A.* 71°18N 156°47W **108** B4
Barrow → *Ireland* 52°25N 6°58W **21** D9
Barrow-in-Furness *U.K.* 54°7N 3°14W **26** D2
Barrow upon Humber *U.K.* 53°41N 0°23W **27** E8
Barrowford *U.K.* 53°51N 2°14W **27** E4
Barry *U.K.* 51°24N 3°16W **29** E7
Barry I. *U.K.* 51°23N 3°16W **29** E7
Barry's Bay *Canada* 45°29N 77°41W **112** C9
Barstow *U.S.A.* 34°54N 117°1W **110** D3
Bartlesville *U.S.A.* 36°45N 95°59W **111** C7
Barton *U.K.* 54°29N 1°38W **26** D5
Barton-upon-Humber *U.K.* 53°41N 0°25W **27** E8
Barú, Volcan *Panama* 8°55N 82°35W **115** F8
Baruun-Urt *Mongolia* 46°46N 113°15E **79** B11
Barwell *U.K.* 52°35N 1°21W **27** G6
Barysaw *Belarus* 54°17N 28°28E **65** A15
Bashkortostan □ *Russia* 54°0N 57°0E **70** D10
Basilan I. *Phil.* 6°35N 122°0E **83** C6
Basildon *U.K.* 51°34N 0°28E **31** C9
Basingstoke *U.K.* 51°15N 1°5W **30** D6
Baskatong, Rés. *Canada* 46°46N 75°50W **113** B10
Basle *Switz.* 47°35N 7°35E **64** E4
Basque Provinces = País Vasco □ *Spain* 42°50N 2°45W **67** A4
Basra *Iraq* 30°30N 47°50E **86** D6
Bass Rock *U.K.* 56°5N 2°38W **25** B10
Bass Str. *Australia* 39°15S 146°30E **98** H8
Bassas da India *Ind. Oc.* 22°0S 39°0E **97** J7
Basse-Terre *Guadeloupe* 16°0N 61°44W **115** D12
Bassein *Burma* 16°45N 94°30E **85** L19
Bassenthwaite L. *U.K.* 54°40N 3°14W **26** C2
Basseterre *St. Kitts & Nevis* 17°17N 62°43W **115** D12
Basti *India* 26°52N 82°55E **85** F13
Bastia *France* 42°40N 9°30E **66** E8
Baston *U.K.* 52°43N 0°21W **27** G8
Bata *Eq. Guin.* 1°57N 9°50E **96** D1
Batabanó, G. de *Cuba* 22°30N 82°30W **115** C8
Batangas *Phil.* 13°35N 121°10E **83** B6
Batatais *Brazil* 20°54S 47°37W **122** D1
Batavia *U.S.A.* 43°0N 78°11W **112** D8
Bataysk *Russia* 47°3N 39°45E **71** E6
Batdambang *Cambodia* 13°7N 103°12E **82** B2
Bath *U.K.* 51°23N 2°22W **30** D4
Bath *Maine, U.S.A.* 43°55N 69°49W **113** D13
Bath *N.Y., U.S.A.* 42°20N 77°19W **112** D9
Bathford *U.K.* 51°24N 2°18W **30** D4
Bathgate *U.K.* 55°54N 3°39W **25** C8
Bathsheba *Barbados* 13°13N 59°32W **114** c
Bathurst *Australia* 33°25S 149°31E **98** G8
Bathurst *Canada* 47°37N 65°43W **109** E13
Bathurst, C. *Canada* 70°34N 128°0W **108** B7
Bathurst Inlet *Canada* 66°50N 108°1W **108** C9
Batley *U.K.* 53°43N 1°38W **27** E5
Batman *Turkey* 37°55N 41°5E **71** G7
Batna *Algeria* 35°34N 6°15E **94** A7
Baton Rouge *U.S.A.* 30°27N 91°11W **111** D8
Batticaloa *Sri Lanka* 7°43N 81°45E **84** R12
Battle *U.K.* 50°55N 0°30E **31** E9
Battle Creek *U.S.A.* 42°19N 85°11W **112** D5
Batu, Kepulauan *Indonesia* 0°30S 98°25E **82** E1
Batu Pahat *Malaysia* 1°50N 102°56E **82** D2
Batumi *Georgia* 41°39N 41°44E **71** F7
Bauld, C. *Canada* 51°38N 55°26W **109** D14
Bauru *Brazil* 22°10S 49°0W **122** D1
Bavaria = Bayern □ *Germany* 48°50N 12°0E **64** D6
Bawdsey *U.K.* 52°1N 1°27E **31** B11
Bawtry *U.K.* 53°26N 1°2W **27** F6
Bay City *U.S.A.* 43°36N 83°54W **112** D6
Bayamo *Cuba* 20°20N 76°40W **115** C9
Bayan Har Shan *China* 34°0N 98°0E **78** E8
Bayan Obo *China* 41°52N 109°59E **79** C10
Baydhabo *Somalia* 3°8N 43°30E **89** G3
Bayern □ *Germany* 48°50N 12°0E **64** D6
Bayeux *France* 49°17N 0°42W **66** B3
Bayonne *France* 43°30N 1°28W **66** E3
Beachley *U.K.* 51°37N 2°39W **30** C3
Beachy Hd. *U.K.* 50°44N 0°15E **31** E9
Beacon *U.S.A.* 41°30N 73°58W **113** E11
Beaconsfield *U.K.* 51°36N 0°38W **31** C7
Beadnell *U.K.* 55°33N 1°38W **26** A5
Beagle, Canal *S. Amer.* 55°0S 68°30W **121** H3
Beaminster *U.K.* 50°48N 2°44W **30** E3
Bear → *U.S.A.* 41°30N 112°8W **110** B4
Bear I. *Arctic* 74°30N 19°0E **54** B8
Bear I. *Ireland* 51°38N 9°50W **20** E3
Bear L. *U.S.A.* 41°59N 111°21W **110** B4
Beardmore Glacier *Antarctica* 84°30S 170°0E **55** E11
Beardstown *U.S.A.* 40°1N 90°26W **112** E2
Béarn *France* 43°20N 0°30W **66** E3
Bearsden *U.K.* 55°55N 4°21W **24** C7
Bearsted *U.K.* 51°16N 0°35E **31** D10
Beatrice *U.S.A.* 40°16N 96°45W **111** B7
Beattock *U.K.* 55°20N 3°28W **25** D9
Beattock Summit *U.K.* 55°25N 3°32W **25** D8
Beauce, Plaine de la *France* 48°10N 1°45E **66** B4
Beaufort Sea *Arctic* 72°0N 140°0W **54** B1
Beaufort West *S. Africa* 32°18S 22°36E **97** L4
Beauharnois *Canada* 45°20N 73°52W **113** C11
Beaulieu *U.K.* 50°48N 1°27W **30** E6
Beauly *U.K.* 57°30N 4°28W **23** H9
Beauly → *U.K.* 57°29N 4°27W **23** H9
Beauly Firth *U.K.* 57°30N 4°20W **23** H9
Beaumaris *U.K.* 53°16N 4°6W **28** A5
Beaumont *U.S.A.* 30°5N 94°6W **111** D8
Beaune *France* 47°2N 4°50E **66** C6
Beauvais *France* 49°25N 2°8E **66** B5
Beaver → *Canada* 55°26N 107°45W **108** D9
Beaver Creek *Canada* 63°0N 141°0W **108** C5
Beaver Dam *U.S.A.* 43°28N 88°50W **112** D3
Beaver Falls *U.S.A.* 40°46N 80°20W **112** E7
Beaver I. *U.S.A.* 45°40N 85°33W **112** C5
Beawar *India* 26°3N 74°18E **84** F9
Bebedouro *Brazil* 21°0S 48°25W **122** D1
Bebington *U.K.* 53°22N 3°0W **27** F3
Beccles *U.K.* 52°27N 1°35E **31** B12
Béchar *Algeria* 31°38N 2°18W **94** B5
Beckermet *U.K.* 54°27N 3°30W **26** D1
Beckfoot *U.K.* 54°50N 3°24W **26** C2
Beckingham *U.K.* 53°24N 0°50W **27** F7
Beckley *U.S.A.* 37°47N 81°11W **112** G7
Bedale *U.K.* 54°18N 1°36W **26** D5
Beddgelert *U.K.* 53°1N 4°6W **28** A5
Bedford *U.K.* 52°8N 0°28W **31** B8
Bedford *Ind., U.S.A.* 38°52N 86°29W **112** F4
Bedford *Va., U.S.A.* 37°20N 79°31W **112** G8
Bedford □ *U.K.* 52°4N 0°28W **31** B8
Bedford Level *U.K.* 52°32N 0°7W **31** A8
Bedlington *U.K.* 55°8N 1°35W **26** B5
Bedworth *U.K.* 52°29N 1°28W **30** B6
Beeford *U.K.* 53°58N 0°17W **27** E8
Beer *U.K.* 50°41N 3°6W **29** F7
Be'er Sheva *Israel* 31°15N 34°48E **86** D3
Beeston *U.K.* 52°56N 1°14W **27** G6
Behchoko *Canada* 62°50N 116°3W **108** C8
Bei Jiang → *China* 23°2N 112°58E **79** G11
Bei Shan *China* 41°30N 96°0E **78** C8
Bei'an *China* 48°10N 126°20E **79** B14
Beighton *U.K.* 53°21N 1°20W **27** F6
Beihai *China* 21°28N 109°6E **79** G10
Beijing *China* 39°53N 116°21E **79** D12
Beinn na Faoghla = Benbecula *U.K.* 57°26N 7°21W **22** H3
Beira *Mozam.* 19°50S 34°52E **97** H6
Beirut *Lebanon* 33°53N 35°31E **86** C3
Beitbridge *Zimbabwe* 22°12S 30°0E **97** J6
Beith *U.K.* 55°45N 4°38W **24** C6
Béja *Tunisia* 36°43N 9°12E **95** A7
Bejaïa *Algeria* 36°42N 5°2E **94** A7
Békéscsaba *Hungary* 46°40N 21°5E **65** E11
Bela *Pakistan* 26°12N 66°20E **84** F5
Belarus ■ *Europe* 53°30N 27°0E **70** D4
Belau = Palau ■ *Palau* 7°30N 134°30E **102** G5
Belbroughton *U.K.* 52°24N 2°7W **30** B4
Belcher Chan. *Canada* 77°15N 95°0W **109** B10
Belcher Is. *Canada* 56°15N 78°45W **109** D12
Beledweyne *Somalia* 4°30N 45°5E **89** G4
Belém *Brazil* 1°20S 48°30W **120** C5
Belep, Îs. *N. Cal.* 19°45S 163°40E **99** D11
Belfast *U.K.* 54°37N 5°56W **19** B10
Belfast *U.S.A.* 44°26N 69°1W **113** C13
Belfast L. *U.K.* 54°40N 5°50W **19** B10
Belford *U.K.* 55°36N 1°49W **26** A5
Belfort *France* 47°38N 6°50E **66** C7
Belgaum *India* 15°55N 74°35E **84** M9
Belgium ■ *Europe* 50°30N 5°0E **64** C3
Belgorod *Russia* 50°35N 36°35E **71** D6
Belgrade *Serbia* 44°50N 20°37E **69** B9
Belitung *Indonesia* 3°10S 107°50E **82** E3
Belize ■ *Cent. Amer.* 17°0N 88°30W **114** D7
Belize City *Belize* 17°25N 88°10W **114** D7
Bell Peninsula *Canada* 63°50N 82°0W **109** C11
Bell Ville *Argentina* 32°40S 62°40W **121** F3
Bella Coola *Canada* 52°25N 126°40W **108** D7
Bellaire *U.S.A.* 40°1N 80°45W **112** E7
Bellary *India* 15°10N 76°56E **84** M10
Belle Fourche → *U.S.A.* 44°26N 102°18W **110** B6
Belle-Île *France* 47°20N 3°10W **66** C2
Belle Isle *Canada* 51°57N 55°25W **109** D14
Belle Isle, Str. of *Canada* 51°30N 56°30W **109** D14
Bellefontaine *U.S.A.* 40°22N 83°46W **112** E6
Belleplaine *Barbados* 13°15N 59°34W **114** c
Belleville *Canada* 44°10N 77°23W **109** E12
Belleville *U.S.A.* 38°31N 89°59W **112** F3
Bellingham *U.K.* 55°9N 2°16W **26** B4
Bellingham *U.S.A.* 48°46N 122°29W **110** A2
Bellingshausen Sea *Antarctica* 66°0S 80°0W **55** C17
Bellinzona *Switz.* 46°11N 9°1E **64** E5
Belmonte *Brazil* 16°0S 39°0W **122** C3
Belmopan *Belize* 17°18N 88°30W **114** D7
Belmullet *Ireland* 54°14N 9°58W **18** C2
Belo Horizonte *Brazil* 19°55S 43°56W **122** C2
Belo Jardim *Brazil* 8°20S 36°26W **122** A3
Belogorsk *Russia* 51°0N 128°20E **77** D13
Beloit *U.S.A.* 42°31N 89°2W **112** D3
Belomorsk *Russia* 64°35N 34°54E **70** B5
Beloretsk *Russia* 53°58N 58°24E **70** D10
Beloye, L. *Russia* 60°10N 37°35E **70** B6
Belper *U.K.* 53°2N 1°29W **27** F6
Belsay *U.K.* 55°6N 1°51W **26** B5
Belton *N. Lincs., U.K.* 53°33N 0°48W **27** E7
Belton *Norfolk, U.K.* 52°35N 1°40E **31** A12
Beltsy *Moldova* 47°48N 27°58E **65** E14
Belturbet *Ireland* 54°6N 7°26W **18** C7
Belvidere *U.S.A.* 42°15N 88°50W **112** D3
Bembridge *U.K.* 50°41N 1°5W **30** E6
Bemidji *U.S.A.* 47°28N 94°53W **111** A8
Ben Cruachan *U.K.* 56°26N 5°8W **24** B5
Ben Dearg *U.K.* 57°47N 4°56W **23** G8
Ben Hope *U.K.* 58°25N 4°36W **23** F8
Ben Lawers *U.K.* 56°32N 4°14W **24** A7
Ben Lomond *U.K.* 56°11N 4°38W **24** B6
Ben Macdhui *U.K.* 57°4N 3°40W **23** H10
Ben Mhor *U.K.* 57°15N 7°18W **22** H3
Ben More *Argyll & Bute, U.K.* 56°26N 6°1W **24** B3
Ben More *Stirling, U.K.* 56°23N 4°32W **24** B6
Ben More Assynt *U.K.* 58°8N 4°52W **23** F8
Ben Nevis *U.K.* 56°48N 5°1W **22** J7
Ben Vorlich *U.K.* 56°21N 4°14W **24** B7
Ben Wyvis *U.K.* 57°40N 4°35W **23** G8
Benares = Varanasi *India* 25°22N 83°0E **85** G13
Benbecula *U.K.* 57°26N 7°21W **22** H3
Bend *U.S.A.* 44°4N 121°19W **110** B2
Benderloch *U.K.* 56°30N 5°22W **24** A5
Bendery *Moldova* 46°50N 29°30E **65** E15
Bendigo *Australia* 36°40S 144°15E **98** H7
Benevento *Italy* 41°8N 14°45E **68** D6
Bengal, Bay of *Ind. Oc.* 15°0N 90°0E **85** M17
Bengbu *China* 32°58N 117°20E **79** E12
Benghazi *Libya* 32°11N 20°3E **95** B10
Bengkulu *Indonesia* 3°50S 102°12E **82** E2
Benguela *Angola* 12°37S 13°25E **97** G2
Beni → *Bolivia* 10°23S 65°24W **120** D3
Beni Mellal *Morocco* 32°21N 6°21W **94** B4
Beni Suef *Egypt* 29°5N 31°6E **95** C12
Benidorm *Spain* 38°33N 0°9W **67** C5
Benin ■ *Africa* 10°0N 2°0E **94** G6
Benin, Bight of *W. Afr.* 5°0N 3°0E **94** H6
Benin City *Nigeria* 6°20N 5°31E **94** G7
Benington *U.K.* 53°0N 0°5E **27** F9
Benjamin Constant *Brazil* 4°40S 70°15W **120** C2
Benoni *S. Africa* 26°11S 28°18E **97** K5
Benson *U.K.* 51°37N 1°6W **30** C6
Bentley *Hants., U.K.* 51°12N 0°52W **31** D7
Bentley *S. Yorks., U.K.* 53°33N 1°8W **27** E6
Bentley Subglacial Trench *Antarctica* 80°0S 115°0W **55** E14
Benton *U.S.A.* 38°0N 88°55W **112** G3
Benton Harbor *U.S.A.* 42°6N 86°27W **112** D4
Benue → *Nigeria* 7°48N 6°46E **94** G7
Benxi *China* 41°20N 123°48E **79** C13
Beppu *Japan* 33°15N 131°30E **81** G2
Berber *Sudan* 18°0N 34°0E **95** E12
Berbera *Somalia* 10°30N 45°2E **89** E4
Berbérati *C.A.R.* 4°15N 15°40E **96** D3
Berbice → *Guyana* 6°20N 57°32W **120** B4
Berdyansk *Ukraine* 46°45N 36°50E **71** E6
Berdychiv *Ukraine* 49°57N 28°30E **71** E4
Bere Alston *U.K.* 50°29N 4°13W **29** G5
Bere Regis *U.K.* 50°45N 2°14W **30** E4
Berea *U.S.A.* 37°34N 84°17W **112** G5
Berens → *Canada* 52°25N 97°2W **108** D10
Berezina → *Belarus* 52°33N 30°14E **70** D5
Bereznik *Russia* 62°51N 42°40E **70** B7
Berezniki *Russia* 59°24N 56°46E **70** C10
Bérgamo *Italy* 45°41N 9°43E **68** B3
Bergen *Norway* 60°20N 5°20E **63** E5
Bergerac *France* 44°51N 0°30E **66** D4
Bering Sea *Pac. Oc.* 58°0N 171°0W **102** B10
Bering Strait *Pac. Oc.* 65°30N 169°0W **108** C3
Berkeley *U.K.* 51°41N 2°27W **30** C4
Berkhamsted *U.K.* 51°45N 0°33W **31** C7
Berkner I. *Antarctica* 79°30S 50°0W **55** D18
Berkshire Downs *U.K.* 51°33N 1°29W **30** C6
Berlin *Germany* 52°31N 13°23E **64** B7
Berlin *U.S.A.* 44°28N 71°11W **113** C12
Bermejo → *Argentina* 26°51S 58°23W **121** E4
Bermuda ☑ *Atl. Oc.* 32°18N 64°45W **52** C6
Bern *Switz.* 46°57N 7°28E **64** E4
Berneray *U.K.* 57°43N 7°11W **22** G3
Berry *France* 46°50N 2°0E **66** C5
Berry Hd. *U.K.* 50°24N 3°29W **29** G7
Bertraghboy B. *Ireland* 53°22N 9°54W **20** B3
Berwick *U.S.A.* 41°3N 76°14W **112** E9
Berwick-upon-Tweed *U.K.* 55°46N 2°0W **26** A5
Berwyn Mts. *U.K.* 52°54N 3°26W **28** B7
Besançon *France* 47°15N 6°2E **66** C7
Bessarabiya *Moldova* 47°0N 28°10E **65** E15
Bessemer *U.S.A.* 46°29N 90°3W **112** B2
Bethel *U.S.A.* 60°48N 161°45W **108** C3
Bethesda *U.K.* 53°10N 4°3W **28** A5
Bethlehem *S. Africa* 28°14S 28°18E **97** K5
Bethlehem *U.S.A.* 40°37N 75°23W **113** E10
Béthune *France* 50°30N 2°38E **66** A5
Betim *Brazil* 19°58S 44°7W **122** C2
Bettiah *India* 26°48N 84°33E **85** F14
Betul *India* 21°58N 77°59E **84** J10
Betws-y-Coed *U.K.* 53°5N 3°48W **28** A6
Beverley *U.K.* 53°51N 0°26W **27** E8
Bewdley *U.K.* 52°23N 2°19W **30** B4
Bexhill *U.K.* 50°51N 0°29E **31** E9
Bexley □ *U.K.* 51°27N 0°9E **31** D9
Beyneu *Kazakhstan* 45°18N 55°9E **71** E10
Beypazarı *Turkey* 40°10N 31°56E **71** F5
Beyşehir Gölü *Turkey* 37°41N 31°33E **71** G5
Béziers *France* 43°20N 3°12E **66** E5
Bhagalpur *India* 25°10N 87°0E **85** G15
Bhaktapur *Nepal* 27°38N 85°24E **85** F14
Bhanrer Ra. *India* 23°40N 79°45E **84** H11
Bharatpur *India* 27°15N 77°30E **84** F10
Bharraig = Barra *U.K.* 57°0N 7°29W **22** J2
Bharuch *India* 21°47N 73°0E **84** J8
Bhatarsaigh = Vatersay *U.K.* 56°55N 7°32W **22** J2
Bhatpara *India* 22°50N 88°25E **85** H16
Bhavnagar *India* 21°45N 72°10E **84** J8
Bhearnaraigh = Berneray *U.K.* 57°43N 7°11W **22** G3
Bhilainagar-Durg *India* 21°13N 81°26E **85** J12
Bhilwara *India* 25°25N 74°38E **84** G9
Bhima → *India* 16°25N 77°17E **84** L10
Bhiwandi *India* 19°20N 73°0E **84** K8
Bhiwani *India* 28°50N 76°9E **84** E10
Bhopal *India* 23°20N 77°30E **84** H10
Bhubaneshwar *India* 20°15N 85°50E **85** J14
Bhuj *India* 23°15N 69°49E **84** H6
Bhusawal *India* 21°3N 75°46E **84** J9
Bhutan ■ *Asia* 27°25N 90°30E **85** F17
Biała Podlaska *Poland* 52°4N 23°6E **65** B12
Białystok *Poland* 53°10N 23°10E **65** B12
Biarritz *France* 43°29N 1°33W **66** E3

Bibury

Bibury U.K. 51°45N 1°49W 30 C5
Bicester U.K. 51°54N 1°9W 30 C6
Bicton U.K. 52°44N 2°48W 27 G3
Bida Nigeria 9°3N 5°58E 94 G7
Biddeford U.S.A. 43°30N 70°28W 113 D12
Biddenden U.K. 51°7N 0°40E 31 D10
Biddulph U.K. 53°7N 2°10W 27 F4
Bideford U.K. 51°1N 4°13W 29 E5
Bideford Bay U.K. 51°5N 4°20W 29 E5
Bidford-on-Avon U.K. 52°11N 1°50W 30 B5
Bié Plateau Angola 12°0S 16°0E 97 G3
Biel Switz. 47°8N 7°14E 64 E4
Bielefeld Germany 52°1N 8°33E 64 B5
Biella Italy 45°34N 8°3E 68 B3
Bielsko-Biala Poland 49°50N 19°2E 65 D10
Bien Hoa Vietnam 10°57N 106°49E 82 B3
Bienville, L. Canada 55°5N 72°40W 109 D12
Big Belt Mts. U.S.A. 46°30N 111°25W 110 A4
Big Rapids U.S.A. 43°42N 85°29W 112 D5
Big Sioux → U.S.A. 42°29N 96°27W 111 B7
Big Spring U.S.A. 32°15N 101°28W 110 D6
Big Trout L. Canada 53°40N 90°0W 109 D11
Bigbury U.K. 50°18N 3°53W 29 G6
Bigbury B. U.K. 50°16N 3°54W 29 G6
Biggar Canada 52°4N 108°0W 108 D9
Biggar U.K. 55°38N 3°32W 25 C8
Biggleswade U.K. 52°5N 0°14W 31 B8
Bighorn → U.S.A. 46°10N 107°28W 110 A5
Bighorn Mts. U.S.A. 44°25N 107°0W 110 B5
Bihar India 25°5N 85°40E 85 G14
Bihar □ India 25°0N 86°0E 85 G15
Bijagós, Arquipélago dos
   Guinea-Biss. 11°15N 16°10W 94 F2
Bijapur India 16°50N 75°55E 84 L9
Bikaner India 28°2N 73°18E 84 E8
Bikini Atoll Marshall Is. 12°0N 167°30E 102 F8
Bila Tserkva Ukraine 49°45N 30°10E 65 D16
Bilaspur India 22°2N 82°15E 85 H13
Bilbao Spain 43°16N 2°56W 67 A4
Bilecik Turkey 40°5N 30°5E 71 F5
Bilhorod-Dnistrovskyy
   Ukraine 46°11N 30°23E 71 E5
Billericay U.K. 51°38N 0°26E 31 C9
Billesdon U.K. 52°38N 0°54W 27 G7
Billingham U.K. 54°36N 1°17W 26 C6
Billinghay U.K. 53°5N 0°17W 27 F8
Billings U.S.A. 45°47N 108°30W 110 A5
Billingshurst U.K. 51°2N 0°27W 31 D8
Bilma Niger 18°50N 13°30E 95 E8
Bilma, Grand Erg de Niger 18°30N 14°0E 95 E8
Biloxi U.S.A. 30°24N 88°53W 111 D9
Bilston U.K. 52°34N 2°4W 27 G4
Bimini Is. Bahamas 25°42N 79°25W 115 B9
Binbrook U.K. 53°26N 0°10W 27 F8
Bingham U.K. 52°57N 0°58W 27 G7
Binghamton U.S.A. 42°6N 75°55W 113 D10
Bingley U.K. 53°51N 1°50W 27 E5
Bioko Eq. Guin. 3°30N 8°40E 96 D1
Biratnagar Nepal 26°27N 87°17E 85 F15
Birchington U.K. 51°22N 1°19E 31 D11
Birdlip U.K. 51°50N 2°5W 30 C4
Birkdale U.K. 53°38N 3°1W 27 E2
Birkenhead U.K. 53°23N 3°2W 27 F2
Birmingham U.K. 52°29N 1°52W 27 H5
Birmingham U.S.A. 33°31N 86°48W 111 D9
Birmingham Int. ✈ (BHX)
   U.K. 52°26N 1°45W 27 H5
Birnin Kebbi Nigeria 12°32N 4°12E 94 F6
Birobidzhan Russia 48°50N 132°50E 77 E14
Birr Ireland 53°6N 7°54W 20 B7
Birtley Northumberland, U.K. 55°6N 2°12W 26 B4
Birtley Tyne & W., U.K. 54°54N 1°34W 26 C5
Biscay, B. of Atl. Oc. 45°0N 2°0W 66 D1
Bishkek Kyrgyzstan 42°54N 74°46E 76 E8
Bishop Auckland U.K. 54°39N 1°40W 26 C5
Bishop's Castle U.K. 52°30N 2°59W 27 H3
Bishop's Cleeve U.K. 51°57N 2°3W 30 C4
Bishop's Frome U.K. 52°8N 2°29W 30 B4
Bishop's Nympton U.K. 51°0N 3°47W 29 F6
Bishop's Stortford U.K. 51°52N 0°10E 31 C9
Bishop's Waltham U.K. 50°57N 1°11W 30 E6
Bishopsteignton U.K. 50°33N 3°33W 29 F6
Bishopstoke U.K. 50°58N 1°19W 30 E6
Biskra Algeria 34°50N 5°44E 94 B7
Bismarck U.S.A. 46°48N 100°47W 110 A6
Bismarck Arch. Papua N. G. 2°30S 150°0E 98 A9
Bissau Guinea-Biss. 11°45N 15°45W 94 F2
Bitola Macedonia 41°1N 21°20E 69 D9
Bitterfontein S. Africa 31°1S 18°32E 97 L3
Bitterroot Range U.S.A. 46°0N 114°20W 110 A4
Bitton U.K. 51°25N 2°27W 30 D4
Biu Nigeria 10°40N 12°3E 95 F8
Biwa-Ko Japan 35°15N 136°10E 81 F5
Biysk Russia 52°40N 85°0E 76 D9
Bizerte Tunisia 37°15N 9°50E 95 A7
Blaby U.K. 52°35N 1°10W 27 G6
Black Combe U.K. 54°16N 3°20W 26 D2
Black Esk → U.K. 55°12N 3°11W 25 D9
Black Forest = Schwarzwald
   Germany 48°30N 8°20E 64 D5
Black Hd. Ireland 53°9N 9°16W 20 B4
Black Hd. U.K. 50°0N 5°7W 29 H3
Black Hills U.S.A. 44°0N 103°45W 110 B6
Black Isle U.K. 57°35N 4°16W 23 G9
Black Mt. = Mynydd Du U.K. 51°52N 3°50W 28 D6
Black Mts. U.K. 51°55N 3°7W 28 D7
Black Range U.S.A. 33°15N 107°50W 110 D5
Black River Jamaica 18°0N 77°50W 114 a
Black River Falls U.S.A. 44°18N 90°51W 112 C2
Black Rock Barbados 13°7N 59°37W 114 c
Black Sea Eurasia 43°30N 35°0E 71 F6
Blackburn U.K. 53°45N 2°29W 27 E4
Blackdown Hills U.K. 50°57N 3°15W 30 E2
Blackmoor Vale U.K. 50°54N 2°28W 30 E4
Blackpool U.K. 53°49N 3°3W 27 E2
Blackrock Ireland 53°18N 6°11W 21 B10
Blacksburg U.S.A. 37°14N 80°25W 112 G8
Blacksod B. Ireland 54°6N 10°0W 18 C1
Blackwater → Meath, Ireland 53°39N 6°41W 19 D8
Blackwater → Waterford,
   Ireland 52°4N 7°52W 20 D7

Blackwater → Armagh, U.K. 54°31N 6°35W 19 B8
Blackwater → Essex, U.K. 51°44N 0°53E 31 C10
Blaenau Ffestiniog U.K. 53°0N 3°56W 28 B6
Blaenavon U.K. 51°46N 3°5W 28 D7
Blagdon U.K. 51°20N 2°43W 30 D3
Blagoevgrad Bulgaria 42°2N 23°5E 69 C10
Blagoveshchensk Russia 50°20N 127°30E 77 D13
Blair Atholl U.K. 56°46N 3°50W 23 J10
Blairgowrie U.K. 56°35N 3°21W 25 A9
Blakeney Gloucs., U.K. 51°46N 2°28W 30 C4
Blakeney Norfolk, U.K. 52°58N 1°1E 31 A11
Blanc, Mont Europe 45°48N 6°50E 66 D7
Blanca, B., Argentina 39°10S 61°30W 121 F3
Blanca, Costa Spain 38°25N 0°10W 67 C5
Blanca Peak U.S.A. 37°35N 105°29W 110 C5
Blanchardstown Ireland 53°23N 6°23W 21 B10
Blanco, C., U.S.A. 42°51N 124°34W 110 B2
Blandford Forum U.K. 50°51N 2°9W 30 E4
Blanquilla, I. Venezuela 11°51N 64°37W 115 E12
Blantyre Malawi 15°45S 35°0E 97 H6
Blarney Ireland 51°56N 8°33W 20 E5
Blaydon U.K. 54°58N 1°42W 26 C5
Blean U.K. 51°18N 1°3E 31 D11
Bleasdale Moors U.K. 53°55N 2°35W 27 E3
Blenheim N.Z. 41°38S 173°57E 99 J13
Bletchingdon U.K. 51°51N 1°15W 30 C6
Bletchley U.K. 51°59N 0°44W 31 C7
Blida Algeria 36°30N 2°49E 94 A6
Blisworth U.K. 52°10N 0°56W 31 B7
Blitar Indonesia 8°5S 112°11E 82 F4
Blockley U.K. 52°1N 1°44W 30 B5
Bloemfontein S. Africa 29°6S 26°7E 97 K5
Blofield U.K. 52°38N 1°26E 31 A11
Blois France 47°35N 1°20E 66 C4
Bloody Foreland Ireland 55°10N 8°17W 18 A5
Bloomington Ill., U.S.A. 40°28N 89°0W 112 E3
Bloomington Ind., U.S.A. 39°10N 86°32W 112 F4
Bloomsburg U.S.A. 41°0N 76°27W 112 E9
Bloxham U.K. 52°1N 1°21W 30 B6
Blue Mountain Pk. Jamaica 18°3N 76°36W 114 a
Blue Mt. U.S.A. 40°30N 76°30W 112 E9
Blue Mts. Jamaica 18°3N 76°36W 114 a
Blue Mts. U.S.A. 45°0N 118°20W 110 A3
Blue Nile → Sudan 15°38N 32°31E 95 E12
Blue Ridge U.S.A. 36°40N 80°50W 111 C10
Blue Stack Mts. Ireland 54°42N 8°12W 18 B5
Bluefield U.S.A. 37°15N 81°17W 112 G7
Bluefields Nic. 12°20N 83°50W 115 E8
Blumenau Brazil 27°0S 49°0W 121 E5
Blundeston U.K. 52°31N 1°42E 31 A12
Blyth Northumberland, U.K. 55°8N 1°31W 26 B5
Blyth Notts., U.K. 53°22N 1°3W 27 F6
Blyth → U.K. 55°8N 1°33W 26 B5
Blyth Bridge U.K. 55°42N 3°22W 25 C9
Blyton U.K. 53°27N 0°42W 27 F7
Bo S. Leone 7°55N 11°50W 94 G3
Bo Hai China 39°0N 119°0E 79 D12
Boa Vista Brazil 2°48N 60°30W 120 B3
Bobcaygeon Canada 44°33N 78°33W 112 C8
Bobo-Dioulasso Burkina Faso 11°8N 4°13W 94 F5
Bóbr → Poland 52°4N 15°4E 64 B8
Bochum Germany 51°28N 7°13E 64 C4
Boddam U.K. 59°56N 1°17W 22 C15
Boden Sweden 65°50N 21°42E 63 D8
Bodiam U.K. 51°0N 0°34E 31 D10
Bodmin U.K. 50°28N 4°43W 29 G4
Bodmin Moor U.K. 50°33N 4°36W 29 G4
Bodø Norway 67°17N 14°24E 63 D6
Bodrog → Hungary 48°11N 21°22E 65 D11
Bodrum Turkey 37°3N 27°30E 71 G4
Bogalusa U.S.A. 30°47N 89°52W 111 D9
Bogda Shan China 43°35N 89°40E 78 C6
Boggeragh Mts. Ireland 52°2N 8°55W 20 D5
Bognor Regis U.K. 50°47N 0°40W 31 E7
Bogor Indonesia 6°36S 106°48E 82 F3
Bogotá Colombia 4°34N 74°0W 120 B2
Bogra Bangla. 24°51N 89°22E 85 G16
Böhmerwald Germany 49°8N 13°14E 64 D7
Bohol Sea Phil. 9°0N 124°0E 83 C6
Boise U.S.A. 43°37N 116°13W 110 B3
Bole China 44°55N 81°37E 78 C5
Bolívar, Pico Venezuela 8°32N 71°2W 115 F10
Bolivia ■ S. Amer. 17°6S 64°0W 120 D3
Bollington U.K. 53°18N 2°6W 27 F4
Bolney U.K. 50°59N 0°12W 31 E8
Bologna Italy 44°29N 11°20E 68 B4
Bologoye Russia 57°55N 34°5E 70 C5
Bolsena, L. di Italy 42°36N 11°56E 68 C4
Bolsover U.K. 53°14N 1°16W 27 F6
Bolt Head U.K. 50°12N 3°48W 29 G6
Bolt Tail U.K. 50°14N 3°52W 29 G6
Bolton U.K. 53°35N 2°26W 27 E4
Bolton Abbey U.K. 53°59N 1°53W 27 E5
Bolton by Bowland U.K. 53°56N 2°20W 27 E4
Bolton-le-Sands U.K. 54°6N 2°48W 26 D3
Bolu Turkey 40°45N 31°35E 71 F5
Bolvadin Turkey 38°45N 31°4E 71 G5
Bolzano Italy 46°31N 11°22E 68 A4
Bom Despacho Brazil 19°43S 45°15W 122 C1
Bom Jesus da Lapa Brazil 13°15S 43°25W 122 B2
Boma Dem. Rep. of the Congo 5°50S 13°4E 96 F2
Bombala Australia 36°56S 149°15E 98 H8
Bombay = Mumbai India 18°56N 72°50E 84 K8
Bomi China 29°50N 95°45E 78 F8
Bomu → C.A.R. 4°40N 22°30E 96 D4
Bon, C. Tunisia 37°1N 11°2E 90 C5
Bonaire W. Indies 12°10N 68°15W 115 E11
Bonar Bridge U.K. 57°54N 4°20W 23 G9
Bonavista Canada 48°40N 53°5W 109 E14
Bonchester Bridge U.K. 55°24N 2°39W 25 D10
Bonchurch U.K. 50°37N 1°11W 30 E6
Bo'ness U.K. 56°1N 3°37W 25 B8
Bongor Chad 10°35N 15°20E 95 F9
Bongos, Massif des C.A.R. 8°40N 22°25E 96 C4
Bonifacio France 41°24N 9°10E 66 F8
Bonn Germany 50°46N 7°6E 64 C4
Bonny, Bight of Africa 3°30N 9°20E 96 D1
Bonnyrigg U.K. 55°52N 3°6W 25 C9
Böön Tsagaan Nuur Mongolia 45°35N 99°9E 78 B8
Boonville U.S.A. 38°3N 87°16W 112 F4

Boosaaso Somalia 11°12N 49°18E 89 E4
Boot U.K. 54°24N 3°13W 26 D2
Boothia, Gulf of Canada 71°0N 90°0W 109 B11
Boothia Pen. Canada 71°0N 94°0W 108 B10
Bootle Cumb., U.K. 54°18N 3°22W 26 D2
Bootle Mersey., U.K. 53°28N 3°1W 27 F2
Borås Sweden 57°43N 12°56E 63 F6
Borborema, Planalto da Brazil 7°0S 37°0W 117 D7
Bordeaux France 44°50N 0°36W 66 D3
Borden I. Canada 78°30N 111°30W 109 B8
Borden Pen. Canada 73°0N 83°0W 109 B11
Borders = Scottish Borders □
   U.K. 55°35N 2°50W 25 C10
Bordon U.K. 51°8N 0°52W 31 D7
Borehamwood U.K. 51°40N 0°15W 31 C8
Boreland U.K. 55°13N 3°17W 25 D9
Borger U.S.A. 35°39N 101°24W 110 C6
Borhoyn Tal Mongolia 43°50N 111°58E 79 C11
Borisoglebsk Russia 51°27N 42°5E 71 D7
Borkou Chad 18°15N 18°50E 95 E9
Borneo E. Indies 1°0N 115°0E 82 D5
Bornholm Denmark 55°10N 15°0E 63 F7
Borohoro Shan China 44°6N 83°10E 78 C5
Boroughbridge U.K. 54°6N 1°24W 26 D6
Borovichi Russia 58°25N 33°55E 70 C5
Borrowdale U.K. 54°31N 3°10W 26 C2
Borth U.K. 52°29N 4°2W 28 C5
Borüjerd Iran 33°55N 48°50E 86 C7
Bosbury U.K. 52°5N 2°26W 30 B4
Boscastle U.K. 50°41N 4°42W 29 F4
Boscobelle Barbados 13°17N 59°35W 114 c
Bose China 23°53N 106°35E 78 G10
Bosham U.K. 50°49N 0°51W 31 E7
Bosnia-Herzegovina ■ Europe 44°0N 18°0E 68 B7
Bosporus Turkey 41°5N 29°3E 71 F4
Bossangoa C.A.R. 6°35N 17°30E 96 C3
Bosten Hu China 41°55N 87°40E 78 C6
Boston U.K. 52°59N 0°2W 27 G8
Boston U.S.A. 42°22N 71°3W 113 D12
Bothel U.K. 54°45N 3°15W 26 C2
Bothnia, G. of Europe 62°0N 20°0E 63 E8
Botletle → Botswana 20°10S 23°15E 97 J4
Botoşani Romania 47°42N 26°41E 65 E14
Botswana ■ Africa 22°0S 24°0E 97 J4
Bottesford U.K. 52°57N 0°48W 27 G7
Botucatu Brazil 22°55S 48°30W 122 D1
Bou Saâda Algeria 35°11N 4°9E 94 A6
Bouaké Ivory C. 7°40N 5°2W 94 G4
Bouar C.A.R. 6°0N 15°40E 96 C3
Bouârfa Morocco 32°32N 1°58W 94 B5
Bougainville I. Papua N. G. 6°0S 155°0E 99 B10
Boulder U.S.A. 40°1N 105°17W 110 B5
Boulogne-sur-Mer France 50°42N 1°36E 66 A4
Bounty Is. Pac. Oc. 48°0S 178°30E 102 M9
Bourbonnais France 46°28N 3°0E 66 C5
Bourg-en-Bresse France 46°13N 5°12E 66 C6
Bourges France 47°9N 2°25E 66 C5
Bourgogne □ France 47°0N 4°50E 66 C6
Bourke Australia 30°8S 145°55E 98 G8
Bourne U.K. 52°47N 0°22W 27 G8
Bournemouth U.K. 50°43N 1°52W 30 E5
Bourton-on-the-Water U.K. 51°52N 1°45W 30 C5
Bouvet I. Antarctica 54°26S 3°24E 52 G10
Bovey Tracey U.K. 50°36N 3°41W 29 F6
Bow → Canada 49°57N 111°41W 108 D8
Bowes U.K. 54°32N 1°59W 26 C5
Bowland, Forest of U.K. 54°0N 2°30W 27 E3
Bowling Green Ky., U.S.A. 36°59N 86°27W 112 G4
Bowling Green Ohio, U.S.A. 41°23N 83°39W 112 E6
Bowmore U.K. 55°45N 6°17W 24 C3
Bowness-on-Solway U.K. 54°57N 3°12W 26 C2
Bowness-on-Windermere
   U.K. 54°22N 2°55W 26 D3
Box U.K. 51°25N 2°15W 30 D4
Box Hill U.K. 51°15N 0°16W 31 D8
Boyle Ireland 53°59N 8°18W 18 D5
Boyne → Ireland 53°43N 6°15W 19 D9
Boyoma, Chutes
   Dem. Rep. of the Congo 0°35N 25°23E 90 F6
Bozeat U.K. 52°14N 0°40W 31 B7
Bozeman U.S.A. 45°41N 111°2W 110 A4
Bozoum C.A.R. 6°25N 16°35E 96 C3
Brač Croatia 43°20N 16°40E 68 C7
Bracadale, L. U.K. 57°20N 6°30W 22 H4
Bracebridge Canada 45°2N 79°19W 112 C8
Bracebridge Heath U.K. 53°12N 0°32W 27 F7
Bräcke Sweden 62°45N 15°26E 63 E7
Brackley U.K. 52°2N 1°8W 30 B6
Bracknell U.K. 51°25N 0°43W 31 D7
Bradford U.K. 53°47N 1°45W 27 E5
Bradford U.S.A. 41°58N 78°38W 112 E8
Bradford on Avon U.K. 51°21N 2°14W 30 D4
Brading U.K. 50°41N 1°8W 30 E6
Bradwell-on-Sea U.K. 51°43N 0°56E 31 C10
Bradworthy U.K. 50°53N 4°24W 29 F5
Braemar U.K. 57°2N 3°26W 23 H11
Braga Portugal 41°35N 8°26W 67 B1
Bragança Brazil 1°0S 47°2W 120 C5
Bragança Portugal 41°48N 6°50W 67 B2
Bragança Paulista Brazil 22°55S 46°32W 122 D1
Brahmanbaria Bangla. 23°58N 91°15E 85 H17
Brahmani → India 20°39N 86°46E 85 J15
Brahmapur India 19°15N 84°54E 85 K14
Brahmaputra → Asia 23°40N 90°35E 85 H16
Braich-y-pwll U.K. 52°47N 4°46W 28 B4
Bräila Romania 45°19N 27°59E 65 F14
Brailsford U.K. 52°58N 1°35W 27 G6
Brainerd U.S.A. 46°22N 94°12W 111 A8
Braintree U.K. 51°53N 0°34E 31 C10
Bramford U.K. 52°4N 1°7E 31 B11
Brampton Canada 43°45N 79°45W 112 D8
Brampton Cambs., U.K. 52°20N 0°14W 31 B8
Brampton Cumb., U.K. 54°57N 2°44W 26 C3
Brancaster U.K. 52°58N 0°38E 31 A10
Branco → Brazil 1°20S 61°50W 120 C3
Brandenburg Germany 52°25N 12°33E 64 B7
Brandenburg □ Germany 52°50N 13°0E 64 B7
Branderburgh U.K. 57°43N 3°17W 23 G11
Brandon Canada 49°50N 99°57W 108 E10
Brandon Durham, U.K. 54°46N 1°37W 26 C5
Brandon Suffolk, U.K. 52°27N 0°38E 31 B10
Brandon B. Ireland 52°17N 10°8W 20 D2

Brandon Mt. Ireland 52°15N 10°15W 20 D2
Branston U.K. 53°12N 0°27W 27 F8
Brantford Canada 43°10N 80°15W 112 D7
Bras d'Or L. Canada 45°50N 60°50W 113 C17
Brasília Brazil 15°47S 47°55W 122 C1
Braşov Romania 45°38N 25°35E 65 F13
Bratislava Slovak Rep. 48°10N 17°7E 65 D9
Bratsk Russia 56°10N 101°30E 77 D11
Bratsk Res. Russia 56°15N 101°45E 77 D11
Brattleboro U.S.A. 42°51N 72°34W 113 D11
Braunschweig Germany 52°15N 10°31E 64 B6
Braunton U.K. 51°7N 4°10W 29 E5
Brava, Costa Spain 41°30N 3°0E 67 B7
Bray Ireland 53°13N 6°7W 21 B10
Bray U.K. 51°30N 0°41W 31 D7
Brazil U.S.A. 39°32N 87°8W 112 F4
Brazil ■ S. Amer. 12°0S 50°0W 120 D4
Brazilian Highlands Brazil 18°0S 46°30W 117 E6
Brazos → U.S.A. 28°53N 95°23W 111 E7
Brazzaville Congo 4°9S 15°12E 96 E3
Breadalbane U.K. 56°30N 4°15W 24 A7
Breage U.K. 50°6N 5°20W 29 G3
Breamish → U.K. 55°35N 2°2W 26 A4
Brechin U.K. 56°44N 2°39W 23 J12
Breckland U.K. 52°30N 0°40E 31 B10
Brecon U.K. 51°57N 3°23W 28 D7
Brecon Beacons △ U.K. 51°50N 3°30W 28 D6
Breda Neths. 51°35N 4°45E 64 C3
Brede U.K. 50°56N 0°36E 31 E10
Bregenz Austria 47°30N 9°45E 64 E5
Breiðafjörður Iceland 65°15N 23°15W 63 A1
Bremen Germany 53°4N 8°47E 64 B5
Bremerhaven Germany 53°33N 8°36E 64 B5
Bremerton U.S.A. 47°34N 122°37W 110 A2
Brendon Hills U.K. 51°6N 3°25W 30 D2
Brennerpass Austria 47°2N 11°30E 64 E6
Brent □ U.K. 51°33N 0°16W 31 C8
Brentwood U.K. 51°37N 0°19E 31 C9
Bréscia Italy 45°33N 10°15E 68 B4
Bressay U.K. 60°9N 1°6W 22 B15
Brest Belarus 52°10N 23°40E 65 B12
Brest France 48°24N 4°31W 66 B1
Bretagne □ France 48°10N 3°0W 66 B2
Breton Sd. U.S.A. 29°35N 89°15W 111 E9
Brewer U.S.A. 44°48N 68°46W 113 C13
Brewood U.K. 52°41N 2°9W 27 G4
Briançon France 44°54N 6°39E 66 D7
Bridestowe U.K. 50°41N 4°7W 29 F5
Bridge U.K. 51°15N 1°8E 31 D11
Bridgefield Barbados 13°9N 59°36W 114 c
Bridgend U.K. 51°30N 3°34W 29 D6
Bridgeport U.S.A. 41°11N 73°12W 113 E11
Bridgeton U.S.A. 39°26N 75°14W 113 F10
Bridgetown Barbados 13°6N 59°37W 114 c
Bridgewater Canada 44°25N 64°31W 109 E13
Bridgnorth U.K. 52°32N 2°25W 27 G4
Bridgwater U.K. 51°8N 2°59W 30 D3
Bridgwater B. U.K. 51°15N 3°15W 30 D2
Bridlington U.K. 54°5N 0°12W 26 D8
Bridlington B. U.K. 54°4N 0°10W 26 D8
Bridport U.K. 50°44N 2°45W 30 E3
Brierfield U.K. 53°49N 2°14W 27 E4
Brierley Hill U.K. 52°29N 2°6W 27 H4
Brigg U.K. 53°34N 0°28W 27 E8
Brigham City U.S.A. 41°31N 112°1W 110 B4
Brighouse U.K. 53°42N 1°46W 27 E5
Brighstone U.K. 50°38N 1°23W 30 E6
Brightlingsea U.K. 51°49N 1°2E 31 C11
Brighton U.K. 50°49N 0°7W 31 E8
Brigstock U.K. 52°27N 0°36W 31 B7
Brill U.K. 51°49N 1°1W 30 C6
Brimfield U.K. 52°18N 2°41W 30 B3
Brindisi Italy 40°39N 17°55E 69 D7
Brinklow U.K. 52°25N 1°22W 30 B6
Brinkworth U.K. 51°33N 1°59W 30 C5
Brisbane Australia 27°25S 153°2E 98 F9
Bristol U.K. 51°26N 2°35W 30 D3
Bristol U.S.A. 58°0N 160°0W 108 D4
Bristol Channel U.K. 51°18N 4°30W 29 E5
Briston U.K. 52°51N 1°4E 31 A11
British Columbia □ Canada 55°0N 125°15W 108 D7
British Isles Europe 54°0N 4°0W 62 D5
British Virgin Is. ☑
   W. Indies 18°30N 64°30W 115 D12
Brittany = Bretagne □ France 48°10N 3°0W 66 B2
Brive-la-Gaillarde France 45°10N 1°32E 66 D4
Brixham U.K. 50°23N 3°31W 29 G6
Brixworth U.K. 52°20N 0°54W 31 B7
Brize Norton U.K. 51°46N 1°34W 30 C5
Brno Czech Rep. 49°10N 16°35E 65 D9
Broad B. U.K. 58°14N 6°18W 22 F5
Broad Chalke U.K. 51°2N 1°56W 30 D5
Broad Haven Ireland 54°20N 9°55W 18 C2
Broad Law U.K. 55°30N 3°21W 25 C9
Broad Sd. U.K. 49°55N 6°21W 29 H1
Broadclyst U.K. 50°46N 3°27W 29 F7
Broadhembury U.K. 50°49N 3°18W 29 F7
Broadstairs U.K. 51°21N 1°27E 31 D11
Broadway U.K. 52°2N 1°50W 30 B5
Broadwindsor U.K. 50°48N 2°47W 30 E3
Brochet Canada 57°53N 101°40W 108 D9
Brock I. Canada 77°52N 114°19W 109 B8
Brocken Germany 51°47N 10°37E 64 C6
Brockenhurst U.K. 50°49N 1°34W 30 E5
Brockville Canada 44°35N 75°41W 113 C10
Brockworth U.K. 51°51N 2°9W 30 C4
Brodeur Pen. Canada 72°30N 88°10W 109 B11
Brodick U.K. 55°35N 5°9W 24 C5
Broken Hill Australia 31°58S 141°29E 98 G7
Bromfield U.K. 52°24N 2°45W 27 H3
Bromham U.K. 51°23N 2°1W 30 D4
Bromley □ U.K. 51°24N 0°2E 31 D9
Brompton U.K. 54°21N 1°25W 26 D6
Bromsgrove U.K. 52°21N 2°2W 30 B4
Bromyard U.K. 52°11N 2°30W 30 B4
Brookings U.S.A. 44°19N 96°48W 111 B7
Brooks Canada 50°35N 111°55W 108 D8
Brooks Range U.S.A. 68°0N 152°0E 108 C5
Broom, L. U.K. 57°55N 5°15W 22 G7
Broome Australia 18°0S 122°15E 98 D3

Broomhill U.K. 55°18N 1°36W 26 B5
Brora U.K. 58°0N 3°52W 23 F10
Brora → U.K. 58°0N 3°51W 23 F10
Broseley U.K. 52°37N 2°29W 27 G4
Brosna → Ireland 53°14N 7°58W 20 B7
Brothertoft U.K. 53°0N 0°7W 27 F8
Brotton U.K. 54°35N 0°56W 26 C7
Brough Cumb., U.K. 54°32N 2°18W 26 C4
Brough E. Riding, U.K. 53°44N 0°36W 27 E7
Brough Hd. U.K. 59°8N 3°20W 23 D11
Broughton Borders, U.K. 55°37N 3°24W 25 C9
Broughton N. Lincs., U.K. 53°34N 0°34W 27 E7
Broughton Northants., U.K. 52°22N 0°46W 31 B7
Broughton-in-Furness U.K. 54°17N 3°13W 26 D2
Broughty Ferry U.K. 56°29N 2°51W 25 B10
Brown Willy U.K. 50°35N 4°37W 29 F4
Brownsville U.S.A. 25°54N 97°30W 111 E7
Brownwood U.S.A. 31°43N 98°59W 110 D7
Broxburn U.K. 55°56N 3°28W 25 C9
Bruay-la-Buissière France 50°29N 2°33E 66 A5
Bruce, Mt. Australia 22°37S 118°8E 98 E2
Brugge Belgium 51°13N 3°13E 64 C2
Brumado Brazil 14°14S 41°40W 122 B2
Brunei ■ Asia 4°50N 115°0E 82 D4
Brunswick Ga., U.S.A. 31°10N 81°30W 111 D10
Brunswick Maine, U.S.A. 43°55N 69°58W 113 D13
Brunton U.K. 55°2N 2°6W 26 B4
Brussels Belgium 50°51N 4°21E 64 C3
Bruton U.K. 51°7N 2°27W 30 D4
Bryan Ohio, U.S.A. 41°28N 84°33W 112 E5
Bryan Tex., U.S.A. 30°40N 96°22W 111 D7
Bryansk Russia 53°13N 34°25E 70 D5
Bryher U.K. 49°57N 6°22W 29 H1
Brynamman U.K. 51°49N 3°51W 28 D6
Brynmawr U.K. 51°48N 3°10W 28 D7
Bucaramanga Colombia 7°0N 73°0W 120 B2
Buchan U.K. 57°32N 2°21W 23 G13
Buchan Ness U.K. 57°29N 1°46W 23 H14
Bucharest Romania 44°27N 26°10E 65 F14
Buckden U.K. 52°18N 0°14W 31 B8
Buckfastleigh U.K. 50°28N 3°48W 29 G6
Buckhannon U.S.A. 39°0N 80°8W 112 F7
Buckhaven U.K. 56°11N 3°3W 25 B9
Buckie U.K. 57°41N 2°58W 23 G12
Buckingham Canada 45°37N 75°24W 113 C10
Buckingham U.K. 52°0N 0°57W 31 C7
Buckinghamshire □ U.K. 51°53N 0°55W 31 C7
Buckley U.K. 53°10N 3°5W 28 A7
Budapest Hungary 47°29N 19°3E 65 E10
Bude U.K. 50°49N 4°34W 29 F4
Bude B. U.K. 50°49N 4°35W 29 F4
Budle B. U.K. 55°37N 1°45W 26 A5
Budleigh Salterton U.K. 50°37N 3°19W 29 F7
Buena Vista U.S.A. 37°44N 79°21W 112 G8
Buenaventura Colombia 3°53N 77°4W 120 B2
Buenos Aires Argentina 34°36S 58°22W 121 F4
Buffalo N.Y., U.S.A. 42°53N 78°53W 112 D8
Buffalo Wyo., U.S.A. 44°21N 106°42W 110 B5
Bug → Poland 52°31N 21°5E 65 B11
Bug → Ukraine 46°59N 31°58E 71 E5
Bugle U.K. 50°24N 4°47W 29 G4
Bugulma Russia 54°33N 52°48E 70 D9
Buguruslan Russia 53°39N 52°26E 70 D9
Builth Wells U.K. 52°9N 3°25W 28 C7
Buir Nur Mongolia 47°50N 117°42E 79 B12
Buji China 22°37N 114°5E 79 a
Bujumbura Burundi 3°16S 29°18E 96 E5
Bukavu Dem. Rep. of the Congo 2°20S 28°52E 96 E5
Bukhara Uzbekistan 39°48N 64°25E 87 B11
Bukittinggi Indonesia 0°20S 100°20E 82 E2
Bulawayo Zimbabwe 20°7S 28°32E 97 J5
Bulford U.K. 51°11N 1°45W 30 D5
Bulgaria ■ Europe 42°35N 25°30E 69 C11
Bullhead City U.S.A. 35°8N 114°32W 110 C4
Bunbury Australia 33°20S 115°35E 98 G2
Bunclody Ireland 52°39N 6°40W 21 D9
Buncrana Ireland 55°8N 7°27W 18 A7
Bundaberg Australia 24°54S 152°22E 98 E9
Bundi India 25°30N 75°35E 84 G9
Bundoran Ireland 54°28N 8°18W 18 C5
Bungay U.K. 52°27N 1°28E 31 B11
Buntingford U.K. 51°56N 0°1W 31 C9
Bunwell U.K. 52°30N 1°9E 31 A11
Buon Ma Thuot Vietnam 12°40N 108°3E 82 B3
Bûr Safâga Egypt 26°43N 33°57E 95 C12
Buraydah Si. Arabia 26°20N 43°59E 86 E5
Burbage Derby, U.K. 53°15N 1°55W 27 F5
Burbage Leics., U.K. 52°32N 1°21W 27 G6
Burbage Wilts., U.K. 51°21N 1°39W 30 D5
Burco Somalia 9°32N 45°32E 89 F4
Burdur Turkey 37°45N 30°17E 71 G5
Bure → U.K. 52°38N 1°43E 31 A12
Burford U.K. 51°49N 1°38W 30 C5
Burgas Bulgaria 42°33N 27°29E 69 C12
Burgess Hill U.K. 50°58N 0°6W 31 E8
Burgh le Marsh U.K. 53°9N 0°15E 27 F9
Burghead U.K. 57°43N 3°30W 23 G11
Burgos Spain 42°21N 3°41W 67 A4
Burgundy = Bourgogne □
   France 47°0N 4°50E 66 C6
Burhanpur India 21°18N 76°14E 84 J10
Burkina Faso ■ Africa 12°0N 1°0W 94 F5
Burley U.K. 50°44N 1°42W 30 E5
Burley U.S.A. 42°32N 113°48W 110 B4
Burley in Wharfedale U.K. 53°54N 1°45W 27 E5
Burlington Colo., U.S.A. 39°18N 102°16W 110 C6
Burlington Iowa, U.S.A. 40°49N 91°14W 111 B8
Burlington N.C., U.S.A. 36°6N 79°26W 111 C11
Burlington Vt., U.S.A. 44°29N 73°12W 113 C11
Burlington Wis., U.S.A. 42°41N 88°17W 112 D3
Burma ■ Asia 21°0N 96°30E 85 J20
Burnham Market U.K. 52°57N 0°44E 31 A10
Burnham-on-Crouch U.K. 51°38N 0°49E 31 C10
Burnham-on-Sea U.K. 51°14N 3°0W 30 D2
Burnie Australia 41°4S 145°56E 98 J8
Burnley U.K. 53°47N 2°14W 27 E4
Burnmouth U.K. 55°50N 2°4W 25 C11

Burnmouth

Burns   **Chesil Beach**

Burns U.S.A. 40°33N 119°3W 110 B3
Burnside → Canada 66°51N 108°4W 108 C9
Burntisland U.K. 56°4N 3°13W 25 B9
Burqin China 47°43N 87°0E 78 B6
Burray U.K. 58°51N 2°54W 23 E12
Burren △ Ireland 53°9N 9°5W 20 B4
Burrow Hd. U.K. 54°41N 4°24W 24 E7
Burry Port U.K. 51°41N 4°15W 28 D5
Bursa Turkey 40°16N 29°5E 71 F4
Burstwick U.K. 53°44N 0°8W 27 E8
Burton U.K. 54°11N 2°43W 26 D3
Burton Agnes U.K. 54°4N 0°18W 26 D8
Burton Bradstock U.K. 50°42N 2°43W 30 E3
Burton Fleming U.K. 54°8N 0°20W 26 D8
Burton Latimer U.K. 52°22N 0°41W 31 B7
Burton upon Stather U.K. 53°39N 0°41W 27 C7
Burton upon Trent U.K. 52°48N 1°38W 27 G5
Buru Indonesia 3°30S 126°30E 83 E7
Burundi ■ Africa 3°15S 30°0E 96 E5
Burwash U.K. 50°59N 0°23E 31 E9
Burwell U.K. 52°17N 0°20E 31 B9
Burwick U.K. 58°45N 2°58W 23 E12
Bury U.K. 53°35N 2°17W 27 F4
Bury St. Edmunds U.K. 52°15N 0°43E 31 B10
Buryatia □ Russia 53°0N 110°0E 77 D11
Busan S. Korea 35°5N 129°0E 79 D14
Büshehr Iran 28°55N 50°55E 87 D7
Bushey U.K. 51°38N 0°22W 31 C8
Busto Arsizio Italy 45°37N 8°51E 68 B3
Buta Dem. Rep. of the Congo 2°50N 24°53E 96 D4
Butare Rwanda 2°31S 29°52E 96 E5
Butaritari Kiribati 3°30N 174°0E 102 G9
Bute U.K. 55°48N 5°2W 24 C5
Bute, Kyles of U.K. 55°55N 6°10W 24 C5
Butembo Dem. Rep. of the Congo 0°9N 29°18E 96 D5
Butler U.S.A. 40°52N 79°54W 112 E8
Buton Indonesia 5°0S 122°45E 83 E6
Butte U.S.A. 46°0N 112°32W 110 A4
Buttermere U.K. 54°32N 3°16W 26 C2
Butterworth Malaysia 5°24N 100°23E 82 C2
Buttevant Ireland 52°14N 8°40W 20 D5
Butuan Phil. 8°57N 125°33E 83 C7
Buurhakaba Somalia 3°12N 44°20E 89 G3
Buxton U.K. 53°16N 1°54W 27 F5
Buyant-Uhaa Mongolia 44°55N 110°11E 79 C11
Buzău Romania 45°10N 26°50E 65 F14
Buzi → Mozam.
Buzuluk Russia 52°48N 52°12E 70 D9
Bydgoszcz Poland 53°10N 18°0E 65 B10
Byfield U.K. 52°10N 1°14W 30 B6
Bylot I. Canada 73°13N 78°34W 109 B12
Byrranga Ra. Russia 75°0N 100°0E 77 B11
Bytom Poland 50°25N 18°54E 65 C10

C

Ca Mau Vietnam 9°7N 105°8E 82 C3
Cabanatuan Phil. 15°30N 120°58E 83 A6
Cabedelo Brazil 7°0S 34°50W 120 C6
Cabimas Venezuela 10°23N 71°25W 120 A2
Cabinda Angola 5°33S 12°11E 96 F2
Cabinda □ Angola 5°0S 12°30E 96 F2
Cabo Frio Brazil 22°51S 42°3W 122 D2
Cabo San Lucas Mexico 22°53N 109°54W 114 C3
Cabonga, Réservoir Canada 47°20N 76°40W 109 E12
Cabora Bassa Dam Mozam. 15°20S 32°50E 97 H6
Cabot Str. Canada 47°15N 59°40W 109 E14
Čačak Serbia 43°54N 20°20E 69 C9
Cáceres Brazil 16°5S 57°40W 120 D4
Cáceres Spain 39°26N 6°23W 67 C2
Cachimbo, Serra do Brazil 9°30S 55°30W 120 C4
Cachoeira Brazil 12°30S 39°0W 122 B3
Cachoeira do Sul Brazil 30°3S 52°53W 121 F4
Cachoeira de Itapemirim Brazil 20°51S 41°7W 122 D2
Cader Idris U.K. 52°42N 3°53W 28 B6
Cadillac U.S.A. 44°15N 85°24W 112 C5
Cádiz Spain 36°30N 6°20W 67 D2
Cádiz, G. de Spain 36°40N 7°0W 67 D2
Caen France 49°10N 0°22W 66 B3
Caenby Corner U.K. 53°24N 0°33W 27 F7
Caerdydd = Cardiff U.K. 51°29N 3°10W 29 E7
Caerfyrddin = Carmarthen U.K. 51°52N 4°19W 28 D5
Caergybi = Holyhead U.K. 53°18N 4°38W 28 A4
Caernarfon U.K. 53°8N 4°16W 28 A5
Caernarfon B. U.K. 53°4N 4°40W 28 A4
Caerphilly U.K. 51°35N 3°13W 29 D7
Caersws U.K. 52°31N 3°26W 28 B7
Caeté Brazil 19°55S 43°40W 122 C2
Caetité Brazil 13°50S 42°32W 122 B2
Cagayan de Oro Phil. 8°30N 124°40E 83 C6
Cágliari Italy 39°13N 9°7E 68 E3
Caguas Puerto Rico 18°14N 66°2W 115 D11
Caha Mts. Ireland 51°45N 9°40W 20 E3
Caherciveen Ireland 51°56N 10°14W 20 E2
Cahir Ireland 52°22N 7°56W 20 D7
Cahore Pt. Ireland 52°33N 6°12W 21 C10
Cahors France 44°27N 1°27E 66 D4
Cairn Gorm U.K. 57°7N 3°39W 23 H10
Cairngorm Mts. U.K. 57°6N 3°42W 23 H10
Cairngorms △ U.K. 57°10N 3°50W 23 H10
Cairnryan U.K. 54°59N 5°1W 24 E5
Cairns Australia 16°57S 145°45E 98 D8
Cairnsmore of Fleet U.K. 54°59N 4°20W 24 E7
Cairo Egypt 30°2N 31°13E 95 B12
Cairo U.S.A. 37°0N 89°11W 112 G3
Caister-on-Sea U.K. 52°40N 1°43E 31 A12
Caistor U.K. 53°30N 0°18W 27 F8
Caithness U.K. 58°25N 3°35W 23 F10
Caithness, Ord of U.K. 58°8N 3°36W 23 F10
Cajamarca Peru 7°5S 78°28W 120 C2
Calabar Nigeria 4°57N 8°20E 94 H7
Calábria □ Italy 39°0N 16°30E 68 E7
Calais France 50°57N 1°56E 66 A4
Calais U.S.A. 45°11N 67°17W 113 C14
Calama Chile 22°30S 68°55W 121 E3
Calamian Group Phil. 11°50N 119°55E 83 B5
Calanscio, Sarīr Libya 27°30N 22°30E 95 C10
Calapan Phil. 13°25N 121°7E 83 B6
Calbayog Phil. 12°4N 124°38E 83 B6
Calcutta = Kolkata India 22°34N 88°21E 85 H16

Caldbeck U.K. 54°45N 3°3W 26 C2
Calder → U.K. 53°44N 1°22W 27 E6
Calder Bridge U.K. 54°27N 3°29W 26 D2
Caldera Chile 27°5S 70°55W 121 E2
Caldew → U.K. 54°54N 2°56W 26 C3
Caldwell U.S.A. 43°40N 116°41W 110 B3
Caledonian Canal U.K. 57°29N 4°15W 23 H9
Calgary Canada 51°0N 114°10W 108 D8
Cali Colombia 3°25N 76°35W 120 B2
Cálida, Costa Spain 37°30N 1°30W 67 D5
California □ U.S.A. 37°30N 119°30W 110 C2
California, G. de Mexico 27°0N 111°0W 114 B2
Callan Ireland 52°32N 7°24W 21 C8
Callander U.K. 56°15N 4°13W 24 B7
Callao Peru 12°3S 77°9W 120 D2
Calne U.K. 51°26N 2°0W 30 D5
Calshot U.K. 50°48N 1°19W 30 E6
Calstock U.K. 50°30N 4°13W 29 F5
Caltanissetta Italy 37°29N 14°4E 68 F6
Calvi France 42°34N 8°45E 66 E8
Calvinia S. Africa 31°28S 19°45E 97 L3
Cam → U.K. 52°21N 0°16E 31 B9
Cam Ranh Vietnam 11°54N 109°12E 82 B3
Camagüey Cuba 21°20N 77°55W 115 C9
Camargue France 43°34N 4°34E 66 E6
Camberley U.K. 51°20N 0°44W 31 D7
Cambo U.K. 55°10N 1°57W 26 B5
Cambodia ■ Asia 12°15N 105°0E 82 B3
Camborne U.K. 50°12N 5°19W 29 G3
Cambrai France 50°11N 3°14E 66 A5
Cambrian Mts. U.K. 52°3N 3°57W 28 C6
Cambridge Jamaica 18°18N 77°54W 114 a
Cambridge U.K. 52°12N 0°8E 31 B9
Cambridge Mass., U.S.A. 42°23N 71°7W 113 D12
Cambridge Md., U.S.A. 38°34N 76°5W 113 F9
Cambridge Ohio, U.S.A. 40°2N 81°35W 112 E7
Cambridge Bay Canada 69°10N 105°0W 108 C9
Cambridgeshire □ U.K. 52°25N 0°7W 31 B8
Camden Ark., U.S.A. 33°35N 92°50W 111 D8
Camden N.J., U.S.A. 39°55N 75°7W 113 F10
Camden □ U.K. 51°32N 0°8W 31 C8
Camel → U.K. 50°31N 4°51W 29 F4
Camelford U.K. 50°37N 4°42W 29 F4
Cameroon ■ Africa 6°0N 12°30E 96 C2
Cameroun, Mt. Cameroon 4°13N 9°10E 96 D1
Cametá Brazil 2°12S 49°30W 120 C5
Camocim Brazil 2°55S 40°50W 120 C5
Campana, I. Chile 48°20S 75°20W 121 G1
Campánia □ Italy 41°0N 14°30E 68 D6
Campbell I. Pac. Oc. 52°30S 169°0E 102 N8
Campbell River Canada 50°5N 125°20W 108 D7
Campbellsville U.S.A. 37°21N 85°20W 112 G5
Campbellton Canada 47°57N 66°43W 109 E13
Campbeltown U.K. 55°26N 5°36W 24 D4
Campeche Mexico 19°51N 90°32W 114 D6
Campeche, Golfo de Mexico 19°30N 93°0W 114 D6
Campina Grande Brazil 7°20S 35°47W 120 C6
Campinas Brazil 22°50S 47°0W 122 D1
Campo Belo Brazil 20°52S 45°16W 122 D1
Campo Grande Brazil 20°25S 54°40W 120 E4
Campobasso Italy 41°34N 14°39E 68 D6
Campos Brazil 21°50S 41°20W 122 D2
Campos Belos Brazil 13°10S 47°3W 122 B1
Can Tho Vietnam 10°2N 105°46E 82 B3
Canada ■ N. Amer. 60°0N 100°0W 108 D10
Canadian → U.S.A. 35°28N 95°3W 111 C7
Canadian Shield Canada 53°0N 75°0W 104 D9
Çanakkale Turkey 40°8N 26°24E 71 F4
Canandaigua U.S.A. 42°54N 77°17W 112 D9
Cananea Mexico 31°0N 110°18W 114 A2
Canaries St. Lucia 13°55N 61°4W 114 b
Canary Is. Atl. Oc. 28°30N 16°0W 94 C2
Canaveral, C. U.S.A. 28°27N 80°32W 111 E10
Canavieiras Brazil 15°39S 39°0W 122 C3
Canberra Australia 35°15S 149°8E 98 H8
Cancún Mexico 21°8N 86°44W 114 C7
Cangzhou China 38°19N 116°52E 79 D12
Caniapiscau → Canada 56°40N 69°30W 109 D13
Caniapiscau, L. Canada 54°10N 69°55W 109 D13
Çankırı Turkey 40°40N 33°37E 71 F5
Canna U.K. 57°3N 6°33W 22 H4
Canna, Sd. of U.K. 57°1N 6°30W 22 H5
Cannes France 43°32N 7°1E 66 E7
Cannington U.K. 51°9N 3°4W 30 D2
Cannock U.K. 52°41N 2°1W 27 G4
Cannock Chase U.K. 52°44N 2°4W 27 G4
Canoas Brazil 29°56S 51°11W 121 E4
Cañon City U.S.A. 38°27N 105°14W 110 C5
Canonbie U.K. 55°5N 2°58W 25 D10
Canora Canada 51°40N 102°30W 108 D9
Canso Canada 45°20N 61°0W 113 C17
Cantabria □ Spain 43°10N 4°0W 67 A4
Cantábrica, Cordillera Spain 43°0N 5°10W 67 A3
Canterbury U.K. 51°16N 1°6E 31 D11
Canton = Guangzhou China 23°6N 113°13E 79 G11
Canton Ill., U.S.A. 40°33N 90°2W 112 E2
Canton N.Y., U.S.A. 44°36N 75°10W 113 C10
Canton Ohio, U.S.A. 40°48N 81°23W 112 E7
Canvey Island U.K. 51°31N 0°37E 31 C10
Cap-de-la-Madeleine Canada 46°22N 72°31W 113 B11
Cap-Haïtien Haiti 19°40N 72°20W 115 D10
Cap Pt. St. Lucia 14°7N 60°57W 114 b
Cape Breton I. Canada 46°0N 60°30W 113 C17
Cape Charles U.S.A. 37°16N 76°1W 113 G10
Cape Coast Ghana 5°5N 1°15W 94 G5
Cape Coral U.S.A. 26°33N 81°57W 111 E10
Cape Fear → U.S.A. 33°53N 78°1W 111 D11
Cape Girardeau U.S.A. 37°19N 89°32W 112 G3
Cape May U.S.A. 38°56N 74°56W 113 F10
Cape Town S. Africa 33°55S 18°22E 97 L3
Cape Verde Is. ■ Atl. Oc. 16°0N 24°0W 91 E1
Cape York Peninsula Australia 12°0S 142°30E 98 C7
Capela Brazil 10°30S 37°0W 122 B3
Capreol Canada 46°43N 80°56W 112 B7
Capri Italy 40°33N 14°14E 68 D6
Caprivi Strip Namibia 18°0S 23°0E 97 H4
Caquetá → Colombia 1°15S 69°15W 120 D3
Caracas Venezuela 10°30N 66°55W 120 A3

Caracol Brazil 9°15S 43°22W 122 A2
Carangola Brazil 20°44S 42°5W 122 D2
Caratasca, L. de Honduras 15°20N 83°40W 115 D8
Caratinga Brazil 19°50S 42°10W 122 C2
Caravelas Brazil 17°45S 39°15W 122 C3
Carbón, L. del Argentina 49°35S 68°21W 121 G3
Carbondale Ill., U.S.A. 37°44N 89°13W 112 G3
Carbondale Pa., U.S.A. 41°35N 75°30W 113 E10
Carbonear Canada 47°42N 53°13W 109 E14
Carcassonne France 43°13N 2°20E 66 E5
Carcross Canada 60°13N 134°45W 108 C6
Cardamon Hills India 9°30N 77°15E 84 Q10
Cárdenas Cuba 23°0N 81°30W 115 C8
Cardiff U.K. 51°29N 3°10W 29 E7
Cardigan U.K. 52°5N 4°40W 28 C4
Cardigan B. U.K. 52°30N 4°30W 28 B4
Cardington U.K. 52°6N 0°25E 31 B8
Cardston Canada 49°15N 113°20W 108 E8
Cariacica Brazil 20°16S 40°25W 122 D2
Caribbean Sea W. Indies 15°0N 75°0W 115 F10
Cariboo Mts. Canada 53°0N 121°0W 108 D7
Caribou U.S.A. 46°52N 68°1W 113 B13
Caribou Mts. Canada 59°12N 115°40W 108 D8
Carinhanha Brazil 14°15S 44°46W 122 B2
Carinhanha → Brazil 14°20S 43°47W 122 B2
Carinthia = Kärnten □ Austria 46°52N 13°30E 64 E8
Carisbrooke U.K. 50°41N 1°19W 30 E6
Cark U.K. 54°11N 2°58W 26 D3
Carleton Place Canada 45°8N 76°9W 113 C9
Carleton Rode U.K. 52°30N 1°7E 31 A11
Carlingford L. U.K. 54°3N 6°9W 19 C9
Carlinville U.S.A. 39°17N 89°53W 112 F3
Carlisle U.K. 54°54N 2°56W 26 C3
Carlisle U.S.A. 40°12N 77°12W 112 E9
Carlisle B. Barbados 13°5N 59°37W 114 c
Carlops U.K. 55°47N 3°20W 25 C9
Carlow Ireland 52°50N 6°56W 21 C9
Carlow □ Ireland 52°43N 6°50W 21 C9
Carlsbad U.S.A. 32°25N 104°14W 110 D6
Carlton U.K. 52°59N 1°5W 27 G6
Carlton Colville U.K. 52°27N 1°43E 31 B12
Carlton Miniott U.K. 54°12N 1°22W 26 D6
Carluke U.K. 55°45N 3°50W 25 C8
Carmacks Canada 62°5N 136°16W 108 C6
Carmarthen U.K. 51°52N 4°19W 28 D5
Carmarthen B. U.K. 51°40N 4°30W 28 D4
Carmarthenshire □ U.K. 51°55N 4°13W 28 D5
Carmaux France 44°3N 2°10E 66 D5
Carmi U.S.A. 38°5N 88°10W 112 F3
Carn Ban U.K. 57°7N 4°15W 23 H9
Carn Eige U.K. 57°17N 5°8W 22 H7
Carnarvon Australia 24°51S 113°42E 98 E1
Carnarvon S. Africa 30°56S 22°8E 97 L4
Carndonagh Ireland 55°16N 7°15W 19 A7
Carnegie, L. Australia 26°5S 122°30E 98 F3
Carnforth U.K. 54°7N 2°45W 26 D3
Carno U.K. 52°34N 3°30W 28 B6
Carnoustie U.K. 56°30N 2°42W 25 A10
Carnsore Pt. Ireland 52°10N 6°22W 21 D10
Caro U.S.A. 43°29N 83°24W 112 D6
Caroline I. Kiribati 9°58S 150°13W 103 H12
Caroline Is. Micronesia 8°0N 150°0E 102 G6
Carondelet Reef Kiribati 5°33S 173°50E 99 B16
Caroní → Venezuela 8°21N 62°43W 120 B3
Carpathians Europe 49°30N 21°0E 65 D11
Carpentaria, G. of Australia 14°0S 139°0E 98 C6
Carpentras France 44°3N 5°2E 66 D6
Carpi Italy 44°47N 10°53E 68 B4
Carrara Italy 44°5N 10°6E 68 B4
Carrauntoohill Ireland 52°0N 9°45W 20 E3
Carrick-on-Shannon Ireland 53°57N 8°7W 18 D5
Carrick-on-Suir Ireland 52°21N 7°24W 21 D8
Carrickfergus U.K. 54°43N 5°49W 19 B10
Carrickmacross Ireland 53°59N 6°43W 19 D8
Carrigaline Ireland 51°48N 8°23W 20 E6
Carrollton U.S.A. 39°18N 90°24W 112 F2
Carron → U.K. 57°53N 4°22W 23 G9
Carron, L. U.K. 57°22N 5°35W 22 H6
Carson City U.S.A. 39°10N 119°46W 110 C3
Carson Sink U.S.A. 39°50N 118°25W 110 C3
Cartagena Colombia 10°25N 75°33W 120 A2
Cartagena Spain 37°38N 0°59W 67 D5
Cartago Colombia 4°45N 75°55W 120 B2
Carter Bar U.K. 55°21N 2°29W 25 D10
Carthage Tunisia 36°52N 10°20E 95 A8
Cartmel U.K. 54°12N 2°57W 26 D3
Cartwright Canada 53°41N 56°58W 109 D14
Caruaru Brazil 8°15S 35°55W 122 A3
Carúpano Venezuela 10°39N 63°15W 120 A3
Cas-gwent = Chepstow U.K. 51°38N 2°41W 28 D8
Casa Grande U.S.A. 32°53N 111°45W 110 D4
Casa Nova Brazil 9°25S 41°5W 122 A2
Casablanca Morocco 33°36N 7°36W 94 B4
Cascade Ra. U.S.A. 47°0N 121°30W 110 A2
Cascavel Ceará, Brazil 4°7S 38°14W 120 C6
Cascavel Paraná, Brazil 24°57S 53°28W 121 E4
Caserta Italy 41°4N 14°20E 68 D6
Cashel Ireland 52°30N 7°53W 20 D7
Casiquiare → Venezuela 2°1N 67°7W 120 B3
Casnewydd = Newport U.K. 51°35N 3°0W 29 D8
Casper U.S.A. 42°51N 106°19W 110 B5
Caspian Depression Eurasia 47°0N 48°0E 71 E8
Caspian Sea Eurasia 43°0N 50°0E 71 F9
Cassiar Mts. Canada 59°30N 130°30W 108 D6
Castell-Nedd = Neath U.K. 51°39N 3°48W 28 D6
Castellammare di Stábia Italy 40°42N 14°29E 68 D6
Castelló de la Plana Spain 39°58N 0°3W 67 C5
Castelsarrasin France 44°2N 1°7E 66 E4
Castilla-La Mancha □ Spain 39°30N 3°30W 67 C4
Castilla y León □ Spain 42°0N 5°0W 67 B3
Castle Acre U.K. 52°42N 0°42E 31 A10
Castle Cary U.K. 51°6N 2°31W 30 D3
Castle Donington U.K. 52°51N 1°20W 27 G6
Castle Douglas U.K. 54°56N 3°56W 25 E8
Castlebar Ireland 53°52N 9°18W 18 D3
Castleblayney Ireland 54°7N 6°44W 19 C8
Castleford U.K. 53°43N 1°21W 27 E6
Castlemaine Harbour Ireland 52°8N 9°50W 20 D3

Castlepollard Ireland 53°41N 7°19W 18 D7
Castlerea Ireland 53°46N 8°29W 18 D5
Castleside U.K. 54°50N 1°52W 26 C5
Castleton Derby., U.K. 53°22N 1°46W 27 F5
Castleton N. Yorks., U.K. 54°28N 0°57W 26 D7
Castletown I. of Man 54°5N 4°38W 19 C12
Castletown Bearhaven Ireland 51°39N 9°55W 20 E3
Castres France 43°37N 2°13E 66 E5
Castries St. Lucia 14°2N 60°58W 114 b
Castro Chile 42°30S 73°50W 121 G2
Castro Alves Brazil 12°46S 39°33W 122 B3
Cat I. Bahamas 24°30N 75°30W 115 C9
Cataguases Brazil 21°23S 42°39W 122 D2
Catalão Brazil 18°10S 47°57W 122 C1
Cataluña □ Spain 41°40N 1°15E 67 B6
Catamarca Argentina 28°30S 65°50W 121 E3
Catanduanes Phil. 13°50N 124°20E 83 B6
Catanduva Brazil 21°5S 48°58W 122 D1
Catánia Italy 37°30N 15°6E 68 F6
Catanzaro Italy 38°54N 16°35E 68 E7
Catcleugh U.K. 55°20N 2°24W 26 B4
Caterham U.K. 51°15N 0°4W 31 D8
Catoche, C. Mexico 21°35N 87°5W 114 C7
Caton U.K. 54°5N 2°42W 26 D3
Catsfield U.K. 50°54N 0°28E 31 E9
Catskill U.S.A. 42°14N 73°52W 113 D11
Catskill Mts. U.S.A. 42°10N 74°25W 113 D10
Catterick U.K. 54°23N 1°37W 26 D5
Catterick Garrison U.K. 54°22N 1°42W 26 D5
Catton U.K. 54°56N 2°16W 26 C4
Cauca → Colombia 8°54N 74°28W 120 B2
Caucaia Brazil 3°40S 38°35W 120 C6
Caucasus Mountains Eurasia 42°50N 44°0E 71 F7
Caulkerbush U.K. 54°54N 3°41W 25 E9
Caura → Venezuela 7°38N 64°53W 120 B3
Cauvery → India 11°9N 78°52E 84 P11
Cavan Ireland 54°0N 7°22W 18 D7
Cavan □ Ireland 54°1N 7°16W 19 C7
Caviana, I. Brazil 0°10N 50°10W 120 B4
Cawood U.K. 53°50N 1°8W 27 E6
Cawston U.K. 52°47N 1°9E 31 A11
Caxias Brazil 4°55S 43°20W 120 C5
Caxias do Sul Brazil 29°10S 51°10W 121 E4
Cayenne Fr. Guiana 5°5N 52°18W 120 B4
Cayman Is. □ W. Indies 19°40N 80°30W 115 D8
Cayman Trench Caribbean 17°0N 83°0W 115 D8
Cayuga L. U.S.A. 42°41N 76°41W 112 D9
Ceará □ Brazil 5°0S 40°0W 120 C6
Cebu Phil. 10°18N 123°54E 83 B6
Cedar City U.S.A. 37°41N 113°4W 110 C4
Cedar L. Canada 53°10N 100°0W 108 D9
Cedar Rapids U.S.A. 41°59N 91°40W 111 E8
Cefalù Italy 38°2N 14°1E 68 E6
Cegléd Hungary 47°11N 19°47E 65 E10
Celaya Mexico 20°31N 100°37W 114 C4
Celebes Sea Indonesia 3°0N 123°0E 83 D6
Celina U.S.A. 40°33N 84°35W 112 E5
Cellar Hd. U.K. 58°25N 6°11W 22 F5
Celtic Sea Atl. Oc. 50°9N 9°34W 62 F4
Cemaes U.K. 53°24N 4°27W 28 A5
Central, Cordillera Colombia 5°0N 75°0W 117 C3
Central African Rep. ■ Africa 7°0N 20°0E 96 C4
Central Bedfordshire □ U.K. 52°5N 0°20W 31 B8
Central Makran Range Pakistan 26°30N 64°15E 84 F4
Central Russian Uplands Europe 54°0N 36°0E 56 E13
Central Siberian Plateau Russia 65°0N 105°0E 72 B12
Centralia Ill., U.S.A. 38°32N 89°8W 112 F3
Centralia Wash., U.S.A. 46°43N 122°58W 110 A2
Cephalonia = Kefalonia Greece 38°15N 20°30E 69 E9
Ceredigion □ U.K. 52°16N 4°15W 28 C5
Cerignola Italy 41°17N 15°53E 68 D6
Cerne Abbas U.K. 50°49N 2°29W 30 E4
Cerrigydrudion U.K. 53°1N 3°33W 28 A6
Cerro de Pasco Peru 10°45S 76°10W 120 D2
Cesena Italy 44°8N 12°15E 68 B5
České Budějovice Czech Rep. 48°55N 14°25E 64 D8
Çeşme Turkey 38°20N 26°23E 71 G4
Ceuta N. Afr. 35°52N 5°18W 67 E3
Ceve-i-Ra Fiji 21°46S 174°31E 99 E13
Cévennes France 44°10N 3°50E 66 D5
Chacewater U.K. 50°15N 5°11W 29 G3
Chachapoyas Peru 6°15S 77°50W 120 C2
Chaco Austral S. Amer. 27°0S 61°30W 121 E3
Chaco Boreal S. Amer. 22°0S 60°0W 121 E4
Chaco Central S. Amer. 24°0S 61°0W 121 E3
Chad ■ Africa 15°0N 17°15E 95 F8
Chad, L. Chad 13°30N 14°30E 95 F8
Chadron U.S.A. 42°50N 103°0W 110 B6
Chagford U.K. 50°40N 3°50W 29 F6
Chaghcharán Afghan. 34°31N 65°15E 87 C11
Chagos Arch. □ Ind. Oc. 6°0S 72°0E 53 E13
Chah Gay Hills Afghan. 29°30N 64°0E 87 D10
Chakradharpur India 22°45N 85°40E 85 H14
Chaleur B. Canada 47°55N 65°30W 113 B15
Chalisgaon India 20°30N 75°10E 84 J9
Challenger Deep Pac. Oc. 11°30N 142°0E 102 F6
Chalon-sur-Saône France 46°48N 4°50E 66 C6
Châlons-en-Champagne France 48°58N 4°20E 66 B6
Chambal → India 26°29N 79°15E 84 F11
Chambersburg U.S.A. 39°56N 77°40W 112 F9
Chambéry France 45°34N 5°55E 66 D6
Chamonix-Mont Blanc France 45°55N 6°51E 66 D7
Champagne France 48°40N 4°20E 66 B6
Champaign U.S.A. 40°7N 88°15W 112 E3
Champlain, L. U.S.A. 44°40N 73°20W 113 C11
Chañaral Chile 26°23S 70°40W 121 E2
Chancery Lane Barbados 13°3N 59°30W 114 c
Chandigarh India 30°43N 76°47E 84 D10
Chandler's Ford U.K. 50°59N 1°22W 30 E6
Chandpur Bangla. 23°8N 90°45E 85 H17
Chandrapur India 19°57N 79°25E 84 K11
Changbai Shan China 42°20N 129°0E 79 C14
Changchun China 43°57N 125°17E 79 C14
Changde China 29°4N 111°35E 79 F11
Changhua Taiwan 24°2N 120°30E 79 G13
Changji China 44°1N 87°19E 78 C6

Changsha China 28°12N 113°0E 79 F11
Changzhi China 36°10N 113°6E 79 D11
Changzhou China 31°47N 119°58E 79 E12
Chania Greece 35°30N 24°4E 69 G11
Channel Is. U.K. 49°19N 2°24W 29 J9
Channel Is. U.S.A. 33°40N 119°15W 110 D2
Channel-Port aux Basques Canada 47°30N 59°9W 109 E14
Chantrey Inlet Canada 67°48N 96°20W 108 C10
Chaoyang China 41°35N 120°22E 79 C13
Chaozhou China 23°42N 116°32E 79 G12
Chapala, L. de Mexico 20°10N 103°20W 114 C4
Chapayevsk Russia 53°0N 49°40E 70 D8
Chapel-en-le-Frith U.K. 53°20N 1°54W 27 F5
Chapel St. Leonards U.K. 53°13N 0°20E 27 F9
Chapleau Canada 47°50N 83°24W 109 E11
Chapra = Chhapra India 25°48N 84°44E 85 G14
Chard U.K. 50°52N 2°58W 30 E3
Chari → Chad 12°58N 14°31E 95 F8
Chārīkār Afghan. 35°0N 69°10E 87 C12
Charing U.K. 51°12N 0°49E 31 D10
Charlbury U.K. 51°53N 1°28W 30 C6
Charleroi Belgium 50°24N 4°27E 64 C3
Charles, C. U.S.A. 37°7N 75°58W 113 G10
Charles City U.S.A. 43°4N 92°41W 111 D8
Charleston Ill., U.S.A. 39°30N 88°10W 112 F3
Charleston Mo., U.S.A. 36°55N 89°21W 112 G3
Charleston S.C., U.S.A. 32°46N 79°56W 111 D11
Charleston W. Va., U.S.A. 38°21N 81°38W 112 F7
Charlestown of Aberlour U.K. 57°28N 3°14W 23 H11
Charleville Australia 26°24S 146°15E 98 F8
Charleville Ireland 52°21N 8°40W 20 D5
Charleville-Mézières France 49°44N 4°40E 66 B6
Charlevoix U.S.A. 45°19N 85°16W 112 C5
Charlotte Mich., U.S.A. 42°34N 84°50W 112 D5
Charlotte N.C., U.S.A. 35°13N 80°50W 111 C10
Charlotte Amalie U.S. Virgin Is. 18°21N 64°56W 115 D12
Charlotte Harbor U.S.A. 26°57N 82°4W 111 E10
Charlottesville U.S.A. 38°2N 78°30W 112 F8
Charlottetown Canada 46°14N 63°8W 113 B16
Charlton I. Canada 52°0N 79°20W 109 D12
Charlton Kings U.K. 51°53N 2°3W 30 C4
Charlwood U.K. 51°9N 0°13W 31 D8
Charminster U.K. 50°44N 2°28W 30 E4
Charmouth U.K. 50°45N 2°54W 30 E3
Charnwood Forest U.K. 52°44N 1°17W 27 G6
Charolles France 46°27N 4°16E 66 C6
Charters Towers Australia 20°5S 146°13E 98 E8
Chartham U.K. 51°14N 1°1E 31 D11
Chartres France 48°29N 1°30E 66 B4
Chascomús Argentina 35°30S 58°0W 121 F4
Châteaubriant France 47°43N 1°23W 66 C3
Châteaulin France 48°11N 4°8W 66 B1
Châteauroux France 46°50N 1°40E 66 C4
Châtellerault France 46°50N 0°30E 66 C4
Chatham = Miramichi Canada 47°2N 65°28W 109 E13
Chatham Canada 42°24N 82°11W 112 D6
Chatham U.K. 51°22N 0°32E 31 D10
Chatham Is. Pac. Oc. 44°0S 176°40W 99 J15
Chatsworth U.K. 53°13N 1°36W 27 F6
Chattanooga U.S.A. 35°3N 85°19W 111 C9
Chatteris U.K. 52°28N 0°2E 31 B9
Chatton U.K. 55°35N 2°0W 26 A5
Chaumont France 48°7N 5°8E 66 B6
Chaykovskiy Russia 56°47N 54°9E 70 C9
Cheadle Gt. Man., U.K. 53°23N 2°12W 27 F4
Cheadle Staffs., U.K. 52°59N 1°58W 27 G5
Cheb Czech Rep. 50°9N 12°28E 64 C7
Cheboksary Russia 56°8N 47°12E 70 C8
Cheboygan U.S.A. 45°39N 84°29W 112 C5
Chech, Erg Africa 25°0N 2°15W 94 D5
Chechenia □ Russia 43°30N 45°29E 71 F8
Chedabucto B. Canada 45°25N 61°8W 113 C17
Cheddar U.K. 51°17N 2°46W 30 D3
Cheddleton U.K. 53°4N 2°2W 27 F4
Cheduba I. Burma 18°45N 93°40E 85 K18
Chegutu Zimbabwe 18°10S 30°14E 97 H6
Chek Lap Kok China 22°18N 113°56E 79 a
Chelm Poland 51°8N 23°30E 65 C12
Chelmer → U.K. 51°44N 0°30E 31 C10
Chelmsford U.K. 51°44N 0°29E 31 C9
Cheltenham U.K. 51°54N 2°4W 30 C4
Chelyabinsk Russia 55°10N 61°24E 76 D7
Chelyuskin, C. Russia 77°30N 103°0E 77 B11
Chemnitz Germany 50°51N 12°54E 64 C7
Chenab → Pakistan 30°23N 71°2E 84 D7
Chengde China 40°59N 117°58E 79 C12
Chengdu China 30°38N 104°2E 78 E9
Chennai India 13°8N 80°19E 84 N12
Cheo, Eilean a' = Skye U.K. 57°15N 6°10W 22 H5
Chepstow U.K. 51°38N 2°41W 28 D8
Cher → France 47°21N 0°29E 66 C4
Cherbourg-Octeville France 49°39N 1°40W 66 B3
Cheremkhovo Russia 53°8N 103°1E 78 A9
Cherepovets Russia 59°5N 37°55E 70 C6
Chergui, Chott ech Algeria 34°21N 0°25E 94 B6
Cheriton U.K. 51°3N 1°8W 30 D6
Cheriton Fitzpaine U.K. 50°51N 3°35W 29 F6
Cherkasy Ukraine 49°27N 32°4E 71 E5
Cherkessk Russia 44°15N 42°5E 71 F7
Chernivtsi Ukraine 48°15N 25°52E 65 D13
Chernobyl Ukraine 51°20N 30°15E 65 C16
Cherokee U.S.A. 42°45N 95°33W 111 B7
Cherrapunji India 25°17N 91°47E 85 G17
Chertsey U.K. 51°23N 0°30W 31 D7
Chervonohrad Ukraine 50°25N 24°10E 65 C13
Cherwell → U.K. 51°44N 1°14W 30 C6
Chesapeake U.S.A. 36°50N 76°17W 112 G9
Chesha B. Russia 67°20N 47°0E 70 A8
Chesham U.K. 51°43N 0°36W 31 C7
Cheshire East □ U.K. 53°15N 2°24W 27 F3
Cheshire West and Chester □ U.K. 53°15N 2°40W 27 F3
Cheshunt U.K. 51°43N 0°1W 31 C8
Chesil Beach U.K. 50°37N 2°33W 30 E3

Chester   Cumberland

Chester U.K. 53°12N 2°53W 27 F3
Chester U.S.A. 39°51N 75°22W 113 F10
Chester-le-Street U.K. 54°51N 1°34W 26 C5
Chesterfield U.K. 53°15N 1°25W 27 F6
Chesterfield, Îs. N. Cal. 19°52S 158°15E 99 D10
Chesterfield Inlet U.S.A. 63°30N 90°45W 108 C10
Chesuncook L. U.S.A. 46°0N 69°21W 113 B13
Chetumal Mexico 18°30N 88°20W 114 D7
Chetwynd Canada 55°45N 121°36W 108 D7
Cheviot, The U.K. 55°29N 2°9W 26 B4
Cheviot Hills U.K. 55°20N 2°30W 26 B3
Chew Bahir Ethiopia 4°40N 36°50E 89 G2
Chew Magna U.K. 51°22N 2°37W 30 D3
Cheyenne U.S.A. 41°8N 104°49W 110 B6
Cheyenne → U.S.A. 44°41N 101°18W 110 B6
Chhapra India 25°48N 84°44E 85 G14
Chhattisgarh □ India 22°0N 82°0E 85 J12
Chi → Thailand 15°11N 104°43E 82 A3
Chiai Taiwan 23°29N 120°25E 79 G13
Chiávari Italy 44°19N 9°19E 68 B3
Chiba Japan 35°30N 140°7E 81 F7
Chibougamau Canada 49°56N 74°24W 109 E12
Chibougamau, L. Canada 49°50N 74°20W 113 A10
Chic-Chocs, Mts. Canada 48°55N 66°0W 113 A14
Chicago U.S.A. 41°52N 87°38W 112 E4
Chichagof I. U.S.A. 57°30N 135°30W 108 D6
Chichester U.K. 50°50N 0°47W 31 E7
Chickasha U.S.A. 35°3N 97°58W 110 C7
Chiclayo Peru 6°42S 79°50W 120 C2
Chico U.S.A. 39°44N 121°50W 110 C2
Chico → Chubut, Argentina 44°0S 67°0W 121 G3
Chico → Santa Cruz, Argentina 50°0S 68°30W 121 G3
Chicopee U.S.A. 42°9N 72°37W 113 D11
Chicoutimi Canada 48°28N 71°5W 113 A12
Chiddingfold U.K. 51°7N 0°37W 31 D7
Chidley, C. Canada 60°23N 64°26W 109 C13
Chieti Italy 42°21N 14°10E 68 C6
Chifeng China 42°18N 118°58E 79 C12
Chihuahua Mexico 28°38N 106°5W 114 B3
Chilapa Mexico 17°36N 99°10W 114 D5
Chilaw Sri Lanka 7°30N 79°50E 84 R11
Childress U.S.A. 34°25N 100°13W 110 D6
Chile ■ S. Amer. 35°0S 72°0W 121 F2
Chilham U.K. 51°15N 0°59E 31 D10
Chililabombwe Zambia 12°18S 27°43E 97 G5
Chilka L. India 19°40N 85°25E 85 K14
Chillán Chile 36°40S 72°10W 121 F2
Chillicothe Ill., U.S.A. 40°55N 89°29W 112 E3
Chillicothe Ohio, U.S.A. 39°20N 82°59W 112 F6
Chilliwack Canada 49°10N 121°54W 108 E7
Chiloé, I. de Chile 42°30S 73°50W 121 G2
Chilpancingo Mexico 17°33N 99°30W 114 D5
Chiltern Hills U.K. 51°40N 0°53W 31 D7
Chilton U.S.A. 44°2N 88°10W 112 C9
Chilung Taiwan 25°3N 121°45E 79 F13
Chilwa, L. Malawi 15°15S 35°40E 97 H7
Chimborazo Ecuador 1°29S 78°55W 120 C2
Chimbote Peru 9°0S 78°35W 120 C2
Chimoio Mozam. 19°4S 33°30E 97 H6
Chin □ Burma 22°0N 93°0E 85 J18
Chin Hills Burma 22°30N 93°30E 85 H18
China ■ Asia 30°0N 110°0E 79 E11
China, Great Plain of Asia 35°0N 115°0E 72 E13
Chinandega Nic. 12°35N 87°12W 114 E7
Chincha Alta Peru 13°25S 76°7W 120 D2
Chindwin → Burma 21°26N 95°15E 85 J19
Chingola Zambia 12°31S 27°53E 97 G5
Chinhoyi Zimbabwe 17°20S 30°8E 97 H6
Chiniot Pakistan 31°45N 73°0E 84 D8
Chinmen Tao Taiwan 24°26N 118°22E 79 G12
Chinon France 47°10N 0°15E 66 C4
Chióggia Italy 45°13N 12°17E 68 B5
Chipata Zambia 13°38S 32°28E 97 G6
Chipman Canada 46°6N 65°53W 113 B15
Chippenham U.K. 51°27N 2°6W 30 D4
Chippewa Falls U.S.A. 44°56N 91°24W 112 C2
Chipping Campden U.K. 52°3N 1°45W 30 B5
Chipping Norton U.K. 51°56N 1°32W 30 C5
Chipping Ongar U.K. 51°42N 0°15E 31 C9
Chipping Sodbury U.K. 51°33N 2°23W 30 C4
Chiquinquira Colombia 5°37N 73°50W 120 B2
Chirbury U.K. 52°35N 3°4W 27 G2
Chirchiq Uzbekistan 41°29N 69°35E 87 A12
Chiredzi Zimbabwe 21°0S 31°38E 97 J6
Chirnside U.K. 55°48N 2°12W 25 C11
Chisasibi Canada 53°50N 79°0W 109 D12
Chiseldon U.K. 51°31N 1°44W 30 C5
Chistopol Russia 55°25N 50°38E 70 C9
Chita Russia 52°0N 113°35E 77 D12
Chitral Pakistan 35°50N 71°56E 84 B7
Chittagong Bangla. 22°19N 91°48E 85 H17
Chitungwiza Zimbabwe 18°0S 31°6E 97 H6
Choiseul St. Lucia 13°47N 61°3W 114 b
Choiseul Solomon Is. 7°0S 156°40E 99 B10
Chōkai-San Japan 39°6N 140°3E 81 D7
Cholet France 47°4N 0°52W 66 C3
Chollerton U.K. 55°4N 2°7W 26 B4
Cholsey U.K. 51°35N 1°8W 30 C6
Choluteca Honduras 13°20N 87°14W 114 E7
Chon Buri Thailand 13°21N 101°1E 82 B2
Ch'ŏngjin N. Korea 41°47N 129°50E 79 C14
Chongqing China 29°35N 106°25E 78 F10
Chongqing Shi □ China 30°0N 108°0E 78 F10
Chonos, Arch. de los Chile 45°0S 75°0W 121 G2
Chorley U.K. 53°39N 2°38W 27 E3
Chorzów Poland 50°18N 18°57E 65 C10
Choybalsan Mongolia 48°4N 114°30E 79 B11
Choyr Mongolia 46°24N 108°30E 79 B10
Christchurch N.Z. 43°33S 172°47E 99 J13
Christchurch U.K. 50°44N 1°47W 30 E5
Christmas I. Ind. Oc. 10°30S 105°40E 102 J2
Chubut → Argentina 43°20S 65°5W 121 G3
Chudleigh U.K. 50°36N 3°36W 29 F6
Chudskoye, L. Russia 58°13N 27°30E 70 C4
Chukchi Sea Russia 68°0N 175°0W 77 C19
Chukot Ra. Russia 68°0N 175°0E 77 C18
Chulmleigh U.K. 50°54N 3°51W 29 F6
Chuncheon S. Korea 37°58N 127°44E 79 D14
Chuquicamata Chile 22°15S 69°0W 121 E3
Chur Switz. 46°52N 9°32E 64 E5
Church Stretton U.K. 52°32N 2°48W 27 G3

Churchdown U.K. 51°52N 2°10W 30 C4
Churchill Canada 58°47N 94°11W 108 D10
Churchill → Man. Canada 58°47N 94°12W 108 D10
Churchill → Nfld. & L., Canada 53°19N 60°10W 109 D13
Churchill, C. Canada 58°46N 93°12W 108 D10
Churchill Falls Canada 53°36N 64°19W 109 D13
Churchill L. Canada 55°55N 108°20W 108 D9
Churchill Pk. Canada 58°10N 125°10W 108 D7
Churu India 28°20N 74°50E 84 E9
Chuska Mts. U.S.A. 36°15N 108°50W 110 C5
Chusovoy Russia 58°22N 57°50E 70 C10
Chuvashia □ Russia 55°30N 47°0E 70 C8
Chuxiong China 25°2N 101°28E 78 F9
Cicero U.S.A. 41°51N 87°44W 112 E4
Ciechanów Poland 52°52N 20°38E 65 B11
Ciego de Ávila Cuba 21°50N 78°50W 115 C9
Cienfuegos Cuba 22°10N 80°30W 115 C8
Cilo Daği Turkey 37°28N 43°55E 71 G7
Cimarron → U.S.A. 36°10N 96°16W 111 C7
Cincinnati U.S.A. 39°9N 84°27N 112 F5
Cinderford U.K. 51°49N 2°30W 30 C3
Cinto, Mte. France 42°24N 8°54E 66 E8
Circle U.S.A. 65°50N 144°4W 108 C5
Circleville U.S.A. 39°36N 82°57W 112 F6
Cirebon Indonesia 6°45S 108°32E 82 F3
Cirencester U.K. 51°43N 1°57W 30 C5
Ciudad Acuña Mexico 29°18N 100°55W 114 B4
Ciudad Bolívar Venezuela 8°5N 63°36W 120 B3
Ciudad del Carmen Mexico 18°38N 91°50W 114 D6
Ciudad del Este Paraguay 25°30S 54°50W 121 E4
Ciudad Guayana Venezuela 8°0N 62°30W 120 B3
Ciudad Guzmán Mexico 19°41N 103°29W 114 D4
Ciudad Juárez Mexico 31°44N 106°29W 114 A3
Ciudad Madero Mexico 22°19N 97°50W 114 C5
Ciudad Mante Mexico 22°44N 98°59W 114 C5
Ciudad Obregón Mexico 27°29N 109°56W 114 B3
Ciudad Real Spain 38°59N 3°55W 67 C4
Ciudad Valles Mexico 21°59N 99°1W 114 C5
Ciudad Victoria Mexico 23°44N 99°8W 114 C5
Civitavécchia Italy 42°6N 11°48E 68 C4
Cizre Turkey 37°19N 42°10E 71 G7
Clackmannan U.K. 56°7N 3°45W 25 B9
Clacton-on-Sea U.K. 51°47N 1°11E 31 C11
Claire, L. Canada 58°35N 112°5W 108 D8
Clara Ireland 53°21N 7°37W 18 C3
Clare U.K. 52°4N 0°34E 31 B10
Clare □ Ireland 52°45N 9°0W 20 C4
Clare → Ireland 53°20N 9°2W 18 C3
Clare I. Ireland 53°47N 10°0W 18 C1
Claremont U.S.A. 43°23N 72°20W 113 D11
Clark Fork → U.S.A. 48°9N 116°15W 110 A3
Clarksburg U.S.A. 39°17N 80°30W 112 F7
Clarksdale U.S.A. 34°12N 90°35W 111 D8
Clarksville U.S.A. 36°32N 87°21W 111 C9
Claverley U.K. 52°32N 2°18W 27 G4
Clay Cross U.K. 53°10N 1°25W 27 F6
Claydon U.K. 52°7N 1°8E 31 B11
Clear, C. Ireland 51°25N 9°32W 20 F3
Clear I. Ireland 51°26N 9°30W 20 F4
Clearfield U.S.A. 41°2N 78°27W 112 E8
Clearwater U.S.A. 27°59N 82°48W 111 E10
Cleator Moor U.K. 54°32N 3°30W 26 C2
Clee Hills U.K. 52°26N 2°35W 27 G3
Cleethorpes U.K. 53°33N 0°3W 27 E8
Cleeve Cloud U.K. 51°56N 2°0W 30 C5
Clent Hills U.K. 52°25N 2°4W 30 B4
Cleobury Mortimer U.K. 52°22N 2°28W 27 H4
Clevedon U.K. 51°26N 2°52W 30 D3
Cleveland Miss., U.S.A. 33°45N 90°43W 111 D8
Cleveland Ohio, U.S.A. 41°29N 81°41W 112 E7
Cleveland Hills U.K. 54°25N 1°11W 26 D6
Clew B. Ireland 53°50N 9°49W 18 C2
Cley U.K. 52°57N 1°2E 31 A11
Clifden Ireland 53°29N 10°1W 18 E1
Cliffe U.K. 51°28N 0°31E 31 D10
Clifford U.K. 52°7N 3°6W 30 B2
Clinton Iowa, U.S.A. 41°51N 90°12W 112 E3
Clinton Okla., U.S.A. 35°31N 98°58W 110 C7
Clinton Colden L. Canada 63°58N 107°27W 108 C9
Clipperton, Î. Pac. Oc. 10°18N 109°13W 103 F17
Clipston U.K. 52°27N 0°58W 31 B7
Clitheroe U.K. 53°53N 2°22W 27 E4
Cleatheroe U.K. 53°53N 2°22W 27 E4
Cleitheroe Ireland 53°48N 6°14W 19 C8
Cloghran Ireland 53°27N 6°14W 21 B10
Clonakilty Ireland 51°37N 8°53W 20 E5
Clonakilty B. Ireland 51°35N 8°51W 20 E5
Cloncurry → Australia 18°37S 140°40E 98 E7
Clondalkin Ireland 53°19N 6°25W 21 B10
Clones Ireland 54°11N 7°15W 19 C7
Clonmel Ireland 52°21N 7°42W 21 D7
Clontarf Ireland 53°22N 6°11W 21 B10
Cloughton U.K. 54°20N 0°26W 26 D8
Clovelly U.K. 51°0N 4°25W 29 F5
Clovis U.S.A. 34°24N 103°12W 110 D6
Clowne U.K. 53°16N 1°17W 27 F6
Cluj-Napoca Romania 46°47N 23°38E 65 E12
Clun Forest U.K. 52°27N 3°7W 27 H2
Clunbury U.K. 52°25N 2°55W 27 H3
Clwyd → U.K. 53°19N 3°31W 28 A6
Clwyd, Firth of U.K. 53°50N 4°30W 24 C6
Clyde, Firth of U.K. 55°55N 4°30W 24 C6
Clyde River Canada 70°30N 68°30W 109 B13
Clydebank U.K. 55°54N 4°23W 24 C7
Clydesdale U.K. 55°43N 3°51W 25 C8
Coalbrookdale U.K. 52°38N 2°30W 27 G4
Coalisland U.K. 54°33N 6°42W 19 B8
Coalville U.K. 52°44N 1°23W 27 G6
Coast Mts. Canada 55°0N 129°20W 108 D7
Coast Ranges U.S.A. 39°0N 123°0W 110 B2
Coatbridge U.K. 55°52N 4°6W 24 C7
Coaticook Canada 45°10N 71°46W 113 C12
Coats I. Canada 62°30N 83°0W 109 C11
Coats Land Antarctica 77°0S 25°0W 55 D1
Coatzacoalcos Mexico 18°7N 94°25W 114 D6
Cobán Guatemala 15°30N 90°21W 114 D6
Cobar Australia 31°27S 145°48E 98 G8
Cobh Ireland 51°51N 8°17W 20 E6
Cobija Bolivia 11°0S 68°50W 120 D3

Cobourg Canada 43°58N 78°10W 112 D8
Cochabamba Bolivia 17°26S 66°10W 120 D3
Cochrane Canada 49°0N 81°0W 109 E11
Cockburn, Canal Chile 54°30S 72°0W 121 H2
Cockburn I. Canada 45°55N 83°22W 112 C6
Cockburn Town Bahamas 24°2N 74°31W 115 C10
Cockerham U.K. 53°58N 2°49W 27 E3
Cockermouth U.K. 54°40N 3°22W 26 C2
Cockfield U.K. 52°10N 0°48E 31 B10
Cockpit Country, The Jamaica 18°15N 77°45W 114 a
Coco → Cent. Amer. 15°0N 83°8W 115 E8
Cocos I. Pac. Oc. 5°25N 87°55W 114 F7
Cocos Is. Ind. Oc. 12°10S 96°55E 102 J1
Cod, C. U.S.A. 42°5N 70°10W 113 D12
Coddenham U.K. 52°9N 1°8E 31 B11
Codó Brazil 4°30S 43°55W 120 C5
Cody U.S.A. 44°32N 109°3W 110 B5
Coeur d'Alene U.S.A. 47°41N 116°46W 110 A3
Coggeshall U.K. 51°52N 0°42E 31 C10
Cognac France 45°41N 0°20W 66 D3
Coigach U.K. 57°59N 5°14W 22 G7
Coigeach, Rubha U.K. 58°6N 5°26W 22 F7
Coimbatore India 11°2N 76°59E 84 P10
Coimbra Portugal 40°15N 8°27W 67 B1
Colatina Brazil 19°32S 40°37W 122 C2
Colchester U.K. 51°54N 0°55E 31 C10
Cold Fell U.K. 54°53N 2°36W 26 C3
Coldstream U.K. 55°39N 2°15W 25 C11
Colebrook U.S.A. 44°54N 71°30W 113 C12
Colebrooke U.K. 50°47N 3°44W 29 F6
Coleford U.K. 51°47N 2°36W 30 C3
Coleraine U.K. 55°8N 6°41W 19 A8
Coleshill U.K. 52°30N 1°41W 27 G5
Colgrave Sd. U.K. 60°36N 0°58W 22 A16
Colima Mexico 19°14N 103°43W 114 D4
Colima, Nevado de Mexico 19°33N 103°38W 114 D4
Coll U.K. 56°39N 6°34W 24 J4
Collier Law U.K. 54°47N 1°59W 26 C5
Collin U.K. 55°4N 3°31W 25 D8
Collingbourne Kingston U.K. 51°18N 1°40W 30 D5
Collingham U.K. 53°8N 0°46W 27 F7
Collingwood Canada 44°29N 80°13W 112 C7
Collooney Ireland 54°11N 8°29W 18 B3
Colmar France 48°5N 7°20E 66 B7
Colne U.K. 53°51N 2°9W 27 E4
Colne → Bucks., U.K. 51°27N 0°32W 31 D7
Colne → Essex, U.K. 51°51N 0°58E 31 C10
Cologne Germany 50°56N 6°57E 64 C4
Colombia ■ S. Amer. 3°45N 73°0W 120 B2
Colombo Sri Lanka 6°56N 79°58E 84 R11
Colonsay U.K. 56°5N 6°12W 24 B3
Colorado □ U.S.A. 39°30N 105°30W 110 C5
Colorado → Argentina 39°50S 62°8W 121 F3
Colorado → N. Amer. 31°45N 114°40W 110 D4
Colorado → U.S.A. 28°36N 95°59W 111 E7
Colorado Plateau U.S.A. 37°0N 111°0W 110 C4
Colorado Springs U.S.A. 38°50N 104°49W 110 C6
Colsterworth U.K. 52°49N 0°37W 27 G7
Coltishall U.K. 52°44N 1°21E 31 A11
Columbia Mo., U.S.A. 38°57N 92°20W 111 C8
Columbia S.C., U.S.A. 34°0N 81°2W 111 D10
Columbia Tenn., U.S.A. 35°37N 87°2W 111 C9
Columbia → N. Amer. 46°15N 124°5W 110 A2
Columbia, District of □ U.S.A. 38°55N 77°0W 112 F9
Columbia Plateau U.S.A. 44°0N 117°30W 110 B3
Columbus Ga., U.S.A. 32°28N 84°59W 111 D10
Columbus Ind., U.S.A. 39°13N 85°55W 112 F5
Columbus Miss., U.S.A. 33°30N 88°25W 111 D9
Columbus Nebr., U.S.A. 41°26N 97°22W 111 B7
Columbus Ohio, U.S.A. 39°58N 83°0W 112 F6
Colville → U.S.A. 70°25N 150°30W 108 B4
Colwell U.K. 55°5N 2°4W 26 B4
Colwich U.K. 52°48N 1°58W 27 G5
Colwyn Bay U.K. 53°18N 3°44W 28 A6
Colyton U.K. 50°44N 3°5W 29 F7
Comayagua Honduras 14°25N 87°37W 114 E7
Combe Martin U.K. 51°12N 4°3W 29 E5
Comber U.K. 54°33N 5°45W 19 B10
Comeragh Mts. Ireland 52°18N 7°34W 21 D7
Comilla Bangla. 23°28N 91°10E 85 H17
Comitán Mexico 16°15N 92°8W 114 D6
Committee B. Canada 68°30N 86°30W 109 C11
Como Italy 45°47N 9°5E 68 B3
Como, L. di Italy 46°0N 9°11E 68 B3
Comodoro Rivadavia Argentina 45°50S 67°40W 121 G3
Comoros ■ Ind. Oc. 12°10S 44°15E 91 H8
Compass Mt. S. Africa 31°45S 24°32E 90 K6
Compiègne France 49°24N 2°50E 66 B5
Conakry Guinea 9°29N 13°49W 94 G3
Conceição da Barra Brazil 18°35S 39°45W 122 C3
Concepción Chile 36°50S 73°0W 121 F2
Concepción Paraguay 23°22S 57°26W 121 E4
Concepción, Est. de Chile 50°30S 74°55W 121 H2
Concepción del Oro Mexico 24°38N 101°25W 114 C4
Concepción del Uruguay Argentina 32°35S 58°20W 121 F4
Conception, Pt. U.S.A. 34°27N 120°28W 110 D2
Conchos → Mexico 29°35N 104°25W 114 B4
Concord Calif., U.S.A. 37°59N 122°2W 110 C2
Concord N.H., U.S.A. 43°12N 71°32W 113 D12
Concordia Argentina 31°20S 58°2W 121 F4
Concordia U.S.A. 39°34N 97°40W 110 C7
Condeúba Brazil 14°52S 42°0W 122 B2
Condover U.K. 52°39N 2°44W 27 G3
Congleton U.K. 53°10N 2°13W 27 F4
Congo ■ Africa 1°0S 16°0E 96 E3
Congo → Africa 6°4S 12°24E 96 F2
Congo, Dem. Rep. of the ■ Africa 3°0S 23°0E 96 E4
Congo Basin Africa 0°10S 24°30E 96 E4
Congresbury U.K. 51°22N 2°48W 30 D3
Coningsby U.K. 53°7N 0°10W 27 F8
Conisbrough U.K. 53°29N 1°14W 27 F6
Coniston Canada 46°29N 80°51W 112 B7
Coniston Water U.K. 54°22N 3°5W 26 D2
Conn, L. Ireland 54°3N 9°15W 18 B2
Connah's Quay U.K. 53°13N 3°4W 28 A7
Connaught □ Ireland 53°43N 9°12W 18 C3
Conneaut U.S.A. 41°57N 80°34W 112 E7

Connecticut □ U.S.A. 41°30N 72°45W 113 E11
Connecticut → U.S.A. 41°16N 72°20W 113 E11
Connellsville U.S.A. 40°1N 79°35W 112 E8
Connemara Ireland 53°29N 9°45W 18 C2
Connemara △ Ireland 53°32N 9°52W 18 C2
Connersville U.S.A. 39°39N 85°8W 112 F5
Conselheiro Lafaiete Brazil 20°40S 43°48W 122 D2
Consett U.K. 54°51N 1°50W 26 C5
Constance, L. Europe 47°35N 9°25E 64 E5
Constanța Romania 44°14N 28°38E 65 F15
Constantine Algeria 36°25N 6°42E 94 A7
Constitución Chile 35°20S 72°30W 121 F2
Contagem Brazil 19°56S 44°3W 122 C2
Contas → Brazil 14°17S 39°1W 122 B3
Contwoyto L. Canada 65°42N 110°50W 108 C8
Conway Ark., U.S.A. 35°5N 92°26W 111 C8
Conway N.H., U.S.A. 43°59N 71°7W 113 D12
Conwy U.K. 53°17N 3°50W 28 A6
Conwy □ U.K. 53°10N 3°44W 28 A6
Conwy → U.K. 53°17N 3°50W 28 A6
Coober Pedy Australia 29°1S 134°43E 98 F6
Cook Inlet U.S.A. 60°0N 152°0W 108 D4
Cook Is. ☑ Pac. Oc. 17°0S 160°0W 103 J12
Cook Strait N.Z. 41°15S 174°29E 99 J13
Cookstown U.K. 54°38N 6°45W 19 B8
Cooktown Australia 15°30S 145°16E 98 D8
Coondapoor India 13°42N 74°40E 84 N9
Coonoor India 11°21N 76°45E 84 P10
Cooper Cr. → Australia 28°29S 137°46E 98 F6
Coos Bay U.S.A. 43°22N 124°13W 110 B2
Cootehill Ireland 54°4N 7°5W 19 C7
Copenhagen Denmark 55°40N 12°26E 63 F6
Copiapó Chile 27°30S 70°20W 121 E2
Copper Harbor U.S.A. 47°28N 87°53W 112 B4
Coppermine → Canada 67°49N 116°4W 108 C8
Coquet → U.K. 55°20N 1°32W 26 B5
Coquet I. U.K. 55°20N 1°36W 26 B5
Coquimbo Chile 30°0S 71°20W 121 E2
Coracora Peru 15°5S 73°45W 120 D2
Coral Harbour Canada 64°8N 83°10W 109 C11
Coral Sea Pac. Oc. 15°0S 150°0E 98 C9
Corbin U.S.A. 36°57N 84°6W 112 G5
Corbridge U.K. 54°58N 2°0W 26 C5
Corby U.K. 52°30N 0°41W 31 A7
Corby Glen U.K. 52°49N 0°30W 27 G7
Cordele U.S.A. 31°58N 83°47W 111 D10
Córdoba Argentina 31°20S 64°10W 121 F3
Córdoba Mexico 18°53N 96°56W 114 D5
Córdoba Spain 37°50N 4°50W 67 D3
Córdoba, Sierra de Argentina 31°10S 64°25W 121 F3
Cordova U.S.A. 60°33N 145°45W 108 C5
Corfe Castle U.K. 50°38N 2°3W 30 E4
Corfe Mullen U.K. 50°46N 2°1W 30 E4
Corfu Greece 39°38N 19°50E 69 E8
Corinth Greece 37°56N 22°55E 69 F10
Corinth U.S.A. 34°56N 88°31W 111 D9
Corinto Brazil 18°20S 44°30W 122 C2
Cork Ireland 51°54N 8°29W 20 E6
Cork □ Ireland 51°57N 8°40W 20 E5
Cork Harbour Ireland 51°47N 8°16W 20 E6
Corner Brook Canada 48°57N 57°58W 109 E14
Corning U.S.A. 42°9N 77°3W 112 D9
Cornwall Canada 45°2N 74°44W 113 C10
Cornwall □ U.K. 50°26N 4°40W 29 G4
Cornwall, C. U.K. 50°8N 5°43W 29 G2
Cornwall I. Canada 77°37N 94°38W 109 B10
Cornwallis I. Canada 75°8N 95°0W 109 B10
Coro Venezuela 11°25N 69°41W 120 A3
Corocoro Bolivia 17°15S 68°28W 120 D3
Coromandel Coast India 12°30N 81°0E 84 N12
Coronation Gulf Canada 68°25N 110°0W 108 B8
Coronel Chile 37°0S 73°10W 121 F2
Coronel Fabriciano Brazil 19°31S 42°38W 122 C2
Coronel Pringles Argentina 38°0S 61°30W 121 F3
Coronel Suárez Argentina 37°30S 61°52W 121 F3
Coropuna, Nevado Peru 15°30S 72°41W 120 D2
Corpus Christi U.S.A. 27°47N 97°24W 110 E7
Corraun Pen. Ireland 53°54N 9°54W 18 C2
Corrib, L. Ireland 53°27N 9°16W 20 B4
Corrientes Argentina 27°30S 58°45W 121 E4
Corrientes, C. Colombia 5°30N 77°34W 120 B2
Corrientes, C. Mexico 20°25N 105°42W 114 C3
Corringham U.K. 53°25N 0°41W 27 F7
Corry U.S.A. 41°55N 79°39W 112 E8
Corse, C. France 43°1N 9°25E 66 E8
Corsham U.K. 51°27N 2°10W 30 D4
Corsica □ France 42°0N 9°0E 66 F8
Corsicana U.S.A. 32°6N 96°28W 111 D7
Corte France 42°19N 9°11E 66 E8
Cortez U.S.A. 37°21N 108°35W 110 C5
Cortland U.S.A. 42°36N 76°11W 113 D9
Corton U.K. 52°31N 1°45E 31 A12
Çorum Turkey 40°30N 34°57E 71 F5
Corumbá Brazil 19°0S 57°30W 120 D4
Corunna = La Coruña Spain 43°20N 8°25W 67 A1
Corvallis U.S.A. 44°34N 123°16W 108 B2
Corve → U.K. 52°22N 2°43W 27 H3
Coseley U.K. 52°33N 2°9W 27 G4
Cosenza Italy 39°18N 16°15E 68 E7
Cosham U.K. 50°51N 1°2W 30 E6
Coshocton U.S.A. 40°16N 81°51W 112 E7
Costa de la Luz Spain 36°15N 5°58W 67 D2
Costa del Azahar Spain 39°39N 0°13E 67 B6
Costa Rica ■ Cent. Amer. 10°0N 84°0W 115 F8
Costa Verde Spain 43°22N 4°14W 67 A3
Costessey U.K. 52°40N 1°13E 31 A11
Cotabato Phil. 7°14N 124°15E 83 C6
Côte d'Azur France 43°25N 7°10E 66 E7
Côte-d'Ivoire = Ivory Coast ■ Africa 7°30N 5°0W 94 G4
Coteau du Missouri U.S.A. 47°0N 100°0W 110 A6
Cotentin France 49°15N 1°30W 66 B3
Cotherstone U.K. 54°35N 1°59W 26 C5
Cotonou Benin 6°20N 2°25E 94 G6
Cotopaxi Ecuador 0°40S 78°30W 120 C2
Cotswold Hills U.K. 51°42N 2°10W 30 C4
Cottbus Germany 51°45N 14°20E 64 C8
Cottenham U.K. 52°18N 0°9E 31 B9
Coudersport U.S.A. 41°46N 78°1W 112 E9
Council Bluffs U.S.A. 41°16N 95°52W 111 B7
Courantyne → S. Amer. 5°50N 57°8W 120 B4
Courtenay Canada 49°45N 125°0W 108 E7

Cove U.K. 56°0N 4°51W 24 B6
Coventry U.K. 52°25N 1°28W 30 B6
Cover → U.K. 54°17N 1°47W 26 D5
Coverack U.K. 50°1N 5°7W 29 G3
Covington U.S.A. 39°5N 84°30W 112 F5
Cowal U.K. 56°5N 5°8W 24 B5
Cowbridge U.K. 51°27N 3°27W 29 E2
Cowdenbeath U.K. 56°7N 3°21W 25 B9
Cowes U.K. 50°45N 1°18W 30 E6
Cowfold U.K. 50°59N 0°16W 31 E8
Cowpen U.K. 55°8N 1°32W 26 B5
Cox's Bazar Bangla. 21°26N 91°59E 85 J17
Cozumel, Isla Mexico 20°30N 86°40W 114 C7
Crab Hill Barbados 13°19N 59°38W 114 c
Cradock S. Africa 32°8S 25°36E 97 L5
Craig U.S.A. 40°31N 107°33W 110 B5
Craigavon U.K. 54°27N 6°23W 19 C9
Crail U.K. 56°16N 2°37W 25 B10
Craiova Romania 44°21N 23°48E 65 F12
Cramlington U.K. 55°6N 1°34W 26 B5
Cranborne Chase U.K. 50°56N 2°6W 30 E4
Cranbrook Canada 49°30N 115°46W 108 E8
Cranbrook U.K. 51°6N 0°34E 31 D10
Crandon U.S.A. 45°34N 88°54W 112 C3
Crane, The Barbados 13°6N 59°27W 114 c
Cranleigh U.K. 51°8N 0°28W 31 D8
Cranwell U.K. 53°3N 0°27W 27 F8
Crateús Brazil 5°10S 40°39W 120 C5
Crato Brazil 7°10S 39°25W 120 C6
Craven Arms U.K. 52°26N 2°50W 27 H3
Crawfordsville U.S.A. 40°2N 86°54W 112 E4
Crawley U.K. 51°7N 0°11W 31 D8
Credenhill U.K. 52°5N 2°48W 30 B3
Crediton U.K. 50°47N 3°40W 29 F6
Cree → Canada 58°57N 105°47W 108 D9
Cree → U.K. 54°55N 4°25W 24 E7
Cree L. Canada 57°30N 106°30W 108 D9
Cremona Italy 45°7N 10°2E 68 B4
Cres Croatia 44°58N 14°25E 68 B6
Crete Greece 35°15N 25°0E 69 G11
Créteil France 48°47N 2°27E 66 B5
Creuse → France 47°0N 0°34E 66 C4
Crewe U.K. 53°6N 2°26W 27 F4
Crewkerne U.K. 50°53N 2°48W 30 E3
Crianlarich U.K. 56°24N 4°37W 24 B6
Criccieth U.K. 52°55N 4°13W 28 B5
Crick U.K. 52°22N 1°8W 30 B6
Crickhowell U.K. 51°52N 3°8W 28 D7
Cricklade U.K. 51°38N 1°50W 30 C5
Crieff U.K. 56°22N 3°50W 25 B8
Criffell U.K. 54°56N 3°39W 25 E8
Crimea □ Ukraine 45°30N 33°10E 71 E5
Crimean Pen. Ukraine 45°0N 34°0E 71 F5
Crișul Alb → Romania 46°42N 21°17E 65 E11
Crișul Negru → Romania 46°42N 21°16E 65 E11
Croagh Patrick Ireland 53°46N 9°40W 18 D2
Croaghan Ireland 53°59N 10°10W 18 D1
Croatia ■ Europe 45°20N 16°0E 68 B7
Croglin U.K. 54°50N 2°39W 26 C3
Crohy Hd. Ireland 54°55N 8°26W 18 B3
Croker, C. Australia 10°58S 132°35E 98 C5
Cromarty U.K. 57°40N 4°2W 23 G9
Cromarty Firth U.K. 57°40N 4°15W 23 G9
Cromdale, Hills of U.K. 57°20N 3°23W 23 H11
Cromer U.K. 52°56N 1°17E 31 A11
Crondall U.K. 51°14N 0°51W 31 D7
Crook U.K. 54°43N 1°45W 26 C5
Crooked I. Bahamas 22°50N 74°10W 115 C10
Crooklands U.K. 54°16N 2°42W 26 D3
Crosby Cumb., U.K. 54°45N 3°25W 26 C2
Crosby Mersey., U.K. 53°30N 3°3W 27 F2
Crosby Ravensworth U.K. 54°33N 2°35W 26 C3
Cross Fell U.K. 54°43N 2°28W 26 C4
Cross Sound U.S.A. 58°0N 135°0W 108 D6
Crosshaven Ireland 51°47N 8°17W 20 E6
Crossmaglen U.K. 54°5N 6°36W 19 C8
Crotone Italy 39°5N 17°8E 68 E7
Crouch → U.K. 51°37N 0°53E 31 C10
Crow Hd. Ireland 51°35N 10°9W 20 E2
Crow Sound U.K. 49°56N 6°16W 29 H1
Crowborough U.K. 51°3N 0°11E 31 D9
Crowland U.K. 52°41N 0°10W 27 G8
Crowle U.K. 53°36N 0°49W 27 E7
Crowsnest Pass Canada 49°40N 114°40W 108 E8
Croyde U.K. 51°7N 4°14W 29 E5
Croydon □ U.K. 51°22N 0°5W 31 D8
Crozet, Îs. Ind. Oc. 46°27S 52°0E 53 G12
Cruden Bay U.K. 57°25N 1°52W 23 H14
Crudgington U.K. 52°46N 2°32W 27 G3
Cruz das Almas Brazil 12°0S 39°6W 122 B3
Cruzeiro Brazil 22°33S 45°0W 122 D2
Cruzeiro do Sul Brazil 7°35S 72°35W 120 C2
Crystal Falls U.S.A. 46°5N 88°20W 112 B3
Cuando → Angola 17°30S 23°15E 97 H4
Cuango → Dem. Rep. of the Congo 3°14S 17°22E 96 E3
Cuanza → Angola 9°21S 13°9E 96 F2
Cuauhtémoc Mexico 28°25N 106°52W 114 B3
Cuba ■ W. Indies 22°0N 79°0W 115 C9
Cubango → Africa 18°50S 22°25E 97 H4
Cuckfield U.K. 51°1N 0°8W 31 D8
Cúcuta Colombia 7°54N 72°31W 120 B2
Cuddalore India 11°46N 79°45E 84 P11
Cuddapah India 14°30N 78°47E 84 M11
Cuenca Ecuador 2°50S 79°9W 120 C2
Cuenca Spain 40°5N 2°10W 67 B4
Cuernavaca Mexico 18°55N 99°15W 114 D5
Cuiabá Brazil 15°30S 56°0W 120 D4
Cuihangcun China 22°27N 113°32E 79 a
Cuillin Hills U.K. 57°13N 6°15W 22 H5
Cuillin Sd. U.K. 57°4N 6°20W 22 H5
Cuito → Angola 18°1S 20°48E 97 H4
Culiacán Mexico 24°50N 107°23W 114 C3
Cullen U.K. 57°42N 2°49W 23 G12
Cullompton U.K. 50°51N 3°24W 29 F7
Culm → U.K. 50°46N 3°31W 29 F6
Culpeper U.S.A. 38°30N 78°0W 112 F9
Cumaná Venezuela 10°30N 64°5W 120 A3
Cumberland U.S.A. 39°39N 78°46W 112 F8
Cumberland → U.S.A. 37°9N 88°25W 111 C9

Cumberland Pen. *Canada* 67°0N 64°0W **109** C13
Cumberland Plateau *U.S.A.* 36°0N 85°0W **111** C10
Cumberland Sd. *Canada* 65°30N 66°0W **109** C13
Cumbernauld *U.K.* 55°57N 3°58W **25** C8
Cumbrae Is. *U.K.* 55°46N 4°54W **24** C6
Cumbria □ *U.K.* 54°42N 2°52W **26** C3
Cumbrian Mts. *U.K.* 54°30N 3°0W **26** D2
Cummertrees *U.K.* 54°59N 3°20W **25** E9
Cumnock *U.K.* 55°28N 4°17W **24** D7
Cumnor *U.K.* 51°44N 1°19W **30** C6
Cumwhinton *U.K.* 54°52N 2°50W **26** C3
Cunene → *Angola* 17°20S 11°50E **97** H2
Cúneo *Italy* 44°23N 7°32E **68** B2
Cunnamulla *Australia* 28°2S 145°38E **98** F8
Cunninghame *U.K.* 55°38N 4°35W **24** C6
Cupar *U.K.* 56°19N 3°1W **25** B9
Curaçao *W. Indies* 12°10N 69°0W **115** E11
Curicó *Chile* 34°55S 71°20W **121** F2
Curitiba *Brazil* 25°20S 49°10W **122** E1
Curlew Mts. *Ireland* 54°0N 8°20W **18** D5
Curry Rivel *U.K.* 51°1N 2°52W **30** D3
Curvelo *Brazil* 18°45S 44°27W **122** C2
Cusco *Peru* 13°32S 72°0W **120** D2
Cuttack *India* 20°25N 85°57E **85** J14
Cuxhaven *Germany* 53°51N 8°41E **64** B5
Cuyahoga Falls *U.S.A.* 41°8N 81°29W **112** E7
Cuyuni → *Guyana* 6°23N 58°41W **120** B4
Cwmbran *U.K.* 51°39N 3°2W **28** D7
Cyclades *Greece* 37°0N 24°30E **69** F11
Cynthiana *U.S.A.* 38°23N 84°18W **112** F5
Cyprus ■ *Asia* 35°0N 33°0E **86** C3
Cyrenaica *Libya* 27°0N 23°0E **95** C10
Czech Rep. ■ *Europe* 50°0N 15°0E **64** D8
Częstochowa *Poland* 50°49N 19°7E **65** C10

D

Da Lat *Vietnam* 11°56N 108°25E **82** B3
Da Nang *Vietnam* 16°4N 108°13E **82** A3
Da Yunhe → *Hopei, China* 39°10N 117°10E **79** D12
Da Yunhe → *Jiangsu, China* 34°26N 120°5E **79** E13
Daba Shan *China* 32°0N 109°0E **79** E10
Dabie Shan *China* 31°20N 115°20E **79** E12
Dadra & Nagar Haveli □ *India* 20°5N 73°0E **84** J8
Dadu *Pakistan* 26°45N 67°45E **84** F5
Daegu *S. Korea* 35°50N 128°37E **79** D14
Daejeon *S. Korea* 36°20N 127°28E **79** D14
Dagestan □ *Russia* 42°30N 47°0E **71** F8
Dagupan *Phil.* 16°3N 120°20E **83** A6
Dahod *India* 22°50N 74°15E **84** H9
Dahongliutan *China* 35°45N 79°20E **78** D4
Daingean *Ireland* 53°18N 7°17W **21** B8
Dajarra *Australia* 21°42S 139°30E **98** E6
Dakar *Senegal* 14°34N 17°29W **94** F2
Dakhla *W. Sahara* 23°50N 15°53W **94** D2
Dakhla, El Wâhât el *Egypt* 25°30N 28°50E **95** C11
Dalandzadgad *Mongolia* 43°27N 104°30E **78** C9
Dalbeattie *U.K.* 54°56N 3°50W **25** E8
Dalhart *U.S.A.* 36°4N 102°31W **110** C6
Dalhousie *Canada* 48°5N 66°26W **113** A14
Dali *China* 25°40N 100°10E **78** F9
Dalian *China* 38°50N 121°40E **79** D13
Daliang Shan *China* 28°0N 102°45E **78** F9
Dalkeith *U.K.* 55°54N 3°4W **25** C9
Dalkey *Ireland* 53°16N 6°6W **21** B10
Dallas *U.S.A.* 32°47N 96°48W **111** D7
Dalles, The *U.S.A.* 45°36N 121°10W **110** A2
Dalmatia *Croatia* 43°20N 17°0E **68** C7
Dalmellington *U.K.* 55°19N 4°23W **24** D7
Daloa *Ivory C.* 7°0N 6°30W **94** G4
Dalry *U.K.* 55°42N 4°43W **24** C6
Dalrymple, L. *Australia* 20°40S 147°0E **98** E8
Dalton *Dumf. & Gall., U.K.* 55°4N 3°24W **25** D9
Dalton *N. Yorks., U.K.* 54°28N 1°32W **26** D5
Dalton-in-Furness *U.K.* 54°10N 3°11W **26** D2
Daly Waters *Australia* 16°15S 133°24E **98** D5
Daman *India* 20°25N 72°57E **84** J8
Damanhûr *Egypt* 31°0N 30°30E **95** B12
Damaraland *Namibia* 20°0S 15°0E **97** H2
Damascus *Syria* 33°30N 36°18E **86** C4
Damerham *U.K.* 50°56N 1°51W **30** E5
Dampier *Australia* 20°41S 116°42E **98** E2
Danakil Desert *Ethiopia* 12°45N 41°0E **89** E3
Danbury *U.S.A.* 41°24N 73°28W **113** E11
Dandong *China* 40°10N 124°20E **79** C13
Danube → *Europe* 45°20N 29°40E **65** F15
Danville *Ill., U.S.A.* 40°8N 87°37W **112** E4
Danville *Ky., U.S.A.* 37°39N 84°46W **112** G5
Danville *Va., U.S.A.* 36°36N 79°23W **111** C11
Daqing *China* 46°35N 125°0E **79** B13
Dar Banda *Africa* 8°0N 23°0E **90** F6
Dar es Salaam *Tanzania* 6°50S 39°12E **96** F7
Darbhanga *India* 26°15N 85°55E **85** F14
Dardanelles *Turkey* 40°17N 26°32E **69** D12
Darent → *U.K.* 51°28N 0°14E **31** D9
Dârfûr *Sudan* 13°40N 24°0E **95** F10
Darhan *Mongolia* 49°37N 106°21E **78** B10
Darién, G. del *Caribbean* 9°0N 77°0W **120** B2
Darjiling *India* 27°3N 88°18E **85** F16
Darling → *Australia* 34°4S 141°54E **98** G7
Darling Ra. *Australia* 32°30S 116°20E **98** G2
Darlington *U.K.* 54°32N 1°33W **26** C5
Darmstadt *Germany* 49°51N 8°39E **64** D5
Darnah *Libya* 32°45N 22°45E **95** B10
Darnley, C. *Antarctica* 68°0S 69°0E **55** C6
Darnley B. *Canada* 69°30N 123°30W **108** C7
Dart → *U.K.* 50°24N 3°39W **29** G6
Dartford *U.K.* 51°26N 0°13E **31** D9
Dartington *U.K.* 50°27N 3°43W **29** G6
Dartmoor △ *U.K.* 50°37N 3°59W **29** F6
Dartmouth *Canada* 44°40N 63°30W **113** C16
Dartmouth *U.K.* 50°21N 3°36W **29** G6
Darton *U.K.* 53°35N 1°31W **27** E5
Darwen *U.K.* 53°42N 2°29W **27** E4
Darwin *Australia* 12°25S 130°51E **98** C5
Dashen, Ras *Ethiopia* 13°8N 38°26E **89** E2
Dasht → *Pakistan* 25°10N 61°40E **84** G2
Daşoguz *Turkmenistan* 41°49N 59°58E **87** A9
Datong *China* 40°6N 113°18E **79** C11
Daugava → *Latvia* 57°4N 24°3E **63** F9
Daugavpils *Latvia* 55°53N 26°32E **63** F9
Dauphin *Canada* 51°9N 100°5W **108** D9
Dauphiné *France* 45°15N 5°25E **66** D6
Daurada, Costa *Spain* 41°12N 1°15E **67** B6
Davangere *India* 14°25N 75°55E **84** M9
Davao *Phil.* 7°0N 125°40E **83** C7
Davenport *U.S.A.* 41°32N 90°35W **112** E2
Daventry *U.K.* 52°16N 1°10W **30** B6
David *Panama* 8°30N 82°30W **115** F8
Davis Str. *N. Amer.* 65°0N 58°0W **104** C14
Dawlish *U.K.* 50°35N 3°28W **29** F7
Dawmat al Jandal *Si. Arabia* 29°55N 39°40E **86** D4
Dawna Ra. *Burma* 16°30N 98°30E **85** L21
Dawros Hd. *Ireland* 54°50N 8°33W **18** B4
Dawson City *Canada* 64°10N 139°30W **108** C6
Dawson Creek *Canada* 55°45N 120°15W **108** D7
Dax *France* 43°44N 1°3W **66** E3
Daxian *China* 31°15N 107°23E **78** E10
Daxue Shan *China* 30°30N 101°30E **78** E9
Dayr az Zawr *Syria* 35°20N 40°5E **86** C5
Dayton *U.S.A.* 39°45N 84°12W **112** F5
Daytona Beach *U.S.A.* 29°13N 81°1W **111** E10
De Aar *S. Africa* 30°39S 24°0E **97** L4
De Pere *U.S.A.* 44°27N 88°4W **112** C3
Dead Sea *Asia* 31°30N 35°30E **86** D3
Deal *U.K.* 51°13N 1°25E **31** D11
Dean, Forest of *U.K.* 51°45N 2°33W **30** C3
Dearham *U.K.* 54°44N 3°25W **26** C2
Dease → *Canada* 59°56N 128°32W **108** D7
Dease Lake *Canada* 58°25N 130°6W **108** D6
Death Valley *U.S.A.* 36°15N 116°50W **110** C3
Deben → *U.K.* 52°0N 1°25E **31** D11
Debenham *U.K.* 52°14N 1°12E **31** B11
Debre Markos *Ethiopia* 10°20N 37°40E **89** E2
Debre Tabor *Ethiopia* 11°50N 38°26E **89** E2
Debrecen *Hungary* 47°33N 21°42E **65** E11
Decatur *Ala., U.S.A.* 34°36N 86°59W **111** D9
Decatur *Ill., U.S.A.* 39°51N 88°57W **112** F3
Decatur *Ind., U.S.A.* 40°50N 84°56W **112** E5
Deccan *India* 18°0N 79°0E **84** L11
Deddington *U.K.* 51°59N 1°18W **30** C6
Dee → *Aberds., U.K.* 57°9N 2°5W **23** H13
Dee → *Dumf. & Gall., U.K.* 54°51N 4°3W **24** E7
Dee → *Wales, U.K.* 53°22N 3°17W **28** A7
Deeping Fen *U.K.* 52°45N 0°15W **27** G8
Deeping St. Nicholas *U.K.* 52°44N 0°12W **27** G8
Deer Lake *Canada* 49°11N 57°27W **109** E14
Defiance *U.S.A.* 41°17N 84°22W **112** E5
Dehra Dun *India* 30°20N 78°4E **84** D11
DeKalb *U.S.A.* 41°56N 88°46W **112** E3
Del Rio *U.S.A.* 29°22N 100°54W **110** E6
Delabole *U.K.* 50°37N 4°46W **29** F4
Delaware *U.S.A.* 40°18N 83°4W **112** E6
Delaware □ *U.S.A.* 39°0N 75°20W **113** F10
Delaware → *U.S.A.* 39°15N 75°20W **113** F10
Delaware B. *U.S.A.* 39°0N 75°10W **111** C12
Delgado, C. *Mozam.* 10°45S 40°40E **96** G8
Delhi *India* 28°39N 77°13E **84** E10
Delice *Turkey* 39°54N 34°2E **71** G5
Delicias *Mexico* 28°13N 105°28W **114** B3
Déline *Canada* 65°11N 123°25W **108** C7
Delphos *U.S.A.* 40°51N 84°21W **112** E5
Delta Junction *U.S.A.* 64°2N 145°44W **108** C5
Demanda, Sierra de la *Spain* 42°15N 3°0W **67** A4
Demavend *Iran* 35°56N 52°10E **87** C8
Deming *U.S.A.* 32°16N 107°46W **110** D5
Demopolis *U.S.A.* 32°31N 87°50W **111** D9
Den Helder *Neths.* 52°57N 4°45E **64** B3
Denbigh *U.K.* 53°12N 3°25W **28** A7
Denbighshire □ *U.K.* 53°8N 3°22W **28** A7
Denby Dale *U.K.* 53°34N 1°40W **27** E5
Denham, Mt. *Jamaica* 18°13N 77°32W **114** a
Denia *Spain* 38°49N 0°8E **67** C6
Denizli *Turkey* 37°42N 29°2E **71** G4
Denmark ■ *Europe* 55°45N 10°0E **63** F6
Denmark Str. *Atl. Oc.* 66°0N 30°0W **54** C6
Dennery *St. Lucia* 13°55N 60°54W **114** b
Denny *U.K.* 56°1N 3°55W **25** B8
Denpasar *Indonesia* 8°39S 115°13E **82** F5
Dent *U.K.* 54°17N 2°27W **26** D4
Denton *Gt. Man., U.K.* 53°27N 2°9W **27** F4
Denton *Lincs., U.K.* 52°53N 0°43W **27** G7
Denton *U.S.A.* 33°13N 97°8W **111** D7
D'Entrecasteaux Is. *Papua N. G.* 9°0S 151°0E **98** B9
Denver *U.S.A.* 39°42N 104°59W **110** C5
Deoghar *India* 24°30N 86°42E **85** G15
Deolali *India* 19°58N 73°50E **84** K8
Deosai Mts. *Pakistan* 35°40N 75°0E **84** B9
Dera Ghazi Khan *Pakistan* 30°5N 70°43E **84** D7
Dera Ismail Khan *Pakistan* 31°50N 70°50E **84** D7
Derbent *Russia* 42°5N 48°15E **71** F8
Derby *Australia* 17°18S 123°38E **98** D3
Derby *U.K.* 52°56N 1°28W **27** G6
Derbyshire □ *U.K.* 53°11N 1°38W **27** F5
Dereham *U.K.* 52°41N 0°57E **31** A10
Derg → *U.K.* 54°44N 7°26W **18** B7
Derg, L. *Ireland* 53°0N 8°20W **20** C6
Deridder *U.S.A.* 30°51N 93°17W **111** D8
Derry = Londonderry *U.K.* 55°0N 7°20W **18** A7
Derrynasaggart Mts. *Ireland* 51°58N 9°15W **20** E4
Derryveagh Mts. *Ireland* 54°56N 8°11W **18** B5
Derwent → *Derby, U.K.* 52°57N 1°28W **27** G6
Derwent → *N. Yorks., U.K.* 53°45N 0°58W **27** E7
Derwent → *Tyne & W., U.K.* 54°58N 1°41W **26** C5
Derwent Water *U.K.* 54°35N 3°9W **26** C2
Des Moines *U.S.A.* 41°35N 93°37W **111** B8
Des Moines → *U.S.A.* 40°23N 91°25W **111** B8
Desborough *U.K.* 52°27N 0°49W **31** B7
Deschutes → *U.S.A.* 45°38N 120°55W **110** A2
Dese *Ethiopia* 11°5N 39°40E **89** E2
Deseado → *Argentina* 47°45S 65°54W **121** G3
Desford *U.K.* 52°37N 1°17W **27** G6
Desolación, I. *Chile* 53°0S 74°0W **121** H2
Dessau *Germany* 51°51N 12°14E **64** C7
Detour, Pt. *U.S.A.* 45°40N 86°40W **112** C4
Detroit *U.S.A.* 42°19N 83°12W **112** D6
Deutsche Bucht *Germany* 54°15N 8°0E **64** A5
Deventer *Neths.* 52°15N 6°10E **64** B4
Deveron → *U.K.* 57°41N 2°32W **23** G12
Devils Lake *U.S.A.* 48°7N 98°52W **110** A7
Devizes *U.K.* 51°22N 1°58W **30** D5
Devon □ *U.K.* 50°50N 3°40W **29** F6
Devon I. *Canada* 75°10N 85°0W **109** B11
Devonport *U.K.* 50°22N 4°11W **29** G5
Dewsbury *U.K.* 53°42N 1°37W **27** E5
Dexter *U.S.A.* 36°48N 89°57W **112** G3
Deyang *China* 31°3N 104°27E **78** E9
Dezfūl *Iran* 32°20N 48°30E **86** C7
Dezhneva, C. *Russia* 66°5N 169°40W **77** C20
Dezhou *China* 37°26N 116°18E **79** D12
Dhahran *Si. Arabia* 26°10N 50°7E **86** E7
Dhaka *Bangla.* 23°43N 90°26E **85** H17
Dhaka □ *Bangla.* 24°25N 90°25E **85** G17
Dhamar *Yemen* 14°30N 44°20E **88** E3
Dhamtari *India* 20°42N 81°35E **85** J12
Dhanbad *India* 23°50N 86°30E **85** H15
Dharwad *India* 15°30N 75°4E **84** M9
Dhaulagiri *Nepal* 28°39N 83°28E **85** E13
Dhenkanal *India* 20°45N 85°35E **85** J14
Dhuburi *India* 26°2N 89°59E **85** F16
Dhule *India* 20°58N 74°50E **84** J9
Diamantina *Brazil* 18°17S 43°40W **122** C2
Diamantina → *Australia* 26°45S 139°10E **98** F6
Diamantino *Brazil* 14°30S 56°30W **120** D4
Dibrugarh *India* 27°29N 94°55E **85** F19
Dickinson *U.S.A.* 46°53N 102°47W **110** A6
Didcot *U.K.* 51°36N 1°14W **30** C6
Diefenbaker, L. *Canada* 51°0N 106°55W **108** D9
Dieppe *France* 49°54N 1°4E **66** B4
Digby *Canada* 44°38N 65°50W **109** E13
Digne-les-Bains *France* 44°5N 6°12E **66** D7
Dijon *France* 47°20N 5°3E **66** C6
Dikson *Russia* 73°40N 80°5E **76** B9
Dili *E. Timor* 8°39S 125°34E **83** F7
Dillingham *U.S.A.* 59°3N 158°28W **108** D4
Dimitrovgrad *Bulgaria* 42°5N 25°35E **69** C11
Dimitrovgrad *Russia* 54°14N 49°39E **70** D8
Dinajpur *Bangla.* 25°33N 88°43E **85** G16
Dinan *France* 48°28N 2°2W **66** B2
Dinant *Belgium* 50°16N 4°55E **64** C3
Dinaric Alps *Croatia* 44°0N 16°30E **68** C7
Dinbych-y-Pysgod = Tenby *U.K.* 51°40N 4°42W **28** D4
Dingle *Ireland* 52°9N 10°17W **20** D2
Dingle B. *Ireland* 52°3N 10°20W **20** D2
Dingle Pen. *Ireland* 52°12N 10°5W **20** D2
Dingwall *U.K.* 57°36N 4°26W **23** G9
Dipolog *Phil.* 8°36N 123°20E **83** C6
Dire Dawa *Ethiopia* 9°35N 41°45E **89** F3
Dirranbandi *Australia* 28°33S 148°17E **98** F8
Disappointment, C. *U.S.A.* 46°18N 124°5W **110** A2
Disappointment, L. *Australia* 23°20S 122°40E **98** E3
Diss *U.K.* 52°23N 1°7E **31** B11
Distington *U.K.* 54°36N 3°32W **26** C1
Distrito Federal □ *Brazil* 15°45S 47°45W **122** C1
Ditchingham *U.K.* 52°28N 1°28E **31** B11
Ditchling Beacon *U.K.* 50°54N 0°6W **31** E8
Dittisham *U.K.* 50°22N 3°37W **29** G6
Ditton Priors *U.K.* 52°30N 2°34W **27** H3
Diu *India* 20°45N 70°58E **84** J7
Divinópolis *Brazil* 20°10S 44°54W **122** D2
Dixon *U.S.A.* 41°50N 89°29W **112** E3
Dixon Entrance *U.S.A.* 54°30N 132°0W **108** D6
Diyarbakır *Turkey* 37°55N 40°18E **71** G7
Dizzard Pt. *U.K.* 50°44N 4°40W **29** F4
Djerba, Î. de *Tunisia* 33°50N 10°48E **95** B8
Djerid, Chott *Tunisia* 33°42N 8°30E **94** B7
Djibouti *Djibouti* 11°30N 43°5E **89** E3
Djibouti ■ *Africa* 12°0N 43°0E **89** E3
Djourab, Erg du *Chad* 16°40N 18°50E **95** E9
Dmitri Laptev Str. *Russia* 73°0N 140°0E **77** B15
Dnepropetrovsk *Ukraine* 48°30N 35°0E **71** E6
Dnieper → *Ukraine* 46°30N 32°18E **71** E5
Dniester → *Europe* 46°18N 30°17E **65** E16
Dniprodzerzhynsk *Ukraine* 48°32N 34°37E **71** E5
Doba *Chad* 8°40N 16°50E **95** G9
Doberai, Jazirah *Indonesia* 1°25S 133°0E **83** E8
Dobrich *Bulgaria* 43°37N 27°49E **69** C12
Dobruja *Europe* 44°30N 28°15E **65** F15
Docking *U.K.* 52°54N 0°38E **31** A10
Doddington *Cambs., U.K.* 52°30N 0°3E **31** B9
Doddington *Northumberland, U.K.* 55°33N 1°54W **26** A5
Dodecanese *Greece* 36°35N 27°0E **69** F12
Dodge City *U.S.A.* 37°45N 100°1W **110** C6
Dodman Pt. *U.K.* 50°13N 4°48W **29** G4
Dodoma *Tanzania* 6°8S 35°45E **96** F7
Doha *Qatar* 25°15N 51°35E **87** E7
Dokdo = Liancourt Rocks *Asia* 37°15N 131°52E **81** E2
Dolbeau-Mistassini *Canada* 48°53N 72°14W **109** E12
Dole *France* 47°7N 5°31E **66** C6
Dolgarrog *U.K.* 53°11N 3°50W **28** A6
Dolgellau *U.K.* 52°45N 3°53W **28** B6
Dolo *Ethiopia* 4°11N 42°3E **89** G3
Dolomites *Italy* 46°23N 11°51E **68** A4
Dolores *Argentina* 36°20S 57°40W **121** F4
Dolphin and Union Str. *Canada* 69°5N 114°45W **108** C8
Dolphinton *U.K.* 55°42N 3°25W **25** C9
Dolton *U.K.* 50°53N 4°2W **29** F5
Dominica ■ *W. Indies* 15°20N 61°20W **115** D12
Dominican Rep. ■ *W. Indies* 19°0N 70°30W **115** D10
Don → *Russia* 47°4N 39°18E **71** E6
Don → *Aberds., U.K.* 57°11N 2°5W **23** H13
Don → *S. Yorks., U.K.* 53°41N 0°52W **27** E7
Don Figuerero Mts. *Jamaica* 18°5N 77°36W **114** a
Donaghadee *U.K.* 54°39N 5°33W **19** B10
Doncaster *U.K.* 53°32N 1°6W **27** E6
Dondra Head *Sri Lanka* 5°55N 80°40E **84** S12
Donegal *Ireland* 54°39N 8°5W **18** B5
Donegal □ *Ireland* 54°53N 8°0W **18** B5
Donegal B. *Ireland* 54°31N 8°49W **18** B4
Donets → *Russia* 47°33N 40°55E **71** E7
Donetsk *Ukraine* 48°0N 37°45E **71** E6
Dong Hoi *Vietnam* 17°29N 106°36E **82** A3
Dongchuan *China* 26°8N 103°1E **78** F9
Dongguan *China* 22°58N 113°44E **79** G11
Dongola *Sudan* 19°9N 30°22E **95** E12
Dongsha Dao *S. China Sea* 20°45N 116°43E **79** G12
Dongting Hu *China* 29°18N 112°45E **79** F11
Donhead *U.K.* 51°1N 2°7W **30** D4
Donington *U.K.* 52°54N 0°12W **27** G8
Donna Nook *U.K.* 53°29N 0°8E **27** F9
Donostia-San Sebastián *Spain* 43°17N 1°58W **67** A5
Doon → *U.K.* 55°27N 4°39W **24** D6
Dorchester *Dorset, U.K.* 50°42N 2°27W **30** E4
Dorchester *Oxon., U.K.* 51°39N 1°10W **30** C6
Dorchester, C. *Canada* 65°27N 77°27W **109** C12
Dordogne → *France* 45°2N 0°36W **66** D3
Dordrecht *Neths.* 51°48N 4°39E **64** C3
Dores do Indaiá *Brazil* 19°27S 45°36W **122** C1
Dorking *U.K.* 51°14N 0°19W **31** D8
Dornie *U.K.* 57°17N 5°31W **22** H6
Dornoch *U.K.* 57°53N 4°2W **23** G9
Dornoch Firth *U.K.* 57°51N 4°4W **23** G9
Döröö Nuur *Mongolia* 48°0N 93°0E **78** B7
Dorset □ *U.K.* 50°45N 2°26W **30** E4
Dorstone *U.K.* 52°3N 2°59W **30** B3
Dortmund *Germany* 51°30N 7°28E **64** C4
Dos Bahías, C. *Argentina* 44°58S 65°32W **121** G3
Dos Hermanas *Spain* 37°16N 5°55W **67** D3
Dothan *U.S.A.* 31°13N 85°24W **111** D9
Douai *France* 50°21N 3°4E **66** A5
Douala *Cameroon* 4°0N 9°45E **96** D1
Doubs → *France* 46°53N 5°1E **66** C6
Douglas *Ireland* 51°52N 8°25W **20** E6
Douglas *I. of Man* 54°10N 4°28W **19** C13
Douglas *U.S.A.* 31°21N 109°33W **110** D5
Dounreay *U.K.* 58°35N 3°44W **23** E10
Dourados *Brazil* 22°9S 54°50W **120** E4
Douro → *Europe* 41°8N 8°40W **67** B1
Dove → *Derby, U.K.* 52°51N 1°36W **27** G5
Dove → *N. Yorks., U.K.* 54°15N 0°55W **26** D7
Dove Dale *U.K.* 53°7N 1°46W **27** F5
Dover *U.K.* 51°7N 1°19E **31** D11
Dover *Del., U.S.A.* 39°10N 75°32W **113** F10
Dover *N.H., U.S.A.* 43°12N 70°56W **113** D12
Dover, Str. of *Europe* 51°0N 1°30E **62** F7
Dover-Foxcroft *U.S.A.* 45°11N 69°13W **113** C13
Doveridge *U.K.* 52°54N 1°49W **27** G5
Dovey = Dyfi → *U.K.* 52°32N 4°3W **28** B5
Dovrefjell *Norway* 62°15N 9°33E **63** E5
Down □ *U.K.* 54°23N 6°2W **19** C9
Downham *U.K.* 52°26N 0°14E **31** B9
Downham Market *U.K.* 52°37N 0°23E **31** A9
Downpatrick *U.K.* 54°20N 5°43W **19** C10
Downpatrick Hd. *Ireland* 54°20N 9°21W **18** C3
Downton *U.K.* 50°59N 1°44W **30** E5
Drâa, Oued → *Morocco* 28°40N 11°10W **94** C3
Draguignan *France* 43°32N 6°27E **66** E7
Drake Passage *S. Ocean* 58°0S 68°0W **55** B17
Drakensberg *S. Africa* 31°0S 28°0E **97** L5
Drammen *Norway* 59°42N 10°12E **63** F6
Drava → *Croatia* 45°33N 18°55E **69** B8
Dresden *Germany* 51°3N 13°44E **64** C7
Dreux *France* 48°44N 1°23E **66** B4
Driffield *U.K.* 54°0N 0°26W **27** D8
Drina → *Bos.-H.* 44°53N 19°21E **69** B8
Drobeta-Turnu Severin *Romania* 44°39N 22°41E **65** F12
Drogheda *Ireland* 53°43N 6°22W **19** D9
Drohobych *Ukraine* 49°20N 23°30E **71** E3
Droitwich *U.K.* 52°16N 2°8W **30** B4
Dromore *U.K.* 54°31N 7°28W **18** B7
Dromore West *Ireland* 54°15N 8°52W **18** C4
Dronfield *U.K.* 53°19N 1°27W **27** F6
Dronning Maud Land *Antarctica* 72°30S 12°0E **55** D3
Drum Hills *Ireland* 52°1N 7°45W **20** D2
Drumheller *Canada* 51°25N 112°40W **108** D8
Drummond I. *U.S.A.* 46°1N 83°39W **112** B5
Drummondville *Canada* 45°55N 72°25W **113** C11
Drumochter, Pass of *U.K.* 56°50N 4°15W **23** J9
Druridge B. *U.K.* 55°17N 1°32W **26** B5
Dry Harbour Mts. *Jamaica* 18°19N 77°24W **114** a
Dryden *Canada* 49°47N 92°50W **108** E10
Drygalski I. *Antarctica* 66°0S 92°0E **55** C7
Du Quoin *U.S.A.* 38°1N 89°14W **112** F3
Duarte, Pico *Dom. Rep.* 19°2N 70°59W **115** D10
Dubai *U.A.E.* 25°18N 55°20E **87** E8
Dubawnt → *Canada* 64°33N 100°6W **108** C9
Dubawnt L. *Canada* 63°8N 101°28W **108** C9
Dubbo *Australia* 32°11S 148°35E **98** G8
Dublin *Ireland* 53°21N 6°15W **21** B10
Dublin *U.S.A.* 32°32N 82°54W **111** D10
Dublin □ *Ireland* 53°24N 6°20W **21** B10
Dublin ✕ **(DUB)** *Ireland* 53°26N 6°15W **21** B10
DuBois *U.S.A.* 41°7N 78°46W **112** E8
Dubrovnik *Croatia* 42°39N 18°6E **69** C8
Dubuque *U.S.A.* 42°30N 90°41W **112** D2
Duddington *U.K.* 52°36N 0°32W **31** A7
Duddon → *U.K.* 54°12N 3°15W **26** D2
Dudinka *Russia* 69°30N 86°13E **77** C9
Dudley *U.K.* 52°31N 2°5W **27** G4
Duffield *U.K.* 52°59N 1°29W **27** G6
Dufftown *U.K.* 57°27N 3°8W **23** H11
Dugi Otok *Croatia* 44°0N 15°3E **68** C6
Duisburg *Germany* 51°26N 6°45E **64** C4
Dukinfield *U.K.* 53°28N 2°6W **27** F4
Dulce → *Argentina* 30°32S 62°33W **121** F3
Duluth *U.S.A.* 46°47N 92°6W **112** B1
Dulverton *U.K.* 51°2N 3°33W **29** E6
Dumaguete *Phil.* 9°17N 123°15E **83** C6
Dumbarton *U.K.* 55°57N 4°33W **24** C6
Dumfries *U.K.* 55°4N 3°37W **25** D8
Dumfries & Galloway □ *U.K.* 55°9N 3°58W **25** D8
Dumyât *Egypt* 31°24N 31°48E **95** B12
Dún Laoghaire *Ireland* 53°17N 6°8W **21** B10
Dunbar *U.K.* 56°0N 2°31W **25** B10
Dunblane *U.K.* 56°11N 3°58W **25** B8
Duncan *U.S.A.* 34°30N 97°57W **110** D7
Duncansby Head *U.K.* 58°38N 3°1W **23** E11
Dunchurch *U.K.* 52°21N 1°17W **30** B6
Dund-Us *Mongolia* 48°1N 91°38E **78** B7
Dundalk *Ireland* 54°1N 6°24W **19** C9
Dundalk Bay *Ireland* 53°55N 6°15W **19** D9
Dundee *U.K.* 56°28N 2°59W **25** B10
Dundrum *Ireland* 53°18N 6°14W **21** B10
Dundrum *U.K.* 54°16N 5°52W **19** C10
Dundrum B. *U.K.* 54°13N 5°47W **19** C10
Dunedin *N.Z.* 45°50S 170°33E **99** K13
Dunfermline *U.K.* 56°5N 3°27W **25** B9
Dungannon *U.K.* 54°31N 6°46W **19** B8
Dungarvan *Ireland* 52°5N 7°37W **21** D7
Dungarvan Harbour *Ireland* 52°4N 7°35W **21** D7
Dungeness *U.K.* 50°54N 0°59E **31** E10
Dunhua *China* 43°20N 128°14E **79** C14
Dunhuang *China* 40°8N 94°36E **78** C7
Dunkeld *U.K.* 56°34N 3°35W **25** A8
Dunkerque *France* 51°2N 2°20E **66** A5
Dunkery Beacon *U.K.* 51°9N 3°36W **29** E6
Dunkirk *U.S.A.* 42°29N 79°20W **112** D8
Dunleer *Ireland* 53°50N 6°24W **19** D9
Dunmanway *Ireland* 51°43N 9°6W **20** E4
Dunmore *U.S.A.* 41°25N 75°38W **113** E10
Dunnet Hd. *U.K.* 58°40N 3°21W **23** E11
Dunoon *U.K.* 55°57N 4°56W **24** C6
Duns *U.K.* 55°47N 2°20W **25** C11
Dunsford *U.K.* 50°41N 3°42W **29** F6
Dunstable *U.K.* 51°53N 0°32W **31** C7
Dunster *U.K.* 51°11N 3°27W **30** D2
Dunston *U.K.* 52°46N 2°7W **27** G4
Dunvegan *U.K.* 57°27N 6°35W **22** H4
Duolun *China* 42°12N 116°28E **79** C12
Duque de Caxias *Brazil* 22°46S 43°18W **122** D2
Durance → *France* 43°55N 4°45E **66** E6
Durango *Mexico* 24°3N 104°39W **114** C4
Durango *U.S.A.* 37°16N 107°53W **110** C5
Durant *U.S.A.* 33°59N 96°25W **111** D7
Durazno *Uruguay* 33°25S 56°31W **121** F4
Durban *S. Africa* 29°49S 31°1E **97** K6
Düren *Germany* 50°48N 6°29E **64** C4
Durgapur *India* 23°30N 87°20E **85** H15
Durham *U.K.* 54°47N 1°34W **26** C5
Durham *U.S.A.* 35°59N 78°54W **111** C11
Durham □ *U.K.* 54°42N 1°45W **26** C5
Durlston Hd. *U.K.* 50°36N 1°57W **30** E5
Durness *U.K.* 58°34N 4°45W **23** E8
Durrës *Albania* 41°19N 19°28E **69** D8
Durrington *U.K.* 51°12N 1°47W **30** D5
Durrow *Ireland* 52°51N 7°24W **21** C8
Dursey I. *Ireland* 51°36N 10°12W **20** E2
Dursley *U.K.* 51°40N 2°21W **30** C4
Dushanbe *Tajikistan* 38°33N 68°48E **87** B12
Düsseldorf *Germany* 51°14N 6°47E **64** C4
Dutch Harbor *U.S.A.* 53°53N 166°32W **108** D3
Duyun *China* 26°18N 107°29E **78** F10
Dvina, N. → *Russia* 64°32N 40°30E **70** B7
Dvina B. *Russia* 65°0N 39°0E **70** B6
Dwarka *India* 22°18N 69°8E **84** H6
Dyce *U.K.* 57°13N 2°12W **23** H13
Dyer, C. *Canada* 66°37N 61°16W **109** C13
Dyersburg *U.S.A.* 36°3N 89°23W **111** C9
Dyfi → *U.K.* 52°32N 4°3W **28** B5
Dymchurch *U.K.* 51°1N 1°0E **31** D11
Dymock *U.K.* 51°59N 2°26W **30** C4
Dzavhan Gol → *Mongolia* 48°54N 93°23E **78** B7
Dzerzhinsk *Russia* 56°14N 43°30E **70** C7
Dzhankoy *Ukraine* 45°40N 34°20E **71** E5
Dzhugdzhur Ra. *Russia* 57°30N 138°0E **77** D14
Dzungarian Basin *China* 44°30N 86°0E **78** C6
Dzungarian Gate *Asia* 45°10N 82°0E **78** B5
Dzüünmod *Mongolia* 47°45N 106°58E **78** B10

E

Eagle *U.S.A.* 64°47N 141°12W **108** C5
Eagle L. *U.S.A.* 46°20N 69°22W **113** B13
Eagle Pass *U.S.A.* 28°43N 100°30W **110** E6
Eagle River *U.S.A.* 47°25N 88°18W **112** B3
Eaglesfield *U.K.* 55°4N 3°12W **25** D9
Eakring *U.K.* 53°9N 0°58W **27** F7
Ealing □ *U.K.* 51°31N 0°20W **31** C8
Earby *U.K.* 53°55N 2°7W **27** E4
Eardisley *U.K.* 52°8N 3°1W **30** B2
Earith *U.K.* 52°22N 0°2E **31** B9
Earl Shilton *U.K.* 52°35N 1°18W **27** G6
Earl Soham *U.K.* 52°14N 1°18E **31** B11
Earls Barton *U.K.* 52°16N 0°45W **31** B7
Earl's Colne *U.K.* 51°56N 0°43E **31** C10
Earlston *U.K.* 55°39N 2°40W **25** C10
Earn → *U.K.* 56°21N 3°18W **25** B9
Earn, L. *U.K.* 56°23N 4°13W **24** B7
Earsdon *U.K.* 55°3N 1°29W **26** B6
Easebourne *U.K.* 51°0N 0°43W **31** E7
Easington *Durham, U.K.* 54°47N 1°21W **26** C6
Easington *E. Riding, U.K.* 53°39N 0°6E **27** E9
Easington Colliery *U.K.* 54°48N 1°19W **26** C6
Easingwold *U.K.* 54°8N 1°11W **26** D6
East Ayrshire □ *U.K.* 55°26N 4°11W **24** C7
East Bengal *Bangla.* 24°0N 90°0E **85** H17
East Bergholt *U.K.* 51°59N 1°3E **31** C11
East Beskids *Europe* 49°20N 22°0E **65** D11
East Brent *U.K.* 51°15N 2°56W **30** D3
East C. = Dezhneva, C. *Russia* 66°5N 169°40W **77** C20
East China Sea *Asia* 30°0N 126°0E **79** F14
East Cowes *U.K.* 50°45N 1°16W **30** E6
East Falkland *Falk. Is.* 51°30S 58°30W **121** H4
East Fen *U.K.* 53°4N 0°5E **27** F9
East Grinstead *U.K.* 51°7N 0°0 **31** D9
East Harling *U.K.* 52°26N 0°56E **31** B10
East Ilsley *U.K.* 51°31N 1°16W **30** C6
East Indies *Asia* 0°0 120°0E **72** J14
East Kilbride *U.K.* 55°47N 4°11W **24** C7
East Lansing *U.S.A.* 42°44N 84°29W **112** D5
East London *S. Africa* 33°0S 27°55E **97** L5
East Lothian □ *U.K.* 55°58N 2°44W **25** C10
East Markham *U.K.* 53°15N 0°53W **27** F7
East Moor *U.K.* 53°16N 1°34W **27** F5
East Pt. *Canada* 46°27N 61°58W **113** B17
East St. Louis *U.S.A.* 38°37N 90°9W **112** F2
East Sea = Japan, Sea of *Asia* 40°0N 135°0E **81** D4
East Siberian Sea *Russia* 73°0N 160°0E **77** B17
East Sussex □ *U.K.* 50°56N 0°19E **31** E9
East Timor ■ *Asia* 8°50S 126°0E **83** F7
East Wittering *U.K.* 50°46N 0°52W **31** E7
East Woodhay *U.K.* 51°21N 1°25W **30** D6
Eastbourne *U.K.* 50°46N 0°18E **31** E9
Eastchurch *U.K.* 51°24N 0°53E **31** D10
Eastern Desert *Egypt* 27°30N 32°30E **95** C12
Eastern Ghats *India* 14°0N 78°50E **84** N11
Eastern Group *Fiji* 17°0S 178°30W **99** D15
Eastleigh *U.K.* 50°58N 1°21W **30** E6

Eastmain

French Creek

Eastmain Canada 52°10N 78°30W 109 D12
Eastmain → Canada 52°27N 78°26W 109 D12
Eastnor U.K. 52°2N 2°23W 30 B4
Easton Dorset, U.K. 50°33N 2°26W 30 E4
Easton Northants., U.K. 52°37N 0°31W 31 A7
Easton Md., U.S.A. 38°47N 76°5W 113 F9
Easton Pa., U.S.A. 40°41N 75°13W 113 E10
Easton-in-Gordano U.K. 51°28N 2°42W 30 D5
Eastport U.S.A. 44°56N 67°0W 113 C14
Eastry U.K. 51°14N 1°19E 31 D11
Eastwood U.K. 53°1N 1°18W 27 F6
Eaton U.K. 52°51N 0°49W 27 G7
Eaton Socon U.K. 52°14N 0°17W 31 B8
Eau Claire U.S.A. 44°49N 91°30W 112 C2
Eau Claire, L. à l' Canada 56°10N 74°25W 109 D12
Ebberston U.K. 54°14N 0°37W 26 D7
Ebbw Vale U.K. 51°46N 3°12W 28 D7
Eberswalde-Finow Germany 52°50N 13°49E 64 B7
Ebetsu Japan 43°7N 141°34E 81 B7
Ebinur Hu China 44°55N 82°55E 78 C5
Ebolowa Cameroon 2°55N 11°10E 96 D2
Ebro → Spain 40°43N 0°54E 67 B6
Ecclefechan U.K. 55°4N 3°16W 25 D9
Eccleshall U.K. 52°52N 2°15W 27 G4
Ech Chéliff Algeria 36°10N 1°20E 94 A6
Echo Bay Canada 66°5N 117°55W 108 C8
Eckington U.K. 53°18N 1°22W 27 F6
Eclipse Sd. Canada 72°38N 79°0W 109 B12
Ecuador ■ S. Amer. 2°0S 78°0W 120 C2
Ed Damazin Sudan 11°46N 34°21E 95 F12
Eday U.K. 59°11N 2°47W 23 D12
Eddrachillis B. U.K. 58°17N 5°14W 22 F7
Eddystone U.K. 50°11N 4°16W 29 G5
Eden → U.K. 54°57N 3°1W 26 C2
Edenbridge U.K. 51°12N 0°5E 31 D9
Edenderry Ireland 53°21N 7°4W 21 B8
Edfu Egypt 24°55N 32°49E 95 D12
Edge Hill U.K. 52°8N 1°26W 30 B6
Edinburgh U.K. 55°57N 3°13W 25 C9
Edinburgh ✈ (EDI) U.K. 55°54N 3°22W 25 C9
Edington U.K. 51°17N 2°5W 30 D4
Edirne Turkey 41°40N 26°34E 71 F4
Edmonton Canada 53°30N 113°30W 108 D8
Edmundbyers U.K. 54°50N 1°58W 26 C5
Edmundston Canada 47°23N 68°20W 109 E13
Edremit Turkey 39°34N 27°0E 86 B1
Edson Canada 53°35N 116°28W 108 D8
Edward, L. Africa 0°25S 29°40E 96 E5
Edward VII Land Antarctica 80°0S 150°0W 55 E13
Edwards Plateau U.S.A. 30°45N 101°20W 110 D6
Effingham U.S.A. 39°7N 88°33W 112 F3
Égadi, Ísole Italy 37°55N 12°16E 68 F5
Eganville Canada 45°32N 77°5W 112 C9
Eger Hungary 47°53N 20°27E 65 E11
Egham U.K. 51°25N 0°32W 31 D7
Eglinton I. Canada 75°48N 118°30W 109 B8
Egremont U.K. 54°29N 3°32W 26 D1
Eğridir Turkey 37°52N 30°51E 71 G5
Eğridir Gölü Turkey 37°53N 30°50E 71 G5
Egton U.K. 54°28N 0°44W 26 D7
Egypt ■ Africa 28°0N 31°0E 95 C12
Eifel Germany 50°15N 6°50E 64 C4
Eigg U.K. 56°54N 6°10W 22 J5
Eil, L. U.K. 56°51N 5°16W 22 J7
Eilat Israel 29°30N 34°56E 86 D3
Eilean Siar □ U.K. 57°30N 7°10W 22 G3
Eindhoven Neths. 51°26N 5°28E 64 C3
Eire = Ireland ■ Europe 53°50N 7°52W 62 E2
Eiriosgaigh = Eriskay U.K. 57°4N 7°18W 22 H3
Eivissa Spain 38°54N 1°26E 67 C6
Ekaterinburg Russia 56°50N 60°30E 76 D7
Ekibastuz Kazakhstan 51°50N 75°10E 76 D8
El Aaiún W. Sahara 27°9N 13°12W 94 C3
El Alamein Egypt 30°48N 28°58E 95 B11
El Centro U.S.A. 32°48N 115°34W 110 D3
El Djouf Mauritania 21°25N 6°40W 94 D4
El Dorado U.S.A. 33°12N 92°40W 111 D8
El Faiyûm Egypt 29°19N 30°50E 95 C12
El Fâsher Sudan 13°33N 25°26E 95 F11
El Fuerte Mexico 26°25N 108°39W 114 B3
El Geneina Sudan 13°27N 22°45E 95 F10
El Gezira □ Sudan 15°0N 33°0E 95 F12
El Gîza Egypt 30°0N 31°12E 95 C12
El Istiwa'iya Sudan 5°0N 28°0E 95 G11
El Jadida Morocco 33°11N 8°17W 94 B4
El Khârga Egypt 25°30N 30°33E 95 C12
El Mahalla el Kubra Egypt 31°0N 31°0E 95 B12
El Mansûra Egypt 31°0N 31°19E 95 B12
El Minyâ Egypt 28°7N 30°33E 95 C12
El Obeid Sudan 13°8N 30°10E 95 F12
El Oued Algeria 33°20N 6°58E 94 B7
El Paso U.S.A. 31°45N 106°29W 110 D5
El Puerto de Santa María Spain 36°36N 6°13W 67 D2
El Reno U.S.A. 35°32N 97°57W 110 C7
El Salvador ■ Cent. Amer. 13°50N 89°0W 114 E7
El Tigre Venezuela 8°44N 64°15W 120 B3
El Uqsur Egypt 25°41N 32°38E 95 C12
Elâzığ Turkey 38°37N 39°14E 71 G6
Elba Italy 42°46N 10°17E 68 C4
Elbasan Albania 41°9N 20°9E 69 D9
Elbe → Europe 53°50N 9°0E 64 B5
Elbert, Mt. U.S.A. 39°7N 106°27W 110 C5
Elbeuf France 49°17N 1°2E 66 B4
Elbląg Poland 54°10N 19°25E 65 A10
Elbrus Russia 43°21N 42°30E 71 F7
Elburz Mts. Iran 36°0N 52°0E 87 B8
Elche Spain 38°15N 0°42W 67 C5
Elda Spain 38°29N 0°47W 67 C5
Eldoret Kenya 0°30N 35°17E 96 D7
Elektrostal Russia 55°41N 38°32E 70 C6
Elephant Butte Res. U.S.A. 33°9N 107°11W 110 D5
Elephant I. Antarctica 61°0S 55°0W 55 C18
Eleuthera I. Bahamas 25°0N 76°20W 115 C9
Elgin U.K. 57°39N 3°19W 23 G11
Elgin U.S.A. 42°2N 88°17W 112 D3
Elgon, Mt. Africa 1°10N 34°30E 96 D6
Elham U.K. 51°9N 1°8E 31 D11
Elishaw U.K. 55°15N 2°14W 26 B4
Elista Russia 46°16N 44°14E 71 E7
Elizabeth U.S.A. 40°39N 74°12W 113 E10

Elizabeth City U.S.A. 36°18N 76°14W 111 C11
Elizabethtown U.S.A. 37°42N 85°52W 112 G5
Elkhart U.S.A. 41°41N 85°58W 112 E5
Elkins U.S.A. 38°55N 79°51W 112 F8
Elko U.S.A. 40°50N 115°46W 110 B3
Elland U.K. 53°41N 1°50W 27 E5
Ellef Ringnes I. Canada 78°30N 102°2W 109 B9
Ellen → U.K. 54°44N 3°30W 26 C2
Ellensburg U.S.A. 46°59N 120°34W 110 A2
Ellerton Barbados 13°7N 59°33W 114 c
Ellesmere U.K. 52°55N 2°53W 27 G3
Ellesmere I. Canada 79°30N 80°0W 109 B12
Ellesmere Port U.K. 53°17N 2°54W 27 F3
Ellington U.K. 55°14N 1°33W 26 B5
Elliot Lake Canada 46°25N 82°35W 112 B6
Ellon U.K. 57°22N 2°4W 23 H13
Ellsworth Land Antarctica 76°0S 89°0W 55 D16
Elmalı Turkey 36°44N 29°56E 71 G4
Elmira U.S.A. 42°6N 76°48W 112 D9
Elmswell U.K. 52°15N 0°55E 31 B10
Eluru India 16°48N 81°8E 85 L12
Ely U.K. 52°24N 0°16E 31 B9
Ely U.S.A. 39°15N 114°54W 110 C4
Elyria U.S.A. 41°22N 82°7W 112 E6
eMalahleni S. Africa 25°51S 29°14E 97 K5
Emämrüd Iran 36°30N 55°0E 87 B8
Embarcación Argentina 23°10S 64°0W 121 E3
Embleton U.K. 55°29N 1°38W 26 B5
Emden Germany 53°21N 7°12E 64 B4
Emerald Australia 37°56S 145°29E 98 E8
Emmen Neths. 52°48N 6°57E 64 B4
Emmonak U.S.A. 62°47N 164°31W 108 C3
Empalme Mexico 27°58N 110°51W 114 B2
Empangeni S. Africa 28°50S 31°52E 97 K6
Empedrado Argentina 28°0S 58°46W 121 E4
Emporia U.S.A. 38°25N 96°11W 111 C7
Emporium U.S.A. 41°31N 78°14W 112 E8
Empty Quarter = Rub' al Khālī Si. Arabia 19°0N 48°0E 89 D4
Ems → Germany 53°20N 7°12E 64 B4
En Nahud Sudan 12°45N 28°25E 95 F11
Enard B. U.K. 58°5N 5°20W 22 F7
Encarnación Paraguay 27°15S 55°50W 121 E4
Encounter B. Australia 35°45S 138°45E 98 H6
Ende Indonesia 8°45S 121°40E 83 F6
Enderbury Kiribati 3°8S 171°5W 102 H10
Enderby U.K. 52°36N 1°13W 27 G6
Enderby Land Antarctica 66°0S 53°0E 55 C5
Endicott U.S.A. 42°6N 76°4W 113 D9
Enewetak Atoll Marshall Is. 11°30N 162°15E 102 F8
Enez Turkey 40°45N 26°5E 71 F4
Enfield □ U.K. 51°38N 0°5W 31 C8
Engadin Switz. 46°45N 10°10E 64 E6
Engels Russia 51°28N 46°6E 71 D8
Enggano Indonesia 5°20S 102°40E 82 F2
England □ U.K. 53°0N 2°0W 62 E6
English → Canada 49°12N 91°5W 108 D10
English Channel Europe 50°0N 2°0W 62 F6
Enid U.S.A. 36°24N 97°53W 110 C7
Ennadai L. Canada 60°58N 101°20W 108 C9
Ennedi Chad 17°15N 22°0E 95 E10
Ennerdale Water U.K. 54°32N 3°24W 26 C2
Ennis Ireland 52°51N 8°59W 20 C5
Enniscorthy Ireland 52°30N 6°34W 21 D9
Enniskillen Ireland 54°21N 7°39W 18 C6
Ennistimon Ireland 52°57N 9°17W 20 C4
Enns → Austria 48°14N 14°32E 64 D8
Enschede Neths. 52°13N 6°53E 64 B4
Ensenada Mexico 31°52N 116°37W 114 A1
Enshi China 30°18N 109°29E 79 C10
Enstone U.K. 51°55N 1°27W 30 C6
Entebbe Uganda 0°4N 32°28E 96 D6
Entre Rios □ Argentina 30°30S 58°30W 121 F4
Enugu Nigeria 6°30N 7°30E 94 G7
Eólie, Ís. Italy 38°30N 14°57E 68 E6
Épernay France 49°3N 3°56E 66 B5
Épinal France 48°10N 6°27E 66 B7
Epping U.K. 51°41N 0°7E 31 C9
Epping Forest U.K. 51°40N 0°5E 31 C9
Epsom U.K. 51°19N 0°16W 31 D8
Epworth U.K. 53°32N 0°48W 27 E7
Equatorial Guinea ■ Africa 2°0N 8°0E 96 D1
Er Rachidia Morocco 31°58N 4°20W 94 B5
Ercyas Dağı Turkey 38°30N 35°30E 86 B3
Erebus, Mt. Antarctica 77°35S 167°0E 55 D11
Ereğli Konya, Turkey 37°31N 34°4E 71 G5
Ereğli Zonguldak, Turkey 41°15N 31°24E 71 F5
Erenhot China 43°48N 112°2E 79 C11
Erfurt Germany 50°58N 11°2E 64 C6
Ergeni Lowlands Russia 47°0N 44°0E 71 E7
Eriboll, L. U.K. 58°30N 4°42W 23 E8
Erie U.S.A. 42°8N 80°5W 112 D7
Erie, L. N. Amer. 42°15N 81°0W 112 D7
Eriskay U.K. 57°4N 7°18W 22 H3
Eritrea ■ Africa 14°0N 38°30E 89 D2
Erlangen Germany 49°36N 11°0E 64 D6
Ermoupoli Greece 37°28N 24°57E 69 F11
Ernakulam India 9°59N 76°22E 84 Q10
Erne → Ireland 54°30N 8°16W 18 C5
Erne, Lower L. U.K. 54°28N 7°47W 18 C6
Erne, Upper L. U.K. 54°14N 7°32W 18 C6
Erode India 11°24N 77°45E 84 P10
Erramala Hills India 15°30N 78°15E 84 M11
Errigal Ireland 55°2N 8°6W 18 A5
Erris Hd. Ireland 54°17N 10°0W 18 B1
Erromango Vanuatu 18°45S 169°5E 99 D12
Erzgebirge Germany 50°27N 12°55E 64 C7
Erzincan Turkey 39°46N 39°30E 71 G6
Erzurum Turkey 39°57N 41°15E 71 G7
Esbjerg Denmark 55°29N 8°29E 63 F5
Escada Brazil 8°22S 35°8W 122 A3
Escanaba U.S.A. 45°45N 87°4W 112 C4
Escuinapa de Hidalgo Mexico 22°50N 105°50W 114 C3
Escuintla Guatemala 14°20N 90°48E 114 E6
Esfahān Iran 32°39N 51°43E 87 C7
Esha Ness U.K. 60°29N 1°38W 22 A14
Esk → Cumb., U.K. 54°20N 3°24W 26 D2
Esk → Dumf. & Gall., U.K. 54°58N 3°2W 25 E9

Esk → N. Yorks., U.K. 54°30N 0°37W 26 D7
Eskdale U.K. 55°12N 3°4W 25 D9
Esker Siding Canada 53°53N 66°25W 109 D13
Eskilstuna Sweden 59°22N 16°32E 63 F7
Eskişehir Turkey 39°50N 30°30E 71 G5
Eslāmābād-e Gharb Iran 34°10N 46°30E 86 C6
Esna Egypt 25°17N 32°30E 95 C12
Esperance Australia 33°45S 121°55E 98 G3
Espinhaço, Serra do Brazil 17°30S 43°30W 122 C2
Espírito Santo □ Brazil 20°0S 40°45W 122 C2
Espíritu Santo Vanuatu 15°15S 166°50E 99 D12
Espoo Finland 60°12N 24°40E 63 E8
Essaouira Morocco 31°32N 9°42W 94 B4
Essen Germany 51°28N 7°2E 64 C4
Essequibo → Guyana 6°50N 58°30W 120 B4
Essex □ U.K. 51°54N 0°27E 31 C9
Esslingen Germany 48°44N 9°18E 64 D5
Estados, I. de Los Argentina 54°40S 64°30W 121 H3
Estância Brazil 11°16S 37°26W 122 B3
Estevan Canada 49°10N 102°59W 108 E9
Eston U.K. 54°34N 1°8W 26 C6
Estonia ■ Europe 58°30N 25°30E 63 F8
Estrela, Serra da Portugal 40°10N 7°45W 67 B2
Estrondo, Serra do Brazil 7°20S 48°0W 120 C5
Etawah India 26°48N 79°6E 84 F11
Etchingham U.K. 51°0N 0°26E 31 D9
Ethiopia ■ Africa 8°0N 40°0E 89 F3
Ethiopian Highlands Ethiopia 10°0N 37°0E 89 F2
Etive, L. U.K. 56°29N 5°10W 24 B5
Etna Italy 37°50N 14°55E 68 F6
Eton U.K. 51°30N 0°36W 31 C7
Etosha Pan Namibia 18°40S 16°30E 97 H3
Ettington U.K. 52°8N 1°35W 30 B5
Ettrick Forest U.K. 55°30N 3°0W 25 C9
Ettrick Water → U.K. 55°31N 2°55W 25 C10
Euclid U.S.A. 41°34N 81°32W 112 E7
Eugene U.S.A. 44°5N 123°4W 110 B2
Euphrates → Asia 31°0N 47°25E 86 D6
Eureka Canada 80°0N 85°56W 109 B11
Eureka U.S.A. 40°47N 124°9W 110 B1
Europa, Île Ind. Oc. 22°20S 40°22E 97 J8
Europa, Picos de Spain 43°10N 4°49W 67 A3
Europe 50°0N 20°0E 56 E10
Eurotunnel Terminal U.K. 51°6N 1°10E 31 D11
Euxton U.K. 53°41N 2°41W 27 E3
Evanston Ill., U.S.A. 42°3N 87°40W 112 D4
Evanston Wyo., U.S.A. 41°16N 110°58W 110 B4
Evansville U.S.A. 37°58N 87°35W 112 G4
Evercreech U.K. 51°9N 2°30W 30 D4
Everest, Mt. Nepal 28°5N 86°58E 85 E15
Everett U.S.A. 47°59N 122°12W 110 A2
Everglades, The U.S.A. 25°50N 81°0W 111 E10
Evesham U.K. 52°6N 1°56W 30 B5
Evia Greece 38°30N 24°0E 69 E11
Évora Portugal 38°33N 7°57W 67 C2
Évreux France 49°3N 1°8E 66 B4
Evros → Greece 41°40N 26°34E 69 D12
Ewe, L. U.K. 57°49N 5°38W 22 G6
Ewell U.K. 51°20N 0°14W 31 D8
Ewhurst U.K. 51°9N 0°25W 31 D8
Exe → U.K. 50°41N 3°29W 29 F7
Exeter U.K. 50°43N 3°31W 29 F6
Exminster U.K. 50°40N 3°29W 29 F7
Exmoor △ U.K. 51°8N 3°42W 29 E6
Exmouth U.K. 50°37N 3°25W 29 F7
Exton U.K. 52°42N 0°38W 27 G7
Extremadura □ Spain 39°30N 6°5W 67 C2
Eyam U.K. 53°17N 1°40W 27 F5
Eyasi, L. Tanzania 3°30S 35°0E 96 E6
Eye Cambs., U.K. 52°37N 0°11W 31 A8
Eye Suffolk, U.K. 52°19N 1°9E 31 B11
Eye Pen. U.K. 58°13N 6°10W 22 F5
Eyemouth U.K. 55°52N 2°5W 25 C11
Eyjafjallajökull Iceland 63°38N 19°36W 63 B2
Eynsham U.K. 51°47N 1°22W 30 C6
Eyre, L. Australia 29°30S 137°26E 98 F6
Eyre Pen. Australia 33°30S 136°17E 98 G6

F

F.Y.R.O.M. = Macedonia ■ Europe 41°53N 21°40E 69 D9
Faenza Italy 44°17N 11°53E 68 B4
Fair Hd. U.K. 55°14N 6°9W 19 A9
Fair Isle U.K. 59°32N 1°38W 22 C14
Fairbanks U.S.A. 64°51N 147°43W 108 C5
Fairfield U.S.A. 38°23N 88°22W 112 F3
Fairford U.K. 51°43N 1°46W 30 C5
Fairlight U.K. 50°52N 0°40E 31 E10
Fairmont U.S.A. 39°29N 80°9W 112 F7
Fairweather, Mt. U.S.A. 58°55N 137°32W 108 D6
Faisalabad Pakistan 31°30N 73°5E 84 D8
Faizabad India 26°45N 82°10E 85 F13
Fakenham U.K. 52°51N 0°51E 31 A10
Falcon Res. U.S.A. 26°34N 99°10W 110 F7
Faldingworth U.K. 53°21N 0°24W 27 F8
Falkirk U.K. 56°0N 3°47W 25 C8
Falkland U.K. 56°16N 3°12W 25 B9
Falkland Is. ☐ Atl. Oc. 51°30S 59°0W 121 H4
Fall River U.S.A. 41°43N 71°10W 113 E12
Falmouth Jamaica 18°30N 77°40W 114 a
Falmouth U.K. 50°9N 5°5W 29 G3
Falmouth B. U.K. 50°6N 5°5W 29 G3
Falstone U.K. 55°11N 2°26W 26 B4
Falun Sweden 60°37N 15°37E 63 E7
Famagusta Cyprus 35°8N 33°55E 86 C3
Fanad Ireland 55°7N 7°36W 18 A6
Fanad Hd. Ireland 55°17N 7°38W 18 A6
Fannich, L. U.K. 57°38N 4°59W 23 G8
Fano Italy 43°50N 13°1E 68 C5
Far East Asia 40°0N 130°0E 72 E14
Farāh Afghan. 32°20N 62°7E 87 C10
Farasān, Si. Arabia 16°45N 41°55E 89 D3
Fareham U.K. 50°51N 1°11W 30 E6
Farewell, C. Greenland 59°48N 43°55W 54 D5
Fargo U.S.A. 46°53N 96°48W 111 A7
Faridabad India 28°26N 77°19E 84 E10
Faridkot India 30°44N 74°45E 84 D9
Faringdon U.K. 51°39N 1°34W 30 C5
Farmington U.S.A. 36°44N 108°12W 110 C5
Farmville U.S.A. 37°18N 78°24W 112 G8

Farnborough U.K. 51°16N 0°45W 31 D7
Farne Is. U.K. 55°38N 1°37W 26 A5
Farnham U.K. 51°13N 0°47W 31 D7
Farnworth U.K. 53°34N 2°25W 27 E4
Faro Canada 62°11N 133°22W 108 C6
Faro Portugal 37°2N 7°55W 67 D2
Faroe Is. ☐ Atl. Oc. 62°0N 7°0W 57 C4
Faslane U.K. 56°5N 4°49W 24 B6
Fataka Solomon Is. 11°55S 170°12E 99 D12
Fatehgarh India 27°25N 79°35E 84 F11
Fatehpur Raj., India 28°0N 74°40E 84 F9
Fatehpur Ut. P., India 25°56N 81°13E 85 G12
Fauldhouse U.K. 55°50N 3°43W 25 C8
Faversham U.K. 51°19N 0°56E 31 D10
Fawley U.K. 50°50N 1°20W 30 E6
Fayetteville Ark., U.S.A. 36°4N 94°10W 111 C8
Fayetteville N.C., U.S.A. 35°3N 78°53W 111 D11
Fazeley U.K. 52°37N 1°40W 27 G5
Fazilka India 30°27N 74°2E 84 D9
Fdérik Mauritania 22°40N 12°45W 94 D3
Feale → Ireland 52°27N 9°37W 20 D3
Fear, C. U.S.A. 33°50N 77°58W 111 D11
Fécamp France 49°45N 0°22E 66 B4
Fehmarn Germany 54°27N 11°7E 64 A6
Feira de Santana Brazil 12°15S 38°57W 122 B3
Felipe Carrillo Puerto Mexico 19°38N 88°3W 114 D7
Felixstowe U.K. 51°58N 1°23E 31 C11
Felton U.K. 55°18N 1°42W 26 B5
Feltwell U.K. 52°30N 0°32E 31 B10
Fenny Bentley U.K. 53°3N 1°45W 27 F5
Fenny Compton U.K. 52°10N 1°23W 30 B6
Fenny Stratford U.K. 52°0N 0°44W 31 C7
Fenyang China 37°18N 111°48E 79 D11
Feodosiya Ukraine 45°2N 35°16E 71 E6
Fergus Falls U.S.A. 46°17N 96°4W 111 A7
Ferkéssédougou Ivory C. 9°35N 5°6W 94 G4
Fermanagh □ U.K. 54°21N 7°40W 18 C6
Fermont Canada 52°47N 67°5W 109 D13
Fermoy Ireland 52°9N 8°16W 20 D6
Fernhurst U.K. 51°3N 0°43W 31 D7
Ferrara Italy 44°50N 11°35E 68 B4
Ferret, C. France 44°38N 1°15W 66 D3
Ferrol Spain 43°29N 8°15W 67 A1
Ferryhill U.K. 54°41N 1°33W 26 C6
Fès Morocco 34°0N 5°0W 94 B5
Fethiye Turkey 36°36N 29°6E 71 G4
Fetlar U.K. 60°36N 0°52W 22 A16
Feuilles → Canada 58°47N 70°4W 109 D12
Feyẕābād Afghan. 37°7N 70°33E 87 B12
Fezzan Libya 27°0N 13°0E 95 C8
Ffestiniog U.K. 52°57N 3°55W 28 B6
Fianarantsoa Madag. 21°26S 47°5E 97 J9
Fife □ U.K. 56°16N 3°1W 25 B9
Fife Ness U.K. 56°17N 2°35W 25 B10
Figeac France 44°37N 2°2E 66 D5
Figueres Spain 42°18N 2°58E 67 A7
Fiji ■ Pac. Oc. 17°20S 179°0E 99 D14
Filby U.K. 52°40N 1°39E 31 A12
Filey U.K. 54°12N 0°18W 26 D8
Filey B. U.K. 54°12N 0°15W 26 D8
Filton U.K. 51°30N 2°34W 30 C3
Fincham U.K. 52°38N 0°30E 31 A9
Findhorn → U.K. 57°38N 3°38W 23 G10
Findlay U.S.A. 41°2N 83°39W 112 E6
Finedon U.K. 52°21N 0°39W 31 B7
Fingal's Cave U.K. 56°27N 6°21W 24 B3
Finglas Ireland 53°23N 6°19W 21 B10
Finike Turkey 36°21N 30°10E 86 B2
Finland ■ Europe 63°0N 27°0E 63 E9
Finland, G. of Europe 60°0N 26°0E 63 F9
Finlay → Canada 57°0N 125°10W 108 D7
Finn → Ireland 54°51N 7°28W 18 B7
Firozabad India 27°10N 78°25E 84 F11
Firozpur India 30°55N 74°40E 84 D9
Fish → Namibia 28°7S 17°10E 97 K3
Fishguard U.K. 52°0N 4°58W 28 D4
Fishtoft U.K. 52°58N 0°1E 27 G9
Fisterra, C. Spain 42°50N 9°19W 67 A1
Fitchburg U.S.A. 42°35N 71°48W 113 D12
Flagstaff U.S.A. 35°12N 111°39W 110 C4
Flamborough U.K. 54°7N 0°7W 26 D8
Flamborough Hd. U.K. 54°7N 0°5W 26 D8
Flandre Europe 50°50N 2°30E 64 C2
Flathead L. U.S.A. 47°51N 114°8W 110 A4
Flattery, C. U.S.A. 48°23N 124°29W 110 A2
Fleet U.K. 51°17N 0°50W 31 D7
Fleetwood U.K. 53°55N 3°1W 27 E2
Flensburg Germany 54°47N 9°27E 64 A5
Flers France 48°47N 0°33W 66 B3
Flimby U.K. 54°42N 3°30W 26 C2
Flin Flon Canada 54°46N 101°53W 108 D9
Flinders → Australia 17°36S 140°36E 98 D7
Flinders I. Australia 40°0S 148°0E 98 H8
Flinders Ranges Australia 31°30S 138°30E 98 G6
Flint U.K. 53°15N 3°8W 28 A7
Flint U.S.A. 43°1N 83°41W 112 D6
Flint I. Kiribati 11°26S 151°48W 103 J12
Flintshire □ U.K. 53°17N 3°17W 28 A7
Flitwick U.K. 52°0N 0°30W 31 C8
Flodden U.K. 55°37N 2°8W 26 A4
Flora U.S.A. 38°40N 88°29W 112 F3
Florence Italy 43°46N 11°15E 68 C4
Florence U.S.A. 34°12N 79°46W 111 D11
Florencia Colombia 1°36N 75°36W 120 B2
Flores Indonesia 8°35S 121°0E 83 F6
Flores Sea Indonesia 6°30S 120°0E 83 F6
Florianópolis Brazil 27°30S 48°30W 121 E5
Florida Uruguay 34°7S 56°10W 121 F4
Florida □ U.S.A. 28°0N 82°0W 111 E10
Florida, Straits of U.S.A. 25°0N 80°0W 115 C9
Florida Keys U.S.A. 24°40N 81°0W 111 F10
Florø Norway 61°35N 5°1E 63 E5
Fly → Papua N. G. 8°25S 143°0E 98 B7
Focșani Romania 45°41N 27°15E 65 F14
Fóggia Italy 41°27N 15°34E 68 D6
Foix France 42°58N 1°38E 66 E4
Foligno Italy 42°57N 12°42E 68 C5

Folkestone U.K. 51°5N 1°12E 31 D11
Fond-du-Lac Canada 59°19N 107°12W 108 D9
Fond du Lac U.S.A. 43°47N 88°27W 112 D3
Fongafale Tuvalu 8°31S 179°13E 99 B14
Fontainebleau France 48°24N 2°40E 66 B5
Fontenay-le-Comte France 46°28N 0°48W 66 C3
Fordham U.K. 52°19N 0°23E 31 B9
Fordingbridge U.K. 50°56N 1°47W 30 E5
Forel, Mt. Greenland 66°52N 36°55W 54 C6
Forest Row U.K. 51°5N 0°3E 31 D9
Forfar U.K. 56°39N 2°53W 23 J12
Forlì Italy 44°13N 12°3E 68 B5
Formartine U.K. 57°20N 2°15W 23 H13
Formby U.K. 53°34N 3°4W 27 E2
Formby Pt. U.K. 53°33N 3°6W 27 E2
Formentera Spain 38°43N 1°27E 67 C6
Formiga Brazil 20°27S 45°25W 122 D1
Formosa Argentina 26°15S 58°10W 121 E4
Formosa Brazil 15°32S 47°20W 122 C1
Forres U.K. 57°37N 3°37W 23 G10
Forsayth Australia 18°33S 143°34E 98 D7
Fort Albany Canada 52°15N 81°35W 109 D11
Fort Augustus U.K. 57°9N 4°42W 23 H8
Fort Chipewyan Canada 58°42N 111°8W 108 D8
Fort Collins U.S.A. 40°35N 105°5W 110 B5
Fort-Coulonge Canada 45°50N 76°45W 112 C9
Fort-de-France Martinique 14°36N 61°5W 115 E12
Fort Dodge U.S.A. 42°30N 94°11W 111 B8
Fort Good Hope Canada 66°14N 128°40W 108 C7
Fort Kent U.S.A. 47°15N 68°36W 113 B13
Fort Lauderdale U.S.A. 26°7N 80°8W 111 E10
Fort Liard Canada 60°14N 123°30W 108 C7
Fort MacKay Canada 57°12N 111°41W 108 D8
Fort Macleod Canada 49°45N 113°30W 108 E8
Fort McMurray Canada 56°44N 111°7W 108 D8
Fort McPherson Canada 67°30N 134°55W 108 C6
Fort Morgan U.S.A. 40°15N 103°48W 110 B6
Fort Myers U.S.A. 26°39N 81°52W 111 E10
Fort Nelson Canada 58°50N 122°44W 108 D7
Fort Nelson → Canada 59°32N 124°0W 108 D7
Fort Peck L. U.S.A. 48°0N 106°26W 110 A5
Fort Providence Canada 61°3N 117°40W 108 C8
Fort Resolution Canada 61°10N 113°40W 108 C8
Fort St. John Canada 56°15N 120°50W 108 D7
Fort Scott U.S.A. 37°50N 94°42W 111 C8
Fort Shevchenko Kazakhstan 44°35N 50°23E 71 F9
Fort Simpson Canada 61°45N 121°15W 108 C7
Fort Smith Canada 60°0N 111°51W 108 C8
Fort Smith U.S.A. 35°23N 94°25W 111 C8
Fort Stockton U.S.A. 30°53N 102°53W 110 D6
Fort Wayne U.S.A. 41°4N 85°9W 112 E5
Fort William U.K. 56°49N 5°7W 22 J7
Fort Worth U.S.A. 32°43N 97°19W 111 D7
Fort Yukon U.S.A. 66°34N 145°16W 108 C5
Fortaleza Brazil 3°45S 38°35W 120 C6
Forth → U.K. 56°9N 3°50W 25 B8
Forth, Firth of U.K. 56°5N 2°55W 25 B10
Fortrose U.K. 57°35N 4°9W 23 G9
Foshan China 23°3N 113°9E 79 G11
Fostoria U.S.A. 41°10N 83°25W 112 E6
Fothergill U.K. 54°43N 3°29W 26 C2
Fotheringhay U.K. 52°32N 0°27W 31 A8
Fougères France 48°21N 1°14W 66 B3
Foula U.K. 60°10N 2°5W 22 a
Foulness I. U.K. 51°36N 0°55E 31 C10
Foulness Pt. U.K. 51°37N 0°58E 31 C10
Foulsham U.K. 52°48N 0°59E 31 A10
Fountainhall U.K. 55°44N 2°53W 25 C11
Fouta Djallon Guinea 11°20N 12°10W 94 F3
Fovant U.K. 51°4N 2°0W 30 D5
Fowey U.K. 50°20N 4°39W 29 G4
Fownhope U.K. 52°0N 2°36W 30 B3
Foxe Basin Canada 66°0N 77°0W 109 C12
Foxe Chan. Canada 65°0N 80°0W 109 C12
Foxe Pen. Canada 65°0N 76°0W 109 C12
Foyle → U.K. 55°3N 7°15W 19 A7
Foyle, Lough U.K. 55°7N 7°4W 19 A7
Foynes Ireland 52°37N 9°7W 20 C4
Foz do Iguaçu Brazil 25°30S 54°30W 121 E4
Framlingham U.K. 52°14N 1°21E 31 B12
Franca Brazil 20°33S 47°30W 122 D1
France ■ Europe 47°0N 3°0E 66 C5
Franceville Gabon 1°40S 13°32E 96 E2
Franche-Comté France 46°50N 5°55E 66 C6
Francis Case, L. U.S.A. 43°4N 98°34W 110 B7
Francistown Botswana 21°7S 27°33E 97 J5
François L. Canada 54°0N 125°30W 108 D7
Frankfort Ind., U.S.A. 40°17N 86°31W 112 E4
Frankfort Ky., U.S.A. 38°12N 84°52W 112 F5
Frankfurt Brandenburg, Germany 52°20N 14°32E 64 B8
Frankfurt Hessen, Germany 50°7N 8°41E 64 C5
Fränkische Alb Germany 49°10N 11°23E 64 D6
Franklin N.H., U.S.A. 43°27N 71°39W 113 D12
Franklin Pa., U.S.A. 41°24N 79°50W 112 E8
Franklin B. Canada 69°45N 126°0W 108 C7
Franklin D. Roosevelt L. U.S.A. 48°18N 118°9W 110 A3
Franklin L. U.S.A. 40°25N 115°22W 110 B3
Franklin Mts. Canada 65°0N 125°0W 108 C7
Franklin Str. Canada 72°0N 96°0W 108 B10
Frant U.K. 51°5N 0°16E 31 D9
Franz Josef Land Arctic 82°0N 55°0E 54 A10
Fraser → Canada 49°7N 123°11W 108 E7
Fraserburgh U.K. 57°42N 2°1W 23 G13
Frederick U.S.A. 39°25N 77°25W 112 F9
Fredericksburg U.S.A. 38°18N 77°28W 112 F9
Fredericktown U.S.A. 37°34N 90°18W 112 G2
Fredericton Canada 45°57N 66°40W 113 C14
Frederikshavn Denmark 57°28N 10°31E 63 F6
Fredonia U.S.A. 42°26N 79°20W 112 D8
Fredrikstad Norway 59°13N 10°57E 63 F6
Free State □ S. Africa 28°30S 27°0E 97 K5
Freeport Bahamas 26°30N 78°47W 115 B9
Freeport Ill., U.S.A. 42°17N 89°36W 112 D3
Freeport Tex., U.S.A. 28°57N 95°21W 111 E7
Freetown S. Leone 8°30N 13°17W 94 G3
Freiburg Germany 47°59N 7°51E 64 E4
Fréjus France 43°25N 6°44E 66 E7
Fremont U.S.A. 41°21N 83°7W 112 E6
French Creek → U.S.A. 41°24N 79°50W 112 E8

French Guiana   Guaratinguetá

French Guiana ☑ S. Amer. 4°0N 53°0W 120 B4
French Polynesia ☑ Pac. Oc. 20°0S 145°0W 103 J13
Frenchman Cr. →
  N. Amer. 40°13N 107°10W 110 A5
Freshwater U.K. 50°41N 1°31W 30 E5
Fresnillo Mexico 23°10N 102°53W 114 C4
Frøsno U.S.A. 36°44N 119°47W 110 C3
Fria, C. Namibia 18°0S 12°0E 90 H5
Fridaythorpe U.K. 54°2N 0°39W 27 D7
Friedrichshafen Germany 47°39N 9°30E 64 E5
Frimley U.K. 51°19N 0°44W 31 D7
Frinton-on-Sea U.K. 51°49N 1°15E 31 C11
Frio, C. Brazil 22°50S 41°50W 117 F6
Frizington U.K. 54°33N 3°28W 26 C2
Frobisher B. Canada 62°30N 66°0W 109 C13
Frobisher L. Canada 56°20N 108°15W 108 D9
Frodsham U.K. 53°18N 2°43W 27 F3
Frome U.K. 51°14N 2°19W 30 D4
Frome → U.K. 50°41N 2°6W 30 E4
Front Range U.S.A. 40°25N 105°45W 110 B5
Front Royal U.S.A. 38°55N 78°12W 112 F8
Frutal Brazil 20°0S 49°0W 122 C1
Frýdek-Místek Czech Rep. 49°40N 18°20E 65 D10
Fuchū Japan 34°34N 133°14E 81 F3
Fuengirola Spain 36°32N 4°41W 67 D3
Fuerte → Mexico 25°54N 109°22W 114 B3
Fuerteventura Canary Is. 28°30N 14°0W 94 C3
Fuhai = Wiay U.K. 57°24N 7°13W 22 H3
Fuji Japan 35°9N 138°39E 81 F6
Fuji-San Japan 35°22N 138°44E 81 F6
Fujian ☐ China 26°0N 118°0E 79 F12
Fujin China 47°16N 132°1E 79 B15
Fukui Japan 36°5N 136°10E 81 E5
Fukuoka Japan 33°39N 130°21E 81 G2
Fukushima Japan 37°44N 140°28E 81 E7
Fukuyama Japan 34°35N 133°20E 81 F3
Fulda Germany 50°32N 9°40E 64 C5
Fulda → Germany 51°25N 9°39E 64 C5
Fulton U.S.A. 43°19N 76°25W 112 D9
Fulwood U.K. 53°47N 2°40W 27 E3
Funabashi Japan 35°45N 140°0E 81 F7
Funchal Madeira 32°38N 16°54W 94 B2
Fundy, B. of Canada 45°0N 66°0W 113 C15
Furnas, Represa de Brazil 20°50S 45°30W 122 D1
Furneaux Group Australia 40°10S 147°50E 98 J8
Fürth Germany 49°28N 10°59E 64 D6
Fury and Hecla Str. Canada 69°56N 84°0W 109 C11
Fushun China 41°50N 123°56E 79 C13
Fustic Barbados 13°16N 59°38W 114 c
Fuxin China 42°5N 121°48E 79 C13
Fuyang China 33°0N 115°48E 79 E12
Fuyong China 22°40N 113°49E 79 a
Fuyu Heilongjiang, China 47°49N 124°27E 79 B13
Fuyu Jilin, China 45°12N 124°43E 79 B13
Fuyun China 47°0N 89°28E 78 B6
Fuzhou China 26°5N 119°16E 79 F12
Fylingdales Moor U.K. 54°25N 0°41W 26 D7
Fyn Denmark 55°20N 10°30E 63 F6
Fyne, L. U.K. 55°59N 5°23W 24 C5

G

Gaalkacyo Somalia 6°30N 47°30E 89 F4
Gabès Tunisia 33°53N 10°2E 95 B8
Gabès, G. de Tunisia 34°0N 10°30E 95 B8
Gabon ■ Africa 0°10S 10°0E 96 E2
Gaborone Botswana 24°45S 25°57E 97 J5
Gabrovo Bulgaria 42°52N 25°19E 69 C11
Gachsārān Iran 30°15N 50°45E 87 D7
Gadarwara India 22°50N 78°50E 84 H11
Gadsden U.S.A. 34°1N 86°1W 111 D9
Gafsa Tunisia 34°24N 8°43E 95 B7
Găgăuzia ☐ Moldova 46°10N 28°40E 65 E15
Gagnoa Ivory C. 6°56N 6°16W 94 G4
Gagnon Canada 51°50N 68°5W 109 D13
Gainesville Fla., U.S.A. 29°40N 82°20W 111 E10
Gainesville Ga., U.S.A. 34°18N 83°50W 111 D10
Gainford U.K. 54°34N 1°43W 26 C5
Gainsborough U.K. 53°24N 0°46W 27 F7
Gairdner, L. Australia 31°30S 136°0E 98 G6
Gairloch U.K. 57°43N 5°41W 22 G6
Gairloch, L. U.K. 57°43N 5°45W 22 G6
Galapagos Ecuador 0°0 91°0W 117 D1
Galashiels U.K. 55°37N 2°49W 25 C10
Galați Romania 45°27N 28°2E 65 F15
Galdhøpiggen Norway 61°38N 8°18E 63 E5
Galena U.S.A. 64°44N 156°56W 108 C4
Galesburg U.S.A. 40°57N 90°22W 112 E2
Galgate U.K. 53°59N 2°46W 27 E3
Galicia ☐ Spain 42°43N 7°45W 67 A2
Galilee, Sea of Israel 32°45N 35°35E 86 C3
Galina Pt. Jamaica 18°24N 76°58W 114 a
Gallan Hd. U.K. 58°15N 7°2W 22 F3
Galle Sri Lanka 6°5N 80°10E 84 R12
Galley Hd. Ireland 51°32N 8°55W 20 E5
Gallinas, Pta. Colombia 12°28N 71°40W 120 A2
Gallipolis U.S.A. 38°49N 82°12W 112 F6
Gällivare Sweden 67°9N 20°40E 63 D8
Galloway U.K. 55°1N 4°29W 24 D7
Galloway, Mull of U.K. 54°39N 4°52W 24 E6
Gallup U.S.A. 35°32N 108°45W 110 C5
Galmpton U.K. 50°23N 3°35W 29 G6
Galmudug Somalia 6°30N 48°0E 89 F4
Galston U.K. 55°36N 4°24W 24 D7
Galty Mts. Ireland 52°22N 8°10W 20 D6
Galtymore Ireland 52°21N 8°11W 20 D6
Galveston U.S.A. 29°18N 94°48W 111 E8
Galway Ireland 53°17N 9°3W 20 B4
Galway ☐ Ireland 53°22N 9°1W 20 B4
Galway B. Ireland 53°13N 9°10W 20 B4
Gambia ■ W. Afr. 13°25N 16°0W 94 F2
Gambia → W. Afr. 13°28N 16°34W 94 F2
Gamlingay U.K. 52°10N 0°11W 31 B8
Gan Jiang → China 29°15N 116°0E 79 F12
Gananoque Canada 44°20N 76°10W 113 C9
Gäncä Azerbaijan 40°45N 46°20E 71 F8
Gand = Gent Belgium 51°2N 3°42E 64 C2
Gandak → India 25°39N 85°13E 85 G14
Gander Canada 48°58N 54°35W 109 E14
Gandhi Sagar India 24°40N 75°40E 84 G9
Gandía Spain 38°58N 0°9W 67 C5

Ganganagar India 29°56N 73°56E 84 E8
Gangdisê Shan China 31°20N 81°0E 78 E5
Ganges → India 23°20N 90°30E 85 H17
Gangneung S. Korea 37°45N 128°54E 79 D14
Gangtok India 27°20N 88°37E 85 F16
Gannett Peak U.S.A. 43°11N 109°39W 110 B5
Gansu ☐ China 36°0N 104°0E 78 D9
Ganzhou China 25°51N 114°56E 79 F11
Gao Mali 16°15N 0°5W 94 E5
Gap France 44°33N 6°5E 66 D7
Gar China 32°10N 79°58E 78 E4
Garanhuns Brazil 8°50S 36°30W 122 A3
Garboldisham U.K. 52°23N 0°57F 31 B10
Garda, L. di Italy 45°40N 10°41E 68 B4
Garden City U.S.A. 37°58N 100°53W 110 C6
Gardēz Afghan. 33°37N 69°9E 87 C12
Gare L. U.K. 56°1N 4°50W 24 B6
Garforth U.K. 53°47N 1°24W 27 E6
Gargrave U.K. 53°59N 2°1W 27 E4
Garioch U.K. 57°18N 2°40W 23 H12
Garissa Kenya 0°25S 39°40E 96 E7
Garmsar Iran 35°20N 52°25E 87 C7
Garonne → France 45°2N 0°36W 66 D3
Garoowe Somalia 8°25N 48°33E 89 F4
Garoua Cameroon 9°19N 13°21E 95 G8
Garron Pt. U.K. 55°3N 5°59W 19 A10
Garry, L. Canada 65°58N 100°18W 108 C9
Garsdale Head U.K. 54°20N 2°20W 26 D4
Garstang U.K. 53°55N 2°46W 27 E3
Gar Japan 41°36N 87°20W 112 E4
Garzê China 31°38N 100°1E 78 E9
Gascogne France 43°45N 0°20E 66 E4
Gascogne, G. de Europe 44°0N 2°0W 66 D2
Gashua Nigeria 12°54N 11°0E 95 F8
Gaspé Canada 48°52N 64°30W 109 E13
Gaspé, C. de Canada 48°48N 64°7W 113 A15
Gaspésie, Pén. de la Canada 48°45N 65°40W 113 A15
Gata, Sierra de Spain 40°20N 6°45W 67 B2
Gatehouse of Fleet U.K. 54°53N 4°12W 24 E7
Gateshead U.K. 54°57N 1°35W 26 C5
Gatineau Canada 45°29N 75°39W 113 C10
Gatineau → Canada 45°27N 75°42W 113 C10
Gatley U.K. 53°24N 2°15W 27 F4
Gävle Sweden 60°40N 17°9E 63 E7
Gawilgarh Hills India 21°15N 76°45E 84 J10
Gawthwaite U.K. 54°16N 3°0W 26 D2
Gaxun Nur China 42°22N 100°30F 78 C9
Gaya India 24°47N 85°4E 85 G14
Gaylord U.S.A. 45°2N 84°41W 112 C5
Gayton U.K. 52°45N 0°36E 31 A10
Gaywood U.K. 52°46N 0°26E 31 A9
Gaza Gaza Strip 31°30N 34°28E 86 D3
Gaza Strip ☐ Asia 31°29N 34°25E 86 D3
Gaziantep Turkey 37°6N 37°23E 71 G6
Gazimağusa 35°8N 33°55E 86 C3
Gdansk Poland 54°22N 18°40E 65 A10
Gdynia Poland 54°35N 18°33E 65 A10
Gebze Turkey 40°47N 29°25E 71 F4
Gedaref Sudan 14°2N 35°28E 95 F13
Gedney U.K. 52°48N 0°4E 27 G9
Gedser Denmark 54°35N 11°55F 63 G6
Geelong Australia 38°10S 144°22E 98 H7
Gejiu China 23°20N 103°10E 78 G9
Gela Italy 37°4N 14°15E 68 F6
Gelibolu Turkey 40°28N 26°43E 71 F4
Gelsenkirchen Germany 51°32N 7°6E 64 C4
General Acha Argentina 37°20S 64°38W 121 F3
General Alvear Argentina 35°0S 67°40W 121 F3
General Carrera, L. S. Amer. 46°35S 72°0W 121 G2
General Pico Argentina 35°45S 63°50W 121 F3
General Santos Phil. 6°5N 125°14E 83 C7
Geneva Switz. 46°12N 6°9E 64 E4
Geneva U.S.A. 42°52N 76°59W 112 D9
Geneva, L. = Léman, L. Europe 46°26N 6°30E 64 E4
Gennargentu, Mti. del Italy 40°1N 9°19E 68 D3
Génova Italy 44°25N 8°57E 68 B3
Génova, G. di Italy 44°0N 9°0E 68 C3
Gent Belgium 51°2N 3°42E 64 C2
George S. Africa 33°58S 22°29E 97 L4
George → Canada 58°49N 66°10W 109 D13
George, L. Australia 29°17N 81°36W 111 E10
George Town Cayman Is. 19°20N 81°24W 115 D8
George Town Malaysia 5°25N 100°20E 82 C2
George V Land Antarctica 69°0S 148°0E 55 C10
Georgetown Guyana 6°50N 58°12W 120 B4
Georgetown Ky., U.S.A. 38°13N 84°33W 112 F5
Georgetown S.C., U.S.A. 33°23N 79°17W 111 D11
Georgia ☐ U.S.A. 32°50N 83°15W 111 D10
Georgia ■ Asia 42°0N 43°0E 71 F7
Georgian B. Canada 45°15N 81°0W 112 C7
Georgiyevsk Russia 44°12N 43°28E 71 F7
Gera Germany 50°53N 12°4E 64 C7
Geraldton Australia 28°48S 114°32E 98 F1
Germany ■ Europe 51°0N 10°0E 64 C6
Germiston S. Africa 26°13S 28°10E 97 K5
Gerrans B. U.K. 50°12N 4°57W 29 G4
Gerrards Cross U.K. 51°35N 0°33W 31 D7
Getafe Spain 40°18N 3°43W 67 B4
Ghadāmis Libya 30°11N 9°29E 95 B7
Ghaghara → India 25°45N 84°40E 85 G14
Ghana ■ W. Afr. 8°0N 1°0W 94 G5
Ghardaïa Algeria 32°20N 3°37E 94 B6
Gharyān Libya 32°10N 13°0E 95 B8
Ghats, Eastern India 14°0N 78°50E 84 N11
Ghats, Western India 14°0N 75°0E 84 N9
Ghazal, Bahr el → Chad 13°0N 15°47E 95 F9
Ghazal, Bahr el →
  South Sudan 9°31N 30°25E 95 G12
Ghaziabad India 28°42N 77°26E 84 E10
Ghazipur India 25°38N 83°35E 85 G13
Ghaznī Afghan. 33°30N 68°28E 87 C12
Ghent = Gent Belgium 51°2N 3°42E 64 C2
Giants Causeway U.K. 55°16N 6°29W 19 A9
Gibraltar ☐ Europe 36°7N 5°22W 67 D3
Gibraltar, Str. of Medit. S. 35°55N 5°40W 67 E3
Gibraltar Pt. U.K. 53°6N 0°19E 27 F9
Gibson Desert Australia 24°0S 126°0E 98 E4
Gifu Japan 35°30N 136°45E 81 F5
Giggleswick U.K. 54°5N 2°17W 26 D4
Gijón Spain 43°32N 5°42W 67 A3
Gila → U.S.A. 32°43N 114°33W 110 D4

Gīlān ☐ Iran 37°0N 50°0E 86 B7
Gilbert Is. Kiribati 1°0N 172°0E 102 G9
Gilgit India 35°50N 74°15E 84 B9
Gilgit-Baltistan ☐ Pakistan 36°30N 73°0E 84 B9
Gillam Canada 56°20N 94°40W 108 D10
Gillette U.S.A. 44°18N 105°30W 110 B5
Gillingham Dorset, U.K. 51°2N 2°18W 30 D4
Gillingham Medway, U.K. 51°23N 0°33E 31 D10
Gilsland U.K. 55°0N 2°34W 26 C3
Gimie, Mt. St. Lucia 13°54N 61°0W 114 b
Girdle Ness U.K. 57°9N 2°3W 23 H13
Giresun Turkey 40°55N 38°30E 71 F6
Girga Egypt 26°17N 31°55E 95 C12
Girona Spain 41°58N 2°46E 67 B7
Gironde → France 45°32N 1°7W 66 D3
Girvan U.K. 55°14N 4°51W 24 D6
Gisborne N.Z. 38°39S 178°5E 99 H14
Gisburn U.K. 53°56N 2°16W 27 E4
Gitega Burundi 3°26S 29°56E 96 E5
Gizhiga Russia 62°3N 160°30E 77 C17
Gjoa Haven Canada 68°38N 95°53W 108 C10
Glace Bay Canada 46°11N 59°58W 113 B18
Glacier Nat. Park △ U.S.A. 48°42N 113°48W 110 A4
Gladstone Australia 23°52S 151°16E 98 E9
Gladstone U.S.A. 45°51N 87°1W 112 C4
Gladwin U.S.A. 43°59N 84°29W 112 D5
Glamorgan, Vale of ☐ U.K. 51°28N 3°25W 29 F7
Glanaruddery Mts. Ireland 52°20N 9°27W 20 D4
Clanton U.K. 55°26N 1°54W 26 B5
Glasgow U.K. 55°51N 4°15W 24 C7
Glasgow Ky., U.S.A. 37°0N 85°55W 112 G5
Glasgow Mont., U.S.A. 48°12N 106°38W 110 A5
Glasgow Int. ✈ (GLA) U.K. 55°51N 4°21W 24 C7
Glasnevin Ireland 53°22N 6°15W 21 B10
Glastonbury U.K. 51°9N 2°43W 30 D3
Glazov Russia 58°9N 52°40E 70 C9
Glemsford U.K. 52°6N 0°40E 31 B10
Glen → U.K. 52°51N 0°7W 27 G8
Glen Affric U.K. 57°17N 5°1W 22 H7
Glen Almond U.K. 56°28N 3°50S 25 B8
Glen Coe U.K. 56°40N 5°0W 22 J7
Glen Etive U.K. 56°37N 5°0W 24 A5
Glen Garry Highl., U.K. 57°3N 5°7W 22 H7
Glen Garry Perth & Kinr., U.K. 56°47N 4°5W 23 J9
Glen Mor U.K. 57°9N 4°37W 23 H8
Glen Moriston U.K. 57°11N 4°52W 23 H8
Glen Orchy U.K. 56°27N 4°52W 24 B6
Glen Orrin U.K. 57°31N 4°45W 23 G8
Glen Oykel U.K. 58°5N 4°50W 23 F8
Glen Roy U.K. 56°56N 4°50W 22 J8
Glen Shee U.K. 56°50N 3°28W 23 J11
Glen Shiel U.K. 57°9N 5°10W 22 H7
Glen Spean U.K. 56°53N 4°40W 23 J8
Glendale Ariz., U.S.A. 33°32N 112°11W 110 D4
Glendale Calif., U.S.A. 34°9N 118°15W 110 D3
Glendive U.S.A. 47°7N 104°43W 110 A6
Gleneagles U.K. 56°17N 3°43W 25 B8
Glenfinnan U.K. 56°53N 5°27W 22 J7
Glengarriff Ireland 51°45N 9°34W 20 E3
Glenkens, The U.K. 55°12N 4°12W 24 D7
Glenluce U.K. 54°52N 4°48W 24 E6
Glennallen U.S.A. 62°7N 145°33W 108 C5
Glennamaddy Ireland 53°37N 8°33W 18 D6
Glenrothes U.K. 56°12N 3°10W 25 B9
Glens Falls U.S.A. 43°19N 73°39W 113 D11
Glenties Ireland 54°48N 8°17W 18 B5
Glenveagh △ Ireland 55°0N 8°1W 18 A5
Gliwice Poland 50°22N 18°41E 65 C10
Globe U.S.A. 33°24N 110°47W 110 D4
Głogów Poland 51°37N 16°5E 64 C9
Glomma → Norway 59°12N 10°57E 63 F6
Glossop U.K. 53°27N 1°56W 27 F5
Gloucester U.K. 51°53N 2°15W 30 C4
Gloucestershire ☐ U.K. 51°46N 2°15W 30 C4
Gloversville U.S.A. 43°3N 74°21W 113 D10
Glyn Ebwy = Ebbw Vale U.K. 51°46N 3°12W 28 D7
Gniezno Poland 52°30N 17°35E 65 B9
Gnosall U.K. 52°48N 2°14W 27 G4
Goa India 15°33N 73°59E 84 M8
Goa ☐ India 15°33N 73°59E 84 M8
Goat Fell U.K. 55°38N 5°11W 24 C5
Gobi Asia 44°0N 110°0E 79 C10
Godalming U.K. 51°11N 0°36W 31 D7
Godavari → India 16°25N 82°18E 85 L13
Goderich Canada 43°45N 81°41W 112 D7
Godhra India 22°49N 73°40E 84 H8
Godmanchester U.K. 52°20N 0°11W 31 B8
Godoy Cruz Argentina 32°56S 68°52W 121 F3
Gods → Canada 56°22N 92°51W 108 D10
Gods L. Canada 54°40N 94°15W 108 D10
Godshill U.K. 50°38N 1°15W 30 E6
Godstone U.K. 51°14N 0°3W 31 D8
Gogama Canada 47°35N 81°43W 112 C7
Goiânia Brazil 16°43S 49°20W 122 C1
Goiás Brazil 15°55S 50°10W 120 D5
Goiás ☐ Brazil 12°10S 48°0W 120 D5
Goio-Erê Brazil 24°12S 53°1W 121 E4
Gold Coast Australia 28°0S 153°25E 98 F9
Gold Coast W. Afr. 4°0N 1°40W 94 H5
Golden Vale Ireland 52°33N 8°17W 20 D6
Goldsboro U.S.A. 35°23N 77°59W 111 C11
Golestān ☐ Iran 37°20N 55°25E 87 B8
Golmud China 36°25N 94°53E 78 D7
Golspie U.K. 57°58N 3°59W 23 G10
Goma Dem. Rep. of the Congo 1°37S 29°10E 96 E5
Gomel Belarus 52°28N 31°0E 65 B16
Gomera Canary Is. 28°7N 17°14W 94 C2
Gómez Palacio Mexico 25°33N 103°30W 114 B4
Gonābād Iran 34°15N 58°45E 87 C9
Gonaïves Haiti 19°20N 72°42W 115 D10
Gonbad-e Kāvūs Iran 37°20N 55°25E 87 B8
Gonda India 27°9N 81°58E 85 F12
Gonder Ethiopia 12°39N 37°30E 89 E2
Gongbei China 22°13N 113°30E 79 a
Gongga Shan China 29°40N 101°55E 78 F9
Good Hope, C. of S. Africa 34°24S 18°30E 97 L3
Goodrich U.S.A. 43°1N 83°6W 112 D6
Goodwood U.K. 50°53N 0°44W 31 E7
Goole U.K. 53°42N 0°53W 27 E7
Goose L. U.S.A. 41°56N 120°26W 110 B2
Gorakhpur India 26°47N 83°23E 85 F13

Gordon U.K. 55°41N 2°34W 25 C10
Gore Ethiopia 8°12N 35°32E 89 F2
Gorebridge U.K. 55°50N 3°2W 25 C9
Gorey Ireland 52°41N 6°18W 21 C10
Gorgān Iran 36°55N 54°30E 87 B8
Goring U.K. 51°31N 1°7W 30 C6
Goring-by-Sea U.K. 50°49N 0°24W 31 E8
Gorleston-on-Sea U.K. 52°35N 1°44E 31 A12
Görlitz Germany 51°9N 14°58E 64 C8
Gorno-Altay ☐ Russia 51°0N 86°0E 76 D9
Gorontalo Indonesia 0°35N 123°5E 83 D6
Gort Ireland 53°3N 8°49W 20 B5
Gorzów Wielkopolski Poland 52°43N 15°15E 64 B8
Gosberton U.K. 52°53N 0°9W 27 G8
Gosforth U.K. 54°26N 3°27W 26 D2
Gosport U.K. 50°48N 1°9W 30 E6
Göta kanal Sweden 58°30N 15°58F 63 F7
Götaland Sweden 57°30N 14°30E 63 F6
Göteborg Sweden 57°43N 11°59E 63 F6
Gotha Germany 50°56N 10°42E 64 C6
Gothenburg = Göteborg
  Sweden 57°43N 11°59E 63 F6
Gotland Sweden 57°30N 18°33E 63 F7
Gotō-Rettō Japan 32°55N 129°5E 81 G1
Göttingen Germany 51°31N 9°55E 64 C5
Gouda Neths. 52°1N 4°42E 64 B3
Goudhurst U.K. 51°6N 0°29E 31 D9
Gouin, Rés. Canada 48°35N 74°40W 113 A10
Goulburn Australia 34°44S 149°44E 98 G8
Goulimine Morocco 28°56N 10°0W 94 C3
Goundam Mali 16°27N 3°40W 94 E5
Gourock U.K. 55°57N 4°49W 24 C6
Governador Valadares
  Brazil 18°15S 41°57W 122 C5
Gower U.K. 51°35N 4°10W 29 D5
Gowna, L. Ireland 53°51N 7°34W 18 D6
Goya Argentina 29°10S 59°10W 121 E4
Gozo Malta 36°3N 14°15E 68 a
Graaff-Reinet S. Africa 32°13S 24°32E 97 L4
Gracias a Dios, C. Honduras 15°0N 83°10W 115 E8
Grafham Water U.K. 52°19N 0°18W 31 B8
Grafton Australia 29°38S 152°58E 98 F9
Grafton U.S.A. 48°25N 97°25W 111 A7
Graham Land Antarctica 65°0S 64°0W 55 C17
Grahamstown S. Africa 33°19S 26°31E 97 L5
Grain Coast W. Afr. 4°20N 10°0W 94 H3
Grainthorpe U.K. 53°27N 0°5E 27 F9
Grampian Mts. U.K. 56°50N 4°0E 23 J9
Gran Canaria Canary Is. 27°55N 15°35W 94 C2
Gran Chaco S. Amer. 25°0S 61°0W 121 E3
Gran Sasso d'Italia Italy 42°27N 13°42E 68 C5
Granada Nic. 11°58N 86°0W 114 E7
Granada Spain 37°10N 3°35W 67 D4
Granada Nic. 37°10N 3°35W 67 D4
Granard Ireland 53°47N 7°30W 18 D6
Granby Canada 45°25N 72°45W 109 E12
Grand → U.S.A. 45°40N 100°45W 110 A6
Grand Bahama I. Bahamas 26°40N 78°30W 115 B9
Grand Canyon U.S.A. 36°3N 112°9W 110 C4
Grand Canyon Nat. Park △
  U.S.A. 36°15N 112°30W 110 C4
Grand Cayman Cayman Is. 19°20N 81°20W 115 D8
Grand Falls Canada 47°3N 67°44W 109 E13
Grand Falls-Windsor
  Canada 48°56N 55°40W 109 E14
Grand Forks U.S.A. 47°55N 97°3W 111 A7
Grand Haven U.S.A. 43°4N 86°13W 112 D4
Grand Island U.S.A. 40°55N 98°21W 110 B7
Grand Junction U.S.A. 39°4N 108°33W 110 C5
Grand L. Canada 45°57N 66°7W 113 C14
Grand Manan I. Canada 44°45N 66°52W 113 C14
Grand-Mère Canada 46°36N 72°40W 113 B11
Grand Rapids Canada 53°12N 99°19W 108 D10
Grand Rapids U.S.A. 42°58N 85°40W 112 D5
Grand St-Bernard, Col du
  Europe 45°50N 7°10E 64 F4
Grand Teton U.S.A. 43°54N 110°50W 110 B4
Grande → Bolivia 15°51S 64°39W 120 D3
Grande → Brazil 11°30S 44°30W 122 B2
Grande, B. Argentina 50°30S 68°20W 121 H3
Grande, Rio → N. Amer. 25°58N 97°9W 111 E7
Grande Baleine → Canada 55°16N 77°47W 109 D12
Grande Prairie Canada 55°10N 118°50W 108 D8
Grange-over-Sands U.K. 54°12N 2°54W 26 D3
Grangemouth U.K. 56°1N 3°42W 25 B8
Grangeville U.S.A. 45°56N 116°7W 110 A3
Grantham U.K. 52°55N 0°38W 27 G7
Grantown-on-Spey U.K. 57°20N 3°36W 23 H10
Grants Pass U.S.A. 42°26N 123°19W 110 B2
Granville U.S.A. 43°24N 73°16W 113 D11
Grasmere U.K. 54°28N 3°1W 26 D2
Grasse France 43°38N 6°56E 66 E7
Grassington U.K. 54°5N 1°59W 26 D5
Graulhet France 43°45N 1°59E 66 E4
Gravesend U.K. 51°26N 0°22E 31 D9
Grayling U.S.A. 44°40N 84°43W 112 C5
Grayrigg U.K. 54°23N 2°39W 26 D3
Grays U.K. 51°28N 0°22E 31 D9
Graz Austria 47°4N 15°27E 64 E8
Great Australian Bight
  Australia 33°30S 130°0E 98 G5
Great Ayton U.K. 54°30N 1°8W 26 D6
Great Baddow U.K. 51°43N 0°31E 31 C10
Great Barrier Reef Australia 18°0S 146°50E 98 D8
Great Basin U.S.A. 40°0N 117°0W 110 B3
Great Bear → Canada 65°0N 126°0W 108 C7
Great Bear L. Canada 65°30N 120°0W 108 B7
Great Bend U.S.A. 38°22N 98°46W 110 C7
Great Bentley U.K. 51°51N 1°4E 31 C11
Great Bernera U.K. 58°14N 6°50W 22 F4
Great Blasket I. Ireland 52°6N 10°32W 20 D1
Great Britain Europe 54°0N 2°15W 62 D5
Great Broughton U.K. 54°26N 1°9W 26 D6
Great Chesterford U.K. 52°4N 0°13E 31 B9
Great Clifton U.K. 54°39N 3°29W 26 C2
Great Dividing Ra. Australia 23°0S 146°0E 98 E8
Great Dunmow U.K. 51°52N 0°23E 31 C9
Great Exuma I. Bahamas 23°30N 75°50W 115 C9
Great Falls U.S.A. 47°30N 111°17W 110 A4
Great Glen = Glen Mor U.K. 57°9N 4°37W 23 H8
Great Harwood U.K. 53°47N 2°24W 27 E4
Great Inagua I. Bahamas 21°0N 73°20W 115 C10

Great Karoo S. Africa 31°55S 21°0E 97 L4
Great Khingan Mts. China 48°0N 121°0E 79 B13
Great Malvern U.K. 52°7N 2°18W 30 B4
Great Massingham U.K. 52°47N 0°40E 31 A10
Great Missenden U.K. 51°42N 0°41W 31 C7
Great Ormes Head U.K. 53°20N 3°52W 28 A6
Great Ouse → U.K. 52°48N 0°21E 31 A9
Great Pedro Bluff Jamaica 17°51N 77°44W 114 a
Great Plains N. Amer. 47°0N 105°0W 110 A6
Great Salt L. U.S.A. 41°15N 112°40W 110 B4
Great Salt Lake Desert
  U.S.A. 40°50N 113°30W 110 B4
Great Sandy Desert Australia 21°0S 124°0E 98 E3
Great Sandy Desert U.S.A. 43°35N 120°15W 110 B2
Great Shefford U.K. 51°28N 1°28W 30 D6
Great Shelford U.K. 52°9N 0°8E 31 B9
Great Shunner Fell U.K. 54°22N 2°14W 26 D4
Great Skellig Ireland 51°47N 10°33W 20 E1
Great Slave L. Canada 61°23N 115°38W 108 C8
Great Snow Mt. Canada 57°26N 124°0W 108 D7
Great Torrington U.K. 50°57N 4°9W 29 F5
Great Victoria Desert
  Australia 29°30S 126°30E 98 F4
Great Wall of China China 38°30N 109°30E 79 D10
Great Waltham U.K. 51°47N 0°28E 31 C9
Great Whernside U.K. 54°10N 1°58W 26 D5
Great Yarmouth U.K. 52°37N 1°44E 31 A12
Greater Antilles W. Indies 17°40N 74°0W 115 D10
Greater London ☐ U.K. 51°31N 0°6W 31 C8
Greater Manchester ☐ U.K. 53°30N 2°15W 27 F4
Greater Sunda Is. Indonesia 7°0S 112°0E 82 F3
Greatham U.K. 54°38N 1°14W 26 C6
Greece ■ Europe 40°0N 23°0E 69 E9
Greeley U.S.A. 40°25N 104°42W 110 B6
Greely Fd. Canada 80°30N 85°0W 109 A11
Green → Ky., U.S.A. 37°54N 87°30W 112 G4
Green → Utah, U.S.A. 38°11N 109°53W 110 C5
Green B. U.S.A. 45°0N 87°30W 112 C4
Green Bay U.S.A. 44°31N 88°0W 112 C4
Green Hammerton U.K. 54°1N 1°18W 27 D6
Green River U.S.A. 41°32N 109°28W 110 B5
Greencastle U.S.A. 39°38N 86°52W 112 F4
Greenfield Ind., U.S.A. 39°47N 85°46W 112 F5
Greenfield Mass., U.S.A. 42°35N 72°36W 113 D11
Greenhead U.K. 54°59N 2°30W 26 C3
Greenland ☑ N. Amer. 66°0N 45°0W 54 C5
Greenland Sea Arctic 73°0N 10°0W 54 B7
Greenlaw U.K. 55°43N 2°27W 25 C11
Greenock U.K. 55°57N 4°46W 24 C6
Greenodd U.K. 54°14N 3°4W 26 D2
Greenore Ireland 54°1N 6°9W 19 C9
Greenore Pt. Ireland 52°14N 6°19W 21 D10
Greensboro U.S.A. 36°4N 79°48W 111 C11
Greensburg Ind., U.S.A. 39°20N 85°29W 112 F5
Greensburg Pa., U.S.A. 40°18N 79°33W 112 E8
Greenstone Pt. U.K. 57°55N 5°37W 22 G6
Greenville Ala., U.S.A. 31°50N 86°38W 111 D9
Greenville Maine, U.S.A. 45°28N 69°35W 113 C13
Greenville Mich., U.S.A. 43°11N 85°15W 112 D5
Greenville Miss., U.S.A. 33°24N 91°4W 111 D8
Greenville Ohio, U.S.A. 40°6N 84°38W 112 E5
Greenville S.C., U.S.A. 34°51N 82°24W 111 D10
Greenwich ☐ U.K. 51°29N 0°1E 31 D9
Greenwood U.S.A. 33°31N 90°11W 111 D8
Greinakha Russia 67°50N 39°47E 70 A6
Grenada ■ W. Indies 12°10N 61°40W 115 E12
Grenoble France 45°12N 5°42E 66 D6
Greta → U.K. 54°9N 2°37W 26 D3
Gretna U.K. 55°0N 3°3W 25 D9
Gretna Green U.K. 55°1N 3°3W 25 D9
Gretton U.K. 52°33N 0°40W 31 A7
Grey Ra. Australia 27°0S 143°30E 98 F7
Greymouth N.Z. 42°29S 171°13E 99 J13
Greystoke U.K. 54°41N 2°51W 26 C3
Greystones Ireland 53°9N 6°5W 21 B10
Griffith Australia 34°18S 146°2E 98 G8
Grimsay U.K. 57°29N 7°14W 22 H3
Grimsby U.K. 53°34N 0°5W 27 E8
Griomasaigh = Grimsay U.K. 57°29N 7°14W 22 H3
Gris-Nez, C. France 50°52N 1°35E 66 A4
Grise Fiord Canada 76°25N 82°57W 109 B11
Grizebeck U.K. 54°16N 3°10W 26 D2
Groningen Neths. 53°15N 6°35E 64 B4
Groote Eylandt Australia 14°0S 136°40E 98 C6
Gros Islet St. Lucia 14°5N 60°58W 114 b
Gros Piton St. Lucia 13°49N 61°5W 114 b
Gros Piton Pt. St. Lucia 13°49N 61°5W 114 b
Grosseto Italy 42°46N 11°8E 68 C4
Grossglockner Austria 47°5N 12°40E 64 E7
Groundhog → Canada 48°45N 82°58W 112 A6
Groznyy Russia 43°20N 45°45E 71 F8
Grudziądz Poland 53°30N 18°47E 65 B10
Gruinard B. U.K. 57°56N 5°35W 22 G6
Guadalajara Mexico 20°40N 103°20W 114 C4
Guadalajara Spain 40°37N 3°12W 67 B4
Guadalcanal Solomon Is. 9°32S 160°12E 99 B11
Guadalete → Spain 36°35N 6°13W 67 D2
Guadalquivir → Spain 36°47N 6°22W 67 D2
Guadarrama, Sierra de Spain 41°0N 4°0W 67 B4
Guadeloupe ☑ W. Indies 16°15N 61°40W 115 D12
Guadiana → Portugal 37°14N 7°22W 67 D2
Guadix Spain 37°18N 3°11W 67 D4
Guafo, Boca del Chile 43°35S 74°0W 121 G2
Guajará-Mirim Brazil 10°50S 65°20W 120 D3
Guajira, Pen. de la Colombia 12°0N 72°0W 120 A2
Gualeguaychú Argentina 33°3S 59°31W 121 F4
Guam ☑ Pac. Oc. 13°27N 144°45E 102 F6
Guamúchil Mexico 25°28N 108°6W 114 B3
Guanajuato Mexico 21°1N 101°15W 114 C4
Guane Cuba 22°10N 84°7W 115 C8
Guangdong ☐ China 23°0N 113°0E 79 G11
Guangxi Zhuang ☐ China 24°0N 109°0E 79 G10
Guangyuan China 32°26N 105°51E 78 E10
Guangzhou China 23°6N 113°13E 79 G11
Guantánamo Cuba 20°10N 75°14W 115 C9
Guantánamo B. Cuba 19°59N 75°10W 115 D10
Guaporé → Brazil 11°55S 65°4W 120 D3
Guaqui Bolivia 16°41S 68°54W 120 D3
Guarapuava Brazil 25°20S 51°30W 121 E4
Guaratinguetá Brazil 22°49S 45°9W 122 D1

Guarulhos Brazil 23°29S 46°33W 122 D1
Guatemala Guatemala 14°40N 90°22W 114 E6
Guatemala ■ Cent. Amer. 15°40N 90°30W 114 D6
Guaviare → Colombia 4°3N 67°44W 120 B3
Guaxupé Brazil 21°10S 47°5W 122 D1
Guayaquil Ecuador 2°15S 79°52W 120 C2
Guayaquil, G. de Ecuador 3°10S 81°0W 120 C1
Guaymas Mexico 27°56N 110°54W 114 B2
Gubkin Russia 51°17N 37°32E 71 D6
Guelph Canada 43°35N 80°20W 112 D7
Guéret France 46°11N 1°51E 66 C4
Guernsey U.K. 49°26N 2°35W 29 J8
Guestling Green U.K. 50°53N 0°39E 31 E10
Guiana Highlands S. Amer. 5°10N 60°40W 117 C4
Guidónia-Montecélio Italy 42°1N 12°45E 68 C5
Guildford U.K. 51°14N 0°34W 31 D7
Guilin China 25°18N 110°15E 79 F11
Guinea ■ W. Afr. 10°20N 11°30W 94 F3
Guinea, Gulf of Atl. Oc. 3°0N 2°30E 90 F4
Guinea-Bissau ■ Africa 12°0N 15°0W 94 F3
Güines Cuba 22°50N 82°0W 115 C8
Guingamp France 48°34N 3°10W 66 B2
Guisborough U.K. 54°33N 1°4W 26 C6
Guiyang China 26°32N 106°40E 78 F10
Guizhou □ China 27°0N 107°0E 78 F10
Gujarat □ India 23°20N 71°0E 84 H7
Gujranwala Pakistan 32°10N 74°12E 84 C9
Gujrat Pakistan 32°40N 74°2E 84 C9
Gulbarga India 17°20N 76°50E 84 L10
Gulf, The = Persian Gulf Asia 27°0N 50°0E 87 E7
Gulfport U.S.A. 30°22N 89°6W 111 D9
Gulian China 52°56N 122°21E 79 A13
Gulu Uganda 2°48N 32°17E 96 D6
Guna India 24°40N 77°19E 84 G10
Gunnison → U.S.A. 39°4N 108°35W 110 C5
Gunsan S. Korea 35°59N 126°45E 79 D14
Guntur India 16°23N 80°30E 85 L12
Gurbantünggüt Desert China 45°8N 87°20E 78 B6
Gurgueia → Brazil 6°50S 43°24W 120 C5
Guri, Embalse de Venezuela 7°50N 62°52W 120 B3
Gurkha Nepal 28°5N 84°40E 85 E14
Gurnard's Hd. U.K. 50°11N 5°37W 29 G2
Gürün Turkey 38°43N 37°15E 71 G6
Gurupi Brazil 11°43S 49°4W 122 B1
Gurupi → Brazil 1°13S 46°6W 120 C5
Gurvan Sayhan Uul Mongolia 43°50N 104°0E 78 C9
Gusau Nigeria 12°12N 6°40E 94 F7
Guwahati India 26°10N 91°45E 85 F17
Guyana ■ S. Amer. 5°0N 59°0W 120 B4
Guyenne France 44°30N 0°40E 66 D4
Gwādar Pakistan 25°10N 62°18E 84 G3
Gwalchmai U.K. 53°16N 4°25W 28 A5
Gwalior India 26°12N 78°10E 84 F11
Gwanda Zimbabwe 20°55S 29°0E 97 J5
Gwangju S. Korea 35°9N 126°54E 79 D14
Gweebarra B. Ireland 54°51N 8°23W 18 B5
Gweedore Ireland 55°3N 8°14W 18 A5
Gweek U.K. 50°5N 5°13W 29 G3
Gwennap U.K. 50°12N 5°11W 29 G3
Gweru Zimbabwe 19°28S 29°45E 97 H5
Gwynedd □ U.K. 52°52N 4°10W 28 B6
Gyaring Hu China 34°50N 97°40E 78 E8
Gydan Peninsula Russia 70°0N 78°0E 76 B8
Gympie Australia 26°11S 152°38E 98 F9
Győr Hungary 47°41N 17°40E 65 E9
Gyumri Armenia 40°47N 43°50E 71 F7

H

Ha'apai Group Tonga 19°47S 174°27W 99 D16
Haarlem Neths. 52°23N 4°39E 64 B3
Hachinohe Japan 40°30N 141°29E 81 C7
Hackney □ U.K. 51°33N 0°3W 31 C8
Hackthorpe U.K. 54°34N 2°42W 26 C3
Ḥadd, Ra's al Oman 22°35N 59°50E 87 F9
Haddenham U.K. 51°46N 0°55W 31 C7
Haddington U.K. 55°57N 2°47W 25 C10
Hadejia Nigeria 12°30N 10°5E 94 F7
Hadleigh U.K. 52°3N 0°58E 31 B10
Hadlow U.K. 51°13N 0°22E 31 D9
Ḥaḍramawt □ Yemen 15°30N 49°30E 89 D4
Hadrian's Wall U.K. 55°0N 2°30W 26 B4
Haeju N. Korea 38°3N 125°45E 79 D14
Hafizabad Pakistan 32°5N 73°40E 84 C8
Hagen Germany 51°21N 7°27E 64 C4
Hagerstown U.S.A. 39°39N 77°43W 112 F9
Hags Hd. Ireland 52°57N 9°28W 20 C4
Hague, C. de la France 49°44N 1°56W 66 B3
Hague, The Neths. 52°7N 4°17E 64 B3
Haguenau France 48°49N 7°47E 66 B7
Haida Gwaii Canada 53°20N 132°10W 108 D6
Haifa Israel 32°46N 35°0E 86 C3
Haikou China 20°1N 110°16E 79 G11
Ḥā'il Si. Arabia 27°28N 41°45E 86 E5
Hailar China 49°10N 119°38E 79 B12
Hailey U.S.A. 43°31N 114°19W 110 B4
Haileybury Canada 47°30N 79°38W 112 B8
Hailsham U.K. 50°52N 0°16E 31 E9
Hailun China 47°28N 126°50E 79 B14
Hainan □ China 19°0N 109°30E 79 H10
Hainan Dao China 19°0N 109°30E 79 H10
Hainan Str. China 20°10N 110°15E 79 G11
Haines Junction Canada 60°45N 137°30W 108 C6
Hainton U.K. 53°21N 0°14W 27 F8
Haiphong Vietnam 20°47N 106°41E 78 G10
Haiti ■ W. Indies 19°0N 72°30W 115 D10
Haji Ibrahim Iraq 36°40N 44°30E 86 B6
Ḥajjah Yemen 15°42N 43°36E 89 D3
Hakkoda-San Japan 40°39N 140°53E 81 C7
Hakodate Japan 41°45N 140°44E 81 C7
Haku-San Japan 36°9N 136°46E 81 E5
Halaib Triangle Africa 22°30N 35°20E 95 D12
Halberstadt Germany 51°54N 11°3E 64 C6
Halberton U.K. 50°54N 3°25W 29 F7
Halden Norway 59°9N 11°23E 63 F6
Haldia India 22°5N 88°3E 85 H16
Haldwani India 29°31N 79°30E 84 E11
Halesowen U.K. 52°27N 2°3W 27 H4
Halesworth U.K. 52°20N 1°31E 31 B12
Halifax Canada 44°38N 63°35W 113 C16
Halifax U.K. 53°43N 1°52W 27 E5
Halkirk U.K. 58°30N 3°29W 23 E11
Hall Beach Canada 68°46N 81°12W 109 C11
Hall Pen. Canada 63°30N 66°0W 109 C13
Halle Germany 51°30N 11°56E 64 C6
Hallow U.K. 52°14N 2°15W 30 B4
Halls Creek Australia 18°16S 127°38E 98 D4
Hallworthy U.K. 50°39N 4°35W 29 F4
Halmahera Indonesia 0°40N 128°0E 83 D7
Halmstad Sweden 56°41N 12°52E 63 F6
Halstead U.K. 51°57N 0°40E 31 C10
Haltwhistle U.K. 54°58N 2°26W 26 C4
Hamadān Iran 34°52N 48°32E 86 C7
Ḥamāh Syria 35°5N 36°40E 86 C4
Hamamatsu Japan 34°45N 137°45E 81 F5
Hamar Norway 60°48N 11°7E 63 E6
Hambantota Sri Lanka 6°10N 81°10E 84 R12
Hambledon U.K. 50°55N 1°5W 30 E6
Hambleton Hills U.K. 54°17N 1°12W 26 D6
Hamburg Germany 53°33N 9°59E 64 B5
Hämeenlinna Finland 61°0N 24°28E 63 E8
Hameln Germany 52°6N 9°21E 64 B5
Hamersley Ra. Australia 22°0S 117°45E 98 E2
Hamhŭng N. Korea 39°54N 127°30E 79 D14
Hami China 42°55N 93°25E 78 C7
Hamilton Canada 43°15N 79°50W 111 B11
Hamilton N.Z. 37°47S 175°19E 99 H14
Hamilton U.K. 55°46N 4°2W 24 C7
Hamilton U.S.A. 39°24N 84°34W 112 F5
Hamm Germany 51°40N 7°50E 64 C4
Hammerfest Norway 70°39N 23°41E 63 C8
Hammersmith and Fulham □ U.K. 51°30N 0°14W 31 D8
Hammond U.S.A. 41°38N 87°30W 112 E4
Hammonton U.S.A. 39°39N 74°48W 113 F10
Hampshire □ U.K. 51°7N 1°23W 30 D6
Hampshire Downs U.K. 51°15N 1°10W 30 D6
Hampton in Arden U.K. 52°26N 1°41W 27 H5
Han Shui → China 30°34N 114°17E 79 E11
Hancock U.S.A. 47°8N 88°35W 112 B3
Handan China 36°35N 114°28E 79 D11
Hanford U.S.A. 36°20N 119°39W 110 C3
Hangayn Nuruu Mongolia 47°30N 99°0E 78 B8
Hangzhou China 30°18N 120°11E 79 E13
Hangzhou Wan China 30°15N 120°45E 79 E13
Hankö Finland 59°50N 22°57E 63 F8
Hanna Canada 51°40N 111°54W 108 D8
Hannibal U.S.A. 39°42N 91°22W 111 C8
Hanningfield Res. U.K. 51°40N 0°31E 31 C10
Hannover Germany 52°22N 9°46E 64 B5
Hanoi Vietnam 21°5N 105°55E 78 G10
Hanover U.S.A. 39°48N 76°59W 112 F9
Hanover, I. Chile 51°0S 74°50W 121 H2
Hans I. Arctic 80°49N 66°38W 109 A13
Hanzhong China 33°10N 107°1E 78 E10
Haora India 22°34N 88°18E 85 H16
Haparanda Sweden 65°52N 24°8E 63 D8
Happy Valley-Goose Bay Canada 53°15N 60°20W 109 D13
Har Hu China 38°20N 97°38E 78 D8
Har Us Nuur Mongolia 48°0N 92°0E 78 B7
Ḥaraḍ Si. Arabia 24°22N 49°0E 86 E7
Harare Zimbabwe 17°43S 31°2E 97 H6
Harbin China 45°48N 126°40E 79 B14
Harbor Beach U.S.A. 43°51N 82°39W 112 D6
Hardangerfjorden Norway 60°5N 6°0E 63 E5
Hardy, Pte. St. Lucia 14°6N 60°56W 114 b
Harer Ethiopia 9°20N 42°8E 89 F3
Harewood U.K. 53°54N 1°30W 27 E6
Hargeisa Somalia 9°30N 44°2E 89 F3
Haridwar India 29°58N 78°9E 84 E11
Haringey □ U.K. 51°34N 0°5W 31 C8
Haringhata → Bangla. 22°0N 89°58E 85 J16
Harīrūd → Asia 37°24N 60°38E 87 B10
Harlech U.K. 52°52N 4°6W 28 B5
Harleston U.K. 52°24N 1°18E 31 B11
Harlingen U.S.A. 26°12N 97°42W 110 E7
Harlow U.K. 51°46N 0°8E 31 C9
Harney L. U.S.A. 43°14N 119°8W 110 B3
Härnösand Sweden 62°38N 17°55E 63 E7
Haroldswick U.K. 60°48N 0°50W 22 A16
Harpenden U.K. 51°49N 0°21W 31 C8
Harricana → Canada 50°56N 79°32W 109 D12
Harrietsham U.K. 51°14N 0°41E 31 D10
Harrington U.K. 54°37N 3°33W 26 C1
Harris U.K. 57°50N 6°55W 22 G4
Harris, Sd. of U.K. 57°44N 7°6W 22 G3
Harrisburg U.S.A. 40°16N 76°53W 112 E9
Harrison, C. Canada 54°55N 57°55W 109 D14
Harrisonburg U.S.A. 38°27N 78°52W 112 F8
Harrisville U.S.A. 44°39N 83°17W 112 C6
Harrogate U.K. 54°0N 1°33W 27 D5
Harrow □ U.K. 51°35N 0°21W 31 C8
Hart U.S.A. 43°42N 86°22W 112 D4
Hartest U.K. 52°8N 0°40E 31 B10
Hartford Conn., U.S.A. 41°46N 72°41W 113 E11
Hartford Ky., U.S.A. 37°27N 86°55W 112 G4
Hartford Wis., U.S.A. 43°19N 88°22W 112 D3
Hartland U.K. 50°59N 4°29W 29 F5
Hartland Pt. U.K. 51°1N 4°32W 29 E4
Hartlebury U.K. 52°20N 2°14W 30 B4
Hartlepool U.K. 54°42N 1°13W 26 C6
Hartley U.K. 55°5N 1°28W 26 B6
Hartpury U.K. 51°55N 2°17W 30 C4
Harvey U.S.A. 41°36N 87°50W 112 E4
Harwell U.K. 51°36N 1°17W 30 C6
Harwich U.K. 51°56N 1°17E 31 C11
Haryana □ India 29°0N 76°10E 84 E10
Harz Germany 51°38N 10°44E 64 C6
Hasa Si. Arabia 25°50N 49°0E 86 E7
Haslemere U.K. 51°5N 0°43W 31 D7
Haslingden U.K. 53°42N 2°19W 27 E4
Hastings U.K. 50°51N 0°35E 31 E10
Hastings U.S.A. 40°35N 98°23W 110 B7
Hat Yai Thailand 7°1N 100°27E 82 C2
Hatay Turkey 36°14N 36°10E 71 G6
Hatfield U.K. 51°46N 0°13W 31 C8
Hatgal Mongolia 50°26N 100°9E 78 A9
Hatherleigh U.K. 50°49N 4°5W 29 F5
Hathersage U.K. 53°20N 1°39W 27 F5
Hathras India 27°36N 78°6E 84 F11
Hatia Bangla. 22°30N 91°5E 85 H17
Hatteras, C. U.S.A. 35°14N 75°32W 111 C11
Hattiesburg U.S.A. 31°20N 89°17W 111 D9
Haugesund Norway 59°23N 5°13E 63 F5
Haughley U.K. 52°14N 0°57E 31 B10
Haut Atlas Morocco 32°30N 5°0W 94 B4
Hauts Plateaux Algeria 35°0N 1°0E 94 B6
Havana = La Habana Cuba 23°8N 82°22W 115 C8
Havant U.K. 50°51N 0°58W 31 E7
Havasu, L. U.S.A. 34°18N 114°28W 110 D4
Havel → Germany 52°50N 12°3E 64 B7
Haverfordwest U.K. 51°48N 4°58W 28 D4
Haverhill U.K. 52°5N 0°28E 31 B9
Haverhill U.S.A. 42°47N 71°5W 113 D12
Haverigg U.K. 54°13N 3°17W 26 D2
Havering □ U.K. 51°34N 0°13E 31 C9
Havre U.S.A. 48°33N 109°41W 110 A5
Havre-St.-Pierre Canada 50°18N 63°33W 109 D13
Hawai'i U.S.A. 19°30N 155°30W 110 J17
Hawai'i □ U.S.A. 19°30N 156°30W 110 H16
Hawaiian Is. Pac. Oc. 20°30N 156°0W 103 E12
Hawes U.K. 54°19N 2°12W 26 D4
Haweswater U.K. 54°31N 2°47W 26 C3
Hawick U.K. 55°26N 2°47W 25 D10
Hawkchurch U.K. 50°48N 2°56W 30 E3
Hawkesbury Canada 45°37N 74°37W 113 C10
Hawkesbury Upton U.K. 51°35N 2°19W 30 C4
Hawkhurst U.K. 51°2N 0°32E 31 D10
Hawkshead U.K. 54°23N 2°59W 26 D3
Haworth U.K. 53°50N 1°58W 27 E5
Hawsker U.K. 54°27N 0°34W 26 D7
Haxby U.K. 54°1N 1°4W 27 D6
Hay Australia 34°30S 144°51E 98 G8
Hay → Canada 60°50N 116°26W 108 C8
Hay-on-Wye U.K. 52°5N 3°8W 28 C7
Hay River Canada 60°51N 115°44W 108 C8
Haydon Bridge U.K. 54°58N 2°14W 26 C4
Hayes → Canada 57°3N 92°12W 108 D10
Hayle U.K. 50°11N 5°26W 29 G3
Hays U.S.A. 38°53N 99°20W 110 C7
Hayton U.K. 54°55N 2°45W 26 C3
Hayward U.S.A. 46°1N 91°29W 112 B2
Haywards Heath U.K. 51°0N 0°5W 31 E8
Hazar Turkmenistan 39°34N 53°16E 71 G9
Hazard U.S.A. 37°15N 83°12W 112 G6
Hazaribag India 23°58N 85°26E 85 H14
Heacham U.K. 52°54N 0°29E 31 A9
Headcorn U.K. 51°10N 0°38E 31 D10
Heanor U.K. 53°1N 1°21W 27 F6
Heard I. Ind. Oc. 53°6S 72°36E 53 G13
Hearst Canada 49°40N 83°41W 109 E11
Heathfield U.K. 50°58N 0°16E 31 E9
Hebburn U.K. 54°59N 1°32W 26 C5
Hebden Bridge U.K. 53°45N 2°0W 27 E5
Hebei □ China 39°0N 116°0E 79 D12
Hebrides U.K. 57°30N 7°0W 56 D4
Hebrides, Sea of the U.K. 57°5N 7°0W 22 H4
Hebron Canada 58°5N 62°30W 109 D13
Hecate Str. Canada 53°10N 130°30W 108 D6
Hechi China 24°40N 108°2E 78 G10
Hechuan China 30°2N 106°12E 78 E10
Heckington U.K. 52°59N 0°17W 27 G8
Hednesford U.K. 52°43N 1°59W 27 G5
Hedon U.K. 53°44N 0°12W 27 E8
Heerlen Neths. 50°55N 5°58E 64 C3
Hefei China 31°52N 117°18E 79 E12
Hegang China 47°20N 130°19E 79 B15
Heidelberg Germany 49°24N 8°42E 64 D5
Heihe China 50°10N 127°30E 79 A14
Heilbronn Germany 49°9N 9°13E 64 D5
Heilongjiang □ China 48°0N 126°0E 79 B14
Heimaey Iceland 63°26N 20°17W 63 B1
Hekla Iceland 63°56N 19°35W 63 B2
Helena U.S.A. 46°36N 112°2W 110 A4
Helensburgh U.K. 56°1N 4°43W 24 B6
Helgoland Germany 54°10N 7°53E 64 A4
Hellifield U.K. 54°1N 2°12W 27 D4
Helmand → Afghan. 31°12N 61°34E 87 D10
Helmsdale U.K. 58°7N 3°39W 23 F10
Helmsley U.K. 54°15N 1°3W 26 D6
Helperby U.K. 54°8N 1°19W 26 D6
Helsby U.K. 53°17N 2°46W 27 F3
Helsingborg Sweden 56°3N 12°42E 63 F6
Helsinki Finland 60°10N 24°55E 63 E9
Helston U.K. 50°6N 5°17W 29 G3
Helvellyn U.K. 54°32N 3°1W 26 C2
Helwân Egypt 29°50N 31°20E 95 C12
Hemel Hempstead U.K. 51°44N 0°28W 31 C8
Hempton U.K. 52°50N 0°50E 31 A10
Hemsworth U.K. 53°37N 1°21W 27 E6
Hemyock U.K. 50°54N 3°15W 29 F7
Henan □ China 34°0N 114°0E 79 E11
Henderson Ky., U.S.A. 37°50N 87°35W 112 G4
Henderson Nev., U.S.A. 36°2N 114°58W 110 C3
Henfield U.K. 50°56N 0°16W 31 E8
Hengduan Shan China 28°30N 98°50E 78 F8
Henggang China 22°39N 114°12E 79 a
Hengyang China 26°59N 112°22E 79 F11
Henley-in-Arden U.K. 52°18N 1°46W 30 B5
Henley-on-Thames U.K. 51°32N 0°54W 31 C7
Henlopen, C. U.S.A. 38°48N 75°6W 113 F10
Henlow U.K. 52°2N 0°17W 31 B8
Henrietta Maria, C. Canada 55°9N 82°20W 109 D11
Henstridge U.K. 50°58N 2°24W 30 E4
Hentiyn Nuruu Mongolia 48°30N 108°30E 79 B10
Herāt Afghan. 34°20N 62°7E 87 C10
Hereford U.K. 52°4N 2°43W 30 B3
Herefordshire □ U.K. 52°8N 2°40W 30 B3
Herford Germany 52°7N 8°39E 64 B5
Herlen → Asia 48°48N 117°0E 79 B12
Herm U.K. 49°30N 2°28W 29 J9
Herma Ness U.K. 60°50N 0°54W 22 A16
Hermosillo Mexico 29°10N 111°0W 114 B2
Hernád → Hungary 47°56N 21°8E 65 D11
Herne Bay U.K. 51°21N 1°8E 31 D11
Herstmonceux U.K. 50°53N 0°20E 31 E9
Hertford U.K. 51°48N 0°4W 31 C8
Hertfordshire □ U.K. 51°51N 0°5W 31 C8
's-Hertogenbosch Neths. 51°42N 5°17E 64 C3
Hessen □ Germany 50°30N 9°0E 64 C5
Hessle U.K. 53°44N 0°24W 27 E8
Hethersett U.K. 52°36N 1°10E 31 A11
Hetton-le-Hole U.K. 54°50N 1°26W 26 C6
Hexham U.K. 54°58N 2°4W 26 C4
Heybridge U.K. 51°45N 0°42E 31 C10
Heysham U.K. 54°3N 2°53W 26 D3
Heytesbury U.K. 51°11N 2°6W 30 D4
Heywood U.K. 53°35N 2°12W 27 E4
Heze China 35°14N 115°20E 79 D12
Hibbing U.S.A. 47°25N 92°56W 111 A8
Hickman U.S.A. 36°34N 89°11W 112 G3
Hidalgo del Parral Mexico 26°56N 105°40W 114 B3
Hierro Canary Is. 27°44N 18°0W 94 C2
Higashiōsaka Japan 34°39N 135°37E 81 F4
High Bentham U.K. 54°7N 2°28W 26 D4
High Ercall U.K. 52°45N 2°35W 27 G3
High Hesket U.K. 54°48N 2°49W 26 C3
High Level Canada 58°31N 117°8W 108 D8
High Pike U.K. 54°42N 3°4W 26 C2
High Prairie Canada 55°30N 116°30W 108 D8
High River Canada 50°30N 113°50W 108 D8
High Veld Africa 27°0S 27°0E 90 J6
High Willhays U.K. 50°40N 4°0W 29 F5
High Wycombe U.K. 51°37N 0°45W 31 C7
Higham Ferrers U.K. 52°19N 0°35W 31 B7
Highbridge U.K. 51°13N 2°58W 30 D3
Highclere U.K. 51°20N 1°21W 30 D6
Highland □ U.K. 57°17N 4°21W 22 H7
Highley U.K. 52°27N 2°23W 27 H4
Hightae U.K. 55°6N 3°26W 25 D9
Highworth U.K. 51°37N 1°43W 30 C5
Hiiumaa Estonia 58°50N 22°45E 63 F8
Ḥijāz Si. Arabia 24°0N 40°0E 86 E4
Hildesheim Germany 52°9N 9°56E 64 B5
Hilgay U.K. 52°34N 0°24E 31 A9
Hillaby, Mt. Barbados 13°12N 59°35W 114 c
Hillcrest Barbados 13°13N 59°31W 114 c
Hillingdon □ U.K. 51°32N 0°27W 31 C8
Hillsborough U.K. 54°28N 6°5W 19 C9
Hillsdale U.S.A. 41°56N 84°38W 112 E5
Hilo U.S.A. 19°44N 155°5W 110 J17
Hilpsford Pt. U.K. 54°3N 3°12W 26 D2
Hilversum Neths. 52°14N 5°10E 64 B3
Himachal Pradesh □ India 31°30N 77°0E 84 D10
Himalaya Asia 29°0N 84°0E 85 E14
Himeji Japan 34°50N 134°40E 81 F4
Hinckley U.K. 52°33N 1°22W 27 G6
Hinderwell U.K. 54°32N 0°45W 26 C7
Hindhead U.K. 51°7N 0°43W 31 D7
Hindley U.K. 53°33N 2°35W 27 E3
Hindu Kush Asia 36°0N 71°0E 87 C12
Hingham U.K. 52°35N 1°0E 31 A10
Hingoli India 19°41N 77°15E 84 K10
Hinkley Pt. U.K. 51°12N 3°8W 30 D2
Hinstock U.K. 52°50N 2°27W 27 G4
Hinton U.S.A. 37°40N 80°54W 112 G7
Hios Greece 38°27N 26°9E 69 E12
Hirosaki Japan 40°34N 140°28E 81 C7
Hiroshima Japan 34°24N 132°30E 81 F3
Hisar India 29°12N 75°45E 84 E9
Hispaniola W. Indies 19°0N 71°0W 115 D10
Histon U.K. 52°16N 0°7E 31 B9
Hitachi Japan 36°36N 140°39E 81 E7
Hitchin U.K. 51°58N 0°16W 31 C8
Hjälmaren Sweden 59°18N 15°40E 63 F7
Hkakabo Razi Burma 28°25N 97°23E 85 E20
Ho Chi Minh City Vietnam 10°58N 106°40E 82 B3
Hoare B. Canada 65°17N 62°30W 109 C13
Hobart Australia 42°50S 147°21E 98 J8
Hobbs U.S.A. 32°42N 103°8W 110 D6
Hodder → U.K. 53°57N 2°27W 27 E4
Hoddesdon U.K. 51°45N 0°1W 31 C8
Hodge → U.K. 54°16N 0°56W 26 D7
Hodgson Canada 51°13N 97°36W 108 D10
Hódmezővásárhely Hungary 46°28N 20°22E 65 E11
Hodna, Chott el Algeria 35°26N 4°43E 94 A6
Hoek van Holland Neths. 52°0N 4°7E 64 B3
Hoff U.K. 54°34N 2°31W 26 C3
Hōfu Japan 34°3N 131°34E 81 F2
Hog's Back U.K. 51°13N 0°38W 31 D7
Hoh Xil Shan China 36°30N 89°0E 78 D6
Hoher Rhön Germany 50°24N 9°58E 64 C5
Hohhot China 40°52N 111°40E 79 C11
Hokkaidō □ Japan 43°30N 143°0E 81 B8
Holbeach U.K. 52°48N 0°1E 27 G9
Holbeach Marsh U.K. 52°52N 0°5E 27 G9
Holderness U.K. 53°45N 0°5W 27 E8
Holetown Barbados 13°11N 59°38W 114 c
Holguín Cuba 20°50N 76°20W 115 C9
Holkham U.K. 52°57N 0°48E 31 A10
Holland U.S.A. 42°47N 86°7W 112 D4
Holland Fen U.K. 53°0N 0°8W 27 G8
Holland on Sea U.K. 51°48N 1°13E 31 C11
Holme U.K. 53°50N 0°46W 27 E7
Holmes Chapel U.K. 53°12N 2°21W 27 F4
Holmfirth U.K. 53°35N 1°46W 27 E5
Holstebro Denmark 56°22N 8°37E 63 F5
Holsworthy U.K. 50°48N 4°22W 29 F5
Holt U.K. 52°55N 1°6E 31 A11
Holy I. Anglesey, U.K. 53°17N 4°37W 28 A4
Holy I. Northumberland, U.K. 55°40N 1°47W 26 A5
Holyhead U.K. 53°18N 4°38W 28 A4
Holywell U.K. 53°16N 3°14W 28 A7
Home B. Canada 68°40N 67°10W 109 C13
Homer U.S.A. 59°39N 151°33W 108 D4
Homs Syria 34°40N 36°45E 86 C4
Honduras ■ Cent. Amer. 14°40N 86°30W 114 E7
Honduras, G. of Caribbean 16°50N 87°0W 114 D7
Hønefoss Norway 60°10N 10°18E 63 E6
Honey L. U.S.A. 40°15N 120°19W 110 B2
Hong Kong □ China 22°11N 114°14E 79 a
Hong Kong Int. ✕ (HKG) China 22°19N 113°57E 79 a
Hongjiang China 27°7N 109°59E 79 F10
Hongshui He → China 23°48N 109°30E 79 G10
Hongze Hu China 33°15N 118°35E 79 E12
Honiara Solomon Is. 9°27S 159°57E 99 B10
Honington U.K. 52°59N 0°35W 27 G7
Honiton U.K. 50°47N 3°11W 29 F7
Honolulu U.S.A. 21°19N 157°52W 103 E12
Honshū Japan 36°0N 138°0E 81 F6
Hoo St. Werburgh U.K. 51°25N 0°35E 31 D10
Hood, Mt. U.S.A. 45°23N 121°42W 110 A2
Hook U.K. 51°17N 0°57W 31 D7
Hook Hd. Ireland 52°7N 6°56W 21 D9
Hooper Bay U.S.A. 61°32N 166°6W 108 C3
Hoopeston U.S.A. 40°28N 87°40W 112 E4
Hoorn Neths. 52°38N 5°4E 64 B3
Hoover Dam U.S.A. 36°1N 114°44W 110 C4
Hope U.S.A. 33°40N 93°36W 111 D8
Hopedale Canada 55°28N 60°13W 109 D13
Horden U.K. 54°46N 1°19W 26 C6
Horley U.K. 51°10N 0°10W 31 D8
Horlivka Ukraine 48°19N 38°5E 71 E6
Hormuz, Str. of The Gulf 26°30N 56°30E 87 E9
Horn, C. = Hornos, C. de Chile 55°50S 67°30W 121 H3
Horn, Is. Wall. & F. Is. 14°16S 178°6W 99 C15
Horn Head Ireland 55°14N 8°0W 18 A6
Hornavan Sweden 66°15N 17°30E 63 D7
Horncastle U.K. 53°13N 0°7W 27 F8
Horndean U.K. 50°55N 1°1W 30 E6
Hornell U.S.A. 42°20N 77°40W 112 D9
Hornepayne Canada 49°14N 84°48W 112 A5
Horningsham U.K. 51°10N 2°15W 30 D4
Hornos, C. de Chile 55°50S 67°30W 121 H3
Hornsea U.K. 53°55N 0°11W 27 E8
Horqin Youyi Qianqi China 46°5N 122°3E 79 B13
Horsforth U.K. 53°50N 1°39W 27 E5
Horsham Australia 36°44S 142°13E 98 H7
Horsham U.K. 51°4N 0°20W 31 D8
Horsham St. Faith U.K. 52°43N 1°14E 31 A11
Horsted Keynes U.K. 51°2N 0°1W 31 D8
Horton → Canada 69°56N 126°52W 108 C7
Horton in Ribblesdale U.K. 54°9N 2°17W 26 D4
Horwich U.K. 53°36N 2°33W 27 E3
Hoste, I. Chile 55°0S 69°0W 121 H3
Hot Springs Ark., U.S.A. 34°31N 93°3W 111 D8
Hot Springs S. Dak., U.S.A. 43°26N 103°29W 110 B6
Hotan China 37°25N 79°55E 78 D4
Hotan He → China 40°22N 80°56E 78 C5
Houghton U.S.A. 47°7N 88°34W 112 B3
Houghton L. U.S.A. 44°21N 84°44W 112 C5
Houghton-le-Spring U.K. 54°51N 1°28W 26 C6
Houghton Regis U.K. 51°54N 0°32W 31 C7
Houlton U.S.A. 46°8N 67°51W 113 B14
Houma U.S.A. 29°36N 90°43W 111 E8
Hounslow □ U.K. 51°28N 0°21W 31 D8
Hourn, L. U.K. 57°7N 5°35W 22 H6
Houston U.S.A. 29°45N 95°21W 111 E7
Hove U.K. 50°50N 0°10W 31 E8
Hoveton U.K. 52°43N 1°25E 31 A11
Hovingham U.K. 54°11N 0°58W 26 D7
Hövsgöl Nuur Mongolia 51°0N 100°30E 78 A9
Howden U.K. 53°45N 0°52W 27 E7
Howe, C. Australia 37°30S 150°0E 98 H9
Howell U.S.A. 42°36N 83°56W 112 D6
Howland I. Pac. Oc. 0°48N 176°38W 102 G10
Howth Ireland 53°23N 6°7W 21 B10
Howth Hd. Ireland 53°22N 6°4W 21 B10
Hoxne U.K. 52°21N 1°12E 31 B11
Hoy U.K. 58°50N 3°15W 23 E11
Høyanger Norway 61°13N 6°4E 63 E5
Hoylake U.K. 53°24N 3°10W 27 F2
Hradec Králové Czech Rep. 50°15N 15°50E 64 C8
Hrodna Belarus 53°42N 23°52E 65 B12
Hron → Slovak Rep. 47°49N 18°45E 65 E10
Hsinchu Taiwan 24°48N 120°58E 79 G13
Huacho Peru 11°10S 77°35W 120 D2
Huai He → China 33°0N 118°30E 79 E12
Huaibei China 34°0N 116°48E 79 E12
Huaihua China 27°32N 109°57E 79 F10
Huainan China 32°38N 116°58E 79 E12
Huallaga → Peru 5°15S 75°30W 120 C2
Huambo Angola 12°42S 15°54E 97 G3
Huancavelica Peru 12°50S 75°5W 120 D2
Huancayo Peru 12°5S 75°12W 120 D2
Huang He → China 37°55N 118°50E 79 D12
Huangshan China 29°42N 118°25E 79 F12
Huangshi China 30°10N 115°3E 79 E12
Huánuco Peru 9°55S 76°15W 120 C2
Huaraz Peru 9°30S 77°32W 120 C2
Huascarán, Nevado Peru 9°7S 77°37W 120 C2
Huasco Chile 28°30S 71°15W 121 E2
Huatabampo Mexico 26°50N 109°38W 114 B3
Hubei □ China 31°0N 112°0E 79 E11
Hubli India 15°22N 75°15E 84 M9
Hucknall U.K. 53°3N 1°13W 27 F6
Huddersfield U.K. 53°39N 1°47W 27 E5
Hudiksvall Sweden 61°43N 17°10E 63 E7
Hudson → U.S.A. 40°42N 74°2W 113 E10
Hudson Bay Canada 60°0N 86°0W 109 D11
Hudson Falls U.S.A. 43°18N 73°35W 113 D11
Hudson Str. Canada 62°0N 70°0W 109 C13
Hue Vietnam 16°30N 107°35E 82 A3
Huelva Spain 37°18N 6°57W 67 D2
Huesca Spain 42°8N 0°25W 67 A5
Hugh Town U.K. 49°55N 6°19W 29 H1
Hughenden Australia 20°52S 144°10E 98 E7
Hugli → India 21°56N 88°4E 85 J16
Huila, Nevado del Colombia 3°0N 76°0W 120 B2
Hull = Kingston upon Hull U.K. 53°45N 0°21W 27 E8
Hull Canada 45°26N 75°43W 113 C10
Hull → U.K. 53°44N 0°20W 27 E8
Hullavington U.K. 51°32N 2°8W 30 C4
Hulme End U.K. 53°8N 1°50W 27 F5
Hulun Nur China 49°0N 117°30E 79 B12
Humaitá Brazil 7°35S 63°1W 120 C3
Humber → U.K. 53°42N 0°27W 27 E8
Humber, Mouth of the U.K. 53°32N 0°8E 27 E9
Humboldt Canada 52°15N 105°9W 108 D9
Humboldt → U.S.A. 39°59N 118°36W 110 B3
Humen China 22°50N 113°40E 79 a
Humphreys Peak U.S.A. 35°21N 111°41W 110 C4
Humshaugh U.K. 55°3N 2°8W 26 B4
Húnaflói Iceland 65°50N 20°50W 63 A1
Hunan □ China 27°30N 112°0E 79 F11
Hunchun China 42°52N 130°28E 79 C15
Hungary ■ Europe 47°20N 19°20E 65 E10
Hungary, Plain of Europe 47°0N 20°0E 56 F10
Hungerford U.K. 51°25N 1°31W 30 D5
Hŭngnam N. Korea 39°49N 127°45E 79 D14
Hunmanby U.K. 54°10N 0°20W 26 D8

Hunsrück

Kasongo

Hunsrück *Germany* 49°56N 7°27E **64** D4
Hunstanton *U.K.* 52°56N 0°29E **31** A9
Huntingdon *U.K.* 52°20N 0°11W **31** B8
Huntington *Ind., U.S.A.* 40°53N 85°30W **112** E5
Huntington *W. Va., U.S.A.* 38°25N 82°27W **112** F6
Huntly *U.K.* 57°27N 2°47W **23** H12
Huntsville *Canada* 45°20N 79°14W **109** F12
Huntsville *Ala., U.S.A.* 34°44N 86°35W **111** D9
Huntsville *Tex., U.S.A.* 30°43N 95°33W **111** D7
Hurghada *Egypt* 27°15N 33°50E **95** C12
Hurley *U.S.A.* 46°27N 90°11W **112** B2
Huron *U.S.A.* 44°22N 98°13W **110** B7
Huron, L. *U.S.A.* 44°30N 82°40W **113** C6
Hursley *U.K.* 51°2N 1°23W **30** D6
Hurstbourne Tarrant *U.K.* 51°17N 1°26W **30** D6
Hurstpierpoint *U.K.* 50°56N 0°11W **31** E8
Húsavík *Iceland* 66°3N 17°21W **63** A2
Husband's Bosworth *U.K.* 52°28N 1°4W **27** H6
Hutchinson *U.S.A.* 38°5N 97°56W **110** C7
Huyton *U.K.* 53°25N 2°51W **27** F3
Huzhou *China* 30°51N 120°8E **79** C13
Hvar *Croatia* 43°11N 16°28E **68** C7
Hwang Ho = Huang He →
China 37°55N 118°50E **79** D12
Hwange *Zimbabwe* 18°18S 26°30E **97** H5
Hwlffordd = Haverfordwest
U.K. 51°48N 4°58W **28** D4
Hyargas Nuur *Mongolia* 49°0N 93°0E **78** B7
Hyde *U.K.* 53°27N 2°4W **27** F4
Hyderabad *India* 17°22N 78°29E **84** L11
Hyderabad *Pakistan* 25°23N 68°24E **84** G6
Hyères *France* 43°8N 6°9E **66** F7
Hyères, Îs. d' *France* 43°0N 6°20E **66** E7
Hyndman Peak *U.S.A.* 43°45N 114°8W **110** B4
Hythe *U.K.* 51°4N 1°5E **31** D11

I

Ialomiţa → *Romania* 44°42N 27°51E **65** F14
Iaşi *Romania* 47°10N 27°40E **65** E14
Ibadan *Nigeria* 7°22N 3°58E **94** G6
Ibagué *Colombia* 4°20N 75°20W **120** B2
Ibarra *Ecuador* 0°21N 78°7W **120** B2
Ibb *Yemen* 14°2N 44°10E **89** E3
Iberian Peninsula *Europe* 40°0N 5°0W **56** H5
Ibiá *Brazil* 19°30S 46°30W **122** C1
Ibiapaba, Sa. da *Brazil* 4°0S 41°30W **120** C5
Ibicaraí *Brazil* 14°51S 39°36W **122** B3
Ibiza = Eivissa *Spain* 38°54N 1°26E **67** C6
Ibotirama *Brazil* 12°13S 43°12W **122** B2
Ibstock *U.K.* 52°42N 1°24W **27** G6
Ica *Peru* 14°0S 75°48W **120** D2
Içá → *Brazil* 2°55S 67°58W **120** C3
Iceland ■ *Europe* 64°45N 19°0W **63** B2
Ichihara *Japan* 35°28N 140°5E **81** F7
Ichinomiya *Japan* 35°18N 136°48E **81** F5
Idaho □ *U.S.A.* 45°0N 115°0W **110** B4
Idaho Falls *U.S.A.* 43°30N 112°2W **110** B4
Idar-Oberstein *Germany* 49°43N 7°16E **64** D4
Idle → *U.K.* 53°27N 0°49W **27** F7
Idlib *Syria* 35°55N 36°36E **86** C4
Idmiston *U.K.* 51°9N 1°42W **30** D5
Ife *Nigeria* 7°30N 4°31E **94** G6
Iforas, Adrar des *Africa* 19°40N 1°40E **94** C5
Igarapava *Brazil* 20°3S 47°47W **122** D1
Igarka *Russia* 67°30N 86°33E **76** C9
Iglésias *Italy* 39°19N 8°32E **68** C3
Iglulik *Canada* 69°20N 81°49W **109** C11
Ignace *Canada* 49°30N 91°40W **112** A2
Igoumenitsa *Greece* 39°32N 20°18E **69** E9
Iguaçu → *Brazil* 25°36S 54°36W **121** E4
Iguaçu, Cat. del *Brazil* 25°41S 54°26W **121** E4
Iguala *Mexico* 18°21N 99°32W **114** D5
Iguatu *Brazil* 6°20S 39°18W **120** C6
Iguidi, Erg *Africa* 27°0N 6°0W **94** C4
Iisalmi *Finland* 63°32N 27°10E **63** E9
Ijebu-Ode *Nigeria* 6°47N 3°58E **94** G6
IJsselmeer *Neths.* 52°45N 5°20E **64** B3
Ikare *Nigeria* 7°32N 5°40E **94** G7
Ikaria *Greece* 37°35N 26°10E **69** F12
Ikeda *Japan* 34°1N 133°48E **81** F3
Ilagan *Phil.* 17°7N 121°53E **83** A6
Ilām *Iran* 33°36N 46°36E **86** C6
Ilchester *U.K.* 51°0N 2°41W **30** D3
Île-de-France □ *France* 49°0N 2°20E **66** B5
Ilebo *Dem. Rep. of the Congo* 4°17S 20°55E **96** E4
Ilemi Triangle *Africa* 5°0N 35°20E **96** C7
Ilesha *Nigeria* 7°37N 4°40E **94** G6
Ilfracombe *U.K.* 51°12N 4°8W **29** E5
Ilhéus *Brazil* 14°49S 39°2W **122** B3
Ili → *Kazakhstan* 45°53N 77°10E **76** E8
Iliamna L. *U.S.A.* 59°30N 155°0W **108** D4
Iligan *Phil.* 8°12N 124°13E **83** C6
Ilkeston *U.K.* 52°58N 1°19W **27** G6
Ilkley *U.K.* 53°56N 1°48W **27** E5
Illapel *Chile* 32°0S 71°10W **121** F2
Iller → *Germany* 48°23N 9°58E **64** D6
Illimani *Bolivia* 16°30S 67°50W **120** D3
Illinois □ *U.S.A.* 40°15N 89°30W **111** B9
Illinois → *U.S.A.* 38°58N 90°28W **111** C8
Ilmen, L. *Russia* 58°15N 31°10E **70** C5
Ilminster *U.K.* 50°55N 2°55W **30** E3
Iloilo *Phil.* 10°45N 122°33E **83** B6
Ilorin *Nigeria* 8°30N 4°35E **94** G6
Imabari *Japan* 34°4N 133°0E **81** F3
Imandra, L. *Russia* 67°30N 33°0E **70** A5
Imatra *Finland* 61°12N 28°48E **63** E9
Imeni Ismail Samani, Pik
Tajikistan 39°0N 72°2E **87** B13
Immingham *U.K.* 53°37N 0°13W **27** E8
Imola *Italy* 44°20N 11°42E **68** B4
Imperatriz *Brazil* 5°30S 47°29W **120** C5
Impéria *Italy* 43°53N 8°3E **68** C3
Imphal *India* 24°48N 93°56E **85** G18
In Salah *Algeria* 27°10N 2°32E **94** C6
Inari *Finland* 68°54N 27°1E **63** D9
Inarijärvi *Finland* 69°0N 28°0E **63** D9
Ince Burun *Turkey* 42°7N 34°56E **71** F5
Incheon *S. Korea* 37°27N 126°40E **79** D14
Incomáti → *Mozam.* 25°46S 32°43E **97** K6
Indalsälven → *Sweden* 62°36N 17°30E **63** E7

India ■ *Asia* 20°0N 78°0E **84** K11
Indian Ocean 5°0S 75°0E **53** E13
Indiana *U.S.A.* 40°37N 79°9W **112** E8
Indiana □ *U.S.A.* 40°0N 86°0W **112** E4
Indianapolis *U.S.A.* 39°46N 86°9W **112** F4
Indigirka → *Russia* 70°48N 148°54E **77** B15
Indira Gandhi Canal *India* 28°0N 72°0E **84** F8
Indo-China *Asia* 15°0N 102°0E **72** G12
Indonesia ■ *Asia* 5°0S 115°0E **82** F5
Indore *India* 22°42N 75°53E **84** H9
Indre → *France* 47°16N 0°11E **66** C4
Indus → *Pakistan* 24°20N 67°47E **84** G5
Ineboli *Turkey* 41°55N 33°40E **71** F5
Inga, Barrage d'
Dem. Rep. of the Congo 5°39S 13°39E **96** F2
Ingatestone *U.K.* 51°40N 0°24E **31** C9
Ingleborough *U.K.* 54°10N 2°22W **26** D4
Ingleton *U.K.* 54°10N 2°27W **26** D4
Ingolstadt *Germany* 48°46N 11°26E **64** D6
Ingraj Bazar *India* 24°58N 88°10E **85** G16
Ingushetia □ *Russia* 43°20N 44°50E **71** F8
Inishbofin *Ireland* 53°37N 10°13W **18** D1
Inisheer *Ireland* 53°3N 9°32W **20** D3
Inishfree B. *Ireland* 55°4N 8°23W **18** A5
Inishkea North *Ireland* 54°9N 10°11W **18** C1
Inishkea South *Ireland* 54°7N 10°12W **18** C1
Inishmaan *Ireland* 53°5N 9°35W **20** B3
Inishmore *Ireland* 53°8N 9°45W **20** B3
Inishowen Pen. *Ireland* 55°14N 7°15W **19** A7
Inishshark *Ireland* 53°37N 10°16W **18** D1
Inishtrahull *Ireland* 55°26N 7°13W **19** A7
Inishturk *Ireland* 53°42N 10°7W **18** D1
Inishvickillane *Ireland* 52°3N 10°37W **20** D1
Inkberrow *U.K.* 52°13N 1°58W **30** B5
Inland Sea *Japan* 34°20N 133°30E **81** F3
Inn → *Austria* 48°35N 13°28E **64** D7
Inner Hebrides *U.K.* 57°0N 6°30W **22** J4
Inner Mongolia = Nei Mongol
Zizhiqu □ *China* 42°0N 112°0E **79** C11
Inner Sound *U.K.* 57°30N 5°55W **22** H6
Innerleithen *U.K.* 55°37N 3°4W **25** D9
Innsbruck *Austria* 47°16N 11°23E **64** E6
Inowrocław *Poland* 52°50N 18°12E **65** B10
Insein *Burma* 16°50N 96°5E **85** L20
Inta *Russia* 66°5N 60°8E **70** A11
Interlaken *Switz.* 46°41N 7°50E **64** E4
Inukjuak *Canada* 58°25N 78°15W **109** D12
Inuvik *Canada* 68°16N 133°40W **108** C6
Inveraray *U.K.* 56°14N 5°5W **24** E3
Inverbervie *U.K.* 56°51N 2°17W **23** J13
Invercargill *N.Z.* 46°24S 168°24E **99** K12
Invergordon *U.K.* 57°41N 4°10W **23** G9
Inverkeithing *U.K.* 56°2N 3°24W **25** B9
Inverness *U.K.* 57°29N 4°13W **23** H9
Inverurie *U.K.* 57°17N 2°23W **23** H13
Ioannina *Greece* 39°42N 20°47E **69** E9
Iona *U.K.* 56°20N 6°25W **24** E3
Ionia *U.S.A.* 42°59N 85°4W **112** D5
Ionian Is. *Greece* 38°40N 20°0E **69** E9
Ionian Sea *Medit. S.* 37°30N 17°30E **69** E7
Ios *Greece* 36°41N 25°20E **69** F11
Iowa □ *U.S.A.* 42°18N 93°30W **111** B8
Iowa City *U.S.A.* 41°40N 91°32W **111** B8
Ipameri *Brazil* 17°44S 48°9W **122** C1
Ipatinga *Brazil* 19°32S 42°30W **122** C2
Ipiales *Colombia* 0°50N 77°37W **120** B2
Ipoh *Malaysia* 4°35N 101°5E **82** D2
Ipswich *Australia* 27°35S 152°40E **98** F9
Ipswich *U.K.* 52°4N 1°10E **31** B11
Iqaluit *Canada* 63°44N 68°31W **109** C13
Iquique *Chile* 20°19S 70°5W **120** E2
Iquitos *Peru* 3°45S 73°10W **120** C2
Iraklio *Greece* 35°20N 25°12E **69** G11
Iran ■ *Asia* 33°0N 53°0E **87** C8
Iranshahr *Iran* 27°15N 60°40E **87** D10
Irapuato *Mexico* 20°41N 101°28W **114** C4
Iraq ■ *Asia* 33°0N 44°0E **86** C5
Irazú, Volcan *Costa Rica* 10°28N 84°42W **115** E8
Irbil *Iraq* 36°15N 44°5E **86** B6
Irchester *U.K.* 52°18N 0°39W **31** B7
Ireland ■ *Europe* 53°50N 7°52W **62** E2
Ireland's Eye *Ireland* 53°24N 6°4W **21** B10
Iringa *Tanzania* 7°48S 35°43E **96** F7
Irish Sea *Europe* 53°38N 4°48W **62** E4
Irkutsk *Russia* 52°18N 104°20E **77** D11
Irlam *U.K.* 53°26N 2°26W **27** F4
Iron Gate *Europe* 44°44N 22°30E **65** F12
Iron Mountain *U.S.A.* 45°49N 88°4W **112** C3
Ironbridge *U.K.* 52°38N 2°30W **27** G3
Ironton *U.S.A.* 38°32N 82°41W **112** F6
Ironwood *U.S.A.* 46°27N 90°9W **112** B2
Irrawaddy → *Burma* 15°50N 95°6E **85** M19
Irt → *U.K.* 54°23N 3°26W **26** D2
Irthlingborough *U.K.* 52°20N 0°37W **31** B7
Irtysh → *Russia* 61°4N 68°52E **76** C7
Irún *Spain* 43°20N 1°52W **67** A5
Irvine *U.K.* 55°37N 4°41W **24** C6
Irvinestown *U.K.* 54°28N 7°39W **18** C6
Isafjörður *Iceland* 66°5N 23°9W **63** A1
Isar → *Germany* 48°48N 12°57E **64** D7
Ischia *Italy* 40°44N 13°57E **68** D6
Isère → *France* 44°59N 4°51E **66** D6
Ishim → *Russia* 57°45N 71°10E **76** D8
Ishinomaki *Japan* 38°32N 141°20E **81** D7
Ishpeming *U.S.A.* 46°29N 87°40W **112** B4
Isiro *Dem. Rep. of the Congo* 2°53S 27°40E **96** D5
Iskenderun *Turkey* 36°32N 36°10E **71** G6
Islamabad *Pakistan* 33°40N 73°10E **84** C8
Island L. *Canada* 53°47N 94°25W **108** D10
Island Pond *U.S.A.* 44°49N 71°53W **113** C12
Islay *U.K.* 55°46N 6°10W **24** D3
Isleham *U.K.* 52°21N 0°25E **31** B9
Islington □ *U.K.* 51°33N 0°5W **31** C8
Islip *U.K.* 51°50N 1°12W **30** C6
Ismâ'iliya *Egypt* 30°37N 32°18E **95** B12
Isparta *Turkey* 37°47N 30°30E **71** G5
Israel ■ *Asia* 32°0N 34°50E **86** C3
Issoire *France* 45°32N 3°15E **66** D5
Issyk Kul *Kyrgyzstan* 42°25N 77°15E **72** D9
İstanbul *Turkey* 41°0N 28°58E **71** F4

Istres *France* 43°31N 4°59E **66** E6
Istria *Croatia* 45°10N 14°0E **68** B5
Itaberaba *Brazil* 12°32S 40°18W **122** B2
Itabira *Brazil* 19°37S 43°13W **122** C2
Itabuna *Brazil* 14°48S 39°16W **122** B3
Itacoatiara *Brazil* 3°8S 58°25W **120** C4
Itaipú, Represa de *Brazil* 25°30S 54°30W **117** F5
Itajaí *Brazil* 27°50S 48°39W **121** E5
Itajubá *Brazil* 22°24S 45°30W **122** D1
Italy ■ *Europe* 42°0N 13°0E **68** C5
Itaperuna *Brazil* 21°10S 41°54W **122** D2
Itapetinga *Brazil* 15°15S 40°15W **122** B3
Itapetininga *Brazil* 23°36S 48°7W **122** D1
Itapicuru → *Brazil* 11°47S 37°32W **122** B3
Itararé *Brazil* 24°6S 49°23W **122** D1
Itaúna *Brazil* 20°4S 44°34W **122** D2
Itchen → *U.K.* 50°55N 1°22W **30** E6
Ithaca *U.S.A.* 42°27N 76°30W **112** D9
Ittoqqortoormiit *Greenland* 70°20N 23°0W **54** B6
Itu *Brazil* 23°17S 47°15W **122** D1
Ivanava *Belarus* 52°7N 25°29E **65** B13
Ivano-Frankivsk *Ukraine* 48°40N 24°40E **65** D13
Ivanovo *Russia* 57°5N 41°0E **70** C7
Iveragh Pen. *Ireland* 51°52N 10°15W **20** D2
Ivinghoe *U.K.* 51°50N 0°37W **31** C7
Ivory Coast ■ *Africa* 7°30N 5°0W **94** G4
Ivujivik *Canada* 62°24N 77°55W **109** C12
Ivybridge *U.K.* 50°23N 3°56W **29** G6
Iwaki *Japan* 37°3N 140°55E **81** E7
Iwakuni *Japan* 34°15N 132°8E **81** F3
Iwo *Nigeria* 7°39N 4°9E **94** G6
Ixworth *U.K.* 52°18N 0°51E **31** B10
Izhevsk *Russia* 56°51N 53°14E **70** C9
Izmayil *Ukraine* 45°22N 28°46E **71** E4
İzmir *Turkey* 38°25N 27°8E **71** G4
İznik Gölü *Turkey* 40°27N 29°30E **71** F4
Izumi-Sano *Japan* 34°23N 135°18E **81** F4

J

Jabalpur *India* 23°9N 79°58E **84** H11
Jaboatão *Brazil* 8°7S 35°1W **120** C6
Jaboticabal *Brazil* 21°15S 48°17W **122** D1
Jacareí *Brazil* 23°20S 46°0W **122** D1
Jackson *Barbados* 13°7N 59°36W **114** c
Jackson *Ky., U.S.A.* 37°33N 83°23W **112** G6
Jackson *Mich., U.S.A.* 42°15N 84°24W **112** D5
Jackson *Miss., U.S.A.* 32°18N 90°12W **111** D8
Jackson *Mo., U.S.A.* 37°23N 89°40W **112** G3
Jackson *Tenn., U.S.A.* 35°37N 88°49W **111** C9
Jacksonville *Ill., U.S.A.* 39°44N 90°14W **112** F2
Jacksonville *Fla., U.S.A.* 30°20N 81°39W **111** D10
Jacmel *Haiti* 18°14N 72°32W **115** D10
Jacobabad *Pakistan* 28°20N 68°29E **84** E6
Jacobina *Brazil* 11°11S 40°30W **122** B2
Jade Mt. *Taiwan* 23°25N 120°52E **79** G13
Jaén *Peru* 5°25S 78°40W **120** C2
Jaén *Spain* 37°44N 3°43W **67** D4
Jaffa = Tel Aviv-Yafo *Israel* 32°4N 34°48E **86** C3
Jaffna *Sri Lanka* 9°45N 80°2E **84** Q12
Jahrom *Iran* 28°30N 53°31E **87** D8
Jaipur *India* 27°0N 75°50E **84** F9
Jakarta *Indonesia* 6°9S 106°52E **82** F3
Jalālābād *Afghan.* 34°30N 70°29E **87** C12
Jalandhar *India* 31°20N 75°40E **84** D9
Jalgaon *India* 21°0N 75°42E **84** J9
Jalna *India* 19°48N 75°38E **84** K9
Jalpaiguri *India* 26°32N 88°46E **85** F16
Jaluit I. *Marshall Is.* 6°0N 169°30E **102** G9
Jämaame *Somalia* 0°4N 42°44E **89** G3
Jamaica ■ *W. Indies* 18°10N 77°30W **114** a
Jamalpur *Bangla.* 24°52N 89°56E **85** G16
Jamalpur *India* 25°18N 86°28E **85** G15
Jambi *Indonesia* 1°38S 103°30E **82** E2
James → *U.S.A.* 42°52N 97°18W **111** B7
James B. *Canada* 54°0N 80°0W **109** D12
Jamestown *N. Dak., U.S.A.* 46°54N 98°42W **110** A7
Jamestown *N.Y., U.S.A.* 42°6N 79°14W **112** D8
Jammu *India* 32°43N 74°54E **84** C9
Jammu & Kashmir □ *India* 34°25N 77°0E **84** B10
Jamnagar *India* 22°30N 70°6E **84** H7
Jamshedpur *India* 22°44N 86°12E **85** H15
Jan Mayen *Arctic* 71°0N 9°0W **54** B7
Janaúba *Brazil* 15°48S 43°19W **122** C2
Janesville *U.S.A.* 42°41N 89°1W **112** D3
Januária *Brazil* 15°25S 44°25W **122** C2
Jaora *India* 23°40N 75°10E **84** H9
Japan ■ *Asia* 36°0N 136°0E **81** G8
Japan, Sea of *Asia* 40°0N 135°0E **81** D4
Japan Trench *Pac. Oc.* 32°0N 142°0E **102** D6
Japurá → *Brazil* 3°8S 65°46W **120** C3
Jari → *Brazil* 1°9S 51°54W **120** C4
Jarrow *U.K.* 54°59N 1°28W **26** C6
Jarvis I. *Pac. Oc.* 0°15S 160°5W **103** H12
Jāsk *Iran* 25°38N 57°45E **87** E9
Jasper *Canada* 52°55N 118°5W **108** D8
Jaú *Brazil* 22°10S 48°30W **122** D1
Jauja *Peru* 11°45S 75°15W **120** D2
Jaunpur *India* 25°46N 82°44E **85** G13
Java *Indonesia* 7°0S 110°0E **82** F3
Java Sea *Indonesia* 4°35S 107°15E **82** E3
Java Trench *Ind. Oc.* 9°0S 105°0E **82** F3
Jawhar *Somalia* 2°48N 45°30E **89** G4
Jaya, Puncak *Indonesia* 3°57S 137°17E **83** F9
Jebel, Bahr el → *South Sudan* 9°30N 30°25E **95** G12
Jedburgh *U.K.* 55°29N 2°33W **25** D10
Jedda *Si. Arabia* 21°29N 39°10E **86** F4
Jeffersonville *U.S.A.* 38°17N 85°44W **112** F5
Jeju *S. Korea* 33°31N 126°32E **79** E14
Jeju-do *S. Korea* 33°29N 126°34E **79** E14
Jelenia Góra *Poland* 50°50N 15°45E **64** C8
Jelgava *Latvia* 56°41N 23°49E **63** F8
Jena *Germany* 50°54N 11°35E **64** C6
Jeonju *S. Korea* 35°50N 127°4E **79** D14
Jequié *Brazil* 13°51S 40°5W **122** B2
Jequitinhonha *Brazil* 16°30S 41°0W **122** C2
Jequitinhonha → *Brazil* 15°51S 38°53W **122** C3
Jérémie *Haiti* 18°40N 74°10W **115** D10
Jerez de la Frontera *Spain* 36°41N 6°7W **67** D2
Jersey *U.K.* 49°11N 2°7W **29** J9
Jersey City *U.S.A.* 40°42N 74°4W **113** E10
Jerseyville *U.S.A.* 39°7N 90°20W **112** F2
Jerusalem *Israel/West Bank* 31°47N 35°10E **86** D3

Jervaulx *U.K.* 54°16N 1°43W **26** D5
Jessore *Bangla.* 23°10N 89°10E **85** H16
Jhang Maghiana *Pakistan* 31°15N 72°22E **84** D8
Jhansi *India* 25°30N 78°36E **84** G11
Jharkhand □ *India* 24°0N 85°50E **85** H14
Jhelum *Pakistan* 33°0N 73°45E **84** C8
Jhelum → *Pakistan* 31°20N 72°10E **84** D8
Jiamusi *China* 46°40N 130°26E **79** B15
Ji'an *Jiangxi, China* 27°6N 114°59E **79** F11
Ji'an *Jilin, China* 41°5N 126°10E **79** C14
Jiangsu □ *China* 33°0N 120°0E **79** C13
Jiangxi □ *China* 27°30N 116°0E **79** D12
Jiaxing *China* 30°49N 120°45E **79** C13
Jiayuguan *China* 39°49N 98°18E **78** D8
Jihlava → *Czech Rep.* 48°55N 16°36E **65** D9
Jijiga *Ethiopia* 9°20N 42°50E **89** F3
Jilib *Somalia* 0°29N 42°46E **89** G3
Jilin *China* 43°44N 126°30E **79** C14
Jilin □ *China* 44°0N 127°0E **79** C14
Jima *Ethiopia* 7°40N 36°47E **89** F2
Jiménez *Mexico* 27°8N 104°54W **114** B4
Jinan *China* 36°38N 117°1E **79** C12
Jinchang *China* 38°30N 102°10E **78** D9
Jincheng *China* 35°29N 112°50E **79** D11
Jinding *China* 22°22N 113°33E **79** a
Jingdezhen *China* 29°20N 117°11E **79** D12
Jingmen *China* 31°0N 112°10E **79** E11
Jinhua *China* 29°8N 119°38E **79** F12
Jining, Nei Monggol Zizhiqu,
China 41°5N 113°0E **79** C11
Jining *Shandong, China* 35°22N 116°34E **79** D12
Jinja *Uganda* 0°25N 33°12E **96** D6
Jinsha Jiang → *China* 28°50N 104°36E **78** F9
Jinxi *China* 40°52N 120°50E **79** C13
Jinzhong *China* 37°42N 112°46E **79** D11
Jinzhou *China* 41°5N 121°3E **79** C13
Jipijapa *Ecuador* 1°0S 80°40W **120** C1
Jishou *China* 28°21N 109°43E **79** F10
Jiujiang *China* 29°42N 115°58E **79** F12
Jiwani *Pakistan* 25°1N 61°44E **87** E10
Jixi *China* 45°20N 130°50E **79** B15
Jīzān *Si. Arabia* 17°0N 42°20E **89** D3
Jizzax *Uzbekistan* 40°6N 67°50E **87** A11
João Pessoa *Brazil* 7°10S 34°52W **120** C6
Jodhpur *India* 26°23N 73°8E **84** F8
Joensuu *Finland* 62°37N 29°49E **63** E9
Jōetsu *Japan* 37°12N 138°10E **81** E6
Johannesburg *S. Africa* 26°11S 28°2E **97** K5
John Crow Mts. *Jamaica* 18°5N 76°25W **114** a
John Day → *U.S.A.* 45°44N 120°39W **110** A3
John o' Groats *U.K.* 58°38N 3°4W **23** E11
Johnson City *U.S.A.* 36°19N 82°21W **111** C10
Johnston Atoll *Pac. Oc.* 17°10N 169°8W **103** F11
Johnstone *U.K.* 55°49N 4°31W **24** C6
Johnstown *U.S.A.* 40°20N 78°55W **112** E8
Johor Bahru *Malaysia* 1°28N 103°46E **82** D2
Joinville *Brazil* 26°15S 48°55W **121** E5
Joliet *U.S.A.* 41°32N 88°5W **112** E3
Joliette *Canada* 46°3N 73°24W **109** E12
Jolo *Phil.* 6°0N 121°0E **83** C6
Jones Sound *Canada* 76°0N 85°0W **109** B11
Jonesboro *U.S.A.* 35°50N 90°42W **111** C8
Jönköping *Sweden* 57°45N 14°8E **63** F6
Jonquière *Canada* 48°27N 71°14W **113** A12
Joplin *U.S.A.* 37°6N 94°31W **111** C8
Jordan ■ *Asia* 31°0N 36°0E **86** D4
Jordan → *Asia* 31°48N 35°32E **86** D3
Jos *Nigeria* 9°53N 8°51E **94** G7
Joseph Bonaparte G.
Australia 14°35S 128°50E **98** C4
Jotunheimen *Norway* 61°35N 8°25E **63** E5
Juan de Fuca, Str. of.
N. Amer. 48°15N 124°0W **110** A2
Juan Fernández, Arch. de
Pac. Oc. 33°50S 80°0W **103** L20
Juàzeiro *Brazil* 9°30S 40°30W **122** A2
Juàzeiro do Norte *Brazil* 7°10S 39°18W **120** C6
Juba *South Sudan* 4°50N 31°35E **95** H12
Juba → *Somalia* 1°30N 42°35E **89** G3
Juchitán de Zaragoza *Mexico* 16°26N 95°1W **114** D5
Juiz de Fora *Brazil* 21°43S 43°19W **122** D2
Juliaca *Peru* 15°25S 70°10W **120** D2
Julianatop *Suriname* 3°40N 56°30W **120** B4
Junagadh *India* 21°30N 70°30E **84** J7
Jundiaí *Brazil* 24°30S 47°0W **122** D1
Juneau *U.S.A.* 58°18N 134°25W **108** D6
Junín *Argentina* 34°33S 60°57W **121** F3
Jur → *South Sudan* 8°45N 29°15E **95** G11
Jura *Europe* 46°40N 6°5E **66** C6
Jura *U.K.* 56°0N 5°50W **24** C3
Jura, Sd. of *U.K.* 55°57N 5°45W **24** C4
Juruá → *Brazil* 2°37S 65°44W **120** C3
Juruena → *Brazil* 7°20S 58°3W **120** C4
Juticalpa *Honduras* 14°40N 86°12W **114** E7
Jutland *Denmark* 56°25N 9°30E **63** F5
Juventud, I. de la *Cuba* 21°40N 82°40W **115** C8
Jyväskylä *Finland* 62°14N 25°50E **63** E9

K

K2 *Pakistan* 35°58N 76°32E **84** B10
Kabardino-Balkaria □ *Russia* 43°30N 43°30E **71** F7
Kābul *Afghan.* 34°28N 69°11E **87** C12
Kabwe *Zambia* 14°30S 28°29E **97** G5
Kachchh, Gulf of *India* 22°50N 69°15E **84** H6
Kachchh, Rann of *India* 24°0N 70°0E **84** H7
Kachin □ *Burma* 26°0N 97°30E **85** G20
Kaçkar *Turkey* 40°45N 41°10E **71** F7
Kadavu *Fiji* 19°0S 178°15E **99** E14
Kade *Ghana* 6°7N 0°56W **94** G5
Kadoma *Zimbabwe* 18°20S 29°52E **97** H5
Kaduna *Nigeria* 10°30N 7°21E **94** F7
Kaesŏng *N. Korea* 37°58N 126°35E **79** D14
Kafue *Zambia* 15°30S 29°0E **97** H5
Kaga Bandoro *C.A.R.* 7°0N 19°10E **96** C3
Kagera → *Uganda* 0°57S 31°47E **96** E6
Kagoshima *Japan* 31°35N 130°33E **81** H2
Kaho'olawe *U.S.A.* 20°33N 156°37W **110** H16
Kahramanmaraş *Turkey* 37°37N 36°53E **71** G6
Kai, Kepulauan *Indonesia* 5°55S 132°45E **83** F8
Kaidu He → *China* 41°46N 86°31E **78** C6

Kaieteur Falls *Guyana* 5°1N 59°10W **120** B4
Kaifeng *China* 34°48N 114°21E **79** E11
Kailua Kona *U.S.A.* 19°39N 155°59W **110** J17
Kainji Res. *Nigeria* 10°1N 4°40E **94** F6
Kairouan *Tunisia* 35°45N 10°5E **95** A8
Kaiserslautern *Germany* 49°26N 7°45E **64** D4
Kaitaia *N.Z.* 35°8S 173°17E **99** H13
Kaiyuan *China* 23°40N 103°12E **78** G9
Kajaani *Finland* 64°17N 27°46E **63** E9
Kakamega *Kenya* 0°20N 34°46E **96** D6
Kakhovka Res. *Ukraine* 47°5N 34°0E **71** E5
Kakinada *India* 16°57N 82°11E **85** L13
Kalaallit Nunaat = Greenland ☑
N. Amer. 66°0N 45°0W **54** C5
Kalahari *Africa* 24°0S 21°30E **97** J4
Kalamata *Greece* 37°3N 22°10E **69** F10
Kalamazoo *U.S.A.* 42°17N 85°35W **112** D5
Kalamazoo → *U.S.A.* 42°40N 86°10W **112** D4
Kalemie *Dem. Rep. of the Congo* 5°55S 29°9E **96** F5
Kalgoorlie-Boulder *Australia* 30°40S 121°22E **98** G3
Kalimantan *Indonesia* 0°0 114°0E **82** E4
Kaliningrad *Russia* 54°42N 20°32E **63** G8
Kalispell *U.S.A.* 48°12N 114°19W **110** A4
Kalisz *Poland* 51°45N 18°8E **65** C10
Kalkaska *U.S.A.* 44°44N 85°11W **112** C5
Kallsjön *Sweden* 63°38N 13°0E **63** E6
Kalmar *Sweden* 56°40N 16°20E **63** F7
Kalmykia □ *Russia* 46°5N 46°1E **71** E8
Kaluga *Russia* 54°35N 36°10E **70** D6
Kalutara *Sri Lanka* 6°35N 80°0E **84** R12
Kalyan *India* 19°15N 73°9E **84** K8
Kama → *Russia* 55°45N 52°0E **70** C9
Kamchatka Pen. *Russia* 57°0N 160°0E **77** D16
Kamensk Uralskiy *Russia* 56°25N 62°2E **76** D7
Kamina *Dem. Rep. of the Congo* 8°45S 25°0E **96** F5
Kamloops *Canada* 50°40N 120°20W **108** D7
Kampala *Uganda* 0°20N 32°30E **96** D6
Kampong Cham *Cambodia* 12°0N 105°30E **82** B3
Kampong Saom *Cambodia* 10°38N 103°30E **82** B2
Kamyanets-Podilskyy
Ukraine 48°45N 26°40E **65** D14
Kamyshin *Russia* 50°10N 45°24E **71** D8
Kananga *Dem. Rep. of the Congo* 5°55S 22°18E **96** F4
Kanash *Russia* 55°30N 47°32E **70** C8
Kanawha → *U.S.A.* 38°50N 82°9W **112** F6
Kanazawa *Japan* 36°30N 136°38E **81** E5
Kanchenjunga *Nepal* 27°50N 88°10E **85** F16
Kanchipuram *India* 12°52N 79°45E **84** N11
Kandahār *Afghan.* 31°32N 65°43E **87** D11
Kandalaksha *Russia* 67°9N 32°30E **70** A5
Kandalaksha, G. of *Russia* 66°0N 35°0E **70** A6
Kandi *Benin* 11°7N 2°55E **94** F6
Kane *U.S.A.* 41°40N 78°49W **112** E8
Kāne'ohe *U.S.A.* 21°25N 157°48W **110** H16
Kangaroo I. *Australia* 35°45S 137°0E **98** H6
Kangiqsualujjuaq *Canada* 58°30N 65°59W **109** D13
Kangiqsujuaq *Canada* 60°0N 70°0W **109** D13
Kangirsuk *Canada* 60°0N 70°0W **109** D13
Kanin Pen. *Russia* 68°0N 45°0E **70** A8
Kankakee *U.S.A.* 41°7N 87°52W **112** E4
Kankakee → *U.S.A.* 41°23N 88°15W **112** E3
Kankan *Guinea* 10°23N 9°15W **94** F4
Kannur *India* 11°53N 75°27E **84** P9
Kannyakumari *India* 8°3N 77°40E **84** Q10
Kano *Nigeria* 12°2N 8°30E **94** F7
Kanpur *India* 26°28N 80°20E **84** F12
Kansas □ *U.S.A.* 38°30N 99°0W **110** C7
Kansas → *U.S.A.* 39°7N 94°37W **111** C8
Kansas City *U.S.A.* 39°6N 94°35W **111** C8
Kansk *Russia* 56°20N 95°37E **77** D10
Kanturk *Ireland* 52°11N 8°54W **20** D5
Kanye *Botswana* 24°55S 25°28E **97** J5
Kaohsiung *Taiwan* 22°35N 120°16E **79** G13
Kaolack *Senegal* 14°5N 16°8W **94** F2
Kapa'a *U.S.A.* 22°5N 159°19W **110** G15
Kapiri Mposhi *Zambia* 13°59S 28°43E **97** G5
Kaposvár *Hungary* 46°25N 17°47E **65** E9
Kaptai L. *Bangla.* 22°40N 92°20E **85** H18
Kapuas → *Indonesia* 0°25S 109°20E **82** E3
Kapuskasing *Canada* 49°25N 82°30W **112** A6
Kara Bogaz Gol *Turkmenistan* 41°0N 53°30E **87** A8
Kara Kum *Turkmenistan* 39°30N 60°0E **87** B9
Kara Sea *Russia* 75°0N 70°0E **76** B7
Karabük *Turkey* 41°12N 32°37E **71** F5
Karachey-Cherkessia □
Russia 43°40N 41°30E **71** F7
Karachi *Pakistan* 24°50N 67°0E **84** G5
Karaganda *Kazakhstan* 49°50N 73°10E **76** E8
Karagiye Depression
Kazakhstan 43°27N 51°45E **71** F9
Karakalpakstan □ *Uzbekistan* 43°0N 58°0E **87** A9
Karakoram *Pakistan* 35°30N 77°0E **84** B10
Karaman *Turkey* 37°14N 33°13E **71** G5
Karamay *China* 45°30N 84°58E **78** B5
Karatax Shan *China* 35°57N 81°0E **78** D5
Karayazı *Turkey* 39°41N 42°9E **71** G7
Karbalā' *Iraq* 32°36N 44°3E **86** C6
Karelia □ *Russia* 65°30N 32°30E **70** A5
Kariba, L. *Zimbabwe* 16°40S 28°25E **97** H5
Kariba Dam *Zimbabwe* 16°30S 28°35E **97** H5
Karimata, Str. of *Indonesia* 2°0S 108°40E **82** E3
Karlovac *Croatia* 45°31N 15°36E **68** B6
Karlskrona *Sweden* 56°10N 15°35E **63** F7
Karlsruhe *Germany* 49°0N 8°23E **64** D5
Karlstad *Sweden* 59°23N 13°30E **63** F6
Karnal *Egypt* 25°43N 32°39E **86** E3
Karnal *India* 29°42N 77°2E **84** E10
Karnataka □ *India* 13°15N 77°0E **84** N10
Karnten □ *Austria* 46°52N 13°30E **64** E8
Karpathos *Greece* 35°37N 27°10E **69** G12
Kars *Turkey* 40°40N 43°5E **71** F7
Karwar *India* 14°55N 74°13E **84** M9
Kasai → *Dem. Rep. of the Congo* 3°30S 16°10E **96** E3
Kasaragod *India* 12°30N 74°58E **84** N9
Kashan *Iran* 34°5N 51°30E **87** C7
Kashi *China* 39°30N 76°2E **78** D4
Kasongo *Dem. Rep. of the Congo* 4°30S 26°33E **96** E5

Kaspiysk

Kaspiysk *Russia* 42°52N 47°40E 71 F8
Kassalâ *Sudan* 15°30N 36°0E 95 E13
Kassel *Germany* 51°18N 9°26E 64 C5
Kastamonu *Turkey* 41°25N 33°43E 71 F5
Kasur *Pakistan* 31°5N 74°25E 84 D9
Kathiawar *India* 22°20N 71°0E 84 H7
Kathmandu *Nepal* 27°45N 85°20E 85 F14
Katihar *India* 25°34N 87°36E 85 G15
Katima Mulilo *Namibia* 17°28S 24°13E 97 H4
Katiola *Ivory C.* 8°10N 5°10W 94 G4
Katowice *Poland* 50°17N 19°5E 65 C10
Katrine, L. *U.K.* 56°15N 4°30W 24 B7
Katsina *Nigeria* 13°0N 7°32E 94 F7
Kattegat *Denmark* 56°40N 11°20E 63 F6
Kaua'i *U.S.A.* 22°3N 159°30W 110 H15
Kauai Channel *U.S.A.* 21°45N 158°50W 110 H15
Kaukauna *U.S.A.* 44°17N 88°17W 112 C3
Kaunakakai *U.S.A.* 21°6N 157°1W 110 H16
Kaunas *Lithuania* 54°54N 23°54E 63 G8
Kavala *Greece* 40°57N 24°28E 69 F11
Kavieng *Papua N. G.* 2°36S 150°51E 98 A9
Kawagoe *Japan* 35°55N 139°29E 81 F6
Kawaguchi *Japan* 35°52N 139°45E 81 F6
Kawardha *India* 22°0N 81°17E 85 J12
Kawasaki *Japan* 35°31N 139°43E 81 F6
Kawawachikamach *Canada* 54°48N 66°50W 109 D13
Kayes *Mali* 14°25N 11°30W 94 F3
Kayseri *Turkey* 38°45N 35°30E 71 G6
Kazan *Russia* 55°50N 49°10E 70 C8
Kazan-Rettō *Pac. Oc.* 25°0N 141°0E 102 E6
Kazanlâk *Bulgaria* 42°38N 25°20E 69 C11
Kea *Greece* 37°35N 24°22E 69 F11
Kea *U.K.* 50°14N 5°6W 29 G3
Keady *U.K.* 54°15N 6°42W 19 C8
Kearney *U.S.A.* 40°42N 99°5W 110 B7
Keban *Turkey* 38°50N 38°50E 71 G6
Keban Baraji *Turkey* 38°41N 38°33E 71 G6
Kebnekaise *Sweden* 67°53N 18°33E 63 D7
Kebri Dehar *Ethiopia* 6°45N 44°17E 89 F3
Kebumen *Indonesia* 7°42S 109°40E 82 F3
Kecskemét *Hungary* 46°57N 19°42E 65 E10
Kediri *Indonesia* 7°51S 112°1E 82 F4
Keelby *U.K.* 53°35N 0°16W 27 E8
Keele *U.K.* 53°0N 2°17W 27 F4
Keene *U.S.A.* 42°56N 72°17W 113 D11
Keeper Hill *Ireland* 52°45N 8°16W 20 C6
Keetmanshoop *Namibia* 26°35S 18°8E 97 K3
Kefalonia *Greece* 38°15N 20°30E 69 E9
Keflavík *Iceland* 64°2N 22°35W 63 B1
Kegworth *U.K.* 52°50N 1°17W 27 G6
Keighley *U.K.* 53°52N 1°54W 27 E5
Keith *U.K.* 57°32N 2°57W 23 G12
Keld *U.K.* 54°24N 2°10W 26 D4
Kelkit → *Turkey* 40°45N 36°32E 71 F6
Kellett, C. *Canada* 72°0N 126°0W 109 B7
Kellogg *U.S.A.* 47°32N 116°7W 110 A3
Kells *Ireland* 53°44N 6°53W 19 D8
Kelowna *Canada* 49°50N 119°25W 108 E8
Kelsale *U.K.* 52°14N 1°31E 31 B12
Kelsall *U.K.* 53°13N 2°43W 27 F3
Kelso *U.K.* 55°36N 2°26W 25 C11
Kelvedon *U.K.* 51°50N 0°43E 31 C10
Kem *Russia* 65°0N 34°38E 70 B5
Kemble *U.K.* 51°40N 1°59W 30 C5
Kemerovo *Russia* 55°20N 86°5E 76 D9
Kemi *Finland* 65°44N 24°34E 63 D8
Kemijoki → *Finland* 65°47N 24°32E 63 D8
Kemp Land *Antarctica* 69°0S 55°0E 55 C5
Kempsey *U.K.* 52°8N 2°12W 30 B4
Kempston *U.K.* 52°7N 0°30W 31 B8
Kempten *Germany* 47°45N 10°17E 64 E6
Kenai *U.S.A.* 60°33N 151°16W 108 C4
Kendal *U.K.* 54°20N 2°44W 26 D3
Kendari *Indonesia* 3°50S 122°30E 83 E6
Kenema *S. Leone* 7°50N 11°14W 94 G3
Kenilworth *U.K.* 52°21N 1°34W 30 B5
Kenitra *Morocco* 34°15N 6°40W 94 B4
Kenmare *Ireland* 51°53N 9°36W 20 E3
Kenmare River → *Ireland* 51°48N 9°51W 20 E2
Kennet → *U.K.* 51°27N 0°57W 31 D7
Kennewick *U.S.A.* 46°12N 119°7W 110 A3
Kenninghall *U.K.* 52°26N 1°0E 31 B11
Kenogami → *Canada* 51°6N 84°28W 109 D11
Kenora *Canada* 49°47N 94°29W 108 E10
Kenosha *U.S.A.* 42°35N 87°49W 112 D4
Kent □ *U.K.* 41°9N 81°22W 112 E7
Kent □ *U.K.* 51°12N 0°40E 31 D10
Kent Pen. *Canada* 68°30N 107°0W 108 C9
Kentisbeare *U.K.* 50°51N 3°20W 29 F7
Kenton *U.S.A.* 40°39N 83°37W 112 E6
Kentucky □ *U.S.A.* 37°0N 84°0W 112 G5
Kentucky → *U.S.A.* 38°41N 85°11W 112 F5
Kentville *Canada* 45°6N 64°29W 109 E13
Kenya ■ *Africa* 1°0N 38°0E 96 D7
Kenya, Mt. *Kenya* 0°10S 37°18E 96 E7
Kerala □ *India* 11°0N 76°15E 84 P10
Kerch *Ukraine* 45°20N 36°20E 71 E6
Kerguelen *Ind. Oc.* 49°15S 69°10E 53 G13
Kericho *Kenya* 0°22S 35°15E 96 E7
Kerinci *Indonesia* 1°40S 101°15E 82 E2
Kermadec Is. *Pac. Oc.* 30°0S 178°15W 99 G15
Kermadec Trench *Pac. Oc.* 30°30S 176°0W 99 G15
Kermān *Iran* 30°15N 57°1E 87 D9
Kermānshāh *Iran* 34°23N 47°0E 86 C6
Kernow = Cornwall □ *U.K.* 50°26N 4°40W 29 G4
Kerrera *U.K.* 56°24N 5°33W 24 E3
Kerrobert *Canada* 51°56N 109°8W 108 D9
Kerry □ *Ireland* 52°7N 9°35W 20 D3
Kerry Hd. *Ireland* 52°25N 9°56W 20 D3
Kessingland *U.K.* 52°26N 1°43E 31 B12
Keswick *U.K.* 54°36N 3°8W 26 C2
Ketchikan *U.S.A.* 55°21N 131°39W 108 D6
Kettering *U.K.* 52°24N 0°43W 31 B7
Kettle Ness *U.K.* 54°33N 0°42W 26 C8
Kettlewell *U.K.* 54°9N 2°3W 26 D4
Kewaunee *U.S.A.* 44°27N 87°31W 112 C4
Keweenaw B. *U.S.A.* 47°0N 88°15W 112 B3
Keweenaw Pen. *U.S.A.* 47°15N 88°15W 112 B3
Keweenaw Pt. *U.S.A.* 47°25N 87°43W 112 B4

Kexby *U.K.* 53°22N 0°42W 27 F7
Key West *U.S.A.* 24°33N 81°48W 111 F10
Keyingham *U.K.* 53°43N 0°7W 27 E8
Keymer *U.K.* 50°55N 0°7W 31 E8
Keynsham *U.K.* 51°24N 2°29W 30 D4
Keyser *U.S.A.* 39°26N 78°59W 112 F8
Keyworth *U.K.* 52°52N 1°5W 27 G6
Khabarovsk *Russia* 48°30N 135°5E 77 E14
Khairpur *Pakistan* 27°32N 68°49E 84 F6
Khambhat *India* 22°23N 72°33E 84 H8
Khambhat, G. of *India* 20°45N 72°30E 84 J8
Khamîs Mushayt *Si. Arabia* 18°18N 42°44E 89 D3
Khan Tengri, Pik *Asia* 42°12N 80°10E 78 C5
Khandyga *Russia* 62°42N 135°35E 77 C14
Khanewal *Pakistan* 30°20N 71°55E 84 D7
Khanka, L. *Asia* 45°0N 132°24E 79 C15
Kharagpur *India* 22°20N 87°25E 85 H15
Kharg *Iran* 29°15N 50°28E 86 D7
Khârga, El Wâhât el *Egypt* 25°10N 30°35E 95 C12
Kharkov *Ukraine* 49°58N 36°20E 71 E6
Khartoum *Sudan* 15°31N 32°35E 95 E12
Khasavyurt *Russia* 43°16N 46°40E 71 F8
Khaskovo *Bulgaria* 41°56N 25°30E 69 D11
Khatanga *Russia* 72°0N 102°20E 77 B11
Khemisset *Morocco* 33°50N 6°1W 94 B4
Khenchela *Algeria* 35°28N 7°11E 94 A7
Kherson *Ukraine* 46°35N 32°35E 71 E5
Khmelnytskyy *Ukraine* 49°23N 27°0E 65 D14
Khojak Pass *Afghan.* 30°51N 66°34E 87 D11
Kholm *Afghan.* 36°45N 67°40E 87 B11
Khon Kaen *Thailand* 16°30N 102°47E 82 A2
Khorāsan *Iran* 34°0N 58°0E 87 C9
Khorramābād *Iran* 33°30N 48°25E 86 C7
Khorramshahr *Iran* 30°29N 48°15E 86 D7
Khouribga *Morocco* 32°58N 6°57W 94 B4
Khūjand *Tajikistan* 40°17N 69°37E 87 B12
Khulna *Bangla.* 22°45N 89°34E 85 H16
Khunjerab Pass *Asia* 36°40N 75°25E 84 A9
Khushab *Pakistan* 32°20N 72°20E 84 C8
Khuzdar *Pakistan* 27°52N 66°30E 84 F5
Khūzestān □ *Iran* 31°0N 49°0E 86 D7
Khvoy *Iran* 38°35N 45°0E 86 B6
Khyber Pakhtunkhwa □ *Pakistan* 34°0N 72°0E 84 B8
Khyber Pass *Afghan.* 34°10N 71°8E 84 B7
Kibworth Beauchamp *U.K.* 52°33N 0°59W 27 G7
Kicking Horse Pass *Canada* 51°28N 116°16W 108 D8
Kidderminster *U.K.* 52°24N 2°15W 30 B4
Kidlington *U.K.* 51°50N 1°15W 30 C6
Kidsgrove *U.K.* 53°5N 2°14W 27 F4
Kidstones *U.K.* 54°13N 2°2W 26 D4
Kidwelly *U.K.* 51°44N 4°18W 28 D5
Kiel *Germany* 54°19N 10°8E 64 A6
Kiel Canal = Nord-Ostsee-Kanal *Germany* 54°12N 9°32E 64 A5
Kielce *Poland* 50°52N 20°42E 65 C11
Kielder *U.K.* 55°14N 2°35W 26 B3
Kieler Bucht *Germany* 54°35N 10°25E 64 A6
Kiev *Ukraine* 50°30N 30°28E 65 C16
Kigali *Rwanda* 1°59S 30°4E 96 E6
Kigoma-Ujiji *Tanzania* 4°55S 29°36E 96 E5
Kikwit *Dem. Rep. of the Congo* 5°0S 18°45E 96 E3
Kīlauea *U.S.A.* 19°25N 155°17W 110 J17
Kilbirnie *U.K.* 55°46N 4°41W 24 C7
Kilbrannan Sd. *U.K.* 55°37N 5°26W 24 C5
Kildare *Ireland* 53°9N 6°55W 21 B9
Kildare □ *Ireland* 53°10N 6°50W 21 B9
Kilfinnane *Ireland* 52°21N 8°28W 20 D6
Kilham *U.K.* 54°4N 0°23W 26 D8
Kilifi *Kenya* 3°40S 39°48E 96 E7
Kilimanjaro *Tanzania* 3°7S 37°20E 96 E7
Kilindini *Kenya* 4°4S 39°40E 96 E7
Kilkee *Ireland* 52°41N 9°39W 20 C3
Kilkeel *U.K.* 54°7N 5°55W 19 C10
Kilkenny *Ireland* 52°39N 7°15W 21 C8
Kilkenny □ *Ireland* 52°35N 7°15W 21 C8
Kilkhampton *U.K.* 50°52N 4°31W 29 F4
Kilkieran B. *Ireland* 53°20N 9°41W 20 B3
Killala *Ireland* 54°13N 9°13W 18 C3
Killala B. *Ireland* 54°16N 9°8W 18 C3
Killaloe *Ireland* 52°48N 8°28W 20 C6
Killarney *Ireland* 52°4N 9°30W 20 D4
Killarney □ *Ireland* 52°0N 9°33W 20 E3
Killary Harbour *Ireland* 53°38N 9°52W 18 D2
Killeen *U.S.A.* 31°7N 97°44W 110 D7
Killin *U.K.* 56°28N 4°19W 24 E7
Killiney *Ireland* 53°15N 6°7W 21 B10
Killinghall *U.K.* 54°2N 1°33W 26 D5
Killorglin *Ireland* 52°6N 9°47W 20 D3
Killybegs *Ireland* 54°38N 8°26W 18 B5
Kilmarnock *U.K.* 55°37N 4°29W 24 C7
Kilrush *Ireland* 52°38N 9°29W 20 C4
Kilsby *U.K.* 52°20N 1°10W 30 B6
Kilsyth *U.K.* 55°59N 4°3W 24 C7
Kilwa Kivinje *Tanzania* 8°45S 39°25E 96 F7
Kilwinning *U.K.* 55°39N 4°43W 24 C6
Kimberley *Australia* 16°20S 127°0E 98 D4
Kimberley *S. Africa* 28°43S 24°46E 97 K4
Kimbolton *U.K.* 52°18N 0°24W 31 B8
Kimch'aek *N. Korea* 40°40N 129°10E 79 C14
Kimmirut *Canada* 62°50N 69°50W 109 C13
Kimry *Russia* 56°55N 37°15E 70 C6
Kinabalu, Gunung *Malaysia* 6°3N 116°14E 82 C5
Kincardine *Canada* 44°10N 81°40W 112 C7
Kincardine Aberds., *U.K.* 56°57N 2°25W 23 J13
Kincardine Fife, *U.K.* 56°4N 3°43W 25 B9
Kinder Scout *U.K.* 53°24N 1°52W 27 F5
Kindersley *Canada* 51°30N 109°10W 108 D9
Kindia *Guinea* 10°0N 12°52W 94 F3
Kindu *Dem. Rep. of the Congo* 2°55S 25°50E 96 E5
Kineshma *Russia* 57°30N 42°5E 70 C7
Kineton *U.K.* 52°10N 1°31W 30 B5
King George I. *Antarctica* 60°0S 60°0W 55 C18
King George Is. *Canada* 57°20N 80°30W 109 D11
King I. *Australia* 39°50S 144°0E 98 H7
King William I. *Canada* 69°10N 97°25W 108 C10
Kingman *U.S.A.* 35°12N 114°4W 110 C4
King's Lynn *U.K.* 52°45N 0°24E 31 B9
King's Sutton *U.K.* 52°1N 1°15W 30 B6
King's Worthy *U.K.* 51°6N 1°17W 30 D6

Kingsbridge *U.K.* 50°17N 3°47W 29 G6
Kingsbury *U.K.* 52°34N 1°40W 27 G5
Kingscourt *Ireland* 53°54N 6°48W 19 D8
Kingskerswell *U.K.* 50°29N 3°35W 29 G6
Kingsland *U.K.* 52°15N 2°48W 30 B3
Kingsteignton *U.K.* 50°33N 3°36W 29 G6
Kingston *Canada* 44°14N 76°30W 109 E12
Kingston *Jamaica* 17°55N 76°50W 114 a
Kingston N.Y., *U.S.A.* 41°56N 73°59W 113 E10
Kingston Pa., *U.S.A.* 41°16N 75°54W 113 E10
Kingston upon Hull *U.K.* 53°45N 0°21W 27 E8
Kingston-upon-Thames □ *U.K.* 51°24N 0°17W 31 D8
Kingstown *St. Vincent* 13°10N 61°10W 115 E12
Kingsville *U.S.A.* 27°31N 97°52W 110 E7
Kingswear *U.K.* 50°21N 3°35W 29 G6
Kingswood *U.K.* 51°27N 2°31W 30 D3
Kington *U.K.* 52°13N 3°1W 30 B2
Kingussie *U.K.* 57°6N 4°2W 23 H9
Kinistino *Canada* 52°57N 105°2W 108 D9
Kinlochleven *U.K.* 56°43N 5°0W 22 J7
Kinnairds Hd. *U.K.* 57°43N 2°1W 23 G13
Kinngait *Canada* 64°14N 76°32W 109 C12
Kinross *U.K.* 56°13N 3°25W 25 B9
Kinsale *Ireland* 51°42N 8°31W 20 E5
Kinsale, Old Hd. of *Ireland* 51°37N 8°33W 20 E5
Kinshasa *Dem. Rep. of the Congo* 4°20S 15°15E 96 E3
Kintore *U.K.* 57°14N 2°20W 23 H13
Kintyre *U.K.* 55°30N 5°35W 24 D4
Kintyre, Mull of *U.K.* 55°17N 5°47W 24 D4
Kippure *Ireland* 53°11N 6°21W 21 B10
Kirensk *Russia* 57°50N 107°55E 77 D11
Kirgiz Steppe *Eurasia* 50°0N 55°0E 71 D10
Kiribati ■ *Pac. Oc.* 3°0S 180°0E 102 H10
Kiritimati *Kiribati* 1°58N 157°27W 103 G12
Kirkbean *U.K.* 54°55N 3°36W 25 E9
Kirkbride *U.K.* 54°54N 3°12W 26 C2
Kirkburton *U.K.* 53°37N 1°42W 27 E5
Kirkby *U.K.* 53°30N 2°54W 27 E3
Kirkby-in-Ashfield *U.K.* 53°6N 1°14W 27 F6
Kirkby Lonsdale *U.K.* 54°12N 2°36W 26 D3
Kirkby Malzeard *U.K.* 54°10N 1°37W 26 D5
Kirkby Stephen *U.K.* 54°29N 2°21W 26 D4
Kirkby Thore *U.K.* 54°37N 2°32W 26 C3
Kirkbymoorside *U.K.* 54°17N 0°56W 26 D7
Kirkcaldy *U.K.* 56°7N 3°9W 25 B9
Kirkcudbright *U.K.* 54°50N 4°2W 24 E7
Kirkham *U.K.* 53°47N 2°53W 27 E3
Kirkintilloch *U.K.* 55°56N 4°8W 24 C7
Kirkland Lake *Canada* 48°9N 80°2W 109 E11
Kırklareli *Turkey* 41°44N 27°15E 86 A1
Kirkoswald *U.K.* 54°46N 2°41W 26 C3
Kirksville *U.S.A.* 40°12N 92°35W 111 B8
Kirkūk *Iraq* 35°30N 44°21E 86 C6
Kirkwall *U.K.* 58°59N 2°58W 23 E12
Kirkwhelpington *U.K.* 55°9N 1°59W 26 B5
Kirov *Russia* 58°35N 49°40E 70 C8
Kirovohrad *Ukraine* 48°35N 32°20E 71 E5
Kirriemuir *U.K.* 56°41N 3°1W 23 J11
Kırşehir *Turkey* 39°14N 34°5E 71 G5
Kirthar Range *Pakistan* 27°0N 67°0E 84 F5
Kirtling *U.K.* 52°12N 0°28E 31 B9
Kirtlington *U.K.* 51°53N 1°15W 30 C6
Kirton *U.K.* 52°56N 0°3W 27 G8
Kirton in Lindsey *U.K.* 53°29N 0°34W 27 F7
Kiruna *Sweden* 67°52N 20°15E 63 D8
Kiryū *Japan* 36°24N 139°20E 81 E6
Kisangani *Dem. Rep. of the Congo* 0°35N 25°15E 96 D5
Kiselevsk *Russia* 54°5N 86°39E 76 D9
Kishanganj *India* 26°3N 88°14E 85 F16
Kishinev *Moldova* 47°2N 28°50E 65 E15
Kisii *Kenya* 0°40S 34°45E 96 E6
Kislovodsk *Russia* 43°50N 42°45E 71 F7
Kismaayo *Somalia* 0°22S 42°32E 89 H3
Kisumu *Kenya* 0°3S 34°45E 96 E6
Kitakyūshū *Japan* 33°50N 130°50E 81 G2
Kitale *Kenya* 1°0N 35°0E 96 D7
Kitami *Japan* 43°48N 143°54E 81 B8
Kitchener *Canada* 43°27N 80°29W 112 D7
Kíthnos *Greece* 37°26N 24°27E 69 F11
Kitimat *Canada* 54°3N 128°38W 108 D7
Kittanning *U.S.A.* 40°49N 79°31W 112 E8
Kitwe *Zambia* 12°54S 28°13E 97 G5
Kivu, L. *Dem. Rep. of the Congo* 1°48S 29°0E 96 E5
Kızıl Irmak → *Turkey* 41°44N 35°58E 71 F6
Kizlyar *Russia* 43°51N 46°40E 71 F8
Kladno *Czech Rep.* 50°10N 14°7E 64 C8
Klagenfurt *Austria* 46°38N 14°20E 64 E8
Klaipėda *Lithuania* 55°43N 21°10E 63 F8
Klamath → *U.S.A.* 41°33N 124°5W 110 B2
Klamath Falls *U.S.A.* 42°13N 121°46W 110 B2
Klang *Malaysia* 3°2N 101°26E 82 D2
Klarälven → *Sweden* 59°23N 13°32E 63 F6
Klerksdorp *S. Africa* 26°53S 26°38E 97 K5
Kluane L. *Canada* 61°15N 138°40W 108 C6
Kluang *Malaysia* 2°3N 103°18E 82 D2
Klyuchevskaya, Sopka *Russia* 55°50N 160°30E 77 D17
Knaresborough *U.K.* 54°1N 1°28W 27 D6
Knebworth *U.K.* 51°52N 0°11W 31 C8
Knighton *U.K.* 52°21N 3°3W 28 C7
Knock *Ireland* 53°48N 8°55W 18 D4
Knockmealdown Mts. *Ireland* 52°14N 7°56W 20 D7
Knossos *Greece* 35°16N 25°10E 69 G11
Knottingley *U.K.* 53°43N 1°16W 27 E6
Knowle *U.K.* 52°23N 1°43W 30 B5
Knoxville *U.S.A.* 35°58N 83°55W 111 C10
Knoydart *U.K.* 57°3N 5°33W 22 H6
Knutsford *U.K.* 53°18N 2°21W 27 F4
Kōbe *Japan* 34°41N 135°13E 81 F4
Koblenz *Germany* 50°21N 7°36E 64 C4
Kocaeli *Turkey* 40°45N 29°50E 71 F4
Koch Bihar *India* 26°22N 89°29E 85 F16
Kochi *India* 9°58N 76°20E 84 Q10
Kōchi *Japan* 33°30N 133°35E 81 G3
Kodiak *U.S.A.* 57°47N 152°24W 108 D4
Kodiak I. *U.S.A.* 57°30N 152°45W 108 D4
Koforidua *Ghana* 6°3N 0°17W 94 G5
Kōfu *Japan* 35°40N 138°30E 81 F6

Kogalym *Russia* 62°16N 74°29E 76 C8
Kohat *Pakistan* 33°40N 71°29E 84 C7
Kohima *India* 25°35N 94°10E 85 G19
Kohtla-Järve *Estonia* 59°20N 27°20E 63 F9
Kokkola *Finland* 63°50N 23°8E 63 E8
Koko Kyunzu *Burma* 14°7N 93°22E 85 M18
Koko Nur *China* 36°40N 100°10E 78 D9
Kokomo *U.S.A.* 40°29N 86°8W 112 E4
Kokopo *Papua N. G.* 4°22S 152°19E 98 A9
Kōkshetaū *Kazakhstan* 53°20N 69°25E 76 D7
Koksoak → *Canada* 58°30N 68°10W 109 D13
Kola Pen. *Russia* 67°30N 38°0E 70 A6
Kolar Gold Fields *India* 12°58N 78°16E 84 N11
Kolguyev, Ostrov *Russia* 69°20N 48°30E 70 A8
Kolhapur *India* 16°43N 74°15E 84 L9
Kolkata *India* 22°34N 88°21E 85 H16
Kollam *India* 8°50N 76°38E 84 Q10
Kolomna *Russia* 55°8N 38°45E 70 C6
Kolomyya *Ukraine* 48°31N 25°2E 71 E4
Kolpino *Russia* 59°44N 30°39E 70 C5
Kolwezi *Dem. Rep. of the Congo* 10°40S 25°25E 96 H5
Kolyma → *Russia* 69°30N 161°0E 77 C17
Kolyma Ra. *Russia* 63°0N 157°0E 77 C16
Komatsu *Japan* 36°25N 136°30E 81 E5
Komi □ *Russia* 64°0N 55°0E 70 B10
Komsomolsk-na-Amur *Russia* 50°30N 137°0E 77 D14
Kondoz *Afghan.* 36°50N 68°50E 87 B12
Kongur Shan *China* 38°34N 75°18E 78 D4
Konin *Poland* 52°12N 18°15E 65 B10
Konosha *Russia* 61°0N 40°5E 70 B7
Konotop *Ukraine* 51°12N 33°7E 71 D5
Konqi He → *China* 40°45N 90°10E 78 C6
Konya *Turkey* 37°52N 32°35E 71 G5
Kootenay L. *Canada* 49°45N 116°50W 108 E8
Kopet Dagh *Asia* 38°0N 58°0E 87 B9
Korçë *Albania* 40°37N 20°50E 69 D9
Korčula *Croatia* 42°56N 16°57E 68 C7
Kordofan *Sudan* 13°0N 29°0E 95 F11
Korea Bay *Korea* 39°0N 124°0E 79 C13
Korea Strait *Asia* 34°0N 129°30E 79 E14
Korhogo *Ivory C.* 9°29N 5°28W 94 G4
Kōriyama *Japan* 37°24N 140°23E 81 E7
Korla *China* 41°45N 86°4E 78 C6
Koror *Palau* 7°20N 134°28E 102 G5
Körös → *Hungary* 46°43N 20°12E 65 E11
Korosten *Ukraine* 50°54N 28°36E 71 D4
Kortrijk *Belgium* 50°50N 3°17E 64 C2
Koryak Ra. *Russia* 61°0N 171°0E 77 C18
Kos *Greece* 36°50N 27°15E 69 F12
Kosciuszko, Mt. *Australia* 36°27S 148°16E 98 H8
Košice *Slovak Rep.* 48°42N 21°15E 65 D11
Kosovo ■ *Europe* 42°30N 21°0E 69 C9
Kôstî *Sudan* 13°8N 32°43E 95 F12
Kostroma *Russia* 57°50N 40°58E 70 C7
Koszalin *Poland* 54°11N 16°8E 64 A9
Kota *India* 25°14N 75°49E 84 G9
Kota Bharu *Malaysia* 6°7N 102°14E 82 C2
Kota Kinabalu *Malaysia* 6°0N 116°4E 82 C5
Kotabumi *Indonesia* 4°49S 104°54E 82 E2
Kotelnich *Russia* 58°22N 48°24E 70 C8
Kotka *Finland* 60°28N 26°58E 63 E9
Kotlas *Russia* 61°17N 46°43E 70 B8
Kotor *Montenegro* 42°25N 18°47E 69 C8
Kotri *Pakistan* 25°22N 68°22E 84 G6
Kotuy → *Russia* 71°54N 102°6E 77 B11
Kotzebue *U.S.A.* 66°53N 162°39W 108 C3
Koudougou *Burkina Faso* 12°10N 2°20W 94 F5
Koumra *Chad* 8°50N 17°35E 95 G9
Kovel *Ukraine* 51°11N 24°38E 70 D8
Kovrov *Russia* 56°25N 41°25E 70 C7
Kowloon *China* 22°19N 114°11E 79 G11
Kozhikode *India* 11°15N 75°43E 84 P9
Kpalimé *Togo* 6°57N 0°44E 94 G6
Kra, Isthmus of *Thailand* 10°15N 99°30E 82 B1
Kragujevac *Serbia* 44°2N 20°56E 69 B9
Krakatoa *Indonesia* 6°10S 105°20E 82 F3
Kraków *Poland* 50°4N 19°57E 65 C10
Kraljevo *Serbia* 43°44N 20°41E 69 C9
Kramatorsk *Ukraine* 48°50N 37°30E 71 E6
Krasnodar *Russia* 45°5N 39°0E 71 E6
Krasnokamensk *Russia* 50°3N 118°0E 77 D12
Krasnokamsk *Russia* 58°4N 55°48E 70 C10
Krasnoturinsk *Russia* 59°46N 60°12E 70 C11
Krasnoyarsk *Russia* 56°8N 93°0E 77 D10
Krasnyy Luch *Ukraine* 48°13N 39°0E 71 E6
Krefeld *Germany* 51°20N 6°33E 64 C4
Kremenchuk *Ukraine* 49°5N 33°25E 71 E5
Kribi *Cameroon* 2°57N 9°56E 96 D1
Krishna → *India* 15°57N 80°59E 85 M12
Kristiansand *Norway* 58°8N 8°1E 63 F5
Kristiansund *Norway* 63°7N 7°45E 63 E5
Krivoy Rog *Ukraine* 47°51N 33°20E 71 E5
Krk *Croatia* 45°8N 14°40E 68 B6
Kronshtadt *Russia* 59°57N 29°51E 70 B4
Kroonstad *S. Africa* 27°43S 27°19E 97 K5
Kropotkin *Russia* 45°28N 40°28E 71 E7
Krugersdorp *S. Africa* 26°5S 27°46E 97 K5
Kruševac *Serbia* 43°35N 21°28E 69 C9
Ksar el Kebir *Morocco* 35°0N 6°0W 94 B4
Ksar el Boukhari *Algeria*
Kuala Belait *Malaysia* 4°35N 114°11E 82 D4
Kuala Lumpur *Malaysia* 3°9N 101°41E 82 D2
Kuala Terengganu *Malaysia* 5°20N 103°8E 82 C2
Kuantan *Malaysia* 3°49N 103°20E 82 D2
Kuching *Malaysia* 1°33N 110°25E 82 D4
Kucing *Malaysia*
Kugluktuk *Canada* 67°50N 115°5W 108 C8
Kuito *Angola* 12°22S 16°55E 97 G3
Kujang *India*
Kukës *Albania*
Kula Kangri *Bhutan/China*
Kulob *Tajikistan* 37°55N 69°50E 87 B12
Kuma → *Russia* 44°55N 47°0E 71 F8
Kumagaya *Japan* 36°9N 139°22E 81 E6
Kumamoto *Japan* 32°45N 130°45E 81 G2
Kumanovo *Macedonia* 42°9N 21°42E 69 C9
Kumasi *Ghana* 6°41N 1°38W 94 G5
Kumba *Cameroon* 4°36N 9°24E 96 D1
Kumbakonam *India* 10°58N 79°25E 84 P11
Kumta *India*
Kunashir, Ostrov *Russia*
Kunlun Shan *Asia* 36°0N 86°30E 78 D6
Kunming *China* 25°1N 102°41E 78 F9
Kuopio *Finland* 62°53N 27°35E 63 E9
Kupang *Indonesia* 10°19S 123°39E 83 F6
Kuqa *China* 41°35N 82°30E 78 C5
Kür → *Azerbaijan* 39°29N 49°15E 71 G8
Kurdistan *Asia* 37°20N 43°30E 86 B5
Kure *Japan* 34°14N 132°32E 81 F3
Kurgan *Russia* 55°26N 65°18E 76 D7
Kuril Is. *Russia* 45°0N 150°0E 77 E16
Kuril-Kamchatka Trench *Pac. Oc.* 44°0N 153°0E 102 C7
Kurnool *India* 15°45N 78°0E 84 M11
Kursk *Russia* 51°42N 36°11E 70 D6
Kuruktag *China* 41°0N 89°0E 78 C6
Kurume *Japan* 33°15N 130°30E 81 G2
Kushiro *Japan* 43°0N 144°25E 81 B9
Kushtia *Bangla.* 23°55N 89°5E 85 H16
Kuskokwim B. *U.S.A.* 59°45N 162°25W 108 D3
Kütahya *Turkey* 39°30N 30°2E 71 G5
Kutaisi *Georgia* 42°19N 42°40E 71 F7
Kuujjuaq *Canada* 58°6N 68°15W 109 D13
Kuujjuarapik *Canada* 55°20N 77°35W 109 D12
Kuwait *Kuwait* 29°30N 48°0E 86 D7
Kuwait ■ *Asia* 29°30N 47°30E 86 D6
Kuybyshev Res. *Russia* 55°2N 49°30E 70 C8
Kuznetsk *Russia* 53°12N 46°40E 70 D8
Kuzomen *Russia* 66°22N 36°50E 70 A6
KwaMashu *S. Africa* 29°45S 30°58E 97 K6
KwaZulu Natal □ *S. Africa* 29°0S 30°0E 97 K6
Kwekwe *Zimbabwe* 18°58S 29°48E 97 H5
Kwun Tong *China* 22°19N 114°13E 79 a
Kyle of Lochalsh *U.K.* 57°17N 5°44W 22 H6
Kyoga, L. *Uganda* 1°35N 33°0E 96 D6
Kyōto *Japan* 35°0N 135°45E 81 F4
Kyrenia *Cyprus* 35°20N 33°20E 86 C3
Kyrgyzstan ■ *Asia* 42°0N 75°0E 76 E8
Kythira *Greece* 36°8N 23°0E 69 F10
Kyūshū *Japan* 33°0N 131°0E 81 G2
Kyustendil *Bulgaria* 42°16N 22°41E 69 C10
Kyzyl *Russia* 51°50N 94°30E 78 A7
Kyzyl Kum *Uzbekistan* 42°30N 65°0E 87 A10
Kyzyl-Orda *Kazakhstan* 44°48N 65°28E 76 E7

L

La Alcarria *Spain* 40°31N 2°45W 67 B4
La Barra *Nic.* 12°54N 83°33W 115 E8
La Ceiba *Honduras* 15°40N 86°50W 114 D7
La Coruña *Spain* 43°20N 8°25W 67 A1
La Crosse *U.S.A.* 43°48N 91°15W 112 D2
La Grande *U.S.A.* 45°20N 118°5W 110 A3
La Grande → *Canada* 53°50N 79°0W 109 D12
La Grange *U.S.A.* 33°2N 85°2W 111 D10
La Habana *Cuba* 23°8N 82°22W 115 C8
La Junta *U.S.A.* 37°59N 103°33W 110 C6
La Línea de la Concepción *Spain* 36°15N 5°23W 67 D3
La Loche *Canada* 56°29N 109°26W 108 D9
La Mancha *Spain* 39°10N 2°54W 67 C4
La Oroya *Peru* 11°32S 75°54W 120 D2
La Palma *Canary Is.* 28°40N 17°50W 94 C2
La Paz *Bolivia* 16°20S 68°10W 120 D3
La Paz *Mexico* 24°10N 110°18W 114 C2
La Perouse Str. *Asia* 45°40N 142°0E 79 B17
La Plata *Argentina* 35°0S 57°55W 121 F4
La Quiaca *Argentina* 22°5S 65°35W 121 E3
La Rioja *Argentina* 29°20S 67°0W 121 E3
La Rioja □ *Spain* 42°20N 2°20W 67 A4
La Roche-sur-Yon *France* 46°40N 1°25W 66 C3
La Rochelle *France* 46°10N 1°9W 66 C3
La Romana *Dom. Rep.* 18°27N 68°57W 115 D11
La Ronge *Canada* 55°5N 105°20W 108 D9
La Sarre *Canada* 48°45N 79°15W 112 A8
La Serena *Chile* 29°55S 71°10W 121 E2
La Seyne-sur-Mer *France* 43°7N 5°52E 66 E6
La Spézia *Italy* 44°7N 9°50E 68 B3
La Tortuga, I. *Venezuela* 11°0N 65°22W 120 A3
La Tuque *Canada* 47°30N 72°50W 109 E12
La Vega *Dom. Rep.* 19°20N 70°30W 115 D10
Labé *Guinea* 11°24N 12°16W 94 F3
Labinsk *Russia* 44°40N 40°48E 71 F7
Laborie *St. Lucia* 13°45N 61°2W 114 b
Labrador *Canada* 53°20N 61°0W 109 D13
Labrador City *Canada* 52°57N 66°55W 109 D13
Labrador Sea *Atl. Oc.* 57°0N 54°0W 109 D14
Labuan *Malaysia* 5°21N 115°13E 82 C5
Lac La Biche *Canada* 54°45N 111°58W 108 D8
Lac-Mégantic *Canada* 45°35N 70°53W 113 C12
Laccadive Is. = Lakshadweep Is. *India* 10°0N 72°30E 72 G9
Laceby *U.K.* 53°33N 0°10W 27 E8
Lacock *U.K.* 51°24N 2°7W 30 D4
Lacombe *Canada* 52°30N 113°44W 108 D8
Laconia *U.S.A.* 43°32N 71°28W 113 D12
Ladakh Ra. *India* 34°0N 78°0E 84 C11
Ladder Hills *U.K.* 57°13N 3°16W 23 H11
Ladock *U.K.* 50°19N 4°58W 29 G4
Ladoga, L. *Russia* 61°15N 30°30E 70 B5
Ladysmith *S. Africa* 28°32S 29°46E 97 K5
Ladysmith *U.S.A.* 45°28N 91°12W 112 C2
Lae *Papua N. G.* 6°40S 147°2E 98 B8
Lafayette, Ind., *U.S.A.* 40°25N 86°54W 112 E4
Lafayette La., *U.S.A.* 30°14N 92°1W 111 D8
Lafia *Nigeria* 8°30N 8°34E 94 G7
Lagan → *U.K.* 54°36N 5°55W 19 B10
Lagarto *Brazil* 10°54S 37°41W 122 B3
Lagdo, L. de *Cameroon* 8°40N 14°0E 95 G8
Laghouat *Algeria* 33°50N 2°59E 94 B6
Lagos *Nigeria* 6°25N 3°27E 94 G6
Lagos *Portugal* 37°5N 8°41W 67 D1
Lahn → *Germany* 50°19N 7°37E 64 C4
Lahore *Pakistan* 31°32N 74°22E 84 D9
Lahti *Finland* 60°58N 25°40E 63 E9
Lairg *U.K.* 58°2N 4°24W 23 F9
Laizhou *China* 37°8N 119°57E 79 C12
Lake Charles *U.S.A.* 30°14N 93°13W 111 D8
Lake City *U.S.A.* 30°11N 82°38W 111 D10
Lake District △ *U.K.* 54°30N 3°21W 26 C2
Lake Havasu City *U.S.A.* 34°27N 114°22W 110 D4

Lakeland   Lyubertsy

Lakeland U.S.A. 28°3N 81°57W 111 E10
Lakenheath U.K. 52°25N 0°32E 31 B10
Lakewood U.S.A. 41°28N 81°47W 112 E7
Lakshadweep Is. India 10°0N 72°30E 72 G9
Lamar U.S.A. 38°5N 102°37W 110 C6
Lambaréné Gabon 0°41S 10°12E 96 E2
Lambay I. Ireland 53°29N 6°1W 21 B10
Lamberhurst U.K. 51°5N 0°24E 31 D9
Lambeth □ U.K. 51°28N 0°6W 31 D8
Lambley U.K. 54°56N 2°30W 26 C4
Lambourn U.K. 51°30N 1°32W 30 C5
Lamesa U.S.A. 32°44N 101°58W 110 D6
Lamma I. China 22°12N 114°7E 79 a
Lammermuir U.K. 55°50N 2°40W 25 D10
Lammermuir Hills U.K. 55°50N 2°40W 25 D10
Lamon B. Phil. 14°30N 122°20E 83 B6
Lampedusa Medit. S. 35°36N 12°40E 68 G5
Lampeter U.K. 52°7N 4°4W 28 C5
Lamu Kenya 2°16S 40°55E 96 E8
Lanark U.K. 55°40N 3°47W 25 C8
Lancang Jiang → China 21°40N 101°10E 78 G9
Lancashire □ U.K. 53°50N 2°48W 27 E3
Lancaster U.K. 54°3N 2°48W 26 D3
Lancaster N.H., U.S.A. 44°29N 71°34W 113 C12
Lancaster Pa., U.S.A. 40°2N 76°19W 112 E9
Lancaster Wis., U.S.A. 42°51N 90°43W 112 D2
Lancaster Sd. Canada 74°13N 84°0W 109 B11
Lanchester U.K. 54°50N 1°44W 26 C5
Lancing U.K. 50°49N 0°19W 31 E8
Landes France 44°0N 1°0W 66 D3
Landkey U.K. 51°3N 4°0W 29 F6
Land's End U.K. 50°4N 5°44W 29 G2
Langholm U.K. 55°9N 3°0W 25 D10
Langport U.K. 51°2N 2°50W 30 D3
Langreo Spain 43°18N 5°40W 67 A3
Langres France 47°52N 5°20E 66 C6
Langres, Plateau de France 47°45N 5°3E 66 C6
Langsa Indonesia 4°30N 97°57E 82 D1
Langstrothdale Chase U.K. 54°14N 2°13W 26 D4
Langtoft U.K. 52°42N 0°20W 27 G8
Langtree U.K. 50°55N 4°13W 29 F5
Languedoc France 43°58N 3°55E 66 E5
Lannion France 48°46N 3°29W 66 B2
L'Annonciation Canada 46°25N 74°55W 113 B10
L'Anse U.S.A. 46°45N 88°27W 112 B3
Lansing U.S.A. 42°44N 84°33W 112 D5
Lantau I. China 22°15N 113°56E 79 a
Lanzhou China 36°1N 103°52E 78 D9
Laoag Phil. 18°7N 120°34E 83 A6
Laois □ Ireland 52°57N 7°27W 21 C7
Laon France 49°33N 3°35E 66 B5
Laos ■ Asia 17°45N 105°0E 82 A3
Lapeer U.S.A. 43°3N 83°19W 112 D6
Lapford U.K. 50°51N 3°48W 29 F6
Lapland Europe 68°7N 24°0E 63 U8
LaPorte U.S.A. 41°36N 86°43W 112 E4
Laptev Sea Russia 76°0N 125°0E 77 B13
L'Aquila Italy 42°22N 13°22E 68 C5
Laramie U.S.A. 41°19N 105°35W 110 B5
Laramie Mts. U.S.A. 42°0N 105°30W 110 B5
Laredo U.S.A. 27°30N 99°30W 110 E7
Largs U.K. 55°47N 4°52W 24 C6
Larisa Greece 39°36N 22°27E 69 E10
Larnaca Cyprus 34°55N 33°38E 86 C3
Larne U.K. 54°51N 5°51W 19 B10
Larne L. U.K. 54°50N 5°48W 19 B10
Larrimah Australia 15°35S 133°12E 98 D5
Larsen Ice Shelf Antarctica 67°0S 62°0W 55 C17
Larvik Norway 59°4N 10°2E 63 F6
Las Cruces U.S.A. 32°19N 106°47W 110 D5
Las Palmas de Gran Canaria
    Canary Is. 28°7N 15°26W 94 C2
Las Tunas Cuba 20°58N 76°59W 115 C9
Las Vegas N. Mex., U.S.A. 35°36N 105°13W 110 C5
Las Vegas Nev., U.S.A. 36°10N 115°8W 110 C3
Lashio Burma 22°56N 97°45E 85 H20
Lassen Pk. U.S.A. 40°29N 121°30W 110 B2
Lastoursville Gabon 0°55S 12°38E 96 E2
Latacunga Ecuador 0°50S 78°35W 120 C2
Latakia Syria 35°30N 35°45E 86 C3
Latina Italy 41°28N 12°52E 68 D5
Latvia ■ Europe 56°50N 24°0E 63 F8
Lauder U.K. 55°43N 2°43W 25 C10
Lauderdale U.K. 55°44N 2°41W 25 C10
Launceston Australia 41°24S 147°8E 98 J8
Launceston U.K. 50°38N 4°22W 29 F5
Laune → Ireland 52°7N 9°47W 20 D3
Laurel U.S.A. 31°41N 89°8W 111 D9
Laurencekirk U.K. 56°50N 2°28W 23 J13
Laurentian Plateau Canada 52°0N 70°0W 104 E12
Lausanne Switz. 46°32N 6°38E 64 E4
Lavagh More Ireland 54°46N 8°6W 18 B5
Laval Canada 45°33N 73°42W 113 C11
Laval France 48°4N 0°48W 66 B3
Lavendon U.K. 52°11N 0°39W 31 B7
Lavenham U.K. 52°6N 0°48E 31 B10
Lavras Brazil 21°20S 45°0W 122 D2
Lawrence Kans., U.S.A. 38°58N 95°14W 111 C7
Lawrence Mass., U.S.A. 42°43N 71°10W 113 D12
Lawton U.S.A. 34°37N 98°25W 110 D7
Laxey U.K. 54°14N 4°23W 19 C13
Laxfield U.K. 52°18N 1°23E 31 B11
Laxford, L. U.K. 58°24N 5°6W 22 F7
Lazio □ Italy 42°10N 12°30E 68 C5
Lazonby U.K. 54°46N 2°42W 26 C3
Le Creusot France 46°48N 4°24E 66 C6
Le Havre France 49°30N 0°5E 66 B4
Le Mans France 48°0N 0°10E 66 C4
Le Puy-en-Velay France 45°3N 3°52E 66 D5
Lea U.K. 53°22N 0°47W 27 F7
Lea → U.K. 51°31N 0°1E 31 C9
Leadenham U.K. 53°3N 0°35W 27 F7
Leamington Canada 42°3N 82°36W 112 D6
Leane, L. Ireland 52°2N 9°32W 20 D3
Leatherhead U.K. 51°18N 0°20W 31 D8
Leavenworth U.S.A. 39°19N 94°55W 111 C8
Lebanon Ind., U.S.A. 40°3N 86°28W 112 E4
Lebanon Ky., U.S.A. 37°34N 85°15W 112 G5
Lebanon Mo., U.S.A. 37°41N 92°40W 111 C8

Lebanon Pa., U.S.A. 40°20N 76°26W 112 E9
Lebanon ■ Asia 34°0N 36°0E 86 C3
Lebu Chile 37°40S 73°47W 121 F2
Lecce Italy 40°23N 18°11E 69 D8
Lechlade U.K. 51°42N 1°41W 30 C5
Ledbury U.K. 52°2N 2°25W 30 B4
Lee → Ireland 51°53N 8°56W 20 E5
Lee-on-the-Solent U.K. 50°48N 1°12W 30 E6
Leech L. U.S.A. 47°10N 94°24W 111 A8
Leeds U.K. 53°48N 1°33W 27 E5
Leeuwarden Neths. 53°15N 5°48E 64 B3
Leeuwin, C. Australia 34°20S 115°9E 98 G2
Leeward Is. Atl. Oc. 16°30N 63°30W 115 D12
Lefkada Greece 38°40N 20°43E 69 E9
Leganés Spain 40°19N 3°45W 67 B4
Legazpi Phil. 13°10N 123°45E 83 B6
Legionowo Poland 52°25N 20°50E 65 B11
Legnica Poland 51°12N 16°10E 64 C9
Leicester U.K. 52°38N 1°8W 27 G6
Leicestershire □ U.K. 52°41N 1°17W 27 G6
Leiden Neths. 52°9N 4°30E 64 B3
Leigh Gt. Man., U.K. 53°30N 2°32W 27 E3
Leigh Hereford, U.K. 52°11N 2°20W 30 B4
Leighton Buzzard U.K. 51°54N 0°38W 31 C7
Leine → Germany 52°43N 9°36E 64 B5
Leinster □ Ireland 53°3N 7°8W 21 B8
Leinster, Mt. Ireland 52°37N 6°46W 21 C9
Leintwardine U.K. 52°22N 2°51W 30 B3
Leipzig Germany 51°18N 12°22E 64 C7
Leiston U.K. 52°12N 1°36E 31 B12
Leith U.K. 55°59N 3°11W 25 C9
Leith Hill U.K. 51°11N 0°22W 31 D8
Leitholm U.K. 55°41N 2°20W 25 C11
Leitrim Ireland 54°0N 8°5W 18 C5
Leitrim □ Ireland 54°8N 8°0W 18 C5
Leixlip Ireland 53°22N 6°30W 21 B9
Leizhou Pen. China 21°0N 110°0E 79 G11
Lelant U.K. 50°11N 5°28W 29 G3
Léman, L. Europe 46°26N 6°30E 64 E4
Lena → Russia 72°52N 126°40E 77 B13
Lenham U.K. 51°14N 0°44E 31 D10
Leninsk-Kuznetskiy Russia 54°44N 86°10E 76 D9
Lennox Hills U.K. 56°3N 4°12W 24 B7
Lens France 50°26N 2°50E 66 A5
Leodhais = Lewis U.K. 58°9N 6°40W 22 D4
Leominster U.K. 52°14N 2°43W 30 B3
Leominster U.S.A. 42°32N 71°46W 113 D12
León Mexico 21°6N 101°41W 114 C4
León Nic. 12°27N 86°51W 114 E7
León Spain 42°38N 5°34W 67 A3
Leonora Australia 28°49S 121°19E 98 F3
Leopoldina Brazil 21°28S 42°40W 122 D2
Lerwick U.K. 60°9N 1°9W 22 B15
Les Cayes Haiti 18°15N 73°46W 115 D10
Les Sables-d'Olonne France 46°30N 1°45W 66 C3
Lesbos Greece 39°10N 26°20E 69 E12
Lesbury U.K. 55°25N 1°36W 26 B5
Leshan China 29°33N 103°41E 78 H9
Leskovac Serbia 43°0N 21°58E 69 C9
Lesosibirsk Russia 58°14N 92°29E 77 D10
Lesotho ■ Africa 29°40S 28°0E 97 K5
Lesser Antilles W. Indies 15°0N 61°0W 115 E12
Lesser Slave L. Canada 55°30N 115°25W 108 C5
Lesser Sunda Is. Indonesia 8°0S 120°0E 83 F6
Leszno Poland 51°50N 16°30E 65 C9
Letchworth Garden City U.K. 51°59N 0°13W 31 C8
Lethbridge Canada 49°45N 112°45W 108 E8
Leti, Kepulauan Indonesia 8°10S 128°0E 83 F7
Leticia Colombia 4°9S 70°0W 120 C2
Letterkenny Ireland 54°57N 7°45W 18 B6
Leuchars U.K. 56°24N 2°53W 25 B10
Leuven Belgium 50°52N 4°42E 64 C3
Leven E. Riding, U.K. 53°53N 0°18W 27 E8
Leven Fife, U.K. 56°12N 3°0W 25 B10
Leven → U.K. 54°31N 1°19W 26 C6
Leven, L. Highl., U.K. 56°42N 5°6W 22 J7
Leven, L. Perth & Kinr., U.K. 56°12N 3°22W 25 B9
Lévis Canada 46°48N 71°9W 113 B12
Lewes U.K. 50°52N 0°1E 31 E9
Lewis U.K. 58°9N 6°40W 22 F4
Lewis, Butt of U.K. 58°31N 6°16W 22 E5
Lewisham □ U.K. 51°27N 0°1W 31 D8
Lewisporte Canada 49°15N 55°3W 109 E14
Lewiston Idaho, U.S.A. 46°25N 117°1W 110 A3
Lewiston Maine, U.S.A. 44°6N 70°13W 113 C12
Lewistown Mont., U.S.A. 47°4N 109°26W 110 A5
Lewistown Pa., U.S.A. 40°36N 77°34W 112 E9
Lexington U.S.A. 38°3N 84°30W 112 F5
Lexington Park U.S.A. 38°16N 76°27W 112 F9
Leyburn U.K. 54°19N 1°48W 26 D5
Leyland U.K. 53°42N 2°43W 27 E3
Leysdown on Sea U.K. 51°24N 0°56E 31 D10
Leyte Phil. 11°0N 125°0E 83 B6
Lhasa China 29°25N 90°58E 78 F7
Lhokseumawe Indonesia 5°10N 97°10E 82 C1
L'Hospitalet de Llobregat Spain 41°21N 2°6E 67 B7
Liancourt Rocks Asia 37°15N 131°52E 81 E2
Lianyungang China 34°40N 119°11E 79 E12
Liaodong Pen. China 40°0N 122°30E 79 D13
Liaoning □ China 41°40N 122°30E 79 C13
Liaotung, G. of China 40°20N 121°10E 79 C13
Liaoyang China 41°15N 122°58E 79 C13
Liaoyuan China 42°58N 125°2E 79 C14
Liard → Canada 61°51N 121°18W 108 C7
Liberal U.S.A. 37°3N 100°55W 110 C6
Liberec Czech Rep. 50°47N 15°7E 64 C8
Liberia ■ W. Afr. 6°30N 9°30W 94 G4
Libourne France 44°55N 0°14W 66 D3
Libreville Gabon 0°25N 9°26E 96 D1
Libya ■ N. Afr. 27°0N 17°0E 95 C9
Libyan Desert Africa 25°0N 25°0E 95 C10
Libyan Plateau Egypt 30°40N 26°30E 95 B11
Lichfield U.K. 52°41N 1°49W 27 G5
Lichinga Mozam. 13°13S 35°11E 97 G7
Liddesdale U.K. 55°14N 2°50W 25 D10
Liechtenstein ■ Europe 47°8N 9°35E 64 E5
Liège Belgium 50°38N 5°35E 64 C3
Liepāja Latvia 56°30N 21°0E 63 F8
Liffey → Ireland 53°21N 6°13W 21 B10

Lifford Ireland 54°51N 7°29W 18 B7
Liguria □ Italy 44°30N 8°50E 68 B3
Ligurian Sea Medit. S. 43°20N 9°0E 68 C3
Lihu'e U.S.A. 21°59N 159°23W 110 H15
Lijiang China 26°55N 100°20E 78 H9
Likasi Dem. Rep. of the Congo 10°55S 26°48E 96 G5
Lille France 50°38N 3°3E 66 A5
Lillehammer Norway 61°8N 10°30E 63 E6
Lilleshall U.K. 52°44N 2°23W 27 G4
Lillongwe Malawi 14°0S 33°48E 97 G6
Lima Peru 12°3S 77°2W 120 D2
Lima U.S.A. 40°44N 84°6W 112 E5
Limassol Cyprus 34°42N 33°1E 86 C3
Limavady U.K. 55°3N 6°56W 19 A8
Limay → Argentina 39°0S 68°0W 121 F3
Limbe Cameroon 4°1N 9°10E 96 D1
Limeira Brazil 22°35S 47°28W 122 D1
Limerick Ireland 52°40N 8°37W 20 C5
Limerick □ Ireland 52°30N 8°50W 20 C5
Limfjorden Denmark 56°55N 9°0E 63 F5
Limnos Greece 39°50N 25°5E 69 E11
Limoges France 45°50N 1°15E 66 D4
Limón Costa Rica 10°0N 83°2W 115 F8
Limousin □ France 45°30N 1°30E 66 D4
Limoux France 43°4N 2°12E 66 E5
Limpopo → Africa 25°5S 33°30E 97 K6
Linares Chile 35°50S 71°40W 121 F2
Linares Mexico 24°52N 99°34W 114 C5
Linares Spain 38°10N 3°40W 67 C4
Linchuan China 27°57N 116°15E 79 F12
Lincoln U.K. 53°14N 0°32W 27 F7
Lincoln Ill., U.S.A. 40°9N 89°22W 112 E3
Lincoln Maine, U.S.A. 45°22N 68°30W 113 C13
Lincoln Nebr., U.S.A. 40°49N 96°41W 111 B7
Lincoln Sea Arctic 84°0N 55°0W 54 A5
Lincolnshire □ U.K. 53°14N 0°32W 27 F7
Lincolnshire Wolds U.K. 53°26N 0°13W 27 F8
Lindale U.K. 54°14N 2°53W 26 D3
Lindesnes Norway 57°58N 7°3E 63 F5
Lindsay Canada 44°22N 78°43W 112 C8
Linfen China 36°3N 111°30E 79 D11
Lingfield U.K. 51°11N 0°1W 31 D8
Lingga, Kepulauan Indonesia 0°10S 104°30E 82 E2
Linhares Brazil 19°25S 40°4W 122 C2
Linhe China 40°48N 107°20E 78 C10
Linkinhorne U.K. 50°32N 4°24W 29 F5
Linköping Sweden 58°28N 15°36E 63 F7
Linnhe, L. U.K. 56°36N 5°25W 24 A5
Linslade U.K. 51°54N 0°41W 31 C7
Linstead Jamaica 18°8N 77°2W 114 a
Linton U.K. 52°6N 0°17E 31 B9
Linton U.S.A. 39°2N 87°10W 112 F4
Linxi China 43°36N 118°2E 79 C12
Linxia China 35°36N 103°10E 78 D9
Linyi China 35°5N 118°21E 79 D12
Linz Austria 48°18N 14°18E 64 D8
Lion, G. du France 43°10N 4°0E 66 E6
Lipa Phil. 13°57N 121°10E 83 B6
Lipari Italy 38°26N 14°58E 68 E6
Lipetsk Russia 52°37N 39°35E 70 D6
Lippe → Germany 51°39N 6°36E 64 C4
Lisbon Portugal 38°42N 9°8W 67 C1
Lisburn U.K. 54°31N 6°3W 19 B9
Liscannor B. Ireland 52°55N 9°24W 20 C4
Lisianski I. U.S.A. 26°2N 174°0W 102 E10
Lisieux France 49°10N 0°12E 66 B4
Liskeard U.K. 50°27N 4°29W 29 G5
Liski Russia 51°3N 39°30E 71 D6
Lismore Australia 28°44S 153°21E 98 F9
Lismore Ireland 52°8N 7°55W 21 D7
Liss U.K. 51°2N 0°54W 31 D7
Listowel Canada 43°44N 80°58W 112 D7
Listowel Ireland 52°27N 9°29W 20 D4
Litani → Lebanon 33°20N 35°15E 86 C3
Litcham U.K. 52°44N 0°47E 31 A10
Litchfield U.S.A. 39°11N 89°39W 112 F3
Litherland U.K. 53°29N 2°59W 27 F3
Lithuania ■ Europe 55°30N 24°0E 63 F8
Little Current Canada 45°55N 82°0W 112 C7
Little Khingan Mts. China 49°0N 127°0E 82 B3
Little Minch U.K. 57°35N 6°45W 22 G4
Little Missouri → U.S.A. 47°36N 102°25W 110 A6
Little Ouse → U.K. 52°22N 1°12E 31 B11
Little Rock U.S.A. 34°45N 92°17W 111 D8
Little Walsingham U.K. 52°54N 0°52E 31 A10
Littlehampton U.K. 50°49N 0°32W 31 E7
Littleport U.K. 52°27N 0°19E 31 B9
Littlestone-on-Sea U.K. 50°58N 0°58E 31 E10
Liupanshui China 26°38N 104°48E 78 F9
Liuwa Plain Zambia 14°20S 22°30E 97 G4
Liuzhou China 24°22N 109°22E 78 G10
Liverpool Canada 44°5N 64°41W 109 E13
Liverpool U.K. 53°25N 3°0W 27 F3
Livingston U.K. 55°54N 3°30W 25 C9
Livingston U.S.A. 45°40N 110°34W 110 A4
Livingstone Zambia 17°46S 25°52E 97 H5
Livonia U.S.A. 42°23N 83°23W 112 D6
Livorno Italy 43°33N 10°19E 68 C4
Lizard U.K. 49°58N 5°13W 29 H3
Lizard Pt. U.K. 49°57N 5°13W 29 H3
Ljubljana Slovenia 46°4N 14°33E 64 E8
Llandeilo U.K. 51°53N 3°59W 28 D6
Llandovery U.K. 51°59N 3°48W 28 D6
Llandrindod Wells U.K. 52°14N 3°22W 28 C7
Llandudno U.K. 53°19N 3°50W 28 A6
Llanelli U.K. 51°41N 4°10W 28 D5
Llanerchymedd U.K. 53°20N 4°23W 28 A5
Llanfair Caereinion U.K. 52°30N 3°20W 28 B7
Llanfair Talhaiarn U.K. 53°13N 3°37W 28 A6
Llanfair-ym-Muallt = Builth Wells
    U.K. 52°9N 3°25W 28 C7
Llanfairfechan U.K. 53°15N 3°58W 28 A6
Llangefni U.K. 53°15N 4°18W 28 A5
Llangollen U.K. 52°58N 3°11W 28 B7
Llanidloes U.K. 52°27N 3°31W 28 C6
Llanllyfni U.K. 53°2N 4°17W 28 A5
Llano Estacado U.S.A. 33°30N 103°0W 110 D6
Llanos S. Amer. 5°0N 71°0W 120 B3
Llanquihue, L. Chile 41°10S 72°50W 121 G2
Llanrhystyd U.K. 52°19N 4°7W 28 C5

Llantrisant U.K. 51°32N 3°22W 29 D7
Llantwit Major U.K. 51°24N 3°29W 29 E7
Llanwrtyd Wells U.K. 52°7N 3°39W 28 C6
Llanyblodwel U.K. 52°48N 3°8W 28 B7
Llanymynech U.K. 52°47N 3°5W 28 B7
Lleida Spain 41°37N 0°39E 67 B6
Lleyn Peninsula U.K. 52°51N 4°36W 28 B4
Llobregat → Spain 41°19N 2°5E 67 B7
Lloret de Mar Spain 41°41N 2°53E 67 B7
Lloydminster Canada 53°17N 110°0W 108 D7
Llullaillaco, Volcán S. Amer. 24°43S 68°30W 121 E3
Lobatse Botswana 25°12S 25°40E 97 K5
Lobito Angola 12°18S 13°35E 97 G2
Loch Lomond and the Trossachs △
    U.K. 56°10N 4°40W 24 B6
Lochaber U.K. 56°59N 5°1W 22 J7
Locharbriggs U.K. 55°7N 3°35W 25 D8
Lochboisdale U.K. 57°9N 7°20W 22 H3
Loches France 47°7N 1°0E 66 C4
Lochgelly U.K. 56°7N 3°19W 25 B9
Lochgilphead U.K. 56°2N 5°26W 24 B5
Lochinver U.K. 58°9N 5°14W 22 F7
Lochmaben U.K. 55°8N 3°27W 25 D9
Lochmaddy U.K. 57°36N 7°10W 22 G3
Lochnagar U.K. 56°57N 3°15W 23 J11
Lochy, L. U.K. 57°0N 4°53W 23 J9
Lock Haven U.S.A. 41°8N 77°28W 112 E9
Lockerbie U.K. 55°7N 3°21W 25 D9
Loddon U.K. 52°32N 1°31E 31 A12
Lodwar Kenya 3°7N 35°36E 96 D7
Łódź Poland 51°45N 19°27E 65 C10
Lofoten Norway 68°30N 13°59E 63 D6
Loftus U.K. 54°34N 0°53W 26 C7
Logan Ohio, U.S.A. 39°32N 82°25W 112 F6
Logan Utah, U.S.A. 41°44N 111°50W 110 B4
Logan W. Va., U.S.A. 37°51N 81°59W 112 G7
Logan, Mt. Canada 60°34N 140°23W 108 C5
Logansport U.S.A. 40°45N 86°22W 112 E4
Logroño Spain 42°28N 2°27W 67 A4
Lohardaga India 23°27N 84°45E 85 H14
Loir → France 47°33N 0°32W 66 C3
Loire → France 47°16N 2°10W 66 C2
Loja Ecuador 3°59S 79°16W 120 C2
Lomami →
    Dem. Rep. of the Congo 0°46N 24°16E 96 D4
Lombárdia □ Italy 45°40N 9°30E 68 B3
Lomblen Indonesia 8°30S 123°32E 83 F6
Lombok Indonesia 8°45S 116°30E 82 F5
Lomé Togo 6°9N 1°20E 94 G6
Lomela →
    Dem. Rep. of the Congo 0°15S 20°40E 96 E4
Lomond, L. U.K. 56°8N 4°38W 24 B6
Łomża Poland 53°10N 22°2E 65 B12
London Canada 42°59N 81°15W 112 D7
London U.K. 51°30N 0°3W 31 D8
London Gateway U.K. 51°31N 0°29E 31 C10
London Gatwick ✈ (LGW)
    U.K. 51°10N 0°11W 31 D8
London Heathrow ✈ (LHR)
    U.K. 51°28N 0°27W 31 D8
London Stansted ✈ (STN) U.K. 51°54N 0°14E 31 C9
Londonderry U.K. 55°0N 7°20W 18 A7
Londonderry □ U.K. 55°0N 7°20W 19 B7
Londonderry, C. Australia 13°45S 126°55E 98 C4
Londrina Brazil 23°18S 51°10W 121 E4
Long, C. U.S.A. 56°4N 9°50W 26 B3
Long Beach U.S.A. 33°46N 118°11W 110 D3
Long Bennington U.K. 52°59N 0°44W 27 G7
Long Branch U.S.A. 40°18N 74°0W 113 E11
Long Clawson U.K. 52°50N 0°56W 27 G7
Long Crendon U.K. 51°46N 0°59W 31 C7
Long Eaton U.K. 52°53N 1°15W 27 G6
Long I. Bahamas 23°20N 75°10W 115 C9
Long I. Ireland 51°30N 9°34W 20 E3
Long I. U.S.A. 40°45N 73°30W 113 E11
Long Itchington U.K. 52°16N 1°22W 30 B6
Long Melford U.K. 52°4N 0°45E 31 B10
Long Mynd, The U.K. 52°35N 2°50W 27 G3
Long Preston U.K. 54°2N 2°14W 27 D4
Long Sutton U.K. 52°48N 0°7E 27 G9
Long Xuyen Vietnam 10°19N 105°28E 82 B3
Longford Ireland 53°43N 7°49W 18 D6
Longford □ Ireland 53°42N 7°45W 18 D6
Longframlington U.K. 55°18N 1°47W 26 B5
Longhoughton U.K. 55°26N 1°37W 26 B5
Longhua China 22°39N 114°0E 79 a
Longlac Canada 49°45N 86°25W 112 A4
Longreach Australia 23°28S 144°14E 98 E7
Longridge U.K. 53°50N 2°35W 27 E3
Longton U.K. 53°44N 2°48W 27 E3
Longtown Cumb., U.K. 55°1N 2°58W 26 B3
Longtown Hereford, U.K. 51°58N 2°59W 30 C3
Longueuil Canada 45°31N 73°29W 113 C11
Longview Tex., U.S.A. 32°30N 94°44W 111 D8
Longview Wash., U.S.A. 46°8N 122°57W 110 A2
Longyan China 25°10N 117°0E 79 F12
Lons-le-Saunier France 46°40N 5°31E 66 C6
Looe U.K. 50°22N 4°28W 29 G5
Loop Hd. Ireland 52°34N 9°56W 20 D3
Lop China 37°3N 80°11E 78 D5
Lop Nur China 40°20N 90°10E 78 C7
Lopez, C. Gabon 0°47S 8°40E 90 G4
Lorain U.S.A. 41°28N 82°11W 112 E6
Loralai Pakistan 30°20N 68°41E 84 D6
Lorca Spain 37°41N 1°42W 67 D5
Lord Howe I. Pac. Oc. 31°33S 159°6E 99 G10
Lord Howe Rise Pac. Oc. 30°0S 162°30E 99 H12
Lordsburg U.S.A. 32°21N 108°43W 110 D5
Lorestān □ Iran 33°30N 48°40E 86 C7
Lorient France 47°45N 3°23W 66 C2
Lorn U.K. 56°26N 5°10W 24 B5
Lorn, Firth of U.K. 56°20N 5°40W 24 B4
Lorraine □ France 48°53N 6°0E 64 D3
Los Alamos U.S.A. 35°53N 106°19W 110 C5
Los Andes Chile 32°50S 70°40W 121 F2
Los Angeles Chile 37°28S 72°23W 121 F2
Los Angeles U.S.A. 34°4N 118°15W 110 D3
Los Roques, Is. Venezuela 11°50N 66°45W 120 A3

Lossiemouth U.K. 57°42N 3°17W 23 G11
Lostwithiel U.K. 50°24N 4°41W 29 G4
Lot → France 44°18N 0°20E 66 D4
Lota Chile 37°5S 73°10W 121 F2
Loubomo Congo 4°9S 12°47E 96 E2
Loughborough U.K. 52°47N 1°11W 27 G6
Lougheed I. Canada 77°26N 105°6W 109 B9
Loughrea Ireland 53°12N 8°33W 20 B5
Loughros More B. Ireland 54°48N 8°32W 18 B4
Louis XIV, Pte. Canada 54°37N 79°45W 109 D12
Louisa U.S.A. 38°7N 82°36W 112 F6
Louisiade Arch. Papua N. G. 11°10S 153°0E 98 C9
Louisiana □ U.S.A. 30°50N 92°0W 111 D8
Louisville U.S.A. 38°15N 85°46W 112 F5
Lourdes France 43°6N 0°3W 66 E3
Louth Ireland 53°58N 6°32W 19 D8
Louth U.K. 53°22N 0°1W 27 F8
Louth □ Ireland 53°56N 6°34W 19 D8
Lovech Bulgaria 43°8N 24°42E 69 C11
Lowell U.S.A. 42°38N 71°19W 113 D12
Lower Beeding U.K. 51°2N 0°15W 31 D8
Lower Saxony = Niedersachsen □
    Germany 52°50N 9°0E 64 B5
Lower Tunguska → Russia 65°48N 88°4E 77 C9
Lowestoft U.K. 52°29N 1°45E 31 B12
Lowther Hills U.K. 55°20N 3°40W 25 D8
Lowick U.K. 55°39N 1°57W 26 A5
Lowther Hills U.K. 55°20N 3°40W 25 D8
Loyauté, Îs. N. Cal. 20°50S 166°30E 99 E12
Lu Wo China 22°33N 114°6E 79 a
Lualaba →
    Dem. Rep. of the Congo 0°26N 25°20E 96 D5
Lu'an China 31°45N 116°29E 79 E12
Luanda Angola 8°50S 13°15E 96 F2
Luangwa → Zambia 14°25S 30°25E 97 G6
Luanshya Zambia 13°3S 28°28E 96 G5
Luapula → Africa 9°26S 28°33E 96 F5
Lubango Angola 14°55S 13°30E 97 G2
Lubbock U.S.A. 33°35N 101°51W 110 D6
Lübeck Germany 53°52N 10°40E 64 B6
Lublin Poland 51°12N 22°38E 65 C12
Lubumbashi
    Dem. Rep. of the Congo 11°40S 27°28E 97 G5
Lucan Ireland 53°22N 6°28W 21 B10
Lucania, Mt. Canada 61°1N 140°27W 108 C5
Lucca Italy 43°50N 10°29E 68 C4
Luce Bay U.K. 54°45N 4°48W 24 E6
Lucea Jamaica 18°27N 78°10W 114 a
Lucena Phil. 13°56N 121°37E 83 B6
Lucknow India 26°50N 81°0E 85 F12
Luda = Dalian China 38°50N 121°40E 79 D13
Lüderitz Namibia 26°41S 15°8E 97 K3
Ludgershall U.K. 51°15N 1°37W 30 D5
Ludgvan U.K. 50°9N 5°30W 29 G2
Ludhiana India 30°57N 75°56E 84 D9
Ludington U.S.A. 43°57N 86°27W 112 D4
Ludlow U.K. 52°22N 2°42W 27 H3
Ludwigsburg Germany 48°53N 9°11E 64 D5
Ludwigshafen Germany 49°29N 8°26E 64 D5
Lufkin U.S.A. 31°21N 94°44W 111 D8
Luga Russia 58°40N 29°55E 70 C4
Lugano Switz. 46°1N 8°57E 64 E5
Lugansk Ukraine 48°38N 39°15E 71 E6
Lugnaquilla Ireland 52°58N 6°28W 21 C10
Lugo Spain 43°2N 7°35W 67 A2
Lugwardine U.K. 52°4N 2°39W 30 B3
Luing U.K. 56°14N 5°39W 24 B4
Luleå Sweden 65°35N 22°10E 63 D8
Luleälven → Sweden 65°35N 22°10E 63 D8
Lundy U.K. 51°10N 4°41W 29 E4
Lune → U.K. 54°0N 2°51W 27 D3
Lüneburger Heide Germany 53°10N 10°12E 64 B6
Lunéville France 48°36N 6°30E 64 D7
Luni → India 24°41N 71°14E 84 G7
Luofu Dem. Rep. of the Congo 0°10S 29°15E 96 E5
Luoyang China 34°40N 112°26E 79 E11
Luray U.S.A. 38°40N 78°28W 112 F8
Lurgan U.K. 54°27N 6°20W 19 B9
Lusaka Zambia 15°28S 28°16E 97 H5
Lūt, Dasht-e Iran 31°30N 58°0E 87 D9
Lutherstadt Wittenberg
    Germany 51°53N 12°39E 64 C7
Luton U.K. 51°53N 0°24W 31 C8
Łutsel K'e Canada 62°24N 110°44W 108 C8
Lutsk Ukraine 50°50N 25°15E 65 C13
Lutterworth U.K. 52°28N 1°12W 27 H6
Luvua → Dem. Rep. of the Congo 6°50S 27°30E 96 F5
Luxembourg Lux. 49°37N 6°9E 64 D4
Luxembourg ■ Europe 49°45N 6°0E 64 D4
Luxor = El Uqsur Egypt 25°41N 32°38E 95 C12
Luzern Switz. 47°3N 8°18E 64 E5
Luzhou China 28°52N 105°20E 78 F10
Luziânia Brazil 16°20S 48°0W 122 C2
Luzon Phil. 16°0N 121°0E 83 A6
Lvov Ukraine 49°50N 24°0E 65 D13
Lyakhov Is. Russia 73°40N 141°0E 77 B15
Lybster U.K. 58°18N 3°15W 23 F11
Lydd U.K. 50°57N 0°55E 31 E10
Lydford U.K. 50°38N 4°8W 29 F5
Lydham U.K. 52°31N 2°58W 27 H3
Lyme B. U.K. 50°42N 2°53W 30 E3
Lyme Regis U.K. 50°43N 2°57W 30 E3
Lyminge U.K. 51°7N 1°6E 31 D11
Lymington U.K. 50°45N 1°32W 30 E5
Lympne U.K. 51°4N 1°2E 31 D11
Lynchburg U.S.A. 37°25N 79°9W 112 G8
Lyndhurst U.K. 50°52N 1°35W 30 E5
Lyneham U.K. 51°31N 1°59W 30 C5
Lynmouth U.K. 51°13N 3°49W 29 E6
Lynn Lake Canada 56°51N 101°3W 108 D9
Lynton U.K. 51°13N 3°50W 29 E6
Lyonnais France 45°45N 4°15E 66 D6
Lyons France 45°46N 4°50E 66 D6
Lysva Russia 58°7N 57°49E 70 C10
Lysychansk Ukraine 48°55N 38°30E 71 E6
Lytchett Minster U.K. 50°44N 2°4W 30 E4
Lytham St. Anne's U.K. 53°45N 3°0W 27 E2
Lythe U.K. 54°31N 0°41W 26 C7
Lyubertsy Russia 55°40N 37°51E 70 C6

M

Ma'ān *Jordan* 30°12N 35°44E **86** D3
Maas → *Neths.* 51°45N 4°32E **64** C3
Maastricht *Neths.* 50°50N 5°40E **64** C3
Mablethorpe *U.K.* 53°20N 0°15E **27** F9
Macaé *Brazil* 22°20S 41°43W **122** D2
McAlester *U.S.A.* 34°56N 95°46W **111** D7
McAllen *U.S.A.* 26°12N 98°14W **110** E7
MacAlpine L. *Canada* 66°32N 102°45W **108** C9
Macapá *Brazil* 0°5N 51°4W **120** B4
Macau *Brazil* 5°15S 36°40W **120** C6
Macau *China* 22°12N 113°33E **79** a
Macclesfield *U.K.* 53°15N 2°8W **27** F4
M'Clintock Chan. *Canada* 72°0N 102°0W **108** B9
M'Clure Str. *Canada* 75°0N 119°0W **109** B8
McComb *U.S.A.* 31°15N 90°27W **111** D8
McCook *U.S.A.* 40°12N 100°38W **110** B6
McDonald Is. *Ind. Oc.* 53°0S 73°0E **53** G13
MacDonnell Ranges *Australia* 23°40S 133°0E **98** E5
Macduff *U.K.* 57°40N 2°31W **23** G12
Macedonia □ *Greece* 40°39N 22°0E **69** D10
Macedonia ■ *Europe* 41°53N 21°40E **69** D9
Maceió *Brazil* 9°40S 35°41W **122** A3
Macgillycuddy's Reeks *Ireland* 51°58N 9°45W **20** E3
Mach *Pakistan* 29°50N 67°20E **84** E5
Machakos *Kenya* 1°30S 37°15E **96** E7
Machala *Ecuador* 3°20S 79°57W **120** C2
Machars, The *U.K.* 54°46N 4°30W **24** E6
Machias *U.S.A.* 44°43N 67°28W **113** C14
Machilipatnam *India* 16°12N 81°8E **85** L12
Machrihanish *U.K.* 55°25N 5°43W **24** D4
Machu Picchu *Peru* 13°8S 72°30W **120** D2
Machynlleth *U.K.* 52°35N 3°50W **28** B6
Mackay *Australia* 21°8S 149°11E **98** E8
Mackay, L. *Australia* 22°30S 129°0E **98** E4
McKeesport *U.S.A.* 40°20N 79°51W **112** E8
Mackenzie *Canada* 55°20N 123°5W **108** D7
Mackenzie → *Canada* 69°10N 134°20W **108** C6
Mackenzie King I. *Canada* 77°45N 111°0W **109** B8
Mackenzie Mts. *Canada* 64°0N 130°0W **108** B6
Mackinaw City *U.S.A.* 45°47N 84°44W **112** C5
McKinley, Mt. *U.S.A.* 63°4N 151°0W **108** C4
McKinley Sea *Arctic* 82°0N 0°0 **54** A7
McMinnville *U.S.A.* 45°13N 123°12W **110** A2
McMurdo Sd. *Antarctica* 77°0S 170°0E **55** D11
Macomb *U.S.A.* 40°27N 90°40W **112** E2
Mâcon *France* 46°19N 4°50E **66** C6
Macon *U.S.A.* 32°51N 83°38W **111** D10
McPherson *U.S.A.* 38°22N 97°40W **110** C7
Macquarie I. *Pac. Oc.* 54°36S 158°55E **102** N7
Macroom *Ireland* 51°54N 8°57W **20** E5
Madagascar ■ *Africa* 20°0S 47°0E **97** J9
Madang *Papua N. G.* 5°12S 145°49E **98** B8
Madeira *Atl. Oc.* 32°50N 17°0W **94** B2
Madeira → *Brazil* 3°22S 58°45W **120** C4
Madeleine, Îs. de la *Canada* 47°30N 61°40W **113** B17
Madeley *U.K.* 53°0N 2°20W **27** F4
Madhya Pradesh □ *India* 22°50N 78°0E **84** H11
Madison *Ind., U.S.A.* 38°44N 85°23W **112** F5
Madison *S. Dak., U.S.A.* 44°0N 97°7W **111** B7
Madison *Wis., U.S.A.* 43°4N 89°24W **112** D3
Madisonville *U.S.A.* 37°20N 87°30W **112** G4
Madiun *Indonesia* 7°38S 111°32E **82** F4
Madley *U.K.* 52°2N 2°51W **30** B3
Madras = Chennai *India* 13°8N 80°19E **84** N12
Madre de Dios → *Bolivia* 10°59S 66°8W **120** D3
Madre de Dios, I. *Chile* 50°20S 75°10W **121** H2
Madre Occidental, Sierra *Mexico* 27°0N 107°0W **114** B3
Madre Oriental, Sierra *Mexico* 25°0N 100°0W **114** C5
Madrid *Spain* 40°24N 3°42W **67** B4
Madura *Indonesia* 7°30S 114°0E **82** F4
Madurai *India* 9°55N 78°10E **84** Q11
Maebashi *Japan* 36°24N 139°4E **81** E6
Maesteg *U.K.* 51°36N 3°40W **29** D6
Mafeking *S. Africa* 25°50S 25°38E **97** K5
Mafia I. *Tanzania* 7°45S 39°50E **96** F7
Magadan *Russia* 59°38N 150°50E **77** D16
Magallanes, Estrecho de *Chile* 52°30S 75°0W **121** H2
Magangué *Colombia* 9°14N 74°45W **120** B2
Magdalena → *Colombia* 11°6N 74°51W **120** A2
Magdeburg *Germany* 52°7N 11°38E **64** B6
Magee Isle *U.K.* 54°48N 5°43W **19** B10
Magelang *Indonesia* 7°29S 110°13E **82** F4
Magellan's Str. = Magallanes, Estrecho de *Chile* 52°30S 75°0W **121** H2
Maggiore, L. *Italy* 45°57N 8°39E **68** B3
Maggotty *Jamaica* 18°9N 77°46W **114** a
Maghâgha *Egypt* 28°38N 30°50E **95** C12
Magherafelt *U.K.* 54°45N 6°37W **19** B8
Maghreb *N. Afr.* 32°0N 4°0W **90** C3
Maghull *U.K.* 53°31N 2°57W **27** E3
Magnetic Pole (North) *Arctic* 85°9N 149°0W **54** A2
Magnetic Pole (South) *Antarctica* 64°8S 138°8E **55** C9
Magnitogorsk *Russia* 53°27N 59°4E **70** D10
Magog *Canada* 45°18N 72°9W **113** C11
Magwe *Burma* 20°10N 95°0E **85** J19
Mahābād *Iran* 36°50N 45°45E **86** B6
Mahajanga *Madag.* 15°40S 46°25E **97** H9
Mahakam → *Indonesia* 0°35S 117°17E **82** E5
Mahalapye *Botswana* 23°1S 26°51E **97** J5
Maḥallāt *Iran* 33°55N 50°30E **87** C7
Mahanadi → *India* 20°20N 86°25E **85** J15
Maharashtra □ *India* 20°30N 75°30E **84** J9
Mahdia *Tunisia* 35°28N 11°0E **95** A8
Mahesana *India* 23°39N 72°26E **84** H8
Mahilyow *Belarus* 53°55N 30°18E **65** B16
Mai-Ndombe, L. *Dem. Rep. of the Congo* 2°0S 18°20E **96** E3
Maiden Bradley *U.K.* 51°9N 2°17W **30** D4
Maiden Newton *U.K.* 50°46N 2°34W **30** E3
Maidenhead *U.K.* 51°31N 0°42W **31** C7
Maidstone *U.K.* 51°16N 0°32E **31** D10
Maiduguri *Nigeria* 12°0N 13°20E **95** F8
Main → *Germany* 50°0N 8°18E **64** C5
Main → *U.K.* 54°48N 6°18W **19** B9
Maine *France* 48°20N 0°15W **66** C3
Maine □ *U.S.A.* 45°20N 69°0W **113** C13
Maine → *Ireland* 52°9N 9°45W **20** D3
Mainland *Orkney, U.K.* 58°59N 3°8W **23** E11
Mainland *Shet., U.K.* 60°15N 1°22W **22** B15
Mainz *Germany* 50°1N 8°14E **64** C5
Maiquetía *Venezuela* 10°36N 66°57W **120** A3
Majorca = Mallorca *Spain* 39°30N 3°0E **67** C7
Majuro *Marshall Is.* 7°9N 171°12E **102** G9
Makale *Indonesia* 3°6S 119°51E **83** E5
Makalu *Nepal* 27°55N 87°8E **78** F6
Makassar *Indonesia* 5°10S 119°20E **83** F5
Makassar, Str. of *Indonesia* 1°0S 118°20E **83** E5
Makgadikgadi Salt Pans *Botswana* 20°40S 25°45E **97** J5
Makhachkala *Russia* 43°0N 47°30E **71** F8
Makhado *S. Africa* 23°1S 29°43E **97** J5
Makran Coast Range *Pakistan* 25°40N 64°0E **84** G4
Makurdi *Nigeria* 7°43N 8°35E **94** G7
Mal B. *Ireland* 52°50N 9°30W **20** C4
Malabar Coast *India* 11°0N 75°0E **84** P9
Malacca, Straits of *Indonesia* 3°0N 101°0E **82** D2
Málaga *Spain* 36°43N 4°23W **67** D3
Malahide *Ireland* 53°26N 6°9W **21** B10
Malaita *Solomon Is.* 9°0S 161°0E **99** B11
Malakal *South Sudan* 9°33N 31°40E **95** G12
Malakula *Vanuatu* 16°15S 167°30E **99** D12
Malang *Indonesia* 7°59S 112°45E **82** F4
Malanje *Angola* 9°36S 16°17E **96** F3
Mälaren *Sweden* 59°30N 17°10E **63** F7
Malatya *Turkey* 38°25N 38°20E **71** G6
Malawi ■ *Africa* 11°55S 34°0E **97** G6
Malawi, L. *Africa* 12°30S 34°30E **97** G6
Malay Pen. *Asia* 7°25N 100°0E **72** H12
Malāyer *Iran* 34°19N 48°51E **86** C7
Malaysia ■ *Asia* 5°0N 110°0E **82** D4
Malden *U.S.A.* 36°34N 89°57W **112** G3
Malden I. *Kiribati* 4°3S 155°1W **103** H12
Maldives ■ *Ind. Oc.* 5°0N 73°0E **73** H9
Maldon *U.K.* 51°44N 0°42E **31** C10
Maldonado *Uruguay* 34°59S 55°0W **121** F4
Malegaon *India* 20°30N 74°38E **84** J9
Malham Tarn *U.K.* 54°6N 2°10W **26** D4
Malheur L. *U.S.A.* 43°20N 118°48W **110** B3
Mali ■ *Africa* 17°0N 3°0W **94** E5
Malin Hd. *Ireland* 55°23N 7°23W **18** A7
Malin Pen. *Ireland* 55°20N 7°17W **19** A7
Malindi *Kenya* 3°12S 40°5E **96** E8
Mallaig *U.K.* 57°0N 5°50W **22** H6
Mallawi *Egypt* 27°44N 30°44E **95** C12
Mallorca *Spain* 39°30N 3°0E **67** C7
Mallow *Ireland* 52°8N 8°39W **20** D5
Malmesbury *U.K.* 51°35N 2°5W **30** C4
Malmö *Sweden* 55°36N 12°59E **63** F6
Malone *U.S.A.* 44°51N 74°18W **113** C10
Malpas *U.K.* 53°1N 2°45W **27** F3
Malpelo, I. de *Colombia* 4°3N 81°35W **115** G8
Malta ■ *Europe* 35°55N 14°26E **68** a
Maltby *U.K.* 53°25N 1°12W **27** F6
Malton *U.K.* 54°8N 0°49W **26** D7
Malvinas, Is. = Falkland Is. ⊠ *Atl. Oc.* 51°30S 59°0W **121** H4
Mamoré → *Bolivia* 10°23S 65°53W **120** D3
Mamoudzou *Mayotte* 12°48S 45°14E **91** H8
Man *Ivory C.* 7°30N 7°40W **94** G4
Man, I. of *U.K.* 54°15N 4°30W **19** C12
Manacles, The *U.K.* 50°2N 5°4W **29** G3
Manado *Indonesia* 1°29N 124°51E **83** D6
Managua *Nic.* 12°6N 86°20W **114** E7
Manaus *Brazil* 3°0S 60°0W **120** C3
Manby *U.K.* 53°21N 0°6E **27** F9
Manchester *U.K.* 53°29N 2°12W **27** F4
Manchester *U.S.A.* 42°59N 71°28W **113** D12
Manchester Int. ✕ (MAN) *U.K.* 53°21N 2°17W **27** F4
Manchuria *China* 45°0N 125°0E **79** C14
Manchurian Plain *China* 47°0N 124°0E **72** D14
Mandal *Norway* 58°2N 7°25E **63** F5
Mandalay *Burma* 22°0N 96°4E **85** J20
Mandan *U.S.A.* 46°50N 100°54W **110** A6
Mandaue *Phil.* 10°20N 123°56E **83** B6
Mandeville *Jamaica* 18°2N 77°31W **114** a
Mandla *India* 22°39N 80°30E **85** H12
Mandsaur *India* 24°3N 75°8E **84** G9
Mandvi *India* 22°51N 69°22E **84** H6
Manea *U.K.* 52°29N 0°10E **31** B9
Manfalût *Egypt* 27°20N 30°52E **95** C12
Manfredónia *Italy* 41°38N 15°55E **68** D6
Mangabeiras, Chapada das *Brazil* 10°0S 46°30W **122** B1
Mangalore *India* 12°55N 74°47E **84** N9
Mangnai *China* 37°52N 91°43E **78** D7
Mangole *Indonesia* 1°50S 125°55E **83** E6
Mangotsfield *U.K.* 51°29N 2°30W **30** D4
Manhattan *U.S.A.* 39°11N 96°35W **111** C7
Manhuaçu *Brazil* 20°15S 42°2W **122** D2
Manica *Mozam.* 18°58S 32°59E **97** H6
Manicoré *Brazil* 5°48S 61°16W **120** C3
Manicouagan → *Canada* 49°30N 68°30W **109** E13
Manicouagan, Rés. *Canada* 51°5N 68°40W **109** D13
Manihiki *Cook Is.* 10°24S 161°1W **103** J11
Manila *Phil.* 14°35N 120°58E **83** B6
Manipur □ *India* 25°0N 94°0E **85** G19
Manisa *Turkey* 38°38N 27°30E **71** G4
Manistee *U.S.A.* 44°15N 86°19W **112** C4
Manistee → *U.S.A.* 44°15N 86°21W **112** C4
Manistique *U.S.A.* 45°57N 86°15W **112** C4
Manitoba □ *Canada* 53°30N 97°0W **108** D10
Manitoba, L. *Canada* 51°0N 98°45W **108** D10
Manitou Is. *U.S.A.* 45°8N 86°0W **112** C4
Manitoulin I. *Canada* 45°40N 82°30W **112** C6
Manitowoc *U.S.A.* 44°5N 87°40W **112** C4
Manizales *Colombia* 5°5N 75°32W **120** B2
Mankato *U.S.A.* 44°10N 94°0W **111** B8
Mannar *Sri Lanka* 9°1N 79°54E **84** Q11
Mannar, G. of *Asia* 8°30N 79°0E **84** Q11
Mannheim *Germany* 49°29N 8°29E **64** D5
Manning *Canada* 56°53N 117°39W **108** D8
Manningtree *U.K.* 51°56N 1°5E **31** C11
Manokwari *Indonesia* 0°54S 134°0E **83** E8
Manosque *France* 43°49N 5°47E **66** E6
Manresa *Spain* 41°48N 1°50E **67** B6
Mansel I. *Canada* 62°0N 80°0W **109** C12
Mansfield *U.K.* 53°9N 1°11W **27** F6
Mansfield *U.S.A.* 40°45N 82°31W **112** E6
Mansfield Woodhouse *U.K.* 53°11N 1°12W **27** F6
Manta *Ecuador* 1°0S 80°40W **120** C1
Mantes-la-Jolie *France* 48°58N 1°41E **66** B4
Mantiqueira, Serra da *Brazil* 22°0S 44°0W **117** F6
Manton *U.K.* 52°38N 0°41W **27** G7
Manton *U.S.A.* 44°25N 85°24W **112** C5
Mántova *Italy* 45°9N 10°48E **68** B4
Manuel Alves → *Brazil* 11°19S 48°28W **122** B1
Manzai *Pakistan* 32°12N 70°15E **84** C7
Manzanillo *Cuba* 20°20N 77°31W **115** C9
Manzanillo *Mexico* 19°3N 104°20W **114** D4
Manzouli *China* 49°35N 117°25E **79** B12
Maó *Spain* 39°53N 4°16E **67** C8
Maoming *China* 21°50N 110°54E **79** G11
Mapam Yumco *China* 30°45N 81°28E **78** E5
Maputo *Mozam.* 25°58S 32°32E **97** K6
Maputo B. *Mozam.* 25°50S 32°45E **90** J7
Maqên *China* 34°24N 100°6E **78** E9
Maqên Gangri *China* 34°55N 99°18E **78** E8
Maquinchao *Argentina* 41°15S 68°50W **121** G3
Maquoketa *U.S.A.* 42°4N 90°40W **112** D2
Mar *U.K.* 57°11N 2°53W **23** H12
Mar, Serra do *Brazil* 25°30S 49°0W **117** F6
Mar Chiquita, L. *Argentina* 30°40S 62°50W **121** F3
Mar del Plata *Argentina* 38°0S 57°30W **121** F4
Mara Rosa *Brazil* 14°1S 49°11W **122** B1
Marabá *Brazil* 5°20S 49°5W **120** C5
Maracá, I. de *Brazil* 2°10N 50°30W **120** B4
Maracaibo *Venezuela* 10°40N 71°37W **120** A2
Maracaibo, L. de *Venezuela* 9°40N 71°30W **120** B2
Maracay *Venezuela* 10°15N 67°28W **120** A3
Maradi *Niger* 13°29N 7°20E **94** F7
Maragogipe *Brazil* 12°46S 38°55W **122** B3
Marajo, I. de *Brazil* 1°0S 49°30W **120** C5
Maranguape *Brazil* 3°55S 38°50W **120** C6
Maranhão □ *Brazil* 5°0S 46°0W **120** C5
Marañón → *Peru* 4°30S 73°35W **120** C2
Marazion *U.K.* 50°7N 5°29W **29** G3
Marbella *Spain* 36°30N 4°57W **67** D3
March *U.K.* 52°33N 0°5E **31** A9
Marche *France* 46°5N 1°20E **66** C4
Marcus I. *Pac. Oc.* 24°20N 153°58E **102** E7
Mardan *Pakistan* 34°20N 72°0E **84** B8
Marden *U.K.* 52°7N 2°42W **30** B3
Mardin *Turkey* 37°20N 40°43E **71** G7
Maree, L. *U.K.* 57°40N 5°26W **22** G7
Mareham le Fen *U.K.* 53°8N 0°4W **27** F8
Marfleet *U.K.* 53°45N 0°17W **27** E8
Margarita, I. de *Venezuela* 11°0N 64°0W **120** A3
Margate *U.K.* 51°23N 1°23E **31** D11
Marghilon *Uzbekistan* 40°27N 71°42E **87** A12
Mārgow, Dasht-e *Afghan.* 30°40N 62°30E **87** D10
Mari El □ *Russia* 56°30N 48°0E **70** C8
Mariana Trench *Pac. Oc.* 13°0N 145°0E **102** F6
Marías, Is. *Mexico* 21°25N 106°28W **114** C3
Maribor *Slovenia* 46°36N 15°40E **64** E8
Marie Byrd Land *Antarctica* 79°30S 125°0W **55** D14
Mariental *Namibia* 24°36S 18°0E **97** J3
Marietta *U.S.A.* 39°25N 81°27W **112** F7
Marília *Brazil* 22°13S 50°0W **120** E4
Marinette *U.S.A.* 45°6N 87°38W **112** C4
Maringá *Brazil* 23°26S 52°2W **121** E4
Marion *Ill., U.S.A.* 37°44N 88°56W **112** G3
Marion *Ind., U.S.A.* 40°32N 85°40W **112** E5
Marion *Ohio, U.S.A.* 40°35N 83°8W **112** E6
Mariupol *Ukraine* 47°5N 37°31E **71** E6
Marka *Somalia* 1°48N 44°50E **89** G3
Markam *China* 29°42N 98°38E **78** F8
Market Bosworth *U.K.* 52°38N 1°24W **27** G6
Market Deeping *U.K.* 52°41N 0°19W **27** G8
Market Drayton *U.K.* 52°54N 2°29W **27** G4
Market Harborough *U.K.* 52°29N 0°55W **27** H7
Market Lavington *U.K.* 51°17N 1°58W **30** D5
Market Rasen *U.K.* 53°24N 0°20W **27** F8
Market Warsop *U.K.* 53°12N 1°9W **27** F6
Market Weighton *U.K.* 53°52N 0°40W **27** E7
Markfield *U.K.* 52°42N 1°17W **27** G6
Markham, Mt. *Antarctica* 83°0S 164°0E **55** E11
Marks Tey *U.K.* 51°52N 0°49E **31** C10
Marlborough *U.K.* 51°25N 1°43W **30** D5
Marlborough Downs *U.K.* 51°27N 1°53W **30** D5
Marlow *U.K.* 51°34N 0°46W **31** C7
Marmara, Sea of *Turkey* 40°45N 28°15E **71** F4
Marmaris *Turkey* 36°50N 28°14E **86** B2
Marmora *Canada* 44°28N 77°41W **112** C9
Marne → *France* 48°47N 2°29E **66** B5
Marnhull *U.K.* 50°57N 2°19W **30** E4
Maroua *Cameroon* 10°40N 14°20E **95** F8
Marple *U.K.* 53°24N 2°4W **27** F4
Marquette *U.S.A.* 46°33N 87°24W **112** B4
Marquis *St. Lucia* 14°2N 60°54W **114** b
Marquises, Îs. *French Polynesia* 9°30S 140°0W **103** H14
Marrakesh *Morocco* 31°9N 8°0W **94** B4
Marree *Australia* 29°39S 138°1E **98** F6
Marsá Matrûh *Egypt* 31°19N 27°9E **95** B11
Marsabit *Kenya* 2°18N 38°0E **96** D7
Marsala *Italy* 37°48N 12°26E **68** F5
Marseilles *France* 43°18N 5°23E **66** E6
Marsh I. *U.S.A.* 29°34N 91°53W **111** E8
Marshall *U.S.A.* 32°33N 94°23W **111** D8
Marshall Is. ■ *Pac. Oc.* 9°0N 171°0E **102** G9
Marshfield *U.K.* 51°28N 2°19W **30** D4
Marshfield *U.S.A.* 44°40N 90°10W **112** C2
Marske-by-the-Sea *U.K.* 54°36N 1°0W **26** C7
Marston Moor *U.K.* 53°58N 1°17W **27** E6
Martaban *Burma* 16°30N 97°35E **85** L20
Martaban, G. of *Burma* 16°5N 96°30E **85** L20
Martapura *Indonesia* 3°22S 114°47E **82** E4
Martham *U.K.* 52°42N 1°37E **31** A12
Martha's Vineyard *U.S.A.* 41°25N 70°38W **113** E12
Martigues *France* 43°24N 5°4E **66** E6
Martinique ⊠ *W. Indies* 14°40N 61°0W **115** E12
Martins Bay *Barbados* 13°12N 59°29W **114** c
Martinsburg *U.S.A.* 39°27N 77°58W **112** F9
Martinsville *U.S.A.* 39°26N 86°25W **112** F4
Martley *U.K.* 52°15N 2°21W **30** B4
Martock *U.K.* 50°58N 2°46W **30** E3
Marwar *India* 25°43N 73°45E **84** G8
Mary *Turkmenistan* 37°40N 61°50E **87** B10
Maryborough *Australia* 25°31S 152°37E **98** F9
Maryland □ *U.S.A.* 39°0N 76°30W **112** F9
Maryport *U.K.* 54°44N 3°28W **26** C2
Marystown *Canada* 47°10N 55°10W **109** E14
Marytavy *U.K.* 50°36N 4°7W **29** F5
Masai Steppe *Tanzania* 4°30S 36°30E **96** E7
Masan *S. Korea* 35°11N 128°32E **79** D14
Masandam, Ra's *Oman* 26°30N 56°30E **89** B6
Masaya *Nic.* 12°0N 86°7W **114** E7
Masbate *Phil.* 12°21N 123°36E **83** B6
Mascara *Algeria* 35°26N 0°6E **94** A6
Maseru *Lesotho* 29°18S 27°30E **97** K5
Masham *U.K.* 54°14N 1°39W **26** D5
Mashhad *Iran* 36°20N 59°35E **87** B9
Mashonaland *Zimbabwe* 16°30S 31°0E **97** H6
Maşīrah, Jazīrat *Oman* 21°0N 58°50E **89** C6
Masjed Soleyman *Iran* 31°55N 49°18E **86** D7
Mask, L. *Ireland* 53°36N 9°22W **18** D3
Mason City *U.S.A.* 43°9N 93°12W **111** B8
Massa *Italy* 44°1N 10°9E **68** B4
Massachusetts □ *U.S.A.* 42°30N 72°0W **113** D11
Massawa *Eritrea* 15°35N 39°25E **89** D2
Massena *U.S.A.* 44°56N 74°54W **113** C10
Massiah Street *Barbados* 13°9N 59°29W **114** c
Massif Central *France* 44°55N 3°0E **66** D5
Massillon *U.S.A.* 40°48N 81°32W **112** E7
Masurian Lakes *Poland* 53°50N 21°0E **65** B11
Masvingo *Zimbabwe* 20°8S 30°49E **97** J6
Mata-Utu *Wall. & F. Is.* 13°17S 176°8W **99** C15
Matabeleland *Zimbabwe* 18°0S 27°0E **97** H5
Matadi *Dem. Rep. of the Congo* 5°52S 13°31E **96** F2
Matagalpa *Nic.* 13°0N 85°58W **114** E7
Matagami *Canada* 49°45N 77°34W **109** E12
Matagami, L. *Canada* 49°50N 77°40W **109** E12
Matagorda I. *U.S.A.* 28°15N 96°30W **111** E7
Matamoros *Coahuila, Mexico* 25°32N 103°15W **114** B5
Matamoros *Tamaulipas, Mexico* 25°53N 97°30W **114** B5
Matane *Canada* 48°50N 67°33W **109** E13
Matanzas *Cuba* 23°0N 81°40W **115** C8
Matara *Sri Lanka* 5°58N 80°30E **84** S12
Mataró *Spain* 41°32N 2°29E **67** B7
Matehuala *Mexico* 23°39N 100°39W **114** C4
Mateke Hills *Zimbabwe* 21°48S 31°0E **97** J6
Matera *Italy* 40°40N 16°36E **68** D7
Mathura *India* 27°30N 77°40E **84** F10
Mati *Phil.* 6°55N 126°15E **83** C7
Matlock *U.K.* 53°9N 1°33W **27** F5
Mato Grosso □ *Brazil* 14°0S 55°0W **120** D4
Mato Grosso, Planalto do *Brazil* 15°0S 55°0W **120** D4
Mato Grosso do Sul □ *Brazil* 18°0S 55°0W **120** D4
Matola *Mozam.* 25°57S 32°27E **97** K6
Matopo Hills *Zimbabwe* 20°36S 28°20E **97** J5
Maṭruḥ *Oman* 23°37N 58°30E **87** F9
Matsu Tao *Taiwan* 26°8N 119°56E **79** F12
Matsue *Japan* 35°25N 133°10E **81** F3
Matsumoto *Japan* 36°15N 138°0E **81** E6
Matsusaka *Japan* 34°34N 136°32E **81** F5
Matsuyama *Japan* 33°45N 132°45E **81** G3
Mattagami → *Canada* 50°43N 81°29W **109** D11
Mattancheri *India* 9°50N 76°15E **84** Q10
Mattawa *Canada* 46°20N 78°45W **112** B8
Matterhorn *Switz.* 45°58N 7°39E **64** F4
Matthew, Î. *N. Cal.* 22°29S 171°15E **99** E13
Mattoon *U.S.A.* 39°29N 88°23W **112** F3
Maturín *Venezuela* 9°45N 63°11W **120** B3
Maubeuge *France* 50°17N 3°57E **66** A6
Maubin *Burma* 16°44N 95°39E **85** L19
Maudin Sun *Burma* 16°0N 94°30E **85** M19
Maui *U.S.A.* 20°48N 156°20W **110** H16
Maumee → *U.S.A.* 41°42N 83°28W **112** E6
Maumturk Mts. *Ireland* 53°32N 9°42W **18** D2
Maun *Botswana* 20°0S 23°26E **97** H4
Mauna Kea *U.S.A.* 19°50N 155°28W **110** J17
Mauna Loa *U.S.A.* 19°30N 155°35W **110** J17
Mauritania ■ *Africa* 20°50N 10°0W **94** E3
Mauritius ■ *Ind. Oc.* 20°0S 57°0E **91** J9
Mawgan *U.K.* 50°4N 5°13W **29** G3
Maxixe *Mozam.* 23°54S 35°17E **97** J7
Maxwellheugh *U.K.* 55°35N 2°26W **25** C11
May, I. of *U.K.* 56°11N 2°32W **25** B10
May Pen *Jamaica* 17°58N 77°15W **114** a
Mayaguana I. *Bahamas* 22°30N 72°44W **115** C10
Mayagüez *Puerto Rico* 18°12N 67°9W **115** D11
Maybole *U.K.* 55°21N 4°42W **24** D6
Mayfield *E. Sussex, U.K.* 51°1N 0°17E **31** D9
Mayfield *Staffs., U.K.* 53°1N 1°47W **27** F5
Mayfield *U.S.A.* 36°44N 88°38W **112** G3
Maykop *Russia* 44°35N 40°10E **71** F7
Maynooth *Ireland* 53°23N 6°34W **21** B9
Mayo *Canada* 63°38N 135°57W **108** C6
Mayo □ *Ireland* 53°53N 9°3W **18** D3
Mayon Volcano *Phil.* 13°15N 123°41E **83** B6
Mayotte ⊠ *Ind. Oc.* 12°50S 45°10E **97** G9
Maysville *U.S.A.* 38°39N 83°46W **112** F6
Māzandarān □ *Iran* 36°30N 52°0E **87** B8
Mazar *China* 36°32N 77°1E **78** D4
Mazār-e Sharīf *Afghan.* 36°41N 67°0E **87** B11
Mazaruni → *Guyana* 6°25N 58°35W **120** B4
Mazatlán *Mexico* 23°13N 106°25W **114** C3
Mazyr *Belarus* 51°59N 29°15E **70** D4
Mbabane *Swaziland* 26°18S 31°6E **97** K6
Mbaïki *C.A.R.* 3°53N 18°1E **96** D3
Mbala *Zambia* 8°46S 31°24E **96** F6
Mbale *Uganda* 1°8N 34°12E **96** D6
Mbandaka *Dem. Rep. of the Congo* 0°1N 18°18E **96** D3
Mbanza Ngungu *Dem. Rep. of the Congo* 5°12S 14°53E **96** F2
Mbeya *Tanzania* 8°54S 33°29E **96** F6
Mbour *Senegal* 14°22N 16°54W **94** F2
Mbuji-Mayi *Dem. Rep. of the Congo* 6°9S 23°40E **96** F4
Mdantsane *S. Africa* 32°56S 27°46E **97** L5
Mead, L. *U.S.A.* 36°0N 114°44W **110** C4
Meadow Lake *Canada* 54°10N 108°26W **108** D9
Meadville *U.S.A.* 41°39N 80°9W **112** E7
Meaford *Canada* 44°36N 80°35W **112** C7
Mealsgate *U.K.* 54°47N 3°13W **26** C2
Mearns, Howe of the *U.K.* 56°52N 2°26W **23** J13
Measham *U.K.* 52°43N 1°31W **27** G5
Meath □ *Ireland* 53°40N 6°57W **19** D8
Meaux *France* 48°58N 2°50E **66** B5
Mecca *Si. Arabia* 21°30N 39°54E **86** F4
Mechelen *Belgium* 51°2N 4°29E **64** C3
Mecklenburg *Germany* 53°33N 11°40E **64** B7
Mecklenburger Bucht *Germany* 54°20N 11°40E **64** A6
Medan *Indonesia* 3°40N 98°38E **82** D1
Médéa *Algeria* 36°12N 2°50E **94** A6
Medellín *Colombia* 6°15N 75°35W **120** B2
Medford *Oreg., U.S.A.* 42°19N 122°52W **110** B2
Medford *Wis., U.S.A.* 45°9N 90°20W **112** C2
Medicine Hat *Canada* 50°0N 110°45W **108** E8
Medina *Si. Arabia* 24°35N 39°52E **86** E4
Mediterranean Sea *Europe* 35°0N 15°0E **90** C5
Médoc *France* 45°10N 0°50W **66** D3
Medstead *U.K.* 51°8N 1°3W **30** D6
Medvezhyegorsk *Russia* 63°0N 34°25E **70** B5
Medway → *U.K.* 51°27N 0°46E **31** D10
Meekatharra *Australia* 26°32S 118°29E **98** F2
Meerut *India* 29°1N 77°42E **84** E10
Meghalaya □ *India* 25°50N 91°0E **85** G17
Meghna → *Bangla.* 22°50N 90°50E **85** H17
Megisti *Greece* 36°8N 29°34E **86** B2
Meharry, Mt. *Australia* 22°59S 118°35E **98** D2
Meighen I. *Canada* 80°0N 99°30W **109** B10
Meiktila *Burma* 20°53N 95°54E **85** J19
Meizhou *China* 24°16N 116°6E **79** G12
Mejillones *Chile* 23°10S 70°30W **121** E2
Mekele *Ethiopia* 13°33N 39°30E **89** E2
Mekhtar *Pakistan* 30°30N 69°15E **84** D6
Meknès *Morocco* 33°57N 5°33W **94** B4
Mekong → *Asia* 9°30N 106°15E **82** C3
Melaka *Malaysia* 2°15N 102°15E **82** D2
Melanesia *Pac. Oc.* 4°0S 155°0E **102** H7
Melbourn *U.K.* 52°4N 0°0 **31** B9
Melbourne *Australia* 37°48S 144°58E **98** H8
Melbourne *U.K.* 52°50N 1°25W **27** G6
Melekeok *Palau* 7°27N 134°38E **102** G5
Mélèzes → *Canada* 57°40N 69°29W **109** D13
Melfort *Canada* 52°50N 104°37W **108** D9
Melilla *N. Afr.* 35°21N 2°57W **67** E4
Melitopol *Ukraine* 46°50N 35°22E **71** E6
Melksham *U.K.* 51°23N 2°8W **30** D4
Melmerby *U.K.* 54°45N 2°35W **26** C3
Melrhir, Chott *Algeria* 34°13N 6°30E **94** B7
Melrose *U.K.* 55°36N 2°43W **25** C10
Melsonby *U.K.* 54°29N 1°42W **26** D5
Melton Constable *U.K.* 52°52N 1°2E **31** A11
Melton Mowbray *U.K.* 52°47N 0°54W **27** G7
Melun *France* 48°32N 2°39E **66** B5
Melville *Canada* 50°55N 102°50W **108** D9
Melville, L. *Canada* 53°30N 60°0W **109** D14
Melville I. *Australia* 11°30S 131°0E **98** C5
Melville I. *Canada* 75°30N 112°0W **109** B8
Melville Pen. *Canada* 68°0N 84°0W **109** C11
Memphis *U.S.A.* 35°8N 90°2W **111** C9
Menai Bridge *U.K.* 53°14N 4°10W **28** A5
Menai Strait *U.K.* 53°11N 4°13W **28** A5
Mende *France* 44°31N 3°30E **66** D5
Mendip Hills *U.K.* 51°17N 2°40W **30** D3
Mendlesham *U.K.* 52°16N 1°6E **31** B11
Mendocino, C. *U.S.A.* 40°26N 124°25W **110** B2
Mendota *U.S.A.* 41°33N 89°7W **112** E3
Mendoza *Argentina* 32°50S 68°52W **121** F3
Menominee *U.S.A.* 45°6N 87°37W **112** C4
Menominee → *U.S.A.* 45°6N 87°35W **112** C4
Menomonie *U.S.A.* 44°53N 91°55W **112** C2
Menorca *Spain* 40°0N 4°0E **67** C8
Mentawai, Kepulauan *Indonesia* 2°0S 99°0E **82** E1
Merced *U.S.A.* 37°18N 120°29W **110** C2
Mercedes *Corrientes, Argentina* 29°10S 58°5W **121** E4
Mercedes *San Luis, Argentina* 33°40S 65°21W **121** F3
Mercedes *Uruguay* 33°12S 58°0W **121** F4
Mercy, C. *Canada* 65°0N 63°30W **109** C13
Mere *U.K.* 51°6N 2°16W **30** D4
Mergui *Burma* 12°26N 98°34E **82** B1
Mérida *Mexico* 20°58N 89°37W **114** C7
Mérida *Spain* 38°55N 6°25W **67** C2
Mérida *Venezuela* 8°24N 71°8W **120** B2
Mérida, Cord. de *Venezuela* 9°0N 71°0W **117** C3
Meriden *U.K.* 52°26N 1°38W **27** H5
Meriden *U.S.A.* 41°32N 72°48W **113** E11
Meridian *U.S.A.* 32°22N 88°42W **111** D9
Merowe Dam *Sudan* 18°35N 31°56E **95** E12
Merrick *U.K.* 55°8N 4°28W **24** D7
Merrill *U.S.A.* 45°11N 89°41W **112** C3
Merritt *Canada* 50°10N 120°45W **108** D7
Merse *U.K.* 55°43N 2°16W **25** C11
Mersea I. *U.K.* 51°47N 0°58E **31** C10
Mersey → *U.K.* 53°25N 3°1W **27** F2
Merseyside □ *U.K.* 53°31N 3°2W **27** E2
Mersin *Turkey* 36°51N 34°36E **71** G5
Merthyr Tydfil *U.K.* 51°45N 3°22W **28** D7
Merton □ *U.K.* 51°25N 0°11W **31** D8
Meru *Kenya* 0°3N 37°40E **96** D7
Meru *Tanzania* 3°15S 36°46E **96** E7
Mesa *U.S.A.* 33°25N 111°50W **110** D4
Mesopotamia *Iraq* 33°30N 44°0E **86** C5
Messina *Italy* 38°11N 15°34E **68** E6
Messina, Str. di *Italy* 38°15N 15°35E **68** F6
Mestre, Espigão *Brazil* 12°30S 46°10W **122** B1
Meta → *S. Amer.* 6°12N 67°28W **120** B3
Meta Incognita Pen. *Canada* 62°45N 68°30W **109** C13
Metheringham *U.K.* 53°9N 0°23W **27** F8
Methwold *U.K.* 52°32N 0°33E **31** A10
Metlakatla *U.S.A.* 55°8N 131°35W **108** D6
Metropolis *U.S.A.* 37°9N 88°44W **112** G3
Metz *France* 49°8N 6°10E **66** B7
Meuse → *Europe* 50°45N 5°41E **64** C3
Mevagissey *U.K.* 50°16N 4°48W **29** G4
Mevagissey B. *U.K.* 50°17N 4°47W **29** G4
Mexborough *U.K.* 53°30N 1°15W **27** E6
Mexiana, I. *Brazil* 0°0 49°30W **120** B5
Mexicali *Mexico* 32°40N 115°30W **114** A1
México *Mexico* 19°24N 99°9W **114** D5

Mexico

Neftekumsk

Mexico ■ *Cent. Amer.* 25°N 105°0W **114** C4
Mexico, G. of *Cent. Amer.* 25°N 90°0W **114** C7
Meymaneh *Afghan.* 35°53N 64°38E **87** C11
Mezen → *Russia* 65°44N 44°22E **70** A7
Mezhdurechensk *Russia* 53°41N 88°33E **76** D9
Mhonadh, Na h-Eileanan = Monach
　Is. *U.K.* 57°32N 7°40W **22** G2
Miami *U.S.A.* 25°46N 80°11W **111** E10
Miāndowāb *Iran* 37°0N 46°5E **86** B6
Mīāneh *Iran* 37°30N 47°40E **86** B6
Mianwali *Pakistan* 32°38N 71°28E **84** C7
Mianyang *China* 31°22N 104°47E **78** E9
Miass *Russia* 54°59N 60°6E **70** D11
Micheldever *U.K.* 51°9N 1°14W **30** D6
Michigan □ *U.S.A.* 44°0N 85°0W **112** B4
Michigan, L. *U.S.A.* 44°0N 87°0W **112** C4
Michipicoten I. *Canada* 47°40N 85°40W **112** B5
Michurinsk *Russia* 52°58N 40°27E **70** D7
Mickle Fell *U.K.* 54°37N 2°18W **26** C4
Mickleover *U.K.* 52°55N 1°33W **27** G5
Mickleton *U.K.* 54°36N 2°2W **26** C4
Micoud *St. Lucia* 13°49N 60°54W **114** b
Micronesia *Pac. Oc.* 11°0N 160°0E **102** G7
Micronesia, Federated States of ■
　Pac. Oc. 9°0N 150°0E **102** G7
Middelburg *S. Africa* 31°30S 25°0E **97** L5
Middle East *Asia* 35°0N 40°0E **72** E5
Middleham *U.K.* 54°17N 1°48W **26** D5
Middlemarsh *U.K.* 50°51N 2°28W **30** E4
Middlesbrough *U.K.* 54°35N 1°13W **26** C6
Middleton *Gt. Man., U.K.* 53°33N 2°12W **27** E4
Middleton *Norfolk, U.K.* 52°43N 0°29E **31** A9
Middleton Cheney *U.K.* 52°5N 1°16W **30** B6
Middleton in Teesdale *U.K.* 54°38N 2°4W **26** C4
Middleton on the Wolds *U.K.* 53°56N 0°35W **27** E7
Middletown *U.K.* 54°17N 6°51W **19** C8
Middletown *N.Y., U.S.A.* 41°27N 74°25W **113** E10
Middletown *Ohio, U.S.A.* 39°31N 84°24W **112** F5
Middlewich *U.K.* 53°12N 2°28W **27** F4
Middlezoy *U.K.* 51°5N 2°54W **30** D3
Midhurst *U.K.* 50°59N 0°44W **31** E7
Midi, Canal du → *France* 43°45N 1°21E **66** E4
Midland *Canada* 44°45N 79°50W **112** C8
Midland *Mich., U.S.A.* 43°37N 84°14W **112** D5
Midland *Tex., U.S.A.* 32°0N 102°3W **110** D6
Midleton *Ireland* 51°55N 8°10W **20** E6
Midsomer Norton *U.K.* 51°17N 2°28W **30** D4
Midway Is. *Pac. Oc.* 28°13N 177°22W **102** E10
Midwest *U.S.A.* 42°0N 90°0W **111** C9
Mieres *Spain* 43°18N 5°48W **67** A3
Mikhaylovka *Russia* 50°3N 43°5E **71** D7
Milan *Italy* 45°28N 9°10E **68** B3
Milborne Port *U.K.* 50°58N 2°28W **30** E4
Mildenhall *U.K.* 52°21N 0°32E **31** B10
Mildura *Australia* 34°13S 142°9E **98** G7
Miles City *U.S.A.* 46°25N 105°51W **110** A5
Milford *U.S.A.* 38°55N 75°26W **113** F10
Milford Haven *U.K.* 51°42N 5°7W **28** D3
Milford on Sea *U.K.* 50°43N 1°35W **30** E5
Milh, Baḩr al *Iraq* 32°40N 43°35E **86** C5
Milk → *U.S.A.* 48°4N 106°19W **110** A5
Millau *France* 44°8N 3°4E **66** D5
Millbrook *U.K.* 50°20N 4°14W **29** G5
Millet *St. Lucia* 13°55N 60°59W **114** b
Millinocket *U.S.A.* 45°39N 68°43W **113** C13
Millom *U.K.* 54°13N 3°16W **26** D2
Milltown Malbay *Ireland* 52°52N 9°24W **20** C4
Millville *U.S.A.* 39°24N 75°2W **113** F10
Milngavie *U.K.* 55°56N 4°19W **24** C7
Milnthorpe *U.K.* 54°14N 2°45W **26** D3
Milos *Greece* 36°44N 24°25E **69** F11
Milton Abbot *U.K.* 50°35N 4°16W **29** F5
Milton Keynes *U.K.* 52°1N 0°44W **31** B7
Milverton *U.K.* 51°1N 3°16W **30** D2
Milwaukee *U.S.A.* 43°2N 87°54W **112** D4
Milwaukee Deep *Atl. Oc.* 19°50N 68°0W **115** D11
Min Jiang → *Fujian, China* 26°0N 119°35E **79** F12
Min Jiang → *Sichuan, China* 28°45N 104°40E **78** F9
Minas *Uruguay* 34°20S 55°10W **121** F4
Minas Gerais □ *Brazil* 18°50S 46°0W **122** C1
Minatitlán *Mexico* 17°59N 94°31W **114** D6
Minchinhampton *U.K.* 51°42N 2°11W **30** C4
Mindanao *Phil.* 8°0N 125°0E **83** C6
Mindoro *Phil.* 13°0N 121°0E **83** B6
Mindoro Str. *Phil.* 12°30N 120°30E **83** B6
Minehead *U.K.* 51°12N 3°29W **30** D2
Mineral Wells *U.S.A.* 32°48N 98°7W **110** D7
Minfeng *China* 37°4N 82°46E **78** D5
Minginish *U.K.* 57°14N 6°15W **22** H5
Mingulay *U.K.* 56°49N 7°39W **22** J2
Minna *Nigeria* 9°37N 6°30E **94** G7
Minneapolis *U.S.A.* 44°57N 93°16W **111** B8
Minnesota □ *U.S.A.* 46°0N 94°15W **111** A8
Minorca = Menorca *Spain* 40°0N 4°0E **67** C8
Minot *U.S.A.* 48°14N 101°18W **110** A6
Minsk *Belarus* 53°52N 27°30E **65** B14
Minster *Kent, U.K.* 51°20N 1°20E **31** D11
Minster *Kent, U.K.* 51°25N 0°50E **31** D10
Minsterley *U.K.* 52°39N 2°54W **27** G3
Minto, L. *Canada* 57°13N 75°0W **109** D12
Miramichi *Canada* 47°2N 65°28W **109** E13
Miramichi B. *Canada* 47°15N 65°0W **113** B15
Mirim, L. *S. Amer.* 32°45S 52°50W **121** F4
Mirnyy *Russia* 62°33N 113°53E **77** C12
Mirpur Khas *Pakistan* 25°30N 69°0E **84** G6
Mirs Bay *China* 22°33N 114°24E **79** a
Mirzapur *India* 25°10N 82°34E **85** G13
Mishawaka *U.S.A.* 41°40N 86°11W **112** E4
Miskolc *Hungary* 48°7N 20°50E **65** D11
Misool *Indonesia* 1°52S 130°10E **83** E8
Miṣrātah *Libya* 32°24N 15°3E **95** B9
Missinaibi → *Canada* 50°43N 81°29W **109** D11
Mississippi □ *U.S.A.* 33°0N 90°0W **111** D9
Mississippi → *U.S.A.* 29°9N 89°15W **111** E9
Mississippi River Delta
　U.S.A. 29°10N 89°15W **111** E9
Missoula *U.S.A.* 46°52N 114°1W **110** A4
Missouri □ *U.S.A.* 38°25N 92°30W **111** C8
Missouri → *U.S.A.* 38°49N 90°7W **111** C8
Mistassini, L. *Canada* 51°0N 73°30W **109** D12
Misterton *Notts., U.K.* 53°27N 0°50W **27** F7

Misterton *Somst., U.K.* 50°52N 2°47W **30** E3
Mitcheldean *U.K.* 51°51N 2°28W **30** C4
Mitchell *U.S.A.* 43°43N 98°2W **110** B7
Mitchell → *Australia* 15°12S 141°35E **98** D7
Mitchelstown *Ireland* 52°15N 8°16W **20** D6
Mito *Japan* 36°20N 140°30E **81** E7
Mitrovicë *Kosovo* 42°54N 20°52E **69** C9
Mitú *Colombia* 1°15N 70°13W **120** B2
Mitumba, Mts.
　Dem. Rep. of the Congo 7°0S 27°30E **96** F5
Miugh Laigh = Mingulay
　U.K. 56°49N 7°39W **22** J2
Miyakonojo *Japan* 31°40N 131°5E **81** H2
Miyazaki *Japan* 31°56N 131°30E **81** H2
Mizen Hd. *Cork, Ireland* 51°27N 9°50W **20** F3
Mizen Hd. *Wicklow, Ireland* 52°51N 6°4W **21** C10
Mizoram □ *India* 23°30N 92°40E **85** H18
Mjøsa *Norway* 60°40N 11°0E **63** E6
Mljet *Croatia* 42°43N 17°30E **68** C7
Mo i Rana *Norway* 66°20N 14°7E **63** D6
Moab *U.S.A.* 38°35N 109°33W **110** C5
Moate *Ireland* 53°24N 7°44W **18** E6
Mobaye *C.A.R.* 4°25N 21°5E **96** D4
Moberly *U.S.A.* 39°25N 92°26W **111** C8
Mobile *U.S.A.* 30°41N 88°3W **111** D9
Mobridge *U.S.A.* 45°32N 100°26W **110** A6
Moçambique *Mozam.* 15°3S 40°42E **97** H8
Mochudi *Botswana* 24°27S 26°7E **97** J5
Mococa *Brazil* 21°28S 47°0W **122** D1
Mocuba *Mozam.* 16°54S 36°57E **97** H7
Modbury *U.K.* 50°21N 3°55W **29** G6
Módena *Italy* 44°40N 10°55E **68** B4
Modesto *U.S.A.* 37°39N 121°0W **110** C2
Modica *Italy* 36°52N 14°46E **68** F6
Moffat *U.K.* 55°21N 3°27W **25** D9
Mogadishu *Somalia* 2°2N 45°25E **89** G4
Mogi-Mirim *Brazil* 22°29S 47°0W **122** D1
Mohammedia *Morocco* 33°44N 7°21W **94** B4
Moher, Cliffs of *Ireland* 52°58N 9°27W **20** C4
Moidart *U.K.* 56°49N 5°41W **22** J6
Moidart, L. *U.K.* 56°47N 5°52W **22** J6
Moisie → *Canada* 50°14N 66°5W **109** D13
Mojave Desert *U.S.A.* 35°0N 116°30W **110** D3
Moji das Cruzes *Brazil* 23°31S 46°11W **122** D1
Mokpo *S. Korea* 34°50N 126°25E **79** E14
Mold *U.K.* 53°9N 3°8W **28** A7
Moldavia = Moldova ■ *Europe* 47°0N 28°0E **65** E15
Molde *Norway* 62°45N 7°9E **63** E5
Moldova ■ *Europe* 47°0N 28°0E **65** E15
Mole → *U.K.* 51°24N 0°21W **31** D8
Molepolole *Botswana* 24°28S 25°28E **97** J5
Mollendo *Peru* 17°0S 72°0W **120** D2
Moloka'i *U.S.A.* 21°8N 157°0W **110** H16
Molopo → *Africa* 28°30S 20°12E **97** K4
Molucca Sea *Indonesia* 0°0 125°0E **83** E6
Moluccas *Indonesia* 1°0S 127°0E **83** E7
Mombasa *Kenya* 4°3S 39°40E **96** E7
Mompós *Colombia* 9°14N 74°26W **120** B2
Mon □ *Burma* 16°0N 97°30E **85** L20
Mona Passage *W. Indies* 18°30N 67°45W **115** D11
Monach Is. *U.K.* 57°32N 7°40W **22** G2
Monaco ■ *Europe* 43°46N 7°23E **66** E7
Monadhliath Mts. *U.K.* 57°10N 4°4W **23** H9
Monaghan *Ireland* 54°15N 6°57W **19** C8
Monaghan □ *Ireland* 54°11N 6°56W **19** C8
Monar, L. *U.K.* 57°26N 5°8W **22** H7
Monar Forest *U.K.* 57°27N 5°10W **22** H7
Monasterevin *Ireland* 53°8N 7°4W **21** B8
Monavullagh Mts. *Ireland* 52°14N 7°35W **21** D7
Monclova *Mexico* 26°54N 101°30W **114** B4
Moncton *Canada* 46°7N 64°51W **113** B15
Moneague *Jamaica* 18°16N 77°7W **114** a
Moneymore *U.K.* 54°41N 6°40W **19** B8
Mongolia ■ *Asia* 47°0N 103°0E **78** B9
Mongolia, Plateau of *Asia* 45°0N 105°0E **72** D12
Mongu *Zambia* 15°16S 23°12E **97** H4
Moniaive *U.K.* 55°12N 3°55W **25** D8
Monifieth *U.K.* 56°30N 2°48W **25** B10
Monmouth *U.K.* 51°48N 2°42W **28** D8
Monmouth *U.S.A.* 40°55N 90°39W **112** E2
Monmouthshire □ *U.K.* 51°48N 2°54W **28** D8
Monnow → *U.K.* 51°49N 2°43W **30** C3
Monroe *La., U.S.A.* 32°30N 92°7W **111** D8
Monroe *Mich., U.S.A.* 41°55N 83°24W **112** E6
Monroe *Wis., U.S.A.* 42°36N 89°38W **112** D3
Monrovia *Liberia* 6°18N 10°47W **94** G3
Mons *Belgium* 50°27N 3°58W **64** C3
Mont-de-Marsan *France* 43°54N 0°31W **66** E3
Mont-Laurier *Canada* 46°35N 75°30W **109** E12
Montana *Bulgaria* 43°27N 23°16E **69** C10
Montaña *Peru* 6°0S 73°0W **120** C2
Montana □ *U.S.A.* 47°0N 110°0W **110** A5
Montargis *France* 47°59N 2°43E **66** C5
Montauban *France* 44°2N 1°21E **66** D4
Montbéliard *France* 47°31N 6°48E **66** C7
Montceau-les-Mines *France* 46°40N 4°23E **66** C6
Monte Azul *Brazil* 15°9S 42°53W **122** C2
Monte-Carlo *Monaco* 43°44N 7°25E **66** E7
Monte Caseros *Argentina* 30°10S 57°50W **121** F4
Monte Cristi *Dom. Rep.* 19°52N 71°39W **115** D10
Montego Bay *Jamaica* 18°28N 77°55W **114** a
Montélimar *France* 44°33N 4°45E **66** D6
Montello *U.S.A.* 43°48N 89°20W **112** D3
Montemorelos *Mexico* 25°12N 99°49W **114** B5
Montenegro ■ *Europe* 42°40N 19°20E **69** C8
Monterey *U.S.A.* 36°37N 121°55W **110** C2
Montería *Colombia* 8°46N 75°53W **120** B2
Monterrey *Mexico* 25°40N 100°19W **114** B4
Montes Claros *Brazil* 16°30S 43°50W **122** C2
Montevideo *Uruguay* 34°50S 56°11W **121** F4
Montgomery *U.K.* 52°34N 3°8W **28** E7
Montgomery *U.S.A.* 32°23N 86°19W **111** D9
Monticello *U.S.A.* 40°45N 86°46W **112** E4
Montluçon *France* 46°22N 2°36E **66** C5
Montmagny *Canada* 46°58N 70°34W **113** B12
Montpelier *Idaho, U.S.A.* 42°19N 111°18W **110** B4
Montpelier *Vt., U.S.A.* 44°16N 72°35W **113** C11
Montpellier *France* 43°37N 3°52E **66** E5
Montréal *Canada* 45°30N 73°33W **113** C11
Montrose *U.K.* 56°44N 2°27W **23** J13
Montrose *U.S.A.* 38°29N 107°53W **110** C5

Montserrat □ *W. Indies* 16°40N 62°10W **115** D12
Monywa *Burma* 22°7N 95°11E **85** H19
Monza *Italy* 45°35N 9°16E **68** B3
Monze, C. *Pakistan* 24°47N 66°37E **84** G5
Moorfoot Hills *U.K.* 55°44N 3°8W **25** C9
Moorhead *U.S.A.* 46°53N 96°45W **111** A7
Moose Jaw *Canada* 50°24N 105°30W **108** D9
Moosehead L. *U.S.A.* 45°38N 69°40W **113** C13
Moosomin *Canada* 50°9N 101°40W **108** D9
Moosonee *Canada* 51°17N 80°39W **109** D11
Mopti *Mali* 14°30N 4°0W **94** F5
Mora *Sweden* 61°2N 14°38E **63** E6
Mora, Na h-Eileanan = Shiant Is.
　U.K. 57°54N 6°22W **22** G5
Moradabad *India* 28°50N 78°50E **84** E11
Morant Bay *Jamaica* 17°53N 76°25W **114** a
Morant Pt. *Jamaica* 17°55N 76°12W **114** a
Moratuwa *Sri Lanka* 6°45N 79°55E **84** R11
Morava → *Serbia* 44°36N 21°4E **69** B9
Morava → *Slovak Rep.* 48°10N 16°59E **65** D9
Moravian Hts. *Czech Rep.* 49°30N 15°40E **56** F9
Moray □ *U.K.* 57°31N 3°18W **23** G11
Moray Firth *U.K.* 57°40N 3°52W **23** G10
Morden *Canada* 49°15N 98°10W **108** D10
Mordvinia □ *Russia* 54°20N 44°30E **70** D7
Moreau → *U.S.A.* 45°18N 100°43W **110** A6
Morebattle *U.K.* 55°31N 2°22W **25** C11
Morecambe *U.K.* 54°5N 2°52W **26** D3
Morecambe B. *U.K.* 54°7N 3°0W **26** D3
Moree *Australia* 29°28S 149°54E **98** F9
Morehead *U.S.A.* 38°11N 83°26W **112** F6
Morelia *Mexico* 19°42N 101°7W **114** D4
Morena, Sierra *Spain* 38°20N 4°0W **67** C3
Moresby I. *Canada* 52°30N 131°40W **108** D6
Moreton-in-Marsh *U.K.* 51°59N 1°41W **30** C5
Moretonhampstead *U.K.* 50°39N 3°46W **29** F6
Morgan City *U.S.A.* 29°42N 91°12W **111** E8
Morgantown *U.S.A.* 39°38N 79°57W **112** F8
Morioka *Japan* 39°45N 141°8E **81** D7
Morlaix *France* 48°36N 3°52W **66** B2
Morley *U.K.* 53°45N 1°36W **27** E5
Morocco ■ *N. Afr.* 32°0N 5°50W **94** B4
Morogoro *Tanzania* 6°50S 37°40E **96** F7
Morón *Cuba* 22°8N 78°39W **115** C9
Mörön *Mongolia* 49°38N 100°9E **78** B9
Morondava *Madag.* 20°17S 44°17E **97** J8
Moroni *Comoros Is.* 11°40S 43°16E **91** H8
Morotai *Indonesia* 2°10N 128°30E **83** D7
Morpeth *U.K.* 55°10N 1°41W **26** B5
Morphou *Cyprus* 35°12N 32°59E **86** C3
Morrinhos *Brazil* 17°45S 49°10W **122** C1
Morris *U.S.A.* 41°22N 88°26W **112** E3
Morte Bay *U.K.* 51°9N 4°14W **29** E5
Morte Pt. *U.K.* 51°11N 4°14W **29** E5
Mortehoe *U.K.* 51°11N 4°12W **29** E5
Mortimer's Cross *U.K.* 52°16N 2°50W **30** B3
Morton Fen *U.K.* 52°49N 0°20W **27** G8
Morvan *France* 47°5N 4°3E **66** C6
Morwenstow *U.K.* 50°54N 4°33W **29** F4
Moscos Is. *Burma* 14°0N 97°30E **85** G20
Moscow *Russia* 55°45N 37°37E **70** C6
Moscow *U.S.A.* 46°44N 117°0W **110** A3
Mosel → *Europe* 50°22N 7°36E **64** C4
Moses Lake *U.S.A.* 47°8N 119°17W **110** A3
Moshi *Tanzania* 3°22S 37°18E **96** E7
Mosjøen *Norway* 65°51N 13°12E **63** D6
Mosselbaai *S. Africa* 34°11S 22°8E **97** L4
Mossley *U.K.* 53°33N 2°1W **27** E4
Mossoró *Brazil* 5°10S 37°15W **120** C6
Most *Czech Rep.* 50°31N 13°38E **64** C7
Mostaganem *Algeria* 35°54N 0°5E **94** A6
Mostar *Bos.-H.* 43°22N 17°50E **69** C7
Mosul *Iraq* 36°15N 43°5E **86** B5
Motcombe *U.K.* 51°1N 2°13W **30** D4
Motherwell *U.K.* 55°47N 3°58W **25** C8
Motihari *India* 26°30N 84°55E **85** F14
Motril *Spain* 36°31N 3°37W **67** D4
Mottisfont *U.K.* 51°2N 1°32W **30** D5
Mouila *Gabon* 1°50S 11°0E **96** E2
Moule à Chique, C. *St. Lucia* 13°43N 60°57W **114** b
Moulins *France* 46°35N 3°19E **66** C5
Moulmein *Burma* 16°30N 97°40E **85** L20
Moulouya, O. → *Morocco* 35°5N 2°25W **94** B5
Moulton *U.K.* 52°17N 0°52W **31** B7
Moundou *Chad* 8°40N 16°10E **95** G9
Moundsville *U.S.A.* 39°55N 80°44W **112** F7
Mount Carmel *U.S.A.* 38°25N 87°46W **112** F4
Mount Desert I. *U.S.A.* 44°21N 68°20W **113** C13
Mount Gambier *Australia* 37°50S 140°46E **98** H7
Mount Hagen *Papua N. G.* 5°52S 144°16E **98** B7
Mount Isa *Australia* 20°42S 139°26E **98** E6
Mount Magnet *Australia* 28°2S 117°47E **98** F2
Mount Pleasant *U.S.A.* 43°36N 84°46W **112** D5
Mount Sterling *U.S.A.* 38°4N 83°56W **112** F6
Mount Vernon *Ind., U.S.A.* 37°56N 87°54W **112** G4
Mount Vernon *Ohio, U.S.A.* 40°23N 82°29W **112** E6
Mountain Ash *U.K.* 51°40N 3°23W **28** D7
Mountain Home *U.S.A.* 43°8N 115°41W **110** B3
Mountain View *U.S.A.* 19°33N 155°7W **110** J17
Mountmellick *Ireland* 53°7N 7°20W **21** B8
Mountrath *Ireland* 53°0N 7°28W **21** C8
Mount's Bay *U.K.* 50°5N 5°31W **29** G2
Mountsorrel *U.K.* 52°44N 1°9W **27** G6
Mourne → *U.K.* 54°52N 7°26W **19** B7
Mourne Mts. *U.K.* 54°10N 6°0W **19** C9
Moville *Ireland* 55°11N 7°3W **19** A7
Moy → *Ireland* 54°8N 9°8W **18** C2
Moyen Atlas *Morocco* 33°0N 5°0W **94** B4
Mozambique ■ *Africa* 19°0S 35°0E **97** H7
Mozambique Chan. *Africa* 17°30S 42°30E **90** H8
Mozdok *Russia* 43°45N 44°48E **71** F7
Mpanda *Tanzania* 6°23S 31°1E **96** F6
Mpumalanga *S. Africa* 29°50S 30°33E **97** K6
Msaken *Tunisia* 35°49N 10°33E **95** A8
Mthatha *S. Africa* 31°36S 28°49E **97** L5
Mtwara-Mikindani *Tanzania* 10°20S 40°20E **96** G8
Muar *Malaysia* 2°3N 102°34E **82** D2
Mubi *Nigeria* 10°18N 13°16E **95** F8
Much Dewchurch *U.K.* 51°58N 2°45W **30** C3
Much Marcle *U.K.* 51°59N 2°29W **30** C4

Much Wenlock *U.K.* 52°35N 2°33W **27** G3
Muchinga Mts. *Zambia* 11°30S 31°30E **97** G6
Muck *U.K.* 56°50N 6°15W **22** J5
Muckle Flugga *U.K.* 60°51N 0°54W **22** A1b
Muckle Roe *U.K.* 60°23N 1°27W **22** B15
Mucuri *Brazil* 18°0S 39°36W **122** C3
Mudanjiang *China* 44°38N 129°30E **79** C14
Mudgee *Australia* 32°32S 149°31E **98** G8
Mufulira *Zambia* 12°32S 28°15E **97** G5
Muğla *Turkey* 37°15N 28°22E **71** G4
Muir of Ord *U.K.* 57°32N 4°28W **23** G9
Mukteswar *India* 30°30N 74°30E **84** D9
Mulanje, Mt. *Malawi* 16°20S 35°0E **97** H7
Mulde → *Germany* 51°53N 12°15E **64** C7
Mulhacén *Spain* 37°4N 3°20W **67** D4
Mulhouse *France* 47°40N 7°20E **66** C7
Mull *U.K.* 56°25N 5°56W **24** B4
Mull, Sound of *U.K.* 56°30N 5°50W **24** A4
Mullagharreirk Mts. *Ireland* 52°20N 9°10W **20** D4
Mullet Pen. *Ireland* 54°13N 10°2W **18** C1
Mullingar *Ireland* 53°31N 7°21W **18** D7
Mullion *U.K.* 50°1N 5°16W **29** G3
Mulroy B. *Ireland* 55°15N 7°46W **18** A6
Multan *Pakistan* 30°15N 71°36E **84** D7
Mumbai *India* 18°56N 72°50E **84** K8
Mumbles Hd. *U.K.* 51°34N 3°59W **29** D6
Muna *Indonesia* 5°0S 122°30E **83** F6
Muncie *U.S.A.* 40°12N 85°23W **112** E5
Mundesley *U.K.* 52°53N 1°26E **31** A11
Mundo Novo *Brazil* 11°50S 40°29W **122** B2
Munger *India* 25°23N 86°30E **85** G15
Munich *Germany* 48°8N 11°34E **64** D6
Munising *U.S.A.* 46°25N 86°40W **112** B4
Münster *Germany* 51°58N 7°37E **64** C4
Munster □ *Ireland* 52°18N 8°44W **20** D5
Murashi *Russia* 59°30N 49°0E **70** C8
Murat → *Turkey* 38°46N 40°0E **71** G7
Murchison → *Australia* 27°45S 114°0E **98** F1
Murcia *Spain* 38°5N 1°10W **67** D5
Murcia □ *Spain* 37°50N 1°30W **67** D5
Mureș → *Romania* 46°15N 20°13E **65** E11
Murfreesboro *U.S.A.* 35°51N 86°24W **111** C9
Müritz *Germany* 53°25N 12°42E **64** B7
Muriaé *Brazil* 21°8S 42°23W **122** D2
Murmansk *Russia* 68°57N 33°10E **70** A5
Murom *Russia* 55°35N 42°3E **70** C7
Muroran *Japan* 42°25N 141°0E **81** B7
Murray *U.S.A.* 36°37N 88°19W **112** G3
Murray → *Australia* 35°20S 139°22E **98** H6
Murray Bridge *Australia* 35°6S 139°14E **98** H6
Murrumbidgee → *Australia* 34°43S 143°12E **98** G7
Murton *U.K.* 54°49N 1°22W **26** C6
Mururoa *French Polynesia* 21°52S 138°55W **103** K14
Murwara *India* 23°46N 80°28E **85** H12
Murzūq *Libya* 25°53N 13°57E **95** C8
Muş *Turkey* 38°45N 41°30E **71** G7
Mûsa, Gebel *Egypt* 28°33N 33°59E **86** D3
Muscat *Oman* 23°37N 58°36E **87** F9
Musgrave Ranges *Australia* 26°0S 132°0E **98** F5
Musina *S. Africa* 22°20S 30°5E **97** J6
Muskegon *U.S.A.* 43°14N 86°16W **112** D4
Muskegon → *U.S.A.* 43°14N 86°21W **112** D4
Muskogee *U.S.A.* 35°45N 95°22W **111** C7
Musselburgh *U.K.* 55°57N 3°2W **25** C9
Musselshell → *U.S.A.* 47°21N 107°57W **110** A5
Mutare *Zimbabwe* 18°58S 32°38E **97** H6
Mutton I. *Ireland* 52°49N 9°32W **20** C3
Muynak *Uzbekistan* 43°44N 59°10E **87** A9
Muz Tag *China* 36°25N 87°25E **78** D6
Muzaffarabad *Pakistan* 34°25N 73°30E **84** B8
Muzaffarnagar *India* 29°26N 77°40E **84** E10
Muztagh-Ata *China* 38°17N 75°7E **78** D4
Mwanza *Tanzania* 2°30S 32°58E **96** E6
Mweelrea *Ireland* 53°39N 9°49W **18** D2
Mwene-Ditu
　Dem. Rep. of the Congo 6°35S 22°27E **96** F4
Mweru, L. *Zambia* 9°0S 28°40E **96** F5
My Tho *Vietnam* 10°29N 106°23E **82** B3
Myanmar = Burma ■ *Asia* 21°0N 96°30E **85** J20
Mycenae *Greece* 37°43N 22°46E **69** F10
Myddle *U.K.* 52°49N 2°47W **27** G3
Myingyan *Burma* 21°30N 95°20E **85** J19
Myitkyina *Burma* 25°24N 97°26E **85** G20
Mymensingh *Bangla.* 24°45N 90°24E **85** G17
Mynydd Du *U.K.* 51°52N 3°50W **28** D6
Mynydd Preseli *U.K.* 51°57N 4°48W **28** D4
Myrtoan Sea *Greece* 37°0N 23°20E **69** F10
Mysore *India* 12°17N 76°41E **84** N10
Mytishchi *Russia* 55°50N 37°50E **70** C6

N

Na Hearadh = Harris *U.K.* 57°50N 6°55W **22** G4
Na Hearadh a Deas = South Harris
　U.K. 57°50N 7°0W **22** G4
Na Hearadh a Tuath = North Harris
　U.K. 58°0N 6°55W **22** F4
Naab → *Germany* 49°1N 12°2E **64** D6
Naas *Ireland* 53°12N 6°40W **21** B9
Naberezhnyye Chelny *Russia* 55°42N 52°19E **70** C9
Nabeul *Tunisia* 36°30N 10°44E **95** A8
Nābulus *West Bank* 32°14N 35°15E **86** C3
Nacala *Mozam.* 14°32S 40°34E **97** G8
Nacogdoches *U.S.A.* 31°36N 94°39W **111** D8
Nacozari de García *Mexico* 30°25N 109°38W **114** A3
Nadiad *India* 22°41N 72°56E **84** H8
Nador *Morocco* 35°14N 2°58W **94** B5
Nafferton *U.K.* 54°1N 0°23W **27** D8
Nafud Desert *Si. Arabia* 28°15N 41°0E **86** D5
Naga *Phil.* 13°38N 123°15E **83** B6
Nagaland □ *India* 26°0N 94°30E **85** G19
Nagano *Japan* 36°40N 138°10E **81** E6
Nagaoka *Japan* 37°27N 138°51E **81** E6
Nagappattinam *India* 10°46N 79°51E **84** P11
Nagasaki *Japan* 32°47N 129°50E **81** G1
Nagaur *India* 27°15N 73°45E **84** F8
Nagercoil *India* 8°12N 77°26E **84** Q10
Nagles Mts. *Ireland* 52°8N 8°30W **20** D6
Nagorno-Karabakh □
　Azerbaijan 39°55N 46°45E **71** F8
Nagoya *Japan* 35°10N 136°50E **81** F5
Nagpur *India* 21°8N 79°10E **84** J11
Nagqu *China* 31°29N 92°3E **78** E7
Naha *Japan* 26°13N 127°42E **79** F14

Nailsea *U.K.* 51°26N 2°44W **30** D3
Nailsworth *U.K.* 51°41N 2°14W **30** C4
Nain *Canada* 56°34N 61°40W **109** D13
Nairn *U.K.* 57°35N 3°53W **23** G10
Nairobi *Kenya* 1°17S 36°48E **96** E7
Naivasha *Kenya* 0°40S 36°30E **96** E7
Najafābād *Iran* 32°40N 51°15E **87** C7
Najd *Si. Arabia* 26°30N 42°0E **86** E5
Najibabad *India* 29°40N 78°20E **84** E11
Najin *N. Korea* 42°12N 130°15E **79** C15
Najrān *Si. Arabia* 17°34N 44°18E **89** D3
Nakhodka *Russia* 42°53N 132°54E **77** E14
Nakhon Ratchasima
　Thailand 14°59N 102°12E **82** B2
Nakhon Sawan *Thailand* 15°35N 100°10E **82** A2
Nakhon Si Thammarat
　Thailand 8°29N 100°0E **82** C2
Nakina *Canada* 50°10N 86°40W **109** D11
Nakuru *Kenya* 0°15S 36°4E **96** E7
Nalchik *Russia* 43°30N 43°33E **71** F7
Nallamalai Hills *India* 15°30N 78°50E **84** M11
Nam Co *China* 30°30N 90°45E **78** E7
Namak, Daryācheh-ye *Iran* 34°30N 52°0E **87** C7
Namaland *Namibia* 26°0S 17°0E **97** K3
Namangan *Uzbekistan* 41°0N 71°40E **87** A12
Namcha Barwa *China* 29°40N 95°10E **78** F8
Namib Desert *Namibia* 22°30S 15°0E **97** J2
Namibe *Angola* 15°7S 12°11E **97** H2
Namibia ■ *Africa* 22°0S 18°9E **97** J3
Nampa *U.S.A.* 43°34N 116°34W **110** B3
Nam'po *N. Korea* 38°52N 125°10E **79** D14
Nampula *Mozam.* 15°6S 39°15E **97** H7
Namumea *Tuvalu* 5°41S 176°9E **99** B14
Namur *Belgium* 50°27N 4°52E **64** C3
Nan Ling *China* 25°0N 112°30E **79** F11
Nanaimo *Canada* 49°10N 124°0W **108** E7
Nanchang *China* 28°42N 115°55E **79** F12
Nanchong *China* 30°43N 106°2E **78** E10
Nancy *France* 48°42N 6°12E **66** B7
Nanda Devi *India* 30°23N 79°59E **84** D11
Nanded *India* 19°10N 77°20E **84** K10
Nandurbar *India* 21°20N 74°15E **84** J9
Nanga Parbat *Pakistan* 35°10N 74°35E **84** B9
Nanjing *China* 32°2N 118°47E **79** E12
Nanning *China* 22°48N 108°20E **78** G10
Nanping *China* 26°38N 118°10E **79** F12
Nansen Sd. *Canada* 81°0N 91°0W **109** A10
Nantes *France* 47°12N 1°33W **66** C3
Nantong *China* 32°1N 120°52E **79** E13
Nantou *China* 22°32N 113°55E **79** a
Nantucket I. *U.S.A.* 41°16N 70°5W **113** E12
Nantwich *U.K.* 53°4N 2°31W **27** F3
Nanuque *Brazil* 17°50S 40°21W **122** C2
Nanyang *China* 33°11N 112°30E **79** E11
Nanyuki *Kenya* 0°2N 37°4E **96** D7
Napa *U.S.A.* 38°18N 122°17W **110** C2
Napier *N.Z.* 39°30S 176°56E **99** H14
Naples *Italy* 40°50N 14°15E **68** D6
Napo → *Peru* 3°20S 72°40W **120** C2
Nappa *U.K.* 53°58N 2°13W **27** E4
Narayanganj *Bangla.* 23°40N 90°33E **85** H17
Narberth *U.K.* 51°47N 4°44W **28** D4
Narbonne *France* 43°11N 3°0E **66** E5
Narborough *U.K.* 52°34N 1°13W **27** G6
Nares Str. *Arctic* 80°0N 70°0W **109** A13
Narmada → *India* 21°38N 72°36E **84** J8
Narodnaya *Russia* 65°5N 59°58E **70** A10
Narva *Estonia* 59°23N 28°12E **63** F9
Narvik *Norway* 68°28N 17°26E **63** D7
Naryan-Mar *Russia* 67°42N 53°12E **70** A9
Nasca *Peru* 14°50S 74°57W **120** D2
Naseby *U.K.* 52°24N 0°59W **31** B7
Nashua *U.S.A.* 42°45N 71°28W **113** D12
Nashville *U.S.A.* 36°10N 86°47W **111** C9
Nasik *India* 19°58N 73°50E **84** K8
Nasirabad *India* 26°15N 74°45E **84** F9
Nasiriyah *Iraq* 31°0N 46°15E **86** D6
Nassau *Bahamas* 25°5N 77°20W **115** B9
Nasser, L. *Egypt* 23°0N 32°30E **95** D12
Natal *Brazil* 5°47S 35°13W **120** C6
Natashquan *Canada* 50°14N 61°46W **109** D13
Natashquan → *Canada* 50°7N 61°50W **109** D13
Natchez *U.S.A.* 31°34N 91°24W **111** D8
Natchitoches *U.S.A.* 31°46N 93°5W **111** D8
Nathdwara *India* 24°55N 73°50E **84** G8
Natitingou *Benin* 10°20N 1°26E **94** F6
Natron, L. *Tanzania* 2°20S 36°0E **96** E7
Natuna Besar, Kepulauan
　Indonesia 4°0N 108°15E **82** D3
Nauru ■ *Pac. Oc.* 1°0S 166°0E **102** H8
Navan *Ireland* 53°39N 6°41W **19** D8
Navarino, I. *Chile* 55°0S 67°40W **121** H3
Navarra □ *Spain* 42°40N 1°40W **67** A5
Navenby *U.K.* 53°6N 0°31W **27** F7
Naver → *U.K.* 58°32N 4°14W **23** E9
Navoiy *Uzbekistan* 40°9N 65°22E **76** E7
Navojoa *Mexico* 27°6N 109°26W **114** B3
Navsari *India* 20°57N 72°59E **84** J8
Nawabshah *Pakistan* 26°15N 68°25E **84** F6
Naxçıvan □ *Azerbaijan* 39°25N 45°26E **71** G8
Naxos *Greece* 37°8N 25°25E **69** F11
Naypyidaw *Burma* 19°44N 96°12E **85** K20
Nazaré *Brazil* 13°2S 39°0W **122** B3
Nazas → *Mexico* 25°12N 104°12W **114** B4
Naze, The *U.K.* 51°53N 1°18E **31** C11
Nazret *Ethiopia* 8°32N 39°22E **89** F2
Ndjamena *Chad* 12°10N 14°59E **95** F8
Ndola *Zambia* 13°0S 28°34E **97** G5
Neagh, Lough *U.K.* 54°37N 6°25W **19** B9
Near Is. *U.S.A.* 52°30N 174°0E **108** C1
Neath *U.K.* 51°39N 3°48W **28** D6
Neblina, Pico da *Brazil* 0°48N 66°0W **120** B3
Nebraska □ *U.S.A.* 41°30N 99°30W **110** B7
Nébrodi, Monti *Italy* 37°54N 14°35E **68** F6
Neckar → *Germany* 49°27N 8°29E **64** D5
Necochea *Argentina* 38°30S 58°50W **121** F4
Needham Market *U.K.* 52°9N 1°4E **31** B11
Needles, The *U.K.* 50°39N 1°35W **30** E5
Neenah *U.S.A.* 44°11N 88°28W **112** C3
Neepawa *Canada* 50°15N 99°30W **108** D10
Neftekumsk *Russia* 44°46N 44°50E **71** F7

Nefteyugansk Russia 61°5N 72°42E 76 C8
Negaunee U.S.A. 46°30N 87°36W 112 B4
Negele Ethiopia 5°20N 39°36E 89 F2
Negombo Sri Lanka 7°12N 79°50E 84 R11
Negra, Pta. Peru 6°6S 81°10W 117 D2
Negril Jamaica 18°22N 78°20W 114 a
Negro → Argentina 41°2S 62°47W 121 G3
Negro → Brazil 3°0S 60°0W 120 C3
Negros Phil. 9°30N 122°40E 83 C6
Nei Mongol Zizhiqu □ China 42°0N 112°0E 79 C11
Neijiang China 29°35N 104°55E 78 F9
Neisse → Europe 52°4N 14°46E 64 B8
Neiva Colombia 2°56N 75°18W 120 B2
Nellore India 14°27N 79°59E 84 M11
Nelson Canada 49°30N 117°20W 108 E8
Nelson N.Z. 41°18S 173°16E 99 J13
Nelson U.K. 53°50N 2°13W 27 E4
Nelson → Canada 54°33N 98°2W 108 D10
Neman → Lithuania 55°25N 21°10E 63 F8
Nen Jiang → China 45°28N 124°30E 79 B13
Nenagh Ireland 52°52N 8°11W 20 C6
Nene → U.K. 52°49N 0°11E 31 A9
Nenjiang China 49°10N 125°10E 79 B14
Neosho → U.S.A. 36°48N 95°18W 111 C7
Nepal ■ Asia 28°0N 84°30E 85 F14
Nephi U.S.A. 39°43N 111°50W 110 C4
Nephin Ireland 54°1N 9°22W 18 C3
Nephin Beg Range Ireland 54°0N 9°40W 18 C2
Nerastro, Sarîr Libya 24°20N 20°37E 95 D10
Neryungri Russia 57°38N 124°28E 77 D13
Ness, L. U.K. 57°15N 4°32W 23 H8
Neston U.K. 53°17N 3°4W 27 F2
Netherbury U.K. 50°46N 2°45W 30 E3
Netherlands ■ Europe 52°0N 5°30E 64 B3
Netherlands Antilles = ABC Islands W. Indies 12°15N 69°0W 115 E11
Netley U.K. 50°52N 1°20W 30 E6
Nettilling L. Canada 66°30N 71°0W 109 C12
Nettlebed U.K. 51°34N 0°59W 31 C7
Nettleham U.K. 53°16N 0°29W 27 F8
Neuchâtel Switz. 47°0N 6°55E 64 E4
Neuchâtel, Lac de Switz. 46°53N 6°50E 64 E4
Neuquén Argentina 38°55S 68°0W 121 F3
Neusiedler See Austria 47°50N 16°47E 65 E9
Neva → Russia 59°56N 30°20E 70 C5
Nevada □ U.S.A. 39°0N 117°0W 110 C3
Nevers France 47°0N 3°9E 66 C5
Nevinnomyssk Russia 44°40N 42°0E 71 F7
New Abbey U.K. 54°59N 3°37W 25 E9
New Alresford U.K. 51°5N 1°8W 30 D6
New Amsterdam Guyana 6°15N 57°36W 120 B4
New Bedford U.S.A. 41°38N 70°56W 113 E12
New Britain Papua N. G. 5°50S 150°20E 98 B9
New Britain U.S.A. 41°40N 72°47W 113 E11
New Brunswick U.S.A. 40°30N 74°27W 113 E10
New Brunswick □ Canada 46°50N 66°30W 113 B14
New Caledonia ☑ Pac. Oc. 21°0S 165°0E 99 E12
New Castle Ind., U.S.A. 39°55N 85°22W 112 F5
New Castle Pa., U.S.A. 41°0N 80°21W 112 E7
New Delhi India 28°36N 77°11E 84 E10
New England U.S.A. 43°0N 71°0W 111 B12
New Forest △ U.K. 50°53N 1°34W 30 E5
New Galloway U.K. 55°5N 4°9W 24 D7
New Georgia Is. Solomon Is. 8°15S 157°30E 99 B10
New Glasgow Canada 45°35N 62°36W 109 E13
New Guinea Oceania 4°0S 136°0E 98 B7
New Hampshire □ U.S.A. 44°0N 71°30W 113 D12
New Haven U.S.A. 41°18N 72°55W 113 E11
New Hebrides = Vanuatu ■ Pac. Oc. 15°0S 168°0E 99 D12
New Holland U.K. 53°42N 0°21W 27 E8
New Iberia U.S.A. 30°1N 91°49W 111 D8
New Ireland Papua N. G. 3°20S 151°50E 98 A9
New Jersey □ U.S.A. 40°0N 74°30W 113 E10
New Lexington U.S.A. 39°43N 82°13W 112 F6
New Liskeard Canada 47°31N 79°41W 109 E12
New London U.S.A. 41°22N 72°6W 113 E11
New Madrid U.S.A. 36°36N 89°32W 112 G3
New Mexico □ U.S.A. 34°30N 106°0W 110 D5
New Mills U.K. 53°23N 2°0W 27 F5
New Milton U.K. 50°45N 1°40W 30 E5
New Orleans U.S.A. 29°57N 90°4W 111 E8
New Philadelphia U.S.A. 40°30N 81°27W 112 E7
New Plymouth N.Z. 39°4S 174°5E 99 H13
New Providence Bahamas 25°25N 77°35W 115 B9
New Quay U.K. 52°13N 4°21W 28 C5
New Radnor U.K. 52°15N 3°9W 28 C7
New Romney U.K. 50°59N 0°57E 31 E10
New Ross Ireland 52°23N 6°57W 21 D9
New Rossington U.K. 53°29N 1°4W 27 F6
New Siberian Is. Russia 75°0N 142°0E 77 B15
New South Wales □ Australia 33°0S 146°0E 98 G8
New York U.S.A. 40°43N 74°0W 113 E11
New York □ U.S.A. 43°0N 75°0W 113 D9
New Zealand ■ Oceania 40°0S 176°0E 99 J14
Newark Del., U.S.A. 39°41N 75°46W 113 F10
Newark N.J., U.S.A. 40°44N 74°10W 113 E10
Newark N.Y., U.S.A. 43°3N 77°6W 112 D9
Newark Ohio, U.S.A. 40°3N 82°24W 112 E6
Newark-on-Trent U.K. 53°5N 0°48W 27 F7
Newberry U.S.A. 46°21N 85°30W 112 B5
Newbiggin-by-the-Sea U.K. 55°11N 1°31W 26 B5
Newbigging U.K. 55°42N 3°34W 25 C8
Newbridge Ireland 53°11N 6°48W 21 B9
Newburgh U.S.A. 41°30N 74°1W 113 E10
Newburn U.K. 54°59N 1°43W 26 C5
Newbury U.K. 51°24N 1°20W 30 D6
Newburyport U.S.A. 42°49N 70°53W 113 D12
Newby Bridge U.K. 54°17N 2°57W 26 D3
Newcastle Australia 33°0S 151°46E 98 G9
Newcastle Canada 47°1N 65°38W 113 B15
Newcastle Ireland 52°27N 9°3W 20 D4
Newcastle S. Africa 27°45S 29°58E 97 K5
Newcastle U.K. 54°13N 5°54W 19 C10
Newcastle Emlyn U.K. 52°2N 4°28W 28 C5
Newcastle-under-Lyme U.K. 53°1N 2°14W 27 F4
Newcastle-upon-Tyne U.K. 54°58N 1°36W 26 C5
Newcastleton U.K. 55°11N 2°49W 25 D10
Newent U.K. 51°56N 2°24W 30 C4
Newfoundland & Labrador □ Canada 52°0N 58°0W 109 D14
Newham □ U.K. 51°31N 0°3E 31 C9
Newhaven U.K. 50°47N 0°3E 31 E9
Newington Kent, U.K. 51°6N 1°7E 31 D11
Newington Kent, U.K. 51°21N 0°41E 31 D10
Newlyn U.K. 50°6N 5°34W 29 G2
Newlyn East U.K. 50°22N 5°5W 29 G3
Newman Australia 23°18S 119°45E 98 E2
Newmarket Ireland 52°13N 9°0W 20 D5
Newmarket U.K. 52°15N 0°25E 31 B9
Newnham U.K. 51°48N 2°27W 30 C4
Newport Ireland 53°53N 9°33W 18 D2
Newport Essex, U.K. 51°59N 0°14E 31 C9
Newport I. of W., U.K. 50°42N 1°17W 30 E6
Newport Newport, U.K. 51°35N 3°0W 29 D8
Newport Pembs., U.K. 52°1N 4°51W 28 C4
Newport Telford & Wrekin, U.K. 52°46N 2°22W 27 G4
Newport Ark., U.S.A. 35°37N 91°16W 111 C8
Newport Ky., U.S.A. 39°5N 84°29W 112 F5
Newport R.I., U.S.A. 41°29N 71°19W 113 E12
Newport Vt., U.S.A. 44°56N 72°13W 113 C11
Newport News U.S.A. 36°58N 76°25W 111 C11
Newport Pagnell U.K. 52°5N 0°43W 31 B7
Newquay U.K. 50°25N 5°6W 29 G3
Newry U.K. 54°11N 6°21W 19 C9
Newton Abbot U.K. 50°32N 3°37W 29 F6
Newton Arlosh U.K. 54°53N 3°14W 26 C2
Newton Aycliffe U.K. 54°37N 1°34W 26 C5
Newton Ferrers U.K. 50°19N 4°3W 29 G5
Newton le Willows U.K. 53°28N 2°38W 27 F3
Newton St. Cyres U.K. 50°46N 3°36W 29 F6
Newton Stewart U.K. 54°57N 4°30W 24 E6
Newtonmore U.K. 57°4N 4°8W 23 H9
Newtown U.K. 52°31N 3°19W 28 B7
Newtown St. Boswells U.K. 55°34N 2°39W 25 C10
Newtownabbey U.K. 54°40N 5°56W 19 B10
Newtownards U.K. 54°36N 5°42W 19 B10
Newtownstewart U.K. 54°43N 7°23W 18 B7
Neyshābūr Iran 36°10N 58°50E 87 B9
Ngamring China 29°14N 87°10E 78 F6
Nganglong Kangri China 33°0N 81°0E 78 E5
Ngaoundéré Cameroon 7°15N 13°35E 96 C2
Ngoring Hu China 34°55N 97°5E 78 E8
Ngorongoro Tanzania 3°11S 35°32E 96 E7
Nguru Nigeria 12°56N 10°29E 95 F8
Nha Trang Vietnam 12°16N 109°10E 82 B3
Nhamundá → Brazil 2°12S 56°41W 120 C4
Niagara Falls Canada 43°7N 79°5W 109 E12
Niagara Falls U.S.A. 43°5N 79°4W 112 D8
Niamey Niger 13°27N 2°6E 94 F6
Nias Indonesia 1°0N 97°30E 82 D1
Nicaragua ■ Cent. Amer. 11°40N 85°30W 114 E7
Nicaragua, L. de Nic. 12°0N 85°30W 114 E7
Nice France 43°42N 7°14E 66 E7
Nicholasville U.S.A. 37°53N 84°34W 112 G5
Nicobar Is. Ind. Oc. 8°0N 93°30E 53 D14
Nicosia Cyprus 35°10N 33°25E 86 C3
Nicoya, Pen. de Costa Rica 9°45N 85°40W 114 F7
Nidd → U.K. 53°59N 1°23W 27 E6
Nidderdale U.K. 54°5N 1°46W 26 D5
Niedersachsen □ Germany 52°50N 9°0E 64 B5
Nieuw Nickerie Suriname 6°0N 56°59W 120 B4
Niğde Turkey 37°58N 34°40E 86 B3
Niger ■ W. Afr. 17°30N 10°0E 94 E7
Niger → W. Afr. 5°33N 6°33E 94 G7
Nigeria ■ W. Afr. 8°30N 8°0E 94 G7
Niigata Japan 37°58N 139°0E 81 E6
Ni'ihau U.S.A. 21°54N 160°9W 110 H14
Nijmegen Neths. 51°50N 5°52E 64 C3
Nikolayev Ukraine 46°58N 32°0E 71 E5
Nikolayevsk-na-Amur Russia 53°8N 140°44E 77 D15
Nikopol Ukraine 47°35N 34°25E 71 E5
Nikšić Montenegro 42°50N 18°57E 69 C8
Nile → Africa 30°10N 31°6E 95 B12
Nimach India 24°30N 74°56E 84 G9
Nîmes France 43°50N 4°23E 66 E6
Nineveh Iraq 36°25N 43°10E 86 B5
Ninfield U.K. 50°53N 0°26E 31 E9
Ningbo China 29°51N 121°28E 79 F13
Ningjing Shan China 31°0N 98°20E 78 E8
Ningxia Hui □ China 38°0N 106°0E 78 D10
Niobrara → U.S.A. 42°46N 98°3W 110 B7
Niort France 46°19N 0°29W 66 C3
Nipawin Canada 53°20N 104°0W 108 D9
Nipigon Canada 49°0N 88°17W 112 A3
Nipigon, L. Canada 49°50N 88°30W 109 E11
Nipissing, L. Canada 46°20N 80°0W 109 E12
Niquelândia Brazil 14°33S 48°23W 122 B1
Niš Serbia 43°19N 21°58E 69 C9
Niterói Brazil 22°53S 43°7W 122 D2
Nith → U.K. 55°14N 3°33W 25 D8
Niton U.K. 50°35N 1°17W 30 E6
Nitra Slovak Rep. 48°19N 18°4E 65 D10
Nitra → Slovak Rep. 47°46N 18°10E 65 E10
Niuafo'ou Tonga 15°30S 175°58W 99 D15
Niue ☑ Pac. Oc. 19°2S 169°54W 99 D17
Nivernais France 47°15N 3°30E 66 C5
Nizamabad India 18°45N 78°7E 84 K11
Nizhnekamsk Russia 55°38N 51°49E 70 C9
Nizhnevartovsk Russia 60°56N 76°38E 76 C8
Nizhniy Novgorod Russia 56°20N 44°0E 70 C7
Nizhniy Tagil Russia 57°55N 59°57E 70 C10
Nizhyn Ukraine 51°5N 31°55E 71 D5
Nizwá Oman 22°56N 57°32E 89 C6
Nkawkaw Ghana 6°36N 0°49W 94 G5
Nkongsamba Cameroon 4°55N 9°55E 96 D1
Noakhali Bangla. 22°48N 91°10E 85 H17
Nobeoka Japan 32°36N 131°41E 81 G2
Noblesville U.S.A. 40°3N 86°1W 112 E5
Nogales Mexico 31°19N 110°56W 114 A2
Nogales U.S.A. 31°21N 110°56W 110 D4
Noirmoutier, Î. de France 46°58N 2°10W 66 C2
Nola C.A.R. 3°35N 16°4E 96 D3
Nome U.S.A. 64°30N 165°25W 108 C3
Nord-Ostsee-Kanal Germany 54°12N 9°32E 64 A5
Nordelph U.K. 52°35N 0°17E 31 A9
Norderstedt Germany 53°42N 10°1E 64 B5
Nordfriesische Inseln Germany 54°40N 8°20E 64 A5
Nordkapp Norway 71°10N 25°50E 63 C9
Nordrhein-Westfalen □ Germany 51°45N 7°30E 64 C4
Nordvik Russia 74°2N 111°32E 77 B12
Nore → Ireland 52°25N 6°58W 21 D9
Norfolk Nebr., U.S.A. 42°2N 97°25W 111 B7
Norfolk Va., U.S.A. 36°50N 76°17W 111 C11
Norfolk □ U.K. 52°39N 0°54E 31 A10
Norfolk Broads △ U.K. 52°45N 1°30E 31 A11
Norfolk I. Pac. Oc. 28°58S 168°3E 99 F12
Norham U.K. 55°43N 2°9W 26 A4
Norilsk Russia 69°20N 88°6E 77 C9
Normal U.S.A. 40°31N 88°59W 112 E3
Norman U.S.A. 35°13N 97°26W 110 C7
Norman Wells Canada 65°17N 126°51W 108 C7
Normandie France 48°45N 0°10E 66 B4
Normanton Australia 17°40S 141°10E 98 D7
Normanton U.K. 53°42N 1°24W 27 E6
Norristown U.S.A. 40°7N 75°21W 113 E10
Norrköping Sweden 58°37N 16°11E 63 F7
Norrland Sweden 62°15N 15°45E 63 E7
Norseman Australia 32°8S 121°43E 98 G3
Norte, Serra do Brazil 11°20S 59°0W 120 D4
North, C. Canada 47°2N 60°20W 113 B17
North Ayrshire □ U.K. 55°45N 4°44W 24 C6
North Battleford Canada 52°50N 108°17W 108 D9
North Bay Canada 46°20N 79°30W 109 E12
North Berwick U.K. 56°4N 2°42W 25 B10
North C. Canada 47°5N 64°0W 113 B15
North C. N.Z. 34°23S 173°4E 99 G13
North Canadian → U.S.A. 35°22N 95°37W 110 C7
North Carolina □ U.S.A. 35°30N 80°0W 111 C11
North Cerney U.K. 51°45N 1°57W 30 C5
North Channel Canada 46°0N 83°0W 112 B6
North Channel U.K. 55°13N 5°52W 24 D4
North Dakota □ U.S.A. 47°30N 100°15W 110 A7
North Dorset Downs U.K. 50°51N 2°30W 30 E4
North Downs U.K. 51°19N 0°21E 31 D9
North Esk → U.K. 56°46N 2°24W 23 J13
North European Plain Europe 55°0N 25°0E 56 E10
North Foreland U.K. 51°22N 1°28E 31 D11
North Harris U.K. 58°0N 6°55W 22 F4
North Hill U.K. 50°33N 4°27W 29 F5
North Hykeham U.K. 53°11N 0°35W 27 F7
North I. N.Z. 38°0S 175°0E 99 H14
North Korea ■ Asia 40°0N 127°0E 79 D14
North Magnetic Pole Arctic 85°9N 149°0W 54 A2
North Minch U.K. 58°5N 5°55W 22 F6
North Molton U.K. 51°3N 3°49W 29 E6
North Ossetia-Alaniya □ Russia 43°30N 44°30E 71 F7
North Petherton U.K. 51°5N 3°1W 30 D2
North Platte U.S.A. 41°8N 100°46W 110 B6
North Platte → U.S.A. 41°7N 100°42W 110 B6
North Pole Arctic 90°0N 0°0 54 A
North Pt. Barbados 13°20N 59°37W 114 c
North Ronaldsay U.K. 59°22N 2°26W 23 D13
North Saskatchewan → Canada 53°15N 105°5W 108 D9
North Sea Europe 56°0N 4°0E 56 D6
North Sea Canal = Nord-Ostsee-Kanal Germany 54°12N 9°32E 64 A5
North Somercotes U.K. 53°27N 0°8E 27 F9
North Sunderland U.K. 55°34N 1°40W 26 A5
North Tawton U.K. 50°48N 3°54W 29 F6
North Thompson → Canada 50°40N 120°20W 108 D7
North Thoresby U.K. 53°28N 0°4W 27 F8
North Tidworth U.K. 51°15N 1°40W 30 D5
North Tyne → U.K. 55°0N 2°8W 26 C4
North Uist U.K. 57°40N 7°15W 22 G3
North Vernon U.S.A. 39°0N 85°38W 112 F5
North Walsham U.K. 52°50N 1°22E 31 A11
North West C. Australia 21°45S 114°9E 98 E1
North West Highlands U.K. 57°33N 4°58W 23 G8
North West River Canada 53°30N 60°10W 109 D13
North York Moors △ U.K. 54°27N 0°51W 26 D7
North Yorkshire □ U.K. 54°15N 1°25W 26 D6
Northallerton U.K. 54°20N 1°26W 26 D6
Northam Australia 31°35S 116°42E 98 G2
Northam U.K. 51°2N 4°13W 29 E5
Northampton U.K. 52°15N 0°53W 31 B7
Northampton U.S.A. 42°19N 72°38W 113 D11
Northamptonshire □ U.K. 52°16N 0°55W 31 B7
Northern Circars India 17°30N 82°30E 85 L13
Northern Ireland □ U.K. 54°45N 7°0W 19 B8
Northern Marianas ☑ Pac. Oc. 17°0N 145°0E 102 F6
Northern Sporades Greece 39°15N 23°30E 69 E10
Northern Territory □ Australia 20°0S 133°0E 98 E5
Northfleet U.K. 51°26N 0°20E 31 D9
Northiam U.K. 50°59N 0°36E 31 E10
Northleach U.K. 51°49N 1°50W 30 C5
Northrepps U.K. 52°54N 1°21E 31 A11
Northumberland □ U.K. 55°12N 2°0W 26 B4
Northumberland △ Northumberland, U.K. 55°15N 2°20W 26 B4
Northumberland Str. Canada 46°20N 64°0W 109 E13
Northwest Territories □ Canada 63°0N 118°0W 108 C9
Northwich U.K. 53°15N 2°31W 27 F3
Northwold U.K. 52°33N 0°36E 31 A10
Norton N. Yorks., U.K. 54°8N 0°47W 26 D7
Norton Suffolk, U.K. 52°16N 0°52E 31 B10
Norton Fitzwarren U.K. 51°1N 3°8W 30 D2
Norton Sd. U.S.A. 63°50N 164°0W 108 C3
Norwalk U.S.A. 41°15N 82°37W 112 E6
Norway ■ Europe 63°0N 11°0E 63 E6
Norway House Canada 53°59N 97°50W 108 D10
Norwegian B. Canada 77°30N 90°0W 109 B11
Norwegian Sea Atl. Oc. 66°0N 1°0E 56 B6
Norwich U.K. 52°38N 1°18E 31 A11
Norwich U.S.A. 42°32N 75°32W 113 D10
Noss Hd. U.K. 58°28N 3°3W 23 F11
Nossa Senhora do Socorro Brazil 10°52S 37°7W 122 B3
Nossob → S. Africa 26°55S 20°45E 97 K4
Notre Dame B. Canada 49°45N 55°30W 109 E14
Nottaway → Canada 51°22N 78°55W 109 D12
Nottingham U.K. 52°58N 1°10W 27 G6
Nottingham I. Canada 63°20N 77°55W 109 C12
Nottinghamshire □ U.K. 53°10N 1°3W 27 F6
Nouâdhibou Mauritania 20°54N 17°0W 94 D2
Nouâdhibou, Râs Mauritania 20°50N 17°0W 94 D2
Nouakchott Mauritania 18°9N 15°58W 94 E2
Nouméa N. Cal. 22°17S 166°30E 99 E12
Nova Friburgo Brazil 22°16S 42°30W 122 D2
Nova Iguaçu Brazil 22°45S 43°28W 122 D2
Nova Scotia □ Canada 45°10N 63°0W 113 C16
Nova Venécia Brazil 18°45S 40°24W 122 C2
Novara Italy 45°28N 8°38E 68 B3
Novaya Zemlya Russia 75°0N 56°0E 76 B6
Novi Pazar Serbia 43°12N 20°28E 69 C9
Novi Sad Serbia 45°18N 19°52E 69 B8
Novocherkassk Russia 47°27N 40°15E 71 E7
Novokuybyshevsk Russia 53°7N 49°58E 70 D8
Novokuznetsk Russia 53°45N 87°10E 76 D9
Novomoskovsk Russia 54°5N 38°15E 70 D6
Novorossiysk Russia 44°43N 37°46E 71 F6
Novoshakhtinsk Russia 47°46N 39°58E 71 E6
Novosibirsk Russia 55°0N 83°5E 76 D9
Novotroitsk Russia 51°10N 58°15E 70 D10
Novyy Urengoy Russia 65°48N 76°52E 76 C8
Nowy Sącz Poland 49°40N 20°41E 65 D11
Noyabrsk Russia 64°34N 76°21E 76 C8
Nu Jiang → China 29°58N 97°25E 78 F8
Nu Shan China 26°0N 99°20E 78 F8
Nubia Africa 21°0N 32°0E 90 D7
Nubian Desert Sudan 21°30N 33°30E 95 D12
Nueces → U.S.A. 27°51N 97°30W 110 E7
Nueltin L. Canada 60°30N 99°30W 108 C10
Nueva Rosita Mexico 27°57N 101°13W 114 B4
Nuevitas Cuba 21°30N 77°20W 115 C9
Nuevo Laredo Mexico 27°30N 99°31W 114 B5
Nuku'alofa Tonga 21°10S 175°12W 99 E16
Nukulaelae Tuvalu 9°23S 179°52E 99 B14
Nukus Uzbekistan 42°27N 59°41E 87 A9
Nullarbor Plain Australia 31°10S 129°0E 98 G4
Numan Nigeria 9°29N 12°3E 95 G8
Numazu Japan 35°7N 138°51E 81 F6
Nunavut □ Canada 66°0N 85°0W 109 C11
Nuneaton U.K. 52°32N 1°27W 27 G6
Nunivak I. U.S.A. 60°10N 166°30W 108 B3
Nunney U.K. 51°12N 2°22W 30 D4
Nuoro Italy 40°20N 9°20E 68 D3
Nuremberg Germany 49°27N 11°3E 64 D6
Nusaybin Turkey 37°3N 41°10E 71 G7
Nuuk Greenland 64°10N 51°35W 54 C5
Nuweveldberge S. Africa 32°10S 21°45E 97 L4
Nyagan Russia 62°30N 65°38E 76 C7
Nyahururu Kenya 0°2N 36°27E 96 D7
Nyainqêntanglha Shan China 30°0N 90°0E 78 F7
Nyâlâ Sudan 12°2N 24°58E 95 F10
Nyalam China 28°32N 86°4E 78 F6
Nyíregyháza Hungary 47°58N 21°47E 65 E11
Nysa Poland 50°30N 17°22E 65 C9
Nzérékoré Guinea 7°49N 8°48W 94 G4

O

Oa, Mull of U.K. 55°35N 6°20W 24 C3
Oadby U.K. 52°36N 1°5W 27 G6
Oahe, L. U.S.A. 44°27N 100°24W 110 A6
O'ahu U.S.A. 21°28N 157°58W 110 H16
Oak Hill U.S.A. 37°59N 81°9W 112 G7
Oak Ridge U.S.A. 36°1N 84°16W 111 C10
Oakengates U.K. 52°41N 2°26W 27 G4
Oakham U.K. 52°40N 0°43W 27 G7
Oakland U.S.A. 37°48N 122°18W 110 C2
Oates Land Antarctica 69°0S 160°0E 55 C11
Oaxaca Mexico 17°3N 96°43W 114 D5
Ob → Russia 66°45N 69°30E 76 C7
Ob, G. of Russia 69°0N 73°0E 76 C8
Oba Canada 49°4N 84°7W 109 E11
Oban U.K. 56°25N 5°29W 24 B5
Oberhausen Germany 51°28N 6°51E 64 C4
Obi, Kepulauan Indonesia 1°23S 127°45E 83 E7
Óbidos Brazil 1°50S 55°30W 120 C4
Obihiro Japan 42°56N 143°12E 81 B8
Obozerskiy Russia 63°34N 40°21E 70 B7
Obshchi Syrt Russia 52°0N 53°0E 56 E16
Ocala U.S.A. 29°11N 82°8W 111 E10
Occidental, Cordillera Colombia 5°0N 76°0W 117 C3
Occidental, Grand Erg Algeria 30°20N 1°0E 94 B6
Ocean City U.S.A. 39°17N 74°35W 113 F10
Oceanside U.S.A. 33°12N 117°23W 110 D3
Ochil Hills U.K. 56°14N 3°40W 25 B8
Ocho Rios Jamaica 18°24N 77°6W 114 a
Oconto U.S.A. 44°53N 87°52W 112 C4
Odawara Japan 35°20N 139°6E 81 F6
Odense Denmark 55°22N 10°23E 63 F6
Oder → Europe 53°33N 14°38E 64 B8
Odessa Ukraine 46°30N 30°45E 71 E5
Odessa U.S.A. 31°52N 102°23W 110 D6
Odiham U.K. 51°15N 0°55W 31 D7
Odintsovo Russia 55°40N 37°16E 70 C6
Odisha □ India 20°0N 84°0E 85 K14
Odzi Zimbabwe 19°0S 32°20E 97 H6
Offa Nigeria 8°13N 4°42E 94 G6
Offaly □ Ireland 53°15N 7°30W 21 B8
Offenbach Germany 50°6N 8°44E 64 C5
Ogaden Ethiopia 7°30N 45°30E 89 F3
Ōgaki Japan 35°21N 136°37E 81 F5
Ogasawara Gunto Pac. Oc. 27°0N 142°0E 102 E6
Ogbomosho Nigeria 8°1N 4°11E 94 G6
Ogden U.S.A. 41°13N 111°58W 110 B4
Ogdensburg U.S.A. 44°42N 75°30W 113 C10
Ogooué → Gabon 1°0S 9°0E 96 E1
Ohio □ U.S.A. 40°15N 82°45W 112 E5
Ohio → U.S.A. 36°59N 89°8W 111 C9
Ohře → Czech Rep. 50°30N 14°10E 64 C8
Ohrid, L. Macedonia 41°8N 20°52E 69 D9
Oil City U.S.A. 41°26N 79°42W 112 E8
Oise → France 49°0N 2°4E 66 B5
Oistins Barbados 13°4N 59°33W 114 c
Oistins B. Barbados 13°4N 59°33W 114 c
Ōita Japan 33°14N 131°36E 81 G2
Ojos del Salado, Cerro Argentina 27°0S 68°40W 121 E3
Oka → Russia 56°20N 43°59E 70 C7
Okara Pakistan 30°50N 73°31E 84 D8
Okavango Delta Botswana 18°45S 22°45E 97 H4
Okayama Japan 34°40N 133°54E 81 F3
Okazaki Japan 34°57N 137°10E 81 F5
Okeechobee, L. U.S.A. 27°0N 80°50W 111 E10
Okehampton U.K. 50°44N 4°0W 29 F5
Okhotsk Russia 59°20N 143°10E 77 D15
Okhotsk, Sea of Asia 55°0N 145°0E 77 D15
Oki-Shotō Japan 36°5N 133°15E 81 E3
Okinawa-Jima Japan 26°32N 128°0E 79 F14
Oklahoma □ U.S.A. 35°20N 97°30W 110 C7
Oklahoma City U.S.A. 35°30N 97°30W 110 C7
Oktyabrskiy Russia 54°28N 53°28E 70 D9
Öland Sweden 56°45N 16°38E 63 F7
Olavarría Argentina 36°55S 60°20W 121 F3
Ólbia Italy 40°55N 9°31E 68 D3
Old Basing U.K. 51°16N 1°3W 30 D6
Old Crow Canada 67°30N 139°55W 108 C6
Old Fletton U.K. 52°33N 0°14W 31 A8
Old Leake U.K. 53°2N 0°5E 27 F9
Old Town U.S.A. 44°56N 68°39W 113 C13
Oldbury U.K. 51°38N 2°33W 30 C3
Oldcastle Ireland 53°46N 7°10W 19 D7
Oldenburg Germany 53°9N 8°13E 64 B5
Oldham U.K. 53°33N 2°7W 27 E4
Oldmeldrum U.K. 57°20N 2°19W 23 H13
Olean U.S.A. 42°5N 78°26W 112 D8
Olekminsk Russia 60°25N 120°30E 77 C13
Olenek → Russia 73°0N 120°10E 77 B13
Oléron, Î. d' France 45°55N 1°15W 66 D3
Ölgiy Mongolia 48°56N 89°57E 78 B6
Olímpia Brazil 20°44S 48°54W 122 D1
Oliveira Brazil 20°39S 44°50W 122 D2
Ollagüe Chile 21°15S 68°10W 120 E3
Ollerton U.K. 53°12N 1°1W 27 F6
Olmaliq Uzbekistan 40°50N 69°35E 76 E7
Olney U.K. 52°10N 0°41W 31 B7
Olney U.S.A. 38°44N 88°5W 112 F3
Olomouc Czech Rep. 49°38N 17°12E 65 D9
Olsztyn Poland 53°48N 20°29E 65 B11
Olt → Romania 43°43N 24°51E 65 G13
Olympia Greece 37°39N 21°39E 69 F9
Olympia U.S.A. 47°3N 122°53W 110 A2
Olympus, Mt. Greece 40°6N 22°23E 69 D10
Olympus, Mt. U.S.A. 47°48N 123°43W 110 A2
Omagh U.K. 54°36N 7°19W 18 B7
Omaha U.S.A. 41°17N 95°58W 111 B7
Oman ■ Asia 23°0N 58°0E 89 C6
Oman, G. of Asia 24°30N 58°30E 87 E9
Ombersley U.K. 52°16N 2°13W 30 B4
Omdurmân Sudan 15°40N 32°28E 95 E12
Ometepec Mexico 16°41N 98°25W 114 D5
Omsk Russia 55°0N 73°12E 76 D8
Ōmuta Japan 33°5N 130°26E 81 G2
Ondangwa Namibia 17°57S 16°4E 97 H3
Öndörhaan Mongolia 47°19N 110°39E 79 B11
Onega → Russia 63°58N 38°2E 70 B6
Onega, L. Russia 61°44N 35°22E 70 B6
Onega B. Russia 64°24N 36°38E 70 B6
Oneida U.S.A. 43°6N 75°39W 113 D10
O'Neill U.S.A. 42°27N 98°39W 110 B7
Oneonta U.S.A. 42°27N 75°4W 113 D10
Onitsha Nigeria 6°6N 6°42E 94 G7
Onny → U.K. 52°24N 2°47W 27 H3
Onslow B. U.S.A. 34°20N 77°15W 111 D11
Ontario U.S.A. 44°2N 116°58W 110 B3
Ontario □ Canada 48°0N 83°0W 109 E11
Ontario, L. N. Amer. 43°20N 78°0W 112 D8
Ontonagon U.S.A. 46°52N 89°19W 112 B3
Oostende Belgium 51°15N 2°54E 64 C2
Opava Czech Rep. 49°57N 17°58E 65 D9
Opole Poland 50°42N 17°58E 65 C9
Oradea Romania 47°2N 21°58E 65 E11
Öræfajökull Iceland 64°2N 16°39W 63 B2
Oral Kazakhstan 51°20N 51°20E 71 D9
Oran Algeria 35°45N 0°39W 94 A5
Orange Australia 33°15S 149°7E 98 G8
Orange France 44°8N 4°47E 66 D6
Orange U.S.A. 38°15N 78°7W 112 F8
Orange → S. Africa 28°41S 16°28E 97 K3
Orange, C. Brazil 4°20N 51°30W 120 B4
Orangeburg U.S.A. 33°30N 80°52W 111 D10
Orangeville Canada 43°55N 80°5W 112 D7
Ordos China 39°50N 110°0E 79 D10
Ordos Desert China 39°0N 109°0E 79 D10
Ordu Turkey 40°55N 37°53E 71 F6
Örebro Sweden 59°20N 15°18E 63 F7
Oregon □ U.S.A. 44°0N 121°0W 110 B2
Orekhovo-Zuyevo Russia 55°50N 38°55E 70 C6
Orel Russia 52°57N 36°3E 70 D6
Orem U.S.A. 40°19N 111°42W 110 B4
Orenburg Russia 51°45N 55°6E 70 D10
Orford U.K. 52°6N 1°33E 31 B12
Orford Ness U.K. 52°5N 1°35E 31 B12
Oriental, Cordillera Colombia 6°0N 73°0W 117 C3
Oriental, Grand Erg Algeria 30°0N 6°30E 94 B7
Orihuela Spain 38°7N 0°55W 67 C5
Orinoco → Venezuela 9°15N 61°30W 120 B3
Oristano Italy 39°54N 8°36E 68 E3
Orizaba Mexico 18°51N 97°6W 114 D5
Orizaba, Pico de Mexico 18°58N 97°15W 114 D5
Orkhon → Mongolia 50°21N 106°0E 78 A10
Orkney □ U.K. 59°2N 3°13W 23 D11
Orkney Is. U.K. 59°0N 3°0W 23 E12
Orlando U.S.A. 28°32N 81°22W 111 E10
Orléanais France 48°0N 2°0E 66 C5
Orléans France 47°54N 1°52E 66 C4
Orléans, Î. d' Canada 46°54N 70°58W 113 B12
Ormara Pakistan 25°16N 64°33E 84 G4
Ormesby St. Margaret U.K. 52°41N 1°41E 31 A12
Ormoc Phil. 11°0N 124°37E 83 B6
Ormskirk U.K. 53°35N 2°54W 27 E3
Örnsköldsvik Sweden 63°17N 18°40E 63 E7
Oronsay U.K. 56°1N 6°15W 24 B3
Orsha Belarus 54°30N 30°25E 70 D5
Ortegal, C. Spain 43°43N 7°52W 67 A2
Oruro Bolivia 18°0S 67°9W 120 D3
Orwell → U.K. 51°59N 1°18E 31 C11
Ōsaka Japan 34°42N 135°30E 81 F4
Osh Kyrgyzstan 40°37N 72°49E 76 E8
Oshakati Namibia 17°45S 15°40E 97 H3
Oshawa Canada 43°50N 78°50W 109 E12
Oshkosh U.S.A. 44°1N 88°33W 112 C3

Oshogbo

Port Erin

Oshogbo Nigeria 7°48N 4°37E 94 G6
Osijek Croatia 45°34N 18°41E 69 B8
Osizweni S. Africa 27°49S 30°7E 97 K6
Oskaloosa U.S.A. 41°18N 92°39W 111 B8
Oskarshamn Sweden 57°15N 16°27E 63 F7
Öskemen Kazakhstan 50°0N 82°36E 76 E9
Oslo Norway 59°54N 10°43E 63 F6
Oslofjorden Norway 59°20N 10°35E 63 F6
Osmaniye Turkey 37°5N 36°10E 71 G6
Osmotherley U.K. 54°22N 1°18W 26 D6
Osnabrück Germany 52°17N 8°3E 64 B5
Osorno Chile 40°25S 73°0W 121 G2
Ossa, Mt. Australia 41°52S 146°3E 98 J8
Ossett U.K. 53°41N 1°34W 27 E5
Ostend = Oostende Belgium 51°15N 2°54E 64 C2
Österdalälven → Sweden 60°30N 16°7E 63 E6
Östersund Sweden 63°10N 14°38E 63 E6
Ostfriesische Inseln Germany 53°42N 7°0E 64 B4
Ostrava Czech Rep. 49°51N 18°18E 65 D10
Ostrołęka Poland 53°4N 21°32E 65 B11
Ostrów Wielkopolski Poland 51°36N 17°44E 65 C9
Ostrowiec-Świętokrzyski Poland 50°55N 21°22E 65 C11
Oswaldtwistle U.K. 53°43N 2°26W 27 E4
Oswego U.S.A. 43°27N 76°31W 112 D9
Oswestry U.K. 52°52N 3°3W 27 G2
Otaru Japan 43°10N 141°0E 81 B7
Otjiwarongo Namibia 20°30S 16°33E 97 J3
Otley U.K. 53°54N 1°41W 27 E5
Otranto Italy 40°9N 18°28E 69 D8
Otranto, Str. of Italy 40°15N 18°40E 69 D8
Ōtsu Japan 35°0N 135°50E 81 F4
Ottawa Canada 45°26N 75°42W 113 C10
Ottawa U.S.A. 41°21N 88°51W 112 E3
Ottawa Is. Canada 59°35N 80°10W 109 D11
Otter → U.K. 50°38N 3°19W 29 F7
Otterburn U.K. 55°14N 2°11W 26 B4
Ottery St. Mary U.K. 50°44N 3°17W 29 F7
Ottumwa U.S.A. 41°1N 92°25W 111 B8
Ouachita → U.S.A. 31°38N 91°49W 111 D8
Ouachita Mts. U.S.A. 34°30N 94°30W 111 D8
Ouagadougou Burkina Faso 12°25N 1°30W 94 F5
Oubangi → Dem. Rep. of the Congo 0°30S 17°50E 96 E3
Oudtshoorn S. Africa 33°35S 22°14E 97 L4
Ouezzane Morocco 34°51N 5°35W 94 B4
Oughterard Ireland 53°26N 9°18W 20 B4
Oujda Morocco 34°41N 1°55W 94 B5
Oulton U.K. 52°30N 1°43E 31 B12
Oulton Broad U.K. 52°28N 1°42E 31 B12
Oulu Finland 65°1N 25°29E 63 D9
Oulujärvi Finland 64°25N 27°15E 63 E9
Oulujoki → Finland 65°1N 25°30E 63 D9
Oundle U.K. 52°29N 0°28W 31 B8
Ourense Spain 42°19N 7°55W 67 A2
Ouro Fino Brazil 22°16S 46°25W 122 D1
Ouro Prêto Brazil 20°20S 43°30W 122 D2
Ouse → E. Sussex, U.K. 50°47N 0°4E 31 E9
Ouse → N. Yorks., U.K. 53°44N 0°55W 27 E7
Outaouais → Canada 45°27N 74°8W 109 E12
Outer Hebrides U.K. 57°30N 7°15W 22 H2
Outjo Namibia 20°5S 16°7E 97 J3
Outwell U.K. 52°37N 0°14E 31 A9
Ovalle Chile 30°33S 71°18W 121 F2
Ovamboland Namibia 18°30S 16°0E 97 H3
Over Wallop U.K. 51°9N 1°36W 30 D5
Overton U.K. 51°15N 1°15W 30 D6
Oviedo Spain 43°25N 5°50W 67 A3
Owatonna U.S.A. 44°5N 93°14W 111 B8
Owen Sound Canada 44°35N 80°55W 109 E11
Owen Stanley Ra. Papua N. G. 8°30S 147°0E 98 B8
Owens → U.S.A. 36°26N 117°57W 110 C3
Owensboro U.S.A. 37°46N 87°7W 112 G4
Owo Nigeria 7°10N 5°39E 94 G7
Owosso U.S.A. 43°0N 84°10W 112 D5
Owston Ferry U.K. 53°29N 0°47W 27 F7
Owyhee → U.S.A. 43°49N 117°2W 110 B3
Oxford U.K. 51°46N 1°15W 30 C6
Oxfordshire □ U.K. 51°48N 1°16W 30 C6
Oxnard U.S.A. 34°12N 119°11W 110 D3
Oyama Japan 36°18N 139°48E 81 E6
Oyem Gabon 1°34N 11°31E 96 D2
Oykel → U.K. 57°56N 4°26W 23 G9
Oyo Nigeria 7°46N 3°56E 94 G6
Ozark Plateau U.S.A. 37°20N 91°40W 111 G8
Ozarks, L. of the U.S.A. 38°12N 92°38W 111 G8

P

Paarl S. Africa 33°45S 18°56E 97 L3
Pab Hills Pakistan 26°30N 66°45E 84 F5
Pabaidh = Pabbay U.K. 57°46N 7°14W 22 G3
Pabbay U.K. 57°46N 7°14W 22 G3
Pabna Bangla. 24°1N 89°18E 85 G16
Pacaraima, Sa. S. Amer. 4°0N 62°30W 120 B3
Pacasmayo Peru 7°20S 79°35W 120 C2
Pachuca Mexico 20°7N 98°44W 114 C5
Pacific Ocean 10°0N 140°0W 103 G14
Padang Indonesia 1°0S 100°20E 82 E2
Padangsidempuan Indonesia 1°30N 99°15E 82 D1
Paddock Wood U.K. 51°11N 0°24E 31 D9
Paderborn Germany 51°42N 8°45E 64 C5
Padiham U.K. 53°48N 2°18W 27 E4
Padre I. U.S.A. 27°10N 97°25W 111 E7
Padstow U.K. 50°33N 4°58W 29 F4
Padstow B. U.K. 50°34N 4°57W 29 F4
Padua Italy 45°25N 11°53E 68 B4
Paducah U.S.A. 37°5N 88°37W 112 G3
Pag Croatia 44°25N 15°3E 68 B6
Pagadian Phil. 7°55N 123°30E 83 C6
Page U.S.A. 36°57N 111°27W 110 C4
Pāhala U.S.A. 19°12N 155°29W 110 J17
Paignton U.K. 50°26N 3°35W 29 G6
Paine Grande, Cerro Chile 50°59S 73°4W 121 H2
Painesville U.S.A. 41°43N 81°15W 112 E7
Painswick U.K. 51°47N 2°10W 30 C4
Painted Desert U.S.A. 36°0N 111°0W 110 C4
Paintsville U.S.A. 37°49N 82°48W 112 G6
País Vasco □ Spain 42°50N 2°45W 67 A4
Paisley U.K. 55°50N 4°25W 24 C7

Paita Peru 5°11S 81°9W 120 C1
Pakistan ■ Asia 30°0N 70°0E 84 F7
Pakxe Laos 15°5N 105°52E 82 A3
Palagruža Croatia 42°24N 16°15E 68 C7
Palakkad India 10°46N 76°42E 84 P10
Palani Hills India 10°14N 77°33E 84 P10
Palanpur India 24°10N 72°25E 84 GR
Palapye Botswana 22°30S 27°7E 97 J5
Palau ■ Palau 7°30N 134°30E 102 G5
Palawan Phil. 9°30N 118°30E 82 C5
Palembang Indonesia 3°0S 104°50E 82 E2
Palencia Spain 42°1N 4°34W 67 A3
Palermo Italy 38°7N 13°22E 68 E5
Palestine U.S.A. 31°46N 95°38W 111 D7
Palgrave U.K. 52°22N 1°8E 31 B11
Pali India 25°50N 73°20E 84 G8
Palikir Micronesia 6°55N 168°9E 102 G7
Palk Strait Asia 10°0N 79°45E 84 Q11
Palm Springs U.S.A. 33°50N 116°33W 110 D3
Palma de Mallorca Spain 39°35N 2°39E 67 C7
Palmares Brazil 8°41S 35°28W 122 A3
Palmas Brazil 10°12S 48°21W 122 B1
Palmas, C. Liberia 4°27N 7°46W 94 H4
Palmeira dos Índios Brazil 9°25S 36°37W 122 A3
Palmer U.S.A. 61°36N 149°7W 108 C5
Palmer Land Antarctica 73°0S 63°0W 55 D18
Palmerston North N.Z. 40°21S 175°39E 99 J14
Palmira Colombia 3°32N 76°16W 120 B2
Palmyra Syria 34°36N 38°15E 86 C4
Palmyra Is. Pac. Oc. 5°52N 162°5W 103 G11
Palopo Indonesia 3°0S 120°16E 83 E6
Palu Indonesia 1°0S 119°52E 83 E5
Palu Turkey 38°45N 40°0E 71 G7
Pamiers France 43°7N 1°39E 66 E4
Pamir Tajikistan 37°40N 73°0E 87 B13
Pamlico Sd. U.S.A. 35°20N 76°0W 111 C11
Pampa U.S.A. 35°32N 100°58W 110 C6
Pampas Argentina 35°0S 63°0W 121 F3
Pamplona-Iruña Spain 42°48N 1°38W 67 A5
Pana U.S.A. 39°23N 89°5W 112 F3
Panaji India 15°25N 73°50E 84 M8
Panamá Panama 9°0N 79°25W 115 F9
Panama ■ Cent. Amer. 8°48N 79°55W 115 F9
Panamá, G. de Panama 8°4N 79°20W 115 F9
Panama, Isthmus of Cent. Amer. 9°0N 79°0W 115 F9
Panama Canal Panama 9°10N 79°37W 115 F9
Panama City U.S.A. 30°10N 85°40W 111 D9
Panay Phil. 11°10N 122°30E 83 B6
Pančevo Serbia 44°52N 20°41E 69 B9
Panevėžys Lithuania 55°42N 24°25E 63 F8
Pangani Tanzania 5°25S 38°58E 96 F7
Pangbourne U.K. 51°29N 1°6W 30 D6
Pangkalpinang Indonesia 2°10S 106°10E 82 E3
Pangnirtung Canada 66°8N 65°43W 109 C13
Pantar Indonesia 8°28S 124°10E 83 F6
Pante Macassar E. Timor 9°30S 123°58E 83 F6
Pantelleria Italy 36°50N 11°57E 68 F4
Panzhihua China 26°33N 101°44E 78 F9
Papa Stour U.K. 60°20N 1°42W 22 B14
Papa Westray U.K. 59°20N 2°55W 23 D12
Papantla Mexico 20°27N 97°19W 114 C5
Papeete Tahiti 17°32S 149°34W 103 J13
Papua □ Indonesia 4°0S 137°0E 83 E9
Papua, G. of Papua N. G. 9°0S 144°50E 98 B7
Papua New Guinea ■ Oceania 8°0S 145°0E 98 B8
Pará □ Brazil 3°20S 52°0W 120 C4
Paracatu Brazil 17°10S 46°50W 122 C1
Paracel Is. S. China Sea 16°0N 112°0E 82 A4
Paragould U.S.A. 36°3N 90°29W 111 C8
Paraguaçu → Brazil 12°45S 38°54W 122 B3
Paraguaná, Pen. de Venezuela 12°0N 70°0W 120 A3
Paraguari Paraguay 25°36S 57°0W 121 E4
Paraguay ■ S. Amer. 23°0S 57°0W 121 E4
Paraguay → Paraguay 27°18S 58°38W 121 E4
Paraíba □ Brazil 7°0S 36°0W 120 C6
Paraíba → Brazil 21°37S 41°3W 122 D2
Parakou Benin 9°25N 2°40E 94 G6
Paramaribo Suriname 5°50N 55°10W 120 B4
Paramushir, Ostrov Russia 50°24N 156°0E 77 D16
Paraná Argentina 31°45S 60°30W 121 F3
Paraná □ Brazil 12°30S 47°48W 122 B1
Paraná □ Brazil 24°30S 51°0W 121 E4
Paraná → Argentina 33°43S 59°15W 121 F4
Paranaguá Brazil 25°30S 48°30W 122 E1
Paranaíba Brazil 20°6S 51°4W 120 E4
Paranaíba → Brazil 20°0S 51°0W 120 E4
Paranapanema → Brazil 22°40S 53°9W 121 E4
Parbhani India 19°8N 76°52E 84 K10
Pardo → Brazil 15°40S 39°0W 122 C3
Pardubice Czech Rep. 50°3N 15°45E 64 C8
Parecis, Serra dos Brazil 13°0S 60°0W 120 D4
Parepare Indonesia 4°0S 119°40E 83 E5
Parima, Serra Brazil 2°30N 64°0W 120 B3
Pariñas, Pta. Peru 4°30S 82°0W 117 D2
Parintins Brazil 2°40S 56°50W 120 C4
Pariparit Kyun Burma 14°52N 93°41E 85 M18
Paris France 48°53N 2°20E 66 B5
Paris U.S.A. 33°40N 95°33W 111 D7
Park Falls U.S.A. 45°56N 90°27W 112 C2
Parkersburg U.S.A. 39°16N 81°34W 112 F7
Parla Spain 40°14N 3°46W 67 B4
Parma Italy 44°48N 10°20E 68 B4
Parnaguá Brazil 10°10S 44°38W 122 B2
Parnaíba Brazil 2°54S 41°47W 120 C5
Parnaíba → Brazil 3°0S 41°50W 120 C5
Pärnu Estonia 58°28N 24°33E 63 F8
Paros Greece 37°5N 25°12E 69 F11
Parracombe U.K. 51°11N 3°56W 29 E6
Parrett → U.K. 51°12N 3°1W 30 D2
Parry Is. Canada 77°0N 110°0W 109 B9
Parry Sound Canada 45°20N 80°0W 109 E12
Parsons U.S.A. 37°20N 95°16W 111 C7
Partney U.K. 53°12N 0°7E 27 F9
Parton U.K. 54°35N 3°33W 26 C1
Partry Mts. Ireland 53°40N 9°28W 18 C3
Paru → Brazil 1°33S 52°38W 120 C4
Pasadena Calif., U.S.A. 34°9N 118°8W 110 D3
Pasadena Tex., U.S.A. 29°43N 95°13W 111 E7
Paschimbanga □ India 23°0N 88°0E 85 H16
Pascua, I. de Chile 27°7S 109°23W 103 K17
Paso Robles U.S.A. 35°38N 120°41W 110 C2
Passage West Ireland 51°52N 8°21W 20 E6

Passau Germany 48°34N 13°28E 64 D7
Passo Fundo Brazil 28°10S 52°20W 121 E4
Passos Brazil 20°45S 46°37W 122 D1
Pastaza → Peru 4°50S 76°52W 120 C2
Pasto Colombia 1°13N 77°17W 120 B2
Patagonia Argentina 45°0S 69°0W 121 G3
Patan India 23°54N 72°14E 84 H8
Pateley Bridge U.K. 54°5N 1°45W 26 D5
Paterson U.S.A. 40°54N 74°9W 113 E10
Pathankot India 32°18N 75°45E 84 C9
Pathfinder Res. U.S.A. 42°28N 106°51W 110 B5
Patiala India 30°23N 76°26E 84 D9
Patkai Bum India 27°0N 95°30E 85 F19
Patmos Greece 37°21N 26°36E 69 F12
Patna India 25°35N 85°12E 85 G14
Patos Brazil 6°55S 37°16W 120 C6
Patos, L. dos Brazil 31°20S 51°0W 121 F4
Patos de Minas Brazil 18°35S 46°32W 122 C1
Patra Greece 38°14N 21°47E 69 E9
Patrington U.K. 53°41N 0°1W 27 E8
Patrocínio Brazil 18°57S 47°0W 122 C1
Patten U.S.A. 46°0N 68°38W 113 C13
Patterdale India 54°32N 2°56W 26 C3
Pau France 43°19N 0°25W 66 E3
Paulatuk Canada 69°25N 124°0W 108 C7
Paulistana Brazil 9°5S 41°9W 122 A2
Paull U.K. 53°44N 0°14W 27 E8
Paulo Afonso Brazil 9°21S 38°15W 122 A3
Pavia Italy 45°7N 9°8E 68 B3
Pavlodar Kazakhstan 52°33N 77°0E 76 D8
Pavlohrad Ukraine 48°30N 35°52E 71 E6
Pávlovo Russia 55°58N 43°5E 70 C7
Pawtucket U.S.A. 41°53N 71°23W 113 E12
Paxton U.S.A. 40°27N 88°6W 112 E3
Payakumbuh Indonesia 0°20S 100°35E 82 E2
Payette U.S.A. 44°5N 116°56W 110 B3
Payne L. Canada 59°30N 74°30W 109 D12
Paysandú Uruguay 32°19S 58°8W 121 F4
Payson U.S.A. 34°14N 111°20W 110 D4
Paz, B. de la Mexico 24°9N 110°25W 114 C2
Pazardzhik Bulgaria 42°12N 24°20E 69 C11
Peace → Canada 59°0N 111°25W 108 D8
Peace River Canada 56°15N 117°18W 108 D8
Peacehaven U.K. 50°48N 0°1E 31 E9
Peak District △ U.K. 53°24N 1°46W 27 F5
Pearl City U.S.A. 21°24N 157°59W 110 H16
Pearl Harbor U.S.A. 21°21N 157°57W 110 H16
Pearl River Bridge China 22°15N 113°48E 79 a
Peasedown U.K. 52°16N 1°27E 31 B11
Peawanuck Canada 55°15N 85°12W 109 D11
Pechora → Russia 65°10N 57°11E 70 A10
Pechora Russia 68°13N 54°15E 70 A9
Pechora B. Russia 68°40N 54°0E 70 A9
Pecos U.S.A. 31°26N 103°30W 110 D6
Pecos → U.S.A. 29°42N 101°22W 110 E6
Pécs Hungary 46°5N 18°15E 65 E10
Pedra Azul Brazil 16°2S 41°17W 122 C2
Pedro Afonso Brazil 9°0S 48°10W 122 A1
Peebles U.K. 55°40N 3°11W 25 C9
Peel I. of Man 54°13N 4°40W 19 C12
Peel → Canada 67°0N 135°0W 108 C6
Peel Fell U.K. 55°18N 2°34W 26 B3
Peel Sd. Canada 73°0N 96°0W 108 B10
Pegswood U.K. 55°11N 1°39W 26 B5
Pegu Yoma Burma 19°0N 96°0E 85 K20
Pegwell Bay U.K. 51°18N 1°24E 31 D11
Peixe Brazil 12°0S 48°40W 122 B1
Pejë Kosovo 42°40N 20°17E 69 C9
Pekalongan Indonesia 6°53S 109°40E 82 F3
Pekanbaru Indonesia 0°30N 101°15E 82 D2
Peking = Beijing China 39°53N 116°21E 79 D12
Pelagie, Is. Italy 35°39N 12°33E 68 G4
Pelée, Mt. Martinique 14°48N 61°10W 115 D12
Peleng Indonesia 1°20S 123°30E 83 E6
Pelješac Croatia 42°55N 17°25E 68 C7
Pelly → Canada 62°47N 137°19W 108 C6
Pelly Bay Canada 68°38N 89°50W 109 C11
Peloponnesos □ Greece 37°10N 22°0E 69 F10
Pelotas Brazil 31°42S 52°23W 121 F4
Pelvoux, Massif du France 44°52N 6°20E 66 D7
Pematangsiantar Indonesia 2°57N 99°5E 82 D1
Pemba Mozam. 12°58S 40°30E 97 G8
Pemba I. Tanzania 5°0S 39°45E 96 F7
Pembridge U.K. 52°13N 2°52W 30 B3
Pembroke Canada 45°50N 77°7W 109 E12
Pembroke U.K. 51°41N 4°55W 28 D3
Pembrokeshire □ U.K. 51°52N 4°56W 28 D3
Pembrokeshire Coast △ U.K. 51°52N 5°2W 28 D3
Pen-bont ar Ogwr = Bridgend U.K. 51°30N 3°34W 29 D6
Pen-y-Ghent U.K. 54°10N 2°14W 26 D4
Penarth U.K. 51°26N 3°11W 29 E7
Peñas, G. de Chile 47°0S 75°0W 121 G2
Pend Oreille, L. U.S.A. 48°10N 116°21W 110 A3
Pendeen U.K. 50°9N 5°41W 29 G2
Pendle Hill U.K. 53°52N 2°19W 27 E4
Pendleton U.S.A. 45°40N 118°47W 110 A3
Penedo Brazil 10°15S 36°36W 122 B3
Penetanguishene Canada 44°50N 79°55W 112 C8
Penfro = Pembroke U.K. 51°41N 4°55W 28 D3
Penicuik U.K. 55°50N 3°13W 25 C9
Peninsular Malaysia □ Malaysia 4°0N 102°0E 82 D2
Penistone U.K. 53°31N 1°37W 27 E5
Penkridge U.K. 52°44N 2°6W 27 G4
Penmarch, Pte. de France 47°48N 4°22W 66 C1
Penn Yan U.S.A. 42°40N 77°3W 112 D9
Pennine, Pte. de France 47°48N 4°22W 66 C1
Pennines U.K. 54°45N 2°27W 26 C4
Pennsylvania □ U.S.A. 40°45N 77°30W 112 E9
Penong Australia 31°56S 133°1E 98 G5
Penrith Australia 33°43N 150°38E 98 A4
Penrith U.K. 54°40N 2°45W 26 C4
Penryn U.K. 50°9N 5°7W 29 G3
Pensacola U.S.A. 30°25N 87°13W 111 D9
Pensacola Mts. Antarctica 84°0S 40°0W 55 E1
Penshurst U.K. 51°10N 0°12E 31 D9
Penticton Canada 49°30N 119°38W 108 E8
Pentire Pt. U.K. 50°35N 4°56W 29 F4
Pentland Firth U.K. 58°43N 3°10W 23 E11

Pentland Hills U.K. 55°48N 3°25W 25 C9
Penwortham U.K. 53°45N 2°46W 27 F3
Penygroes U.K. 53°3N 4°17W 28 A5
Penza Russia 53°15N 45°5E 70 D8
Penzance U.K. 50°7N 5°33W 29 G2
Peoria U.S.A. 40°42N 89°36W 112 E3
Perabumulih Indonesia 3°27S 104°15E 82 E2
Perdido, Mte. Spain 42°40N 0°5E 67 A6
Pereira Colombia 4°49N 75°43W 120 B2
Pergamino Argentina 33°52S 60°30W 121 F3
Péribonka → Canada 48°45N 72°5W 109 E12
Périgueux France 45°10N 0°42E 66 D4
Perm Russia 58°0N 56°10E 70 C10
Pernambuco □ Brazil 8°0S 37°0W 120 C6
Pernik Bulgaria 42°35N 23°2E 69 C10
Perpignan France 42°42N 2°53E 66 E5
Perranporth U.K. 50°20N 5°11W 29 G3
Perranzabuloe U.K. 50°18N 5°9W 29 G3
Perryton U.S.A. 36°24N 100°48W 110 C6
Perryville U.S.A. 37°43N 89°52W 112 G3
Persepolis Iran 29°55N 52°50E 87 D8
Pershore U.K. 52°7N 2°4W 30 B4
Persian Gulf Asia 27°0N 50°0E 87 E7
Perth Australia 31°57S 115°52E 98 G2
Perth Canada 44°55N 76°15W 109 E14
Perth U.K. 56°24N 3°26W 25 B9
Perth & Kinross □ U.K. 56°45N 3°55W 23 J9
Peru ■ S. Amer. 4°0S 75°0W 120 C2
Peru U.S.A. 40°45N 86°4W 112 E4
Peru-Chile Trench Pac. Oc. 20°0S 72°0W 103 K20
Perúgia Italy 43°7N 12°23E 68 C5
Pervomaysk Ukraine 48°10N 30°46E 71 E5
Pervouralsk Russia 56°59N 59°59E 70 C10
Pésaro Italy 43°54N 12°55E 68 C5
Pescara Italy 42°28N 14°13E 68 C6
Peshawar Pakistan 34°2N 71°37E 84 B7
Pesqueira Brazil 8°20S 36°42W 122 A3
Petah Tiqwa Israel 32°6N 34°53E 86 C3
Peterborough Canada 44°20N 78°20W 109 E12
Peterborough U.K. 52°35N 0°15W 31 A8
Peterchurch U.K. 52°2N 2°56W 30 B3
Peterculter U.K. 57°6N 2°16W 23 H13
Peterhead U.K. 57°31N 1°48W 23 G14
Peterlee U.K. 54°47N 1°20W 26 C6
Petersburg Alaska, U.S.A. 56°48N 132°50W 108 D6
Petersburg Va., U.S.A. 37°14N 77°24W 112 G9
Petersfield U.K. 51°1N 0°56W 31 D7
Petit Piton St. Lucia 13°51N 61°5W 114 b
Petitot → Canada 60°14N 123°29W 108 C7
Petitsikapau L. Canada 54°37N 66°25W 109 D13
Peto Mexico 20°8N 88°55W 114 C7
Petoskey U.S.A. 45°22N 84°57W 112 C5
Petra Jordan 30°20N 35°22E 86 D3
Petrolândia Brazil 9°5S 38°20W 122 A3
Petrolina Brazil 9°24S 40°30W 122 A2
Petropavl Kazakhstan 54°53N 69°13E 76 D7
Petropavlovsk-Kamchatskiy Russia 53°3N 158°43E 77 D16
Petrópolis Brazil 22°33S 43°9W 122 D2
Petrozavodsk Russia 61°41N 34°20E 70 B5
Petworth U.K. 51°0N 0°36W 31 E7
Pevensey U.K. 50°49N 0°23E 31 E9
Pevensey Levels U.K. 50°50N 0°20E 31 E9
Pewsey U.K. 51°20N 1°45W 30 D5
Pewsey, Vale of U.K. 51°22N 1°40W 30 D5
Pforzheim Germany 48°52N 8°41E 64 D5
Phalodi India 27°12N 72°24E 84 F8
Phan Rang-Thap Cham Vietnam 11°34N 109°0E 82 B3
Phan Thiet Vietnam 11°1N 108°9E 82 B3
Phi Phi, Ko Thailand 7°45N 98°46E 82 C1
Philadelphia U.S.A. 39°57N 75°9W 113 E10
Philippine Sea Pac. Oc. 18°0N 125°0E 72 G14
Philippine Trench Pac. Oc. 12°0N 126°6E 83 B7
Philippines ■ Asia 12°0N 123°0E 83 B6
Phillips U.S.A. 45°42N 90°24W 112 C2
Phitsanulok Thailand 16°50N 100°12E 82 A2
Phnom Penh Cambodia 11°33N 104°55E 82 B2
Phoenix U.S.A. 33°26N 112°4W 110 D4
Phoenix Is. Kiribati 3°30S 172°0W 99 A16
Phuket Thailand 7°53N 98°24E 82 C1
Piacenza Italy 45°1N 9°40E 68 B3
Piatra Neamţ Romania 46°56N 26°21E 65 E14
Piauí □ Brazil 7°0S 43°0W 120 C5
Piauí → Brazil 6°38S 42°42W 120 C5
Piave → Italy 45°32N 12°44E 68 B5
Picardie □ France 49°50N 3°0E 66 B5
Pichilemu Chile 34°22S 72°0W 121 F2
Pickering U.K. 54°15N 0°46W 26 D7
Pickering, Vale of U.K. 54°14N 0°45W 26 D7
Picos Brazil 7°5S 41°28W 120 C5
Picton Canada 44°1N 77°9W 112 C9
Pidley U.K. 52°23N 0°3W 31 B8
Pidurutalagala Sri Lanka 7°10N 80°50E 84 R12
Piedmont □ U.S.A. 34°42N 82°28W 111 D10
Piedras Negras Mexico 28°42N 100°31W 114 B4
Piemonte □ Italy 45°0N 8°0E 68 B2
Pierre U.S.A. 44°22N 100°21W 110 B6
Pietermaritzburg S. Africa 29°35S 30°25E 97 K6
Pikes Peak U.S.A. 38°50N 105°3W 110 C5
Pikeville U.S.A. 37°29N 82°31W 112 G6
Pilar Paraguay 26°50S 58°20W 121 E4
Pilcomayo → Paraguay 25°21S 57°42W 121 E4
Pilibhit India 28°40N 79°50E 84 E11
Pilica → Poland 51°52N 21°17E 65 C11
Pilling U.K. 53°56N 2°54W 27 E3
Pilton U.K. 51°10N 2°36W 30 D3
Pimentel Peru 6°45S 79°55W 120 C2
Pinar del Río Cuba 22°26N 83°40W 115 C8
Pinatubo, Mt. Phil. 15°8N 120°21E 83 A6
Pinchbeck U.K. 52°50N 0°9W 27 G8
Pinckneyville U.S.A. 38°5N 89°23W 112 F3
Pindus Mts. Greece 40°0N 21°0E 69 E9
Pine Bluff U.S.A. 34°13N 92°1W 111 D8
Pinega → Russia 64°30N 44°19E 70 B8
Pingdingshan China 33°43N 113°27E 79 E11
P'ingtung Taiwan 22°38N 120°30E 79 G13
Pingxiang Guangxi Zhuangzu, China 22°6N 106°46E 78 G10
Pingxiang Jiangxi, China 27°43N 113°48E 79 F11

Pinheiro Brazil 2°31S 45°5W 120 C5
Pinhoe U.K. 50°44N 3°28W 29 F7
Pinsk Belarus 52°10N 26°1E 70 D4
Piombino Italy 42°55N 10°32E 68 C4
Piotrków Trybunalski Poland 51°23N 19°43E 65 C10
Pipmuacan, Rés. Canada 49°45N 70°30W 113 A12
Piracicaba Brazil 22°45S 47°40W 122 D1
Pirapora Brazil 17°20S 44°56W 122 C2
Píreas Greece 37°57N 23°42E 69 F10
Pirmasens Germany 49°12N 7°36E 64 D4
Pisa Italy 43°43N 10°23E 68 C4
Pisagua Chile 19°40S 70°15W 120 D2
Pishan China 37°30N 78°33E 78 D4
Pistóia Italy 43°55N 10°54E 68 C4
Pit → U.S.A. 40°47N 122°6W 110 B2
Pitcairn I. Pac. Oc. 25°5S 130°5W 103 K14
Piteå Sweden 65°20N 21°25E 63 D8
Piteşti Romania 44°52N 24°54E 65 F13
Pitlochry U.K. 56°42N 3°44W 23 J10
Pittsburg U.S.A. 37°25N 94°42W 111 C8
Pittsburgh U.S.A. 40°26N 79°58W 112 E8
Pittsfield U.S.A. 42°27N 73°15W 113 D11
Piura Peru 5°15S 80°38W 120 C1
Placentia Canada 47°20N 54°0W 109 E14
Placentia B. Canada 47°0N 54°40W 109 E14
Placetas Cuba 22°15N 79°44W 115 C9
Plainview U.S.A. 34°11N 101°43W 110 D6
Plata, Río de la → S. Amer. 34°45S 57°30W 121 F4
Platte → U.S.A. 39°16N 94°50W 111 C8
Plattsburgh U.S.A. 44°42N 73°28W 113 C11
Plauen Germany 50°30N 12°8E 64 C7
Playa del Carmen Mexico 20°37N 87°4W 114 C7
Plenty, B. of N.Z. 37°45S 177°0E 99 H14
Plessisville Canada 46°14N 71°47W 113 B12
Pleven Bulgaria 43°26N 24°37E 69 C11
Płock Poland 52°32N 19°40E 65 B10
Ploiești Romania 44°57N 26°5E 65 F14
Plovdiv Bulgaria 42°8N 24°44E 69 C11
Plymouth U.K. 50°22N 4°10W 29 G5
Plymouth Ind., U.S.A. 41°21N 86°19W 112 E4
Plymouth Wis., U.S.A. 43°45N 87°59W 112 D4
Plympton U.K. 50°23N 4°5W 29 G5
Plymstock U.K. 50°21N 4°7W 29 G5
Plynlimon = Pumlumon Fawr U.K. 52°28N 3°46W 28 C6
Plzeň Czech Rep. 49°45N 13°22E 64 D7
Po → Italy 44°57N 12°4E 68 B5
Pocatello U.S.A. 42°52N 112°27W 110 B4
Pocklington U.K. 53°56N 0°46W 27 E7
Poços de Caldas Brazil 21°50S 46°33W 122 D1
Podgorica Montenegro 42°30N 19°19E 69 C8
Podolsk Russia 55°25N 37°30E 70 C6
Pohang S. Korea 36°1N 129°23E 79 D14
Pohnpei Micronesia 6°55N 158°10E 102 G7
Point Hope U.S.A. 68°21N 166°47W 108 C3
Point L. Canada 65°15N 113°4W 108 C8
Point Pleasant U.S.A. 38°51N 82°8W 112 F6
Pointe-à-Pitre Guadeloupe 16°15N 61°32W 114 b
Pointe-Noire Congo 4°48S 11°53E 96 E2
Poitiers France 46°35N 0°20E 66 C4
Poitou France 46°40N 0°10W 66 C3
Pokhara Nepal 28°14N 83°58E 85 E13
Poland ■ Europe 52°0N 20°0E 65 C10
Polatsk Belarus 55°30N 28°50E 70 C4
Polden Hills U.K. 51°7N 2°50W 30 D3
Polegate U.K. 50°49N 0°16E 31 E9
Polesworth U.K. 52°37N 1°36W 27 G6
Polevskoy Russia 56°26N 60°11E 70 C11
Polokwane S. Africa 23°54S 29°25E 97 J5
Polperro U.K. 50°20N 4°32W 29 G4
Polruan U.K. 50°19N 4°38W 29 G4
Poltava Ukraine 49°35N 34°35E 71 E5
Polynesia Pac. Oc. 10°0S 162°0W 103 F11
Pomeranian Lakes Poland 53°40N 16°37E 65 B9
Ponca City U.S.A. 36°42N 97°5W 111 C7
Ponce Puerto Rico 18°1N 66°37W 115 D11
Pond Inlet Canada 72°40N 77°0W 109 B12
Ponferrada Spain 42°32N 6°35W 67 A2
Ponta Grossa Brazil 25°7S 50°10W 121 E4
Pontardawe U.K. 51°43N 3°51W 28 D6
Pontardulais U.K. 51°43N 4°3W 28 D5
Pontarlier France 46°54N 6°20E 66 C7
Pontchartrain, L. U.S.A. 30°5N 90°5W 111 D9
Ponte Nova Brazil 20°25S 42°54W 122 D2
Pontefract U.K. 53°42N 1°18W 27 E6
Ponteland U.K. 55°3N 1°45W 26 B5
Pontevedra Spain 42°26N 8°40W 67 A1
Pontiac Ill., U.S.A. 40°53N 88°38W 112 E3
Pontiac Mich., U.S.A. 42°38N 83°18W 112 D6
Pontianak Indonesia 0°3S 109°15E 82 E3
Pontine Mts. Turkey 41°0N 36°45E 71 F6
Pontivy France 48°5N 2°58W 66 B2
Pontrilas U.K. 51°56N 2°52W 30 C3
Pontypool U.K. 51°42N 3°2W 28 D7
Pontypridd U.K. 51°36N 3°20W 28 D7
Ponziane, Ísole Italy 40°55N 12°57E 68 D5
Poole U.K. 50°43N 1°59W 30 E5
Poole Harbour U.K. 50°41N 2°0W 30 E5
Pooley Bridge U.K. 54°37N 2°48W 26 C3
Poopó, L. de Bolivia 18°30S 67°35W 120 D3
Popayán Colombia 2°27N 76°36W 120 B2
Poplar Bluff U.S.A. 36°46N 90°24W 111 G8
Popocatépetl, Volcán Mexico 19°2N 98°38W 114 D5
Porbandar India 21°44N 69°43E 84 J6
Porcupine → U.S.A. 66°34N 145°19W 108 C5
Pori Finland 61°29N 21°48E 63 E8
Porlock U.K. 51°13N 3°35W 29 E6
Port Alberni Canada 49°14N 124°50W 108 E7
Port Antonio Jamaica 18°10N 76°26W 114 a
Port Arthur U.S.A. 29°54N 93°56W 111 E8
Port-au-Prince Haiti 18°40N 72°20W 115 D10
Port Augusta Australia 32°30S 137°50E 98 G6
Port Carlisle U.K. 54°57N 3°11W 26 C2
Port-Cartier Canada 50°2N 66°50W 109 D13
Port-de-Paix Haiti 19°50N 72°50W 115 D10
Port Elgin Canada 44°25N 81°25W 112 C7
Port Elizabeth S. Africa 33°58S 25°40E 97 L5
Port Ellen U.K. 55°38N 6°11W 24 C3
Port Erin I. of Man 54°5N 4°45W 19 C12

Port-Gentil

Rochester

Port-Gentil *Gabon* 0°40S 8°50E **96** E1
Port Glasgow *U.K.* 55°56N 4°41W **24** C6
Port Harcourt *Nigeria* 4°40N 7°10E **94** H7
Port Hawkesbury *Canada* 45°36N 61°22W **109** E13
Port Hedland *Australia* 20°25S 118°35E **98** E2
Port Hope Simpson *Canada* 52°33N 56°18W **109** D14
Port Huron *U.S.A.* 42°58N 82°26W **112** D6
Port Isaac *U.K.* 50°35N 4°50W **29** F4
Port Isaac B. *U.K.* 50°36N 4°50W **29** F4
Port Lincoln *Australia* 34°42S 135°52E **98** G6
Port Louis *Mauritius* 20°10S 57°30E **91** H9
Port McNeill *Canada* 50°35N 127°6W **108** D7
Port Macquarie *Australia* 31°25S 152°25E **98** G9
Port Maria *Jamaica* 18°22N 76°54W **114** a
Port Morant *Jamaica* 17°54N 76°19W **114** a
Port Moresby *Papua N. G.* 9°24S 147°8E **98** B8
Port Nolloth *S. Africa* 29°17S 16°52E **97** K3
Port of Spain *Trin. & Tob.* 10°40N 61°31W **120** A3
Port Pirie *Australia* 33°10S 138°1E **98** G6
Port Said *Egypt* 31°16N 32°18E **95** B12
Port St. Lucie *U.S.A.* 27°18N 80°21W **111** E10
Port St. Mary *U.K.* 54°5N 4°44W **19** C12
Port Shepstone *S. Africa* 30°44S 30°28E **97** L6
Port Sudan *Sudan* 19°32N 37°9E **95** E13
Port Talbot *U.K.* 51°35N 3°47W **29** D6
Port Vila *Vanuatu* 17°45S 168°18E **99** D12
Port Washington *U.S.A.* 43°23N 87°53W **112** D4
Port William *U.K.* 54°46N 4°35W **24** E6
Portadown *U.K.* 54°25N 6°27W **19** C9
Portaferry *U.K.* 54°23N 5°33W **19** C10
Portage *U.S.A.* 43°33N 89°28W **112** D3
Portage la Prairie *Canada* 49°58N 98°18W **108** E10
Portarlington *Ireland* 53°9N 7°14W **21** B8
Porth Tywyn = Burry Port
  U.K. 51°41N 4°15W **28** D5
Porthcawl *U.K.* 51°29N 3°42W **29** E6
Porthleven *U.K.* 50°4N 5°19W **29** G3
Porthmadog *U.K.* 52°55N 4°8W **28** B5
Portishead *U.K.* 51°29N 2°46W **30** D3
Portknockie *U.K.* 57°42N 2°51W **23** G12
Portland *Maine, U.S.A.* 43°39N 70°16W **113** D12
Portland *Oreg., U.S.A.* 45°32N 122°37W **110** A2
Portland, I. of *U.K.* 50°33N 2°26W **30** E4
Portland Bight *Jamaica* 17°52N 77°5W **114** a
Portland Bill *U.K.* 50°31N 2°28W **29** F9
Portland Pt. *Jamaica* 17°42N 77°11W **114** a
Portlaoise *Ireland* 53°2N 7°18W **21** B8
Portmarnock *Ireland* 53°26N 6°8W **21** B10
Portmore *Jamaica* 17°53N 76°53W **114** a
Porto *Portugal* 41°8N 8°40W **67** B1
Pôrto Alegre *Brazil* 30°5S 51°10W **121** F4
Porto Esperança *Brazil* 19°37S 57°29W **120** D4
Porto Nacional *Brazil* 10°40S 48°30W **122** B1
Porto-Novo *Benin* 6°23N 2°42E **94** G6
Porto Seguro *Brazil* 16°26S 39°5W **122** C3
Porto Tôrres *Italy* 40°50N 8°24E **68** D3
Porto-Vecchio *France* 41°35N 9°16E **66** F8
Porto Velho *Brazil* 8°46S 63°54W **120** C3
Porton *U.K.* 51°8N 1°43W **30** D5
Portpatrick *U.K.* 54°51N 5°7W **24** E5
Portree *U.K.* 57°25N 6°12W **22** H5
Portrush *U.K.* 55°12N 6°40W **19** A8
Portslade *U.K.* 50°50N 0°12W **31** E8
Portsmouth *U.K.* 50°48N 1°6W **30** E6
Portsmouth *N.H., U.S.A.* 43°5N 70°45W **113** D12
Portsmouth *Ohio, U.S.A.* 38°44N 82°57W **112** F6
Portsmouth *Va., U.S.A.* 36°58N 76°23W **111** C11
Portsoy *U.K.* 57°41N 2°41W **23** G12
Portstewart *U.K.* 55°11N 6°43W **19** A8
Porttipahdan tekojärvi *Finland* 68°5N 26°40E **63** D9
Portugal ■ *Europe* 40°0N 8°0W **67** C1
Portumna *Ireland* 53°6N 8°14W **20** B6
Posadas *Argentina* 27°30S 55°50W **121** E4
Posse *Brazil* 14°4S 46°18W **122** B1
Postmasburg *S. Africa* 28°18S 23°5E **97** K4
Potchefstroom *S. Africa* 26°41S 27°7E **97** K5
Potenza *Italy* 40°38N 15°48E **68** D6
Poti *Georgia* 42°10N 41°38E **71** F7
Potiskum *Nigeria* 11°39N 11°2E **95** F8
Potomac → *U.S.A.* 38°0N 76°23W **112** F9
Potosí *Bolivia* 19°38S 65°50W **120** D3
Potsdam *Germany* 52°23N 13°3E **64** B7
Potsdam *U.S.A.* 44°40N 74°59W **113** C10
Potter Heigham *U.K.* 52°42N 1°34E **31** A12
Potterne *U.K.* 51°20N 2°0W **30** D4
Potters Bar *U.K.* 51°42N 0°11W **31** C8
Potterspury *U.K.* 52°5N 0°52W **31** B7
Pottstown *U.S.A.* 40°15N 75°39W **113** E10
Pottsville *U.S.A.* 40°41N 76°12W **113** E9
Pottuvil *Sri Lanka* 6°55N 81°50E **84** R12
Poughkeepsie *U.S.A.* 41°42N 73°56W **113** E11
Poulaphouca Res. *Ireland* 53°8N 6°30W **21** B10
Poulton-le-Fylde *U.K.* 53°51N 2°58W **27** E3
Poundstock *U.K.* 50°44N 4°36W **29** F4
Pouso Alegre *Brazil* 22°14S 45°57W **122** D1
Powder → *U.S.A.* 46°45N 105°26W **110** A5
Powell *U.S.A.* 36°57N 111°29W **110** C4
Powell River *Canada* 49°50N 124°35W **108** E7
Powers *U.S.A.* 45°41N 87°32W **112** C4
Powick *U.K.* 52°10N 2°14W **30** B4
Powys □ *U.K.* 52°20N 3°20W **28** E7
Poyang Hu *China* 29°5N 116°20E **79** D12
Poza Rica *Mexico* 20°33N 97°27W **114** C5
Poznań *Poland* 52°25N 16°55E **65** B9
Pozuoli *Italy* 40°49N 14°7E **68** D6
Prado *Brazil* 17°20S 39°13W **122** C3
Prague *Czech Rep.* 50°4N 14°25E **64** C8
Praia *C. Verde Is.* 15°2N 23°34W **91** E1
Praia Grande *Brazil* 24°0S 46°24W **122** D1
Prairie du Chien *U.S.A.* 43°3N 91°9W **112** D2
Prata *Brazil* 19°25S 48°54W **122** C1
Prato *Italy* 43°53N 11°6E **68** C4
Pratt *U.S.A.* 37°39N 98°44W **110** C7
Prawle Pt. *U.K.* 50°12N 3°44W **29** G6
Praya *Indonesia* 8°39S 116°17E **82** F5
Prees *U.K.* 52°54N 2°39W **27** F3
Preesall *U.K.* 53°55N 2°57W **27** E3
Prescott *Canada* 44°45N 75°30W **113** C10
Prescott *U.S.A.* 34°33N 112°28W **110** D4
Presidencia Roque Sáenz Peña
  Argentina 26°45S 60°30W **121** E3

Presidente Prudente *Brazil* 22°5S 51°25W **120** E4
Presidio *U.S.A.* 29°34N 104°22W **110** E6
Prespa, L. *Macedonia* 40°55N 21°0E **69** D9
Presque Isle *U.S.A.* 46°41N 68°1W **113** B13
Prestatyn *U.K.* 53°20N 3°24W **28** A7
Prestbury *U.K.* 51°54N 2°2W **30** C4
Presteigne *U.K.* 52°17N 3°0W **28** C7
Preston *Borders, U.K.* 55°49N 2°19W **25** C11
Preston *Dorset, U.K.* 50°38N 2°26W **30** E4
Preston *Lancs., U.K.* 53°46N 2°42W **27** E3
Preston *U.S.A.* 42°6N 111°53W **110** B4
Prestonpans *U.K.* 55°58N 2°58W **25** C10
Prestwich *U.K.* 53°32N 2°17W **27** E4
Prestwick *U.K.* 55°29N 4°37W **24** D6
Pretoria *S. Africa* 25°44S 28°12E **97** K5
Pribilof Is. *U.S.A.* 57°0N 170°0W **108** D2
Price *U.S.A.* 39°36N 110°49W **110** C4
Prieska *S. Africa* 29°40S 22°42E **97** K4
Prilep *Macedonia* 41°21N 21°32E **69** D9
Prince Albert *Canada* 53°15N 105°50W **108** D9
Prince Albert Pen. *Canada* 72°30N 116°0W **108** B8
Prince Albert Sd. *Canada* 70°25N 115°0W **108** B8
Prince Alfred, C. *Canada* 74°20N 124°40W **109** B7
Prince Charles I. *Canada* 67°47N 76°12W **109** C12
Prince Charles Mts. *Antarctica* 72°0S 67°0E **55** D6
Prince Edward I. □ *Canada* 46°20N 63°20W **113** B16
Prince Edward Is. *Ind. Oc.* 46°35S 38°0E **53** G11
Prince George *Canada* 53°55N 122°50W **108** D7
Prince Gustaf Adolf Sea
  Canada 78°30N 107°0W **109** B9
Prince of Wales I. *Canada* 73°0N 99°0W **108** B10
Prince of Wales I. *U.S.A.* 55°47N 132°50W **108** D6
Prince Patrick I. *Canada* 77°0N 120°0W **109** B8
Prince Rupert *Canada* 54°20N 130°20W **108** D6
Prince William Sd. *U.S.A.* 60°40N 147°0W **108** C5
Princes Risborough *U.K.* 51°43N 0°49W **31** C7
Princeton *Ill., U.S.A.* 41°23N 89°28W **112** E3
Princeton *Ind., U.S.A.* 38°21N 87°34W **112** F4
Princeton *Ky., U.S.A.* 37°7N 87°53W **112** G4
Princeton *W. Va., U.S.A.* 37°22N 81°6W **112** G7
Princetown *U.K.* 50°33N 4°0W **29** F5
Príncipe *São Tomé & Príncipe* 1°37N 7°25E **90** F4
Pripet → *Europe* 51°20N 30°15E **65** C16
Pripet Marshes *Europe* 52°10N 27°10E **65** B15
Prishtinë *Kosovo* 42°40N 21°13E **69** C9
Privas *France* 44°45N 4°37E **66** D6
Prizren *Kosovo* 42°13N 20°45E **69** C9
Probolinggo *Indonesia* 7°46S 113°13E **82** F4
Probus *U.K.* 50°17N 4°58W **29** G4
Progreso *Mexico* 21°20N 89°40W **114** C7
Prome *Burma* 18°49N 95°13E **85** K19
Propriá *Brazil* 10°13S 36°51W **122** B3
Provence *France* 43°40N 5°46E **66** E6
Providence *U.S.A.* 41°49N 71°24W **113** E12
Providencia, I. de *Caribbean* 13°25N 81°26W **115** E8
Provins *France* 48°33N 3°15E **66** B5
Provo *U.S.A.* 40°14N 111°39W **110** B4
Prudhoe *U.K.* 54°57N 1°52W **26** C5
Prudhoe Bay *U.S.A.* 70°18N 148°22W **108** B5
Pruszków *Poland* 52°9N 20°49E **65** B11
Prut → *Romania* 45°28N 28°10E **65** F15
Pruzhany *Ukraine* 50°30N 32°24E **71** D5
Przemyśl *Poland* 49°50N 22°45E **65** D12
Pskov *Russia* 57°50N 28°25E **70** C4
Puddletown *U.K.* 50°44N 2°20W **30** E4
Pudsey *U.K.* 53°47N 1°40W **27** E5
Puducherry *India* 11°59N 79°50E **84** P11
Puebla *Mexico* 19°3N 98°12W **114** D5
Pueblo *U.S.A.* 38°16N 104°37W **110** C6
Puerto Aisén *Chile* 45°27S 73°0W **121** G2
Puerto Barrios *Guatemala* 15°40N 88°32W **114** D7
Puerto Cabello *Venezuela* 10°28N 68°1W **120** A3
Puerto Cabezas *Nic.* 14°0N 83°30W **115** E8
Puerto Carreño *Colombia* 6°12N 67°22W **120** B3
Puerto Cortés *Honduras* 15°51N 88°0W **114** D7
Puerto Deseado *Argentina* 47°55S 66°0W **121** G3
Puerto La Cruz *Venezuela* 10°13N 64°38W **120** A3
Puerto Madryn *Argentina* 42°48S 65°4W **121** G3
Puerto Maldonado *Peru* 12°30S 69°10W **120** D3
Puerto Montt *Chile* 41°28S 73°0W **121** G2
Puerto Plata *Dom. Rep.* 19°48N 70°45W **115** D10
Puerto Princesa *Phil.* 9°46N 118°45E **83** C5
Puerto Rico ☑ *W. Indies* 18°15N 66°45W **115** D11
Puerto Rico Trench *Atl. Oc.* 19°50N 66°0W **115** D11
Puerto San Julián *Argentina* 49°18S 67°43W **121** G3
Puerto Suárez *Bolivia* 18°58S 57°52W **120** D4
Puerto Wilches *Colombia* 7°21N 73°54W **120** B2
Puertollano *Spain* 38°43N 4°7W **67** C3
Puffin I. *Ireland* 51°50N 10°24W **20** E2
Puget Sound *U.S.A.* 47°50N 122°30W **110** A2
Pukapuka *Cook Is.* 10°53S 165°49W **103** J11
Pula *Croatia* 44°54N 13°57E **68** B5
Pulacayo *Bolivia* 20°25S 66°41W **120** E3
Pulaski *U.S.A.* 37°3N 80°47W **111** C10
Pulborough *U.K.* 50°58N 0°30W **31** E8
Pulham Market *U.K.* 52°26N 1°13E **31** B11
Pulham St. Mary *U.K.* 52°26N 1°16E **31** B11
Pulumon Fawr *U.K.* 52°28N 3°46W **28** C6
Pune *India* 18°29N 73°57E **84** K8
Punjab □ *India* 31°0N 76°0E **84** D9
Punjab □ *Pakistan* 32°0N 72°30E **84** E9
Puno *Peru* 15°55S 70°3W **120** D2
Punta Arenas *Chile* 53°10S 71°0W **121** H2
Puntland *Somalia* 9°0N 50°0E **89** F4
Punxsutawney *U.S.A.* 40°57N 78°59W **112** E8
Purbeck, Isle of *U.K.* 50°39N 1°59W **30** E5
Purfleet *U.K.* 51°29N 0°16E **31** D9
Puri *India* 19°50N 85°58E **85** K14
Purley on Thames *U.K.* 51°29N 1°3W **30** D6
Purnia *India* 25°45N 87°31E **85** G15
Puruliya *India* 23°17N 86°24E **85** H15
Purus → *Brazil* 3°42S 61°28W **120** C3
Putian *China* 25°23N 119°0E **79** F12
Putorana, Gory *Russia* 69°0N 95°0E **77** C10
Puttalam *Sri Lanka* 8°1N 79°55E **84** Q11
Puttgarden *Canada* 60°2N 77°10W **109** C12
Puy-de-Dôme *France* 45°46N 2°57E **66** D5
Puyehue *Chile* 40°40S 72°37W **121** G2

Pwllheli *U.K.* 52°53N 4°25W **28** B5
Pyatigorsk *Russia* 44°2N 43°6E **71** F7
Pyinmana *Burma* 19°45N 96°12E **85** K20
P'yŏngyang *N. Korea* 39°0N 125°30E **79** D14
Pyramid L. *U.S.A.* 40°1N 119°35W **110** C3
Pyrénées *Europe* 42°45N 0°18E **66** E4

Q

Qaanaaq *Greenland* 77°30N 69°10W **54** B4
Qā'emshahr *Iran* 36°30N 52°53E **87** B8
Qaidam Basin *China* 37°0N 95°0E **78** D8
Qamdo *China* 31°15N 97°6E **78** E8
Qandyaghash *Kazakhstan* 49°28N 57°25E **71** E10
Qaqortoq *Greenland* 60°43N 46°0W **54** C5
Qarqan He → *China* 39°30N 88°30E **78** D6
Qarshi *Uzbekistan* 38°53N 65°48E **87** B11
Qatar ■ *Asia* 25°30N 51°15E **87** E7
Qattâra Depression *Egypt* 29°30N 27°30E **95** C11
Qazvin *Iran* 36°15N 50°0E **86** B7
Qena *Egypt* 26°10N 32°43E **95** C12
Qeqertarsuaq *Greenland* 69°15N 53°38W **54** C5
Qeshm *Iran* 26°55N 56°10E **87** E9
Qianshan *China* 22°15N 113°31E **79** a
Qi'ao Dao *China* 22°25N 113°38E **79** a
Qiemo *China* 38°8N 85°32E **78** D6
Qijiaojing *China* 43°28N 91°36E **78** C7
Qilian Shan *China* 38°30N 96°0E **78** D8
Qingdao *China* 36°5N 120°20E **79** D13
Qinghai □ *China* 36°0N 98°0E **78** D8
Qinhuangdao *China* 39°56N 119°30E **79** D12
Qinling Shandi *China* 33°50N 108°10E **79** C10
Qinzhou *China* 21°58N 108°38E **78** G10
Qiqihar *China* 47°26N 124°0E **79** B13
Qira *China* 37°0N 80°48E **78** D5
Qitai *China* 44°2N 89°35E **78** C6
Qitaihe *China* 45°48N 130°51E **79** B15
Qom *Iran* 34°40N 51°0E **87** C7
Qostanay *Kazakhstan* 53°10N 63°35E **76** D7
Quadring *U.K.* 52°54N 0°10W **27** G8
Quang Ngai *Vietnam* 15°13N 108°58E **82** A3
Quanzhou *China* 24°55N 118°34E **79** G12
Quaqtaq *Canada* 60°55N 69°40W **109** C13
Quartu Sant'Elena *Italy* 39°15N 9°10E **68** E3
Québec *Canada* 46°52N 71°13W **113** B12
Québec □ *Canada* 48°0N 74°0W **109** E12
Queen Charlotte Sd. *Canada* 51°0N 128°0W **108** D7
Queen Elizabeth Is. *Canada* 76°0N 95°0W **109** B10
Queen Elizabeth Land
  Antarctica 85°0S 60°0W **55** E18
Queen Maud G. *Canada* 68°15N 102°30W **108** C9
Queenborough *U.K.* 51°25N 0°46E **31** D10
Queensbury *U.K.* 53°46N 1°50W **27** E5
Queensferry *U.K.* 55°59N 3°23W **25** C9
Queensland □ *Australia* 22°0S 142°0E **98** E7
Queenstown *N.Z.* 45°1S 168°40E **99** K12
Queenstown *S. Africa* 31°52S 26°52E **97** L5
Queimadas *Brazil* 11°0S 39°38W **122** B3
Quelimane *Mozam.* 17°53S 36°58E **97** H7
Quendale, B. of *U.K.* 59°53N 1°20W **22** C15
Querétaro *Mexico* 20°36N 100°23W **114** C4
Quesnel *Canada* 53°0N 122°30W **108** D7
Quesnel L. *Canada* 52°30N 121°20W **108** D7
Quetta *Pakistan* 30°15N 66°55E **84** D5
Quetzaltenango *Guatemala* 14°50N 91°30W **114** E6
Quezon City *Phil.* 14°37N 121°2E **83** B6
Qui Nhon *Vietnam* 13°40N 109°13E **82** B3
Quibdó *Colombia* 5°42N 76°40W **120** B2
Quilán, C. *Chile* 43°15S 74°30W **121** G2
Quilpie *Australia* 26°35S 144°11E **98** F7
Quimper *France* 48°0N 4°9W **66** B1
Quincy *Ill., U.S.A.* 39°56N 91°23W **111** C8
Quincy *Mass., U.S.A.* 42°14N 71°0W **113** D12
Quito *Ecuador* 0°15S 78°35W **120** C2
Qujing *China* 25°32N 103°41E **78** F9
Qulsary *Kazakhstan* 46°59N 54°1E **71** E9
Qŭnghirot *Uzbekistan* 43°2N 58°50E **87** A9
Quorndon *U.K.* 52°45N 1°10W **27** G6
Qŭqon *Uzbekistan* 40°31N 70°56E **87** A12
Quseir *Egypt* 26°7N 34°16E **95** C12
Quzhou *China* 28°57N 118°54E **79** F12

R

Raahe *Finland* 64°40N 24°28E **63** E8
Raasay *U.K.* 57°25N 6°4W **22** H5
Raasay, Sd. of *U.K.* 57°30N 6°8W **22** H5
Raba *Indonesia* 8°36S 118°55E **83** F5
Rabat *Morocco* 34°2N 6°48W **94** B4
Rabaul *Papua N. G.* 4°24S 152°18E **98** A9
Rābigh *Si. Arabia* 22°50N 39°5E **89** C2
Race, C. *Canada* 46°40N 53°5W **109** E14
Rach Gia *Vietnam* 10°5N 105°5E **82** B3
Racine *U.S.A.* 42°44N 87°47W **112** D4
Rackheath *U.K.* 52°40N 1°22E **31** A11
Radcliffe *U.K.* 53°34N 2°18W **27** E4
Radcliffe on Trent *U.K.* 52°57N 1°2W **27** G6
Radford *U.S.A.* 37°8N 80°34W **112** G7
Radley *U.K.* 51°41N 1°14W **30** C6
Radnor Forest *U.K.* 52°17N 3°10W **28** C7
Radom *Poland* 51°23N 21°12E **65** C11
Radstock *U.K.* 51°17N 2°26W **30** D4
Rae Bareli *India* 26°18N 81°20E **85** F12
Rae Isthmus *Canada* 66°40N 87°30W **109** C11
Rafaela *Argentina* 31°10S 61°30W **121** F3
Rafsanjān *Iran* 30°30N 56°5E **87** D9
Ragusa *Italy* 36°55N 14°44E **68** F6
Rahimyar Khan *Pakistan* 28°30N 70°25E **84** E7
Raichur *India* 16°10N 77°20E **84** L10
Raigarh *India* 21°56N 83°25E **85** J13
Rainbow Lake *Canada* 58°30N 119°23W **108** D8
Rainier, Mt. *U.S.A.* 46°52N 121°46W **110** A2
Rainworth *U.K.* 53°7N 1°7W **27** F6
Rainy L. *Canada* 48°30N 93°10W **108** E10
Raipur *India* 21°17N 81°45E **85** J12
Raj Nandgaon *India* 21°5N 81°5E **85** J12

Rajahmundry *India* 17°1N 81°48E **85** L12
Rajapalaiyam *India* 9°25N 77°35E **84** Q10
Rajasthan □ *India* 26°45N 73°30E **84** F8
Rajkot *India* 22°15N 70°56E **84** H7
Rajshahi *Bangla.* 24°22N 88°39E **85** G16
Rakhine □ *Burma* 19°0N 94°15E **85** K18
Raleigh *U.S.A.* 35°47N 78°39W **111** C11
Rame Head *U.K.* 50°19N 4°13W **29** G5
Ramgarh *India* 23°40N 85°35E **85** H14
Ramna Stacks *U.K.* 60°35N 1°24W **22** A15
Râmnicu Vâlcea *Romania* 45°9N 24°21E **65** F13
Rampside *U.K.* 54°5N 3°9W **26** C1
Rampur *India* 28°50N 79°5E **84** E11
Ramree I. *Burma* 19°0N 93°40E **85** K19
Ramsbottom *U.K.* 53°38N 2°19W **27** E4
Ramsbury *U.K.* 51°26N 1°36W **30** D5
Ramsey *I. of Man* 54°20N 4°22W **19** C13
Ramsey *Cambs., U.K.* 52°27N 0°7W **31** B8
Ramsey *Essex, U.K.* 51°55N 1°13E **31** C11
Ramsgate *U.K.* 51°20N 1°25E **31** D11
Rancagua *Chile* 34°10S 70°50W **121** F2
Ranchi *India* 23°19N 85°27E **85** H14
Randalstown *U.K.* 54°45N 6°19W **19** B9
Randers *Denmark* 56°29N 10°1E **63** F6
Rangoon *Burma* 16°45N 96°20E **85** L20
Rangpur *Bangla.* 25°42N 89°22E **85** G16
Rankin Inlet *Canada* 62°30N 93°0W **108** C10
Rannoch *U.K.* 56°40N 4°20W **23** J9
Rannoch, L. *U.K.* 56°41N 4°20W **23** J9
Rannoch Moor *U.K.* 56°38N 4°48W **23** J8
Rantoul *U.S.A.* 40°19N 88°9W **112** E3
Rapa *French Polynesia* 27°35S 144°20W **103** K13
Rapallo *Italy* 44°21N 9°14E **68** B3
Raper, C. *Canada* 69°44N 67°6W **109** C13
Rapid City *U.S.A.* 44°5N 103°14W **110** B6
Rarotonga *Cook Is.* 21°30S 160°0W **103** K12
Ra's al Khaymah *U.A.E.* 25°50N 55°59E **87** E9
Rasht *Iran* 37°20N 49°40E **86** B7
Rat Islands *U.S.A.* 52°0N 178°0E **108** D1
Ratangarh *India* 28°5N 74°35E **84** E9
Rathcoole *Ireland* 53°17N 6°29W **21** B10
Rathdrum *Ireland* 52°56N 6°14W **21** C10
Rathkeale *Ireland* 52°32N 8°56W **20** D5
Rathlin I. *U.K.* 55°18N 6°14W **19** A9
Rathmelton *Ireland* 55°2N 7°39W **18** A6
Ratlam *India* 23°20N 75°0E **84** H9
Ratnagiri *India* 16°57N 73°18E **84** L8
Raton *U.S.A.* 36°54N 104°24W **110** C6
Rattray Hd. *U.K.* 57°38N 1°50W **23** G14
Rauma *Finland* 61°10N 21°30E **63** E8
Raunds *U.K.* 52°21N 0°32W **31** B7
Raurkela *India* 22°14N 84°50E **85** H14
Ravenglass *U.K.* 54°22N 3°24W **26** D2
Ravenna *Italy* 44°25N 12°12E **68** B5
Ravenstonedale *U.K.* 54°26N 2°25W **26** D4
Ravi → *Pakistan* 30°35N 71°49E **84** D7
Rawalpindi *Pakistan* 33°38N 73°8E **84** C8
Rawlins *U.S.A.* 41°47N 107°14W **110** B5
Rawmarsh *U.K.* 53°27N 1°21W **27** F6
Rawson *Argentina* 43°15S 65°5W **121** G3
Rawtenstall *U.K.* 53°42N 2°17W **27** E4
Ray, C. *Canada* 47°33N 59°15W **109** E14
Rayleigh *U.K.* 51°36N 0°37E **31** C10
Rayong *Thailand* 12°40N 101°20E **82** B2
Raz, Pte. du *France* 48°2N 4°47W **66** C1
Ré, Î. de *France* 46°12N 1°30W **66** C3
Reading *U.K.* 51°27N 0°58W **31** D7
Reading *U.S.A.* 40°20N 75°56W **113** E10
Reay Forest *U.K.* 58°22N 4°55W **23** F8
Rebiana Desert *Libya* 24°30N 21°0E **95** D10
Recife *Brazil* 8°0S 35°0W **122** B3
Reconquista *Argentina* 29°10S 59°45W **121** E4
Red → *U.S.A.* 31°1N 91°45W **111** D8
Red Bluff *U.S.A.* 40°11N 122°15W **110** B2
Red Deer *Canada* 52°20N 113°50W **108** D8
Red Dial *U.K.* 54°49N 3°10W **26** D2
Red L. *U.S.A.* 48°8N 94°45W **111** A8
Red Lake *Canada* 51°3N 93°49W **108** D10
Red Oak *U.S.A.* 41°1N 95°14W **111** B7
Red River of the North →
  N. Amer. 49°0N 97°15W **108** D10
Red Sea *Asia* 25°0N 36°0E **89** C2
Red Wing *U.S.A.* 44°34N 92°31W **111** B8
Redbridge □ *U.K.* 51°35N 0°7E **31** C9
Redcar *U.K.* 54°37N 1°4W **26** D6
Redding *U.S.A.* 40°35N 122°24W **110** B2
Redditch *U.K.* 52°18N 1°55W **30** B5
Rede → *U.K.* 55°9N 2°13W **26** B4
Redesmouth *U.K.* 55°8N 2°13W **26** B4
Redhill *U.K.* 51°14N 0°9W **31** D8
Redlynch *U.K.* 51°0N 1°41W **30** E5
Redmile *U.K.* 52°55N 0°48W **27** G7
Redmire *U.K.* 54°19N 1°55W **26** D5
Redon *France* 47°40N 2°6W **66** C2
Redruth *U.K.* 50°14N 5°14W **29** G3
Ree, L. *Ireland* 53°35N 8°0W **18** D6
Reedham *U.K.* 52°34N 1°34E **31** A12
Reepham *U.K.* 52°46N 1°6E **31** A11
Reese → *U.S.A.* 40°48N 117°4W **110** B3
Reeth *U.K.* 54°23N 1°56W **26** D5
Regensburg *Germany* 49°1N 12°6E **64** D7
Réggio di Calábria *Italy* 38°6N 15°39E **68** E6
Réggio nell'Emília *Italy* 44°43N 10°36E **68** B4
Regina *Canada* 50°27N 104°35W **108** D9
Reichenbach *Germany* 50°37N 12°17E **64** C7
Reigate *U.K.* 51°14N 0°12W **31** D8
Reims *France* 49°15N 4°1E **66** B6
Reina Adelaida, Arch. *Chile* 52°20S 74°0W **121** H2
Reindeer L. *Canada* 57°15N 102°15W **108** D9
Remanso *Brazil* 9°41S 42°4W **122** A2
Renfrew *Canada* 45°30N 76°40W **112** C9
Renfrew *U.K.* 55°52N 4°24W **24** C7
Rennell *Solomon Is.* 11°40S 160°10E **99** C11
Rennes *France* 48°7N 1°41W **66** B3
Reno *U.S.A.* 39°31N 119°48W **110** C3
Repton *U.K.* 52°50N 1°33W **27** G5
Republican → *U.S.A.* 39°4N 96°48W **111** C7
Repulse Bay *Canada* 66°30N 86°30W **109** C11
Resistencia *Argentina* 27°30S 59°0W **121** E4
Resolute *Canada* 74°42N 94°54W **109** B10

Resolution I. *Canada* 61°30N 65°0W **109** C13
Reston *U.K.* 55°51N 2°10W **25** C11
Retford *U.K.* 53°19N 0°56W **27** F7
Rethimno *Greece* 35°18N 24°30E **69** G11
Réunion ☑ *Ind. Oc.* 21°0S 56°0E **91** J9
Reus *Spain* 41°10N 1°5E **67** B6
Reutlingen *Germany* 48°29N 9°12E **64** D5
Revda *Russia* 56°48N 59°57E **70** C10
Revelstoke *Canada* 51°0N 118°10W **108** D8
Revilla Gigedo, Is. de *Pac. Oc.* 18°40N 112°0W **114** D2
Rewa *India* 24°33N 81°25E **85** G12
Rewari *India* 28°15N 76°40E **84** E10
Rexburg *U.S.A.* 43°49N 111°47W **110** B4
Rey Malabo *Eq. Guin.* 3°45N 8°50E **96** D1
Reykjavík *Iceland* 64°10N 21°57W **63** B1
Reynosa *Mexico* 26°7N 98°18W **114** B5
Rēzekne *Latvia* 56°30N 27°17E **63** F9
Rhayader *U.K.* 52°18N 3°29E **28** C7
Rheidol → *U.K.* 52°25N 4°5W **28** C5
Rheine *Germany* 52°17N 7°26E **64** B4
Rheinland-Pfalz □ *Germany* 50°0N 7°0E **64** C4
Rhine → *Europe* 51°52N 6°2E **64** C4
Rhinelander *U.S.A.* 45°38N 89°25W **112** C3
Rhinns Pt. *U.K.* 55°40N 6°29W **24** C3
Rhins, The *U.K.* 54°52N 5°3W **24** E5
Rhode Island □ *U.S.A.* 41°40N 71°30W **113** E12
Rhodes *Greece* 36°15N 28°10E **69** F13
Rhodope Mts. *Bulgaria* 41°40N 24°20E **69** D11
Rhondda □ *U.K.* 51°39N 3°31W **28** D6
Rhône → *France* 43°28N 4°42E **66** E6
Rhosllanerchrugog *U.K.* 53°1N 3°3W **28** A7
Rhossili *U.K.* 51°34N 4°17W **29** D5
Rhossili B. *U.K.* 51°32N 4°14W **29** D5
Rhum = Rùm *U.K.* 57°0N 6°20W **22** J5
Rhydaman = Ammanford
  U.K. 51°48N 3°59W **28** D6
Rhyl *U.K.* 53°20N 3°29W **28** A7
Rhymney *U.K.* 51°46N 3°17W **28** D7
Riau, Kepulauan □ *Indonesia* 0°30N 104°20E **82** D2
Ribble → *U.K.* 53°52N 2°25W **27** E4
Ribeirão Prêto *Brazil* 21°10S 47°50W **122** D1
Riberalta *Bolivia* 11°0S 66°0W **120** D3
Riccall *U.K.* 53°50N 1°3W **27** E6
Rice Lake *U.S.A.* 45°30N 91°44W **112** C2
Richards Bay *S. Africa* 28°48S 32°6E **97** K6
Richfield *U.S.A.* 38°46N 112°5W **110** C4
Richland *U.S.A.* 46°17N 119°18W **110** A3
Richland Center *U.S.A.* 43°21N 90°23W **112** D2
Richlands *U.S.A.* 37°6N 81°48W **112** G7
Richmond *U.K.* 54°25N 1°43W **26** D5
Richmond *Ind., U.S.A.* 39°50N 84°53W **112** F5
Richmond *Ky., U.S.A.* 37°45N 84°18W **112** G5
Richmond *Va., U.S.A.* 37°33N 77°27W **112** G9
Richmond-upon-Thames □
  U.K. 51°27N 0°17W **31** D8
Rickmansworth *U.K.* 51°38N 0°29W **31** C8
Ridgecrest *U.S.A.* 35°38N 117°40W **110** C3
Ridgway *U.S.A.* 41°25N 78°44W **112** E8
Ridsdale *U.K.* 55°9N 2°9W **26** B4
Rievaulx *U.K.* 54°16N 1°7W **26** D6
Rift Valley *Africa* 7°0N 30°0E **90** G7
Rīga *Latvia* 56°53N 24°8E **63** F8
Riga, G. of *Latvia* 57°40N 23°45E **63** F8
Rigestan *Afghan.* 30°15N 65°0E **87** D11
Rigolet *Canada* 54°10N 58°23W **109** D14
Rijeka *Croatia* 45°20N 14°21E **68** B6
Rillington *U.K.* 54°9N 0°42W **26** D7
Rímini *Italy* 44°3N 12°33E **68** B5
Rimouski *Canada* 48°27N 68°30W **109** E13
Ringmer *U.K.* 50°53N 0°5E **31** E9
Ringwood *U.K.* 50°50N 1°47W **30** E5
Rio Branco *Brazil* 9°58S 67°49W **120** C3
Rio Claro *Brazil* 22°19S 47°35W **122** D1
Rio Cuarto *Argentina* 33°10S 64°25W **121** F3
Rio de Janeiro *Brazil* 22°54S 43°12W **122** D2
Rio de Janeiro □ *Brazil* 22°50S 43°0W **122** D2
Rio Gallegos *Argentina* 51°35S 69°15W **121** H3
Rio Grande *Brazil* 32°0S 52°20W **121** F4
Rio Grande de Santiago →
  Mexico 21°36N 105°26W **114** C3
Rio Grande do Norte □ *Brazil* 5°40S 36°0W **120** C6
Rio Grande do Sul □ *Brazil* 30°0S 53°0W **121** E4
Rio Largo *Brazil* 9°28S 35°50W **122** A3
Rio Muni □ *Eq. Guin.* 1°30N 10°0E **96** D2
Riohacha *Colombia* 11°33N 72°55W **120** A2
Ripley *Derby, U.K.* 53°3N 1°24W **27** F6
Ripley *N. Yorks., U.K.* 54°3N 1°34W **26** D5
Ripon *U.K.* 54°9N 1°31W **26** D6
Ripon *U.S.A.* 43°51N 88°50W **112** D3
Risca *U.K.* 51°37N 3°5W **29** D7
Rishton *U.K.* 53°46N 2°26W **27** E4
Rivera *Uruguay* 31°0S 55°50W **121** F4
Riverhead *U.S.A.* 40°55N 72°40W **113** E11
Riverside *U.S.A.* 33°59N 117°22W **110** D3
Riverton *U.S.A.* 43°2N 108°23W **110** B5
Riviera = Côte d'Azur *France* 43°25N 7°10E **66** E7
Rivière-du-Loup *Canada* 47°50N 69°30W **113** B13
Rivne *Ukraine* 50°40N 26°10E **65** C14
Riyadh *Si. Arabia* 24°41N 46°42E **86** E6
Rize *Turkey* 41°0N 40°30E **71** F7
Rizhao *China* 35°25N 119°30E **79** D12
Roade *U.K.* 52°9N 0°53W **31** B7
Roanne *France* 46°3N 4°4E **66** C6
Roanoke → *U.S.A.* 35°57N 76°42W **111** C11
Roanoke *U.S.A.* 37°16N 79°56W **112** G8
Roberton *U.K.* 55°25N 2°54W **25** D10
Roberval *Canada* 48°32N 72°15W **109** E12
Robin Hood's Bay *U.K.* 54°26N 0°31W **26** D7
Robson, Mt. *Canada* 53°10N 119°10W **108** D8
Roca, C. da *Portugal* 38°40N 9°31E **67** C1
Rocester *U.K.* 52°57N 1°50W **27** G5
Rocha *Uruguay* 34°30S 54°25W **121** F4
Rochdale *U.K.* 53°38N 2°9W **27** E4
Roche *U.K.* 50°24N 4°50W **29** G4
Rochefort *France* 45°56N 0°57W **66** D3
Rochester *Medway, U.K.* 51°23N 0°31E **31** D10
Rochester *Northumberland,*
  U.K. 55°17N 2°17W **26** B4
Rochester *Minn., U.S.A.* 44°1N 92°28W **111** B8
Rochester *N.H., U.S.A.* 43°18N 70°59W **113** D12

Rochester N.Y., U.S.A. 43°10N 77°37W 112 D9
Rochford U.K. 51°34N 0°43E 31 C10
Rock Hill U.S.A. 34°56N 81°1W 111 D10
Rock Island U.S.A. 41°30N 90°34W 112 E2
Rock Springs U.S.A. 41°35N 109°14W 110 B5
Rockall Atl. Oc. 57°37N 13°42W 56 D3
Rockcliffe U.K. 54°57N 3°0W 26 C3
Rockford U.S.A. 42°16N 89°6W 112 D3
Rockhampton Australia 23°22S 150°32E 98 E9
Rockingham U.K. 52°31N 0°43W 31 A7
Rockingham Forest U.K. 52°29N 0°42W 31 B7
Rockland U.S.A. 44°6N 69°7W 113 C13
Rocky Mount U.S.A. 35°57N 77°48W 111 C11
Rocky Mts. N. Amer. 49°0N 115°0W 108 D7
Rodez France 44°21N 2°33E 66 D5
Roding → U.K. 51°31N 0°6E 31 C9
Rodrigues Ind. Oc. 19°45S 63°20E 53 E13
Roe → U.K. 55°6N 6°59W 19 A8
Roes Welcome Sd. Canada 65°0N 87°0W 109 C11
Rogans Seat U.K. 54°26N 2°7W 26 D4
Rogate U.K. 51°0N 0°50W 31 D7
Rogers City U.S.A. 45°25N 83°49W 112 C6
Rohri Pakistan 27°45N 68°51E 84 F6
Rojo, C. Mexico 21°33N 97°20W 114 C5
Rolla U.S.A. 37°57N 91°46W 111 C8
Roma Australia 26°32S 148°49E 98 F8
Romaine → Canada 50°18N 63°47W 109 D13
Romania ■ Europe 46°0N 25°0E 65 F12
Romans-sur-Isère France 45°3N 5°3E 66 D6
Rome Italy 41°54N 12°28E 68 D5
Rome Ga., U.S.A. 34°15N 85°10W 111 D9
Rome N.Y., U.S.A. 43°13N 75°27W 113 D10
Romney U.S.A. 39°21N 78°45W 112 F8
Romney Marsh U.K. 51°2N 0°54E 31 D10
Romorantin-Lanthenay France 47°21N 1°45E 66 C4
Romsey U.K. 51°0N 1°29W 30 E6
Rona U.K. 57°34N 5°59W 22 G6
Roncador, Serra do Brazil 12°30S 52°30W 120 D4
Rondônia □ Brazil 11°0S 63°0W 120 D3
Rondonópolis Brazil 16°28S 54°38W 120 D4
Ronge, L. la Canada 55°6N 105°17W 108 D9
Ronne Ice Shelf Antarctica 77°30S 60°0W 55 D18
Roosevelt → Brazil 7°35S 60°20W 120 C3
Roosevelt I. Antarctica 79°30S 162°0W 55 D12
Ropsley U.K. 52°54N 0°30W 27 G8
Roquetas de Mar Spain 36°46N 2°36W 67 D4
Roraima □ Brazil 2°0N 61°30W 120 B3
Roraima, Mt. Venezuela 5°10N 60°40W 120 B3
Rosario Argentina 33°0S 60°40W 121 F3
Rosario Mexico 22°58N 105°53W 114 C3
Rosario de la Frontera Argentina 25°50S 65°0W 121 E3
Roscommon Ireland 53°38N 8°11W 18 D5
Roscommon □ Ireland 53°49N 8°23W 18 D5
Roscrea Ireland 52°57N 7°49W 20 C7
Roseau Dominica 15°17N 61°24W 115 D12
Roseburg U.S.A. 43°13N 123°20W 110 B2
Rosedale Abbey U.K. 54°21N 0°52W 26 D7
Rosehearty U.K. 57°42N 2°7W 23 G13
Rosenheim Germany 47°51N 12°7E 64 F7
Rosetown Canada 51°35N 107°59W 108 D9
Roseville U.S.A. 38°45N 121°17W 110 C3
Roslavl Russia 53°57N 32°55E 70 D5
Ross Ice Shelf Antarctica 80°0S 180°0E 55 E12
Ross-on-Wye U.K. 51°54N 2°34W 30 C3
Ross River Canada 62°30N 131°30W 108 C6
Ross Sea Antarctica 74°0S 178°0E 55 D11
Russell Pt. U.K. 54°42N 8°47W 27 E2
Rossan Pt. Ireland 54°42N 8°47W 18 B4
Rosses, The Ireland 55°2N 8°20W 18 A5
Rossignol L. Canada 44°12N 65°10W 113 C15
Rosslare Ireland 52°17N 6°24W 21 D10
Rosslare Harbour Ireland 52°15N 6°20W 21 D10
Rossosh Russia 50°15N 39°28E 71 D6
Rostock Germany 54°5N 12°8E 64 A7
Rostov Russia 47°15N 39°45E 71 E6
Roswell Ga., U.S.A. 34°2N 84°22W 111 D10
Roswell N. Mex., U.S.A. 33°24N 104°32W 110 D6
Rote Indonesia 10°50S 123°0E 83 F6
Rothbury U.K. 55°19N 1°58W 26 B5
Rothbury Forest U.K. 55°19N 1°50W 26 B5
Rother → U.K. 50°59N 0°45E 31 E10
Rotherham U.K. 53°26N 1°20W 27 F6
Rothes U.K. 57°32N 3°13W 23 G11
Rothesay U.K. 55°50N 5°3W 24 C5
Rothwell Northants., U.K. 52°25N 0°48W 31 B7
Rothwell W. Yorks., U.K. 53°45N 1°28W 27 E6
Rotorua N.Z. 38°9S 176°16E 99 H14
Rotterdam Neths. 51°55N 4°30E 64 C3
Rottingdean U.K. 50°48N 0°4W 31 E8
Rotuma Fiji 12°25S 177°5E 99 C14
Roubaix France 50°40N 3°10E 66 A5
Rouen France 49°27N 1°4E 66 B4
Round Mt. Australia 30°26S 152°16E 98 G9
Rousay U.K. 59°10N 3°2W 23 D11
Roussillon France 42°30N 2°35E 66 E5
Rouyn-Noranda Canada 48°20N 79°0W 109 E12
Rovaniemi Finland 66°29N 25°41E 63 D9
Rovigo Italy 45°4N 11°47E 68 B4
Rowanburn U.K. 55°5N 2°55W 25 D10
Roxas Phil. 11°36N 122°49E 83 B6
Roxburgh U.K. 55°35N 2°28W 25 C10
Roxby U.K. 53°38N 0°38W 27 E7
Royal Canal Ireland 53°30N 7°13W 21 B8
Royal Leamington Spa U.K. 52°18N 1°31W 30 B5
Royal Tunbridge Wells U.K. 51°7N 0°16E 31 D9
Royal Wootton Bassett U.K. 51°33N 1°54W 30 C5
Royale, Isle U.S.A. 48°0N 88°54W 112 B3
Royan France 45°37N 1°2W 66 D3
Royston U.K. 52°3N 0°0 31 B8
Royton U.K. 53°34N 2°8W 27 E4
Rub' al Khālī Si. Arabia 19°0N 48°0E 89 D4
Rubery U.K. 52°24N 2°1W 30 B4
Rubh a' Mhail U.K. 55°56N 6°8W 24 C3
Rubha Hunish U.K. 57°42N 6°20W 22 G5
Rubtsovsk Russia 51°30N 81°10E 76 D9
Ruby L. U.S.A. 40°10N 115°28W 110 B3
Rudnyy Kazakhstan 52°57N 63°7E 76 D7
Rudston U.K. 54°6N 0°20W 26 D8
Rufford U.K. 53°38N 2°50W 27 E3

Rufiji → Tanzania 7°50S 39°15E 96 F7
Rugby U.K. 52°23N 1°16W 30 B6
Rugeley U.K. 52°46N 1°55W 27 G5
Rügen Germany 54°22N 13°24E 64 A7
Ruhr → Germany 51°27N 6°43E 64 C4
Ruki → Dem. Rep. of the Congo 0°5N 18°17E 96 E3
Rukwa, L. Tanzania 8°0S 32°20E 96 F6
Rùm U.K. 57°0N 6°20W 22 J5
Rùm, Sound of U.K. 56°55N 6°14W 22 J5
Rumania = Romania ■ Europe 46°0N 25°0E 65 F12
Rumford U.S.A. 44°33N 70°33W 113 C10
Runaway Bay Jamaica 18°27N 77°20W 114 a
Runcorn U.K. 53°21N 2°44W 27 F3
Rundu Namibia 17°52S 19°43E 97 H3
Rungwe Tanzania 9°11S 33°32E 96 G7
Ruo Shui → China 41°0N 100°16E 78 C9
Ruoqiang China 38°55N 88°10E 78 D6
Rupert → U.S.A. 42°37N 113°41W 110 B4
Rupert → Canada 51°29N 70°45W 109 D12
Ruse Bulgaria 43°48N 25°59E 69 C12
Rush Ireland 53°31N 6°6W 21 A10
Rushden U.K. 52°18N 0°35W 31 B7
Rushville Ill., U.S.A. 40°7N 90°34W 112 E2
Rushville Ind., U.S.A. 39°37N 85°27W 112 F5
Ruskington U.K. 53°3N 0°22W 27 F8
Russellville U.S.A. 35°17N 93°8W 111 C8
Russia ■ Eurasia 62°0N 105°0E 77 C11
Rustavi Georgia 41°30N 45°0E 71 F8
Rustenburg S. Africa 25°41S 27°14E 97 K5
Rutherglen U.K. 55°49N 4°13W 24 C7
Ruthin U.K. 53°6N 3°19W 28 A7
Ruthwell U.K. 55°0N 3°25W 25 D9
Rutog China 33°27N 79°42E 78 E4
Ruvuma → Tanzania 10°29S 40°28E 96 G8
Ruwenzori Africa 0°30N 29°55E 96 D5
Rwanda ■ Africa 2°0S 30°0E 96 E5
Ryan, L. U.K. 55°0N 5°2W 24 E5
Ryazan Russia 54°40N 39°40E 70 D6
Rybachi Pen. Russia 69°43N 32°0E 70 A5
Rybinsk Russia 58°5N 38°50E 70 C6
Rybinsk Res. Russia 58°30N 38°25E 70 C6
Rydal U.K. 54°27N 2°59W 26 D3
Ryde U.K. 50°43N 1°9W 30 E6
Rye U.K. 50°57N 0°45E 31 E10
Rye → U.K. 54°11N 0°44W 26 D7
Rye Bay U.K. 50°52N 0°49E 31 E10
Ryhope U.K. 54°53N 1°21W 26 C6
Ryton U.K. 52°22N 1°25W 30 B6
Ryukyu Is. Japan 26°0N 126°0E 79 F14
Rzeszów Poland 50°5N 21°58E 65 C11
Rzhev Russia 56°20N 34°20E 70 C5

S

Saale → Germany 51°56N 11°54E 64 C6
Saar → Europe 49°41N 6°32E 64 D4
Saarbrücken Germany 49°14N 6°59E 64 D4
Saaremaa Estonia 58°30N 22°30E 63 F8
Sabadell Spain 41°28N 2°7E 67 B7
Sabah □ Malaysia 6°0N 117°0E 82 C5
Sabhā Libya 27°9N 14°29E 95 C8
Sabinas Mexico 27°51N 101°7W 114 B4
Sabinas Hidalgo Mexico 26°30N 100°10W 114 B4
Sabine → U.S.A. 29°59N 93°47W 111 E8
Sable, C. Canada 43°29N 65°38W 113 D15
Sable, C. U.S.A. 25°9N 81°8W 111 E10
Sable I. Canada 44°0N 60°0W 109 E14
Sachsen □ Germany 50°55N 13°10E 64 C7
Sachsen-Anhalt □ Germany 52°0N 12°0E 64 C7
Saco U.S.A. 43°30N 70°27W 113 D12
Sacramento U.S.A. 38°35N 121°29W 110 C2
Sacramento → U.S.A. 38°3N 121°56W 110 C2
Sacramento Mts. U.S.A. 32°30N 105°30W 110 D5
Sado Japan 38°0N 138°25E 81 D6
Safford U.S.A. 32°50N 109°43W 110 D5
Saffron Walden U.K. 52°1N 0°16E 31 B9
Safi Morocco 32°18N 9°20W 94 B4
Saga Japan 33°15N 130°16E 81 G1
Sagaing Burma 21°52N 95°59E 85 J19
Sagar India 23°50N 78°44E 84 H11
Saginaw U.S.A. 43°26N 83°56W 112 D6
Saginaw B. U.S.A. 43°50N 83°40W 112 D6
Sagua la Grande Cuba 22°50N 80°10W 115 C8
Saguenay → Canada 48°22N 71°0W 113 A12
Sagunt Spain 39°42N 0°18W 67 C5
Sahara Africa 23°0N 5°0E 94 D6
Saharanpur India 29°58N 77°33E 84 E10
Sahel Africa 16°0N 5°0E 94 E5
Sahiwal Pakistan 30°45N 73°8E 84 D8
Saidpur Bangla. 25°48N 89°0E 85 G16
St. Abb's Head U.K. 55°55N 2°8W 25 C11
St. Agnes Corn., U.K. 50°19N 5°13W 29 H3
St. Agnes Corn., U.K. 49°54N 6°21W 29 H1
St. Agnes Hd. U.K. 50°19N 5°15W 29 G3
St. Albans U.K. 51°45N 0°19W 31 C8
St. Albans Vt., U.S.A. 44°49N 73°5W 113 C11
St. Albans W. Va., U.S.A. 38°23N 81°50W 112 F7
St. Alban's Head U.K. 50°34N 2°4W 30 E5
St. Andrews U.K. 56°20N 2°47W 25 B10
St. Ann's U.K. 55°14N 3°28W 25 D9
St. Ann's Bay Jamaica 18°26N 77°12W 114 a
St. Anthony Canada 51°22N 55°35W 109 D14
St. Asaph U.K. 53°15N 3°27W 28 A7
St-Augustin Canada 51°13N 58°38W 109 D14
St. Augustine U.S.A. 29°54N 81°19W 111 E10
St. Austell U.K. 50°20N 4°47W 29 G4
St. Bees U.K. 54°30N 3°35W 26 C1
St. Bees Hd. U.K. 54°31N 3°38W 26 C1
St. Blazey U.K. 50°22N 4°43W 29 G4
St. Brides B. U.K. 51°49N 5°9W 28 D3
St-Brieuc France 48°30N 2°46W 66 B2
St. Buryan U.K. 50°4N 5°37W 29 G2
St. Catharines Canada 43°10N 79°15W 112 D8
St. Catherine's Pt. U.K. 50°34N 1°18W 30 E6
St. Charles U.S.A. 38°47N 90°29W 112 F2
St. Clair, L. N. Amer. 42°27N 82°39W 112 D6
St. Clears U.K. 51°49N 4°31W 28 D4
St. Cloud U.S.A. 45°34N 94°10W 111 A8
St. Columb Major U.K. 50°26N 4°58W 29 G4
St. Croix U.S. Virgin Is. 17°45N 64°45W 115 D12

St. David's U.K. 51°53N 5°16W 28 D3
St. David's Head U.K. 51°54N 5°19W 28 D3
St Denis France 48°56N 2°20E 66 B5
St-Dizier France 48°38N 4°56E 66 B6
St. Dominick U.K. 50°29N 4°16W 29 G6
St. Elias, Mt. U.S.A. 60°18N 140°56W 108 C5
St. Elias Mts. N. Amer. 60°33N 139°28W 108 D6
St. Enoder U.K. 50°22N 4°59W 29 G4
St. Erth U.K. 50°9N 5°26W 29 G3
St-Étienne France 45°27N 4°22E 66 D6
St-Félicien Canada 48°40N 72°25W 113 A11
St-Flour France 45°2N 3°6E 66 D5
St. Gallen Switz. 47°26N 9°22E 64 E4
St-Gaudens France 43°6N 0°44E 66 E4
St. George U.S.A. 37°6N 113°35W 110 C4
St-Georges Canada 46°8N 70°40W 113 B12
St. George's Grenada 12°5N 61°43W 115 E12
St. George's Channel Europe 52°0N 6°0W 21 E11
St. Germans U.K. 50°23N 4°19W 29 G5
St. Helena Atl. Oc. 15°58S 5°42W 52 E9
St. Helens U.K. 53°27N 2°44W 27 F3
St. Helens U.S.A. 46°12N 122°12W 110 A2
St. Helens, Mt. U.S.A. 46°12N 122°12W 110 A2
St. Helier U.K. 49°10N 2°7W 29 J9
St-Hyacinthe Canada 45°40N 72°50W 109 E12
St. Ignace U.S.A. 45°52N 84°44W 112 C5
St. Issey U.K. 50°30N 4°57W 29 G4
St. Ives Cambs., U.K. 52°20N 0°4W 31 B8
St. Ives Corn., U.K. 50°12N 5°30W 29 G3
St. Ives B. U.K. 50°13N 5°27W 29 G3
St-Jean, L. Canada 48°40N 72°0W 113 A12
St-Jérôme Canada 45°47N 74°0W 113 C11
St. John Canada 45°20N 66°8W 109 E13
St. John → N. Amer. 45°12N 66°5W 113 C14
St. John's Antigua & B. 17°6N 61°51W 115 D12
St. John's Canada 47°35N 52°40W 109 E15
St. Johns U.S.A. 43°0N 84°33W 112 D5
St. Johns → U.S.A. 30°24N 81°24W 111 D10
St. John's Pt. Ireland 54°34N 8°27W 18 B5
St. Johnsbury U.S.A. 44°25N 72°1W 113 C11
St. Joseph Mich., U.S.A. 42°6N 86°29W 112 D4
St. Joseph Mo., U.S.A. 39°46N 94°50W 111 C8
St. Joseph, L. Canada 51°10N 90°35W 109 D10
St. Just U.K. 50°7N 5°42W 29 G2
St. Keverne U.K. 50°3N 5°6W 29 G3
St. Kilda U.K. 57°49N 8°34W 22 b
St. Kitts & Nevis ■ W. Indies 17°20N 62°40W 115 D12
St. Lawrence → Canada 49°30N 66°0W 109 E13
St. Lawrence, Gulf of Canada 48°25N 62°0W 109 E13
St. Lawrence I. U.S.A. 63°30N 170°30W 108 B2
St. Levan U.K. 50°2N 5°41W 29 G2
St-Lô France 49°7N 1°5W 66 B3
St-Louis Senegal 16°8N 16°27W 94 E2
St. Louis U.S.A. 38°37N 90°11W 112 F2
St. Lucia ■ W. Indies 14°0N 60°57W 114 b
St. Mabyn U.K. 50°30N 4°47W 29 F4
St. Magnus B. U.K. 60°25N 1°35W 22 B14
St-Malo France 48°39N 2°1W 66 B2
St-Marc Haiti 19°10N 72°41W 115 D10
St. Margaret's-at-Cliffe U.K. 51°9N 1°23E 31 D11
St-Martin ☑ W. Indies 18°5N 63°5W 115 D12
St. Martins Barbados 13°5N 59°28W 114 c
St. Martin's U.K. 49°58N 6°17W 29 H1
St. Mary Bourne U.K. 51°15N 1°24W 30 D6
St. Mary's Corn., U.K. 49°55N 6°18W 29 H1
St. Mary's Orkney, U.K. 58°54N 2°54W 23 E12
St. Marys U.S.A. 41°26N 78°34W 112 E8
St. Mary's Sd. U.K. 49°53N 6°19W 29 H1
St. Matthew I. U.S.A. 60°24N 172°42W 108 C2
St. Mawes U.K. 50°10N 5°1W 29 G3
St. Merryn U.K. 50°32N 5°1W 29 F3
St. Michael's Mount U.K. 50°7N 5°29W 29 G3
St. Minver U.K. 50°33N 4°53W 29 F4
St. Moritz Switz. 46°30N 9°51E 64 E5
St-Nazaire France 47°17N 2°12W 66 C2
St. Neots U.K. 52°14N 0°15W 31 B8
St-Omer France 50°45N 2°15E 66 A5
St. Osyth U.K. 51°47N 1°5E 31 C11
St. Paul U.S.A. 44°56N 93°5W 111 B8
St. Paul, Î. Ind. Oc. 38°55S 77°34E 53 F13
St. Peter Port U.K. 49°26N 2°33W 29 J8
St. Petersburg Russia 59°55N 30°20E 70 C5
St. Petersburg U.S.A. 27°46N 82°40W 111 E10
St-Pierre-et-Miquelon ☑ N. Amer. 46°55N 56°10W 109 E14
St-Quentin France 49°50N 3°16E 66 B5
St. Stephen Canada 45°16N 67°17W 113 C14
St. Stephen U.K. 50°21N 4°53W 29 G4
St. Teath U.K. 50°35N 4°45W 29 F4
St. Thomas Canada 42°45N 81°10W 112 D7
St-Tropez France 43°17N 6°38E 66 E7
St. Tudy U.K. 50°33N 4°45W 29 F4
St. Vincent, G. Australia 35°0S 138°0E 98 G6
St. Vincent & the Grenadines ■ W. Indies 13°0N 61°10W 115 E12
Ste. Genevieve U.S.A. 37°59N 90°2W 112 G2
Ste-Marie Canada 46°26N 71°0W 113 B12
Saintes France 45°45N 0°37W 66 D3
Saintfield U.K. 54°28N 5°49W 19 C10
Saintonge France 45°40N 0°50W 66 D3
Saipan N. Marianas 15°12N 145°45E 102 F6
Saitama Japan 35°54N 139°38E 81 F7
Sajama Bolivia 18°7S 69°0W 120 D3
Sakākah Si. Arabia 30°0N 40°8E 86 D5
Sakakawea, L. U.S.A. 47°30N 101°25W 110 A6
Sakarya Turkey 40°48N 30°25E 71 F5
Sakata Japan 38°55N 139°50E 81 D6
Sakha □ Russia 66°0N 130°0E 77 C13
Sakhalin Russia 51°0N 143°0E 77 D15
Sakurajima Japan 31°35N 130°39E 81 H2
Sala Sweden 59°58N 16°35E 63 F7
Sala-y-Gómez Pac. Oc. 26°28S 105°28W 103 K17
Salado → La Pampa, Argentina 37°30S 67°0W 121 F3
Salado → Santa Fe, Argentina 31°40S 60°41W 121 F3
Salālah Oman 16°56N 53°59E 89 D5
Salamanca Spain 40°58N 5°39W 67 B3
Salamanca U.S.A. 42°10N 78°43W 112 D8
Salar de Uyuni Bolivia 20°30S 67°45W 120 E3
Salavat Russia 53°21N 55°55E 70 D10

St. David's U.K. 51°53N 5°16W 28 D3
Salaverry Peru 8°15S 79°0W 120 C2
Salayar Indonesia 6°7S 120°30E 83 F6
Salcombe U.K. 50°14N 3°47W 29 H6
Saldanha S. Africa 33°0S 17°58E 97 L3
Sale Australia 38°6S 147°6E 98 H8
Salé Morocco 34°3N 6°48W 94 B4
Sale U.K. 53°26N 2°19W 27 F4
Salekhard Russia 66°30N 66°35E 76 C7
Salem India 11°40N 78°11E 84 P11
Salem Ind., U.S.A. 38°36N 86°6W 112 F4
Salem Mass., U.S.A. 42°31N 70°53W 113 D12
Salem Ohio, U.S.A. 40°54N 80°52W 112 E7
Salem Oreg., U.S.A. 44°56N 123°2W 110 B2
Salem Va., U.S.A. 37°18N 80°3W 112 G7
Salerno Italy 40°41N 14°47E 68 D6
Salford U.K. 53°30N 2°18W 27 F4
Salford Priors U.K. 52°10N 1°53W 30 B5
Salida U.S.A. 38°32N 106°0W 110 C5
Salina U.S.A. 38°50N 97°37W 110 C7
Salina Cruz Mexico 16°10N 95°12W 114 D5
Salinas Ecuador 2°10S 80°58W 120 C1
Salinas U.S.A. 36°40N 121°39W 110 C2
Salinas → U.S.A. 36°45N 121°48W 110 C2
Salinas Grandes Argentina 30°0S 65°0W 121 E3
Salisbury U.K. 51°4N 1°47W 30 D5
Salisbury U.S.A. 38°22N 75°36W 113 F10
Salisbury I. Canada 63°30N 77°0W 109 C12
Salisbury Plain U.K. 51°14N 1°55W 30 D5
Salmon U.S.A. 45°11N 113°54W 110 A4
Salmon → U.S.A. 45°51N 116°47W 110 A3
Salmon Arm Canada 50°40N 119°15W 108 D8
Salmon River Mts. U.S.A. 44°50N 115°30W 110 B4
Salon-de-Provence France 43°39N 5°6E 66 E6
Salsk Russia 46°28N 41°30E 71 E7
Salt → U.S.A. 33°23N 112°19W 110 D4
Salt Lake City U.S.A. 40°45N 111°53W 110 B4
Salta Argentina 24°57S 65°25W 121 E3
Saltash U.K. 50°24N 4°14W 29 G5
Saltburn-by-the-Sea U.K. 54°35N 0°58W 26 C7
Saltcoats U.K. 55°38N 4°47W 24 C6
Saltee Is. Ireland 52°7N 6°37W 21 D9
Saltfleet U.K. 53°25N 0°11E 27 F9
Saltfleetby U.K. 53°23N 0°10E 27 F9
Saltillo Mexico 25°25N 101°0W 114 B4
Salton Sea U.S.A. 33°15N 115°45W 110 D3
Saltwood U.K. 51°4N 1°2E 31 D11
Salvador Brazil 13°0S 38°30W 122 B3
Salween → Burma 16°31N 97°37E 78 G8
Salyan Azerbaijan 39°33N 48°59E 71 G8
Salzburg Austria 47°48N 13°2E 64 E7
Salzgitter Germany 52°9N 10°19E 64 B6
Samar Phil. 12°0N 125°0E 83 B7
Samara Russia 53°8N 50°6E 70 D9
Samarinda Indonesia 0°30S 117°9E 82 E5
Samarqand Uzbekistan 39°40N 66°55E 87 B11
Sambalpur India 21°28N 84°4E 85 J14
Sambhal India 28°35N 78°37E 84 E11
Sambhar India 26°52N 75°6E 84 F9
Samoa ■ Pac. Oc. 14°0S 172°0W 99 C16
Samos Greece 37°45N 26°50E 69 F12
Samothraki Greece 40°28N 25°28E 69 D11
Sampford Courtenay U.K. 50°47N 3°58W 29 F6
Samsun Turkey 41°15N 36°22E 71 F6
Samui, Ko Thailand 9°30N 100°0E 82 C2
San → Poland 50°45N 21°51E 65 C11
San Ambrosio Pac. Oc. 26°28S 79°53W 103 K20
San Andres, I. de Caribbean 12°42N 81°46W 115 E8
San Andres Mts. U.S.A. 33°0N 106°30W 110 D5
San Andrés Tuxtla Mexico 18°27N 95°13W 114 D5
San Angelo U.S.A. 31°28N 100°26W 110 D6
San Antonio Chile 33°40S 71°40W 121 F2
San Antonio U.S.A. 29°25N 98°29W 110 E7
San Antonio → U.S.A. 28°30N 96°54W 111 E7
San Antonio Oeste Argentina 40°40S 65°0W 121 G3
San Bernardino U.S.A. 34°7N 117°19W 110 D3
San Bernardino Str. Phil. 12°30N 124°10E 83 B6
San Bernardo Chile 33°40S 70°50W 121 F2
San Blas, C. U.S.A. 29°40N 85°21W 111 E9
San Carlos Phil. 10°29N 123°25E 83 B6
San Carlos de Bariloche Argentina 41°10S 71°25W 121 G2
San Carlos de Bolivar Argentina 36°15S 61°6W 121 F3
San Cristóbal Argentina 30°20S 61°10W 121 F3
San Cristóbal Solomon Is. 10°30S 161°0E 99 C11
San Cristóbal Venezuela 7°46N 72°14W 120 B2
San Cristóbal de las Casas Mexico 16°45N 92°38W 114 D6
San Diego U.S.A. 32°42N 117°9W 110 D3
San Felipe Venezuela 10°20N 68°44W 120 A3
San Félix Pac. Oc. 26°23S 80°0W 103 K20
San Fernando Chile 34°30S 71°0W 121 F2
San Fernando Spain 36°28N 6°17W 67 D2
San Fernando de Apure Venezuela 7°54N 67°15W 120 B3
San Francisco U.S.A. 37°46N 122°23W 110 C2
San Francisco, C. de Colombia 6°18N 77°29W 117 C3
San Francisco de Macorís Dom. Rep. 19°19N 70°15W 115 D10
San Gottardo, P. del Switz. 46°33N 8°33E 64 E5
San Ignacio Bolivia 16°20S 60°55W 120 D3
San Joaquín → U.S.A. 38°4N 121°51W 110 C2
San Jorge, G. Argentina 46°0S 66°0W 121 G3
San José Costa Rica 9°55N 84°2W 115 F8
San Jose Phil. 12°27N 121°4E 83 B6
San Jose U.S.A. 37°20N 121°53W 110 C2
San José de Chiquitos Bolivia 17°53S 60°50W 120 D3
San José de Jáchal Argentina 30°15S 68°46W 121 F3
San José de Mayo Uruguay 34°27S 56°40W 121 F4
San José del Cabo Mexico 23°3N 109°41W 114 C3
San Juan Argentina 31°30S 68°30W 121 F3
San Juan Puerto Rico 18°28N 66°7W 115 D11
San Juan → Nic. 10°56N 83°42W 115 E8
San Juan → U.S.A. 37°16N 110°26W 110 C4
San Juan de la Maguana Dom. Rep. 18°49N 71°12W 115 D10
San Juan de los Morros Venezuela 9°55N 67°21W 120 B3
San Juan Mts. U.S.A. 37°30N 107°0W 110 C5

San Lorenzo, Mte. Argentina 47°40S 72°20W 121 G2
San Lucas, C. Mexico 22°52N 109°53W 114 C3
San Luis Argentina 33°20S 66°20W 121 F3
San Luis Obispo U.S.A. 35°17N 120°40W 110 C2
San Luis Potosí Mexico 22°9N 100°59W 114 C4
San Marcos U.S.A. 29°53N 97°56W 110 E7
San Marino ■ Europe 43°56N 12°25E 68 C5
San Matías, G. Argentina 41°30S 64°0W 121 G3
San Miguel El Salv. 13°30N 88°12W 114 E7
San Miguel de Tucumán Argentina 26°50S 65°20W 121 E3
San Nicolás Argentina 33°25S 60°10W 121 F3
San Pedro Ivory C. 4°50N 6°33W 94 H4
San Pedro de las Colonias Mexico 25°45N 102°59W 114 B4
San Pedro de Macorís Dom. Rep. 18°30N 69°18W 115 D11
San Pedro Sula Honduras 15°30N 88°0W 114 D7
San Pietro Italy 39°8N 8°17E 68 E3
San Rafael Argentina 34°40S 68°21W 121 F3
San Remo Italy 43°49N 7°46E 68 C2
San Salvador El Salv. 13°40N 89°10W 114 E7
San Salvador de Jujuy Argentina 24°10S 64°48W 121 E3
San Salvador I. Bahamas 24°0N 74°30W 115 C10
San Severo Italy 41°41N 15°23E 68 D6
San Valentin, Mte. Chile 46°30S 73°30W 121 G2
Sana' = Sanaa Yemen 15°27N 44°12E 89 D3
Sanaa Yemen 15°27N 44°12E 89 D3
Sanaga → Cameroon 3°35N 9°38E 96 D1
Sanandaj Iran 35°18N 47°1E 86 C6
Sancti Spíritus Cuba 21°52N 79°33W 115 C9
Sancy, Puy de France 45°23N 2°50E 66 D5
Sandakan Malaysia 5°53N 118°4E 82 C5
Sanday U.K. 59°16N 2°31W 23 D12
Sandbach U.K. 53°9N 2°21W 27 F4
Sandgate U.K. 51°4N 1°10E 31 D11
Sandhurst U.K. 51°21N 0°48W 31 D7
Sandown U.K. 50°40N 1°10W 30 E6
Sandpoint U.S.A. 48°17N 116°33W 110 A3
Sandray U.K. 56°53N 7°31W 22 J2
Sandringham U.K. 52°51N 0°31E 31 A10
Sandusky U.S.A. 41°27N 82°42W 112 E6
Sandwich U.K. 51°16N 1°21E 31 D11
Sandy U.K. 52°8N 0°17W 31 B8
Sandy L. Canada 53°2N 93°0W 108 D10
Sanford, Mt. U.S.A. 62°13N 144°8W 108 C5
Sangihe, Pulau Indonesia 3°35N 125°30E 83 D7
Sangli India 16°55N 74°33E 84 L9
Sangre de Cristo Mts. U.S.A. 37°30N 105°20W 110 C5
Sanikiluaq Canada 56°32N 79°14W 109 D12
Sankt Pölten Austria 48°12N 15°38E 64 D8
Sankuru → Dem. Rep. of the Congo 4°17S 20°25E 96 E4
Sanliurfa Turkey 37°12N 38°50E 71 G6
Sanlúcar de Barrameda Spain 36°46N 6°21W 67 D2
Sanmenxin China 34°47N 111°12E 79 E11
Sanming China 26°15N 117°40E 79 F12
Sanndraigh = Sandray U.K. 56°53N 7°31W 22 J2
Sanquhar U.K. 55°22N 3°54W 25 D8
Sant Feliu de Guixols Spain 41°45N 3°1E 67 B7
Santa Ana El Salv. 14°0N 89°31W 114 E7
Santa Ana U.S.A. 33°46N 117°52W 110 D3
Santa Barbara U.S.A. 34°25N 119°42W 110 D3
Santa Catarina □ Brazil 27°25S 48°30W 121 E5
Santa Clara Cuba 22°20N 80°0W 115 C9
Santa Coloma de Gramenet Spain 41°27N 2°13E 67 B7
Santa Cruz Bolivia 17°43S 63°10W 120 D3
Santa Cruz de Tenerife Canary Is. 28°28N 16°15W 94 C2
Santa Cruz Is. Solomon Is. 10°30S 166°0E 99 C12
Santa Cruz Mts. Jamaica 17°58N 77°43W 114 a
Santa Fé Argentina 31°35S 60°41W 121 F3
Santa Fe U.S.A. 35°41N 105°57W 110 C5
Santa Inês, I. Chile 54°0S 73°0W 121 H2
Santa Isabel Solomon Is. 8°0S 159°0E 99 B10
Santa Maria Brazil 29°40S 53°48W 121 E4
Santa Maria U.S.A. 34°57N 120°26W 110 D2
Santa Maria → Mexico 31°0N 107°14W 114 A3
Santa Marta Colombia 11°15N 74°13W 120 A2
Santa Marta, Sierra Nevada de Colombia 10°55N 73°50W 120 A2
Santa Rosa Argentina 36°40S 64°17W 121 F3
Santa Rosa U.S.A. 38°26N 122°43W 110 C2
Santai China 31°5N 104°58E 78 E9
Santana do Livramento Brazil 30°55S 55°30W 121 F4
Santander Spain 43°27N 3°51W 67 A4
Santanilla, Is. Honduras 17°22N 83°57W 115 D8
Santarém Brazil 2°25S 54°42W 120 C4
Santarém Portugal 39°12N 8°42W 67 C1
Santiago Chile 33°26S 70°40W 121 F2
Santiago de Compostela Spain 42°52N 8°37W 67 A1
Santiago de Cuba Cuba 20°0N 75°49W 115 D9
Santiago de los Caballeros Dom. Rep. 19°30N 70°40W 115 D10
Santiago del Estero Argentina 27°50S 64°15W 121 E3
Santo Amaro Brazil 12°30S 38°43W 122 B3
Santo André Brazil 23°39S 46°29W 122 D1
Sant' Antioco Italy 39°4N 8°27E 68 E3
Santo Antônio de Jesus Brazil 12°58S 39°16W 122 B3
Santo Domingo Dom. Rep. 18°30N 69°59W 115 D11
Santo Domingo de los Colorados Ecuador 0°15S 79°9W 120 C2
Santorini Greece 36°23S 25°27E 69 F11
Santos Brazil 24°0S 46°20W 122 D1
Santos Dumont Brazil 22°55S 43°10W 122 D2
Sanxiang China 22°21N 113°25E 79 a
Sanya China 18°14N 109°29E 79 H10
São Bernardo do Campo Brazil 23°45S 46°34W 122 D1
São Borja Brazil 28°39S 56°0W 121 E4
São Caitano Brazil 8°21S 36°6W 122 A3

São Carlos

São Carlos *Brazil* 22°0S 47°50W **122 D1**
São Francisco → *Brazil* 10°30S 36°24W **122 B3**
São Gonçalo *Brazil* 22°48S 43°5W **122 D2**
São João da Boa Vista *Brazil* 22°0S 46°52W **122 D1**
São João de Meriti *Brazil* 22°48S 43°22W **122 D2**
São João del Rei *Brazil* 21°8S 44°15W **122 D2**
São João do Piauí *Brazil* 8°21S 42°15W **122 A2**
São José do Rio Preto *Brazil* 20°50S 49°20W **122 D1**
São José dos Campos *Brazil* 23°7S 45°52W **122 D1**
São Lourenço *Brazil* 22°7S 45°3W **122 D2**
São Luís *Brazil* 2°39S 44°15W **120 C5**
São Marcos → *Brazil* 18°15S 47°37W **122 C1**
São Marcos, B. de *Brazil* 2°0S 44°0W **120 C5**
São Mateus *Brazil* 18°44S 39°50W **122 C3**
São Paulo *Brazil* 23°32S 46°38W **122 D1**
São Paulo □ *Brazil* 22°0S 49°0W **120 E5**
São Roque, C. de *Brazil* 5°30S 35°16W **120 C6**
São Sebastião do Paraiso *Brazil* 20°54S 46°59W **122 D1**
São Tomé *São Tomé & Príncipe* 0°10N 6°39E **90 F4**
São Tomé & Príncipe ■ *Africa* 0°12N 6°39E **91 F4**
São Vicente *Brazil* 23°57S 46°23W **122 D1**
São Vicente, C. de *Portugal* 37°0N 9°0W **67 D1**
Saône → *France* 45°44N 4°50E **66 D6**
Sapele *Nigeria* 5°50N 5°40E **94 G7**
Sapporo *Japan* 43°0N 141°21E **81 B7**
Saqqez *Iran* 36°15N 46°20E **86 B6**
Sar-e Pol *Afghan.* 36°10N 66°0E **87 B11**
Saraburi *Thailand* 14°30N 100°55E **82 B2**
Sarajevo *Bos.-H.* 43°52N 18°26E **69 C8**
Saranac Lakes *U.S.A.* 44°20N 74°28W **113 C10**
Saransk *Russia* 54°10N 45°10E **70 D8**
Sarapul *Russia* 56°28N 53°48E **70 C9**
Sarasota *U.S.A.* 27°20N 82°32W **111 E10**
Saratoga Springs *U.S.A.* 43°5N 73°47W **113 D11**
Saratov *Russia* 51°30N 46°2E **71 D8**
Sarawak □ *Malaysia* 2°0N 113°0E **82 D4**
Sarda → *India* 27°21N 81°23E **85 F12**
Sardinia □ *Italy* 40°0N 9°0E **68 D3**
Sargasso Sea *Atl. Oc.* 27°0N 72°0W **104 G13**
Sargodha *Pakistan* 32°10N 72°40E **84 C8**
Sarh *Chad* 9°5N 18°23E **95 G9**
Sārī *Iran* 36°30N 53°4E **87 B8**
Sariwon *N. Korea* 38°31N 125°46E **79 D14**
Sark *U.K.* 49°25N 2°22W **29 J9**
Sarlat-la-Canéda *France* 44°54N 1°13E **66 D4**
Sarmiento *Argentina* 45°35S 69°5W **121 G3**
Sarnia *Canada* 42°58N 82°23W **109 E11**
Sarqan *Kazakhstan* 45°24N 79°55E **78 B4**
Sarreguemines *France* 49°5N 7°4E **66 B7**
Sarthe → *France* 47°33N 0°31W **66 C3**
Sasebo *Japan* 33°10N 129°43E **81 G1**
Saskatchewan □ *Canada* 54°40N 106°0W **108 D9**
Saskatchewan → *Canada* 53°37N 100°40W **108 D9**
Saskatoon *Canada* 52°10N 106°38W **108 D9**
Sássari *Italy* 40°43N 8°34E **68 D3**
Sassnitz *Germany* 54°29N 13°39E **64 A7**
Satmala Hills *Maharashtra, India* 20°15N 74°40E **84 J9**
Satmala Hills *Telangana, India* 19°45N 78°45E **84 K11**
Satna *India* 24°35N 80°50E **85 G12**
Satpura Ra. *India* 21°25N 76°10E **84 J10**
Satu Mare *Romania* 47°46N 22°55E **65 E12**
Saudi Arabia ■ *Asia* 26°0N 44°0E **89 B3**
Sault Ste. Marie *Canada* 46°30N 84°20W **112 B5**
Saumur *France* 47°15N 0°5W **66 C3**
Saundersfoot *U.K.* 51°43N 4°42W **28 D4**
Saurimo *Angola* 9°40S 20°12E **96 F4**
Sava → *Serbia* 44°50N 20°26E **69 B9**
Savai'i *Samoa* 13°28S 172°24W **99 C16**
Savanna-la-Mar *Jamaica* 18°10N 78°10W **114 a**
Savannah *U.S.A.* 32°5N 81°6W **111 D10**
Savannah → *U.S.A.* 32°2N 80°53W **111 D10**
Savannakhet *Laos* 16°30N 104°49E **82 A2**
Savoie □ *France* 45°26N 6°25E **66 D7**
Savona *Italy* 44°17N 8°30E **68 B3**
Sawatch Range *U.S.A.* 39°0N 106°30W **110 C5**
Sawbridgeworth *U.K.* 51°48N 0°9E **31 C9**
Sawel Mt. *U.K.* 54°50N 7°2W **19 B7**
Sawston *U.K.* 52°8N 0°10E **31 B9**
Sawtry *U.K.* 52°27N 0°17W **31 B8**
Sawu *Indonesia* 10°35S 121°50E **83 F6**
Sawu Sea *Indonesia* 9°30S 121°50E **83 F6**
Saxilby *U.K.* 53°16N 0°38W **27 F7**
Saxlingham Nethergate *U.K.* 52°32N 1°18E **31 A11**
Saxmundham *U.K.* 52°13N 1°30E **31 B12**
Saxony = Sachsen □ *Germany* 50°55N 13°10E **64 C7**
Sayan Mts. *Russia* 54°0N 96°0E **77 D10**
Saydā *Lebanon* 33°35N 35°25E **86 C3**
Sayre *U.S.A.* 41°59N 76°32W **112 E9**
Sázava → *Czech Rep.* 49°53N 14°24E **64 D8**
Scafell Pike *U.K.* 54°27N 3°14W **26 D2**
Scalby *U.K.* 54°18N 0°26W **26 D8**
Scalloway *U.K.* 60°9N 1°17W **22 B15**
Scalpay *Highl., U.K.* 57°18N 6°0W **22 H6**
Scalpay *W. Isles, U.K.* 57°52N 6°40W **22 G4**
Scamblesby *U.K.* 53°17N 0°5W **27 F8**
Scandicci *Italy* 43°45N 11°11E **68 C4**
Scandinavia *Europe* 64°0N 12°0E **56 B8**
Scapa Flow *U.K.* 58°53N 3°3W **23 E11**
Scarba *U.K.* 56°11N 5°43W **24 E3**
Scarborough *U.K.* 54°17N 0°24W **26 D8**
Scariff I. *Ireland* 51°44N 10°15W **20 E2**
Scarning *U.K.* 52°41N 0°54E **31 A10**
Scarp *U.K.* 58°1N 7°8W **22 F2**
Schaffhausen *Switz.* 47°42N 8°39E **64 E5**
Schelde → *Belgium* 51°15N 4°16E **64 C3**
Schenectady *U.S.A.* 42°49N 73°57W **113 D11**
Schiehallion *U.K.* 56°40N 4°6W **24 A7**
Schleswig *Germany* 54°31N 9°34E **64 A5**
Schleswig-Holstein □ *Germany* 54°30N 9°30E **64 A5**
Schreiber *Canada* 48°45N 87°20W **112 A4**
Schwäbische Alb *Germany* 48°20N 9°30E **64 D5**
Schwarzwald *Germany* 48°30N 8°20E **64 D5**
Schwerin *Germany* 53°36N 11°22E **64 B6**
Schwyz *Switz.* 47°2N 8°39E **64 E5**
Scilly, Is. of *U.K.* 49°56N 6°22W **29 H1**
Scioto → *U.S.A.* 38°44N 83°1W **112 F6**
Scole *U.K.* 52°22N 1°10E **31 B11**

Scone *U.K.* 56°25N 3°24W **25 B9**
Scopwick *U.K.* 53°8N 0°24W **27 F8**
Scotia Sea *Antarctica* 56°5S 56°0W **55 B18**
Scotland □ *U.K.* 57°0N 4°0W **62 C5**
Scott I. *Antarctica* 67°0S 179°0E **55 C11**
Scottish Borders □ *U.K.* 55°35N 2°50W **25 C10**
Scottsbluff *U.S.A.* 41°52N 103°40W **110 B6**
Scottsburg *U.S.A.* 38°41N 85°47W **112 F5**
Scrabster *U.K.* 58°36N 3°33W **23 E10**
Scranton *U.S.A.* 41°25N 75°40W **113 E10**
Scremerston *U.K.* 55°44N 2°0W **26 A5**
Scunthorpe *U.K.* 53°36N 0°39W **27 E7**
Scutari *Albania* 42°4N 19°32E **69 C8**
Scutari *Turkey* 41°1N 29°0E **86 A2**
Seaford *U.K.* 50°47N 0°7E **31 E9**
Seaford *U.S.A.* 38°39N 75°37W **113 F10**
Seaforth, L. *U.K.* 57°52N 6°36W **22 G4**
Seaham *U.K.* 54°50N 1°20W **26 C6**
Seahouses *U.K.* 55°34N 1°39W **26 A5**
Seal → *Canada* 59°4N 94°48W **108 D10**
Seamer *U.K.* 54°15N 0°26W **26 D8**
Seascale *U.K.* 54°24N 3°29W **26 D2**
Seaton *Cumb., U.K.* 54°40N 3°31W **26 C1**
Seaton *Devon, U.K.* 50°42N 3°5W **29 F7**
Seaton Delaval *U.K.* 55°5N 1°33W **26 B5**
Seattle *U.S.A.* 47°36N 122°19W **110 A2**
Sebastián Vizcaino, B. *Mexico* 28°0N 114°30W **114 B2**
Şebinkarahisar *Turkey* 40°22N 38°28E **71 F6**
Sedalia *U.S.A.* 38°42N 93°14W **111 C8**
Sedan *France* 49°43N 4°57E **66 B6**
Sedbergh *U.K.* 54°20N 2°31W **26 D3**
Sedgefield *U.K.* 54°40N 1°26W **26 C6**
Seend *U.K.* 51°21N 2°4W **30 D4**
Segesta *Italy* 37°56N 12°50E **68 F5**
Ségou *Mali* 13°30N 6°16W **94 F4**
Segovia *Spain* 40°57N 4°10W **67 B3**
Séguéla *Ivory C.* 7°55N 6°40W **94 G4**
Sehore *India* 23°10N 77°5E **84 H10**
Seil *U.K.* 56°18N 5°38W **24 E3**
Seine → *France* 49°26N 0°26E **66 B4**
Sekondi-Takoradi *Ghana* 4°58N 1°45W **94 H5**
Selborne *U.K.* 51°6N 0°56W **31 D7**
Selby *U.K.* 53°47N 1°5W **27 E6**
Selebi-Phikwe *Botswana* 21°58S 27°48E **97 J5**
Selenge Mörön → *Asia* 52°16N 106°16E **78 A10**
Selkirk *Canada* 50°10N 96°55W **108 D10**
Selkirk *U.K.* 55°33N 2°50W **25 C10**
Selkirk Mts. *Canada* 51°15N 117°40W **108 D8**
Sellafield *U.K.* 54°25N 3°29W **26 D2**
Selma *U.S.A.* 32°25N 87°1W **111 D9**
Selsey *U.K.* 50°44N 0°47W **31 E7**
Selsey Bill *U.K.* 50°43N 0°47W **31 E7**
Selvas *Brazil* 6°30S 67°0W **120 C3**
Selwyn L. *Canada* 60°0N 104°30W **108 C9**
Selwyn Mts. *Canada* 63°0N 130°0W **108 C6**
Semarang *Indonesia* 7°0S 110°26E **82 F4**
Semey *Kazakhstan* 50°30N 80°10E **76 D9**
Semnan *Iran* 35°40N 53°23E **87 C8**
Sena Madureira *Brazil* 9°5S 68°45W **120 C3**
Sendai *Japan* 38°15N 140°53E **81 D7**
Seneca L. *U.S.A.* 42°40N 76°54W **112 D9**
Senegal ■ *W. Afr.* 14°30N 14°30W **94 F3**
Sénégal → *W. Afr.* 15°48N 16°32W **94 E2**
Senegambia *Africa* 12°45N 12°0W **90 E2**
Senhor-do-Bonfim *Brazil* 10°30S 40°10W **122 B2**
Senja *Norway* 69°25N 17°30E **63 D7**
Senkaku Is. *E. China Sea* 25°45N 123°30E **79 F13**
Senlis *France* 49°13N 2°35E **66 B5**
Sennen *U.K.* 50°4N 5°42W **29 G2**
Sens *France* 48°12N 3°18E **66 B5**
Seoul *S. Korea* 37°31N 126°58E **79 D14**
Seph → *U.K.* 54°18N 1°9W **26 D6**
Sept-Îles *Canada* 50°13N 66°22W **109 D13**
Seram *Indonesia* 3°10S 129°0E **83 E7**
Seram Sea *Indonesia* 2°30S 128°30E **83 E7**
Serang *Indonesia* 6°8S 106°10E **82 F3**
Serbia ■ *Europe* 43°20N 20°0E **69 B9**
Serdar *Turkmenistan* 39°4N 56°23E **87 B9**
Seremban *Malaysia* 2°43N 101°53E **82 D2**
Serengeti Plain *Tanzania* 2°40S 35°0E **96 E7**
Sergipe □ *Brazil* 10°30S 37°30W **122 B3**
Sergiyev Posad *Russia* 56°20N 38°10E **70 C6**
Serhetabat *Turkmenistan* 35°20N 62°18E **87 C10**
Serifos *Greece* 37°9N 24°30E **69 F11**
Serov *Russia* 59°29N 60°35E **70 C11**
Serowe *Botswana* 22°25S 26°43E **97 J5**
Serra *Brazil* 20°7S 40°18W **122 D2**
Serra de Mesa, Barragem de *Brazil* 14°30S 48°30W **122 B1**
Serrinha *Brazil* 11°39S 39°0W **122 B3**
Sète *France* 43°25N 3°42E **66 E5**
Sete Lagoas *Brazil* 19°27S 44°16W **122 C2**
Sétif *Algeria* 36°9N 5°26E **94 A7**
Settat *Morocco* 33°0N 7°40W **94 B4**
Settle *U.K.* 54°5N 2°16W **26 D4**
Setúbal *Portugal* 38°30N 8°58W **67 C1**
Setúbal, B. de *Portugal* 38°40N 8°56W **67 C1**
Seul, Lac *Canada* 50°20N 92°30W **108 D10**
Sevan, L. *Armenia* 40°30N 45°20E **71 F8**
Sevastopol *Ukraine* 44°35N 33°30E **71 F5**
Seven → *U.K.* 54°12N 0°52W **26 D7**
Sevenoaks *U.K.* 51°16N 0°11E **31 D9**
Severn → *Canada* 56°2N 87°36W **109 D11**
Severn → *U.K.* 51°35N 2°40W **30 C3**
Severn Beach *U.K.* 51°33N 2°39W **30 C3**
Severn Stoke *U.K.* 52°6N 2°12W **30 B4**
Severnaya Zemlya *Russia* 79°0N 100°0E **77 B10**
Severodvinsk *Russia* 64°27N 39°58E **70 B6**
Severomorsk *Russia* 69°5N 33°27E **70 A5**
Sevier → *U.S.A.* 39°4N 113°6W **110 C4**
Sevier L. *U.S.A.* 38°54N 113°9W **110 C4**
Seville *Spain* 37°23N 5°58W **67 D2**
Seward *U.S.A.* 60°7N 149°27W **108 C5**
Seward Peninsula *U.S.A.* 65°30N 166°0W **108 C3**
Seychelles ■ *Ind. Oc.* 5°0S 56°0E **91 G9**
Seyðisfjörður *Iceland* 65°16N 13°57E **63 A3**
Seydişehir *Turkey* 37°25N 31°51E **71 G5**
Seymour *U.S.A.* 38°58N 85°53W **112 F5**

Sfântu Gheorghe *Romania* 45°52N 25°48E **65 F13**
Sfax *Tunisia* 34°49N 10°48E **95 B8**
Sha Tin *China* 22°23N 114°12E **79 a**
Shaanxi □ *China* 35°0N 109°0E **79 D10**
Shabeelle → *Somalia* 2°0N 44°0E **89 G3**
Shache *China* 38°20N 77°10E **78 D4**
Shaftesbury *U.K.* 51°0N 2°11W **30 D4**
Shahjahanpur *India* 27°54N 79°57E **84 F11**
Shajing *China* 22°44N 113°48E **79 a**
Shakhty *Russia* 47°40N 40°16E **71 E7**
Shaki *Nigeria* 8°41N 3°21E **94 G6**
Shaldon *U.K.* 50°32N 3°31W **29 F6**
Shaluli Shan *China* 30°40N 99°55E **78 E8**
Shamo, L. *Ethiopia* 5°45N 37°30E **89 F2**
Shan □ *Burma* 21°30N 98°30E **85 J21**
Shandong □ *China* 36°0N 118°0E **79 D12**
Shandong Pen. *China* 37°0N 121°0E **79 D13**
Shanghai *China* 31°15N 121°26E **79 E13**
Shangqiu *China* 34°26N 115°36E **79 E12**
Shangrao *China* 28°25N 117°59E **79 F12**
Shanklin *U.K.* 50°38N 1°11W **30 E6**
Shannon → *Ireland* 52°35N 9°30W **20 C4**
Shannon ✈ (SNN) *Ireland* 52°42N 8°57W **20 C5**
Shannon, Mouth of the *Ireland* 52°30N 9°55W **20 D3**
Shantou *China* 23°18N 116°40E **79 G12**
Shanxi □ *China* 37°0N 112°0E **79 D11**
Shaoguan *China* 24°48N 113°35E **79 G11**
Shaoxing *China* 30°0N 120°35E **79 F13**
Shaoyang *China* 27°14N 111°25E **79 F11**
Shap *U.K.* 54°32N 2°40W **26 C3**
Shapinsay *U.K.* 59°3N 2°51E **23 D12**
Shaqra' *Si. Arabia* 25°15N 45°16E **86 E6**
Sharjah *U.A.E.* 25°23N 55°26E **87 E8**
Shark B. *Australia* 25°30S 113°32E **98 F1**
Sharm el Sheikh *Egypt* 27°53N 34°18E **86 F3**
Sharon *U.S.A.* 41°14N 80°31W **112 E7**
Sharpness *U.K.* 51°43N 2°28W **30 C4**
Sharya *Russia* 58°22N 45°20E **70 C8**
Shasta, Mt. *U.S.A.* 41°25N 122°12W **110 B2**
Shawano *U.S.A.* 44°47N 88°36W **112 C3**
Shawbury *U.K.* 52°48N 2°39W **27 G3**
Shawinigan *Canada* 46°35N 72°50W **109 E12**
Shawnee *U.S.A.* 35°20N 96°55W **111 C7**
Shebbear *U.K.* 50°51N 4°15W **29 F5**
Sheboygan *U.S.A.* 43°46N 87°45W **112 D4**
Sheelin, L. *Ireland* 53°48N 7°20W **18 D7**
Sheep Haven *Ireland* 55°11N 7°52W **18 A6**
Sheerness *U.K.* 51°26N 0°47E **31 D10**
Sheffield *U.K.* 53°23N 1°28W **27 F6**
Shefford *U.K.* 52°2N 0°20W **31 B8**
Shehy Mts. *Ireland* 51°47N 9°15W **20 E4**
Shekou *China* 22°30N 113°55E **79 a**
Shelburne *Canada* 43°47N 65°20W **113 D15**
Shelby *U.S.A.* 48°30N 111°51W **110 A4**
Shelbyville *Ill., U.S.A.* 39°24N 88°48W **112 F3**
Shelbyville *Ind., U.S.A.* 39°31N 85°47W **112 F5**
Shelikhov G. *Russia* 59°30N 157°0E **77 D16**
Shenandoah *U.S.A.* 40°49N 76°12W **113 E9**
Shenandoah → *U.S.A.* 39°19N 77°44W **112 F9**
Shendi *Sudan* 16°46N 33°22E **95 E12**
Shenfield *U.K.* 51°38N 0°22E **31 C9**
Shenyang *China* 41°48N 123°27E **79 C13**
Shenzhen *China* 22°32N 114°5E **79 a**
Shenzhen Bao'an Int. ✈ (SZX) *China* 22°41N 113°49E **79 a**
Shenzhen Wan *China* 22°27N 113°55E **79 a**
Shepparton *Australia* 36°23S 145°26E **98 H8**
Sheppey, I. of *U.K.* 51°25N 0°48E **31 D10**
Shepshed *U.K.* 52°47N 1°18W **27 G6**
Shepton Mallet *U.K.* 51°11N 2°33W **30 D3**
Sherborne *U.K.* 50°57N 2°31W **30 E3**
Sherborne St. John *U.K.* 51°17N 1°7W **30 D6**
Sherbrooke *Canada* 45°28N 71°57W **113 C12**
Sherburn *U.K.* 54°11N 0°32W **26 D7**
Sherburn in Elmet *U.K.* 53°48N 1°15W **27 E6**
Shere *U.K.* 51°13N 0°27W **31 D8**
Sherfield English *U.K.* 51°1N 1°34W **30 D5**
Sheridan *U.S.A.* 44°48N 106°58W **110 B5**
Sheriff Hutton *U.K.* 54°5N 1°0W **26 D7**
Sheringham *U.K.* 52°56N 1°13E **31 A11**
Sherkin I. *Ireland* 51°28N 9°26W **20 F4**
Sherman *U.S.A.* 33°38N 96°36W **111 D7**
Sherston *U.K.* 51°34N 2°14W **30 C4**
Sherwood Forest *U.K.* 53°6N 1°7W **27 F6**
Shetland □ *U.K.* 60°30N 1°30W **22 B15**
Shetland Is. *U.K.* 60°30N 1°30W **22 B15**
Sheung Shui *China* 22°31N 114°7E **79 a**
Sheyenne → *U.S.A.* 47°2N 96°50W **111 A7**
Shiant Is. *U.K.* 57°54N 6°22W **22 G5**
Shibām *Yemen* 15°59N 48°36E **89 D4**
Shiel, L. *U.K.* 56°48N 5°34W **22 J6**
Shifnal *U.K.* 52°39N 2°23W **27 G4**
Shihezi *China* 44°15N 86°2E **78 C6**
Shijiazhuang *China* 38°2N 114°28E **79 D11**
Shikarpur *Pakistan* 27°57N 68°39E **84 F6**
Shikoku □ *Japan* 33°30N 133°30E **81 G3**
Shilbottle *U.K.* 55°23N 1°40W **26 B5**
Shildon *U.K.* 54°38N 1°38W **26 C5**
Shiliguri *India* 26°45N 88°25E **85 F16**
Shillelagh *Ireland* 52°45N 6°32W **21 C9**
Shillingstone *U.K.* 50°53N 2°15W **30 E4**
Shillong *India* 25°35N 91°53E **85 G17**
Shimla *India* 31°2N 77°9E **84 D10**
Shimoga *India* 13°57N 75°32E **84 N9**
Shimonoseki *Japan* 33°58N 130°55E **81 G2**
Shin, L. *U.K.* 58°5N 4°30W **23 F8**
Shinyanga *Tanzania* 3°45S 33°27E **96 E6**
Shipdham *U.K.* 52°38N 0°54E **31 A10**
Shiphoirt, L. = Seaforth, L. *U.K.* 57°52N 6°36W **22 G4**
Shipley *U.K.* 53°50N 1°47W **27 E5**
Shipston-on-Stour *U.K.* 52°3N 1°37W **30 B5**
Shipton under Wychwood *U.K.* 51°51N 1°36W **30 C5**
Shīrāz *Iran* 29°42N 52°30E **87 D8**
Shire → *Africa* 17°42S 35°19E **97 H7**
Shirebrook *U.K.* 53°12N 1°13W **27 F6**
Shivpuri *India* 25°26N 77°42E **84 G10**
Shizuishan *China* 39°15N 106°50E **78 D10**

Shizuoka *Japan* 34°57N 138°24E **81 F6**
Shoeburyness *U.K.* 51°32N 0°49E **31 C10**
Shoreham-by-Sea *U.K.* 50°50N 0°16W **31 E8**
Shreveport *U.S.A.* 32°31N 93°45W **111 D8**
Shrewsbury *U.K.* 52°43N 2°45W **27 G3**
Shrewton *U.K.* 51°12N 1°54W **30 D5**
Shrirampur *India* 22°44N 88°21E **85 H16**
Shrivenham *U.K.* 51°36N 1°38W **30 C5**
Shropshire □ *U.K.* 52°36N 2°45W **27 G3**
Shuangliao *China* 43°29N 123°30E **79 C13**
Shuangyashan *China* 46°28N 131°5E **79 B15**
Shule *China* 39°25N 76°3E **78 D4**
Shule He → *China* 40°20N 92°50E **78 C7**
Shumagin Is. *U.S.A.* 55°7N 160°30W **108 D4**
Shumen *Bulgaria* 43°18N 26°55E **69 C12**
Shunān *Japan* 34°3N 131°50E **81 F2**
Shuqrā' *Yemen* 13°22N 45°44E **89 E4**
Shwebo *Burma* 22°30N 95°45E **85 H19**
Shymkent *Kazakhstan* 42°18N 69°36E **87 A12**
Si Kiang = Xi Jiang → *China* 22°5N 113°20E **79 G11**
Siahan Range *Pakistan* 27°30N 64°40E **84 F4**
Sialkot *Pakistan* 32°32N 74°30E **84 C9**
Šiauliai *Lithuania* 55°56N 23°15E **63 F8**
Šibenik *Croatia* 43°48N 15°54E **68 C6**
Siberia *Russia* 60°0N 100°0E **72 B11**
Siberut *Indonesia* 1°30S 99°0E **82 E1**
Sibi *Pakistan* 29°30N 67°54E **84 E5**
Sibiu *Romania* 45°45N 24°9E **65 F13**
Sible Hedingham *U.K.* 51°59N 0°37E **31 C10**
Sibolga *Indonesia* 1°42N 98°45E **82 D1**
Sibsey *U.K.* 53°2N 0°1E **27 F9**
Sibu *Malaysia* 2°18N 111°49E **82 D4**
Sibuyan Sea *Phil.* 12°30N 122°20E **83 B6**
Sichuan □ *China* 30°30N 103°0E **78 E9**
Sicily *Italy* 37°30N 14°30E **68 F6**
Sicily, Str. of *Medit. S.* 37°35N 11°56E **68 F4**
Sicuani *Peru* 14°21S 71°10W **120 D2**
Sidbury *U.K.* 50°42N 3°14W **29 F7**
Sidi-bel-Abbès *Algeria* 35°13N 0°39W **94 A5**
Sidlaw Hills *U.K.* 56°32N 3°2W **25 B9**
Sidlesham *U.K.* 50°47N 0°47W **31 E7**
Sidmouth *U.K.* 50°40N 3°15W **29 F7**
Sidney *Nebr., U.S.A.* 41°8N 102°59W **110 B6**
Sidney *Ohio, U.S.A.* 40°17N 84°9W **112 E5**
Sidra = Surt *Libya* 31°11N 16°39E **95 B9**
Siedlce *Poland* 52°10N 22°20E **65 B12**
Siegen *Germany* 50°51N 8°0E **64 C5**
Siena *Italy* 43°19N 11°21E **68 C4**
Sierra Blanca Peak *U.S.A.* 33°23N 105°49W **110 D5**
Sierra Leone ■ *W. Afr.* 9°0N 12°0W **94 G3**
Sierra Nevada *Spain* 37°3N 3°15W **67 D4**
Sierra Nevada *U.S.A.* 39°0N 120°30W **110 C2**
Sierra Vista *U.S.A.* 31°33N 110°18W **110 D4**
Sifnos *Greece* 37°0N 24°45E **69 F11**
Sighty Crag *U.K.* 55°7N 2°38W **26 B3**
Sikar *India* 27°33N 75°10E **84 F9**
Sikasso *Mali* 11°18N 5°35W **94 F4**
Sikeston *U.S.A.* 36°53N 89°35W **112 G3**
Sikhote Alin Ra. *Russia* 45°0N 136°0E **77 E14**
Sikkim □ *India* 27°50N 88°30E **85 F16**
Silesia *Poland* 51°0N 16°30E **64 C9**
Silifke *Turkey* 36°22N 33°58E **71 G5**
Siling Co *China* 31°50N 89°20E **78 E6**
Silloth *U.K.* 54°52N 3°23W **26 C2**
Silsden *U.K.* 53°55N 1°55W **27 E5**
Silver City *U.S.A.* 32°46N 108°17W **110 D5**
Silvermine Mts. *Ireland* 52°47N 8°15W **20 C6**
Silverstone *U.K.* 52°5N 1°2W **30 B6**
Silverton *U.K.* 50°49N 3°29W **29 F7**
Simao *China* 22°47N 101°5E **78 G9**
Simcoe, L. *Canada* 44°25N 79°20W **112 C8**
Simeulue *Indonesia* 2°45N 95°45E **82 D1**
Simferopol *Ukraine* 44°55N 34°3E **71 F5**
Simi *Greece* 36°35N 27°50E **69 F12**
Simonsbath *U.K.* 51°8N 3°46W **29 E6**
Simonside *U.K.* 55°17N 1°59W **26 B5**
Simplonpass *Switz.* 46°15N 8°3E **64 E5**
Simpson Desert *Australia* 25°0S 137°0E **98 F6**
Simpson Pen. *Canada* 68°34N 88°45W **109 C11**
Sinai *Egypt* 29°0N 34°0E **95 C12**
Sincelejo *Colombia* 9°18N 75°24W **120 B2**
Sinclair's B. *U.K.* 58°31N 3°5W **23 E11**
Sind Sagar Doab *Pakistan* 32°0N 71°30E **84 D7**
Sindh □ *Pakistan* 26°0N 69°0E **84 G6**
Sines *Portugal* 37°56N 8°51W **67 D1**
Singapore ■ *Asia* 1°17N 103°51E **82 D2**
Singaraja *Indonesia* 8°7S 115°6E **82 F5**
Singida *Tanzania* 4°49S 34°48E **96 E6**
Singkawang *Indonesia* 1°0N 108°57E **82 D3**
Singleton *U.K.* 50°55N 0°46W **31 E7**
Sinkiang □ *China* 42°0N 86°0E **78 C6**
Sinop *Turkey* 42°1N 35°11E **71 F6**
Sintra *Portugal* 38°47N 9°25W **67 C1**
Sion *Switz.* 46°14N 7°20E **64 E4**
Sion Mills *U.K.* 54°48N 7°29W **18 B7**
Sioux City *U.S.A.* 42°30N 96°24W **111 B7**
Sioux Falls *U.S.A.* 43°33N 96°44W **111 B7**
Sioux Lookout *Canada* 50°10N 91°50W **108 D10**
Siping *China* 43°8N 124°21E **79 C13**
Sir James MacBrien, Mt. *Canada* 62°7N 127°41W **108 C7**
Siracusa *Italy* 37°4N 15°17E **68 F6**
Sirajganj *Bangla.* 24°25N 89°47E **85 G16**
Sīrjān *Iran* 29°30N 55°45E **87 D8**
Sirsa *India* 29°33N 75°4E **84 E9**
Sirte = Surt *Libya* 31°11N 16°39E **95 B9**
Sīstān *Asia* 30°50N 61°0E **87 D10**
Sitapur *India* 27°38N 80°45E **85 F12**
Sitges *Spain* 41°17N 1°47E **67 B6**
Sitka *U.S.A.* 57°3N 135°20W **108 D6**
Sittingbourne *U.K.* 51°21N 0°45E **31 D10**
Sittwe *Burma* 20°18N 92°45E **85 J18**
Sivas *Turkey* 39°43N 36°58E **71 G6**
Sivrihisar *Turkey* 39°30N 31°35E **71 G5**
Siwa *Egypt* 29°11N 25°31E **95 C11**
Siwalik Range *Nepal* 28°0N 83°0E **85 F13**
Siwan *India* 26°13N 84°21E **85 F14**
Six Cross Roads *Barbados* 13°7N 59°28W **114 c**
Sixmilebridge *Ireland* 52°44N 8°46W **20 C5**
Sizewell *U.K.* 52°12N 1°37E **31 B12**

Sjælland *Denmark* 55°30N 11°30E **63 F6**
Skagerrak *Denmark* 57°30N 9°0E **63 F5**
Skagway *U.S.A.* 59°28N 135°19W **108 D6**
Skeena → *Canada* 54°9N 130°5W **108 D6**
Skegness *U.K.* 53°9N 0°20E **27 F9**
Skeleton Coast *Namibia* 20°0S 13°0E **97 J2**
Skellefteå *Sweden* 64°45N 20°50E **63 E8**
Skellefteälven → *Sweden* 64°45N 21°10E **63 E8**
Skellingthorpe *U.K.* 53°15N 0°37W **27 F7**
Skelmersdale *U.K.* 53°33N 2°48W **27 E3**
Skelmorlie *U.K.* 55°52N 4°53W **24 C6**
Skelton *Cleve., U.K.* 54°34N 0°58W **26 C7**
Skelton *Cumb., U.K.* 54°43N 2°51W **26 C3**
Skerries, The *U.K.* 53°25N 4°36W **28 A4**
Skiathos *Greece* 39°12N 23°30E **69 E10**
Skibbereen *Ireland* 51°33N 9°16W **20 E4**
Skiddaw *U.K.* 54°39N 3°9W **26 C2**
Skien *Norway* 59°12N 9°35E **63 F5**
Skikda *Algeria* 36°50N 6°58E **94 A7**
Skipsea *U.K.* 53°58N 0°13W **27 E8**
Skipton *U.K.* 53°58N 2°3W **27 E4**
Skiros *Greece* 38°55N 24°34E **69 E11**
Skopelos *Greece* 39°9N 23°47E **69 E10**
Skopje *Macedonia* 42°1N 21°26E **69 C9**
Skovorodino *Russia* 54°0N 124°0E **77 D13**
Skowhegan *U.S.A.* 44°46N 69°43W **113 C13**
Skull *Ireland* 51°32N 9°34W **20 E3**
Skye *U.K.* 57°15N 6°10W **22 H5**
Slaidburn *U.K.* 53°58N 2°26W **27 E4**
Slaney → *Ireland* 52°26N 6°33W **21 D9**
Slatina *Romania* 44°28N 24°22E **65 F13**
Slave → *Canada* 61°18N 113°39W **108 C8**
Slave Coast *W. Afr.* 6°0N 2°30E **94 G6**
Slave Lake *Canada* 55°17N 114°43W **108 D8**
Sleaford *U.K.* 53°0N 0°24W **27 F7**
Sleat, Sd. of *U.K.* 57°5N 5°47W **22 H6**
Sledmere *U.K.* 54°4N 0°35W **26 D7**
Sleeper Is. *Canada* 58°30N 81°0W **109 D11**
Sleights *U.K.* 54°27N 0°40W **26 D7**
Slieve Aughty *Ireland* 53°4N 8°30W **20 B5**
Slieve Bloom *Ireland* 53°4N 7°40W **21 B7**
Slieve Donard *U.K.* 54°11N 5°55W **19 C10**
Slieve Gamph *Ireland* 54°6N 9°0W **18 C4**
Slieve Gullion *U.K.* 54°7N 6°26W **19 C9**
Slieve League *Ireland* 54°40N 8°42W **18 B4**
Slieve Mish *Ireland* 52°12N 9°50W **20 D3**
Slievenamon *Ireland* 52°25N 7°34W **21 D7**
Sligo *Ireland* 54°16N 8°28W **18 C5**
Sligo □ *Ireland* 54°8N 8°42W **18 C4**
Sligo B. *Ireland* 54°18N 8°40W **18 C4**
Sliven *Bulgaria* 42°42N 26°19E **69 C12**
Slough *U.K.* 51°30N 0°36W **31 C7**
Slovak Rep. ■ *Europe* 48°30N 20°0E **65 D10**
Slovenia ■ *Europe* 45°58N 14°30E **64 F8**
Slovyansk *Ukraine* 48°55N 37°36E **71 E6**
Słupsk *Poland* 54°30N 17°3E **65 A9**
Slutsk *Belarus* 53°2N 27°31E **70 D4**
Slyne Hd. *Ireland* 53°25N 10°10W **18 E1**
Smallwood Res. *Canada* 54°5N 64°30W **109 D13**
Smederevo *Serbia* 44°40N 20°57E **69 B9**
Smerwick Harbour *Ireland* 52°12N 10°23W **20 D2**
Smethwick *U.K.* 52°30N 1°57W **27 G5**
Smiths Falls *Canada* 44°55N 76°0W **113 C9**
Smoky → *Canada* 56°10N 117°21W **108 D8**
Smoky Hill → *U.S.A.* 39°4N 96°48W **111 C7**
Smolensk *Russia* 54°45N 32°5E **70 D5**
Snaefell *I. of Man* 54°16N 4°27W **19 C13**
Snainton *U.K.* 54°14N 0°35W **26 D7**
Snaith *U.K.* 53°42N 1°1W **27 E6**
Snake → *U.S.A.* 46°12N 119°2W **110 A3**
Snape *U.K.* 52°10N 1°30E **31 B12**
Snettisham *U.K.* 52°53N 0°31E **31 A10**
Snizort, L. *U.K.* 57°33N 6°28W **22 G5**
Snøhetta *Norway* 62°19N 9°16E **63 E5**
Snow Hill *U.S.A.* 38°11N 75°24W **113 F10**
Snowdon *U.K.* 53°4N 4°5W **28 A5**
Snowdonia △ *U.K.* 53°7N 3°59W **28 A6**
Snowy Mts. *Australia* 36°30S 148°20E **98 H8**
Sobat → *South Sudan* 9°22N 31°33E **95 G12**
Sobradinho, Represa de *Brazil* 9°30S 42°0W **122 A2**
Sobral *Brazil* 3°50S 40°20W **120 C5**
Soc Trang *Vietnam* 9°37N 105°50E **82 C3**
Sochi *Russia* 43°35N 39°40E **71 F6**
Société, Îs. de la *French Polynesia* 17°0S 151°0W **103 J12**
Socorro *U.S.A.* 34°4N 106°54W **110 D5**
Socotra *Yemen* 12°30N 54°0E **89 E5**
Söderhamn *Sweden* 61°18N 17°10E **63 E7**
Sofia *Bulgaria* 42°45N 23°20E **69 C10**
Sognefjorden *Norway* 61°10N 5°50E **63 E5**
Sohâg *Egypt* 26°33N 31°43E **95 C12**
Soham *U.K.* 52°21N 0°21E **31 B9**
Soissons *France* 49°25N 3°19E **66 B5**
Sokhumi *Georgia* 43°0N 41°0E **71 F7**
Sokodé *Togo* 9°0N 1°11E **94 G6**
Sokoto *Nigeria* 13°2N 5°16E **94 F7**
Sol, Costa del *Spain* 36°30N 4°30W **67 D3**
Solapur *India* 17°43N 75°56E **84 L9**
Soldotna *U.S.A.* 60°29N 151°3W **108 C4**
Soledad *Colombia* 10°55N 74°46W **120 A2**
Solent, The *U.K.* 50°45N 1°25W **30 E6**
Solihull *U.K.* 52°26N 1°47W **27 H5**
Solikamsk *Russia* 59°38N 56°50E **70 C10**
Solingen *Germany* 51°10N 7°5E **64 C4**
Sóller *Spain* 39°46N 2°43E **67 C7**
Sologne *France* 47°40N 1°45E **66 C4**
Solomon Is. ■ *Pac. Oc.* 6°0S 155°0E **99 B10**
Solomon Sea *Papua N. G.* 7°0S 150°0E **98 B9**
Solon *China* 46°32N 121°10E **79 B13**
Solothurn *Switz.* 47°13N 7°32E **64 E4**
Solway Firth *U.K.* 54°49N 3°35W **26 C1**
Somali Pen. *Africa* 7°0N 46°0E **90 F8**
Somalia ■ *Africa* 7°0N 47°0E **89 F4**
Somaliland □ *Somalia* 10°0N 46°0E **89 E4**
Sombrerete *Mexico* 23°38N 103°39W **114 C4**
Somerby *U.K.* 52°42N 0°50W **27 G7**
Somerset *U.S.A.* 37°5N 84°36W **112 G5**
Somerset □ *U.K.* 51°9N 3°0W **30 D2**
Somerset I. *Canada* 73°30N 93°0W **108 B10**

Somerset I.

Somersham   Taza

Somersham U.K. 52°24N 0°1W 31 B0
Somerton U.K. 51°2N 2°43W 30 D3
Somme → France 50°11N 1°38E 66 A4
Songhua Hu China 43°35N 126°50F 79 C14
Songhua Jiang → China 47°45N 132°30E 79 B15
Songkhla Thailand 7°13N 100°37E 82 C2
Sonid Youqi China 42°45N 112°48E 79 C11
Sonning U.K. 51°28N 0°54W 31 D7
Sonora → Mexico 29°5N 110°55W 114 B2
Sonoran Desert U.S.A. 33°40N 113°30W 110 D4
Sonoyta Mexico 31°51N 112°50W 114 A2
Sopot Poland 54°27N 18°31E 65 A10
Sorel-Tracy Canada 46°0N 73°10W 113 C11
Soria Spain 41°43N 2°32W 67 B4
Sorocaba Brazil 23°31S 47°27W 122 D1
Soroya Norway 70°40N 22°30E 63 C8
Sosnowiec Poland 50°20N 19°10E 65 C10
Soufrière St. Lucia 13°51N 61°3W 114 b
Soufrière Bay St. Lucia 13°51N 61°4W 114 b
Sound, The U.K. 50°20N 4°10W 29 G5
Souris → N. Amer. 49°40N 99°34W 108 E9
Sousse Tunisia 35°50N 10°38E 95 A8
South African ■ Africa 32°0S 23°0E 97 L4
South America 10°0S 60°0W 117 E5
South Australia □ Australia 32°0S 139°0E 98 G6
South Ayrshire □ U.K. 55°18N 4°41W 24 D6
South Bend U.S.A. 41°41N 86°15W 112 E4
South Benfleet U.K. 51°33N 0°36E 31 C10
South Brent U.K. 50°25N 3°51W 29 G6
South Carolina □ U.S.A. 34°0N 81°0W 111 D10
South Cave U.K. 53°47N 0°37W 27 E7
South China Sea Asia 10°0N 113°0E 82 C4
South Dakota □ U.S.A. 44°15N 100°0W 110 B7
South Dorset Downs U.K. 50°40N 2°26W 30 E4
South Downs △ U.K. 50°50N 0°50W 31 E7
South East C. Australia 43°40S 146°50E 98 J8
South Elkington U.K. 53°23N 0°4W 27 F0
South Esk → U.K. 56°43N 2°31W 23 J12
South Foreland U.K. 51°8N 1°24E 31 D11
South Georgia Antarctica 54°30S 37°0W 55 B1
South Harris U.K. 57°50N 7°0W 22 G4
South Hayling U.K. 50°47N 0°58W 31 E7
South I. N.Z. 44°0S 170°0E 99 J13
South Korea ■ Asia 36°0N 128°0E 79 D14
South Lanarkshire □ U.K. 55°37N 3°53W 25 C8
South Magnetic Pole Antarctica 64°8S 138°8E 55 C9
South Molton U.K. 51°1N 3°51W 29 E6
South Nahanni → Canada 61°3N 123°21W 108 C7
South Negril Pt. Jamaica 18°16N 78°22W 114 a
South Orkney Is. Antarctica 63°0S 45°0W 55 C18
South Ossetia □ Georgia 42°21N 44°2E 71 F7
South Petherton U.K. 50°57N 2°46W 30 E3
South Petherwin U.K. 50°36N 4°24W 29 F5
South Platte → U.S.A. 41°7N 100°42W 110 B6
South Pole Antarctica 90°0S 0°0E 55 E
South Pt. Barbados 13°2N 59°32W 114 c
South Ronaldsay U.K. 58°48N 2°58W 23 E12
South Sandwich Is. Antarctica 57°0S 27°0W 55 B1
South Saskatchewan → Canada 53°15N 105°5W 108 D9
South Shetland Is. Antarctica 62°0S 59°0W 55 C18
South Shields U.K. 55°0N 1°25W 26 C6
South Sudan ■ Africa 8°0N 30°0E 95 G11
South Tawton U.K. 50°44N 3°55W 29 F6
South Tyne → U.K. 54°59N 2°8W 26 C4
South Uist U.K. 57°20N 7°15W 22 H3
South Woodham Ferrers U.K. 51°39N 0°37E 31 C10
South Yorkshire □ U.K. 53°27N 1°36W 27 F5
Southam U.K. 52°18N 1°23W 30 B6
Southampton U.K. 50°54N 1°23W 30 E5
Southampton I. Canada 64°30N 84°0W 109 C11
Southborough U.K. 51°9N 0°16E 31 D9
Southend-on-Sea U.K. 51°32N 0°44E 31 C10
Southern Alps N.Z. 43°41S 170°11E 99 J13
Southern Indian L. Canada 57°10N 98°30W 108 D10
Southern Ocean 62°0S 60°0E 53 H13
Southern Uplands U.K. 55°28N 3°52W 25 D8
Southery U.K. 52°31N 0°24E 31 A9
Southminster U.K. 51°40N 0°51E 31 C10
Southport U.K. 53°39N 3°0W 27 E2
Southwark □ U.K. 51°29N 0°6W 31 D8
Southwell U.K. 53°4N 0°57W 27 F7
Southwick U.K. 50°50N 0°13W 31 E8
Southwold U.K. 52°20N 1°41E 31 B12
Sovetsk Russia 55°6N 21°50E 63 F8
Sowerby U.K. 54°14N 1°21W 26 D6
Soweto S. Africa 26°14S 27°52E 97 K5
Spain ■ Europe 39°0N 4°0W 67 B4
Spalding U.K. 52°48N 0°9W 27 G8
Spanish Canada 46°12N 82°20W 112 B6
Spanish Town Jamaica 18°0N 76°57W 114 a
Sparkford U.K. 51°2N 2°33W 30 D3
Sparks U.S.A. 39°32N 119°45W 110 C3
Sparta Greece 37°5N 22°25E 69 F10
Sparta U.S.A. 43°56N 90°49W 112 D8
Spartanburg U.S.A. 34°56N 81°57W 111 D10
Spartivento, C. Italy 37°55N 16°4E 68 F7
Speightstown Barbados 13°15N 59°39W 114 c
Speke U.K. 53°21N 2°52W 27 F3
Spencer U.S.A. 43°9N 95°9W 111 B7
Spencer G. Australia 34°0S 137°20E 98 G6
Spennymoor U.K. 54°42N 1°36W 26 C5
Sperrin Mts. U.K. 54°50N 7°0W 19 B7
Spey → U.K. 57°40N 3°6W 23 G11
Spilsby U.K. 53°10N 0°6E 27 F9
Spithead U.K. 50°45N 1°10W 30 E6
Split Croatia 43°31N 16°26E 68 C7
Spofforth U.K. 53°57N 1°27W 27 E6
Spokane U.S.A. 47°40N 117°24W 110 A3
Spooner U.S.A. 45°50N 91°53W 112 C2
Spratly Is. S. China Sea 8°20N 112°0E 82 C4
Spree → Germany 52°32N 13°12E 64 B7
Spring Hall Barbados 13°18N 59°36W 114 c
Springbok S. Africa 29°42S 17°54E 97 K3
Springfield Ill., U.S.A. 39°48N 89°39W 112 F3
Springfield Mass., U.S.A. 42°6N 72°35W 113 D11
Springfield Mo., U.S.A. 37°13N 93°17W 111 C8
Springfield Ohio, U.S.A. 39°55N 83°49W 112 F6
Springfield Oreg., U.S.A. 44°3N 123°1W 110 B2

Springhill Canada 45°40N 64°4W 113 C15
Springs S. Africa 26°13S 28°25E 97 K5
Sproatley U.K. 53°47N 0°11W 27 E8
Spurn Hd. U.K. 53°35N 0°8E 27 E9
Srebrenica Bos.-H. 44°6N 19°18E 69 B8
Sredinny Ra. Russia 57°0N 160°0E 77 D16
Sri Lanka ■ Asia 7°30N 80°50E 84 R12
Srikakulam India 18°14N 83°58E 85 K13
Srinagar India 34°5N 74°50E 84 B9
Stacks Mts. Ireland 52°20N 9°34W 20 D3
Staffa U.K. 56°27N 6°21W 24 D3
Stafford U.K. 52°49N 2°7W 27 G4
Staffordshire □ U.K. 52°53N 2°10W 27 G4
Staindrop U.K. 54°36N 1°47W 26 C5
Staines-upon-Thames U.K. 51°26N 0°29W 31 D8
Stainforth U.K. 53°37N 1°0W 27 E7
Stainmore Forest U.K. 54°29N 2°5W 26 D4
Stainton U.K. 53°18N 0°24W 27 F8
Staithes U.K. 54°34N 0°46W 26 C7
Stakhanov Ukraine 48°35N 38°40E 71 E6
Stalbridge U.K. 50°57N 2°23W 30 E4
Stalham U.K. 52°47N 1°31E 31 A12
Stallingborough U.K. 53°35N 0°12W 27 E8
Stalybridge U.K. 53°28N 2°3W 27 F4
Stamford U.K. 52°39N 0°29W 27 G8
Stamford U.S.A. 41°3N 73°32W 113 E11
Stamford Bridge U.K. 54°0N 0°54W 27 E7
Stamfordham U.K. 55°3N 1°53W 26 B5
Standish U.K. 53°35N 2°41W 27 E3
Standish U.S.A. 43°59N 83°57W 112 DG
Stanford on Teme U.K. 52°18N 2°25W 30 D4
Stanhope U.K. 54°45N 2°1W 26 C4
Stanley Falk. Is. 51°40S 59°51W 121 H4
Stanley U.K. 54°53N 1°41W 26 C5
Stannington U.K. 55°7N 1°40W 26 B5
Stanovoy Ra. Russia 55°0N 130°0E 77 D13
Stansted Mountfitchet U.K. 51°52N 0°11E 31 C9
Stanwix U.K. 54°55N 2°56W 26 C3
Stapleford U.K. 52°57N 1°16W 27 G6
Staplehurst U.K. 51°9N 0°34E 31 D10
Stara Zagora Bulgaria 42°26N 25°39E 69 C11
Staraya Russa Russia 57°58N 31°23E 70 C5
Starbuck I. Kiribati 5°37S 155°55W 103 H12
Start B. U.K. 50°13N 3°39W 29 G6
Start Pt. U.K. 50°13N 3°39W 29 G6
Staryy Oskol Russia 51°19N 37°55E 71 D6
State College U.S.A. 40°48N 77°52W 112 E9
Staten, I. = Estados, I. de Los Argentina 54°40S 64°30W 121 H3
Staunton U.K. 51°57N 2°17W 30 C4
Staunton U.S.A. 38°9N 79°4W 112 F8
Stavanger Norway 58°57N 5°40E 63 F5
Staveley Cumb., U.K. 54°23N 2°48W 26 D3
Staveley Derby, U.K. 53°16N 1°21W 27 F6
Stavropol Russia 45°5N 42°0E 71 E7
Steiermark □ Austria 47°26N 15°0E 64 E8
Steinkjer Norway 64°1N 11°31E 63 E6
Stellarton Canada 45°32N 62°30W 113 C16
Stellenbosch S. Africa 33°58S 18°50E 97 L3
Stenhousemuir U.K. 56°2N 3°48W 25 B8
Steornabhaigh = Stornoway U.K. 58°13N 6°23W 22 F5
Stephenville Canada 48°31N 58°35W 109 E14
Steppe Asia 50°0N 50°0E 72 C7
Sterling Colo., U.S.A. 40°37N 103°13W 110 B6
Sterling Ill., U.S.A. 41°48N 89°42W 112 E3
Sterlitamak Russia 53°40N 56°0E 70 D10
Stettler Canada 52°19N 112°40W 108 D6
Steubenville U.S.A. 40°22N 80°37W 112 E7
Stevenage U.K. 51°55N 0°13W 31 C8
Stevens Point U.S.A. 44°31N 89°34W 112 C3
Stevenston U.K. 55°39N 4°45W 24 C6
Stewart Canada 55°56N 129°57W 108 D7
Stewart → Canada 63°19N 139°26W 108 C6
Stewart I. N.Z. 46°58S 167°54E 99 K12
Stewarton U.K. 55°40N 4°32W 24 C6
Steyning U.K. 50°53N 0°18W 31 E8
Steyr Austria 48°3N 14°25E 64 D8
Stikine → Canada 56°40N 132°30W 108 D6
Stillington U.K. 54°6N 1°6W 26 D6
Stillwater U.S.A. 36°7N 97°4W 111 A8
Stiperstones U.K. 52°36N 2°55W 27 G3
Stirling U.K. 56°8N 3°57W 25 B8
Stirling □ U.K. 56°12N 4°18W 24 B7
Stobo U.K. 55°38N 3°17W 25 C9
Stockbridge U.K. 51°7N 1°29W 30 D6
Stockholm Sweden 59°19N 18°4E 63 F7
Stockport U.K. 53°25N 2°9W 27 F4
Stocksbridge U.K. 53°29N 1°35W 27 F5
Stockton U.S.A. 37°58N 121°17W 110 C2
Stockton-on-Tees U.K. 54°35N 1°19W 26 D6
Stoer, Pt. of U.K. 58°16N 5°23W 22 F7
Stoke U.K. 51°26N 0°41E 31 D10
Stoke Ferry U.K. 52°34N 0°31E 31 A10
Stoke Fleming U.K. 50°19N 3°37W 29 G6
Stoke Mandeville U.K. 51°47N 0°47W 31 C7
Stoke-on-Trent U.K. 53°1N 2°11W 27 F4
Stoke Prior U.K. 52°19N 2°4W 30 B4
Stokesley U.K. 54°28N 1°12W 26 D6
Stone Bucks., U.K. 51°48N 0°52W 31 C7
Stone Staffs., U.K. 52°55N 2°9W 27 G4
Stonehaven U.K. 56°59N 2°12W 23 J13
Stonehouse U.K. 51°45N 2°16W 30 C4
Stonham Aspal U.K. 52°12N 1°9E 31 B11
Stony Stratford U.K. 52°3N 0°50W 31 B7
Stony Tunguska → Russia 61°50N 90°13E 77 C10
Stora Lulevatten Sweden 67°10N 19°30E 63 D7
Store Bælt Denmark 55°20N 11°0E 63 F6
Stornberg → Africa 31°16S 26°17E 97 L5
Stornoway U.K. 58°13N 6°23W 22 F5
Storsjön Sweden 63°9N 14°30E 63 E6
Stort → U.K. 51°46N 0°2E 31 C9
Storuman Sweden 65°5N 17°10E 63 D7
Stotfold U.K. 52°1N 0°13W 31 B8
Stour → Dorset, U.K. 50°43N 1°47W 30 E5
Stour → Kent, U.K. 51°18N 1°22E 31 D11
Stour → Suffolk, U.K. 51°57N 1°4E 31 C11
Stour → Worcs., U.K. 52°21N 2°17W 30 B4

Stourbridge U.K. 52°28N 2°8W 27 H4
Stourport-on-Severn U.K. 52°21N 2°17W 30 B4
Stow U.K. 55°42N 2°50W 25 C10
Stow Bardolph U.K. 52°38N 0°24E 31 A9
Stow-on-the-Wold U.K. 51°56N 1°42W 30 C5
Stowmarket U.K. 52°12N 1°0E 31 B10
Strabane U.K. 54°50N 7°27W 18 B7
Stradbroke U.K. 52°19N 1°16E 31 B11
Stralsund Germany 54°18N 13°4E 64 A7
Strangford L. U.K. 54°30N 5°37W 19 C10
Stranraer U.K. 54°54N 5°1W 24 E5
Strasbourg France 48°35N 7°42E 66 B7
Stratford Canada 43°23N 81°0W 112 D7
Stratford St. Mary U.K. 51°58N 1°0E 31 C10
Stratford-upon-Avon U.K. 52°12N 1°42W 30 B5
Strath Avon → U.K. 57°18N 3°23W 23 H11
Strath Dearn U.K. 57°20N 4°0W 23 H9
Strath Glass U.K. 57°22N 4°42W 23 H8
Strath Halladale U.K. 58°30N 3°51W 23 F10
Strath Naver → U.K. 58°24N 4°12W 23 F9
Strath of Kildonan U.K. 58°14N 3°56W 23 F10
Strath Spey → U.K. 57°9N 3°49W 23 H10
Strath Tay U.K. 56°40N 3°48W 25 A8
Strathaven U.K. 55°40N 4°5W 24 C7
Strathbogie U.K. 57°25N 2°45W 23 H12
Strathmore Angus, U.K. 56°37N 3°7W 23 J11
Strathmore Highl., U.K. 58°22N 4°40W 23 F8
Strathpeffer U.K. 57°35N 4°32W 23 H8
Strathroy Canada 42°58N 81°38W 112 D7
Strathy Pt. U.K. 58°36N 4°1W 23 F9
Stratton U.K. 50°49N 4°32W 29 F4
Stratton St. Margaret U.K. 51°35N 1°44W 30 C5
Streatley U.K. 51°31N 1°8W 30 C6
Street U.K. 51°8N 2°44W 30 D3
Strensall U.K. 54°3N 1°4W 26 DG
Stretford U.K. 53°28N 2°17W 27 F4
Stroma U.K. 58°41N 3°7W 23 E11
Strómboli Italy 38°47N 15°13E 68 E6
Stromeferry U.K. 57°21N 5°33W 22 H6
Stromness U.K. 58°58N 3°17W 23 E11
Stronsay U.K. 59°7N 2°35W 23 D12
Stroud U.K. 51°45N 2°13W 30 C4
Stuart I. Canada 54°30N 124°30W 108 D7
Studland U.K. 50°39N 1°58W 30 E5
Studley U.K. 52°16N 1°53W 30 B5
Sturgeon Bay U.S.A. 44°50N 87°23W 112 C4
Sturgeon Falls Canada 46°25N 79°57W 112 B8
Sturminster Marshall U.K. 50°47N 2°5W 30 E4
Sturminster Newton U.K. 50°55N 2°18W 30 E4
Sturt Stony Desert Australia 28°30S 141°0E 98 F6
Sturton U.K. 53°19N 0°39W 27 F7
Stuttgart Germany 48°48N 9°11E 64 D5
Stuttgart U.S.A. 34°30N 91°33W 111 D8
Suakin Sudan 19°8N 37°20E 95 E13
Subotica Serbia 46°6N 19°39E 69 A8
Suceava Romania 47°38N 26°16E 65 E14
Suck → Ireland 53°17N 8°3W 20 B6
Sucre Bolivia 19°0S 65°15W 120 D3
Sudan ■ Africa 15°0N 30°0E 95 E11
Sudbury Canada 46°30N 81°0W 112 B7
Sudbury Derby, U.K. 52°54N 1°45W 27 G5
Sudbury Suffolk, U.K. 52°2N 0°45E 31 B10
Sudd South Sudan 8°20N 30°0E 95 G12
Sudeten Europe 50°20N 16°45E 65 C9
Suez Egypt 29°58N 32°31E 95 C12
Suez, G. of Egypt 28°40N 33°0E 95 C12
Suez Canal Egypt 31°0N 32°20E 95 B12
Suffolk □ U.K. 52°16N 1°0E 31 B11
Sugluk Canada 62°14N 75°38W 109 C12
Suhar Oman 24°20N 56°40E 87 E9
Suihua China 46°32N 126°55E 79 B14
Suining China 30°26N 105°35E 78 E10
Suir → Ireland 52°16N 7°9W 21 D8
Sukabumi Indonesia 6°56S 106°50E 82 F3
Sukhona → Russia 61°15N 46°39E 70 C6
Sukkur Pakistan 27°42N 68°54E 84 F6
Sulaiman Range Pakistan 30°30N 69°50E 84 D6
Sulawesi Indonesia 2°0S 120°0E 83 E6
Sullana Peru 4°52S 80°39W 120 C1
Sullom Voe U.K. 60°27N 1°20W 22 B15
Sulu Arch. Phil. 6°0N 121°0E 83 C6
Sulu Sea E. Indies 8°0N 120°0E 83 C6
Sumare Brazil 22°49S 47°16W 122 D1
Sumatra Indonesia 0°40N 100°20E 82 D2
Sumba Indonesia 9°45S 119°35E 83 F5
Sumbawa Indonesia 8°26S 117°30E 82 F5
Sumburgh Hd. U.K. 59°52N 1°17W 22 C15
Summer L. U.S.A. 42°50N 120°45W 110 B2
Summerside Canada 46°24N 63°47W 109 E13
Sumqayit Azerbaijan 40°34N 49°38E 71 F8
Sumter U.S.A. 33°55N 80°21W 111 D10
Sumy Ukraine 50°57N 34°50E 71 D5
Sun Valley U.S.A. 43°42N 114°21W 110 B4
Sunart, L. U.K. 56°43N 5°42W 22 J6
Sunbury U.S.A. 40°52N 76°48W 112 E9
Sunda, Selat Indonesia 6°20S 105°30E 82 F3
Sunda Is. Indonesia 5°0S 105°0E 102 H2
Sundarbans Asia 22°0N 89°0E 85 J16
Sunderland U.K. 54°55N 1°23W 26 C6
Sundsvall Sweden 62°23N 17°17E 63 E7
Sungaipenuh Indonesia 2°1S 101°20E 82 E2
Sunk Island U.K. 53°39N 0°6W 27 E8
Sunninghill U.K. 51°24N 0°39W 31 D7
Sunshine Coast Australia 26°30S 153°0E 98 F9
Superior U.S.A. 46°44N 92°6W 112 B1
Superior, L. N. Amer. 47°0N 87°0W 112 B4
Sür Lebanon 33°19N 35°16E 86 C3
Sura → Russia 56°6N 46°0E 70 C8
Surabaya Indonesia 7°17S 112°45E 82 F4
Surakarta Indonesia 7°35S 110°48E 82 F4
Surat India 21°12N 72°55E 84 J8
Surgut Russia 61°14N 73°20E 76 C8
Surigao Phil. 9°47N 125°29E 83 C7
Suriname ■ S. Amer. 4°0N 56°0W 120 B4
Surrey □ U.K. 51°15N 0°31W 31 D7
Surt Libya 31°11N 16°39E 95 B9
Surt, Khalīj Libya 31°40N 18°30E 95 B9
Surtsey Iceland 63°20N 20°30W 63 B1

Susquehanna → U.S.A. 39°33N 76°5W 113 F9
Sussex Canada 45°45N 65°37W 113 C15
Sutherland U.K. 58°12N 4°50W 23 F8
Sutlej → Pakistan 29°23N 71°3E 84 C7
Sutterton U.K. 52°55N 0°6W 27 G8
Sutton □ U.K. 51°21N 0°11W 31 D8
Sutton Bridge U.K. 52°47N 0°10E 27 G9
Sutton Coldfield U.K. 52°35N 1°49W 27 G5
Sutton Courtenay U.K. 51°39N 1°16W 30 C6
Sutton in Ashfield U.K. 53°8N 1°16W 27 F6
Sutton on-Sea U.K. 53°19N 0°16E 27 F9
Sutton Scotney U.K. 51°9N 1°20W 30 D6
Suva Fiji 18°6S 178°30E 99 D14
Suwałki Poland 54°8N 22°59E 65 A12
Suwarrow Is. Cook Is. 13°15S 163°5W 103 J11
Suzhou China 31°19N 120°38E 79 E13
Svalbard Arctic 78°0N 17°0E 54 B8
Svealand Sweden 60°20N 15°0E 63 E7
Sverdrup Chan. Canada 79°56N 96°25W 109 B10
Sverdrup Is. Canada 79°0N 97°0W 109 B10
Svir → Russia 60°30N 32°48E 70 B5
Swadlincote U.K. 52°47N 1°33W 27 G5
Swaffham U.K. 52°39N 0°42E 31 A10
Swakopmund Namibia 22°37S 14°30E 97 J2
Swan Hill Australia 35°20S 143°33E 98 H7
Swan River Canada 52°10N 101°16W 108 D9
Swanage U.K. 50°36N 1°58W 30 C5
Swansea U.K. 51°37N 3°57W 29 D6
Swansea B. U.K. 51°32N 3°57W 29 D6
Swartberge S. Africa 33°20S 22°0E 90 K6
Swaziland ■ Africa 26°30S 31°30E 97 K6
Sweden ■ Europe 57°0N 15°0E 63 F7
Sweetwater U.S.A. 32°28N 100°25W 110 D6
Swellendam S. Africa 34°1S 20°26E 97 L4
Swift Current Canada 50°20N 107°45W 108 D9
Swilly, L. Ireland 55°12N 7°33W 18 A6
Swindon U.K. 51°34N 1°46W 30 C6
Swineshead U.K. 52°57N 0°10W 27 G8
Swinford Ireland 53°57N 8°58W 18 D4
Swinton Borders, U.K. 55°43N 2°15W 25 C11
Swinton Gt. Man., U.K. 53°31N 2°20W 27 F4
Swinton S. Yorks., U.K. 53°29N 1°20W 27 F6
Switzerland ■ Europe 46°30N 8°0E 64 E5
Swords Ireland 53°28N 6°13W 21 B10
Sydney Australia 33°52S 151°12E 98 G9
Sydney Canada 46°7N 60°7W 113 B17
Syktyvkar Russia 61°45N 50°40E 70 B9
Sylhet Bangla. 24°54N 91°52E 85 G17
Symington U.K. 55°36N 3°36W 25 C8
Symonds Yat U.K. 51°51N 2°38W 30 C3
Syracuse U.S.A. 43°3N 76°9W 113 D9
Syrdarya → Kazakhstan 46°3N 61°0E 76 E7
Syria ■ Asia 35°0N 38°0E 86 C4
Syrian Desert Asia 32°0N 40°0E 86 C4
Syston U.K. 52°42N 1°3W 27 G6
Syzran Russia 53°12N 48°30E 70 D8
Szczecin Poland 53°27N 14°27E 64 B8
Szechwan = Sichuan □ China 30°30N 103°0E 78 E9
Szeged Hungary 46°16N 20°10E 65 E11
Székesfehérvár Hungary 47°15N 18°25E 65 E10
Szekszárd Hungary 46°22N 18°42E 65 E10
Szolnok Hungary 47°10N 20°15E 65 E11
Szombathely Hungary 47°14N 16°38E 65 E9

T
Tabas Iran 33°35N 56°55E 87 C9
Tablas I. Phil. 12°25N 122°2E 83 B6
Table B. S. Africa 33°35S 18°25E 97 L3
Table Mt. S. Africa 33°58S 18°26E 97 L3
Tabora Tanzania 5°2S 32°50E 96 F6
Tabrīz Iran 38°7N 46°20E 86 B6
Tabuaeran Kiribati 3°51N 159°22W 103 G12
Tabūk Si. Arabia 28°23N 36°36E 86 D4
Tacheng China 46°40N 82°58E 78 B5
Tacloban Phil. 11°15N 124°58E 83 B6
Tacna Peru 18°0S 70°20W 120 D2
Tacoma U.S.A. 47°14N 122°26W 110 A2
Tacuarembó Uruguay 31°45S 56°0W 121 F4
Tadcaster U.K. 53°53N 1°16W 27 E6
Tademaït, Plateau du Algeria 28°30N 2°30E 94 C6
Tadley U.K. 51°21N 1°7W 30 D6
Taganrog Russia 47°12N 38°50E 71 E6
Taguatinga Brazil 12°27S 46°22W 122 B1
Tagus → Europe 38°40N 9°24W 67 C1
Tahiti French Polynesia 17°37S 149°27W 103 J13
Tahoe, L. U.S.A. 39°6N 120°2W 110 C2
Tahoua Niger 14°57N 5°16E 94 F7
Tahta Egypt 26°44N 31°32E 95 C12
Tai Hu China 31°5N 120°10E 79 E13
Tai Po China 22°27N 114°10E 79 a
Tai'an China 36°12N 117°8E 79 D12
Taibei = T'aipei Taiwan 25°4N 121°29E 79 D14
Taichung Taiwan 24°9N 120°37E 79 G13
Tain U.K. 57°49N 4°4W 23 G9
Tainan Taiwan 23°0N 120°10E 79 G13
T'aipei Taiwan 25°4N 121°29E 79 D14
Taiping Malaysia 4°51N 100°44E 82 D2
Taitao, Pen. de Chile 46°30S 75°0W 121 G2
T'aitung Taiwan 22°43N 121°4E 79 G13
Taiwan ■ Asia 23°30N 121°0E 79 G13
Taiwan Str. Asia 24°40N 120°0E 79 G13
Taiyuan China 37°52N 112°33E 79 D11
Taizhou China 32°28N 119°55E 79 E12
Ta'izz Yemen 13°35N 44°2E 89 E3
Tajikistan ■ Asia 38°30N 70°0E 87 B12
Tak Thailand 16°52N 99°8E 82 A1
Takamatsu Japan 34°20N 134°5E 81 F4
Takaoka Japan 36°47N 137°0E 81 E5
Takasaki Japan 36°20N 139°0E 81 E6
Takeshima = Liancourt Rocks Asia 37°15N 131°52E 81 E2
Taklamakan Desert China 38°0N 83°0E 78 D5
Talara Peru 4°38S 81°18W 120 C1
Talaud, Kepulauan Indonesia 4°30N 126°50E 83 D7
Talavera de la Reina Spain 39°55N 4°46W 67 C3
Talca Chile 35°28S 71°40W 121 F2
Talcahuano Chile 36°40S 73°10W 121 F1
Taldyqorghan Kazakhstan 45°10N 78°45E 76 E8
Talgarth U.K. 52°0N 3°14W 28 D7

Taliabu Indonesia 1°50S 125°0E 83 E6
Tallaght Ireland 53°17N 6°22W 21 B10
Tallahassee U.S.A. 30°27N 84°17W 111 D10
Tallinn Estonia 59°22N 24°48E 63 F8
Taloyoak Canada 69°32N 93°32W 108 C10
Taltal Chile 25°23S 70°33W 121 E2
Tamale Ghana 9°22N 0°50W 94 G5
Tamana Kiribati 2°30S 175°59E 99 A13
Tamanrasset Algeria 22°50N 5°30E 94 D7
Tamar → U.K. 50°27N 4°15W 29 G5
Tambov Russia 52°45N 41°28E 70 D7
Tame → U.K. 52°44N 1°43W 27 G5
Tamil Nadu □ India 11°0N 77°0E 84 P10
Tampa U.S.A. 27°56N 82°27W 111 E10
Tampa B. U.S.A. 27°50N 82°30W 111 E10
Tampere Finland 61°30N 23°50E 63 E8
Tampico Mexico 22°13N 97°51W 114 C5
Tamworth Australia 31°7S 150°58E 98 G9
Tamworth U.K. 52°39N 1°41W 27 G5
Tana → Kenya 2°32S 40°31E 96 E8
Tana → Norway 70°30N 28°14E 63 C9
Tana, L. Ethiopia 13°5N 37°30E 89 E2
Tanami Desert Australia 18°50S 132°0E 98 D5
Tanana → U.S.A. 65°10N 151°58W 108 C4
Tandil Argentina 37°15S 59°6W 121 F4
Tandragee U.K. 54°21N 6°24W 19 C9
Tanezrouft Algeria 23°9N 0°11E 94 D6
Tanga Tanzania 5°5S 39°2E 96 F7
Tanganyika, L. Africa 6°40S 30°0E 96 F6
Tanggula Shan China 32°40N 92°10E 78 E7
Tanggula Shankou China 32°42N 92°27E 78 E7
Tangier Morocco 35°50N 5°49W 94 A4
Tangjia China 22°22N 113°35E 79 a
Tangra Yumco China 31°0N 86°38E 78 E6
Tangshan China 39°38N 118°10E 79 D12
Tanimbar, Kepulauan Indonesia 7°30S 131°30E 83 E6
Tanjungbalai Indonesia 2°55N 99°44E 82 D1
Tanjungpandan Indonesia 2°43S 107°38E 82 E3
Tanjungredeb Indonesia 2°9N 117°29E 82 D5
Tanna Vanuatu 19°30S 169°20E 99 D12
Tannu Ola Asia 51°0N 94°0E 77 D10
Tanta Egypt 30°45N 30°57E 95 B12
Tanworth U.K. 52°20N 1°50W 30 B5
Tanzania ■ Africa 6°0S 34°0E 96 F6
Tanzhou China 22°16N 113°28E 79 a
Taolanaro Madag. 25°2S 47°0E 97 K9
Taonan China 45°22N 122°40E 79 B13
Taos U.S.A. 36°24N 105°36W 110 C5
Tapachula Mexico 14°54N 92°17W 114 E6
Tapajós → Brazil 2°24S 54°41W 120 C4
Tapti → India 21°8N 72°41E 84 J8
Taquaritinga Brazil 21°24S 48°30W 122 D1
Tarakan Indonesia 3°20N 117°35E 82 D5
Taransay U.K. 57°54N 7°0W 22 G3
Táranto Italy 40°28N 17°14E 68 D7
Táranto, G. di Italy 40°8N 17°20E 68 D7
Tarasaigh = Taransay U.K. 57°54N 7°0W 22 G3
Tarawa Kiribati 1°30N 173°0E 102 G9
Taraz Kazakhstan 42°54N 71°22E 87 A12
Tarbagatay, Khrebet Kazakhstan 48°0N 83°0E 76 E9
Tarbat Ness U.K. 57°52N 3°47W 23 G10
Tarbela Dam Pakistan 34°8N 72°52E 84 B8
Tarbert Argyll & Bute, U.K. 55°52N 5°25W 24 C5
Tarbert W. Isles, U.K. 57°54N 6°49W 22 G4
Tarbes France 43°15N 0°3E 66 E4
Tarcoola Australia 30°44S 134°36E 98 G5
Taree Australia 31°50S 152°30E 98 G9
Tarfaya Morocco 27°55N 12°55W 94 C3
Târgoviște Romania 44°55N 25°27E 65 F13
Târgu Jiu Romania 45°5N 23°19E 65 F12
Târgu Mureș Romania 46°31N 24°38E 65 E13
Tarija Bolivia 21°30S 64°40W 120 E3
Tarim Basin China 40°0N 84°0E 78 C5
Tarim He → China 39°30N 88°30E 78 D6
Tarleton U.K. 53°41N 2°50W 27 E3
Tarn → France 44°5N 1°6E 66 E4
Tarnów Poland 50°3N 21°0E 65 C11
Taroudannt Morocco 30°30N 8°52W 94 B4
Tarporley U.K. 53°10N 2°40W 27 F3
Tarragona Spain 41°5N 1°17E 67 B6
Tarsus Turkey 36°58N 34°55E 71 G5
Tartu Estonia 58°20N 26°44E 63 F9
Tartūs Syria 34°55N 35°55E 86 C3
Tashkent Uzbekistan 41°20N 69°10E 87 A12
Tasiilaq Greenland 65°40N 37°20W 54 C6
Tasikmalaya Indonesia 7°18S 108°12E 82 F3
Tasman Sea Pac. Oc. 36°0S 160°0E 99 H10
Tasmania □ Australia 42°0S 146°30E 98 J8
Tassili n'Ajjer Algeria 25°47N 8°1E 94 C7
Tatar Str. Russia 50°0N 141°0E 77 E14
Tatarstan □ Russia 55°30N 51°30E 70 C9
Tatinnai L. Canada 57°16N 91°0W 108 D10
Tatra Slovak Rep. 49°20N 20°0E 65 D11
Tattenhall U.K. 53°7N 2°46W 27 F3
Tatuí Brazil 23°25S 47°53W 122 D1
Tatvan Turkey 38°31N 42°15E 71 G7
Taubaté Brazil 23°0S 45°36W 122 D1
Tauern Austria 47°15N 12°40E 64 E7
Taungdwingyi Burma 20°50N 97°0E 85 J20
Taunton U.K. 51°1N 3°5W 30 D2
Taunton U.S.A. 41°54N 71°6W 113 E12
Taunus Germany 50°13N 8°34E 64 C5
Taurus Mts. Turkey 37°0N 32°30E 71 G5
Tavan Bogd Uul Mongolia 49°10N 87°49E 78 B6
Tavistock U.K. 50°33N 4°9W 29 F5
Taw → U.K. 51°4N 4°4W 29 E5
Tawas City U.S.A. 44°16N 83°31W 112 C6
Tawau Malaysia 4°20N 117°55E 82 D5
Taxkorgan Tajik Zizhixian China 37°49N 75°14E 78 D4
Tay → U.K. 56°37N 3°38W 25 A8
Tay, Firth of U.K. 56°25N 3°8W 25 B9
Tay, L. U.K. 56°32N 4°8W 24 B7
Taylor, Mt. U.S.A. 35°14N 107°37W 110 C5
Taylorville U.S.A. 39°33N 89°18W 112 F3
Tayport U.K. 56°27N 2°52W 25 B10
Taz → Russia 67°32N 78°40E 76 C8
Taza Morocco 34°16N 4°6W 94 B5

Tbilisi — Union City

Tbilisi _Georgia_ 41°43N 44°50E 71 F7
Tebay _U.K._ 54°26N 2°35W 26 D3
Tébessa _Algeria_ 35°22N 8°8E 94 A7
Tees → _U.K._ 54°37N 1°10W 26 C4
Teesdale _U.K._ 54°37N 2°10W 26 C4
Teesside _U.K._ 54°36N 1°15W 26 C6
Tegal _Indonesia_ 6°52S 109°8E 82 F3
Tegid, L. = Bala, L. _U.K._ 52°53N 3°37W 28 B6
Tegucigalpa _Honduras_ 14°5N 87°14W 114 E7
Tehrān _Iran_ 35°41N 51°25E 87 C7
Tehuantepec _Mexico_ 16°21N 95°13W 114 D5
Tehuantepec, G. de _Mexico_ 15°50N 95°12W 114 D5
Tehuantepec, Istmo de _Mexico_ 17°15N 94°30W 114 D6
Teifi → _U.K._ 52°5N 4°41W 28 C4
Teign → _U.K._ 50°32N 3°32W 29 F6
Teignmouth _U.K._ 50°33N 3°31W 29 F6
Tejen _Turkmenistan_ 37°23N 60°31E 87 B10
Tekirdağ _Turkey_ 40°58N 27°30E 71 F4
Tel Aviv-Jaffa _Israel_ 32°4N 34°48E 86 C3
Tela _Honduras_ 15°40N 87°28W 114 D7
Telangana □ _India_ 17°30N 78°30E 84 K11
Telegraph Creek _Canada_ 58°0N 131°10W 108 D6
Teles Pires → _Brazil_ 7°21S 58°3W 120 C4
Telford _U.K._ 52°40N 2°27W 27 G4
Tell City _U.S.A._ 37°57N 86°46W 112 G4
Telpos Iz _Russia_ 63°16N 59°13E 70 B10
Teluk Intan _Malaysia_ 4°3N 101°0E 82 D2
Tema _Ghana_ 5°41N 0°0 94 G5
Teme → _U.K._ 52°11N 2°13W 30 B4
Temirtau _Kazakhstan_ 50°5N 72°56E 76 D8
Témiscaming _Canada_ 46°44N 79°5W 112 B8
Temple _U.S.A._ 31°6N 97°21W 111 D7
Temple Combe _U.K._ 51°0N 2°24W 30 D4
Temple Ewell _U.K._ 51°8N 1°17E 31 D11
Temple Sowerby _U.K._ 54°38N 2°36W 26 C3
Templemore _Ireland_ 52°47N 7°51W 20 C7
Temuco _Chile_ 38°45S 72°40W 121 F2
Tenali _India_ 16°15N 80°35E 85 L12
Tenbury Wells _U.K._ 52°19N 2°35W 30 B3
Tenby _U.K._ 51°40N 4°42W 28 D4
Tenerife _Canary Is._ 28°15N 16°35W 94 C2
Tengchong _China_ 25°0N 98°28E 78 G8
Tengger Desert _China_ 38°0N 104°10E 78 D9
Tennant Creek _Australia_ 19°30S 134°15E 98 D5
Tennessee □ _U.S.A._ 36°0N 86°30W 111 C9
Tennessee → _U.S.A._ 37°4N 88°34W 111 C9
Tenterden _U.K._ 51°4N 0°42E 31 D10
Teófilo Otoni _Brazil_ 17°50S 41°30W 122 C2
Tepic _Mexico_ 21°30N 104°54W 114 C4
Teraina _Kiribati_ 4°43N 160°25W 103 G12
Téramo _Italy_ 42°39N 13°42E 68 C5
Teresina _Brazil_ 5°9S 42°45W 120 C5
Termiz _Uzbekistan_ 37°15N 67°15E 87 B11
Ternate _Indonesia_ 0°45N 127°25E 83 D7
Terni _Italy_ 42°34N 12°37E 68 C5
Ternopil _Ukraine_ 49°30N 25°40E 65 D13
Terrace _Canada_ 54°30N 128°35W 108 D7
Terrassa _Spain_ 41°34N 2°1E 67 B7
Terre Haute _U.S.A._ 39°28N 87°25W 112 F4
Terschelling _Neths._ 53°25N 5°20E 64 B3
Teruel _Spain_ 40°22N 1°8W 67 B5
Tesiyn Gol → _Mongolia_ 50°40N 93°20E 78 A7
Teslin _Canada_ 60°10N 132°43W 108 C6
Test → _U.K._ 50°56N 1°29W 30 E6
Tetbury _U.K._ 51°38N 2°10W 30 C4
Tete _Mozam._ 16°13S 33°33E 97 H6
Tetney _U.K._ 53°29N 0°1W 27 F8
Tétouan _Morocco_ 35°35N 5°21W 94 A4
Tetovo _Macedonia_ 42°1N 20°59E 69 C9
Teuco → _Argentina_ 25°35S 60°11W 121 E3
Teutoburger Wald _Germany_ 52°5N 8°22E 64 B5
Teviot → _U.K._ 55°29N 2°38W 25 D10
Teviotdale _U.K._ 55°25N 2°50W 25 D10
Teviothead _U.K._ 55°20N 2°56W 25 D10
Tewkesbury _U.K._ 51°59N 2°9W 30 C4
Texarkana _U.S.A._ 33°26N 94°3W 111 D8
Texas □ _U.S.A._ 31°40N 98°30W 110 D7
Texel _Neths._ 53°5N 4°50E 64 B3
Teynham _U.K._ 51°20N 0°50E 31 D10
Tezpur _India_ 26°40N 92°45E 85 F18
Thabana Ntlenyana _Lesotho_ 29°30S 29°16E 97 K5
Thabazimbi _S. Africa_ 24°40S 27°21E 97 J5
Thailand ■ _Asia_ 16°0N 102°0E 82 A2
Thailand, G. of _Asia_ 11°30N 101°0E 82 B2
Thal Desert _Pakistan_ 31°10N 71°30E 84 D7
Thalassery _India_ 11°45N 75°30E 84 P9
Thame → _U.K._ 51°45N 0°58W 31 C7
Thame → _U.K._ 51°39N 1°9W 30 C6
Thames → _Canada_ 42°20N 82°25W 112 D6
Thames → _U.K._ 51°29N 0°34E 31 D10
Thane _India_ 19°12N 72°59E 84 K8
Thanet, I. of _U.K._ 51°21N 1°20E 31 D11
Thanjavur _India_ 10°48N 79°12E 84 P11
Thar Desert _India_ 28°0N 72°0E 84 F8
Thargomindah _Australia_ 27°58S 143°46E 98 F7
Thasos _Greece_ 40°40N 24°40E 69 D11
Thatcham _U.K._ 51°24N 1°15W 30 D6
Thatta _Pakistan_ 24°42N 67°55E 84 G5
Thaxted _U.K._ 51°57N 0°22E 31 C9
The Pas _Canada_ 53°45N 101°15W 108 D9
Theale _U.K._ 51°26N 1°5W 30 D6
Thebes _Egypt_ 25°40N 32°35E 95 C12
Thelon → _Canada_ 64°16N 96°4W 108 C9
Thermopolis _U.S.A._ 43°39N 108°13W 110 B5
Thermopylae _Greece_ 38°48N 22°35E 69 E10
Thessalon _Canada_ 46°20N 83°30W 112 B6
Thessaloniki _Greece_ 40°38N 22°58E 69 D10
Thetford _U.K._ 52°25N 0°45E 31 B9
Thetford Mines _Canada_ 46°8N 71°18W 109 E12
Thiers _France_ 45°52N 3°33E 66 D5
Thiès _Senegal_ 14°50N 16°51W 94 F2
Thika _Kenya_ 1°1S 37°5E 96 E7
Thimphu _Bhutan_ 27°31N 89°45E 85 F16
Thionville _France_ 49°20N 6°10E 66 B7
Thira = Santorini _Greece_ 36°23N 25°27E 69 F11
Thirlmere _U.K._ 54°32N 3°4W 26 C2
Thirsk _U.K._ 54°14N 1°19W 26 D6
Thiruvananthapuram _India_ 8°41N 77°0E 84 Q10
Thlewiaza → _Canada_ 60°29N 94°40W 108 D9

Thomasville _U.S.A._ 30°50N 83°59W 111 D10
Thompson _Canada_ 55°45N 97°52W 108 D10
Thornaby on Tees _U.K._ 54°33N 1°18W 26 C6
Thornbury _U.K._ 51°36N 2°31W 30 C3
Thorndon _U.K._ 52°17N 1°9E 31 B11
Thorne _U.K._ 53°37N 0°57W 27 E7
Thorney _U.K._ 52°37N 0°6W 31 A8
Thornham _U.K._ 52°58N 0°35E 31 A10
Thornhill _U.K._ 54°37N 3°13W 26 C2
Thornton _U.K._ 53°52N 2°59W 27 E5
Thornton Dale _U.K._ 54°15N 0°42W 26 D7
Thorpe _U.K._ 52°38N 1°22E 31 A11
Thorpe le Soken _U.K._ 51°51N 1°11E 31 C11
Thrace _Europe_ 41°0N 27°0E 69 D12
Thrace, Sea of _Greece_ 40°30N 25°0E 69 D11
Thrapston _U.K._ 52°24N 0°32W 31 B7
Three Gorges Dam _China_ 30°45N 111°15E 79 E11
Threlkeld _U.K._ 54°37N 3°3W 26 C2
Threshfield _U.K._ 54°4N 2°1W 26 D4
Thrissur _India_ 10°30N 76°18E 84 P10
Thunder B. _U.S.A._ 45°0N 83°20W 112 C6
Thunder Bay _Canada_ 48°20N 89°15W 112 A3
Thüringer Wald _Germany_ 50°35N 11°0E 64 C6
Thurlby _U.K._ 52°45N 0°22W 27 G8
Thurles _Ireland_ 52°41N 7°49W 20 C7
Thurmaston _U.K._ 52°40N 1°5W 27 G6
Thursby _U.K._ 54°51N 3°2W 26 C2
Thurso _U.K._ 58°36N 3°32W 23 E10
Thurso → _U.K._ 58°36N 3°32W 23 E10
Thurston I. _Antarctica_ 72°0S 100°0W 55 D16
Tian Shan _Asia_ 40°30N 76°0E 78 C4
Tianjin _China_ 39°7N 117°12E 79 D12
Tianjun _China_ 38°0N 98°30E 78 D8
Tianmen _China_ 30°39N 113°9E 79 E11
Tianshui _China_ 34°32N 105°40E 78 E10
Tiaret _Algeria_ 35°20N 1°21E 94 A6
Tibastī, Sarīr _Libya_ 22°50N 18°30E 95 D9
Tiber → _Italy_ 41°44N 12°14E 68 D5
Tiberias, L. = Galilee, Sea of _Israel_ 32°45N 35°35E 86 C3
Tibesti _Chad_ 21°0N 17°30E 95 D9
Tibet = Xizang Zizhiqu □ _China_ 32°0N 88°0E 78 E6
Tibet, Plateau of _Asia_ 32°0N 86°0E 72 E10
Tiburón, I. _Mexico_ 29°0N 112°25W 114 B2
Ticehurst _U.K._ 51°3N 0°25E 31 D9
Ticino → _Italy_ 45°9N 9°14E 68 B3
Tickhill _U.K._ 53°26N 1°6W 27 F6
Ticonderoga _U.S.A._ 43°51N 73°26W 113 D11
Tideswell _U.K._ 53°17N 1°47W 27 F5
Tieling _China_ 42°20N 123°55E 79 C13
Tierra de Campos _Spain_ 42°10N 4°50W 67 A3
Tierra del Fuego, I. Grande de _Argentina_ 54°0S 69°0W 121 H3
Tiffin _U.S.A._ 41°7N 83°11W 112 E6
Tignish _Canada_ 46°58N 64°2W 113 B15
Tigris → _Asia_ 31°0N 47°25E 86 D6
Tijuana _Mexico_ 32°32N 117°1W 114 A1
Tikhoretsk _Russia_ 45°56N 40°5E 71 E7
Tikhvin _Russia_ 59°35N 33°30E 70 C5
Tikrīt _Iraq_ 34°35N 43°37E 86 C5
Tiksi _Russia_ 71°40N 128°45E 77 B13
Tilburg _Neths._ 51°31N 5°6E 64 C3
Tilbury _U.K._ 51°27N 0°22E 31 D9
Till → _U.K._ 55°41N 2°13W 26 A4
Tillicoultry _U.K._ 56°9N 3°45W 25 B8
Tilmanstone _U.K._ 51°12N 1°18E 31 D11
Tilt → _U.K._ 56°46N 3°51W 23 J10
Timaru _N.Z._ 44°23S 171°14E 99 J13
Timișoara _Romania_ 45°43N 21°15E 65 F11
Timmins _Canada_ 48°28N 81°25W 109 E11
Timor _Asia_ 9°0S 125°0E 83 F7
Timor Leste = East Timor ■ _Asia_ 8°50S 126°0E 83 F7
Timor Sea _Ind. Oc._ 12°0S 127°0E 72 K14
Tingewick _U.K._ 51°59N 1°2W 30 C6
Tingri _China_ 28°34N 86°38E 78 F6
Tinogasta _Argentina_ 28°5S 67°32W 121 E3
Tinos _Greece_ 37°33N 25°8E 69 F11
Tintagel _U.K._ 50°39N 4°46W 29 F4
Tintagel Hd. _U.K._ 50°40N 4°47W 29 F4
Tipperary _Ireland_ 52°28N 8°10W 20 D6
Tipperary □ _Ireland_ 52°37N 7°55W 20 C7
Tipton _U.K._ 52°32N 2°4W 27 G4
Tiptree _U.K._ 41°46N 91°8W 112 E2
Tiptree _U.K._ 51°48N 0°46E 31 C10
Tiranë _Albania_ 41°18N 19°49E 69 D8
Tiraspol _Moldova_ 46°55N 29°35E 65 E15
Tirebolu _Turkey_ 40°58N 38°45E 71 F6
Tiree _U.K._ 56°31N 6°55W 24 A2
Tiree, Passage of _U.K._ 56°30N 6°30W 24 B2
Tirich Mir _Pakistan_ 36°15N 71°55E 84 A7
Tirol □ _Austria_ 47°3N 10°43E 64 E6
Tiruchchirappalli _India_ 10°45N 78°45E 84 P11
Tirunelveli _India_ 8°45N 77°45E 84 Q10
Tiruppur _India_ 11°5N 77°22E 84 P10
Tisa → _Serbia_ 45°15N 20°17E 69 B9
Tisbury _U.K._ 51°4N 2°5W 30 D4
Tisdale _Canada_ 52°50N 104°0W 108 D9
Titchfield _U.K._ 50°50N 1°15W 30 E6
Titicaca, L. _S. Amer._ 15°30S 69°30W 120 D3
Titusville _U.S.A._ 41°38N 79°41W 112 E8
Tiverton _U.K._ 50°54N 3°29W 29 F7
Tivoli _Italy_ 41°58N 12°45E 68 D5
Tizi-Ouzou _Algeria_ 36°42N 4°3E 94 A6
Tlaxiaco _Mexico_ 17°25N 97°35W 114 D5
Tlemcen _Algeria_ 34°52N 1°21W 94 B5
Toamasina _Madag._ 18°10S 49°25E 97 H9
Toba, Danau _Indonesia_ 2°30N 98°30E 82 D1
Toba Kakar _Pakistan_ 31°30N 69°0E 84 D6
Tobago _Trin. & Tob._ 11°10N 60°30W 120 A3
Tobermory _Canada_ 45°12N 81°40W 112 C7
Tobermory _U.K._ 56°38N 6°5W 24 A3
Tobol → _Russia_ 58°10N 68°12E 76 D7
Tobolsk _Russia_ 58°15N 68°10E 70 D7
Tocantins → _Brazil_ 1°45S 49°10W 120 C5
Toddington _U.K._ 51°57N 0°32W 31 C7
Todmorden _U.K._ 53°43N 2°6W 27 E5
Todos os Santos, B. de _Brazil_ 12°48S 38°38W 122 B3
Toe Hd. _U.K._ 57°50N 7°8W 22 D2
Togliatti _Russia_ 53°32N 49°24E 70 D8
Togo ■ _W. Afr._ 8°30N 1°35E 94 G6

Tok _U.S.A._ 63°20N 142°59W 108 C5
Tokachi-Dake _Japan_ 43°17N 142°5E 81 B8
Tokat _Turkey_ 40°22N 36°35E 71 F6
Tokelau Is. ☑ _Pac. Oc._ 9°0S 171°45W 99 B16
Tokushima _Japan_ 34°4N 134°34E 81 F4
Tōkyō _Japan_ 35°43N 139°45E 81 F6
Toledo _Spain_ 39°50N 4°2W 67 C3
Toledo _U.S.A._ 41°39N 83°33W 112 E6
Toledo, Montes de _Spain_ 39°33N 4°20W 67 C3
Toliara _Madag._ 23°21S 43°40E 97 J8
Tolima _Colombia_ 4°40N 75°19W 120 B2
Tollesbury _U.K._ 51°45N 0°51E 31 C10
Toluca _Mexico_ 19°17N 99°40W 114 D5
Tomah _U.S.A._ 43°59N 90°30W 112 D2
Tomakomai _Japan_ 42°38N 141°36E 81 B7
Tombador, Serra do _Brazil_ 12°0S 58°0W 120 D4
Tombigbee → _U.S.A._ 31°8N 87°57W 111 D9
Tombouctou _Mali_ 16°50N 3°0W 94 E5
Tomini, Teluk _Indonesia_ 0°10S 121°0E 83 E6
Tomintoul _U.K._ 57°15N 3°23W 23 H11
Tomsk _Russia_ 56°30N 85°5E 76 D9
Tonbridge _U.K._ 51°11N 0°17E 31 D9
Tone → _U.K._ 50°58N 3°20W 29 F7
Tong _U.K._ 52°40N 2°17W 27 G4
Tonga ■ _Pac. Oc._ 19°50S 174°30W 99 D16
Tonga Trench _Pac. Oc._ 18°0S 173°0W 99 D16
Tongareva _Cook Is._ 9°0S 158°0W 103 H12
Tongatapu Group _Tonga_ 21°0S 175°0W 99 E16
Tongchuan _China_ 35°6N 109°3E 79 D10
Tonghua _China_ 41°42N 125°58E 79 C14
Tongliao _China_ 43°38N 122°18E 79 C13
Tongling _China_ 30°55N 117°48E 79 E12
Tongue _U.K._ 58°29N 4°25E 79 E13
Tongue → _U.S.A._ 46°25N 105°52W 110 A5
Tonk _India_ 26°6N 75°54E 84 F9
Tonkin, G. of _Asia_ 20°0N 108°0E 78 G10
Tonlé Sap _Cambodia_ 13°0N 104°0E 82 B2
Tonopah _U.S.A._ 38°4N 117°14W 110 C3
Toowoomba _Australia_ 27°32S 151°56E 98 F9
Topeka _U.S.A._ 39°3N 95°40W 111 C7
Topolobampo _Mexico_ 25°36N 109°3W 114 B3
Topsham _U.K._ 50°41N 3°28W 29 F7
Tor B. _U.K._ 50°25N 3°33W 29 G6
Torbay □ _U.K._ 50°26N 3°33W 29 G6
Torbay _U.K._ 50°27N 3°32W 29 G6
Torne älven → _Europe_ 65°50N 24°12E 63 D8
Torneträsk _Sweden_ 68°24N 19°15E 63 D7
Tornio _Finland_ 65°50N 24°12E 63 D8
Toro, Cerro del _Chile_ 29°10S 69°50W 121 E3
Toronto _Canada_ 43°39N 79°20W 112 D8
Torpoint _U.K._ 50°23N 4°13W 29 G5
Torquay _U.K._ 50°27N 3°32W 29 G6
Torre del Greco _Italy_ 40°47N 14°22E 68 D6
Torrejón de Ardoz _Spain_ 40°27N 3°29W 67 B4
Torrelavega _Spain_ 43°20N 4°5W 67 A3
Torremolinos _Spain_ 36°38N 4°30W 67 D3
Torrens, L. _Australia_ 31°0S 137°50E 98 G6
Torrent _Spain_ 39°27N 0°28W 67 C5
Torreón _Mexico_ 25°33N 103°26W 114 B4
Torres Strait _Australia_ 9°50S 142°20E 98 C7
Torridge → _U.K._ 51°0N 4°13W 29 E5
Torridon, L. _U.K._ 57°35N 5°50W 22 G6
Torthorwald _U.K._ 55°6N 3°32W 25 D8
Tortosa _Spain_ 40°49N 0°31E 67 B6
Toruń _Poland_ 53°2N 18°39E 65 B10
Torver _U.K._ 54°20N 3°6W 26 D2
Tory I. _Ireland_ 55°16N 8°13W 18 A5
Toscana □ _Italy_ 43°25N 11°0E 68 C4
Toshka, Buheirat en _Egypt_ 22°50N 31°0E 95 D12
Totland _U.K._ 50°41N 1°32W 30 E5
Totley _U.K._ 53°20N 1°32W 27 F5
Totnes _U.K._ 50°26N 3°42W 29 G6
Totton _U.K._ 50°55N 1°29W 30 E6
Tottori _Japan_ 35°30N 134°15E 81 F4
Toubkal, Djebel _Morocco_ 31°0N 8°0W 94 B4
Tougourt _Algeria_ 33°6N 6°4E 94 B7
Toul _France_ 48°40N 5°53E 66 B6
Toulon _France_ 43°10N 5°55E 66 E6
Toulouse _France_ 43°37N 1°27E 66 E4
Touraine _France_ 47°20N 0°30E 66 C4
Tournai _Belgium_ 50°35N 3°25E 64 C2
Tournon-sur-Rhône _France_ 45°4N 4°50E 66 D6
Tours _France_ 47°22N 0°40E 66 C4
Towanda _U.S.A._ 41°46N 76°27W 112 E9
Towcester _U.K._ 52°8N 0°59W 31 B7
Town Yetholm _U.K._ 55°33N 2°17W 25 C11
Townsville _Australia_ 19°15S 146°45E 98 D8
Towraghondi _Afghan._ 35°13N 62°16E 84 B3
Towson _U.S.A._ 39°24N 76°36W 112 F9
Toyama _Japan_ 36°40N 137°15E 81 E5
Toyohashi _Japan_ 34°45N 137°25E 81 F5
Toyota _Japan_ 35°3N 137°7E 81 F5
Trabzon _Turkey_ 41°0N 39°45E 71 F6
Trafalgar, C. _Spain_ 36°10N 6°2W 67 D2
Trail _Canada_ 49°5N 117°40W 108 E8
Tralee _Ireland_ 52°16N 9°42W 20 D3
Tralee B. _Ireland_ 52°17N 9°55W 20 D3
Tramore _Ireland_ 52°10N 7°10W 21 D8
Tramore B. _Ireland_ 52°9N 7°10W 21 D8
Tranent _U.K._ 55°57N 2°57W 25 C10
Trang _Thailand_ 7°33N 99°38E 82 C1
Transantarctic Mts. _Antarctica_ 85°0S 170°0W 55 E12
Transnistria □ _Moldova_ 47°20N 29°15E 65 E15
Transylvania _Romania_ 46°30N 24°0E 65 E12
Transylvanian Alps _Romania_ 45°30N 25°0E 65 F13
Trápani _Italy_ 38°1N 12°29E 68 E5
Trasimeno, L. _Italy_ 43°8N 12°6E 68 C5
Traverse City _U.S.A._ 44°46N 85°38W 112 C5
Trawbreaga B. _Ireland_ 55°20N 7°25W 18 A7
Trawsfynydd _U.K._ 52°54N 3°55W 28 B6
Tredegar _U.K._ 51°47N 3°14W 28 D7
Trefaldwyn = Montgomery _U.K._ 52°34N 3°8W 28 B7
Trefynwy = Monmouth _U.K._ 51°48N 2°42W 28 D8
Tregaron _U.K._ 52°14N 3°56W 28 C5
Treharris _U.K._ 51°40N 3°16W 28 D7
Treinta y Tres _Uruguay_ 33°16S 54°17W 121 F4
Trelew _Argentina_ 43°10S 65°20W 121 G3
Trent → _U.K._ 53°41N 0°42W 27 E7
Trentham _U.K._ 52°58N 2°11W 27 G4

Trento _Italy_ 46°4N 11°8E 68 A4
Trenton _Canada_ 44°10N 77°34W 112 C9
Trenton _U.S.A._ 40°14N 74°46W 113 E10
Tres Arroyos _Argentina_ 38°26S 60°20W 121 F3
Três Corações _Brazil_ 21°44S 45°15W 122 D1
Três Lagoas _Brazil_ 20°50S 51°43W 120 E4
Três Pontas _Brazil_ 21°23S 45°29W 122 D1
Tres Puntas, C. _Argentina_ 47°0S 66°0W 121 G3
Três Rios _Brazil_ 22°6S 43°15W 122 D2
Tresco _U.K._ 49°57N 6°20W 29 H1
Treviso _Italy_ 45°40N 12°15E 68 B5
Trevose Hd. _U.K._ 50°32N 5°3W 29 F3
Trier _Germany_ 49°45N 6°38E 64 D4
Trieste _Italy_ 45°40N 13°46E 68 B5
Trim _Ireland_ 53°33N 6°48W 19 D8
Trimdon _U.K._ 54°42N 1°24W 26 C6
Trimley _U.K._ 51°59N 1°20E 31 C11
Trincomalee _Sri Lanka_ 8°38N 81°15E 84 Q12
Trindade _Atl. Oc._ 20°20S 29°50W 52 F8
Trinidad _Bolivia_ 14°46S 64°50W 120 D3
Trinidad _Cuba_ 21°48N 80°0W 115 C9
Trinidad _U.S.A._ 37°10N 104°31W 110 C6
Trinidad & Tobago ■ _W. Indies_ 10°30N 61°20W 115 E12
Trinity → _U.S.A._ 29°45N 94°43W 111 E8
Trinity B. _Canada_ 48°20N 53°10W 109 E14
Trinity Is. _U.S.A._ 56°33N 154°25W 108 D4
Tripoli _Lebanon_ 34°31N 35°50E 86 C3
Tripoli _Libya_ 32°49N 13°7E 95 B8
Tripolitania _Libya_ 31°0N 13°0E 95 B8
Tripura □ _India_ 24°0N 92°0E 85 H18
Tristan da Cunha _Atl. Oc._ 37°6S 12°20W 52 F9
Trnava _Slovak Rep._ 48°23N 17°35E 65 D9
Trois-Rivières _Canada_ 46°25N 72°34W 113 C11
Trollhättan _Sweden_ 58°17N 12°20E 63 F6
Trombetas → _Brazil_ 1°55S 55°35W 120 C4
Tromsø _Norway_ 69°40N 18°56E 63 D7
Tronador _Argentina_ 41°10S 71°50W 121 G2
Trondheim _Norway_ 63°36N 10°25E 63 E6
Trondheimsfjorden _Norway_ 63°35N 10°30E 63 E6
Troon _U.K._ 55°33N 4°39W 24 C6
Trossachs, The _U.K._ 56°14N 4°24W 24 B7
Trostan _U.K._ 55°3N 6°10W 19 A9
Trotternish _U.K._ 57°32N 6°15W 22 G5
Trou Gras Pt. _St. Lucia_ 13°51N 60°53W 114 b
Trout L. _N.W.T., Canada_ 60°40N 121°14W 108 C7
Trout L. _Ont., Canada_ 51°20N 93°15W 108 D10
Trowbridge _U.K._ 51°18N 2°12W 30 D4
Troy _Turkey_ 39°57N 26°12E 71 G4
Troy _Ala., U.S.A._ 31°48N 85°58W 111 D9
Troy _N.Y., U.S.A._ 42°44N 73°41W 113 D11
Troy _Ohio, U.S.A._ 40°2N 84°12W 112 E5
Troyes _France_ 48°19N 4°3E 66 B6
Trujillo _Honduras_ 16°0N 86°0W 114 D7
Trujillo _Peru_ 8°6S 79°0W 120 C2
Trujillo _Venezuela_ 9°22N 70°38W 120 B2
Truk _Micronesia_ 7°25N 151°46E 102 G7
Trull _U.K._ 51°0N 3°6W 30 E2
Trumpington _U.K._ 52°10N 0°7E 31 B9
Truro _Canada_ 45°21N 63°14W 109 E13
Truro _U.K._ 50°16N 5°4W 29 G3
Tsavo _Kenya_ 2°59S 38°28E 96 E7
Tseung Kwan _China_ 22°19N 114°15E 79 a
Tshikapa _Dem. Rep. of the Congo_ 6°28S 20°48E 96 F4
Tsiigehtchic _Canada_ 67°15N 134°0W 108 C6
Tsimlyansk Res. _Russia_ 48°0N 43°0E 71 E7
Tskhinvali _Georgia_ 42°14N 44°1E 71 F7
Tsuchiura _Japan_ 36°5N 140°15E 81 E7
Tsuen Wan _China_ 22°22N 114°6E 79 a
Tsugaru Str. _Japan_ 41°35N 141°0E 81 C7
Tsumeb _Namibia_ 19°9S 17°44E 97 H3
Tsuruoka _Japan_ 38°44N 139°50E 81 D6
Tsushima _Japan_ 34°20N 129°20E 81 F1
Tuam _Ireland_ 53°31N 8°51W 18 D4
Tuamotu, Îs. _French Polynesia_ 17°0S 144°0W 103 J13
Tuapse _Russia_ 44°5N 39°10E 71 F6
Tubarão _Brazil_ 28°30S 49°0W 121 E5
Tübingen _Germany_ 48°31N 9°4E 64 D5
Tubruq _Libya_ 32°7N 23°55E 95 B10
Tubuaï, Îs. _French Polynesia_ 25°0S 150°0W 103 K13
Tucson _U.S.A._ 32°13N 110°58W 110 D4
Tucumcari _U.S.A._ 35°10N 103°44W 110 C6
Tucupita _Venezuela_ 9°2N 62°3W 120 B3
Tucuruí _Brazil_ 3°42S 49°44W 120 C5
Tucuruí, Represa de _Brazil_ 4°0S 49°30W 120 C5
Tuen Mun _China_ 22°23N 113°57E 79 a
Tuguegarao _Phil._ 17°35S 121°42E 83 A6
Tuktoyaktuk _Canada_ 69°27N 133°2W 108 C6
Tula _Russia_ 54°13N 37°38E 70 D6
Tulancingo _Mexico_ 20°5N 98°22W 114 C5
Tulare _U.S.A._ 36°13N 119°21W 110 C3
Tulcán _Ecuador_ 0°48N 77°43W 120 B2
Tulcea _Romania_ 45°13N 28°46E 65 F15
Tulita _Canada_ 64°57N 125°30W 108 C7
Tulla _Ireland_ 52°53N 8°46W 20 C5
Tullamore _Ireland_ 53°16N 7°31W 21 B7
Tulle _France_ 45°16N 1°46E 66 D4
Tullow _Ireland_ 52°49N 6°45W 21 C9
Tulsa _U.S.A._ 36°10N 95°55W 111 C7
Tumaco _Colombia_ 1°50N 78°45W 120 B2
Tumbes _Peru_ 3°37S 80°27W 120 C1
Tummel → _U.K._ 56°42N 4°5W 23 J9
Tummel, L. _U.K._ 56°43N 3°55W 23 J10
Tumucumaque, Serra _Brazil_ 2°0N 55°0W 120 B4
Tunis _Tunisia_ 36°50N 10°11E 95 A8
Tunisia ■ _Africa_ 33°30N 9°10E 95 A7
Tunja _Colombia_ 5°33N 73°25W 120 B2
Tunstall _U.K._ 52°9N 1°27E 31 B11
Tupaciguara _Brazil_ 18°35S 48°42W 122 C1
Tupelo _U.S.A._ 34°16N 88°43W 111 D9
Tupiza _Bolivia_ 21°30S 65°40W 120 E3
Turfan Basin _China_ 42°40N 89°25E 78 C6
Turgutlu _Turkey_ 38°30N 27°43E 71 G4
Turin _Italy_ 45°3N 7°40E 68 B2
Turkana, L. _Africa_ 3°30N 36°5E 96 D7
Turkey ■ _Eurasia_ 39°0N 36°0E 71 G6
Türkmenabat _Turkmenistan_ 39°6N 63°34E 87 B10
Türkmenbashi _Turkmenistan_ 40°5N 53°5E 87 A8
Turkmenistan ■ _Asia_ 39°0N 59°0E 87 B9

Turks & Caicos Is. ☑ _W. Indies_ 21°20N 71°20W 115 C10
Turku _Finland_ 60°30N 22°19E 63 E8
Turnberry _U.K._ 55°18N 4°49W 24 D6
Turneffe Is. _Belize_ 17°20N 87°50W 114 D7
Turpan _China_ 43°58N 89°10E 78 C6
Turriff _U.K._ 57°32N 2°27W 23 G13
Tuscaloosa _U.S.A._ 33°12N 87°34W 111 D9
Tuscany = Toscana □ _Italy_ 43°25N 11°0E 68 C4
Tutbury _U.K._ 52°51N 1°41W 27 G5
Tuticorin _India_ 8°50N 78°12E 84 Q11
Tutuila _Amer. Samoa_ 14°19S 170°50W 99 C16
Tutume _Botswana_ 20°30S 27°5E 97 J5
Tuul Gol → _Mongolia_ 48°30N 104°25E 78 B9
Tuva □ _Russia_ 51°30N 95°0E 77 D10
Tuvalu ■ _Pac. Oc._ 8°0S 178°0E 99 B14
Tuxford _U.K._ 53°14N 0°54W 27 F7
Tuxpan _Mexico_ 20°57N 97°24W 114 C5
Tuxtla Gutiérrez _Mexico_ 16°45N 93°7W 114 D6
Tuz Gölü _Turkey_ 38°42N 33°18E 71 G5
Tuzla _Bos.-H._ 44°34N 18°41E 69 B8
Tver _Russia_ 56°55N 35°59E 70 C6
Tweed → _U.K._ 55°45N 2°0W 25 C11
Tweedmouth _U.K._ 55°45N 2°0W 26 A5
Tweedshaws _U.K._ 55°27N 3°29W 25 D9
Twenty _U.K._ 52°47N 0°17W 27 G8
Twin Falls _U.S.A._ 42°34N 114°28W 110 B4
Two Harbors _U.S.A._ 47°2N 91°40W 112 B2
Two Rivers _U.S.A._ 44°9N 87°34W 112 C4
Twyford _Hants., U.K._ 51°1N 1°19W 30 D6
Twyford _Wokingham, U.K._ 51°28N 0°51W 31 D7
Tychy _Poland_ 50°9N 18°59E 65 C10
Tydd St. Mary _U.K._ 52°45N 0°7E 27 G9
Tyler _U.S.A._ 32°21N 95°18W 111 D7
Tyndrum _U.K._ 56°26N 4°42W 24 B6
Tyne → _U.K._ 54°59N 1°32W 26 C5
Tyne & Wear □ _U.K._ 55°6N 1°17W 26 B6
Tynemouth _U.K._ 55°1N 1°26W 26 B6
Tyrol = Tirol □ _Austria_ 47°3N 10°43E 64 E6
Tyrone □ _U.K._ 54°38N 7°11W 19 B7
Tyrrhenian Sea _Medit. S._ 40°0N 12°30E 68 E5
Tyumen _Russia_ 57°11N 65°29E 76 D7
Tywardreath _U.K._ 50°21N 4°42W 29 G4
Tywi → _U.K._ 51°48N 4°21W 28 D5
Tywyn _U.K._ 52°35N 4°5W 28 B5
Tzaneen _S. Africa_ 23°47S 30°9E 97 J6

U

U.S.A. = United States of America ■ _N. Amer._ 37°0N 96°0W 110 C7
U.S. Virgin Is. ☑ _W. Indies_ 18°20N 65°0W 115 D12
Uaupés → _Brazil_ 0°2N 67°16W 120 B3
Ubá _Brazil_ 21°8S 43°0W 122 D2
Ubaitaba _Brazil_ 14°18S 39°20W 122 B3
Ube _Japan_ 33°56N 131°15E 81 G2
Uberaba _Brazil_ 19°50S 47°55W 122 C1
Uberlândia _Brazil_ 19°0S 48°20W 122 C1
Ubon Ratchathani _Thailand_ 15°15N 104°50E 82 A2
Ucayali → _Peru_ 4°30S 73°30W 120 C2
Uckfield _U.K._ 50°58N 0°7E 31 E9
Udagamandalam _India_ 11°30N 76°44E 84 P10
Udaipur _India_ 24°36N 73°44E 84 G8
Uddingston _U.K._ 55°49N 4°5W 24 C7
Údine _Italy_ 46°3N 13°14E 68 A5
Udmurtia □ _Russia_ 57°30N 52°30E 70 C9
Udon Thani _Thailand_ 17°29N 102°46E 82 A2
Udupi _India_ 13°25N 74°42E 84 N9
Uele → _Dem. Rep. of the Congo_ 3°45N 24°45E 96 D4
Ufa _Russia_ 54°45N 55°55E 70 D10
Uffculme _U.K._ 50°54N 3°20W 29 F7
Ufford _U.K._ 52°8N 1°23E 31 B11
Uganda ■ _Africa_ 2°0N 32°0E 96 D6
Ugborough _U.K._ 50°22N 3°53W 29 G6
Uibhist a Deas = South Uist _U.K._ 57°20N 7°15W 22 H3
Uibhist a Tuath = North Uist _U.K._ 57°40N 7°15W 22 G3
Uig _U.K._ 57°35N 6°21W 22 G5
Uinta Mts. _U.S.A._ 40°45N 110°30W 110 B4
Uitenhage _S. Africa_ 33°40S 25°28E 97 L5
Ujjain _India_ 23°9N 75°43E 84 H9
Ukhta _Russia_ 63°34N 53°41E 70 B9
Ukiah _U.S.A._ 39°9N 123°13W 110 C2
Ukraine ■ _Europe_ 49°0N 32°0E 71 E5
Ulaan-Uul _Mongolia_ 46°4N 100°49E 78 B9
Ulaangom _Mongolia_ 50°5N 92°10E 78 A7
Ulan Bator _Mongolia_ 47°55N 106°53E 78 B10
Ulan Ude _Russia_ 51°45N 107°40E 77 D11
Ulceby Cross _U.K._ 53°15N 0°7E 27 F9
Ulhasnagar _India_ 19°15N 73°10E 84 K8
Uliastay _Mongolia_ 47°56N 97°28E 78 B8
Ullapool _U.K._ 57°54N 5°9W 22 G7
Ulleungdo _S. Korea_ 37°30N 130°30E 81 E2
Ullswater _U.K._ 54°34N 2°52W 26 C3
Ulm _Germany_ 48°23N 9°58E 64 D5
Ulsan _S. Korea_ 35°20N 129°15E 79 D14
Ulster □ _U.K._ 54°35N 6°30W 19 B9
Ulukhaktok _Canada_ 70°44N 117°44W 108 B8
Ulungur He → _China_ 47°1N 87°24E 78 B6
Uluru _Australia_ 25°23S 131°5E 98 F5
Ulva _U.K._ 56°29N 6°13W 24 B3
Ulverston _U.K._ 54°13N 3°5W 26 D2
Ulyanovsk _Russia_ 54°20N 48°25E 70 D8
Uman _Ukraine_ 48°40N 30°12E 71 E5
Umeå _Sweden_ 63°45N 20°20E 63 E8
Umeälven → _Sweden_ 63°45N 20°20E 63 E8
Umlazi _S. Africa_ 29°59S 30°54E 97 K6
Umm al Qaywayn _U.A.E._ 25°30N 55°35E 87 E8
Umm I. _U.S.A._ 53°15N 168°20W 108 D3
Umuahia _Nigeria_ 5°31N 7°26E 94 G7
Unalakleet _U.S.A._ 63°52N 160°47W 108 C3
Unalaska _U.S.A._ 53°53N 166°32W 108 D3
Unalaska I. _U.S.A._ 53°35N 166°50W 108 D3
'Unayzah _Si. Arabia_ 26°6N 43°58E 86 E5
Uncía _Bolivia_ 18°25S 66°40W 120 D3
Ungava, Pén. d' _Canada_ 60°0N 74°0W 109 C12
Ungava B. _Canada_ 59°30N 67°30W 109 D13
União dos Palmares _Brazil_ 9°10S 36°2W 122 A3
Unimak I. _U.S.A._ 54°45N 164°0W 108 D3
Union City _U.S.A._ 36°26N 89°3W 112 G3

Uniontown   **White**

Uniontown U.S.A. 39°54N 79°44W 112 F8
United Arab Emirates ■ Asia 23°50N 54°0E 87 F8
United Kingdom ■ Europe 53°0N 2°0W 62 E6
United States of America ■
 N. Amer. 37°0N 96°0W 110 C7
Unst U.K. 60°44N 0°53W 22 A16
Unzen-Dake Japan 32°46N 130°17E 81 G2
Upavon U.K. 51°18N 1°48W 30 D5
Upington S. Africa 28°25S 21°15E 97 K4
'Upolu Samoa 13°58S 172°0W 99 C16
Upper Heyford U.K. 51°56N 1°15W 30 C6
Upper Klamath L. U.S.A. 42°25N 121°55W 110 B2
Uppingham U.K. 52°30N 0°43W 27 G7
Uppsala Sweden 59°53N 17°38E 63 F7
Upton U.K. 53°1N 2°54W 27 D
Upton-upon-Severn U.K. 52°3N 2°12W 30 B4
Upwey U.K. 50°39N 2°29W 30 E4
Ur Iraq 30°55N 46°25E 86 D6
Ural Kazakhstan 47°0N 51°48E 71 E9
Ural Mts. Eurasia 60°0N 59°0E 70 C10
Uranium City Canada 59°34N 108°37W 108 D9
Uraricoera → Brazil 3°2N 60°30W 120 B3
Urbana Ill., U.S.A. 40°7N 88°12W 112 E3
Urbana Ohio, U.S.A. 40°7N 83°45W 112 E6
Ure → U.K. 54°5N 1°20W 26 D5
Urganch Uzbekistan 41°40N 60°41E 87 A10
Urmia Iran 37°40N 45°0E 86 B6
Urmia, L. Iran 37°50N 45°30E 86 B6
Urmston U.K. 53°27N 2°21W 27 F4
Uruaçu Brazil 14°30S 49°10W 122 D1
Uruapan Mexico 19°24N 102°3W 114 D4
Urubamba → Peru 10°43S 73°48W 120 D2
Uruguai → Brazil 26°0S 53°30W 121 E4
Uruguaiana Brazil 29°50S 57°0W 121 E4
Uruguay ■ S. Amer. 32°30S 56°30W 121 F4
Uruguay → S. Amer. 34°12S 58°18W 117 G5
Ürümqi China 43°45N 87°45E 78 C6
Usa → Russia 66°16N 59°49E 70 A10
Uşak Turkey 38°43N 29°28E 71 G4
Usakos Namibia 21°54S 15°31E 97 J3
Usedom Germany 53°55N 14°2E 64 B8
Ushant France 48°28N 5°6W 66 B1
Ushuaia Argentina 54°50S 68°23W 121 H3
Usk → U.K. 51°33N 2°58W 29 D8
Usolye Sibirskoye Russia 52°48N 103°40E 77 D11
Uspallata, P. de Argentina 32°37S 69°22W 121 F3
Usselby U.K. 53°26N 0°21W 27 F8
Ussuriysk Russia 43°48N 131°59E 81 D2
Ust-Ilimsk Russia 58°3N 102°39E 77 D11
Ust Kut Russia 56°50N 105°42E 77 D11
Ústí nad Labem Czech Rep. 50°41N 14°3E 64 C8
Ústica Italy 38°42N 13°11E 68 E5
Usu China 44°27N 84°40E 78 C5
Usumacinta → Mexico 18°24N 92°38W 114 D6
Utah □ U.S.A. 39°20N 111°30W 110 C4
Utah L. U.S.A. 40°12N 111°48W 110 B4
Utica U.S.A. 43°6N 75°14W 113 D10
Utrecht Neths. 52°5N 5°8E 64 B3
Utsunomiya Japan 36°30N 139°50E 81 E6
Uttar Pradesh □ India 27°0N 80°0E 84 F12
Uttaradit Thailand 17°36N 100°5E 82 A2
Uttarakhand □ India 30°0N 79°30E 84 D11
Uttoxeter U.K. 52°54N 1°52W 27 G5
Uusikaupunki Finland 60°47N 21°25E 63 E8
Uvalde U.S.A. 29°13N 99°47W 110 E7
Uvira Dem. Rep. of the Congo 3°22S 29°3E 96 E5
Uvs Nuur Mongolia 50°20N 92°30E 78 A7
Uyuni Bolivia 20°28S 66°47W 120 E3
Uzbekistan ■ Asia 41°30N 65°0E 87 A10
Uzhhorod Ukraine 48°36N 22°18E 65 D12

V
Vaal → S. Africa 29°4S 23°38E 97 K4
Vaasa Finland 63°6N 21°38E 63 E8
Vadakara India 11°35N 75°40E 84 P9
Vadodara India 22°20N 73°10E 84 H8
Vadsø Norway 70°3N 29°50E 63 C9
Vaduz Liech. 47°8N 9°31E 64 E5
Váh → Slovak Rep. 47°43N 18°7E 65 D9
Vail U.S.A. 39°40N 106°20W 110 C5
Vaila U.K. 60°12N 1°36W 22 B14
Val-d'Or Canada 48°7N 77°47W 109 E12
Valdai Hills Russia 57°0N 33°30E 70 C5
Valdés, Pen. Argentina 42°30S 63°45W 121 G3
Valdez U.S.A. 61°7N 146°16W 108 C5
Valdivia Chile 39°50S 73°14W 121 F2
Valdosta U.S.A. 30°50N 83°17W 111 D10
Vale of Glamorgan □ U.K. 51°28N 3°25W 29 E7
Valença Brazil 13°20S 39°5W 122 B3
Valence France 44°57N 4°54E 66 D6
Valencia Spain 39°27N 0°23W 67 C5
Valencia Venezuela 10°11N 68°0W 120 A3
Valencia □ Spain 39°20N 0°40W 67 C5
Valencia, G. de Spain 39°30N 0°20E 67 C6
Valencia I. Ireland 51°54N 10°22W 20 E2
Valenciennes France 50°20N 3°34E 66 A5
Valera Venezuela 9°19N 70°37W 120 B2
Valladolid Mexico 20°41N 88°12W 114 C7
Valladolid Spain 41°38N 4°43W 67 B3
Valledupar Colombia 10°29N 73°15W 120 A2
Vallejo U.S.A. 38°7N 122°14W 110 C2
Vallenar Chile 28°30S 70°50W 121 E2
Valletta Malta 35°54N 14°31E 68 G6
Valley U.K. 53°16N 4°34W 28 A4
Valley U.S.A. 46°55N 98°0W 110 A7
Valparaíso Chile 33°2S 71°40W 121 F2
Van Turkey 38°30N 43°20E 71 G7
Van, L. Turkey 38°30N 43°0E 71 G7
Van Buren U.S.A. 47°10N 67°58W 113 B13
Van Wert U.S.A. 40°52N 84°35W 112 E5
Vanadzor Armenia 40°48N 44°30E 71 F7
Vancouver Canada 49°15N 123°7W 108 E7
Vancouver U.S.A. 45°38N 122°40W 110 A2
Vancouver I. Canada 49°50N 126°0W 108 E7
Vandalia U.S.A. 38°58N 89°6W 112 F3
Vanderhoof Canada 54°0N 124°0W 108 D7
Vänern Sweden 58°47N 13°30E 63 F6
Vännäs Sweden 63°58N 19°48E 63 E7
Vannes France 47°40N 2°47W 66 C2
Vanrhynsdorp S. Africa 31°36S 18°44E 97 L3

Vantaa Finland 60°18N 24°56E 63 E8
Varna Levu Fiji 16°33S 179°15E 99 D14
Vanuatu ■ Pac. Oc. 15°0S 168°0E 99 D12
Varanasi India 25°22N 83°0E 85 G13
Varangerfjorden Norway 70°3N 29°25E 63 C9
Varberg Sweden 57°6N 12°20E 63 F6
Vardø Norway 70°23N 31°5E 63 C10
Varese Italy 45°48N 8°50E 68 B3
Varginha Brazil 21°33S 45°25W 122 D1
Varna Bulgaria 43°13N 27°56E 69 C12
Vasa Barris → Brazil 11°10S 37°10W 122 B3
Västerås Sweden 59°37N 16°38E 63 F7
Västervik Sweden 57°43N 16°33E 63 F7
Vaté Vanuatu 17°40S 168°25E 99 D12
Vatersay U.K. 56°55N 7°32W 22 J2
Vatican City ■ Europe 41°54N 12°27E 68 D6
Vatnajökull Iceland 64°30N 16°48W 63 B2
Vättern Sweden 58°25N 14°30E 63 F6
Vaughn U.S.A. 34°36N 105°13W 110 D5
Vava'u Group Tonga 18°40S 174°0W 99 D16
Vega Norway 65°40N 11°55E 63 D6
Vegreville Canada 53°30N 112°5W 108 D8
Vélez-Málaga Spain 36°48N 4°5W 67 D3
Velhas → Brazil 17°13S 44°49W 122 C2
Velikiy Novgorod Russia 58°30N 31°25E 70 C5
Velikiye Luki Russia 56°25N 30°32E 70 C5
Veliko Tŭrnovo Bulgaria 43°6N 25°41E 69 C11
Velikonda Range India 14°45N 79°10E 84 M11
Vellore India 12°57N 79°10E 84 N11
Velsk Russia 61°10N 42°5E 70 D7
Vendée □ France 46°50N 1°35W 66 C3
Vendôme France 47°47N 1°3E 66 C4
Venézia, G. di Italy 45°15N 13°0E 68 B5
Venezuela ■ S. Amer. 8°0N 66°0W 120 B3
Venezuela, G. de Venezuela 11°30N 71°0W 120 A2
Vengurla India 15°53N 73°45E 84 M8
Venice Italy 45°27N 12°21E 68 B5
Ventnor U.K. 50°36N 1°12W 30 E6
Ventoux, Mt. France 44°10N 5°17E 66 D6
Ventspils Latvia 57°25N 21°32E 63 F8
Veracruz Mexico 19°11N 96°8W 114 D5
Veraval India 20°53N 70°27E 84 J7
Vercelli Italy 45°19N 8°25E 68 B3
Verde → U.S.A. 33°33N 111°40W 110 D4
Verdun France 49°9N 5°24E 66 B6
Vereeniging S. Africa 26°38S 27°57E 97 K5
Verkhoyansk Russia 67°35N 133°25E 77 C14
Verkhoyansk Ra. Russia 66°0N 129°0E 77 C13
Vermont □ U.S.A. 44°0N 73°0W 113 D11
Vernal U.S.A. 40°27N 109°32W 110 B5
Vernon Canada 50°20N 119°15W 108 D8
Vernon U.S.A. 34°9N 99°17W 110 D7
Verona Italy 45°27N 10°59E 68 B4
Versailles France 48°48N 2°7E 66 B5
Vert, C. Senegal 14°45N 17°30W 94 F2
Verviers Belgium 50°37N 5°52E 64 C3
Verwood U.K. 50°52N 1°52W 30 E5
Veryan U.K. 50°13N 4°56W 29 G4
Veryan B. U.K. 50°13N 4°51W 29 G4
Vesoul France 47°40N 6°11E 66 C7
Vesterålen Norway 68°45N 15°0E 63 D6
Vestfjorden Norway 67°55N 14°0E 63 D6
Vesuvio Italy 40°49N 14°26E 68 D6
Veszprém Hungary 47°8N 17°57E 65 E9
Vianópolis Brazil 16°40S 48°35W 122 C1
Viaréggio Italy 43°52N 10°14E 68 C4
Vichada → Colombia 4°55N 67°50W 120 B3
Vichy France 46°9N 3°26E 66 C5
Vickerstown U.K. 54°6N 3°15W 26 D2
Vicksburg U.S.A. 32°21N 90°53W 111 D8
Victoria Canada 48°30N 123°25W 108 E7
Victoria China 22°17N 114°11E 79 a
Victoria U.S.A. 28°48N 97°0W 111 E7
Victoria □ Australia 37°0S 144°0E 98 H7
Victoria, L. Africa 1°0S 33°0E 96 E6
Victoria Falls Zimbabwe 17°58S 25°52E 97 H5
Victoria I. Canada 71°0N 111°0W 108 B8
Victoria Ld. Antarctica 75°0S 160°0E 55 D11
Victoria Str. Canada 69°31N 100°30W 108 B9
Victoriaville Canada 46°4N 71°56W 113 B12
Vidin Bulgaria 43°59N 22°50E 69 C10
Viedma, L. Argentina 49°30S 72°30W 121 G2
Vienna Austria 48°12N 16°22E 64 D9
Vienne France 45°31N 4°53E 66 D6
Vienne → France 47°13N 0°5E 66 C4
Vientiane Laos 17°58N 102°36E 82 A2
Vierge Pt. St. Lucia 13°49N 60°53W 114 b
Vierzon France 47°13N 2°5E 66 C5
Vietnam ■ Asia 19°0N 106°0E 82 A3
Vieux Fort St. Lucia 13°46N 60°58W 114 b
Vigévano Italy 45°19N 8°51E 68 B3
Vigo Spain 42°12N 8°41W 67 A1
Vijayawada India 16°31N 80°39E 85 L12
Vikna Norway 64°55N 10°58E 63 D6
Vila Nova de Gaia Portugal 41°8N 8°37W 67 B1
Vila Velha Brazil 20°20S 40°17W 122 D2
Vilaine → France 47°30N 2°27W 66 C2
Vilhelmina Sweden 64°35N 16°39E 63 E7
Vilhena Brazil 12°40S 60°5W 120 D3
Vilkitski Str. Russia 78°0N 103°0E 77 B11
Villa Bella Bolivia 10°25S 65°22W 120 D3
Villa Maria Argentina 32°20S 63°10W 121 F3
Villach Austria 46°37N 13°51E 64 E7
Villahermosa Mexico 17°59N 92°55W 114 D6
Villajoyosa Spain 38°30N 0°12W 67 C5
Villarrica Paraguay 25°40S 56°30W 121 E4
Villavicencio Colombia 4°9N 73°37W 120 B2
Ville-Marie Canada 47°20N 79°30W 112 B8
Villeneuve-sur-Lot France 44°24N 0°42E 66 D4
Vilnius Lithuania 54°38N 25°19E 63 G9
Vilyuy → Russia 64°24N 126°26E 77 C13
Vilyuysk Russia 63°40N 121°35E 77 C13
Viña del Mar Chile 33°0S 71°30W 121 F2
Vincennes U.S.A. 38°41N 87°32W 112 F4
Vindhya Ra. India 22°50N 77°0E 84 H10
Vineland U.S.A. 39°29N 75°2W 113 F10
Vinnytsya Ukraine 49°15N 28°30E 65 D15
Virden Canada 49°50N 100°56W 108 E9
Vire France 48°50N 0°53W 66 B3
Virgenes, C. Argentina 52°19S 68°21W 121 H3

Virgin → U.S.A. 36°28N 114°21W 110 C4
Virgin Is. (British) ☑ W. Indies 18°30N 64°30W 115 D12
Virgin Is. (U.S.) ☑ W. Indies 18°20N 65°0W 115 D12
Virginia S. Africa 28°8S 26°55E 97 K5
Virginia U.S.A. 47°31N 92°32W 111 A8
Virginia □ U.S.A. 37°30N 78°45W 112 G8
Virginia Beach U.S.A. 36°49N 76°9W 111 C11
Viroqua U.S.A. 43°34N 90°53W 112 D2
Vis Croatia 43°4N 16°10E 68 C7
Visalia U.S.A. 36°20N 119°18W 110 C3
Visby Sweden 57°37N 18°18E 63 F7
Viscount Melville Sd. Canada 74°10N 108°0W 109 B9
Vishakhapatnam India 17°45N 83°20E 85 L13
Vistula → Poland 54°22N 18°55E 65 A10
Vitebsk Belarus 55°10N 30°15E 70 C5
Viterbo Italy 42°25N 12°6E 68 C5
Viti Levu Fiji 17°30S 177°30E 99 D14
Vitim → Russia 59°26N 112°34E 77 D12
Vitória Brazil 20°20S 40°22W 122 D2
Vitória da Conquista Brazil 14°51S 40°51W 122 B2
Vitoria-Gasteiz Spain 42°50N 2°41W 67 A4
Vittória Italy 36°57N 14°32E 68 F6
Vizianagaram India 18°6N 83°30E 85 K13
Vladikavkaz Russia 43°0N 44°35E 71 F7
Vladimir Russia 56°15N 40°30E 70 C7
Vladivostok Russia 43°10N 131°53E 77 E14
Vlissingen Neths. 51°26N 3°34E 64 C2
Vlorë Albania 40°32N 19°28E 69 D8
Vltava → Czech Rep. 50°21N 14°30E 64 D8
Voe U.K. 60°21N 1°16W 22 B15
Vogelsberg Germany 50°31N 9°12E 64 C5
Vohimena, Tanjon' i Madag. 25°36S 45°8E 97 K9
Voi Kenya 3°25S 38°32E 96 E7
Vojvodina □ Serbia 45°20N 20°0E 69 B9
Volga → Russia 46°0N 48°30E 71 E8
Volga Hts. Russia 51°0N 46°0E 71 D8
Volgodonsk Russia 47°33N 42°5E 71 E7
Volgograd Russia 48°40N 44°25E 71 E7
Volgograd Res. Russia 50°0N 45°20E 71 D8
Vologda Russia 59°10N 39°45E 70 C6
Volos Greece 39°24N 22°59E 69 E10
Volsk Russia 52°5N 47°22E 70 D8
Volta → Ghana 5°46N 0°41E 94 G6
Volta, L. Ghana 7°30N 0°0 04 G5
Volta Redonda Brazil 22°31S 44°5W 122 D2
Volzhskiy Russia 48°56N 44°46E 71 E7
Vorkuta Russia 67°48N 64°20E 70 A11
Voronezh Russia 51°40N 39°10E 70 D6
Vosges France 48°20N 7°10E 66 B7
Vostok I. Kiribati 10°5S 152°23W 103 J12
Votkinsk Russia 57°0N 53°55E 70 C9
Vratsa Bulgaria 43°15N 23°30E 69 C10
Vryburg S. Africa 26°55S 24°45E 97 K4
Vryheid S. Africa 27°45S 30°47E 97 K6
Vung Tau Vietnam 10°21N 107°4E 82 B3
Vyazma Russia 55°10N 34°15E 70 C5
Vyborg Russia 60°43N 28°47E 70 B4
Vychegda → Russia 61°18N 46°36E 70 B8
Vyrnwy, L. U.K. 52°48N 3°31W 28 B6
Vyshniy Volochek Russia 57°30N 34°30E 70 C5

W
Waal → Neths. 51°37N 5°0E 64 C3
Wabasca → Canada 58°22N 115°20W 108 D8
Wabash U.S.A. 40°48N 85°49W 112 E5
Wabash → U.S.A. 37°48N 88°2W 112 G3
Waco U.S.A. 31°33N 97°9W 111 D7
Wad Medani Sudan 14°28N 33°30E 95 F12
Waddesdon U.K. 51°51N 0°55W 31 C7
Waddingham U.K. 53°27N 0°32W 27 F7
Waddington U.K. 53°10N 0°32W 27 F7
Waddington, Mt. Canada 51°23N 125°15W 108 D7
Wadebridge U.K. 50°31N 4°51W 29 F4
Wadhurst U.K. 51°3N 0°20E 31 D9
Wadi Halfa Sudan 21°53N 31°19E 95 D12
Wager B. Canada 65°26N 88°40W 109 C11
Wagga Wagga Australia 35°7S 147°24E 98 H8
Wah Pakistan 33°45N 72°40E 84 C8
Wahiawā U.S.A. 21°30N 158°2W 110 H15
Waigeo Indonesia 0°20S 130°40E 83 E8
Wailuku U.S.A. 20°53N 156°30W 110 H16
Wainfleet All Saints U.K. 53°7N 0°15E 27 F9
Wakayama Japan 34°15N 135°15E 81 F4
Wake I. Pac. Oc. 19°18N 166°36E 102 F8
Wakefield Jamaica 18°26N 77°42W 114 a
Wakefield U.K. 53°41N 1°29W 27 E6
Wakkanai Japan 45°28N 141°35E 81 A7
Walberswick U.K. 52°19N 1°40E 31 B12
Wałbrzych Poland 50°45N 16°18E 64 C9
Walbury Hill U.K. 51°21N 1°28W 30 D6
Waldron U.K. 50°56N 0°13E 31 E9
Wales □ U.K. 52°19N 4°43W 28 C4
Walgett Australia 30°0S 148°5E 98 G8
Walker L. U.S.A. 38°42N 118°43W 110 C3
Walla Walla U.S.A. 46°4N 118°20W 110 A3
Wallaceburg Canada 42°34N 82°23W 112 D6
Wallachia Romania 44°35N 25°0E 65 F13
Wallasey U.K. 53°25N 3°2W 27 F2
Wallingford U.K. 51°35N 1°8W 30 C6
Wallis & Futuna, Is. ☑ Pac. Oc. 13°18S 176°10W 99 C15
Walls U.K. 60°14N 1°33W 22 B14
Wallsend U.K. 54°59N 1°31W 26 C5
Walmer U.K. 51°11N 1°25E 31 D11
Walney, I. of U.K. 54°6N 3°15W 26 D2
Walpole U.K. 52°45N 0°13E 31 A9
Walsall U.K. 52°35N 1°58W 27 G5
Walsenburg U.S.A. 37°38N 104°47W 110 C6
Walsoken U.K. 52°41N 0°11E 31 A9
Waltham Abbey U.K. 51°41N 0°1E 31 C9
Waltham Forest □ U.K. 51°35N 0°0 31 C9
Walton-on-the-Naze U.K. 51°51N 1°17E 31 C11
Walvis Bay Namibia 23°0S 14°28E 97 J2
Wamba Dem. Rep. of the Congo 2°10N 27°57E 96 D5
Wanborough U.K. 51°33N 1°42W 30 C5

Wandsworth □ U.K. 51°27N 0°11W 31 D8
Wanganui N.Z. 39°56G 175°3E 99 H14
Wanleweyne Somalia 2°37N 44°54E 89 G3
Wansbeck → U.K. 55°10N 1°32W 26 B5
Wantage U.K. 51°35N 1°25W 30 C6
Wanxian China 30°42N 108°20E 78 E10
Wanzai China 22°12N 113°31E 79 a
Wapakoneta U.S.A. 40°34N 84°12W 112 E5
Warangal India 17°58N 79°35E 84 L11
Warboys U.K. 52°24N 0°4W 31 B8
Ward Ireland 53°26N 6°20W 21 B10
Wardha India 20°45N 78°39E 84 J11
Wardington U.K. 52°7N 1°17W 30 B6
Wardle U.K. 53°7N 2°35W 27 F3
Ward's Stone U.K. 54°1N 2°36W 27 D3
Ware U.K. 51°49N 0°0 31 C8
Wareham U.K. 50°42N 2°7W 30 E4
Wark U.K. 55°6N 2°14W 26 B4
Warkworth U.K. 55°21N 1°37W 26 B5
Warley U.K. 52°30N 1°59W 27 H5
Warminster U.K. 51°12N 2°10W 30 D4
Warragul Australia 30°24S 145°21E 98 G8
Warren Mich., U.S.A. 42°28N 83°1W 112 D6
Warren Ohio, U.S.A. 41°14N 80°49W 112 E7
Warren Pa., U.S.A. 41°51N 79°9W 112 E8
Warrenpoint U.K. 54°6N 6°15W 19 C9
Warri Nigeria 5°30N 5°41E 94 G7
Warrington U.K. 53°24N 2°35W 27 F3
Warrnambool Australia 38°25S 142°30E 98 H7
Warsaw Poland 52°14N 21°0E 65 B11
Warsaw U.S.A. 41°14N 85°51W 112 E5
Warta → Poland 52°35N 14°39E 64 B8
Warwick Australia 28°10S 152°1E 98 G9
Warwick U.K. 52°18N 1°35W 30 B5
Warwick U.S.A. 41°42N 71°28W 113 E12
Warwickshire □ U.K. 52°14N 1°38W 30 B5
Wasatch Ra. U.S.A. 40°0N 111°30W 110 B4
Wash, The U.K. 52°58N 0°20E 31 A9
Washburn U.S.A. 46°40N 90°54W 112 B2
Washford U.K. 51°9N 3°21W 30 D2
Washington U.K. 54°55N 1°30W 26 C6
Washington D.C., U.S.A. 38°53N 77°2W 112 F9
Washington Ind., U.S.A. 38°40N 87°10W 112 F4
Washington Pa., U.S.A. 40°10N 80°15W 112 E7
Washington □ U.S.A. 47°30N 120°30W 110 A2
Washington, Mt. U.S.A. 44°16N 71°18W 113 C12
Washington I. U.S.A. 45°23N 86°54W 112 C4
Wasilla U.S.A. 61°35N 149°26W 108 C5
Waskaganish Canada 51°30N 78°40W 109 D12
Wast Water U.K. 54°26N 3°18W 26 D2
Watampone Indonesia 4°29S 120°25E 83 E6
Watchet U.K. 51°10N 3°19W 30 D2
Waterbeach U.K. 52°16N 0°12E 31 B9
Waterbury U.S.A. 41°33N 73°3W 113 E11
Waterford Ireland 52°15N 7°8W 21 D8
Waterford □ Ireland 52°10N 7°40W 21 D7
Waterford Harbour Ireland 52°8N 6°58W 21 D9
Watergate B. U.K. 50°26N 5°4W 29 G3
Waterloo Canada 43°30N 80°32W 112 D7
Waterloo Ill., U.S.A. 38°20N 90°9W 112 F2
Waterloo Iowa, U.S.A. 42°30N 92°21W 111 B8
Watersmeet U.S.A. 46°16N 89°11W 112 B3
Watertown N.Y., U.S.A. 43°59N 75°55W 113 D10
Watertown S. Dak., U.S.A. 44°54N 97°7W 111 B7
Watertown Wis., U.S.A. 43°12N 88°43W 112 D3
Watford U.K. 51°40N 0°24W 31 C8
Watlington Norfolk, U.K. 52°40N 0°24E 31 A9
Watlington Oxon., U.K. 51°38N 1°0W 30 C6
Watrous Canada 51°40N 105°25W 108 D9
Watsa Dem. Rep. of the Congo 3°4N 29°30E 96 D5
Watseka U.S.A. 40°47N 87°44W 112 E4
Watson Lake Canada 60°6N 128°49W 108 C7
Watton U.K. 52°34N 0°51E 31 A10
Wau South Sudan 7°45N 28°1E 95 G11
Waukegan U.S.A. 42°22N 87°50W 112 D4
Waukesha U.S.A. 43°1N 88°14W 112 D3
Waupaca U.S.A. 44°21N 89°5W 112 C3
Waupun U.S.A. 43°38N 88°44W 112 D3
Wausau U.S.A. 44°58N 89°38W 112 C3
Wautoma U.S.A. 44°4N 89°18W 112 C3
Wauwatosa U.S.A. 43°2N 88°0W 112 D4
Waveney → U.K. 52°35N 1°39E 31 A12
Waver → U.K. 54°50N 3°15W 26 C2
Wawa Canada 47°59N 84°47W 112 B5
Waycross U.S.A. 31°13N 82°21W 111 D10
Wayne U.S.A. 38°13N 82°27W 112 F6
Waynesboro U.S.A. 38°4N 78°53W 112 F8
Waynesburg U.S.A. 39°54N 80°11W 112 F7
Wazirabad Pakistan 32°30N 74°8E 84 C9
Weald, The U.K. 51°4N 0°20E 31 D9
Wear → U.K. 54°55N 1°23W 26 C6
Weardale U.K. 54°44N 2°5W 26 C4
Wearhead U.K. 54°45N 2°13W 26 C4
Weaver → U.K. 53°17N 2°35W 27 F3
Weaverham U.K. 53°16N 2°35W 27 F3
Webster Springs U.S.A. 38°29N 80°25W 112 F7
Weddell Sea Antarctica 72°30S 40°0W 55 D1
Wedmore U.K. 51°13N 2°48W 30 D3
Wednesbury U.K. 52°34N 2°1W 27 G4
Wednesfield U.K. 52°37N 2°2W 27 G4
Weedon Bec U.K. 52°15N 1°5W 30 B6
Weifang China 36°44N 119°7E 79 D12
Weihai China 37°30N 122°6E 79 D13
Weipa Australia 12°40S 141°50E 98 C7
Welch U.S.A. 37°26N 81°35W 112 G7
Weldon U.S.A. 55°17N 1°45W 26 B5
Welford Northants., U.K. 52°25N 1°3W 30 B6
Welford W. Berkshire, U.K. 51°23N 1°24W 30 C5
Welkom S. Africa 28°0S 26°46E 97 K5
Welland Canada 43°0N 79°15W 112 D8
Welland → U.K. 52°51N 0°5W 27 G7
Wellesley Is. Australia 16°42S 139°30E 98 D6
Wellingborough U.K. 52°19N 0°41W 31 B7
Wellington N.Z. 41°19S 174°46E 99 J13
Wellington Somst., U.K. 50°58N 3°13W 30 E2
Wellington Telford & Wrekin, U.K. 52°42N 2°30W 27 G3
Wellington, I. Chile 49°30S 75°0W 121 G2
Wellington Chan. Canada 75°0N 93°0W 109 B10
Wells U.K. 51°13N 2°39W 30 D3
Wells-next-the-Sea U.K. 52°57N 0°51E 31 A10

Wellsboro U.S.A. 41°46N 77°10W 112 E9
Wellsville U.S.A. 42°7N 77°57W 112 D9
Welney U.K. 52°31N 0°15E 31 A9
Wels Austria 48°9N 14°1E 64 D8
Welshpool U.K. 52°39N 3°8W 28 B7
Welton U.K. 53°18N 0°29W 27 F7
Welwyn Garden City U.K. 51°48N 0°12W 31 C8
Wem U.K. 52°52N 2°44W 27 G3
Wembury U.K. 50°19N 4°6W 29 G5
Wemindji Canada 53°0N 78°49W 109 D12
Wemyss Bay U.K. 55°52N 4°53W 24 CC
Wenatchee U.S.A. 47°25N 120°19W 110 A2
Wendover U.K. 51°45N 0°44W 31 C7
Wenlock Edge U.K. 52°30N 2°43W 27 H3
Wensleydale U.K. 54°17N 2°0W 26 D4
Wensu China 41°15N 80°10E 78 C5
Wensum → U.K. 52°40N 1°15E 31 A11
Wenzhou China 28°0N 120°38E 79 F13
Weobley U.K. 52°11N 2°50W 30 B3
Werrington U.K. 50°39N 4°23W 29 F5
Weser → Germany 53°36N 8°28E 64 B5
West Antarctica Antarctica 80°0S 90°0W 55 D15
West Auckland U.K. 54°38N 1°43W 26 C5
West Bank ■ Asia 32°6N 35°13E 86 C3
West Bend U.S.A. 43°25N 88°11W 112 D3
West Bengal = Paschimbanga □ India 23°0N 88°0E 85 H16
West Berkshire □ U.K. 51°25N 1°17W 30 D6
West Beskids Europe 49°30N 19°0E 65 D10
West Bridgford U.K. 52°55N 1°8W 27 G6
West Bromwich U.K. 52°32N 1°59W 27 G5
West Burra U.K. 60°5N 1°21W 22 B15
West Calder U.K. 55°51N 3°33W 25 C8
West Coker U.K. 50°55N 2°40W 30 E3
West Falkland Falk. Is. 51°40S 60°0W 121 H3
West Fen U.K. 53°5N 0°5W 27 F8
West Frankfort U.S.A. 37°54N 88°55W 111 C9
West Grinstead U.K. 50°58N 0°19W 31 E8
West Haddon U.K. 52°20N 1°3W 30 B6
West Kirby U.K. 53°23N 3°11W 27 F2
West Linton U.K. 55°46N 3°21W 25 C9
West Lulworth U.K. 50°37N 2°14W 30 E4
West Malling U.K. 51°17N 0°26E 31 D9
West Meon U.K. 61°1N 1°5W 30 D6
West Mersea U.K. 51°46N 0°56E 31 C10
West Midlands □ U.K. 52°26N 2°0W 27 H5
West Moors U.K. 50°49N 1°53W 30 E5
West Palm Beach U.S.A. 26°43N 80°3W 111 E10
West Point U.S.A. 37°32N 76°48W 112 G9
West Rasen U.K. 53°23N 0°24W 27 F8
West Seneca U.S.A. 42°51N 78°48W 112 D8
West Siberian Plain Russia 62°0N 75°0E 72 B9
West Sussex □ U.K. 50°55N 0°30W 31 E7
West Virginia □ U.S.A. 38°45N 80°30W 112 F7
West Yorkshire □ U.K. 53°45N 1°40W 27 E5
Westbourne U.K. 50°52N 0°55W 31 E7
Westbrook U.S.A. 43°41N 70°22W 113 D12
Westbury Shrops., U.K. 52°41N 2°55W 27 G3
Westbury Wilts., U.K. 51°15N 2°11W 30 D4
Westbury-on-Severn U.K. 51°50N 2°25W 30 C4
Wester Ross U.K. 57°37N 4°51W 22 G6
Westerham U.K. 51°16N 0°5E 31 D9
Western Australia □ Australia 25°0S 118°0E 98 F2
Western Ghats India 14°0N 75°0E 84 N9
Western Isles = Eilean Siar □ U.K. 57°30N 7°10W 22 G3
Western Sahara ■ Africa 25°0N 13°0W 94 D3
Westerwald Germany 50°38N 7°56E 64 C4
Westfield U.K. 50°55N 0°35E 31 E10
Westhill U.K. 57°9N 2°19W 23 H13
Westhoughton U.K. 53°33N 2°31W 27 E3
Westmeath □ Ireland 53°33N 7°34W 18 D6
Westminster U.K. 39°34N 76°59W 112 F9
Westmoreland Barbados 13°13N 59°37W 114 c
Weston U.S.A. 52°51N 2°1W 27 G4
Weston U.S.A. 39°2N 80°28W 112 F7
Weston-super-Mare U.K. 51°21N 2°58W 30 D3
Westport Ireland 53°48N 9°31W 18 D2
Westray U.K. 59°18N 3°0W 23 D11
Westruther U.K. 55°45N 2°35W 25 C10
Westward Ho! U.K. 51°2N 4°15W 29 E5
Wetar Indonesia 7°48S 126°30E 83 F7
Wetaskiwin Canada 52°55N 113°24W 108 D8
Wetherby U.K. 53°56N 1°23W 27 E6
Wetwang U.K. 54°1N 0°35W 27 D7
Wewak Papua N. G. 3°38S 143°41E 98 A7
Wexford Ireland 52°20N 6°28W 21 D10
Wexford □ Ireland 52°20N 6°25W 21 D10
Wexford Harbour Ireland 52°20N 6°25W 21 D10
Wey → U.K. 51°22N 0°27W 31 D8
Weybourne U.K. 52°57N 1°9E 31 A11
Weybridge U.K. 51°22N 0°27W 31 D8
Weymm Canada 49°40N 103°50W 108 E9
Weymouth U.K. 50°37N 2°28W 30 E4
Wha Ti Canada 63°8N 117°16W 108 C8
Whale Cove Canada 62°10N 92°34W 108 C10
Whales, B. of Antarctica 78°0S 160°0W 55 D12
Whalley U.K. 53°49N 2°24W 27 E4
Whalsay U.K. 60°22N 0°59W 22 B16
Whalton U.K. 55°8N 1°46W 26 B5
Whangarei N.Z. 35°43S 174°21E 99 H13
Whaplode U.K. 52°42N 0°3W 27 G8
Wharfe → U.K. 53°51N 1°9W 27 E6
Wharfedale U.K. 54°6N 2°1W 26 D4
Wheatley Hill U.K. 54°45N 1°23W 26 C6
Wheeler Pk. U.S.A. 38°57N 114°15W 110 C4
Wheeling U.S.A. 40°4N 80°43W 112 E7
Whernside U.K. 54°14N 2°24W 26 D4
Whicham U.K. 54°15N 3°21W 26 D2
Whimple U.K. 50°46N 3°20W 29 F7
Whipsnade U.K. 52°43N 0°6W 27 G8
Whitburn U.K. 55°52N 3°40W 25 C8
Whitby U.K. 54°29N 0°37W 26 D7
Whitchurch Devon, U.K. 50°32N 4°9W 29 F5
Whitchurch Hants., U.K. 51°14N 1°20W 30 D6
Whitchurch Shrops., U.K. 52°59N 2°40W 27 G3
White → Ark., U.S.A. 33°57N 91°5W 111 D8
White → Ind., U.S.A. 38°25N 87°45W 112 F4
White → Utah, U.S.A. 40°4N 109°41W 110 B5

White Esk → U.K. 55°13N 3°11W 25 D9
White Horse, Vale of U.K. 51°37N 1°30W 30 C5
White Horse Hill U.K. 51°34N 1°33W 30 C5
White Mts. Calif., U.S.A. 37°30N 118°15W 110 C3
White Mts. N.H., U.S.A. 44°15N 71°15W 111 B12
White Nile → Sudan 15°38N 32°31E 95 E12
White Sea Russia 66°30N 38°0E 70 A6
Whiteadder Water → U.K. 55°51N 2°25W 25 C11
Whitecourt Canada 54°10N 115°45W 108 D8
Whitefish Pt. U.S.A. 46°45N 84°59W 112 B5
Whitehall U.S.A. 44°22N 91°19W 112 C2
Whitehaven U.K. 54°33N 3°35W 26 C1
Whitehorse Canada 60°43N 135°3W 108 C6
Whitesand B. U.K. 50°21N 4°18W 29 G5
Whitewater U.S.A. 42°50N 88°44W 112 D3
Whithorn U.K. 54°44N 4°26W 24 E7
Whitley Bay U.K. 55°3N 1°27W 26 B6
Whitstable U.K. 51°21N 1°3E 31 D11
Whittington Derby., U.K. 53°16N 1°26W 27 F6
Whittington Shrops., U.K. 52°52N 3°0W 27 E2
Whittlesey U.K. 52°33N 0°8W 31 A8
Whittlesford U.K. 52°7N 0°9E 31 B9
Whitwell Derby., U.K. 53°17N 1°12W 27 F6
Whitwell I. of W., U.K. 50°36N 1°15W 30 E6
Whitwick U.K. 52°45N 1°22W 27 G6
Whitworth U.K. 53°39N 2°11W 27 E4
Wholdaia L. Canada 60°43N 104°20W 108 C9
Whyalla Australia 33°2S 137°30E 98 G6
Wiarton Canada 44°40N 81°10W 112 C7
Wiay U.K. 57°24N 7°13W 22 H3
Wichita U.S.A. 37°42N 97°20W 111 C7
Wichita Falls U.S.A. 33°54N 98°30W 110 D7
Wick U.K. 58°26N 3°5W 23 F11
Wickford U.K. 51°36N 0°33E 31 C10
Wickham U.K. 50°54N 1°11W 30 E6
Wickham Market U.K. 52°9N 1°23E 31 B11
Wicklow Ireland 52°59N 6°3W 21 C10
Wicklow □ Ireland 52°57N 6°25W 21 C10
Wicklow Hd. Ireland 52°58N 6°0W 21 C11
Wicklow Mts. △ Ireland 53°6N 6°21W 21 B11
Wickwar U.K. 51°36N 2°23W 30 C4
Widdrington U.K. 55°15N 1°35W 26 B5
Widecombe U.K. 50°34N 3°49W 29 F6
Widemouth U.K. 50°47N 4°34W 29 F4
Widnes U.K. 53°23N 2°45W 27 F3
Wiener Neustadt Austria 47°49N 16°16E 64 E9
Wiesbaden Germany 50°4N 8°14E 64 C5
Wigan U.K. 53°33N 2°38W 27 E3
Wight, Isle of □ U.K. 50°41N 1°17W 30 E6
Wigmore U.K. 52°19N 2°51W 30 B3
Wigston U.K. 52°35N 1°6W 27 G6
Wigton U.K. 54°50N 3°10W 26 C2
Wigtown U.K. 54°53N 4°27W 24 E7
Wigtown B. U.K. 54°46N 4°15W 24 E7
Wilhelm, Mt. Papua N. G. 5°50S 145°1E 98 B8
Wilhelmshaven Germany 53°31N 8°7E 64 B5
Wilkes-Barre U.S.A. 41°15N 75°53W 113 E10
Wilkes Land Antarctica 69°0S 120°0E 55 D9
Wilkins Ice Shelf Antarctica 70°30S 72°0W 55 D17
Willemstad Curaçao 12°5N 68°55W 115 E11
Willenhall U.K. 52°36N 2°2W 27 G4
Willesborough U.K. 51°8N 0°56E 31 D10
Williams Lake Canada 52°10N 122°10W 108 D7
Williamsburg U.S.A. 37°16N 76°43W 112 G9
Williamson U.S.A. 37°41N 82°17W 112 G6
Williamsport U.S.A. 41°15N 77°1W 112 E9
Willingdon U.K. 50°47N 0°17E 31 E9
Williston U.S.A. 48°9N 103°37W 110 A6
Williston L. Canada 56°0N 124°0W 108 D7
Williton U.K. 51°9N 3°19W 30 D2
Willmar U.S.A. 45°7N 95°3W 111 A7
Willoughby U.K. 53°13N 0°12E 27 F9
Wilmington U.K. 50°47N 3°7W 29 F7
Wilmington Del., U.S.A. 39°45N 75°33W 113 F10
Wilmington N.C., U.S.A. 34°14N 77°55W 111 D11
Wilmslow U.K. 53°19N 2°13W 27 F4
Wilnecote U.K. 52°36N 1°39W 27 G5
Wilton U.K. 51°5N 1°51W 30 D5
Wiltshire □ U.K. 51°18N 1°53W 30 D5
Wimblington U.K. 52°31N 0°4E 31 A9
Wimborne Minster U.K. 50°48N 1°59W 30 E5
Wincanton U.K. 51°3N 2°24W 30 D4
Winchelsea U.K. 50°55N 0°43E 31 E10
Winchester U.K. 51°4N 1°18W 30 D6
Winchester Ky., U.S.A. 37°59N 84°11W 112 G6
Winchester Va., U.S.A. 39°11N 78°10W 112 F8
Wind → U.S.A. 43°12N 108°12W 110 B5
Wind River Range U.S.A. 43°0N 109°30W 110 B5
Windermere U.K. 54°23N 2°55W 26 C3
Windhoek Namibia 22°35S 17°4E 97 J3
Windrush → U.K. 51°43N 1°24W 30 C6
Windsor Canada 42°18N 83°0W 109 E11
Windsor U.K. 51°29N 0°36W 31 D7
Windward Is. W. Indies 13°0N 61°0W 115 E12
Windward Passage Caribbean 20°0N 74°0W 115 D10
Wing U.K. 51°53N 0°43W 31 C7
Wingham U.K. 51°16N 1°13E 31 D11
Winisk → Canada 55°17N 85°5W 109 D11
Winkleigh U.K. 50°50N 3°58W 29 F6

Winkler Canada 49°10N 97°56W 108 E10
Winneba Ghana 5°25N 0°36W 94 G5
Winnebago, L. U.S.A. 44°0N 88°26W 112 D3
Winnemucca U.S.A. 40°58N 117°44W 110 B3
Winnipeg Canada 49°54N 97°9W 108 E10
Winnipeg, L. Canada 52°0N 97°0W 108 D10
Winnipegosis L. Canada 52°30N 100°0W 108 C9
Winona U.S.A. 44°3N 91°39W 111 B8
Winooski U.S.A. 44°29N 73°11W 113 C11
Winsford U.K. 53°12N 2°31W 27 F3
Winslow U.K. 51°57N 0°52W 31 C7
Winslow U.S.A. 35°2N 110°42W 110 C4
Winster U.K. 53°9N 1°39W 27 F5
Winston-Salem U.S.A. 36°6N 80°15W 111 C10
Winterborne Abbas U.K. 50°42N 2°33W 30 E3
Winterthur Switz. 47°30N 8°44E 64 E5
Winterton N. Lincs., U.K. 53°39N 0°37W 27 E7
Winterton Norfolk, U.K. 52°43N 1°41E 31 A12
Winton Australia 22°24S 143°3E 98 E7
Wirksworth U.K. 53°6N 1°35W 27 F5
Wirral U.K. 53°25N 3°0W 27 F2
Wisbech U.K. 52°41N 0°9E 31 A9
Wisborough Green U.K. 51°2N 0°30W 31 D7
Wisconsin □ U.S.A. 44°45N 89°30W 111 B9
Wisconsin Rapids U.S.A. 44°23N 89°49W 112 C3
Wishaw U.K. 55°46N 3°54W 25 C8
Wiske → U.K. 54°19N 1°27W 26 D6
Witham U.K. 51°48N 0°40E 31 C10
Witham → U.K. 52°59N 0°2W 27 G8
Withern U.K. 53°18N 0°8E 27 F9
Withernsea U.K. 53°44N 0°1E 27 E9
Witley U.K. 51°9N 0°39W 31 D7
Witney U.K. 51°48N 1°28W 30 C6
Wittersham U.K. 51°0N 0°43E 31 D10
Wiveliscombe U.K. 51°2N 3°19W 30 D2
Wivenhoe U.K. 51°51N 0°59E 31 C10
Wkra → Poland 52°27N 20°44E 65 B11
Włocławek Poland 52°40N 19°3E 65 B10
Woburn U.K. 51°59N 0°36W 31 C7
Woburn Sands U.K. 52°1N 0°39W 31 B7
Wodonga Australia 36°5S 146°50E 98 H8
Woking U.K. 51°19N 0°34W 31 D7
Wokingham U.K. 51°24N 0°49W 31 D7
Wolf Rock U.K. 49°57N 5°49W 29 H2
Wolfsburg Germany 52°25N 10°48E 64 B6
Wolin Poland 53°50N 14°37E 64 B8
Wollaston L. Canada 58°7N 103°10W 108 D9
Wollaston Pen. Canada 69°30N 115°0W 108 C8
Wollongong Australia 34°25S 150°54E 98 G9
Wolsingham U.K. 54°44N 1°52W 26 C5
Wolverhampton U.K. 52°35N 2°7W 27 G4
Wolverton U.K. 52°3N 0°47W 31 B7
Wolviston U.K. 54°38N 1°18W 26 C6
Wombwell U.K. 53°32N 1°25W 27 E6
Wŏnsan N. Korea 39°11N 127°27E 79 D14
Wonston U.K. 51°8N 1°18W 30 D6
Woodbridge U.K. 52°6N 1°20E 31 B11
Woodbury U.K. 50°41N 3°24W 29 F7
Woodhall Spa U.K. 53°10N 0°12W 27 F8
Woodhouse U.K. 53°22N 1°21W 27 F6
Woodley U.K. 51°27N 0°53W 31 D7
Woodroffe, Mt. Australia 26°20S 131°45E 98 F5
Woods, L. of the N. Amer. 49°15N 94°45W 108 E10
Woodstock N.B., Canada 46°11N 67°37W 109 E13
Woodstock Ont., Canada 43°10N 80°45W 112 D7
Woodstock U.K. 51°51N 1°20W 30 C6
Woodstock U.S.A. 42°19N 88°27W 112 D3
Wookey U.K. 51°13N 2°41W 30 D3
Wookey Hole U.K. 51°14N 2°40W 30 D3
Wool U.K. 50°40N 2°12W 30 E4
Woolacombe U.K. 51°10N 4°13W 29 E5
Wooler U.K. 55°33N 2°1W 26 A4
Woonsocket U.S.A. 42°0N 71°31W 113 E11
Wootton Wawen U.K. 52°16N 1°47W 30 B5
Worcester S. Africa 33°39S 19°27E 97 L3
Worcester U.K. 52°11N 2°12W 30 B4
Worcester U.S.A. 42°16N 71°48W 113 D12
Worcestershire □ U.K. 52°13N 2°10W 30 B4
Worfield U.K. 52°34N 2°21W 27 G4
Workington U.K. 54°39N 3°33W 26 C1
Worksop U.K. 53°18N 1°7W 27 F6
Worms Germany 49°37N 8°21E 64 D5
Wortham U.K. 52°21N 1°3E 31 B11
Worthing Barbados 13°5N 59°35W 114 c
Worthing U.K. 50°49N 0°21W 31 E7
Worthington U.S.A. 43°37N 95°36W 111 B7
Wotton under Edge U.K. 51°37N 2°20W 30 C4
Wragby U.K. 53°18N 0°17W 27 F8
Wrangel I. Russia 71°0N 180°0E 77 B19
Wrangell U.S.A. 56°28N 132°23W 108 D6
Wrangell Mts. U.S.A. 61°30N 142°0W 108 C5
Wrangle U.K. 53°3N 0°7E 27 F9
Wrath, C. U.K. 58°38N 5°1W 22 E7
Wrekin, The U.K. 52°41N 2°32W 27 G3
Wrentham U.K. 52°23N 1°40E 31 B12
Wrexham U.K. 53°3N 3°0W 28 A8
Wrexham □ U.K. 53°1N 2°58W 28 D3
Wrigley Canada 63°16N 123°37W 108 C7
Writtle U.K. 51°44N 0°25E 31 C9
Wrocław Poland 51°5N 17°5E 65 C9

Wroughton U.K. 51°31N 1°47W 30 C5
Wroxham U.K. 52°42N 1°24E 31 A11
Wu Jiang → China 29°40N 107°20E 78 F10
Wuhai China 39°39N 106°48E 78 D10
Wuhan China 30°31N 114°18E 79 E11
Wuhu China 31°22N 118°21E 79 E12
Wutongqiao China 29°22N 103°50E 78 F9
Wuwei China 37°57N 102°34E 78 D9
Wuxi China 31°33N 120°18E 79 E13
Wuyi Shan China 27°0N 117°0E 79 F12
Wuzhong China 38°2N 106°12E 78 D10
Wuzhou China 23°30N 111°18E 79 G11
Wye U.K. 51°10N 0°57E 31 D10
Wye → U.K. 51°38N 2°40W 30 C3
Wylye → U.K. 51°5N 1°51W 30 D5
Wymondham Leics., U.K. 52°45N 0°43W 27 G7
Wymondham Norfolk, U.K. 52°35N 1°7E 31 A11
Wyndham Australia 15°33S 128°3E 98 D4
Wyoming □ U.S.A. 43°0N 107°30W 110 B5
Wyre → U.K. 53°52N 2°57W 27 E3
Wyre Forest U.K. 52°24N 2°24W 27 H4

X

Xaçmaz Azerbaijan 41°31N 48°42E 71 F8
Xai-Xai Mozam. 25°6S 33°31E 97 J6
Xalapa Mexico 19°32N 96°55W 114 D5
Xankändi Azerbaijan 39°52N 46°49E 71 G8
Xenia U.S.A. 39°41N 83°56W 112 F6
Xi Jiang → China 22°5N 113°20E 79 G11
Xiaguan China 25°32N 100°16E 78 F9
Xiamen China 24°25N 118°4E 79 G12
Xi'an China 34°15N 109°0E 79 E10
Xiang Jiang → China 28°55N 112°50E 79 F11
Xiangfan China 32°2N 112°8E 79 E11
Xianggang = Hong Kong □ China 22°11N 114°14E 79 a
Xiangtan China 27°51N 112°54E 79 F11
Xiantao China 30°25N 113°25E 79 E11
Xianyang China 34°20N 108°40E 78 E10
Xichang China 27°51N 102°19E 78 F9
Xigazê China 29°5N 88°45E 78 F6
Xilinhot China 43°52N 116°2E 79 C12
Ximiao China 40°59N 100°12E 78 C9
Xinghua China 32°58N 119°48E 79 E12
Xingu → Brazil 1°30S 51°53W 120 C4
Xingyi China 25°3N 104°59E 78 F9
Xining China 36°34N 101°40E 78 D9
Xinwen China 22°47N 113°40E 79 a
Xinxiang China 35°18N 113°50E 79 D11
Xinyang China 32°6N 114°3E 79 E11
Xinyi China 34°23N 118°21E 79 E12
Xique-Xique Brazil 10°50S 42°40W 122 B2
Xixiang China 22°34N 113°52E 79 a
Xizang Zizhiqu □ China 32°0N 88°0E 78 E6
Xuanhua China 40°40N 115°2E 79 C12
Xuwen China 20°20N 110°10E 79 G11
Xuzhou China 34°18N 117°10E 79 E12

Y

Y Drenewydd = Newtown U.K. 52°31N 3°19W 28 B7
Y Fenni = Abergavenny U.K. 51°49N 3°1W 28 D7
Y Gelli Gandryll = Hay-on-Wye U.K. 52°5N 3°8W 28 C7
Y Trallwng = Welshpool U.K. 52°39N 3°8W 28 C7
Ya'an China 29°58N 103°5E 78 F9
Yablonovyy Ra. Russia 53°0N 114°0E 77 D12
Yacuiba Bolivia 22°0S 63°43W 120 E3
Yakeshi China 49°17N 120°44E 79 B13
Yakima U.S.A. 46°36N 120°31W 110 A2
Yakutat U.S.A. 59°33N 139°44W 108 D6
Yakutsk Russia 62°5N 129°50E 77 C13
Yala Thailand 6°33N 101°18E 82 C2
Yalong Jiang → China 26°40N 101°55E 78 F9
Yalta Ukraine 44°30N 34°10E 71 F5
Yalu Jiang → China 39°55N 124°19E 79 D13
Yamagata Japan 38°15N 140°15E 81 D7
Yamaguchi Japan 34°10N 131°32E 81 F2
Yamal Pen. Russia 71°0N 70°0E 76 B7
Yambol Bulgaria 42°30N 26°30E 69 C12
Yamethin Burma 20°29N 96°18E 85 J20
Yamoussoukro Ivory C. 6°49N 5°17W 94 G4
Yampa → U.S.A. 40°32N 108°59W 110 B5
Yamuna → India 25°30N 81°53E 85 G12
Yamzho Yumco China 28°48N 90°35E 78 F7
Yan'an China 36°35N 109°26E 78 D10
Yanbu 'al Bahr Si. Arabia 24°5N 38°5E 86 E4
Yancheng China 33°23N 120°8E 79 E13
Yangambi Dem. Rep. of the Congo 0°47N 24°24E 96 D4
Yangjiang China 21°50N 111°59E 79 G11
Yangquan China 37°58N 113°31E 79 D11
Yangtse → China 31°48N 121°10E 79 E13

Yangzhou China 32°21N 119°26E 79 E12
Yanji China 42°59N 129°30E 79 C14
Yankton U.S.A. 42°53N 97°23W 111 B7
Yanqi China 42°5N 86°35E 78 C6
Yantai China 37°34N 121°22E 79 D13
Yantian China 22°35N 114°16E 79 a
Yaoundé Cameroon 3°50N 11°35E 96 D2
Yap Pac. Oc. 9°30N 138°10E 102 G5
Yapen Indonesia 1°50S 136°0E 83 E9
Yaqui → Mexico 27°37N 110°39W 114 B2
Yaraka Australia 24°53S 144°3E 98 E7
Yarcombe U.K. 50°51N 3°5W 29 F7
Yare → U.K. 52°35N 1°38E 31 A12
Yaren Nauru 0°33S 166°55E 102 H8
Yarkant He → China 40°26N 80°59E 78 C5
Yarkhun → Pakistan 36°17N 72°30E 84 A8
Yarm U.K. 54°31N 1°21W 26 C6
Yarmouth Canada 43°50N 66°7W 109 E13
Yarmouth U.K. 50°42N 1°29W 30 E6
Yaroslavl Russia 57°35N 39°55E 70 C6
Yarrow U.K. 55°33N 3°1W 25 C9
Yarumal Colombia 6°58N 75°24W 120 B2
Yāsūj Iran 30°31N 51°31E 87 D7
Yate U.K. 51°32N 2°25W 30 C4
Yathkyed L. Canada 62°40N 98°0W 108 C10
Yatsushiro Japan 32°30N 130°40E 81 G2
Yatton U.K. 51°23N 2°49W 30 D3
Yavari → Peru 4°21S 70°2W 120 C2
Yaxley U.K. 52°31N 0°16W 31 A8
Yazd Iran 31°55N 54°27E 87 D8
Yazoo → U.S.A. 32°22N 90°54W 111 D8
Yazoo City U.S.A. 32°51N 90°25W 111 D8
Yealmpton U.K. 50°21N 4°1W 29 G5
Yecheng China 37°54N 77°26E 78 D4
Yelets Russia 52°40N 38°30E 70 D6
Yell U.K. 60°35N 1°5W 22 A15
Yell Sd. U.K. 60°33N 1°15W 22 A15
Yellow = Huang He → China 37°55N 118°50E 79 D12
Yellow Sea China 35°0N 123°0E 79 D13
Yellowhead Pass Canada 52°53N 118°25W 108 D8
Yellowknife Canada 62°27N 114°29W 108 C8
Yellowstone → U.S.A. 47°59N 103°59W 110 A6
Yellowstone Nat. Park △ U.S.A. 44°40N 110°30W 110 B5
Yemen ■ Asia 15°0N 44°0E 89 E3
Yenisey → Russia 71°50N 82°40E 76 B9
Yeo → U.K. 51°24N 2°54W 30 D3
Yeola India 20°2N 74°30E 84 J9
Yeovil U.K. 50°57N 2°38W 30 E3
Yerevan Armenia 40°10N 44°31E 71 F7
Yes Tor U.K. 50°41N 4°0W 29 F5
Yeu, Î. d' France 46°42N 2°20W 66 C2
Yevpatoriya Ukraine 45°15N 33°20E 71 E5
Yeysk Russia 46°40N 38°12E 71 E6
Yibin China 28°45N 104°32E 78 F9
Yichang China 30°40N 111°20E 79 E11
Yichun China 47°44N 128°52E 79 B14
Yilehuli Shan China 51°20N 124°20E 79 A13
Yinchuan China 38°30N 106°15E 78 D10
Yingkou China 40°37N 122°18E 79 C13
Yining China 43°58N 81°10E 78 C5
Yixing China 31°21N 119°48E 79 E12
Yiyang China 28°35N 112°18E 79 F11
Yogyakarta Indonesia 7°49S 110°22E 82 F4
Yokkaichi Japan 34°55N 136°38E 81 F5
Yokohama Japan 35°27N 139°28E 81 F6
Yokosuka Japan 35°20N 139°40E 81 F6
Yonago Japan 35°25N 133°19E 81 F3
Yong'an China 25°59N 117°25E 79 F12
Yongzhou China 26°17N 111°37E 79 F11
Yonkers U.S.A. 40°56N 73°52W 113 E11
Yonne → France 48°23N 2°58E 66 B5
York U.K. 53°58N 1°6W 27 E6
York U.S.A. 39°58N 76°44W 112 F9
York, C. Australia 10°42S 142°31E 98 C7
York, Vale of U.K. 54°15N 1°25W 26 D6
Yorkshire Dales △ U.K. 54°12N 2°10W 26 D4
Yorkshire Wolds U.K. 54°8N 0°31W 26 D7
Yorkton Canada 51°11N 102°28W 108 D9
Yosemite Nat. Park △ U.S.A. 37°45N 119°40W 110 C3
Yoshkar Ola Russia 56°38N 47°55E 70 C8
Youghal Ireland 51°56N 7°52W 20 E7
Youghal B. Ireland 51°55N 7°49W 20 E7
Youlgreave U.K. 53°11N 1°40W 27 F6
Youngstown U.S.A. 41°6N 80°39W 112 E7
Yoxall U.K. 52°46N 1°47W 27 G5
Yoxford U.K. 52°16N 1°31E 31 B12
Yozgat Turkey 39°51N 34°47E 71 G5
Yr Wyddgrug = Mold U.K. 53°9N 3°8W 28 A7
Yreka U.S.A. 41°44N 122°38W 110 B2
Ystalyfera U.K. 51°46N 3°48W 28 D6
Ythan → U.K. 57°19N 1°59W 23 H14
Yu Jiang → China 23°22N 110°3E 79 G11
Yuan Jiang → China 28°55N 111°50E 79 F11
Yuanping China 38°42N 112°46E 79 D11
Yuba City U.S.A. 39°8N 121°37W 110 C2
Yucatán Mexico 19°30N 89°0W 114 D7
Yucatan Channel Caribbean 22°0N 86°30W 114 C7

Yuen Long China 22°26N 114°2E 79 a
Yueyang China 29°21N 113°5E 79 F11
Yukon → U.S.A. 62°32N 163°54W 108 C3
Yukon Territory □ Canada 63°0N 135°0W 108 C6
Yulin China 38°20N 109°30E 79 D10
Yuma U.S.A. 32°43N 114°37W 110 D4
Yumen China 39°50N 97°30E 78 D8
Yungas Bolivia 17°0S 66°0W 120 D3
Yunling Shan China 28°30N 98°50E 78 F8
Yunnan □ China 25°0N 102°0E 78 G9
Yurimaguas Peru 5°55S 76°7W 120 C2
Yushu China 33°5N 96°55E 78 E8
Yutian China 36°52N 81°42E 78 D5
Yuxi China 24°30N 102°35E 78 G9
Yuzhno-Sakhalinsk Russia 46°58N 142°45E 77 E15
Yuzhou China 34°10N 113°28E 79 E11
Yvetot France 49°37N 0°44E 66 B4

Z

Zāb al Kabīr → Iraq 36°1N 43°24E 86 B5
Zābol Iran 32°0N 67°0E 87 D10
Zabrze Poland 50°18N 18°50E 65 C10
Zacatecas Mexico 22°47N 102°35W 114 C4
Zadar Croatia 44°8N 15°14E 68 B6
Zagaoua Chad 15°30N 22°24E 95 E10
Zagazig Egypt 30°40N 31°30E 95 B12
Zagreb Croatia 45°50N 15°58E 68 B7
Zagros Mts. Iran 33°45N 48°5E 86 C7
Zāhedān Iran 29°30N 60°50E 87 D10
Zahlah Lebanon 33°52N 35°50E 86 C3
Zakynthos Greece 37°47N 20°54E 69 F9
Zalantun China 48°0N 122°43E 79 B13
Zambezi → Africa 18°35S 36°20E 97 H7
Zambia ■ Africa 15°0S 28°0E 97 G5
Zamboanga Phil. 6°59N 122°3E 83 C6
Zamora Mexico 19°59N 102°16W 114 D4
Zamora Spain 41°30N 5°45W 67 B3
Zamość Poland 50°43N 23°15E 65 C12
Zanda China 31°32N 79°50E 78 E4
Zanesville U.S.A. 39°56N 82°1W 112 F6
Zanjan Iran 36°40N 48°35E 86 B7
Zanzibar Tanzania 6°12S 39°12E 96 F7
Zaouiet Reggâne Algeria 26°32N 0°3E 94 C6
Zaoyang China 32°10N 112°45E 79 E11
Zaozhuang China 34°50N 117°35E 79 E12
Zapala Argentina 39°0S 70°5W 121 F2
Zaporozhye Ukraine 47°50N 35°10E 71 E6
Zaragoza Spain 41°39N 0°53W 67 B5
Zaranj Afghan. 30°55N 61°55E 87 D10
Zárate Argentina 34°7S 59°0W 121 F4
Zaria Nigeria 11°0N 7°40E 94 F7
Zarzis Tunisia 33°31N 11°2E 95 B8
Zaskar Mts. India 33°15N 77°30E 84 C10
Zaysan, L. Kazakhstan 48°0N 83°0E 76 E9
Zeebrugge Belgium 51°19N 3°12E 64 C2
Zeil, Mt. Australia 23°30S 132°23E 98 E5
Zelenograd Russia 56°1N 37°12E 70 C6
Zenica Bos.-H. 44°10N 17°57E 69 B7
Zhangjiabian China 22°33N 113°28E 79 a
Zhangjiakou China 40°48N 114°55E 79 C11
Zhangye China 38°50N 100°23E 78 D9
Zhangzhou China 24°30N 117°35E 79 G12
Zhanjiang China 21°15N 110°20E 79 G11
Zhaoqing China 23°0N 112°20E 79 G11
Zhaotong China 27°20N 103°44E 78 F9
Zhejiang □ China 29°0N 120°0E 79 F13
Zhengzhou China 34°45N 113°34E 79 E11
Zhezqazghan Kazakhstan 47°44N 67°40E 76 E7
Zhigansk Russia 66°48N 123°27E 77 C13
Zhlobin Belarus 52°55N 30°0E 70 D5
Zhob Pakistan 31°20N 69°31E 84 D6
Zhongdian China 27°48N 99°42E 78 F8
Zhongshan China 22°26N 113°20E 79 a
Zhuhai China 22°17N 113°34E 79 a
Zhumadian China 32°59N 114°2E 79 E11
Zhuzhou China 27°49N 113°12E 79 F11
Zhytomyr Ukraine 50°20N 28°40E 65 C15
Zibo China 36°47N 118°3E 79 D12
Zielona Góra Poland 51°57N 15°31E 64 C8
Zigong China 29°15N 104°48E 78 F9
Ziguinchor Senegal 12°35N 16°20W 94 F2
Žilina Slovak Rep. 49°12N 18°42E 65 D10
Zimbabwe ■ Africa 19°0S 30°0E 97 H5
Zinder Niger 13°48N 9°0E 94 F7
Ziway, L. Ethiopia 8°0N 38°50E 89 F2
Zlatoust Russia 55°10N 59°40E 70 C10
Zlín Czech Rep. 49°14N 17°40E 65 D9
Zonguldak Turkey 41°28N 31°50E 71 F5
Zrenjanin Serbia 45°22N 20°23E 69 B9
Zug Switz. 47°10N 8°31E 64 E5
Zunyi China 27°42N 106°53E 78 F10
Zürich Switz. 47°22N 8°32E 64 E5
Zuwārah Libya 32°58N 12°1E 95 B8
Zvishavane Zimbabwe 20°17S 30°2E 97 J6
Zwelitsha S. Africa 32°55S 27°22E 97 L5
Zwickau Germany 50°44N 12°30E 64 C7
Zwolle Neths. 52°31N 6°6E 64 B4

Published in Great Britain in 2015 by Philip's, a division of Octopus Publishing Group Limited (www.octopusbooks.co.uk) Carmelite House 50 Victoria Embankment London EC4Y 0DZ

An Hachette UK Company (www.hachette.co.uk)

Ninety-eighth edition

Copyright © 2015 Philip's Reprinted 2016

ISBN 978-1-84907-353-0 (HARDBACK EDITION)
ISBN 978-1-84907-354-7 (PAPERBACK EDITION)

Printed in Hong Kong

A CIP catalogue record for this book is available from the British Library.

Philip's World Atlases are published in association with The Royal Geographical Society (with The Institute of British Geographers).

The Society was founded in 1830 and given a Royal Charter in 1859 for 'the advancement of geographical science'. Today it is a leading world centre for geographical learning – supporting education, teaching, research and expeditions, and promoting public understanding of the subject.

Further information about the Society and how to join may be found on its website at: **www.rgs.org**

PHOTOGRAPHIC ACKNOWLEDGEMENTS

Satellite images in the atlas are courtesy of the following: China RSGS p. 14tl; DigitalGlobe p. 12; ESA p. 15; NASA pp. 9t, 9tc, 9bc, 10, 11bl, 11br, 13, 116; NPA Satellite Mapping, CGG (www.cgg.com) pp. 6, 11t, 14tr, 16b, 49, 88, 123, 130; Tower Hamlets Local History Library and Archives p. 16t; USGS pp. 8, 9b, 14bl, 14br. Front cover/p. 1: Shutterstock/leonello calvetti